Ex Líbrís

*Lendy Manning*

# LENIN

## A NEW BIOGRAPHY

# LENIN

## A NEW BIOGRAPHY

# Dmitri Volkogonov

Translated and edited by Harold Shukman

THE FREE PRESS

New York · London · Toronto · Sydney · Tokyo · Singapore

The Free Press
A Division of Simon & Schuster, Inc.
866 Third Avenue, New York, N. Y. 10022

Printed in the United States of America

printing number
10 9 8 7 6 5 4 3 2


**Library of Congress Cataloging-in-Publication Data**

Volkogonov, Dmitriĭ Antonovich.
    Lenin: a new biography / Dmitri Volkogonov.
        p.    cm.
    Includes bibliographical references and index.
    ISBN 0-02-933435-7
    1. Lenin, Vladimir Il'ich, 1870-1924. 2. Heads of state - Soviet Union - Biography.
    3. Soviet Union - History - 1917-1936. I. Title.
    DK254.L4V587  1994
    947.084'1'092 - dc20
    [B]                                                                94 - 31752
                                                                            CIP

# Contents

# *Illustrations*

Unless otherwise indicated, all illustrations originate from the Central Committee Archives (RTsKLIDNI).

1 The house in Simbirsk where Lenin was born in 1870.
2 The town centre of Simbirsk, 1867.
3 Lenin's maternal grandfather, Alexander Dmitrievich Blank.
4 Lenin's father, Ilya Nikolaevich Ulyanov.
5 The Ulyanov family in 1879.
6 Alexander Ulyanov in his teens.
7 Lenin aged seventeen in 1887.
8 Lenin's sister Olga.
9 Lenin's sister Anna.
10 Lenin's brother Dmitri.
11 Sergei Nechaev. (*Internationaal Instituut Voor Sociale Geschiedenis, Amsterdam*)
12 Lenin at the age of twenty as a student in Samara.
13 Lenin photographed by the police after his arrest in St Petersburg in 1896.
14 Yuli Martov in the police photograph taken when he was arrested with Lenin in 1896.
15 Georgi Plekhanov, the 'father of Russian Marxism'.
16 Alexander Helphand, alias 'Parvus', under arrest in St Petersburg in 1905. (*David King Collection*)
17 Inessa Armand in 1902.
18 Lenin playing chess on Capri in 1908 with Alexander Bogdanov, watched by Maxim Gorky.

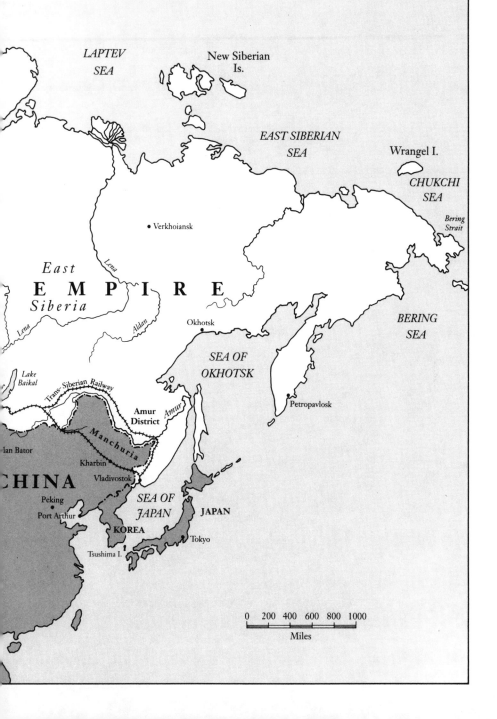

# RUSSIAN EMPIRE CIRCA 1900

OCEAN

*LAPTEV SEA*

New Siberian Is.

*EAST SIBERIAN SEA*

Wrangel I.

*CHUKCHI SEA*

*Bering Strait*

• Verkhoiansk

*East*
**E M P I R E**
*Siberia*

*Lena*

*Lena*

*Aldan*

Okhotsk

*BERING SEA*

*SEA OF OKHOTSK*

Petropavlosk

Lake Baikal

Trans-Siberian Railway

Amur District

*Amur*

*Manchuria*

lan Bator

Kharbin

Vladivostok

**HINA**

Peking

*SEA OF JAPAN*

**JAPAN**

Port Arthur

**KOREA**

Tokyo

Tsushima I.

0   200  400  600  800  1000

Miles

# Abbreviations

| | |
|---|---|
| AMB | Archives of the Ministry of Security |
| AMBRF | Archives of the Ministry of Security of the Russian Federation |
| APRF | Archives of the President of the Russian Federation |
| ECCI | Executive Committee of the Communist International |
| GARF | State Archives of the Russian Federation |
| GPU | State Political Administration |
| KGB | Committee of State Security |
| NKGB | People's Commissariat of State Security |
| NKVD | People's Commissariat of the Interior |
| OGPU | Combined State Political Administration |
| *PSS* | V.I. Lenin, *Polnoe sobranie sochinenii* (Complete Works), 5th edition, 55 vols., Moscow, 1970–85 |
| RTsKhIDNI | Russian Centre for the Preservation and Study of Recent Historical Documentation |
| TsAKGB | Central KGB Archives |
| TsAMBRF | Central Interior Ministry Archives of the Russian Federation |
| TsAMO | Central Archives of the Ministry of Defence |
| TsGALI | Central State Archives of Literature and Art |
| TsGASA | Central State Archives of the Soviet Army |
| TsGoA | Central State Special Archive |
| TsGVIA | Central State Military History Archives |
| TsIK | Central Executive Committee |
| TsKhSD | Centre for the Preservation of Contemporary Documentation |
| VTsIK | All-Russian Central Executive Committee |

# Chronological Table

Until February 1918 dates in Russia conformed to the Julian or Old Style Calendar, which by the twentieth century was lagging thirteen days behind the Gregorian Western Calendar, or New Style. Thus, the February Revolution of 1917 took place in March according to the Western calendar and the Bolsheviks seized power on 25 October 1917, when in the West the date was 7 November. In the text we have used New Style dates, adding Old Style where any ambiguity might arise. In the following table, all dates are according to New Style.

| | | |
|---|---|---|
| 1870 | 22 April | Vladimir Ilyich Ulyanov (Lenin) born. |
| 1879 | 7 November | Lev Davydovich Bronshtein (Trotsky) born. |
| | 21 December | Iosif Vissarionovich Dzhugashvili (Stalin) born. |
| 1880 | January | Georgy Plekhanov flees Russia for Western Europe. |
| 1881 | 13 March | Tsar Alexander II assassinated. |
| 1883 | September | Plekhanov forms Marxist 'Emancipation of Labour Group' in Geneva. |
| 1886 | 24 January | Ilya Nikolaevich Ulyanov (Lenin's father) dies. |
| 1887 | 20 May | Alexander Ulyanov (Lenin's brother) hanged. |
| | 25 August | Lenin enters Kazan University. |
| | 17 December | Arrested in student protest demonstration. |
| 1891 | November | Passes law examination as external student at St Petersburg University. |

| | | |
|---|---|---|
| 1892 | | Practises as defence lawyer in Samara. |
| 1894 | September | First published work, 'What are the "Friends of the People" and how they Fight Against the Social Democrats'. |
| 1895 | May–September | Goes abroad and meets Plekhanov. |
| | 21 December | Arrested in St Petersburg. |
| 1897 | 10 February | Exiled for three years to Siberia. |
| 1898 | March | Russian Social Democratic Labour Party (RSDLP) founded in Minsk. |
| | 22 July | Lenin marries Nadezhda Konstantinovna Krupskaya in Shushenskoe, Siberia. |
| 1900 | 10 February | Lenin's exile ends. |
| | March | Arrives in St Petersburg. |
| | 3 June | Arrested for ten days. |
| | 20 June | Visits Krupskaya in exile in Ufa. |
| | 29 July | Leaves Russia for Western Europe. |
| 1901 | Winter | Socialist Revolutionary Party (PSR) founded. |
| 1902 | March | Lenin's *What is to Be Done?* published. |
| | April–May | Lenin in London. |
| 1903 | 30 July–23 August | Second Congress of RSDLP in Brussels and London. |
| | | Bolshevik–Menshevik split. |
| | December | Lenin resigns from *Iskra*. |
| 1904 | 9 February | Russo–Japanese war breaks out. |
| | 14 March | Lenin resigns from Party Central Committee. |
| 1905 | 22 January | 'Bloody Sunday' in St Petersburg. |
| | 23 January | Strikes begin throughout Russia. |
| | 25 April–10 May | Third Congress of RSDLP in London. |
| | 27 May | Russian fleet sunk in Straits of Tsushima, off Japan. |
| | June | Mutiny on battleship *Potemkin* in Black Sea. |
| | 15 July | Vyacheslav Plehve, Minister of Interior, assassinated in St Petersburg. |
| | 5 September | Russo–Japanese Treaty of Portsmouth, USA. |
| | mid-October | General strike in Russia. |
| | 25 October | Constitutional Democratic party (Kadets) formed. |
| | 26 October | St Petersburg Soviet of Workers' Deputies formed with Trotsky as deputy leader. |
| | 30 October | Nicholas II issues manifesto promising civil |

|      |               | rights and a legislative assembly, the State Duma. |
|------|---------------|---------------------------------------------------|
|      | 21 November   | Lenin arrives in St Petersburg. |
|      | 16 December   | St Petersburg Soviet arrested. |
|      | 21 December   | Bolshevik-led armed uprising in Moscow crushed by army. |
| 1906 | 23 April–8 May | Fourth Congress of RSDLP in Stockholm. |
|      | 10 May        | First State Duma opens in St Petersburg. |
|      | 21 July       | Duma dissolved; Peter Stolypin appointed Prime Minister. |
| 1907 | January–April | Lenin resides in Kokkala, Finland. |
|      | 5 March       | Second Duma opens. |
|      | 15 June       | Second Duma dissolved. |
|      | 13 April–1 June | Fifth Congress of RSDLP in London. |
|      | 20 November   | Third Duma opens, based on new electoral law. |
|      | December      | Lenin takes up residence in Switzerland. |
| 1908 | December      | Moves to Paris. |
| 1909 |               | Meets Inessa Armand in Paris. |
| 1912 | June          | Moves to Cracow in Austrian Poland. |
|      | 28 November   | Fourth Duma opens. |
| 1913 | May           | Lenin moves to Poronin. |
|      | July          | Accompanies Krupskaya to Berne for her surgery. |
| 1914 | 30 July       | Russia mobilizes. |
|      | 1 August      | Germany declares war on Russia. |
|      | 3 August      | First World War begins. |
|      | August        | St Petersburg renamed Petrograd. |
|      | August        | Russia invades Austrian Galicia and East Prussia. |
|      | 8 August      | Lenin arrested in Austrian Poland as Russian spy. |
|      | 19 August     | Released. |
|      | September     | Russian forces defeated in East Prussia. |
|      | September     | Lenin leaves Austria for Switzerland |
| 1915 | 22 July       | Russian forces withdraw from Poland |
|      | 4 September   | Nicholas II takes over supreme command of Russian forces. |
|      | September     | Lenin participates in conference of anti-war socialists at Zimmerwald, Switzerland. |

| | | |
|---|---|---|
| 1916 | April | Second meeting of anti-war socialists at Kienthal, Switzerland. |
| | 30 December | Rasputin murdered in Petrograd. |
| 1917 | 8 March | Start of February Revolution in Petrograd. |
| | 12 March | Petrograd Soviet formed. |
| | 14 March | Moscow Soviet formed. |
| | 15 March | Provisional Government formed. Nicholas II abdicates. |
| | 25 March | Stalin and other Bolsheviks arrive in Petrograd from Siberian exile. |
| | 16 April | Lenin arrives in Petrograd from Switzerland. |
| | 17 April | Lenin issues his 'April Theses'. |
| | May | Bolshevik Red Guards organized. |
| | May | Trotsky returns to Russia from New York. |
| | 16 June | First Congress of Soviets opens. |
| | 4 July | Provisional Government issues orders to arrest Lenin and other leading Bolsheviks. |
| | 13 July | Lenin flees to Finland. |
| | 17 July | Bolsheviks attempt coup in Petrograd – 'July Days'. |
| | 18 July | Lenin goes into hiding. |
| | 24 July | Alexander Kerensky becomes Prime Minister. |
| | August | Sixth Bolshevik Party Congress in Petrograd. |
| | mid-September | Kornilov campaign against Soviets launched and crushed. |
| | 8 October | Trotsky becomes Chairman of Petrograd Soviet. |
| | 23 October | Lenin returns secretly to Petrograd for Central Committee meeting to vote on armed uprising. |
| | 6 November | Armed uprising by Bolshevik Red Guards. |
| | 7 November | Trotsky declares seizure of power at Second Congress of Soviets, where Lenin's decrees on land and peace are passed. |
| | 17 November | Sovnarkom given supreme legislative power by TsIK. |
| | November | First phase of civil war opens in Ukraine. |
| | 25 November | Elections to Constituent Assembly begin. |
| | 3 December | Soviet–German armistice talks open at Brest-Litovsk. |

| | | |
|---|---|---|
| | 15 December | Russian–German armistice signed. |
| | 20 December | Cheka (Extra-ordinary Commission for Combating Counter-revolution and Sabotage) established. |
| | December | Don Cossacks revolt, (White) Volunteer Army formed under Generals Kaledin and Kornilov. |
| 1918 | 9 January | Peace talks reopen at Brest-Litovsk. |
| | 14 January | Attempt on Lenin's life in Petrograd. |
| | 18 January | Constituent Assembly convened and is forcibly dispersed by Bolsheviks. |
| | 22 January | Ukraine declares independence. |
| | 9 February | Ukraine and Central Powers sign treaty. |
| | 18 February | Germans resume war against Russia. |
| | 3 March | Treaty of Brest-Litovsk signed by Soviet Russia and Germany. Bolshevik troops enter Ukrainian capital, Kiev. |
| | 9 March | Allied expeditionary force lands at Murmansk. |
| | 10 March | Capital of Soviet Russia transferred from Petrograd to Moscow. |
| | 13 March | Trotsky appointed People's Commissar for War. Begins formation of Red Army. |
| | 4 April | Japanese expeditionary force lands at Vladivostok. |
| | June | British expeditionary force lands at Archangel. |
| | 12 June | Tsar's brother, Grand Duke Michael, murdered near Perm in the Urals. |
| | 16 June | Lenin reintroduces death penalty. |
| | 4 July | Constitution approved by Fifth Congress of Soviets. |
| | 6 July | Count Mirbach, German Ambassador to Moscow assassinated. |
| | 17 July | Tsar Nicholas II and his family executed in Yekaterinburg. |
| | 30 August | Lenin shot and wounded in Moscow. Uritsky, Head of Petrograd Cheka, murdered. |
| | 4 September | Lenin orders hostage-taking. Red Terror begins. |

| | September | Red Army captures Kazan and Simbirsk from Whites in Volga campaign. |
|---|---|---|
| | Early November | Kaiser Wilhelm II abdicates. |
| | 6 November | Soviet embassy expelled from Berlin for revolutionary agitation. |
| | 11 November | Allies and Central Powers sign Armistice. |
| | 13 November | Soviet Government renounces Treaty of Brest-Litovsk. |
| | December | French intervention forces land at Odessa. |
| 1919 | 11 April | Concentration camps created in Soviet Russia. |
| | 2–6 March | First Congress of Communist International (Comintern). |
| | March | Opening of civil war in Urals. |
| 1920 | 26 April | Poland invades Soviet territory. |
| | 8 May | Polish army captures Kiev in Ukraine. |
| | June | Red Army repels Poles. |
| | July | Red Army reaches Warsaw and is repelled. |
| | 21 July–6 August | Second Congress of Communist International in Moscow. |
| | August | Red Army retreats from Poland. |
| | 24 September | Inessa Armand dies in the Caucasus. |
| | November | White forces in mass evacuation from Crimea to Turkey. |
| 1921 | 1–18 March | Anti-Bolshevik uprising on Kronstadt island. |
| | 8 March | Tenth Bolshevik Party Congress in Moscow. NEP announced. |
| 1922 | April | Stalin appointed to newly created post of General Secretary of the Party. |
| | 26 May | Lenin suffers his first stroke. |
| | Summer | Convalesces at Gorki. |
| | 16 December | Second stroke. |
| | 25 December | Dictates his 'Letter to the Congress', or 'Testament'. |
| 1923 | 10 March | Third stroke. |
| | 17–25 April | Twelfth Bolshevik Party Congress. |
| | 18 October | Lenin visits Moscow and Kremlin for last time. |
| 1924 | 21 January | Lenin dies. |
| | 27 January | Lenin's mummified body installed in Mausoleum. |

# Editor's Preface

With the demise of the Soviet Union an era of Russian history was closed. It was an era that began in 1917 with the seizure of power by the Bolshevik Communist Party and ended with the disgrace and eviction of the same Party in August 1991, followed by the formal termination of the Soviet state itself at the end of the same year. From its inception to its end the Soviet state was identified with Lenin, whether alive or dead. Without him, it is generally accepted, there would have been no October revolution. Following the revolution, his name, his image, his words and his philosophy embellished, informed, exhorted and inspired generations of ordinary Soviet citizens, and especially those raised to positions of authority. He was made into an icon, a totem of ideological purity and guidance beyond questioning. All other Party leaders were found to be fallible in due course, many of the 1917 cohort in the great purge of 1936–38, and most famously Stalin in 1956 when Khrushchev debunked his 'cult of personality' at the Twentieth Party Congress. But Lenin remained untouched. As more and more topics of Soviet history were re-examined during Gorbachev's enlightened leadership, and the Bolshevik old guard, exterminated in the 1930s, were rehabilitated, it became obvious that the spotlight must sooner or later fall on the last dark place on the stage – that occupied by Lenin.

A new reading of Lenin was made possible not only because Dmitri Volkogonov was granted access to the archives in the 1980s, but also, indeed chiefly, because Leninism itself had totally collapsed in the former Soviet Union. As the author of this book himself confesses, even after he had spent years collecting the incriminating evidence for his major study of Stalin, mostly written before 1985 and published in 1988, Lenin was the 'last bastion' in his mind to fall. Lenin has at last passed into history. No longer is he the prop of a powerful regime, the object of an ideology, or the central myth of a political culture. To engage in debate about Lenin and to assess his actions is no longer to challenge the legitimacy of an existing political system. Like him, it too has become history.

Books about Lenin have been coming out in the West almost from the moment the world first became aware of him in 1917. Even more abundantly, Soviet historians pumped out publications on allegedly every aspect of his life, and eye-witnesses of every degree added their own testimony in books with such titles as 'They Knew Lenin', 'Lenin Knew Them', 'They Saw Lenin', 'Lenin Saw Them', and so on, with variations on the theme effected by altering Lenin's name: 'They Knew Ilyich', 'Ilyich Knew Them', etc., etc. Yet another book on Vladimir Ilyich Lenin therefore requires a word of justification.

Western books (including two by the undersigned) have largely been based on the published sources, many of them of Soviet origin. On the other hand, Soviet books from the outset have been apologist and ideological in content and purpose. From the end of the 1920s, when Stalin's authority was complete, Soviet historians (like authors of creative literature, playwrights and film-makers) were strictly forbidden to write 'objectively', that is, from any other point of view than that laid down by the Central Committee of the Communist Party of the Soviet Union. Now that the Central Committee has evaporated together with the Party, there are virtually no taboos on historical research left; Russian historians may if they wish differ in their assessment of any events they choose to analyse, but access to a widening pool of hitherto concealed data will at least ensure that their interpretations are based on the full facts. Areas which have been closed to them, and only partially known to Western scholars, and which have now been opened up in this book, include the complete documentation of Lenin's genealogy, his financial operations – German involvement in the funding of Bolshevik activity during the First World War and Soviet funding of foreign Communist Parties after it – the nature of his friendship with Inessa Armand, and the effects of his illness on his political judgment, to mention a few.

The opening of the Party and other archives of Soviet history has been a gradual and intermittent process. Numerous efforts made to publish inventories and collections of documents have met with varied success, and so far it is fair to say the process is still at an early stage. Although with the failure of the attempted coup in August 1991 the Russian state took over from the Communist Party control of all the archival collections within its boundaries, the new state has barely formulated rules on the release of documents for publication, and the picture remains unclear. Nevertheless, even the minutes of the Politburo for the 1930s have been seen by Western and Russian scholars alike, and much valuable material is now appearing in two new journals devoted to the publication of extracts from the archives, *Istoricheskii arkhiv* and *Istochnik*, and a new series of miscellanies called 'Unknown Russia' (*Neizvestnaya Rossiya*), as well as an increasing amount of similar material in journals which have survived from the Soviet era. Subject to the rules and regulations of the Russian Archive Commission (Rosarkhiv), all the documents cited in this book can be seen at the various locations indicated. Documents from the Archives of the President of the Russian Federation (APRF) have been transferred from the Kremlin to the archives of the former Central Committee (RTsKhIDNI) and TsKhSD).

The first researcher to gain access to the most secret archives was Dmitri Volkogonov. As the Director of the Institute of Military History and a serving Colonel-General, he had for years collected material for his biography of Stalin. Its publication in 1988 made him a pariah among his fellow senior officers, whose patience with him finally ran out in June 1991, when the draft of a new history of the Second World War, edited under his aegis, was discussed at his Institute and condemned. Accused of blackening the name of the army, as well as that of the Communist Party and the Soviet state, and personally attacked by Minister of Defence Yazov, Volkogonov resigned. When the attempted coup followed two months later, Volkogonov was the government's natural choice to supervise the control and declassification of the Party and State archives.

The author's original Russian version of this book is considerably longer than this English rendition, and the two main principles that I applied in editing it deserve a mention. As a Russian historian suddenly able to write freely about this subject, Volkogonov ranged far beyond the history of his subject, particularly into philosophical reflection and into the backgrounds of topics which, while of special

interest to his Russian readers, tended either to be excessively familiar
to a Western reader, or to slow down the general chronological drift
underlying the shifting narrative. I felt an English reader might
become impatient at times for a return to the book's central theme.
My first rule was therefore to try to preserve as much as possible of
the material – published as well as unpublished – either emanating
from or pertaining to Lenin himself. My second principle was to
preserve material demonstrating Volkogonov's own thesis, namely
that Stalin, his system and his successors, all derived directly from
Lenin, his theories and practices.

Among the questions Russian historians have yet to confront is that
of continuity. For many years, Western scholars have debated the
extent to which the Soviet system inherited features of the tsarist
empire. Some have argued that strong, centralized government by a
self-appointed oligarchy was a Russian tradition, that a passive population, inclined towards collective rather than individualistic action
and fed on myths of a special destiny and of rewards to come only in
the distant future (if not only after death), was also characteristically
Russian. Others, especially those closest in time to the events of 1917,
have suggested that the liberal and democratic aspirations of the
February 1917 revolution, when Nicholas II abdicated, had viable if
shallow roots that would have become strong and stable, but for the
intervention of the Bolsheviks.

Whatever their differences of emphasis, all schools, whether
Western or Soviet, have agreed that the Bolshevik seizure of power,
and the period of turmoil that immediately followed it, diverted the
country irredeemably from any previously supposed path of development. The destruction of the liberal political intelligentsia by Lenin
meant that the constitutional option was a dead letter; the decimation
of the peasants' political leadership left them exposed to the
Bolsheviks' violent exploitation of their economic potential; heavy-
handed Bolshevik management of the trade unions prefigured their
reduction to obedient servants of the regime; Lenin's suppression of
the free press set the scene for the censorship of information by the
Communist Party that is erroneously taken to be the hallmark of
Stalinism; Lenin's immediate resort to the prison, the concentration
camp, exile, the firing squad, hostages and blackmail, and his creation
of an entire system of punishment to replace that of the tsars, set the

new order on a path of violence and universal suspicion that was to become typical of twentieth-century tyrannies thereafter.

In the view of Dmitri Volkogonov, the question of whether or not Soviet history was a continuation in any sense of Russian history is of less importance than the question of whether Soviet history is itself a continuum. In this book, he shows that between Lenin and Stalin there was neither an ideological discontinuity, nor a difference of method. And, indeed, it is his contention that, while the methods employed by Stalin's successors were much more moderate, they were just as motivated by the impulses of their legendary founder as their monstrous predecessor had been.

Among writers on the history of the Soviet Union – whether Westerners or Russian émigrés – it was not uncommon to trace events back and to seek a point at which 'things might have gone differently'. Many have wondered whether, had Lenin not died so early in the life of the regime, the country might have developed along less militaristic and politically sterile lines. Perhaps the New Economic Policy, allowing peasants – more or less – to work for themselves, and permitting a degree of latitude in cultural life, would have continued and led to a more tolerant order of things. In the early years of *glasnost* this idea was widely debated by Russian as well as Western scholars. Among the latter were many who could not accept that any good could have come from Lenin and his creations, while some still retained a lingering doubt that such an intelligent man as Lenin could possibly have initiated and carried through the inhuman collectivization and the great terror of the 1930s. In Russia, as long as the Soviet state continued to exist, Lenin remained a virtually unblemished icon.

Dmitri Volkogonov has now demolished the icon, and he has firmly committed himself to the view that Russia's only hope in 1917 lay in the liberal and social democratic coalition that emerged in the February revolution. He has, in other words, concluded that there was no salvation to be found in any of the policies practised by Lenin, and he has taken his account further to show how Lenin's malign influence was imbibed by all subsequent Soviet leaders. Indeed, the Party leaders, he shows, quoted Lenin and referred to his teaching, not just when mouthing their pious platitudes for the populace, but even when they were closeted in the privacy of the Politburo. Having absorbed a philosophy that had failed almost before it was put into practice, it should have caused little surprise that the practitioners of Leninism in the modern age would ultimately share a similar fate.

# Introduction

The massive steel door swung open and I was ushered into a large lobby, from which a similar reinforced door led to the Communist holy of holies, Lenin's archives. The former Central Committee building on Staraya Square in central Moscow is a vast grey edifice the size of an entire city block. Along its endless corridors are the identical wood-panelled offices where the Party hierarchs once sat, dozens of meeting rooms of all sizes, a great reading room lined with catalogues and indexes to the Party's meticulously preserved records. And deep in its basement, reminiscent of a nuclear bomb-shelter, on special shelves in special metal boxes, I was shown all the written traces to be found of the man still regarded by some as a genius, by others as the scourge of the century.

Despite the fact that there have been five editions of his collected works in Russian (the fourth of which was translated into many foreign languages), these are Lenin's unpublished documents, numbering 3724 in all. Another 3000 or so were merely signed by him. Why were they hidden away? Could it be that his halo would have been tarnished by publishing, for instance, his instructions in November 1922 to punish Latvia and Estonia for supporting the Whites by such means as *'catching them out'* with more and more evidence, by penetrating their borders 'in hot pursuit' and 'then hanging 100–1000 of their officials and rich folk...'?[1] Perhaps such documents were concealed because there was no one left who could explain them. As the Anarchist veteran Prince Kropotkin wrote to Lenin in December 1920, when the Bolsheviks had seized a large group of hostages whom they would 'destroy mercilessly' (in the words of *Pravda*) should an attempt be made on the life of any of the Soviet leaders: 'Is there none among you to remind his comrades and to persuade them that such measures are a return to the worst times of the Middle Ages and the religious wars, and that they are not worthy of people who have undertaken to create the future society?'[2] Lenin read the letter and marked it 'For the archives.'

Of course, our view of Lenin has changed not only because we have found there is more than the stories that inspired us for decades. We began to doubt his infallibility above all because the 'cause', which he launched and for which millions paid with their lives, has suffered a major historical defeat. It is hard to write this. As a former Stalinist who has made the painful transition to a total rejection of Bolshevik totalitarianism, I confess that Leninism was the last bastion to fall in my mind. As I saw more and more closed Soviet archives, as well as the large Western collections at Harvard University and the Hoover Institution in California, Lenin's profile altered in my estimation: gradually the creator and prophet was edged out by the Russian Jacobin. I realised that none of us knew Lenin; he had always stood before us in the death-mask of the earthly god he had never been.

After my books on Stalin and Trotsky,[3] I set about the final part of the trilogy with the aim of rethinking Lenin. He had always been multi-faceted, but after his death his image was channelled into the single dimension of a saint, and the more we saw him as such, the more we distanced ourselves from the historical Lenin who was still, I think, the greatest revolutionary of the century.

The intellectual diet of Leninism was as compulsory for every Soviet citizen as the Koran is for an observing Muslim. On 1 January 1990 in the Soviet Union there were more than 653 million copies of Lenin's writings in 125 languages – perhaps the only area of abundance achieved by Communist effort. Thus were millions of people educated in Soviet dogmatics, and we are still not fully aware how impoverished and absurd our idol-worship will look to the twenty-first century.

To write about Lenin is above all to express one's view of Leninism. In 1926, two years after Lenin's death, Stalin produced a collection called *The Foundations of Leninism*. Leninism, we were told, came down to making possible the revolutionary destruction of the old world and the creation on its ruins of a new and radiant civilization. How? By what means? By means of unlimited dictatorship. It was here that the original sin of Marxism in its Leninist version was committed – not that Marx, to give him his due, was much taken with the idea of dictatorship. Lenin, however, regarded it as Marxism's chief contribution on the question of the state. In fact, according to him, the dictatorship of the proletariat constituted the basic content of the socialist revolution. His assertion that 'only by struggle and war' can the 'great questions of humanity' be resolved gave priority to the destructive tendency.[4]

Thus armed, Lenin and his successors assumed that in the name of the happiness of future generations, everything was permitted and moral: the export of revolution, civil war, unbridled violence, social experimentation. The vitality and, let it not be denied, the appeal of much of Leninism derived from the perpetual human longing for the perfect and just world. The Russian revolutionaries, including Lenin, rightly exposed the age-old evils of human existence, the exploitation, inequality, lack of freedom. But having acquired the opportunity to abolish these evils, the Leninists established a new, barely disguised form of exploitation to be carried out by the state. Instead of social and ethnic inequality came bureaucratic inequality; in place of class unfreedom came total unfreedom. The Leninist version of Marxism was made flesh in this vast country, becoming something like a secular religion in the process.

In the last analysis, the Leninist promise of great progress turned into great backwardness. The founders of the Russian Marxist movement, George Plekhanov, Vera Zasulich and Lev Deich, in their 'Open Letter to the Petrograd Workers' of 28 October 1917, wrote prophetically that 'the revolution is the greatest historic disaster, it will provoke a civil war which in the end will force it to retreat far from the conquests of February 1917'.[5] For that matter, on the eve of the Bolshevik coup of October 1917 other Bolsheviks were not confident of success and were alarmed by Lenin's radicalism, which with maniacal persistence was pushing the masses towards armed uprising against the Provisional Government. At the Central Committee on 16 October 1917, where the issue of the uprising was discussed, Lenin made a note, which reads: '"We dare not win", that's the main point of all their speeches.'[6] A man of enormous will, Lenin succeeded in turning his party in the direction of violence and coercion as a way of dealing with the problems of peace, land and freedom.

Leninism was not restrained by national limits. With the aid of

Comintern, established in Moscow in March 1919 and virtually an international section of the Russian Communist Party, he attempted to initiate revolutions wherever the possibility existed, and sometimes where it did not. In July 1920 he cabled Stalin in Kharkov: 'The situation in Comintern is splendid. Zinoviev, Bukharin and I believe that we ought to encourage revolution in Italy right now. My own opinion is that we need to sovietize Hungary for the purpose, and maybe also Czecho[slovakia] and Romania.'[7] Emissaries were sent east and west, and on Lenin's orders the Finance Commissariat made available millions of gold roubles 'for the needs of the world revolution'.[8] Meanwhile Soviet citizens were dying in their hundreds of thousands from famine and disease. For Lenin, the revolution was everything, and it could not be achieved without countless victims.

It is impossible to think of Lenin without contemplating his brainchild, his party. Perhaps the idea of the mighty revolutionary organization is central to Leninism, but his accomplishment was not merely that he created a party with a disciplined organization, but that he was rapidly able to erect it into a state system. The Party soon acquired a monopoly of power, of thought and of life itself. It became a Leninist order, in whose name its 'leaders' and their 'comrades-in-arms' were to rule the country for decades to come. It was an ideal backbone for a totalitarian regime, but as soon as Soviet society began its rapid change in the second half of the 1980s, the Party, like a fish cast onto the bank, began to expire. Its rapid and amazingly painless disintegration after the attempted coup of August 1991 revealed its absolute inability to survive in conditions of an emerging civil society.

If the chief feature of a dictator is unlimited personal power – and Lenin had such power – we ought to see him as a dictator. Yet he was not. Certainly he regarded dictatorship as a positive virtue contributing to the success of the revolution, and certainly he saw the Bolshevik leaders as 'dictators' in their allocated areas of responsibility: at the 10 July 1919 session of the Politburo, Alexei Rykov was appointed 'dictator for military supply'.[9] Power for Lenin was dictatorship, but he exercised it remotely, through a flexible mechanism of ideological and organizational structures.

Little is known of Lenin's private life. This is not only because of the Marxist postulate of the primacy of the social above the personal, but also because of the desire of the revolutionary hierarchs to keep the personal lives of their leaders secret from the masses. While every detail of the life of a minor functionary was regarded as essential information, the life of a Politburo member and his family was seen as a state secret. Their salaries, numbers of servants and automobiles, as well as the size of their houses and dachas – all such information was untouchable in 'special files'. Nobody in Russia ever learnt, for example, what financial support Lenin had received during the years of his voluntary exile in Europe, from 1900 to 1905 and from 1906 to 1917, or who had financed the Party before the revolution, or why Lenin had never worked, in the usual meaning of the word, or how he had travelled through Germany at the height of the war, or whether the Bolsheviks had ever received financial help from Germany, Russia's enemy, before the revolution. On 21 August 1918 Lenin wrote to his emissary in Sweden, Vatslav Vorovsky: 'No one asked the Germans for help, but there were negotiations on *when* and *how* they, the Germans, would carry out their plan to advance . . . There was a coincidence of interests. We would have been idiots not to have exploited it.'[10] The new regime's relations with Germany, after the separate peace of Brest-Litovsk of March 1918, were shrouded in secrecy. In February 1921, Lenin received a cipher from the Soviet legation in Berlin reporting on the results of talks with the Germans, in the course of which agreement had been reached on the rehabilitation of the German war industry, contravening the Versailles prohibition. The German firm Blohm and Voss was ready to build submarines, Albatrosswerke aircraft, and Krupp artillery pieces on Soviet soil. Lenin responded: '. . . I think, yes. Tell them so. Secret.'[11]

Soviet biographies of Lenin are countless and uniformly eulogistic, singing the praises of his genius, his perfection and his greatness. Within a year of the Bolshevik seizure of power, Grigory Zinoviev virtually mapped out the first official biography and set the tone that would become almost statutory, in a speech in which he employed such terms as 'the apostle of Communism' and 'Leader, by the grace of God'.[12] The published memoirs of Lenin's wife, Nadezhda Krupskaya, who knew him better than anyone, were different, though they too bear the stamp of the era, 'the midnight of the epoch'. The exception to the rule is perhaps her memoirs about the last period of his life which, like those of his sister, Maria, were never published.

The five editions of Lenin's collected works vary substantially. The first came out between 1920 and 1926 and numbered twenty volumes. The second and third (which differed only in the quality of their bindings) were published in thirty volumes between 1930 and 1932. The fourth, known as the Stalin Edition and the one translated into foreign languages, including English, came out between 1941 and 1957 in thirty-five volumes. The fifth, described as the Complete Edition and the one to which we refer most often in this book, was published between 1958 and 1965 and benefited to some extent from the somewhat liberal climate of Khrushchev's early years. It ran to fifty-five volumes, while the sixth, which was in preparation when the August 1991 events occurred, was planned to have at least seventy. Lenin is inexhaustible. The most serious Soviet work on him is a twelve-volume 'Biographical Chronicle' which provides not merely the basic contours of the man-god's life, but also thousands of names and facts. It also contains many cuts, silences and distorted interpretations. The biographies written in the West are immeasurably more useful, although they lack the original source material, especially on the Soviet period.

One of the most interesting published accounts of Lenin was written by Trotsky when Lenin died in 1924.[13] It formed part of the material he collected for many years for a 'big book' on Lenin. In April 1929, exiled in Constantinople, he wrote to Alexandra Ramm, his translator in Berlin: 'My book *Lenin and His Successors* cannot appear earlier than two or three months after my autobiography has come out.' And three months later he wrote that he was writing another book on 'Lenin (a biography, personal portrait, memoirs and correspondence)'.[14] Five years later Trotsky wrote to his supporter, M. Parizhanin: 'My work on Lenin has not yet and will not soon move beyond the preparatory stage. I won't be able to send the first chapters for translation before July.'[15] Lenin dead was no less useful to Trotsky, for personal reasons, than he was to Stalin. Both of them knew more about their patron than anyone else, but the 'big book on Lenin', alas, was never completed or published.

Trotsky first met Lenin in 1902, and their relationship went from mutual admiration to deep mutual rejection and back to close alliance. Trotsky could have recalled that, at the time of the 1905 revolution, Lenin in a fit of frustration had called him a *balalaika*, a poseur, base careerist, rogue, scoundrel, liar, crook, swine, and more. That was

Lenin's style, but it did not prevent him from writing in 1917, 'Bravo, Comrade Trotsky!' or from calling him 'the best Bolshevik'. Trotsky, for his own part, was never short of an insulting epithet to throw back.

Stalin also knew a lot about Lenin, notably from the Soviet rather than the émigré period. The archives show that Stalin received no fewer than 150 personal notes, cables, letters and orders from Lenin. But many of them are fragments of telegram tape, second copies of typescript and other indirect evidence. I have alluded in my book on Stalin to the dubious authenticity of such materials. After becoming supreme dictator, and with the help of his yes-men, Stalin introduced some significant falsifications into the correspondence with Lenin, which had grown rapidly with his appointment to the post of General Secretary of the Communist Party in 1922. After his own authorized biography had appeared, it seems Stalin also planned to bring out a book on Lenin, though he never did.[16]

Perhaps it was another leading Bolshevik, Lev Kamenev, who received the most correspondence, 350 letters and memoranda by my reckoning, most of them still unpublished. He was much trusted by Lenin, even on personal matters, for example on Lenin's relationship with his mistress Inessa Armand at the time he and Lenin were sharing an apartment in Poland. Kamenev's knowledge of Lenin is important because he was the first editor, with Lenin's direct participation, of Lenin's collected works (1920–26). Kamenev, however, wrote little, and left nothing to compare in size with the heritage of his constant friend Zinoviev.

Grigory Yevseyevich Zinoviev and his wife Z.I. Lilina were close family friends of Lenin, and Zinoviev probably received more personal letters from Lenin than any other leader. The new Communist top brass were not modest: once in power, they took up residence in the Kremlin, expropriated palaces and estates, gave cities their names, erected monuments to themselves, surrounded themselves with body-guards and doctors, and quickly set about publishing their collected works. Zinoviev's best work on Lenin was possibly his introduction to the study of Leninism, in which he exhorted his readers to 'study Lenin at first-hand! To know Lenin is to know the road to the victory of the world revolution.'[17] In the early 1930s, when Zinoviev's days were numbered, he wrote several chapters of a book on Lenin, hoping it would save him. Stalin would not so much as look at what his prisoner had written, for he had long ago decided the fate of Zinoviev, and Kamenev too.

Most of Lenin's biographers have understandably concentrated on his social and political rôle, but it is also important to balance that against his strictly human, moral and intellectual qualities, and to do so without forgetting the historical context. The historical Lenin was a child of his time: troubled, cruel, expectant, alarming. History neither accuses nor justifies, it is a means to understand, to discern the patterns that characterize a distant age. We say the word 'Lenin' and we see in our mind's eye a man whose high forehead and large bald patch suggest the embodiment of intellect – as well as the commonplace.

Gleb Krzhizhanovsky, an early associate of Lenin's who held high office in the Soviet government, made an attempt in his book *Velikii Lenin* to define the essence of Lenin's genius (to which the book was dedicated), but was more successful in describing his subject's exterior appearance. It was, he wrote, simple and modest: 'Short of stature and wearing his usual cloth cap, he could easily have passed unnoticed in any factory district. All one could say of his appearance was that he had a pleasant, swarthy face with a touch of the Asiatic. In a rough country coat he could just as easily have passed in a crowd of Volga peasants.' Clearly, this description was intended to stress the 'folksiness', the 'depth', the 'link with the lower orders', but Krzhizhanovsky also noticed an important element: Lenin's eyes, the mirror of the human mind. Those eyes, he wrote, 'were unusual, piercing, full of inner strength and energy, dark, dark brown . . .'[18] It was a feature noticed by many, especially by the writer A.I. Kuprin in his graphic description, 'Instant Photography'. Lenin, he wrote, 'is short, broad-shouldered and lean. He looks neither repellent, militant nor deep-thinking. He has high cheekbones and slanting eyes . . . The dome of his forehead is broad and high, though not as exaggerated as it appears in foreshortened photographs . . . He has traces of hair on his temples, and his beard and moustache still show how much of a fiery redhead he was in his youth. His hands are large and ugly . . . I couldn't stop looking at his eyes . . . they are narrow; besides which he tends to screw them up, no doubt a habit of concealing short sight, and this, and the rapid glances beneath his eyebrows, gives him an occasional squint and perhaps a look of cunning. But what surprised me most was their colour ... Last summer in the Paris zoo, seeing the eyes of a lemur, I said to myself in amazement: at last I've found the colour of Lenin's eyes! The only difference being that the lemur's pupils were bigger and more restless, while Lenin's were no more than pinpricks from which blue sparks seemed to fly.'[19] The writer Ariadna Tyrkova, who had seen Lenin at close quarters more than once, drew a simpler picture: 'Lenin was an evil man. And he had the evil eyes of a wolf.'[20]

A physical detail, while of no decisive significance to Lenin's political portrait, may nevertheless highlight his main characteristic, namely his powerful mind, a mind that was too often not merely pragmatic, flexible and sophisticated, but also malevolent and perfidious. His radical pragmatism explains the actions he took to bring about the defeat of his own country in the First World War in order to get his party into power. His radicalism compelled him to accept the loss of entire national regions of the former tsarist empire, although when complete disintegration was threatened he cast aside his internationalism and started defending that empire, by then transformed into its Soviet form.

It was power, not love of fatherland, that prompted him to save Russia. He had, after all, shown his contempt – to put it mildly – for Russia and the Russians. Writing in the autumn of 1920 to Jan Berzin, a Central Committee member of Latvian origin, about publishing Communist propaganda, he complained that things were going badly. He advised Berzin to invite two Swiss comrades from Zurich, and to pay them 'arch-generously'. He went on: 'Hand out the work to Russian idiots: send the cuttings here, but not occasional issues (as these idiots have been doing until now).'[21] Without a blush, he could call his fellow-countrymen idiots who could only be trusted to do the simplest tasks, while left-wingers from Zurich had to be paid 'arch-generously'. This is only a short note, but a very eloquent one, and similar evidence of Lenin's attitude to Russianness is abundant, though of course well hidden in the archives.

In the middle of 1922 the civil war was over and Russia lay in ruins. It seemed that at last the cruelty would end. Lenin pointed out that 'although coercion is not our ideal', the Bolsheviks could not live without it, even where ideas, views and the human spirit are concerned. He recommended the death penalty, commuted in mitigating circumstances to deprivation of liberty or deportation abroad, 'for propaganda or agitation or belonging to or aiding organizations supporting that part of the international bourgeoisie that does not recognize the ... Communist system'.[22] This proposal was later incorporated into the infamous Article 58 of the Criminal Code, under which millions constructed and then filled the concentration camps. Lenin is the source of the totalitarian ideology of intolerance. By creating the Cheka, the punitive organ of the dictatorship and his favourite brainchild, Lenin influenced the outlook of the Communists who soon came to believe that the amoral was moral, if it was in the Party's interest. S.I. Gusev, a member of the Party Central Control Commission, addressing the XIV Congress in December 1925, declared: 'Lenin once taught us that every member of the Party must be an agent of the Cheka, that is, we must watch and inform ... I believe every member of the Party should inform. If we suffer from anything, it is not from denunciation, but from non-denunciation. We might be the best of friends, but once we start to differ in politics, we must not only break off our friendships, we must go further and start informing.'[23] Leninist doctrine had donned the police agent's cloak.

It is often said that, as he felt death approaching, Lenin was horrified by what he had done and was willing to rethink much. It may be so, but it is impossible to prove. Even had he wanted to change things, which is doubtful, he took his intentions with him to the grave. It is also said that Lenin failed to build 'true socialism', even with the aid of the New Economic Policy. But if one looks closely at his understanding of this 'new policy', one can clearly discern old Bolshevik features. NEP, as far as Lenin was concerned, was bridled capitalism, and it could be 'slapped down' at any time. When reports started coming in about profiteering by traders, the so-called '*Nepmen*', Lenin reacted quickly: '... we need a number of *model* trials with the *harshest* sentences. The Justice Commissariat obviously doesn't understand that the New Economic Policy requires *new* methods of applying punishment of *new harshness*.'[24]

Lenin never concealed his belief that the new world could only be built with the aid of physical violence. In March 1922 he wrote to Kamenev: 'It is the biggest mistake to think that NEP will put an end to the terror. We shall return to the terror, and to economic terror.'[25]

And indeed there was to be enough terror of every kind. After many decades we Russians condemned it, refusing for shame to answer the question of who had started it and who had made it into a sacred object of revolutionary method. I do not doubt that Lenin wanted earthly happiness for the people, at least for those he called 'the proletariat'. But he regarded it as normal to build this 'happiness' on blood, coercion and the denial of freedom.

# 1

## *Distant Sources*

Vladimir Ilyich Lenin did not appear fully fledged on the scene as the leader of the radical wing of Russian social democracy. At the end of the nineteenth century, when he was not quite thirty, he was merely one among many. Julius Martov, who collaborated closely with him in St Petersburg and Western Europe between 1895 and 1903, recalled that Lenin cut a rather different figure then from the one he was to present later on. There was less self-confidence, nor did he show the scorn and contempt which, in Martov's view, would shape his particular kind of political leadership. But Martov also added significantly: 'I never saw in him any sign of personal vanity.'[1]

Lenin himself was not responsible for the absurdly inflated cult that grew up around his name throughout the Soviet period, although he was not entirely blameless. When in August 1918, for instance, it was decided to erect a monument at the spot in Moscow where an attempt had recently been made on his life, he did not protest, and only a year after the Bolshevik seizure of power he was posing for sculptors. In 1922 monuments were raised to him in his home province of Simbirsk, in Zhitomir and Yaroslavl. He regarded all this as normal: in place of monuments to the tsars, let there be statues of the leaders of the revolution. His purpose was rather to affirm the Bolshevik idea than to glorify personalities. Everyone had to don ideological garb, the uniform of dehumanized personality, and Lenin and Leninism were the main components of the costume. The deification of the cult figure was the work of the system which he had created and by which he was more needed dead than alive.

Vladimir Ilyich Ulyanov began to use the alias and pseudonym 'Lenin', probably derived from the River Lena in Siberia, at an early stage. His very first writings, in 1893, appeared, unsigned, in mimeo-graphed form. He first used a signature, 'V.U.', at the end of 1893, and then a year later he signed himself 'K. Tulin', a name derived from the town of Tula. In 1898 he used the pseudonym 'Vl. Ilyin' when reviewing a book on the world market by Parvus (Alexander Helphand), translated from German. In August 1900, in a private letter, he signed himself 'Petrov', a name he continued to use in correspondence with other Social Democrats until January 1901, when he signed a letter to Plekhanov with the alias 'Lenin'. He seems not to have settled into this alias straight away, and still went on using 'Petrov' and 'V.U.', as well as his proper name, for some time. He also adopted the name 'Frei' for part of 1901, and in 1902 'Jacob Richter' vied for a while with 'Lenin'. But from June of that year, it appears he became comfortable at last with the name by which the world would one day come to know him.

It is difficult to imagine Lenin as young. We are familiar with the photograph of the chubby little boy and high school student with intelligent eyes, yet he seems to have stepped straight from his youth into mature adulthood. Alexander Potresov, another early collabor-ator, who knew him well at the age of twenty-five, recalled that 'he was only young according to his identity papers. You would have said he couldn't be less than forty or thirty-five. The faded skin, complete baldness, apart from a few hairs on his temples, the red beard, the sly, slightly shifty way he would watch you, the older man's hoarse voice . . . It wasn't surprising that he was known in the St Petersburg Union of Struggle as "the old man".'[2]

It is worth noting that both Lenin and his father lost their consider-able mental powers much earlier than might be thought normal. I am not suggesting a necessary connection, but it is true that both men died of brain disease, his father from a brain haemorrhage at the age of fifty-four, and Lenin from cerebral sclerosis at fifty-three. Lenin always looked much older than his years. His brain was in constant high gear, and he was usually having a 'row' with someone, 'row' being one of his favourite words. It may not be a sign of his genius, but the fact is that, even when he was relatively young, Lenin always looks like a tired old man. Be that as it may, let us look at his origins, his antecedents and his background.

## Genealogy

Simbirsk, where Lenin was born on 23 April 1870, was the small leafy capital of the province of the same name. At the end of 1897 it had a population of 43,000 inhabitants, of whom 8.8 per cent were of gentry (or noble) status, 0.8 per cent clergy families, 3.2 per cent merchants, 57.5 per cent ordinary town-dwellers or lower middle-class, 11 per cent peasants, 17 per cent military and the remaining 2 per cent unclassified. It had two high schools, one each for boys and girls, a cadet school, a religious school and seminary, a trade school, a midwifery school, schools for the Chuvash and Tatar minorities, several parish schools, the Karamzin Library, and the Goncharov Public Library. It had a vodka distillery, a winery, a brewery, a candle factory and flour-mill. There were a number of charitable institutions. Founded on the high side of the middle Volga in 1648 as a defence against nomadic raids, the town was soon transformed into a typical, sleepy, unhurried provincial Russian town.

In time Simbirsk became a Bolshevik shrine, renamed Ulyanovsk. A local historian, Z. Mindubaev, has written that the transformation of the ancient town into a 'grandiose Leninist altar' was accompanied by a 'huge pogrom' which flattened everything. With astonishing mindlessness, the 'builders' tore down ancient churches, cathedrals and monasteries. Even the church where Lenin was baptized was razed, as was a house in which Pushkin had once stayed early in the nineteenth century. The cathedral which had been erected at about the same time in memory of the fallen of Simbirsk in the war of 1812 was cleared in the 1920s to make way for a monument to Lenin. Streets were renamed after Marx and Engels, Liebknecht, Rosa Luxemburg, Plekhanov and Bebel. At the height of the famine of 1921, when the Volga region was ravaged, the local authorities allocated funds for a statue of Marx. The cemetery of the Pokrovsky Monastery was bulldozed to make way for a cosy square, leaving only one grave – that of Lenin's father, Ilya Nikolaevich Ulyanov, with its cross removed.[3]

The twelve-volume 'Biographical Chronicle' of Lenin's life, while it attempts (with little success) to catalogue every fact and account for virtually every waking moment of his life, is extremely laconic about his birth and background: 'April 10 (22 New Style[4]) 1870 Vladimir Ilyich Ulyanov (Lenin) was born. His father, Ilya Nikolaevich, was an inspector and later the director of the province's schools. He came of poor town-dwellers of Astrakhan. His father had been a serf. Lenin's mother, Maria Alexandrovna, was the daughter of a doctor, A.D. Blank. The Ulyanov family lived in Simbirsk (still called Ulyanovsk in late 1994), in a wing of Pribylovskaya's house on Streletsky Street (now Ulyanov Street) No. 17a.'[5] Other information about the family has to be gleaned in fragments from the twelve volumes, most of which consist of references to Lenin 'making plans', or 'destroying his opponents intellectually', reading, writing or making a speech. Consisting of several thousand pages, it is a chronicle that presents the portrait of a political robot, not a human being.

Similar information is to be found in the official biography of Lenin, compiled by a brigade of scholars under P.N. Pospelov. All eight editions of this work, beginning with the first in 1960, can be found in any Soviet library, but it is doubtful if any have ever been consulted voluntarily. The people may have resigned themselves to believing assurances that the Party was in the hands of 'outstanding leaders of the Leninist type', but they always retained the lingering suspicion that this idea was exaggerated. Most people were therefore rather indifferent to the official image of Lenin. Only a few individuals, perhaps while preparing for an exam or writing a dissertation, were actually required to pore over a volume of Lenin's works. As for Party leaders themselves, the majority of those I have known never read a word of Lenin beyond the 'Party minimum'.[6] What was regarded as the proper Leninist text to read was laid down in directives and confidential letters from the Central Committee. They were all being led by a Lenin they did not know.

In order to establish Lenin's genealogy, we have to resort to books published in the 1920s, as well as to foreign publications and a range of Russian archives. The large Ulyanov family had many branches. Lenin's parents married in 1863 in Penza, capital of the province of that name to the west of the lower Volga, where Lenin's father was working as a teacher of physics and mathematics. After a spell in Nizhni Novgorod, in the centre of European Russia, the family moved to Simbirsk. There is almost nothing in the official biographies about

Lenin's grandparents, especially their ethnic origin, not that this would tell us anything about his intellectual capacities, social position or moral qualities. But there has been a great reluctance to discuss the Ulyanov family tree, no doubt because it was felt that the leader of the Russian revolution must be a Russian.

The Russian Empire, however, was a crucible of the most varied national and racial ingredients, as was to be expected in so vast a territory. I dwell on this aspect of Lenin's biography because his ethnic background was carefully covered up to make sure that he was seen to have been, if not of 'proletarian', at least of 'poor peasant' origin. But if the 'Chronicle' was able to show – as it does – that his father's father had been a serf, why was it not possible to reveal the background of his father's mother, and his mother's parents?

Lenin's mother, Maria Alexandrovna, was the fourth daughter of Alexander Dmitrievich Blank, a doctor and a baptized Jew from Zhitomir. He had taken as his patronymic the name of his godfather at his baptism, Dmitri Baranov, dropped his original patronymic of Moishevich, and adopted the Christian name of Alexander in place of his original first name, Srul, the Yiddish form of Israel. According to research done by David Shub and S.M. Ginsburg, Lenin's grandfather was the son of Moishe Itskovich Blank, a Jewish merchant from Starokonstantinov in the province of Volynia, who was married to a Swedish woman called Anna Karlovna Ostedt.[7] Shub asks how a Jew could have become a police doctor, and later the owner of an estate. Referring among other things to the archives of the Holy Synod, Shub concluded that conversion to Orthodox Christianity removed many barriers to a career in state service. 'There were,' he writes, 'baptized Jews in the reign of Nicholas I who occupied far higher positions than police doctor ... Many such Jews were ennobled and thus achieved all the rights and privileges of that class.'[8]

In St Petersburg, Alexander Blank married Anna Grigorievna Groschopf, the daughter of prosperous Germans. The Blanks were evidently well off, since they were able to make several trips to Europe, notably to take the waters in Karlsbad in the Czech part of Austria-Hungary. Alexander Blank worked in various towns and provincial capitals of the Russian interior, for the most part in the Volga region, as district physician, police doctor and hospital doctor, finally occupying the prestigious post of hospital medical inspector of the state arms factory in Zlatoust, in the province of Chelyabinsk, Western Siberia. In 1847, having attained the civil service rank of State Counsellor, he retired and registered himself as a member of the nobility of Kazan, a major city on the Volga and centre of Tatar culture in the region. There he bought the estate of Kokushkino.[9] This had been made possible by the large dowry his wife had brought with her. Anna Grigorievna never learned to speak fluent Russian and never abandoned her Lutheran religion. In Kokushkino she would raise five daughters: Anna, Lyubov, Sofia, Maria (Lenin's mother) and Yekaterina.

Kokushkino was not the 'smallholding' of the official biographies, but was rather a small landowner's estate where, until 1861, Blank owned serfs. This normal feature of the time was something Soviet historians were never allowed to mention. It was a busy, well populated place, and Blank was evidently a strong-willed and rather impulsive man. He was obsessed with the idea that hydrotherapy was a panacea, and wrote a book on it, stating that 'water inside and out' could sustain everyone in good health. He used to make his tearful daughters wrap themselves in wet sheets for the night, with the result that they couldn't wait to grow up and marry to escape their father's crazy experiments.

Anna Groschopf died young, and after her death her sister, Yekaterina, came to Kokushkino to take on the job of raising the children. She was an educated woman, and it was from her that Lenin's mother acquired her ability to play the piano, to sing and to speak German, English and French. A frequent visitor to Kokushkino was Karl Groschopf, Yekaterina's brother and a senior official in the department of foreign trade. His visits would occasion musical evenings, and the Blank girls were much attracted to their educated and exuberant uncle. Life on the estate was very much that of a typical, moderately well-off landowning family, with a strong German cultural tinge, thanks to the Groschopf connection. Unlike his Soviet biographers, Lenin never tried to hide his 'landowner' origins; indeed in April 1891 he signed an order inscribing his mother in the gentry register of Simbirsk province.[10] And at the end of his exile in 1900, when he applied to the police department to allow his wife, Nadezhda Krupskaya, to serve out the remainder of her own term of exile in Pskov, he signed himself 'hereditary nobleman Vladimir Ulyanov'.[11] Lenin's origins on his mother's side were far from 'proletarian', a fact which underlines the absurdity of the Bolshevik practice of evaluating a person by their social class. This criterion reached grotesque proportions in the 1920s and 1930s, when people even committed suicide on discovering a 'bourgeois' or 'landowner' skeleton in their past. The Party leaders were, of course, excused as a 'revolutionary exception'.

Lenin's paternal lineage was plainly plebeian, and the 'Biographical Chronicle' makes much of the fact that his grandfather had been a serf. But this was not actually true. Lenin's grandfather, Nikolai Vasilievich, was a Russian town-dweller[12] of Astrakhan who earned his living as a tailor. He was the son of a serf, but at an early age had been released to work away from the village, and had never returned home, becoming a town-dweller – as distinct from a peasant, merchant or nobleman – by social status. It was Lenin's great-grandfather, Vasili Nikitich Ulyanov, who had been a serf.[13] He had remained single until he turned fifty, and it was only then, having saved up some money, that he married. His bride, who was almost twenty years his junior, was Anna Alexeevna Smirnova, a baptized Kalmyk, whose ethnic origin was responsible for Lenin's somewhat Asiatic appearance. Five children resulted from this late marriage: Alexander, Vasili, Ilya (Lenin's father), Maria and Feodosia. Ilya was the youngest child, and was born when his father was already past sixty and his mother was forty-three. His father died in 1836, leaving his wife, the five-year-old Ilya (Alexander had died in infancy), and his two daughters to his seventeen-year-old son, Vasili, to look after.

Vasili rose to the occasion and displayed exemplary enterprise, becoming a salesman for Sapozhnikov Brothers, a large commercial firm in Astrakhan. His willingness to work and his loyalty earned his employers' trust, and he was able to look after his mother and younger brother, supporting Ilya through his studies at Kazan University until he became a teacher of mathematics, sending him money 'for settling down', 'for the wedding', 'for the move' and so on. Vasili, a bachelor all his life, and a diligent and enthusiastic salesman, may also have sent his cash assets to Ilya shortly before he died at a date historians have been unable to establish.[14]

It would not be worth dwelling on the Ulyanov family tree had the official picture not been so obscured by a mass of unnecessary trivia and painted in the colours of 'class consciousness', and had so much not been passed over in silence, distorted and blatantly falsified. A brief account, however, may suffice to show that Lenin's background reflected the face of the entire empire. He had a general idea about his origins, but, although he was Russian by culture and language, his country was not his highest value – not that he particularly felt himself to be a German, a Swede, a Jew or a Kalmyk. He may have described himself as a Russian when filling in forms, but in his outlook he was an internationalist and cosmopolitan, for whom the revolution, power and the Party were to be immeasurably more precious than Russia itself. It is only important to clarify this matter because the Bolsheviks found it necessary to suppress evidence of the perfectly natural mixture of nationalities in Russia in order to present their leader as ethnically 'pure'.

Lenin's antecedents were Russian, Kalmyk, Jewish, German and Swedish, and possibly others, symbolizing Russian history, as it were: a Slavic beginning, Asiatic expansion, a Jewish accretion to the national intellect, and German or West European culture. Genetic selection in history is spontaneous and mysterious. But here a digression is called for. When Lenin died, the Central Committee Secretariat commissioned his elder sister, Anna Yelizarova, to collect all the materials she could find and to write a definitive account of the Ulyanovs. Anna, who was one of the founders of the Lenin Institute, set to work, and soon discovered what I also found: namely, that there was a mass of material in the St Petersburg police department archives about her mother's descent, as well as other materials which M.S. Olminsky, chairman of the Commission for the Study of the History of the Party (*Istpart*), helped her locate. Some eight years later she had still not divulged her discoveries to anyone. But in 1932, two years before she died, she suddenly revealed her findings to Stalin, and said she wanted to publish them. She knew that her grandfather, Moishe Itskovich Blank, had been born in Starokonstantinov, that his two sons, Abel and Srul, had converted to Christianity and changed their names to Dmitri and Alexander, and that in 1820 both had been admitted into the St Petersburg Medical-Surgical Academy, from which they graduated in 1824.[15]

In her letter to Stalin, Anna wrote: 'It's probably no secret for you that the research on our grandfather shows that he came from a poor Jewish family, that he was, as his baptismal certificate says, the son of

"Zhitomir *meshchanin* Moishe Blank".' She went on to suggest that 'this fact could serve to help combat anti-semitism'. Paradoxically for a Marxist who believed in the primacy of environmental over inherited factors, she also asserted the dubious proposition that Lenin's Jewish origins 'are further confirmation of the exceptional abilities of the Semitic tribe, [confirmation] always shared by Ilyich [Lenin] . . . Ilyich always valued the Jews highly.'[16] Anna's claim explains, for instance, why Lenin frequently recommended giving foreigners, especially Jews, intellectually demanding tasks, and leaving the elementary work to the 'Russian fools'.[17] According to General A.A. Yepishev, former chief of the army's main political directorate, who heard it from Stalin's personal assistant Poskrebyshev, Anna's sister Maria handed the letter to Stalin and waited while he read it carefully. His response was categorical and fierce: 'Absolutely not one word about this letter!' But a little over a year later, Anna approached Stalin again, asserting that 'in the Lenin Institute, as well as in the Institute of the Brain . . . they have long recognized the great gifts of this nation and the extremely beneficial effects of its blood on the progeny of mixed marriages. Ilyich himself rated their revolutionary qualities highly, their "tenacity" in the struggle, as he put it, contrasting it with the more sluggish and unstable character of the Russians. He often pointed out that the great [attributes of] organization and the strength of the revolutionary bodies in the south and west [of Russia] arose precisely from the fact that 50 per cent of their members were of that nationality.'[18] But Stalin, the Russified Georgian, could not allow it to be known that Lenin had Jewish roots, and his strict prohibition remained firmly in place.

In November 1937, the writer Marietta Shaginyan published an article in the Moscow journal *Novy mir* as the first part of her research into the genealogy of the Ulyanovs. Somehow the article went unnoticed, but in 1938 she published her work as a novel based on fact, entitled *The Ulyanov Family*, and dealing with the origins of the family up to the birth of Lenin. The reaction was harsh. The book was first read by a small group of senior members of the Soviet Writers' Union, who condemned it as an 'ideologically dangerous' work of 'petty bourgeois' character. A month later, on 9 August 1938, the presidium of the Union convened and passed a resolution which declared that 'in applying pseudo-scientific research methods to

Lenin's so-called "family tree", M.S. Shaginyan gives a distorted representation of the national character of Lenin, the greatest proletarian
revolutionary, a genius of mankind, who was raised up by the Russian
people and who is its national pride'.[19] Those responsible for writing,
publishing and distributing the book were dealt with severely. In 1972,
all documents on Lenin's origins, 284 pages in all, were transferred
from the various archives which held them to the Central Committee
special collections, where they remained.

The German branch of Lenin's family tree is also interesting.
According to Leonhard Haas, the Swiss historian and former director
of the Swiss Federal Archives, the Groschopfs, all of whom were
wealthy bourgeois, came from northern Germany and could boast
several notable personalities throughout German history: Lenin's
great-grandfather, J.G. Groschopf, was a representative of Schade, a
German trading company. Other ancestors and descendants of Lenin's
forebears include I. Hoeffer, a well-known theologian; Ernst Curtius,
the tutor of Kaiser Friedrich III; and Field Marshal Walter Model,
who earned the title of 'the Führer's Fireman' as an audacious commander in the Wehrmacht's assault on Moscow in 1941.[20] The
Swedish branch, who were mostly artisans – wigmakers, hatters, tailors
– issued from a rich jeweller, one K.F. Estedt, who lived in Uppsala
and supplied the court of King Gustavus IV in the late eighteenth
century.

Having settled in Simbirsk in 1869, the Ulyanovs lived the life of
most civil service families or bourgeoisie of the period. Like most
provincial towns at that time, social life in Simbirsk was not especially
stimulating. Trade and commerce were the dominant activities, while
various educational and cultural establishments provided spiritual and
intellectual nourishment. Both Ulyanov parents, however, had high
aspirations for their children, and their efforts left their mark.
Vladimir, who was born in April 1870, had two brothers and three
sisters: Anna (born 1864), Alexander (1866), Olga (1871), Dmitri
(1874) and Maria (1878). Another brother, Nikolai, born in 1873,
died in infancy, and another sister, also called Olga, died at birth in
1868. (The second Olga died at the age of twenty.) Lenin's mother
did not attend university, but was nevertheless well educated, thanks
to the efforts of her aunt, Yekaterina Groschopf. Much has been
written about the education of Lenin and his siblings, some of it

accurate, but also much that is sugar-coated and exaggerated. Some authors have almost suggested that Lenin's genius emerged while he was still in nappies. I do not intend to recount the domestic life of the family in detail, but to pick out some salient features that are sometimes missed.

The young Vladimir – invariably known in the family as Volodya – was a gifted and capable child, qualities enhanced by the comfortable, supportive atmosphere of the home, thanks to his father's successful career. The family lived in a good house, the three eldest children each had a room of their own, there was a cook, a nanny, and servants to deal with the domestic chores. Lenin himself recalled that the family lacked for nothing. An outstanding teacher and advocate of state education, his father rose to become director of the province's schools in a few years. He was well regarded by the authorities and was awarded several decorations, including the Order of Stanislav, First Class, finally achieving the rank of State Counsellor, corresponding on the Table of Ranks to the title of general. Having become a hereditary noble through his service career, he thus conferred the same privileged status on his family. The Ulyanovs' life was stable and secure – until, that is, Ilya Nikolaevich died in 1886, and, out of the blue, the eldest son, Alexander, was arrested and hanged in the following year.

Volodya was always top of his class, but he showed none of the 'revolutionary free-thinking' described by many of his biographers. It is surely one of the most striking ironies of modern Russian history that the headmaster of his high school should have been Fedor Mikhailovich Kerensky, father of the future 'hero' of the February revolution of 1917 who was to be the last obstacle to the Bolshevik seizure of power in October. Kerensky *père* often publicly expressed his admiration for the ability and diligence shown by Volodya Ulyanov. Volodya, meanwhile, was acquiring a strong intellectual foundation as a result of family support and encouragement from his teachers. He was also acquiring deep self-confidence and a sense of superiority over his peers. He was the family favourite, accustomed to being the centre of attention. Not that he was vain, but neither did he conceal his moral 'right' to the primacy he believed was his, and even at that early stage he seems to have shown intolerance of other people's views.

One of Alexander's school friends, V.V. Vodovozov, recalled that he realised, after visiting the Ulyanovs, that it would he impossible to become a close friend of Vladimir, whom he thought rude in argument, excessively self-confident and self-important, and puffed up by being thought a genius within the family and an infallible authority outside it.[21]

## Vladimir and Alexander

Lenin's intellectual and political self-definition still lay in the future, but one of the most decisive landmarks along the way was the fate of his brother Alexander. The age difference of four years between Alexander and Volodya meant that, as children, the younger boy very much looked up to his elder as a superior being, a hero figure, a rôle which Alexander evidently played with relish. Alexander, moreover, as the eldest child, and perhaps the brightest, also set a pattern of behaviour and activity at home that was bound to encourage his juniors to do their best intellectually: in his teens he edited a family weekly to which everyone was expected to contribute.[22] The sudden and traumatic removal of such an admired and loved member of the family was bound to have a powerful effect on the lives of the others.

The execution of Alexander was a tragedy that struck at the entire family. In the young Lenin, it sparked a surge of rebellion, although it was not as literal and direct as post-revolutionary myth would have us believe. It was customary among Soviet historians to quote the words he is reported to have uttered to his sister Maria, then aged all of nine, when news of Alexander's execution reached the family: 'No, we will not go that way. That's not the way.'[23] According to the official accounts, the fate of Lenin's brother 'reinforced his revolutionary views'.[24] He may well have spoken those words to his little sister, but the fact is that at this age he held no revolutionary views whatsoever, and he could not have distinguished one revolutionary 'way' from another.

The death of his father, undoubtedly a major tragedy and economic disaster for the family, has also been depicted in official Soviet literature as an event of ideological significance in the life of the young

Lenin. Most writers followed Nadezhda Krupskaya's clumsy assertion of 1938 that Lenin's father's views exerted a revolutionary influence on his children: 'As a teacher, Ilya Nikolaevich read Dobrolyubov with particular interest. Dobrolyubov conquered the honest heart of Ilya Nikolaevich and defined his work as schools director and as the mentor of his son, Lenin, and his other children, all of whom became revolutionaries.'[25] This is far from the truth.

A well educated, cultivated man of his time, Ilya Ulyanov was also deeply pious and rather conservative. His eldest daughter, Anna, recalled that he 'had never been a revolutionary and wanted to protect the young from that way of thinking. He much admired Alexander II whose reign, especially its first phase, was for him "a bright period".'[26] The 1860s had been a period of 'great reforms', when the serfs had been emancipated, a measure of local self-government introduced in the provinces, the judiciary allowed to become a free professional corporation, universities and schools expanded and given greater autonomy: in a word, Russia had been launched on a path of reform in the general direction, if not of liberal democracy, then at least of social modernization. The climate of reform, combined with the government's fear of going too far, too fast, also gave rise to a revolutionary movement, whose members – mainly students – felt that nothing would change fundamentally for the better unless the whole political structure was demolished, or at least the tsar was removed. To support the reformist trend was to be progressive, to oppose it reactionary, and to dismiss both sides of the argument revolutionary. Ilya Ulyanov definitely belonged to the first category.

Ilya's youngest daughter, Maria, also attested to his civic loyalty: '[He] was not a revolutionary, and we don't know enough to say what his attitudes were to the revolutionary activities of the young.'[27] It would, however, be safe to assume that, as a teacher with a profound sense of vocation, he did much to create a democratic, humane atmosphere in the household. The harmony between husband and wife, their concern for the children, the equality between the siblings, the culture of hard work and diligence, all helped to form an extremely favourable soil for the seeds of free thinking, should they fall there. Ilya Ulyanov, in other words, created the preconditions for his children, above all Alexander and Vladimir, to be receptive to radical ideas. Ilya Ulyanov did not make Lenin a revolutionary; he and his wife merely cultivated in their children the ability to change, to feel the need for change. When Lenin's father died in January 1886, Vladimir was not yet sixteen.

Even before she had buried her husband, Maria Ulyanov applied for a pension for herself and her children, and a little later asked the Kazan schools district for a special grant. From now on she would live only on her pension and the rent from Kokushkino, of which she was a joint owner. In September 1886 the Simbirsk district court confirmed that Ilya's estate should pass to Maria and her children.

In April 1887, when Lenin reached the age of seventeen, he registered for military service,[28] but as he was now the eldest son and potential breadwinner, he was exempted.[29] He was not in fact the family breadwinner. On the contrary, thanks to his mother's pension, and with her strong encouragement, he pursued his studies.

If it was the family culture that created the preconditions for Lenin to become radically minded, it was the fate of his brother Alexander that provided the catalyst. It is doubtful if Alexander's tragic end changed Lenin's revolutionary direction, since there was none to change. Vladimir's supposed words to his sister on hearing of his brother's execution also raise a question. 'No, we will not go that way.' Why 'we'? He belonged to no secret society or circle. Perhaps Maria misremembered his words after so many years, or perhaps the heavy weight of Soviet experience suggested the words to her mind. In any case, it is hard, in purely human terms, to believe that Vladimir's response to the news of his brother's death would prompt him to pronounce the slogan that would make him forever a 'proper' revolutionary.

Alexander was a gifted youth, as the gold medal he attained on graduating from high school indicated. At school he had shown an interest in zoology and acquired three European languages, and at St Petersburg University, which he entered in 1883, he quickly became one of the top students. A month before his father's premature death he won the University gold medal for work on annelid worms. Nothing indicated that he had been seized by the forces of social protest.

In his first years at university, Alexander was indifferent, if not sceptical, towards the political circles, but he became more involved when friends introduced him to the writings of Marx, Engels and

Plekhanov. For them, Marxism emphasized the need for violence to change the existing conditions. One of the more radical members of the group, P. Shevyrev, declared that only by the removal of tyrants could life be reorganized on just principles. At first Alexander, who was wrapped up in his scientific plans and discoveries, merely listened, but gradually he was won over by the apparent logic of his friends' radicalism, and came to feel it was morally unacceptable to stand aside from 'the ideas of progress and revolution', as they put it.

While Alexander was at university his contacts with Vladimir were sporadic, limited to the occasional letter with greetings to all. And when he came home on vacation, there was no particular intimacy between them. They were a close-knit family, but the children tended to pair off, and Vladimir was closest to his sister Olga, though he deferred to Alexander's intelligence. Anna, the eldest sister, recalled once talking with Alexander after their father had died, and asking him: 'How do you like our Volodya?' Her brother replied: 'He's obviously very gifted, but we don't really get on.' Anna was intrigued, but Alexander refused to explain.[30] This may be the only hint in all the apologist literature that relations between the siblings might not have been entirely flawless.

The 1880s in Russia were a time of harsh reaction against the assassination in 1881 of the 'tsar-liberator', Alexander II. Students in particular were more closely watched and harassed by the police than ever before, and Alexander's entry into a group of conspirators who were planning the assassination of Alexander III is commonly explained by the violent dispersal by the police of a student demonstration in memory of the radical thinker Dobrolyubov on 17 November 1886. The arrest and deportation to Siberia of several student friends confronted Alexander with the moral question of how to behave in such circumstances. According to Shevyrev's view: 'When the government takes our closest friends by the throat, it is especially immoral to refuse to struggle, and under the present circumstances real struggle with tsarism can only mean terrorism.' Of this dilemma Nikolai Valentinov, an early Bolshevik who knew Lenin well during the time of his first period abroad, between 1900 and 1905, and a valuable historical source in himself, wrote: 'Painfully sensitive to suggestions of immorality, Alexander, after agonizing hesitation, began to share these views, and once he did so, he became an advocate of systematic, frightening terrorism, capable of shaking the autocracy.'[31]

The group of conspirators under Shevyrev's leadership grew. Their watch on the tsar's route from the palace to St Isaac's Cathedral began on 26 February 1887, but they were utterly inexperienced, and when on 1 March the police intercepted a letter from one of them, the entire group was arrested. The Ulyanov family was devastated, but placed their hope in the emperor's clemency. Alexander's mother rushed to St Petersburg and handed in a letter to Alexander III which said, among other things, that she would purge her son's heart of its criminal schemes and resurrect the healthy human instincts he had always lived by, if only the tsar would show mercy.

The drama caught the attention of society, and received much publicity. Maria Ulyanova's entreaties failed, however, not only because of the tsar's intransigence, but because Alexander refused to ask for clemency. Those who found it possible to do so had their death sentences commuted to hard labour. The trial was very short, lasting only from 15 to 19 March. Five unrepentant comrades were sentenced to hang. Even when Alexander was saying goodbye to his mother there was still the chance of salvation, but he told her in a quiet, firm voice, 'I cannot do it after everything I said in court. It would be insincere.' Alexander's lawyer, Knyazev, was present at this meeting, and after the October revolution he recalled that Alexander had explained: 'Imagine, Mama, two men facing each other at a duel. One of them has already shot at his opponent, the other has yet to do so, when the one who has shot asks him not to. No, I cannot behave like that!'

Alexander had proved himself to be extraordinarily brave. His last wish was that his mother should bring him a volume of Heine to read. On the morning of 8 May 1887 the prisoners were told they were to be hanged in the courtyard of Shlisselburg Fortress in two hours' time. This was their last chance to appeal for clemency, but even now these young people, misguided as history may judge them to have been, proved themselves morally worthy of the nation's memory. They were not fanatics, they believed that their country's future could only be altered by revolutionary acts against tyrants. Alexander's group seemed then and seems now naive, but it is impossible not to admire their willingness to sacrifice their lives in the name of freedom.

The day Alexander was hanged, Vladimir was doing his geometry and arithmetic exams, for which he got his usual top marks. The family still believed the widespread rumour that the death sentence would be commuted at the last minute. His mother's last words to him were, 'Be brave, be brave.'[32] She was in deep mourning for a long time, comforted perhaps by the fact that, as she told her children, before his execution Alexander had bowed before the cross and so would receive God's forgiveness.

Vladimir Ulyanov was shaken by his brother's death. Later he would learn that Alexander had had a hand in formulating the programme of the Narodnaya Volya (People's Will) terrorist faction, a document bearing the stamp of Marxist influence, but simplistic and 'barracks-minded'. Still reeling from the shock of the family tragedy, Vladimir was, however, less concerned with the young terrorists' ideas than with the stoicism and strength of will they had shown. The sharp turn that now took place in his mind was not about methods of struggle – terror or a mass movement. He still had no views on this issue. But, somewhere in the depths of his mind, the soil was now prepared for the notion that nothing would be achieved on the way to revolution without radicalism, plus the will to succeed, and it was this that became the nucleus of his outlook. His remark 'We will not go that way' meant – if he said it – that he realized it was not necessary to be a bomb-thrower oneself, like the unfortunate Alexander, nor was it necessary to man the barricades oneself, or put down rebellion oneself, or go to the front in a civil war oneself. And he never would do any of these things himself. The action of individual units was not important. The main thing was to command huge, virtually unwitting masses. It was a more effective way, if less noble than Alexander's.

## The Forerunners

The list of those who have been proposed as Lenin's ideological precursors is long, and it starts with the radical nineteenth-century philosopher Nikolai Chernyshevsky. Arrested in 1862 for seditious agitation, Chernyshevsky was to spend the next twenty years in prison and in

Siberian exile, where he served seven years of hard labour. Before his deportation from St Petersburg, however, he managed in 1864 to write his novel *What is to be Done?* and to have it smuggled out and published. It was to inspire an entire generation of Russian youth with ideas of self-emancipation and the duty to bring knowledge to the peasants. Other suggested early sources of Lenin's revolutionary awakening include various Populist thinkers and Plekhanov's Marxist 'Emancipation of Labour' Group. It is interesting to note what Lenin himself thought of the origins of his political thinking. In an essay on Lenin in 1933, Karl Radek, a brilliant pamphlet-writer and juggler of paradoxes, wrote: 'When Vladimir Ilyich once saw me looking at a collection of his 1903 articles . . . his face lit up with a cunning grin and he said with a chuckle, "Interesting to see what fools we were." '[33]

The sources of Lenin's political outlook were complex, and there can be no argument about the formative effect of his brother's death, which sent a ray of white light through the prism of his mind, a ray which, to paraphrase Winston Churchill, was refracted by that prism into red.[34] The 'prism' was in fact a constellation of circumstances. The first of these was the government's treatment of Vladimir and his family. When Lenin entered Kazan University in 1887, he went with a glowing testimonial from his headmaster in Simbirsk, Fedor Kerensky, who wanted to protect him from adverse association with his brother's notoriety: 'Neither in school nor outside did Ulyanov ever give occasion, either by word or deed, to arouse an unfavourable opinion among the school authorities or his teachers.'[35] Even when Lenin was expelled from the university in the December of his first year for taking part in a student demonstration, Kerensky, both to defend the young man and to justify his confidence in him, wrote: '[Vladimir Ulyanov] might have lost the balance of his mind as a result of the fatal catastrophe that has shattered the unhappy family and, no doubt, has also influenced the impressionable youth disastrously.'[36] But on the first occasion when Lenin attended a student meeting, during his first term at the university, he had already been 'marked' by the authorities.

The administrator of the Kazan educational region noted that, two days before the demonstration took place, 'Ulyanov was up to no good: he was spending his time in the smoking-room, chatting and whispering . . .' It seems that the 'demonstration' amounted to little

more than running up and down a corridor,[37] but in view of the fact
that he was the brother of a condemned 'state criminal', Ulyanov was
not merely expelled but also sent away from Kazan to the family estate
at Kokushkino.

By labelling him as unreliable and suspect, the expulsion effectively
excluded the young Lenin from the state educational system
altogether. When his mother applied for him to be reinstated at
Kazan, the Director of the Police Department in St Petersburg, P.N.
Durnovo, noted, 'We can scarcely do anything for Ulyanov.'[38] The
Director of the Education Department was more emphatic: 'Isn't this
the brother of *that* Ulyanov? He's also from Simbirsk high school.
Yes, it's clear from the end of the document. He should certainly not
be admitted.'[39] By thus ostracizing him, the tsarist authorities were
steadily narrowing Lenin's range of choices. His solidarity with his
dead brother became more firmly fixed. The letters he wrote, in which
he respectfully requested 'Your Excellency's permission to enter the
Imperial Kazan University', or had 'the honour most humbly to
request Your Excellency to allow me to go abroad to a foreign university', and which he signed 'Nobleman Ulyanov', were at first unsuccessful.[40] The spirit of protest grew as the regime rejected him.

Expulsion did not mean Lenin now had to earn his living as a
docker or shop assistant, like his grandfather. He was 'exiled' to
Kokushkino, and the family then moved to their farm at Alakaevka,
about thirty miles from Samara. His mother acquired the property of
some two hundred acres in early 1889 for the sum of 7500 roubles.
Lenin now immersed himself in reading a wide range of Western and
Russian social-political literature, including Marx's *Capital*. The police
kept their eye on him, but he gave them no trouble. Apart from
attending an illegal meeting and occasionally seeing some Marxists,
it is difficult to find any evidence of the so-called 'revolutionary period
in Samara'. It would be more accurate to describe this time as one
of intensive preparation for the examinations to enter St Petersburg
University as an external student. By the time he reached the age
of twenty-two, Lenin had acquired a first-class diploma from
St Petersburg and been accepted as a lawyer's assistant on the Samara
circuit. He was not destined to succeed at this profession and he soon
cooled towards the busy life of a defence attorney. The few cases he
was given to handle were only petty thefts or property claims, and he

accomplished even these with variable success, although he did defend his own interests twice, winning on both occasions. In one case he sued his peasant neighbours for damage to the Ulyanov estate, and, much later, during a period of residence in Paris, he sued a vicomte who ran him over when he was riding his bicycle. His legal career was not something Lenin was ever keen to recall.

Returning to the question of his revolutionary roots, the time at Kokushkino was one of intensive study of the widest range of ideas. In conversation with Valentinov in 1904 in Geneva – one of the many European cities where he spent seventeen years as an émigré, with a brief interval back in Russia during the 1905 revolution – Lenin recalled reading non-stop from early morning until late at night. His favourite author was Chernyshevsky, whose every word published in the journal *Sovremennik* he read. 'I became acquainted with the works of Marx, Engels and Plekhanov,' he stated, 'but it was only Cherny-shevsky who had an overwhelming influence on me, beginning with his novel *What is to be Done?*. Chernyshevsky's great service was not only that he showed that every right-thinking and really decent person must be a revolutionary, but something more important: what kind of revolutionary, what his principles ought to be, how he should aim for his goal, what means and methods he should employ to realize it . . .'[41]

Valentinov suggests that it was Chernyshevsky, who had in Lenin's own words 'ploughed him over' before he had read Marx, who made the young man into a revolutionary. It is a view contested by the Menshevik writer Mark Vishnyak, who pointed out that Lenin read Chernyshevsky a month or two after the execution of his brother, and therefore 'the soil was ready for ploughing over', and it was the news of that event, Vishnyak claimed, that gave Lenin the charge he had needed, not Chernyshevsky's 'talentless and primitive novel'.[42] These two views boil down to the same conclusion, namely that Chernyshev-sky was Lenin's John the Baptist thanks to the tragedy of Alexander.[43] Chernyshevsky, whatever else Lenin took from him, made it possible for the young man to absorb a profound hostility towards liberalism, as one of his earliest works (1894) shows. 'Who are the "friends of the people" and how do they fight against the social democrats?' was published (unsigned) in mimeographed form in St Petersburg, and in it Lenin repeatedly cited Chernyshevsky and called his judgments 'the foresight of genius', while the 'loathsome' compromise of the 'liberals and landowners' could only hamper 'the open struggle of the classes' in Russia.[44] He wanted to use Chernyshevsky's writings in his attacks on the liberal bourgeoisie, particularly in order to expose the existence of 'an entire chasm' between the socialists and the democrats.[45]

In effect, Lenin used Chernyshevsky to 'russify' Western Marxism, which had too much of the liberal and democratic and too little 'class war'. The split that was to take place among the Russian social democrats would be precisely over attitudes to democracy, to legal, parliamentary means of struggle, to the place of political parties in a democracy and the strength of liberal persuasion. Lenin's forebears were, thus, those thinkers who fostered notions which reinforced the coercive, harsh, class elements in Marxism. It would therefore be true to say that Lenin was guided by pragmatic considerations in becoming a revolutionary. While worshipping classical Marxism, he could borrow concepts and ideas, arguments and rebuttals from Chernyshevsky, Peter Tkachev, Sergei Nechaev, Mikhail Bakunin, Carl Clausewitz, Peter Struve, Peter Lavrov and Alexander Herzen. He reinforced his 'mainline' Marxism with everything that made that teaching uncompromising, harsh and radical. Recalling the first weeks of the Soviet regime, Krupskaya wrote: 'Closely studying the experience of the Paris Commune, the first proletarian state in the world, Ilyich remarked on the pernicious effect of the mild attitude of the workers and proletarian masses and the workers' government towards their manifest enemies. And therefore, when speaking about struggling with enemies, Ilyich always "tightened the screws", so to speak, fearing the excessive mildness of the masses, as well as his own.'[46]

The presence of Nechaev among the names of Lenin's sources should give pause. Both Marx and Engels had condemned Nechaev's doctrine of individual terror – just as Lenin himself would on numerous occasions. But Nechaev was more than an advocate of terror, he was synonymous with conspiratorial politics, entailing secret plans for the overthrow and merciless extermination of hated authorities and governments. In the terminology of the time, such tactics were called Blanquist, after Louis Auguste Blanqui, a radical activist in France during the 1830s and 1840s. While condemning this approach, Lenin would unhesitatingly resort to it at decisive moments. As Plekhanov wrote in 1906: 'From the very beginning, Lenin was more of a

Blanquist than a Marxist. He imported his Blanquist contraband under the flag of the strictest Marxist orthodoxy.'[47] The Bolshevik Vladimir Bonch-Bruevich recalled Lenin discussing Nechaev, who had been depicted by Dostoevsky in his novel *The Possessed*, which fictionalized the murder of a student by Nechaev and his 'Secret Reprisal' group: 'Even the revolutionary milieu was hostile to Nechaev, forgetting, Lenin said, "that he had possessed a special talent as an organizer, a conspirator, and a skill which he could wrap up in staggering formulations."' He also approvingly quoted Nechaev's reply to the question of which of the Romanovs should be killed: 'The entire House of Romanov!'[48]

Vladimir Voitinsky, an economist and active Bolshevik in 1905, recalled discussing Lenin's abandonment of liberalism in conversations at the time. Lenin used to talk about the need to combat 'liberal pompous triviality'. 'Revolution,' Lenin would say, 'is a tough business. You can't make it wearing white gloves and with clean hands ... The Party's not a ladies' school ... a scoundrel might be what we need just because he is a scoundrel.'[49] Nechaev's famous dictum, 'Everything that helps the revolution is moral. Everything that hinders it is immoral and criminal,' was echoed by Lenin at the III Congress of Communist Youth in 1919 when he said that everything is moral that promotes the victory of Communism. In 1918 he declared to Maria Spiridonova, the *doyenne* of terrorists and a member of the Socialist Revolutionary Party, that there was no room for morality in politics, only pragmatism.

Lenin adopted Marxism as a weapon, 'freeing' it of its 'liberal', 'democratic' trivialities, because the steel fist of the proletarian dictatorship had no need of gloves. Following the Bolsheviks' forcible dispersal of the Constituent Assembly in January 1918, Plekhanov, 'the father of Russian Marxism', could write in his last article: 'The tactics of the Bolsheviks are the tactics of Bakunin, and in many cases those of Nechaev, pure and simple.'[50] The question of who were Lenin's ideological forebears, therefore, is answered simply: he used anything and anyone if it helped him achieve his aim.

## The Discovery of Marxism

There may be many reasons why Lenin became captivated by Marxism. In my opinion, his powerful and already extremely well informed mind was searching for a universal explanation of human existence. In any event, some time on the eve of 1889, when the family was still living in Kazan, he got hold of the first volume of *Capital*. It must have been a revelation simply in terms of the scale of its grasp, regardless of its rôle in history. Hegel once remarked on the 'attraction of the distance', and for the young Lenin, with his radical outlook, *Capital*'s historical distance captured his imagination, seeming to lead to the solution to all of life's eternal and 'accursed' questions of justice, freedom, equality, oppression and exploitation. But who introduced Lenin to Marxism?

At the time he was expelled from university, there was a convinced young Marxist, called Nikolai Fedoseev, living in Kazan. Lenin was to meet him only once, nearly ten years later, when they were both on their way to exile in Siberia. Fedoseev had compiled a reading list for social democrats, and Lenin told Gorky in 1908, when they were together on Capri, that 'it was the best reference book anyone had yet put together', and that it had helped him find his way through political literature, opening the path for him to Marxism.[51] Lenin's first known writing was a piece written in 1893 called 'New Economic Movements in Peasant Life', in effect a review of V.E. Postnikov's book *The South Russian Economy*.[52] The article, which was unsigned, read like a schoolboy's attempt at Marxist analysis. There is little of Lenin's own ideas in it and it was rejected by the journal, *Russkaya mysl'*. He had greater success with a second review-article, also written in 1893 and similarly unsigned, called 'On the So-called Question of Markets', in which he contrasted Marxist and Populist (Narodnik) ideas on the development of capitalism in Russia, in effect arguing that 'class' and impersonal historic need had replaced the 'critically thinking individual'. This article was also not published, but Lenin read it at a meeting of Marxist students in St Petersburg in the autumn of 1893, and received the praise of the engineering students present.

Lenin soon went beyond the guidelines of Fedoseev's catalogue, and it is evident from his earliest, as well as his later, works that two main ideas in Marxism dominated his thinking: classes and class struggle, and the dictatorship of the proletariat. No other Marxist theorist took these concepts as far as Lenin, despite the fact that Marx had said very little about the dictatorship. As a social democrat, Lenin did not limit himself to commenting on and recapitulating the interpretations given by Marx and Engels, but formulated his own 'classical' definitions. For instance, on rural poverty, he asked, 'What is the class war?' and gave the answer, 'It is the struggle of one part of the people against another, the mass of the rightless, oppressed and toiling against the privileged, oppressing and parasitic, it is the struggle of the workers or proletarians against the owners or the bourgeoisie'.[53] Like so many other thinkers and revolutionaries, Lenin would fall into the trap of thinking that it was only necessary to take everything from the 'haves' and redistribute it 'fairly' and all would be well. It was the eternal mirage. As the philosopher Nikolai Berdyaev observed: 'Many times in history the lower orders have risen up and tried to sweep away all hierarchical and qualitative differences in society and to install mechanical equality . . . But class is quantity and man is quality. Class warfare, elevated to an "idea", conceals the qualitative image of man . . . Thus the idea of class kills the idea of man. This murder is carried out theoretically in Marxism . . .'[54]

The context in which Lenin acquired his Marxism was the debate with romantic Populism. In one of his early works, 'What is the Legacy we are Rejecting?', he rightly criticized N.K. Mikhailovsky, one of the leading exponents of liberal Populism, for the Populist refusal to accept capitalism in Russia and for the Populist idealization of the peasant commune.[55] One can already detect in this article echoes that will soon become a hallmark of Leninist usage – 'rubbish', 'slander', 'trivial trick' – often as a substitute for real argument. It seems never to have occurred to Lenin to ask himself whether the dictatorship of the proletariat was compatible with the justice Marxism cherished as a fundamental idea. By what right should one class unconditionally command another? Could such a dictatorship achieve priority over the highest value, namely liberty?

Such questions did not trouble the young Lenin. When he accepted Marxism it was finally and irrevocably. He never questioned the sociopolitical concept of the doctrine, which was based in the last analysis on coercion as the solution to all contradictions in the interests of

one class. He was never troubled by the viciousness and narrowness
of this way of building the new society. It was not therefore surprising
that when he became the ruler of that new society, his main preoccupation was with the punitive organs, the Cheka (the political police)
and the State Political Administration, or GPU. Indeed, reading the
minutes of Lenin's Politburo after the seizure of power, it quickly
becomes clear that there was scarcely a session that did not review
measures for tightening the dictatorship of the proletariat – that is,
the dictatorship of the Party – by widening the powers of the punitive
bodies, legislating terror, ensuring the immunity of the new caste of
'untouchables' and the class 'purity' of its members. Thus, on 14 May
1921 the Politburo, with Lenin's active encouragement, adopted a
decision to widen the powers of the Cheka 'in the use of the highest
form of punishment', i.e. the death penalty;[56] in January 1922 a further
step was taken to strengthen the punitive function of the dictatorship
and the guarantee of the 'class line' by the creation of the GPU, whose
chief task was to struggle against counter-revolution using the widest
range of physical and psychological force. And the courts 'must include
people chosen by the Cheka'.[57]

As for the way these bodies were to act, Lenin himself set the style.
When a cipher arrived from the Red Army in the Far East in August
1921 announcing the arrest of Baron Ungern von Sternberg, one of
the leaders of the White forces in the Trans-Baikal region, Lenin
personally raised the question of a trial at the Politburo. Naturally
there were no objections, and he merely had to dictate the Politburo
resolution as that of the highest Party tribunal: 'The accusations must
be sound, and if the proof is conclusive and beyond doubt, then a
public trial should be set, conducted with the greatest despatch, and
[Ungern] should be shot.'[58] So much for a 'trial'!

Nikolai Fedoseev could never have dreamed that the young man
he met briefly in a station waiting-room in Siberia in 1897, as their
paths into exile crossed, would turn out to be a major figure in
twentieth-century history. The correspondence between the two men
leaves no doubt that it was Fedoseev who had, however imperceptibly,
given Vladimir Ulyanov another shove in the direction of revolution.
When Lenin heard in the summer of 1898 that Fedoseev had killed
himself at Verkholensk in Eastern Siberia, he was genuinely saddened.
The death of the exile was embellished by romantic tragedy when his

fiancée, Maria Gofengauz, living at Archangel in forced settlement, and with whom Lenin was acquainted, also killed herself. Lenin often recalled Fedoseev warmly. Gorky wrote that on one occasion, when Fedoseev was mentioned, Lenin became animated and said excitedly that if he'd lived, 'he'd no doubt have been a great Bolshevik'.[59]

For Lenin, Marxism meant above all one thing, and that was revolution. It was the revolutionary message of the doctrine that attracted him in the first place. He absorbed its ideas and propositions as a convinced pragmatist, and was less interested in the early humanistic writings of Marx and Engels than he was in those concerned with the class struggle. He plunged into the Marxist world of categories, laws, principles, legends and myths, and regarded Plekhanov with reverence, which may explain why the ideas he drew from Marxism were free of a purely 'Western' vision of historical evolution. He was entranced by Plekhanov's *On the Monistic View of History*, published under the pseudonym of N. Beltov, a book in which, Potresov wrote, the author 'brought the ten commandments of Marxism down from Mount Sinai and handed them to the Russian young', and, as Nicolaevsky echoed, 'introduced the Russian intelligentsia, above all the students, who were the avant-garde of the revolutionary army at the time, to undiluted revolutionary Marxism'.[60] Plekhanov wrote that 'Chernyshevsky never missed an opportunity to mock the Russian liberals and to state in print that . . . he . . . had nothing in common with them. Cowardice, short-sightedness, narrow views, inactivity and garrulous boastfulness, these were the distinguishing features he saw in the liberals'. Plekhanov had taken as the epigraph for his book an extract from a letter Chernyshevsky had written to his wife in October 1862 when he was in the Peter-Paul Fortress in St Petersburg: 'Our life together belongs to history: in hundreds of years from now our names will still be dear to people, and they will remember them with gratitude . . .'[61] Lenin must have felt an affinity with these words. He was not vain or ambitious, he simply believed in his historic mission. Plekhanov's works brought Lenin still closer to Chernyshevsky, and finally led him to the social democratic Bible, the works of Marx.

Plekhanov and Lenin would part in due course for reasons usually ascribed to differences over organization. I believe that this was a secondary cause, and that the real reason for their split was over attitudes to liberty. As early as the end of the century, Lenin, like

Chernyshevsky before him, was already defining the main enemies of the working class as liberalism and so-called 'Economism', a sort of Russian trade unionism which encouraged the workers to organize and fight for a better economic life, while the intelligentsia would struggle for their political and civil rights. In Lenin's view, and that of his followers, the liberals and 'Economists', by leading the workers away from political struggle, were denying them the opportunity to aim for socialist revolution. The Marxism preached by Lenin and the Bolsheviks had no place for liberalism and 'Economism', which in fact held the key to democratic change in Russia. To the end of his life, Lenin was therefore sympathetic to the early Plekhanov and openly hostile to the later one, who was to call Lenin's 1917 policy 'delirious'. It is interesting to note that when in April 1922 the Politburo discussed the publication of Plekhanov's works, Lenin insisted that only one volume be compiled, and only of his early, 'revolutionary' writings.[62]

If Lenin was not fond of late Plekhanov, he positively hated the Plekhanov of the revolutionary era. Plekhanov had seen through Lenin, he understood the essence and the danger of his line. In his 1910 article 'A Comedy of Errors', published in his *Dnevnik sotsial-demokrata*, he wrote that 'only Lenin could have gone so far as "to ask myself in which month we should begin the armed uprising . . ."'. Lenin's plans, which boiled down to a seizure of power, Plekhanov called utopian.[63] And indeed, as soon as the Bolsheviks had power in their hands, they quickly forgot many of their slogans and promises. Power for Lenin was the goal and the means to bring about his utopian designs.

While absorbing Marxism from the writings of the doctrine's founders, Lenin also took up ideas from a wide range of thinkers and writers, a fact suggesting perhaps a developed ability to comprehend and, by applying his own 'ferment', to absorb, digest and make those ideas his own. He was, however, never able to assimilate the ideas of the liberals, who proclaimed the rule of law, or the 'Economists', who wanted the workers to flourish, or the Western democrats, who put parliamentary government above all else. Lenin's 'discovery' of Marxism was thus extremely selective; he saw in it only what he wanted to see. Even Trotsky, who after October 1917 and to the end of his days described himself as a Leninist, criticized Lenin at the turn of the century for his lack of 'flexibility of thought', his belittling of the

rôle of theory, which could lead to a 'dictatorship *over* the proletariat'.[64]

By the turn of the century Lenin had acquired the conviction that,
as far as his opponents were concerned, his theoretical position was
unassailable, and henceforth he exhibited a rare hostility to everything
that would not fit the Procrustean bed of his preconceptions. In a
letter to Maxim Gorky in 1908 – the famous writer was a major
benefactor of the revolutionary movement and had a close, if complex,
relationship with Lenin after 1907 – on the philosophical work of the
Bolshevik Alexander Bogdanov, Lenin wrote: 'After reading it, I got
into a rage and became unusually furious: it became clear to me that
he has taken an arch-wrong path.' He went on: 'I became frenzied
with indignation.' What had made him so angry was that the Bolsheviks might draw their teaching on the dialectic 'from the putrid
well of some French "positivists" or other'.[65] His Marxism was, however, plainly one-sided, Blanquist, super-revolutionary. Like a man
'with the truth in his pocket,' Viktor Chernov, leader of the Socialist
Revolutionaries, wrote, 'he did not value the creative search for truth,
he had no respect for the convictions of others, no feeling for the
freedom that is integral to any individual spiritual creativity. On the
contrary, he was open to the purely Asiatic idea of making the press,
speech, the rostrum, even thought itself, the monopoly of a single
party which he raised to the rank of a ruling caste.'[66]

Marx and Engels were theorists. Lenin turned their teaching into
a catechism of class struggle. As the writer Alexander Kuprin observed:
'For Lenin, Marx was indisputable. There isn't a speech in which he
does not lean on his Messiah, as on the fixed centre of the universe.
But there can be no doubt that if Marx were to look down from where
he is on Lenin and his Russian, sectarian, Asiatic Bolshevism, he would
repeat his famous remark, "Excuse me, monsieur, but I am no
Marxist." '[67]


## Nadezhda Krupskaya

Russian social democrats subordinated the moral side of their political
programmes to the practical interests of the moment. Vera Zasulich,

a leading member of the Russian social democratic movement, once remarked that Marxism had 'no official system of morals'.[68] The proletariat and everyone who called themselves socialists valued above all solidarity and loyalty to the ideal: 'Whatever serves Communism is moral.' The Communists – the author of these lines included – saw wisdom of the highest order in this precept, not a fundamentally immoral approach which could be used to justify any crime against humanity along with the most trivial political malpractice. Such justification was made not only in the midnight of the Stalin era, but in the earlier years of the Soviet regime, and the later.

In November 1920, at the height of the civil war in Russia, the head of the Cheka, Felix Dzerzhinsky, informed Lenin that '403 Cossack men and women, aged between fourteen and seventeen, have arrived without documentation in Orel from Grozny to be imprisoned in the concentration camp for rebellion. They cannot be accommodated as Orel is overcrowded.'[69] Lenin was not moved to halt the crime against 'men and women aged between fourteen and seventeen', and merely wrote 'For the archives' on the document, thus establishing the tradition that, no matter how callous, cruel and immoral an act of the regime might be, it would be recorded and stored in the archives for a history that would never be written as long as that regime lasted. The doctrine of force as a universal means was sufficient justification for such laconic gestures. From an early stage, Lenin had surrounded himself with people who were receptive to such an approach, energetic, bold and capable people whom he taught to be morally indiscriminate. The domestic Lenin was, however, rather different. Alexander Potresov, who saw him at close quarters between 1895 and 1903, wrote that 'at home Lenin was a modest, unpretentious, virtuous family man, engaged in a good-natured, sometimes comic, daily war with his mother-in-law, the only person in his immediate environment who could stand up to him'.[70]

Throughout his life, Lenin's family circle consisted mostly of women: mother, sisters, wife and mother-in-law. In the absence of any children of his own, he himself was the constant object of their care and concern. He differed from his Party comrades in his puritanical restraint, steadiness and constancy, and would have been a model husband, had it not been for the ten-year relationship he began in 1910 with a lively woman revolutionary called Inessa Armand.

In none of the mass of writing about Lenin is there any mention of an affair of the heart in his youth. It appears that his preoccupation with books and revolutionary dreams left no room for the normal feelings that usually occupy the mind of any young man. There is no broken first marriage, no stormy romance, no love at first sight, no unhappy love affair. Yet there was something like an undying love. When he returned to St Petersburg in January 1894, Lenin established contacts, legal and illegal, with the local Marxists. With little to do, he was free to spend time with his new acquaintances. One day in February, at the apartment of an engineer called Klasson, a group of Marxists gathered in the cosy sitting-room, among them two young women, Apollinaria Yakubova and Nadezhda Krupskaya. At first, Lenin spent time with both of them, then he started visiting Nadezhda's home on the Nevsky Prospekt on a more regular basis. Nadezhda lived with her mother, Yelizaveta Vasilievna, the widow of an army officer whose career had been cut short when he was cashiered for reading Chernyshevsky and Herzen, and who apparently belonged to the revolutionary organization Land and Freedom. He had been dismissed and even put on trial, then after several years of indecision was exonerated, but banned from public service. When he died, the family had moved to St Petersburg, where they lived on his pension. Nadezhda taught at a Sunday evening school for workers.

Her mother made tea while the young people talked about Plekhanov, Potresov, the book the young man – who was already quite bald – was writing, the need to establish contact with European social democrats. We do not know what Yelizaveta thought of her future son-in-law, except that she remained independent of him all her life, and was known to have been openly critical of 'people who don't do any real work'.[71] The clever young man kept appearing at the apartment, but he seemed more interested in politics than in Nadezhda.

Lenin was also friends with Apollinaria Yakubova, and sometimes the three of them would go out together. When he was arrested in December 1895 for being part of a Marxist propaganda circle – an almost routine event for men of Lenin's cast of mind at the time – both young women tried to visit him at the pre-trial prison on Shpalernaya Street. Lenin wrote Nadezhda a coded message, saying they should walk past the prison at 2.15 so that he could catch a glimpse of them through the window.[72] It is difficult to establish the nature of the relations between these three young people, especially as the almost hundred-year-old 'conspiracy' about this area of their lives has destroyed almost any trace.

Apollinaria was a teacher, like Nadezhda, and a Marxist, and Lenin apparently proposed to her, but was rejected in favour of K.M. Takhtarev, the editor of the journal *Rabochaya mysl'*.[73] Also like Nadezhda, she was exiled to Siberia in 1896. She and Lenin maintained a correspondence, notably when Lenin was in Munich after 1900 and she was in London, in which he reminded her of their 'old friendship',[74] and they met several times in London in 1902 and 1903, where he was then living and working on his Party newspaper, *Iskra*. There is some evidence that, before Lenin became acquainted with Inessa Armand, he had an affair with a Frenchwoman in Paris. When Viktor Tikhomirnov, a researcher from the Marx-Engels-Lenin Institute, met the ex-Bolshevik émigré G.A. Alexinsky in Paris in 1935 to discuss some Lenin documents, Alexinsky showed him letters of an extremely personal nature that Lenin had written to a woman writer, and which the recipient preferred not to send to Moscow as long as Krupskaya was still alive. She was then living on a Soviet pension which she had been receiving via Dzerzhinsky and later Menzhinsky, successive heads of the Soviet secret police.[75] The letters remained in Paris and their whereabouts are now unknown.

Exile to remote parts of Siberia was the usual punishment for a wide range of activities regarded as seditious by the government, whether taking part in a Marxist study circle or fomenting a strike and joining a demonstration. After a series of interrogations in prison in the capital, therefore, Lenin was exiled for three years to Siberia under police surveillance in February 1897. He soon began to correspond with Krupskaya. At the same time, his mother launched a campaign of requests to the police on her son's behalf, starting with an application to allow him to travel at his own expense, because of his poor state of health, followed by one asking them to delay his departure from the capital, then for him to stay in Moscow for a week as she herself was ill, then to extend his stay there, and so on. She also wrote to the governor-general of Eastern Siberia asking him to 'allocate Krasnoyarsk or one of the southern towns of Yenisei province' as her son's place of exile, again because of his poor state of health. Lenin reinforced her efforts on his own behalf, advancing the same reason.[76] All of their requests, except one, were conceded by the 'blood-stained tsarist regime'.[77] Lenin would not be so lenient when he came to power, even where former social democrat comrades were involved. In a note to Stalin dated 17 July 1922, he proposed that a number of them, including Potresov, be expelled from the country forthwith: '. . . several hundred of such gentlemen should be put across the border without mercy . . . Get the lot of them out of Russia.'[78] He believed in general that 'repressions against the Mensheviks should be stepped up and our courts should be told to do this'.[79]

How his attitudes had changed! Exile in Shushenskoe had been little more than an enforced three-year vacation. He had thought it normal to request a nicer place to live 'in view of my poor health', nobody made him do any work, he was under no restraints. Many other exiles, Julius Martov, for instance, thought it beneath their dignity as revolutionaries to beg for favours or a nicer place. Lenin, however, for all his 'poor state of health', wrote home to the family that 'apart from hunting and swimming, most of my time is spent on long walks'.[80] He was also sleeping 'extraordinarily long', and although it was 'impossible to find [domestic] help, and unthinkable in the summer', he was 'satisfied with the apartment and the food', had 'filled out and got a suntan', and was living 'as before, peacefully and unrebellious'. He compared his present abode favourably with Spitz, the Swiss resort where the family was then on holiday.[81]

The life of a political exile under the tsar was immeasurably easier than that installed by the Soviet regime, whose prisoners first had to build their own camps and then fill them. The tsar's exiles – we are not speaking of prisoners, but of those expelled from European Russia and made to remain in a designated place for a period – could pay each other visits in different locations, arrange meetings, write books and political programmes, entertain their relations and even start families. In July 1897, for example, Lenin received an invitation to attend the wedding of his friends V.V. Starkov and A.M. Rozenberg, the sister of the Marxist organizer G.M. Krzhizhanovsky. Perhaps it was such an event that prompted the correspondence between Lenin and Nadezhda Krupskaya, who by then was herself in exile, for the same offence, in Ufa in the southern Urals. In January 1898, Lenin applied to the police department to allow his 'fiancée', Krupskaya, to continue her exile in Shushenskoe. Krupskaya recalled that she also requested transfer to Shushenskoe, 'and for that reason I said I was his "fiancée"'.[82] While a large number of Nadezhda's letters to Vladimir seem to have been preserved, his letters to her appear not to have been.

At the beginning of May 1898, after a long journey by rail, boat and horse-drawn transport, Krupskaya arrived in Shushenskoe with her mother, who would accompany the couple wherever fate despatched them. According to Lenin, his future mother-in-law had barely set eyes on him before she exclaimed, 'They really wanted you well out of the way, didn't they?'[83] He wrote to his mother that Nadezhda had 'imposed a tragi-comic condition: if we don't get married *right away* (!), she's off back to Ufa. I'm not at all disposed to go along with this, so we've already started having "rows" (mostly about applying for the papers without which we can't get married).'[84]

There were a number of formalities to be observed. Lenin applied to the Minusinsk district prefect and then to higher provincial authorities for the necessary papers, but old Russia had more than its fair share of bureaucracy, and nearly two months passed before the papers arrived. Nadezhda's mother insisted they have the full religious ceremony, and despite the fact that Lenin was by now twenty-eight and Nadezhda a year older, and that both of them were long-standing atheists, they felt compelled to submit. Lenin invited a few exile-friends to the wedding, and on 10 July 1898 the modest ceremony took place, witnessed by two local peasants called Yermolaev and Zhuravlev. Congratulatory greetings arrived from Apollinaria, who was in exile near Krasnoyarsk. Also, on the very day of the wedding, the couple received a letter from Y. M. Lyakhovsky with the news that Fedoseev had committed suicide in Verkholensk, and had wanted Lenin to know that he had done so not with disappointment, but 'wholehearted faith in life'.[85] Another letter arrived soon afterwards with the news that Fedoseev's fiancée had also killed herself.

The Ulyanovs' marriage, a union of two mature people, was itself mature, practical, quiet and devoid of either passionate love or emotional upheavals. Unlike her mother, Nadezhda was an obliging, even-tempered and balanced woman. Exceptionally intelligent and hard-working, she at once assumed her rôle as assistant to the man who was working hard, through his writing and contacts, to establish himself as a dominant force in the Russian Marxist revolutionary movement while still in Siberian exile. After the wedding, the couple moved from the house of a certain A.D. Zyryanov to that of a peasant woman called A.P. Petrova. Lenin's work on his first major book, *The Development of Capitalism in Russia*, began to make more rapid progress. Between jaunts on the river, hunting and walking in the forest, he consumed a vast amount of economic, philosophical and historical literature, which was sent to order by his mother, Potresov and Pavel Axelrod, a close associate of Plekhanov's. The first book he read in Shushenskoe was *The World Market and the Agricultural Crisis* by Alexander Helphand, who wrote under the alias of Parvus, and who would emerge in a far more significant rôle in Lenin's life in later years.

Nadezhda settled straight away into serving as her husband's work-mate, helping him select material, rewriting passages, listening as he read her some of his chapters, though rarely offering critical comment. They were destined to be childless, though neither apparently ever confided their disappointment to anyone. Perhaps there was a clue in the letter he wrote to his mother from Pskov, having left Shushenskoe and Nadezhda temporarily: 'Nadya must still rest: the doctor found, as she wrote to me a week ago, that her (woman's) illness requires sustained treatment and that she must rest for 4–6 weeks (I sent her more money, I got 100 roubles from Vodovozova), as the treatment is going to cost quite a bit.'[86] Later, when they were abroad, Nadezhda contracted exophthalmic goitre, or Graves' Disease, and had to undergo surgery. Lenin, again writing to his mother, reported that 'Nadya was very poorly, very high temperature and delirium, and it gave me quite a scare'.[87] It is worth noting, perhaps, that between them, all of the Ulyanov siblings produced only two children – Dmitri had a son and a daughter, Olga, who is still alive at the time of writing (1994). Nadezhda says nothing about this in her memoirs, although occasionally she allows the pain of her personal unfulfilment to break through when describing the lives of others. She commented, for instance, that Vera Zasulich, with whom she was extremely close and who lived alone, missed not having a family: 'She had an enormous need for a family. One had only to see how lovingly she played with Dimka's fair-haired little boy.'[88] 'Dimka' was Lenin's brother Dmitri, the sole parent of his generation of Ulyanovs.

Krupskaya's prominent place in Soviet history is, obviously enough, explained by the fact that she was Lenin's wife. It might be argued that she also played a part in her own right, as witnessed by the eleven editions of her collected writings on education that were published by 1963. But all of her ideas on Communist education were based on her husband's comments, and do not merit special attention. Her memoirs, however, do have historical value, especially when she is dealing with Lenin's last years and his illness. Her notes entitled 'The last six months of the life of V.I. Lenin', read together with the memoirs of Lenin's sister Maria, give the fullest account of that fateful period, and draw aside the veil on many hitherto unknown details, though neither of these women could reveal everything they knew, and their most informative reminiscences remained under lock and key in the Party archives.[89]

The marriage which began without strong love became closer over the years, but Nadezhda was in effect Lenin's shadow, her life having meaning only because she was linked to him. When they went abroad, she soon adapted to the leisurely pace her husband set, as the letters Lenin wrote to his mother between 1900 and 1914 indicate: 'I still follow my summer style of life, walking, swimming and doing nothing'; from Finland he wrote: 'The rest here is wonderful, swimming, walks, no people around, nothing to do. Having no people around and nothing to do is best of all for me'; from France: 'We're going to Brittany for a holiday, probably this Saturday'; from Poland to his mother in Vologda: 'It's already spring here: the snow's all gone, it's very warm, we go without galoshes, the sun's shining especially bright above Cracow, it's hard to think that this is "wet" Cracow. Too bad you and Manyasha [Maria] have to live in that miserable dump!'[90]

## Inessa Armand

The telegram lay on the desk in front of Lenin, but he seemed unable to grasp its message, and had to read it several times: 'Top priority. To Lenin, Sovnarkom, Moscow. Unable to save Comrade Inessa Armand sick with cholera STOP She died 24 September [1920] STOP

Sending body to Moscow signed Nazarov.'[91] The shock was all the greater because earlier that very day Ordzhonikidze, his emissary in the Caucasus, had told him that Inessa was fine, when Lenin had asked him to see that she and her son were being taken care of. Nor could he forget that it had been at his insistence that she went to the south for a rest. She had wanted to go to France, but he had dissuaded her. It was so absurd, so senseless. Why hadn't the doctors been able to help? Why cholera? He was shattered. As Alexandra Kollontai, a senior Bolshevik who knew them both well, said later: 'He could not survive Inessa Armand. The death of Inessa precipitated the illness which was fatal.'[92]

Lenin had no close friends. It would be hard to find someone, apart from his mother, for whom he showed greater concern than Inessa Armand. In his last letter to her, around the middle of August 1920, he had written:

Dear friend,

I was sad to learn that you [he addressed her formally as *Vy*] are overtired and not happy with your work and the people around you (or your colleagues at work). Can't I do something for you, get you into a sanatorium? I'll do anything with great pleasure. If you go to France I will, of course, help with that, too: I'm a bit concerned, in fact I'm afraid, I'm really afraid you could get into trouble . . . They'll arrest you and keep you there a long time . . . You must be careful. Wouldn't it be better to go to Norway (where many of them speak English), or Holland? Or Germany as a Frenchwoman, a Russian (or a Canadian?). Best not to go to France where they could put you inside for a long time and are not even likely to exchange you for anyone. Better not go to France.

I've had a marvellous holiday, got tanned, didn't read a line or take a single phone call. The hunting used to be good, but it's been all ruined. I hear your name everywhere: 'Things were all right with them here,' and so on. If you don't fancy a sanatorium, why not go to the South? To Sergo [Ordzhonikidze] in the Caucasus? Sergo will arrange rest, sunshine, interesting work, he can fix it all up. Think about it.

He signed off conventionally as 'Yours, Lenin'.[93]

Lenin had been hearing Inessa's name everywhere because he was close to the Armand family estate in the village of Yeldigino in Moscow province. What there was to hunt in August is unclear.

On the same day he wrote, as head of the Soviet government: [To whom it may concern] 'I request that you help in every way possible to arrange the best accommodation and treatment for the writer, Comrade Inessa Fedorovna Armand, and her elder son. I request that you give complete trust and all possible assistance to these Party comrades with whom I am personally acquainted.'[94] He also cabled Ordzhonikidze, asking him to put himself out over Inessa's safety and accommodation in Kislovodsk, and ordered his secretaries to help see her off to the Caucasus. Although Russia was still enduring the civil war, the Bolshevik leadership were accustomed to frequent holidays. Hence Lenin could insist on the fateful trip.

For a decade, since they had met in Paris in 1909, Inessa Armand had occupied an enormous space in the life of a man whose dedication to the Great Idea left little or no room for anything else. She had succeeded in touching chords hidden deep in his near-puritanical heart. He had felt a constant need to be with her, write to her, talk to her. His wife did not stand in their way. As Alexandra Kollontai recalled in the 1920s, in conversation with her colleague at the Soviet legation in Norway, Marcel Body, Krupskaya was 'au courant'. She knew how closely 'Lenin was attached to Inessa and many times expressed the intention of leaving', but Lenin had persuaded her to stay.[95]

This appears to have been one of those rare triangles in which all three people involved behaved decently. Feelings of attachment and love do not readily lend themselves to rational explanation. If Lenin's life was filled with the turbulence of politics and revolutionary activity, on the personal level it had been monotonous, flat, boring. Inessa entered his life in emigration like a comet. It is pointless to speculate what it was about her that attracted him. She was extremely beautiful, elegant and full of creative energy, and that was perhaps enough. Also, she was open and passionate about everything she did, whether it was caring for her children or the revolution or the routine Party jobs she was asked to do. She was an exceptional person, emotional, responsive and exciting. For all his old-fashioned views on family life, Lenin was unable to suppress the strong feelings she evoked in him. For the historian, however, it is as difficult to write about feelings as it is to try to convey in words the sound of a symphony.

In her later memoirs, Krupskaya often refers to Inessa, but usually in passing and in another context: 'Inessa's entire entourage lived in her house. We lived at the other end of the village and ate with everyone else'; 'Vladimir Ilyich wrote a speech, Inessa translated it'; 'all our people in Paris were then feeling strongly drawn to Russia: Inessa, Safarov and others were getting ready to go back'; 'It was good to be busy in Serenburg. Soon Inessa came to join us'; 'Our entire life was filled with Party concerns and affairs, more like student life than family life, and we were glad of Inessa.'[96] To Krupskaya's credit, having once decided the tone of her relationship with Inessa, as a Party comrade, she never changed it. Inessa's presence was an inevitability which she accepted with dignity. Occasionally, she abandons her own conventions and writes in greater detail: 'For hours we would walk along the leaf-strewn forest lanes. Usually we were in a threesome, Vladimir Ilyich and Inessa and I . . . Sometimes we would sit on a sunny slope, covered with shrubs. Ilyich would sketch outlines of his speeches, getting the text right, while I learned Italian . . . Inessa would be sewing a skirt and enjoying the warmth of the autumn sunshine.'[97] It was perhaps during such walks that Inessa would talk about her origins, her parents and the dramas in her life.

She was born, according to the register of the 18th arrondissement, in Paris at 2 p.m. on 8 May 1874 at 63, Rue de la Chapelle, and was named Inessa-Elisabeth. She was the daughter of Theodore Stephan, a French opera singer aged twenty-six, and an English-French mother, Nathalie Wild, aged twenty-four, of no profession. Her parents were not married at the time of her birth,[98] but they legalized their relationship later at St Mary's parish church in Stoke Newington, London. Inessa's father died young, leaving his family of three small daughters penniless. Her mother became a singing teacher in London. The turning point in Inessa's life was a trip to Moscow in 1879 with her grandmother and aunt, who taught music and French, and who together were capable of giving the girl a good education. The archives tell us little about her life, and the best Russian account so far to emerge is Pavel Podlyashchuk's *Tovarishch Inessa*, first published in 1963 and revised with new material in 1987. This has been superseded by Ralph Carter Elwood's *Inessa Armand: Revolutionary and Feminist*, published in 1992.

A gifted young woman, fluent in French, Russian and English, and an excellent pianist, Inessa became a governess. She took after her handsome father in looks, attracting the attention of a good many men, and in October 1893, at the age of nineteen, she married Alexander Evgenievich Armand, the son of a wealthy merchant. The wedding took place in the village of Pushkino, outside Moscow, in the presence of members of Moscow's business élite, to which the Armands themselves belonged.[99]

Everything seemed as it should in a successful, wealthy family. Inessa had a handsome, good husband, children, trips to the South and abroad. In the course of eight years she gave birth to five children, three boys and two girls. Despite her preoccupation with her family, she managed to read a great deal and was drawn to the social and political writings of Lavrov, Mikhailovsky and Rousseau. By the late 1890s she had also become seriously concerned with feminist issues, an interest she retained all her life. To all appearances, she was living in harmony with her husband, when suddenly, on the eve of the 1905 revolution, she left him, taking the children with her. She had been consumed by passion for another man, her husband's younger brother Vladimir.

Everyone suffered in this great family drama, yet there were apparently no dreadful scenes, mutual recriminations or arm-twisting. Inessa was exercising her commitment to the principle of 'free love'. Two weeks before she died in 1920 she would confide to her diary: 'For romantics, love occupies first place in their lives, it comes before everything else.'[100] By this time she had come to see love with different eyes, but she was recalling herself as a younger woman, when her dramatic departure from the marital home shifted her life onto a completely unexpected course.

Her life with the young Vladimir did not last long. Since 1903 she had become involved in illegal propaganda activities on behalf of the Russian Social Democratic Labour Party in Moscow, and in 1907 she was arrested (for the third time) and exiled to the North above Archangel. Vladimir followed her, but he soon developed tuberculosis and went to Switzerland for treatment. There was, however, no cure to be found, and two weeks after she had fled from exile abroad to join him, at the beginning of 1909, he died.

With the financial help of her ever-tolerant husband, who was also caring for the children, Inessa, now aged thirty-five, enrolled to study economics at the New University in Brussels. In the same year, in Paris, she met Lenin, whose name was well known to her, as a member of the Party since 1903, and thereafter for a decade she occupied a special place in his life, as the voluminous correspondence between them shows. The official version has always insisted that their friendship, although personal, was essentially one of Party comrades, lacking any suggestion of intimacy. Unofficially, it was always believed that Lenin was simply 'obliged' to love only Krupskaya, and would never have lowered himself to the rôle of adulterer.*

We have already seen that the Party leadership learned in the 1930s that there was a female acquaintance of Lenin's in Paris who possessed a number of his intimate letters to her, which she would not consent to have published while Krupskaya was alive. This woman had been receiving a generous pension from the Soviet government, thanks entirely to her earlier friendship with Lenin.

While many of Lenin's letters to Armand concerning Party matters have been published, those of a more intimate nature appear either to have vanished or to have suffered cuts at the hands of his editors. The following lines were removed from a letter he wrote to her in 1914: 'Please bring when you come (i.e. bring with you) all our letters (sending them by registered mail is not convenient: a registered letter can easily be opened by friends. And so on . . .) Please bring all the letters, come yourself and we'll talk about it.'[102] In this letter Lenin used the familiar form of address, *ty*. This period was the peak of their friendship, and it is most likely that he wanted Inessa to bring him the letters so he could destroy them. Inessa's Western biographer, Carter Elwood, is of the opinion that Lenin may have wanted her to bring the letters because they contained potentially embarrassing comments about fellow Bolsheviks.[103] Whatever the reason, there can be little doubt that theirs was a uniquely close friendship.

Krupskaya was Lenin's loyal comrade, his uncomplaining wife and dedicated helper. As well as Graves' Disease she had a weak heart, which was perhaps one reason why she was childless. The writer Ilya

---

* For decades the Party archives also concealed evidence that both Marx and Engels fathered illegitimate children – Marx by his housekeeper Elena Denmuth.[101]

Ehrenburg is reputed to have said: 'One look at Krupskaya, and you can see that Lenin wasn't interested in women.' This was not so. It is quite possible, moreover, that what Ehrenburg found unappealing might have brought Lenin warm comfort. In any event, once Lenin met Inessa, they were virtually inseparable. She followed the Ulyanovs everywhere, always finding lodgings nearby and meeting both Lenin and Krupskaya frequently. She became almost an integral part of their family relations, and, as Alexander Solzhenitsyn has noted perceptively, Krupskaya saw her task as ensuring Lenin's peace of mind by always giving Inessa a warm and friendly reception.[104]

Lenin and Inessa shared a deep feeling. They had their secrets, as Inessa herself wrote from Paris in December 1913 in a letter which, naturally, remained hidden in the archives as utterly unsuitable for the Party's propaganda purposes. The Ulyanovs had been living in Cracow in Austrian Poland since October, remaining there until May 1914. The letter was a very long one, and we reproduce only extracts from it here. She uses the familiar form throughout:

Saturday morning.

My dear, Here I am in Ville Lumière and my first impression is one of disgust. Everything about the place grates – the grey of the streets, the over-dressed women, the accidentally overheard conversations, even the French language ... It was sad that Arosa was so temporary, somehow transitory. Arosa was so close to Cracow, while Paris is, well, so final. We have parted, parted, you and I, my dear! And it is so painful. I know, I just feel that you won't be coming here. As I gazed at the familiar places, I realised all too clearly, as never before, what a large place you occupied in my life, here in Paris, so that all our activity here is tied by a thousand threads to the thought of you. I wasn't at all in love with you then, though even then I did love you. Even now I would manage without the kisses, if only I could see you, to talk with you occasionally would be such a joy – and it couldn't cause pain to anyone. Why did I have to give that up? You ask me if I'm angry that it was you who 'carried out' the separation. No, I don't think you did it for yourself.

There was much that was good in Paris in my relations with

N.K. [Krupskaya]. In one of our last chats she told me I had
become dear and close to her only recently . . . Only at
Longjumeau and then last autumn over the translations and so
on. I have become rather accustomed to you. I so loved not
just listening to you, but looking at you as you spoke. First of
all, your face is so animated, and secondly it was easy for me
to look at you because you didn't notice . . .

In the last part of the letter, marked 'Sunday evening', Inessa writes
at length about a forthcoming lecture she is to give, and asks:

When you write to me about business matters, give me some
indication of what the KZO [the Committee of Russian Social
Democratic Party Organizations Abroad] may talk about and
what it may not . . .

   Well, my dear, that's enough for today, I want to send this
off. There was no letter from you yesterday! I'm rather afraid
my letters are not reaching you – I sent you three letters (this
is the fourth) and a telegram. Is it possible you haven't received
them? I get the most unlikely ideas thinking about it. I've also
written to N.K., to your brother, and to Zina [Zinaida Lilina,
the wife of Zinoviev]. Has nobody received anything? I send
you a big kiss.
   Your Inessa.[105]

The tone, eloquence and content of this letter leave little doubt about
the nature of Inessa's feelings. Her remark that she would be satisfied
if she could just see Lenin, and that 'it couldn't cause pain to anyone',
places a question mark over Lenin's reasons for leaving Paris in June
1912. Plainly Inessa's presence in the Ulyanov family orbit had at first
met Krupskaya's natural resistance. The fact that the three-cornered
relationship was not a simple one is evidenced by the frequent cuts
in the letters made by various Soviet editors, tasked with maintaining
Lenin's purity. Many of these excised parts have simply vanished. Not
all of them, however.
   Lenin's letter to Inessa of 13 January 1917, when he was still in
Switzerland, was published in volume 49 of the fifth edition of his
works. Following the words, 'Dear friend,' the following lines were
removed: 'Your latest letters were so full of sadness and evoked such

gloomy thoughts in me and aroused such feelings of guilt, that I can't come to my senses . . .'[106] The letter goes on in the same vein. Plainly, Lenin the puritan found the bond, which went well beyond platonic friendship, a hard one to bear. For Inessa too, accustomed as she was to yielding completely to her emotions, the secrecy and deceit were unbearable.

There are many such cuts in the 'complete' works. A week after the above letter, on 23 January 1917, Lenin wrote again:

Dear friend
    . . . Apparently the lack of reply to several of my latest letters indicates – in connection with something else – a certain changed mood, a decision, your situation. At the end of your last letter a word was repeated twice. I went and checked. Nothing. I don't know what to think, whether you are offended at something or were too distracted by the move or something else . . . I'm afraid to ask, as I know you don't like questions, and so I've decided to think that you don't like being questioned and that's that. So, I'm sorry for [the questions] and won't repeat them, of course.[107]

This rigmarole could only be understood by the two people concerned, and plainly they had to take Krupskaya's presence into consideration.

Lenin's sojourn in Cracow was terminated on 26 July (8 August) 1914 when he was arrested in Nowy Targ on suspicion of spying. The authorities quickly released him, however, when a number of social democrats, notably Victor Alder in Vienna, but also Feliks Kon and Yakov Ganetsky, interceded, explaining that he was a sworn enemy of tsarism, with which Austria was now at war. Lenin's two weeks in Austrian police custody became in Soviet historiography an act of vast revolutionary importance, for he was alleged to have spent the time 'reflecting on the tasks and tactics now facing the Bolshevik Party; talking to imprisoned peasants, giving them legal advice on how to expedite their cases, writing requests and statements for them and so on'.[108]

The Austrians did not yet realise that Lenin would become their ally. He hated both tsar and Kaiser, but, as he wrote to one of his trusted agents, Alexander Shlyapnikov, in October 1914, 'tsarism is a hundred times worse than kaiserism'.[109] Yet even what they already knew about him prompted the Austrian authorities to cable the Nowy Targ prosecutor to 'free Vladimir Ulyanov at once'.[110] Within a couple of weeks Lenin and Krupskaya were in Zurich and shortly after in Berne, where Lenin was soon reunited with Inessa. According to the official version, he suggested she give lectures, 'work to unite the left socialist women of different countries', helped her prepare a publication for women workers, and even 'criticized her outline of the brochure', appointed her to take part in the International Socialist Youth Conference, and gave her a host of Party missions to perform. This version does not, however, report that she was a frequent visitor at the Ulyanovs, that they often went for walks together, that she played the piano for Lenin, and that she joined the couple on holiday in Serenburg.

It was here in Switzerland in March 1915 that Krupskaya's mother died. As Krupskaya recalled, the old lady had wanted to return to Russia, 'but we had no one there to look after her'. She had often quarrelled with Lenin, but on the whole they had maintained a civil relationship. 'We cremated her in Berne,' Krupskaya wrote. 'Vladimir Ilyich and I sat in the cemetery and after two hours they brought us a metal jug still warm with her ashes, and showed us where to bury them.'[111] Yelizaveta Vasilievna nevertheless found her way back to Russia eventually: on 21 February 1969 the Central Committee Secretariat arranged for her ashes to be taken to Leningrad.

After Inessa had left for Paris, she and Lenin conducted a lively correspondence. He signed himself variously as 'Ivan', 'Basil', or sometimes even 'Lenin'. Apart from their personal relationship, Lenin had come to rely on her in Party affairs to a considerable extent as well. In January 1917, for some reason, he decided Switzerland was likely to be drawn into the war, in which case, he told her, 'the French will capture Geneva straight away ... Therefore I'm thinking of giving you the Party funds to look after (to carry on you in a bag made for the purpose, as the banks won't give money out during the war) ...'[112]

In 1916 and 1917, up to the time Lenin left for Russia, he wrote to Inessa more often than to anyone else. When he heard about the February revolution, it was to her that he wrote first, and she was among those who left Switzerland for Russia, via Germany, in the famous 'sealed train'. Her children were in Russia, and it was of them she was thinking as the train from Stockholm to Petrograd carried them on the last leg of the journey.

The revolution soon took its toll on Inessa. She had never been able to work at half-steam, and in Petrograd and later in Moscow she held important posts in the Central Committee and the Moscow Provincial Economic Council, and she worked without respite. In 1919 she went to France to negotiate the return of Russian soldiers, and she wrote for the newspapers. Her meetings with Lenin became less frequent; he was at the epicentre of the storm that raged in Russia. Occasionally, however, they managed a telephone conversation. His address book contained her Moscow address, which he visited only two or three times: 3/14 Arbat, apartment 12, corner of Denezhny and Glazovsky Streets, temporary telephone number 31436.[113]

Sometimes he rang or sent a note, such as the one he wrote in February 1920: 'Dear Friend, I wanted to telephone you [the polite form] when I heard you were ill, but the phone doesn't work. Give me the number and I'll tell them to repair it.'[114] On another occasion he wrote: 'Please say what's wrong with you. These are appalling times: there's typhus, influenza, Spanish 'flu, cholera. I've just got up and I'm not going out. Nadia [Krupskaya] has a temperature of 39 and wants to see you. What's your temperature? Don't you need some medicine? I beg you to tell me frankly. You must get well!'[115] He telephoned the Sovnarkom Secretariat and told them to get a doctor to see Inessa, then wrote again: 'Has the doctor been, you have to do exactly as he says. The phone's out of order again. I told them to repair it and I want your daughters to call me and tell me how you are. You must do everything the doctor tells you. (Nadia's temperature this morning was 37.3, now it's 38).' 'To go out with a temperature of 38 or 39 is sheer madness,' he wrote. 'I beg you earnestly not to go out and to tell your daughters *from me* that I want them to watch you and *not to let you out*: 1) until your temperature is back to normal, 2) with the doctor's permission. I want an exact reply on this. (This morning, 16 February, Nadezhda Konstantinovna had a temperature of 39.7, now in the evening it's 38.2. The doctors were here: it's quinsy. They'll cure her. I am *completely* healthy). Yours, Lenin. Today, the 17th, Nadezhda Konstantinovna's temperature is already down to 37.3.'[116]

Volume 48 of the Complete Works contains a letter from Lenin to Inessa from which the following was cut: 'Never, never have I written that I respect only three women! Never!! I wrote to you [familiar form] that my experience of the *most complete* friendship and *absolute* trust was limited to only two or three women. These are completely mutual, completely mutual business relations...'[117] It seems certain he had Inessa and Krupskaya in mind. There had been other women, of course, who had left a fleeting trace in his heart: Krupskaya's friend Yakubova, the pianist Ekaterina K., and the mystery woman in Paris with the pension from the Soviet government. The relations between Lenin, Krupskaya and Inessa were, as we have seen, both of a personal and a practical nature.

The revolution inevitably distanced Inessa from Lenin, although their feelings for each other remained strong. She was worn out by the privation, the burdens and the cheerless struggle. Not that she lost her revolutionary ideals or regretted the past, but at a certain point her strength began to flag. Lenin gave support occasionally, telephoning, writing notes, helping her children, but she felt he was doing so from habit. The Bolshevik leader no longer belonged to himself, or to Krupskaya, still less to her; he was completely possessed by the revolution. Sometimes his concerns were extraordinary, considering his Jacobin priorities: 'Comrade Inessa, I rang to find out what size of galoshes you take. I hope to get hold of some. Write and tell me how your health is. What's wrong with you? Has the doctor been?'[118] He sent her English newspapers, and several times sent physicians to see her. By 1920, however, Inessa was utterly exhausted. She wrote to Lenin: 'My dear friend, Things here are just as you saw them and there's simply no end to the overwork. I'm beginning to give up, I sleep three times more than the others and so on...'[119]

An invaluable insight into Inessa's mental state during her 'restcure' in the North Caucasus is provided by a diary which she kept in the last month of her life, and which by a miracle survives in the archives. The last, fragmented, hastily pencilled notes tell us more about their relationship than a thousand pages of Lenin's biography:

1 September 1920. Now I have time, I'm going to write every day, although my head is heavy and I feel as if I've turned into a stomach that craves food the whole time ... I also feel a wild desire to be alone. It exhausts me even when people around me are speaking, never mind if I have to speak myself. Will this feeling of inner death ever pass? I hardly ever laugh or smile now

because I'm prompted to by a feeling of joy, but just because one should smile sometimes. I am also surprised by my present indifference to nature. I used to be so moved by it. And I find I like people much less now. I used to approach everyone with a warm feeling. Now I'm indifferent to everyone. The main thing is I'm bored with almost everyone. I only have warm feelings left for the children and V.I. In all other respects it's as if my heart has died. As if, having given up all my strength, all my passion to V.I. and the work, all the springs of love have dried up in me, all my sympathy for people, which I used to have so much of. I have none left, except for V.I. and my children, and a few personal relations, but only in work. And people can feel this deadness in me, and they pay me back in the same coin of indifference or even antipathy (and people used to love me) . . . I'm a living corpse, and it's dreadful!

The devastating sincerity of this self-analysis, this confession, almost suggests Inessa knew she had only three weeks to live. The little diary contains only four more entries. On 3 September she voices her concern for her children:

I'm weak in this respect, not at all like a Roman matron who would readily sacrifice her children in the interests of the republic. I cannot . . . The war is going to go on for a long time, at some point our foreign comrades will revolt . . . Our lives at this time are nothing but sacrifice. There is no personal life because our strength is used up all the time for the common cause . . .

On 9 September she returned to the theme of her first entry:

It seems to me that as I move among people I'm trying not to reveal my secret to them that I am a dead person among the living, a living corpse . . . My heart remains dead, my soul is silent, and I can't completely hide my sad secret . . . As I have no warmth anymore, as I no longer radiate warmth, I can't give happiness to anyone anymore . . .

On 11 September, just two weeks before her death, her last diary entry dwells once more on love, her favourite and eternal theme, and shows the influence Lenin had had on her life. They loved each other, but he had managed to persuade her that 'proletarian interests' took priority over personal feelings. She wrote:

The importance of love, compared to social life, is becoming altogether small, it cannot be compared to the social cause. True, in my own life love still occupies a big place, it makes me suffer a lot, and takes up a lot of my thoughts. But still not for a minute do I cease to recognize that, however painful for me, love and personal relationships are nothing compared to the needs of the struggle . . .'[120]

If there were other entries, they were either lost or censored. There is evidence that some pages were torn out of the diary.

It was some time before Inessa's body could be brought to Moscow, and the archives contain a file of telegrams between the capital and Vladikavkaz. The Central Committee became involved, and Lenin himself demanded that the body be sent to Moscow as soon as possible. There were no suitable goods vans. A death was nothing unusual at that time – people were being buried without coffins. But Moscow was demanding a railcar and a coffin. As long as the local authorities were not threatened with revolutionary justice, they could not find a railcar. Inessa died on 24 September 1920, but her body did not reach Moscow until 11 October.

In a large, ugly lead coffin (not open, as she had been dead for some time), she lay in state in a small hall in the House of Soviets. Only a few people came. Some wreaths had been laid, including one of white hyacinths, with a ribbon inscribed 'To Comrade Inessa from V.I. Lenin'.[121] At the burial at the Kremlin wall the next day, Lenin was almost unrecognizable. Angelica Balabanova, a Comintern official and seasoned revolutionary, was there: 'Not only his face but his whole body expressed so much sorrow that I dared not greet him, not even with the slightest gesture. It was clear that he wanted to be alone with his grief. He seemed to have shrunk: his cap almost covered his face, his eyes seemed drowned in tears held back with effort. As our circle moved, following the movement of the people, he too moved, without offering resistance, as if he were grateful for being brought nearer to the dead comrade.'[122] Witnesses recalled that he looked as if he might fall. His sad eyes saw nothing, his face was frozen in an expression of permanent grief.

Lenin saw that Inessa was given a proper, if modest, tombstone. Inessa's family now had no one, and to Lenin's credit, as long as he was healthy, he (and Krupskaya, when he too was dead) did what he could to get Inessa's five children back on their feet. In December 1921, for instance, Lenin cabled Theodore Rothstein, a former émigré who had returned to Russia in 1920 after twenty years in England, where he had been involved in forming the Communist Party of Great

Britain, and was now a Comintern official: 'I request that you do something for Varya Armand [Inessa's youngest daughter] and if necessary send her here, but not alone and with a warm dress . . .'[123]

Inessa had died tragically early, but she had been prepared for such an eventuality. In February 1919 she went with a Russian Red Cross delegation to France to work among the remnants of the Russian Expeditionary Corps being held there. She wrote to her elder daughter, known as Little Inessa (Inusya):

> Here I am in [Petrograd] . . . We spent the night here and are now moving on . . . I'm enclosing a letter for Sasha, another for Fedya [her sons] and a third one for Ilyich. *Only you* are to know about this last one. Give the first and second ones to them straight away, but *keep the third one yourself for the time being.* When we get back I'll tear it up. If something happens to me (not that I think there's any special danger about this trip, but anything can happen on the journey, so just in case), *then you must give the letter personally to Vl. Il.* The way to do it is to go to *Pravda* where Marya Ilyinichna [Lenin's sister] works, give her the letter and say that it's from me and is *personal* for V.I. Meanwhile, hang onto it . . . It's sealed in an envelope.'[124]

Inessa returned to Moscow in May 1919, and the contents of that letter to Lenin has joined the other secrets of their relationship. Whatever they may have been, we can say with certainty that Inessa had been perhaps the brightest ray of sunshine in his life.

## Financial Secrets

Some 'professional revolutionaries' lived quite well. One would search the Soviet sources in vain for any account of where Lenin and his family found the money to live on after their father died, yet they could travel abroad almost at will, and lived in Germany, Switzerland and France. For seventeen years Lenin lived in the capital cities of Europe and stayed in some of the most congenial resorts. What was the source of the funds that he needed not merely for his activities as leader of the Bolsheviks, but also for 'doing nothing'?

The Bolsheviks had a rule that only the highest Party authorities should know the details of the Party's finances; often only the General Secretary himself. Millions of Communists – as they called themselves after October 1917 – dutifully paid their dues without the least notion of where their money was going. Not even the government knew how much was being spent on ostentatious Party occasions such as congresses, support for foreign Communist Parties and illegal groups, and funding Comintern right up to 1943. The Central Committee reviewed the budget for Comintern annually. For instance, on 20 April 1922 the Politburo accepted a forecast budget of 3,150,600 gold roubles for Comintern activities for the year. There was no discussion, despite the fact that other complex matters of state expenditure were on the agenda, such as reparations which Soviet Russia had agreed to pay to Poland under the terms of the Treaty of Riga, and the allocation of gold to the intelligence services for special purposes.[125] A week later, Zinoviev, as chairman of Comintern, tabled a paper on the budget, and the previous week's forecast was revised upwards by a further reserve of 400,000 gold roubles as a first instalment. Zinoviev explained that he needed 100,000 gold roubles at once 'for agitation among the Japanese troops'.[126] The passion for financial secrecy was, however, born long before, and it extended to the official account of Lenin's early life as well.

Hired in January 1892 as an assistant to the barrister A.N. Khardin, the young Ulyanov stuck the job for barely eighteen months. He acted as defence counsel in a few cases, mostly of petty theft – personal items from a merchant's suitcase, bread from a warehouse – in his own words barely enough 'to cover the selection of court papers'. At the time of the revolution of 1917, Lenin, aged forty-seven, had spent all of two years in paid work. How was the impression formed in the Soviet public mind that, contrary to the 'materialistic philosophy of history', questions of Lenin's everyday life and existence counted for nothing alongside the worldwide issues of the revolution? The first historian to raise the question of Lenin and money was the émigré and former Bolshevik and Menshevik Nikolai Valentinov, who based the various accounts he published, mostly after the Second World War, on first-hand knowledge and scrupulous research.

After the death of Ilya Ulyanov, his widow, as the widow of a State Counsellor and holder of the Order of Stanislav First Class, received a pension of 100 roubles a month. This compares with the eight roubles a month that Lenin received from the state as an exile in Shushenskoe, and that he found adequate for rent, simple food, and laundry.[127] Could all the Ulyanovs have lived on their mother's pension, even though it was a good one by contemporary standards, and study, travel, go abroad? She went abroad herself three times, to Switzerland, France and Sweden, on two occasions with her daughter Maria. And Maria in addition went abroad five times, sometimes for lengthy periods. The elder daughter, Anna, also went abroad several times, staying in Germany and France for almost two years. Tickets, hotels, food, purchases and unforeseen expenses on long trips, all took considerable funds, certainly more than the pension would stand. Anna and Maria and Lenin's wife all testified that they lived on the mother's pension and on what their father had managed to save in his lifetime. But this does not square with the reality, and Krupskaya herself says so: 'They are writing about our lives as if we were in penury. It's not true. We were never in the position of not being able to afford bread. Were there such people among the émigrés? There were some who had had no income for two years and got no money from Russia, and they really starved. We were not like that. We lived simply, that's the truth.'[128]

Neither in Russia nor abroad did Lenin suffer deprivation. He lived on his mother's resources, his 'Party salary', the donations of various benefactors at various times. Pamphlets and articles printed for illegal distribution inside Russia earned precious little, while the émigré market for such works was scarcely more rewarding. His mother owned part of the estate at Kokushkino which the family had put at the disposal of a certain Anna Alexandrovna Veretennikova, who paid Lenin's mother her admittedly not very large share of the rent regularly. The sale of the estate helped to fill the family's coffers. In February 1889 Lenin's mother acquired a farm at Alakaevka in Samara province. Her agent for the purchase was Mark Yelizarov, Anna's future husband. For 7500 roubles the family had acquired just over 200 acres, much of it non-arable. The original intention had been to carry on a farming business, with Vladimir in charge, and in fact in their first year they acquired some livestock, and sowed some wheat, buckwheat and sunflowers. But Vladimir soon became bored as 'farm manager', and began, in Nikolai Valentinov's words, 'to live on the farm like a carefree squire staying at his summer home. He would ensconce himself in the lime-tree avenue and prepare for the state exams at St Petersburg University, study Marxism and write his first work, an article called "New Economic Movements in Peasant Life".[129] The article describes the exploitation of peasants and land, criticizes many of the ills of capitalism in the countryside, such as money-lending, leasehold, the increasing number of 'kulaks', or rich peasants. Yet when Lenin was put off by his own experience of farming, the family leased out land to a kulak, one Mr Krushvits, who paid rent to the Ulyanovs for several years, substantially supplementing their income.

There may have been another reason for leasing out the land. The peasants of the region were extremely poor, and those around Alakaevka especially so. Numbering thirty-four households, together they had about 160 acres of arable, roughly the same as the Ulyanovs. Farming in the midst of such appalling poverty may have been felt by the budding Marxist as an uncomfortable moral position, especially as he himself had sued his peasant neighbours for letting their cattle wander onto his crops. None of this prevented the family from summering at Alakaevka every year, reminding Krushvits of his responsibilities, and collecting their rent. Eventually it was decided to sell the farm, and a document composed by Vladimir in his mother's name shows the sale having been made to S.R. Dannenberg in July 1893.[130]

Maria Alexandrovna had evidently decided it was better to realize her assets and keep the money in the bank, together with what she had been given by her late husband's brother, and live on the interest. Meanwhile, no one in the family was earning anything. Vladimir soon gave up legal practice, and Anna, Dmitri and Maria were long-term students, and showed no inclination to supplement the family income. As Valentinov wrote: 'the money deposited in the bank and converted into state bonds, together with the pension, constituted a special "family fund", which Lenin's very thrifty mother capably managed over many years. They all dipped into this fund ... They certainly were not rich, but over this long period there was *enough* ...'[131] Enough, for instance, for Vladimir to be able to write to his mother from Geneva: 'I had hoped Manyasha [Maria] would come ... but she keeps putting it off. It would be good if she came in the second half of October, as we could pop down to Italy together ... Why can't Mitya [Dmitri] also come here? Yes, invite him, too, we'll have a great time together.'[132]

Such a secure material environment must have played a significant part in Lenin's intellectual development, enabling him to run his own life, decide for himself where to live, where to go, what to do. Had he been the 'proletarian' some authors would have liked him to be, his position among the leaders of the Russian social democratic movement would have been immeasurably less important. He would not have had time for self-education, literary work or Party 'rows'.

After the failure of the 1905 revolution, when revolutionaries – including Lenin – who had returned hopefully from Europe now had to retrace their steps, an important source of support for Lenin and Krupskaya in their various stopping-places was the Party fund, a source that was never revealed in published documents, but whose existence Lenin himself confirmed in a letter to his mother in 1908: 'I still get the salary I told you about in Stockholm.'[133] In fact, references to money abound in Lenin's voluminous correspondence with his mother and sisters, usually reporting that he had received a draft, or asking for money to be sent urgently, and so on.[134]

Another, and rather more bountiful, source of income was the Party. The Russian Social Democratic Labour Party (RSDLP) was set up, rather shakily, at its First Congress in 1898 by a handful of provincial organizers. It was quickly decimated by the police, but its name remained as the banner for whoever was capable of gathering revolutionary-minded workers and intellectuals for the purpose of building a large and powerful revolutionary party. In February 1900, as soon as he had completed his term of exile in Siberia, Lenin departed for Europe, where he launched a newspaper, *Iskra* (The Spark), and began recruiting his own agents. These he sent back into Russia, both to distribute his message via *Iskra* and to obtain the allegiance of local forces.

By 1903 it seemed Lenin and his closest comrades had gathered sufficient backing to hold a new Party Congress, called the Second, for the sake of keeping the already well established name. This took place in the summer of 1903 in Brussels, moving to London when the Russian secret police proved too intrusive. Far from consolidating the Party's forces, however, the Second Congress witnessed their split into Leninists and anti-Leninists, or Bolsheviks (Majorityites) and

Mensheviks (Minorityites). These new labels came about as the result
of one particular vote which gave Lenin a minuscule majority.

In the period following this fiasco, with the resulting contest for
various resources and Party assets such as printing facilities and,
especially, money, Lenin had to devote a great deal of attention to
establishing his own, Bolshevik, fund. He needed it to maintain his
'professional revolutionaries', to conduct meetings and congresses,
support his own publishing activities, and finance agitation inside
Russia. The 'professional revolutionaries' of course knew about this
fund, which in the final analysis Lenin personally controlled, since he
was the creator of the Bolshevik wing of the Party, as well as its
ideologist and chief organizer. For instance, Lev Trotsky, who was
then on very bad terms with Lenin, wrote in June 1909 to his brother-
in-law Lev Kamenev, who was Lenin's right-hand man: 'Dear Lev
Borisovich, I have to ask a favour which will give you no pleasure.
You must dig up 100 roubles and cable it to me. We're in a terrible
situation which I will not describe: enough to say that we have not
paid the grocer for April, May, June . . .' Kamenev left it up to Lenin
to decide whether or not to provide Trotsky with the money, but
there is no indication of the outcome.[135]

At times the Bolsheviks had very considerable funds at their disposal, some of it legitimate in origin, some of it not. Some came from
local Party committees in Russia, who in turn gathered it from their
members and supporters: on the eve of the 1905 revolution, there
were probably 10,000 paid-up members of the Party altogether. In
his memoirs, the former Bolshevik A.D. Naglovsky wrote that in the
summer of 1905 he was sent by the Kazan committee to Geneva to
hand over 20,000 roubles to Lenin and await instructions.[136] In fact,
the origins of such money were tortuous. Lenin himself frankly admitted after the revolution: 'The old Bolshevik was right when he
explained what Bolshevism was to the Cossack who'd asked him if it
was true the Bolsheviks stole. "Yes," he said, "we steal what has
already been stolen."'[137]

At the 4th Congress of the RSDLP in 1906, at which the two
factions were meant to have reunited, a fierce struggle took place
between the Bolsheviks and Mensheviks over whether such 'expropriations' in the interests of the revolution should be countenanced.
The Bolsheviks proposed that armed raids on banks be allowed. The

Mensheviks opposed this vigorously, and succeeded in passing their own resolution. Nevertheless, the robberies continued, with Lenin's knowledge. Krupskaya, who was well informed on the subject, wrote frankly that 'the Bolsheviks thought it permissible to seize tsarist treasure and allowed expropriations'.[138] At the centre of this bandit venture stood the Bolsheviks Iosif Dzhugashvili (Stalin) and Semyon Ter-Petrosyan (Kamo). The operation was run by Leonid Krasin, a highly qualified electrical engineer.

The biggest 'expropriation' took place at midday on 26 July 1907 on Yerevan Square in Tiflis (Tbilisi), Georgia. As two carriages carrying banknotes to the bank entered the square, a man in an officer's uniform jumped out of a phaeton and starting shouting orders. From nowhere, a gang of 'expropriators' emerged, throwing bombs and firing shots. Three people fell dead by the carriages, and many more were wounded. Sacks containing 340,000 roubles were rapidly thrown into the phaeton, and in three or four minutes the square was deserted.[139]

The stolen banknotes were of large denominations, and the Bolsheviks were not able to convert them all even by the time of the revolution. Those who attempted to do so, as Krupskaya recalled, were arrested. 'In Stockholm they picked up Strauyan of the Zurich group, in Munich, Olga Ravich of the Geneva group and Bogdasaryan and Khodzhamiryan who had just left Russia, and Semashko in Geneva. The Swiss burghers were terrified to death. All they could talk about was the Russian expropriators.'[140] The Tiflis operation was the most ambitious of all those carried out by the radical wing of the RSDLP. Other 'expropriations' included the seizure of large sums from the steamship *Nikolai I* in the port of Baku, and the robbery of post offices and railway ticket offices. Officially, the Bolshevik Centre was not involved, but part of the loot was sent by Dzhugashvili and Ter-Petrosyan to the Bolsheviks,[141] and Lenin paid small 'Party salaries' – sums ranging from 200 to 600 French francs – to the dozen or so members of his inner Party nucleus, the Bolshevik Centre.[142]

There are many unpublished documents in the Lenin archives concerning financial affairs, some of them requiring careful deciphering. One thing is clear enough, however: Bolshevik money was under Lenin's control. He taught himself to handle money and to keep all kinds of bills and invoices, and detailed lists of his own expenses, often

of trivial amounts. There is, for instance, a 'personal budget' for 3
July 1901 to 1 March 1902, running to thirteen pages.[143] Money
figures in much of his correspondence with the family. His earnings
from the pamphlets and newspaper articles he wrote for the revolutionary press formed a small, if not negligible, part of Lenin's income,
as his literary output was of interest to only a few people. It was
his family and Party 'injections' taken from the donations of rich
sympathizers that supported him.

Formally, Lenin stood aside from the 'expropriations', preferring,
as in many of his ventures, to remain off-stage. His speeches and
editorials, whether published in his own weekly, *Proletarii*, founded
in 1906, or in other revolutionary organs, however, reveal a more
'balanced' position on the 'expropriations' than a simple prohibition.
For instance, six months after the 4th Congress, which had condemned 'partisan actions', he wrote: 'When I see social democrats
proudly and smugly declaring, "We are not anarchists, we're not
thieves or robbers, we are above all that, we condemn partisan warfare," I ask myself if these people realize what they are saying.'[144] He
had earlier stated that the combat groups must be free to act, but with
'the least harm to the personal safety of ordinary citizens and the
maximum harm to the personal safety of spies, active Black Hundreds,
the authorities, the police, troops, the navy and so on and so forth.[145]
The Black Hundreds were ultra-rightist organizations, with such
names as the Union of Russian Men, the Russian Monarchist Union,
the Society for Active Struggle against Revolution and Anarchy.
Rabidly anti-Semitic and anti-Western, they organized virulent press
campaigns, as well as violent physical attacks, against the liberal and
socialist movements.

In 1911, Kamo (Ter-Petrosyan) was in Lenin's sitting-room in
Paris, eating almonds and recounting the details of his arrest in Berlin
in 1907, when the authorities had caught him trying to transport
explosives and weapons. He had spent the last four years in prison in
Germany, feigning insanity. Krupskaya recalled that 'Ilyich listened
and felt so sorry for this selflessly brave, childishly naive man with
such a burning heart, willing to do great deeds ... during the civil
war Kamo found his niche and again performed miracles of hero-
ism.'[146] Kamo did not know that he and his ilk were merely blind
tools of the Bolshevik Centre, needed to acquire money 'for the revol-

ution' by whatever means. For the Bolsheviks violence and 'exes' were part of a wide range of methods to be used as the need arose. It is likely, however, that the 'exes' were one of the main sources of the Party's pre-revolutionary funds, under the control of Lenin's trustees Krasin, Bogdanov, Kamenev, Zinoviev, Ganetsky and a few others. This explains how his mother's 'injections' into her son's personal budget were regularly topped up by his 'Party salary', which though not great, was no less than the average wage of a European worker. According to Valentinov, the maximum Party salary for the Bolshevik leaders was fixed at 350 Swiss francs.[147] This was the amount Lenin stated he received every month, while not declining the money his mother went on sending him right up to her death in 1916.

A major source of funding, both to the Party coffers and for Lenin's personal needs, came from private benefactors. At the turn of the century the Russian social democrats, like the liberals, enjoyed a certain degree of sympathy, not only from sections of the intelligentsia, but also from a number of industrialists, who looked to the revolutionaries for liberation from the conservative attitudes of the autocracy. The relationship sometimes took on bizarre form. The 'N. Schmidt affair', for instance, sometimes seemed like a detective story, and even now aspects of it are unclear, as the papers relating to the case were carefully concealed for many years. The official version has always been that the 'affair' took place for the good of the Bolshevik cause. In Krupskaya's words, the funds which came from this source provided a 'sound material base'.[148]

The Schmidt affair began with the millionaire Savva Morozov, the head of a large merchant dynasty in Moscow. His relatives were known as patrons of the arts and social enterprises. One was a celebrated collector of ceramics, while another collected rare Russian and foreign paintings. Both collections ended up as Soviet state property. The Morozovs built hospitals, founded courses to eradicate illiteracy, supported theatres. The well-known newspaper *Russkie vedomosti* (Russian News) depended on Savva Morozov's largesse for many years. At the beginning of the century, under the influence of Maxim Gorky, he gave money to publish the social democratic paper *Iskra* and to help social democratic organizations. His motivation was probably less social than religious or spiritual, expressing a desire to support not only culture but also the oppressed. A somewhat confused individual, his mind haphazard and unstable, he was terrified of going insane, and in Cannes in May 1905, in a moment of deep depression, he killed himself. Through Gorky, he left a large amount in his will to the Bolsheviks – 100,000 roubles, according to some sources.

Savva's nephew, Nikolai Pavlovich Schmidt, owned a large furniture factory in Moscow, and also supported the social democrats. During the armed uprising in Moscow in December 1905 he was arrested for supporting the 'insurgents', and in February 1907, aged twenty-three, he killed himself in prison in suspicious circumstances. It is still unclear why he should have done this, just before he was to be released on his family's surety. In any event, he left part of his estate to revolutionary causes, although not exclusively to the Bolsheviks. According to the law, his estate should have gone to his two sisters, Yekaterina and the sixteen-year-old Yelizaveta, and a younger brother, but then two of Nikolai's young Bolshevik acquaintances, Nikolai Andrikanis and Viktor Taratuta, entered the scene.

It seems that these two had been deputed to ensure that Nikolai's money came to the Bolsheviks. Their assignment was to court, conquer and marry the girls, nothing less. Taratuta, whom Lenin knew well, and his comrade performed their rôles to perfection, and both girls were swept away by the romance of 'preparing for revolution' in Russia. Soon, however, Andrikanis began having second thoughts about handing over the inheritance to the Party. Lenin wrote (the text in the archive is in the hand of Inessa Armand) that 'one of the sisters, Yekaterina Schmidt (married to Mr Andrikanis), questioned giving the money to the Bolsheviks. The conflict was settled by arbitration in Paris in 1908, with the good offices of members of the Socialist Revolutionary Party . . . The judgment was that the Schmidt money should go to the Bolsheviks.'[149] In 1909 the two newly married couples arrived in Paris.

Andrikanis, however, would only part with a small amount. When it was decided that he should be 'tried' by a Party court, he simply left the Party, which had to be content with the crumbs 'Person X', as he was codenamed, had deigned to cast its way.[150] In order to act before the funds of the younger sister, Yelizaveta (who was still a minor, and whose financial affairs were in the hands of a trustee), were also cut off, a session of the Bolshevik Centre was held in Paris on 21 February 1909. Zinoviev, who took the minutes, recorded: 'In

January 1908 Yelizaveta X told the Bolshevik Centre . . . that in carrying out her brother's will as correctly as possible, she considered herself morally obliged to give the Bolshevik Centre the half-share of her brother's property that had come to her legally. That half, which she inherited by law, includes eighty-three shares in Company X and about 47,000 roubles of available capital.' The document is signed by N. Lenin, Grigorii (Zinoviev), Marat (V. Shantser), V. Sergeev (Taratuta), Maximov (A. Bogdanov), Y. Kamenev.[151]

It was agreed that the money should be transferred after sale of the shares. In November, Taratuta and Yelizaveta came back to Paris and handed Lenin more than a quarter of a million francs. By now the Bolsheviks had received more than half a million francs, as documents written and signed by Lenin indicate: 'In accordance with the decision and calculations of the executive commission of the Bolshevik Centre (plus the editorial board of *Proletarii*) of 11 November 1909, I have received from Ye. X. two hundred and seventy thousand nine hundred and eighty four (275,984) francs.'[152] He issued a receipt to Yelizaveta and Taratuta, stating : 'We, the undersigned, acting in the matter of the money with power of attorney from Comrade Vishnevsky, in concluding the case conducted by the entire Bolshevik Centre, and in taking over the remainder of the money, accept before you the obligation to answer to the Party collegially for the fate of this money. Signed N. Lenin, Gr. Zinoviev.'[153]

This was not the end of the affair. After various vain attempts to reunite the Party, the Mensheviks raised the question of uniting the Party funds. The question was, who was to control the capital, which of course contained more than just the Schmidt inheritance. After long and heated argument, it was agreed in 1910 that the Party's resources be handed over to three depositors, the well-known German social democrats Clara Zetkin, Karl Kautsky and Franz Mehring, and in due course a substantial part was deposited in a bank under their names. But the reunification turned out to be a fiction, with the Party carrying on its in-fighting as before. The trustees found themselves pressured and accused by both wings of the Party, as only they had the authority to disburse the money. Lenin demanded they hand all the money back to the Bolshevik Centre. Kautsky replied, on 2 October 1911: 'Comrade Ulyanov, I have received your letter. You will receive a reply once I have consulted Madame Zetkin and Mr

Mehring. You probably know that he has retired as a depositor owing to illness. As a result of this, the depositors can take no decision if there is a difference of opinion.' He added a postscript: 'My work is suffering from the great waste of time and energy spent on this hopeless matter. Therefore I can no longer continue my functions. With Party greetings, K. Kautsky.'[154]

Clara Zetkin tried to break the deadlock by suggesting that all the money be returned as the property of the entire Party. A tug-of-war ensued, involving lawyers, long drawn-out correspondence, and caustic comments addressed to the depositors. In a letter to G.L. Shklovsky on Zetkin's position, Lenin wrote: '"Madame" had lied so much in her reply, that she's got herself even more confused . . .'[155] The case went to court, and a typical letter from Krupskaya, written on 23 May 1912 under Lenin's instructions, to their lawyer, a certain Duclos, reads:

> Sir,
> My husband, Mr Ulyanov, has left for a few days and has asked me to acquaint you with the enclosed documents. A letter from the three depositors dated 30 June 1911. A memorandum from the manager of the National Bank's agency in Paris dated 7 July 1911 concerning the despatch of a cheque to Mrs Zetkin for the sum of 24,455 marks and 30 Swedish bonds. A decision of the RSDLP of January 1912 concerning the sum held by Mrs Zetkin.
> Signed N. Ulyanova.'[156]

Zetkin held her ground, handing out some money for various meetings, and the row only subsided after the First World War had intervened. The money at issue, however, was the smaller part of the Schmidt inheritance, the greater part having remained all the time in the hands of the Bolshevik Centre, i.e. Lenin's, as the chief controller of the Party's finances. In August 1909, for instance, he sent an order to the National Discount Bank in Paris to sell stock held in his name and to issue a cheque for 25,000 francs to A.I. Lyubimov, a member of the Bolshevik Centre.[157] Thus, the true 'depositor' of the Party funds was Lenin himself, and to a great extent the Bolsheviks in emigration depended financially on him.

The Mensheviks, fully aware of the murky background of the

Schmidt affair, tried to depict Taratuta as a 'Party pimp' who was securing Lenin's finances by sleazy methods. When Taratuta complained about attacks on him by Bogdanov – another member of the Bolshevik Centre, but by now Lenin's rival – Lenin secured a special resolution of the Bolshevik Centre, amounting to a Party indulgence and emphasizing that what had happened 'in no way evokes the slightest weakening of the trust the Bolshevik Centre has in Comrade Viktor [Taratuta]'.[158] After 1917 Taratuta continued to enjoy Lenin's trust and confidence.

Lenin had other sources of funds beyond Morozov, Schmidt and Gorky. In 1890, for example, he had met A.I. Yeremasov, a young entrepreneur from Syzran in the province of Simbirsk, who had been involved with local revolutionary circles.[159] At the end of 1904 Lenin asked him to help fund the Bolshevik newspaper *Vpered* in Paris.[160]

There were many others. The relationship between Lenin and Maxim Gorky was a special one. Gorky, who was internationally famous before the revolution, for his play *The Lower Depths* (1902), his novel *The Mother* (1906) and his three-part autobiography, gave the Bolsheviks much material help. This did not not prevent him from taking an independent position at critical moments, as the essays he published in 1917–1918 in his own newspaper, *Novaya zhizn'* (New Life), show.[161] Their correspondence was voluminous, and there is hardly one letter from Lenin in which he does not complain about money. Among other things, he asked Gorky to donate some of his royalties to supporting this or that Bolshevik publication, 'to help drum up subscriptions', 'to find a little cash to expand *Pravda*', or nudged him with such hints as, 'I'm sure you won't refuse to help *Prosveshchenie*', 'hasn't "the merchant" started giving yet?', or 'Because of the war, I'm in desperate need of a wage and so I would ask you, if it's possible and won't put you out too much, to help speed up the publication of the brochure'.[162] While Gorky helped the Bolsheviks with both money and influence, in November 1917 he could still refer to Lenin darkly as 'not an omnipotent magician, but a cold-blooded trickster who spares neither the honour nor the lives of the proletariat'.[163]

From the little we have so far seen of Lenin's financial affairs, it is plain that he was not in need, although he was always ready to raise the issue. Biographers have frequently quoted his letter from Zurich

to Shlyapnikov in Stockholm in the autumn of 1916, in which he
wrote: 'As for myself, I need a salary. Otherwise we'll simply perish,
I mean it!! The cost of living is diabolical, and we've nothing to live
on. You've got to drag the money *by force* out of [Gorky] who has two
of my brochures (he must pay, *now*, and a bit more!) . . . If this doesn't
happen, I swear I won't make it, and I am really, really serious . . .'[164]

Perhaps the death of Lenin's mother in July 1916, which had so
shaken him, explains the dramatic tone of this letter. He was, after
all, still controlling the Party finances, which, though depleted, were
accessible to him. Furthermore, before the war broke out Krupskaya
had inherited money from an aunt in Novocherkassk, Lenin's sisters
Anna and Maria were still sending occasional remittances, and even
when they returned to Russia in April 1917, Lenin and Krupskaya
were not without funds. The fact is, Lenin, whether in Russia or
abroad, was never short of money. He could decide whether to live
in Bern or Zurich, he could travel to London, Berlin or Paris, visit
Gorky on Capri, or write to Anna, 'I'm on holiday in Nice. It's sheer
luxury here: sunny, warm, dry, the southern sea. In a few days I return
to Paris'.[165] Doss-houses and attics were not for him. He wrote to
Anna in December 1908 on arriving in Paris, 'We've found a good
apartment, fashionable and expensive: 840 francs plus about 60 francs
tax, and about the same for the concierge per year. Cheap by Moscow
prices (4 rooms, kitchen, larder, water, gas), but it's expensive here.'[166]

Lenin was punctilious about keeping accounts and planning his
budget. He kept notes of what he had spent on food, train fares,
mountain holidays and so on,[167] and carried these slips of paper around
with him from country to country, city to city, long after their 'expiry
date', until he finally ensconced himself in the Kremlin, whereupon
he handed them over to the Central Party Archive.

He loved dealing with financial matters. In June 1921 he ordered
1878 boxes of valuable objects to be brought into the Kremlin.[168]
Perhaps it made him feel more secure. On 15 October of that year
the Politburo ordered that no expenditure of the gold reserve was to
take place without its – i.e. Lenin's – authority.[169] He loved holidays
in expensive resorts, and he often went to the theatre and cinema.
All this was perfectly natural behaviour, especially for the hereditary
nobleman Lenin described himself as,[170] and there was no need for
him to make a big secret of it. What remains a mystery, however, is

not the financial details of his everyday life, but how he, like his comrades Trotsky and Stalin – none of them ever having worked for a living, and none of them having anything in common with the working class – could think they had the right to determine the fate of a great nation, and to carry out their bloody, monstrous experiment.

# 2

## Master of the Order

At the turn of the century, Russia was entering a period of turbulence. Peasants rioted against a system which piled debts on them and taxed their basic necessities excessively; workers went on strike for better conditions and wages and against police harassment; students were demanding autonomy for their universities and civil liberties for everyone; the professional classes – doctors, lawyers, teachers – were becoming increasingly vociferous in their demand for representative government; and the national minorities in the empire's borderlands were organizing liberation movements. In 1904 the country stumbled into a war against Japan over control of Chinese territory in Manchuria, 6000 miles from European Russia, and by the middle of 1905 Russia's resources appeared exhausted, and humiliation seemed certain. The whole of 1905 was consumed in strikes and demonstrations, and mutinous action in parts of the army and navy, and by the autumn Tsar Nicholas II was ready to concede reform: the creation of a State Duma, or parliament, and various promises of social legislation.

It was against this background of rising political activity that Lenin emerged from his exile in Siberia and threw himself into reorganizing the Russian Social Democratic Labour Party as a revolutionary body, prepared to overthrow the existing order. To justify the rôle of those who were to do the overthrowing, he created the idea of the 'professional revolutionary'. In his extended essay *What is to be Done?*, a title he took from Chernyshevsky, he wrote that an 'organization of revolutionaries must chiefly and above all include people whose profession is revolutionary activity',[1] one of his main arguments being that it was 'far harder to catch a dozen clever people than a hundred fools'. By 'clever people' he meant professional revolutionaries.[2]

Published in Stuttgart in 1902,[3] *What is to be done?* was Lenin's grand plan to create a conspiratorial organization. Advancing the idea of an 'all-Russian political newspaper' as the basis for such a party, he envisaged a 'network of agents' – or 'collaborators, if this is a more acceptable term' – who would provide 'the greatest certainty of success in the event of a rising'.[4]

He would certainly succeed in building his strictly disciplined organization, but after it had seized power he would find it difficult to discern where the Party ended and the security organs began. In April 1922, for instance, it was the Politburo that gave the state security organ, the GPU, the power to shoot bandit elements on the spot. In May they ordered that Patriarch Tikhon, the head of the Orthodox Church, be put on trial for allegedly obstructing the expropriation of Church property, and in the same month this élite of 'professional revolutionaries' sentenced eleven priests to be executed for the same reason. In August 1921 it was Lenin who initiated the creation of a commission to maintain surveillance on incoming foreigners, notably those involved in the American famine relief programme.[5]

The illegal, conspiratorial character of the Party predetermined the mutual penetration, if not fusion, of this 'social' organization and the state security organs. The process occurred officially and 'legally'. One of Lenin's most trusted agents, Yakov Ganetsky, wrote to Lenin on 10 October 1919 proposing 'the closest possible ties between the Party organizations and the extraordinary [security] commissions . . . and to oblige all Party members in responsible posts to report to the . . . commissions any information they obtain by both private and official means and which might serve to combat counter-revolution and espionage. They should also actively help the . . . commissions by taking part in solving cases . . . being present at interrogations and so on.'[6] Lenin could hardly have made the point clearer, when he stated, 'A good Communist is a good Chekist [secret policeman] at the same time.'[7]

## Theorist of Revolution

As had become their custom, late on the morning of 10 January 1905 Lenin and Krupskaya were making their way to the city library in

Geneva, where they were then residing. On the steps they ran into Anatoly Lunacharsky and his wife, who told them the wonderful news that revolution had broken out in St Petersburg. They all ran to Lepeshinsky's émigré restaurant, where the events were already being discussed excitedly. Lenin proposed a joint meeting with the Mensheviks, on condition that only one speaker from each side take the floor, and two days later the two irreconcilable factions met. Lunacharsky spoke for the Bolsheviks, Fedor Dan for the Mensheviks. But each side was more intent on preventing the other from scoring a success than on discussing realities. When Dan hinted darkly at 'splitters', Lenin gave a signal and the Bolsheviks walked out.[8]

Everything Lenin had written until now had been devoted to the problems of preparing for revolution: creating a party, formulating its programme, exposing tsarism. Now it was necessary to write about the revolution itself. Even if it was somewhat embarrassing that the popular workers' leader Father Gapon, who had built up a large following in St Petersburg, was closer to events than 'real' revolutionaries, Lenin was fascinated by the priest, who seemed to have been pushed into the revolution only by the suffering he shared with his flock. Gapon in fact had since 1904 been working in close cooperation with the secret police, whose object had been to divert the workers from revolution by helping them in their struggle for economic gains. Lenin did not believe Gapon was a provocateur and he inscribed his 1905 Geneva pamphlet, 'Two Tactics of Social Democracy in the Democratic Revolution', 'To Georgy Gapon with respect, from the author'.[9] In an article in the January issue of *Vpered* entitled 'The Priest Gapon', he wrote: 'Gapon may be a sincere Christian socialist and perhaps it was precisely Bloody Sunday that pushed him onto a fully revolutionary path.' He concluded that a cautious attitude was called for.[10] 'Bloody Sunday', 22 January 1905, had been the occasion of a huge procession of workers and their families, led by Gapon, towards the Winter Palace, to petition the tsar for help. Troops guarding the approaches to the city centre were ordered to fire into the crowds, after repeated warnings, and some eight hundred were killed and many more wounded. It was an event which not only shocked world opinion, but also triggered the violence and disorder of the rest of the year.

*       *       *

It would appear, from everything that has been written about him by Soviet historians, that there was no field of social life which Lenin did not 'enrich', 'refine', 'formulate' or 'illuminate'. But let us dwell here only on his theory of socialist revolution, such as it was.

Analysing the entrails of capitalism, Marx had stressed that the coming of proletarian revolution depended wholly on the material conditions of hired labour. For him, revolution was a social fruit that must ripen. While agreeing in principle with this idea, Lenin, believing that only the conscious activity of individuals could guarantee the success of the revolution, shifted the stress onto forcing the process by energizing the masses, by organizations and parties. In principle, he regarded the improvement of the workers' conditions and the realization of socialist goals by evolutionary, reformist means, as impossible. For him the main thing was to create the institution of control. In January 1917 he wrote that contemporary society was ripe for socialism, ripe for control 'from a single centre'.[11] Reforms, he wrote, were 'a side effect of the revolutionary class struggle'.[12] Throughout his writings, he speaks of the decisive rôle of the conscious masses, classes, parties, leaders. Circumstances were important only in order to legitimize the settling of these problems by force of will.

Even though the First World War, and Russia's fortunes in it, dramatically altered the political situation, and led to the downfall of the tsar and the formation of a liberal Provisional Government, Lenin must have known the Mensheviks were right when they said in 1917 that Russia was not ripe for socialist revolution. Yet he was prepared to exploit the opportunity for his own party to seize power in October. The alternative was for the Bolsheviks to occupy the position of an extreme wing with little influence in the forthcoming Constituent Assembly, planned by the Provisional Government and actually convened in January 1918. Lenin therefore leapfrogged the classic Marxist scheme, ignoring 'objective conditions', as well as a host of home-grown and European Social Democrats who were committed to a parliamentary process. He was cleverer than they, for he recognized that the war had not only been the chief cause of the February revolution which finished off the Russian Empire, but would also dash the hopes that had been aroused then. He exploited the war by moving it in effect from the trenches of the Eastern front to the Russian plains in the shape of revolution and civil war, and in doing so, he altered the disposition of political forces. It was this strategy that led to the redrawing of the map of the world, brought into being mighty movements in all continents, and held the minds of statesmen in tension and fear as to whether the world revolution would occur.

Like all the Russian leaders, Lenin was hypnotized by the French Revolution. Peppering their articles and speeches with terms like 'Girondistes', 'Jacobins', 'commissars', 'Convention', 'Thermidor', 'Vendée', they were not merely paying homage to the French revolutionaries, but were also emulating them, as they tried to remake history for themselves. In a telegram of 30 August 1918, the day he was nearly assassinated by the Socialist Revolutionary Fanya Kaplan, Lenin told Trotsky in Sviyazhsk to use the most extreme measures against senior commanders who showed lack of strength: 'They should be told that from now on we are applying the model of the French Revolution and will put on trial and even shoot . . . the army commander at Kazan and the other top commanders.'[13] The French revolutionaries applied terror in the name of liberty, of course, whereas Lenin did so in the name of power.

At the height of the First World War, Lenin came to the unexpected conclusion that 'the victory of socialism is possible first in a few or even one individual capitalist country'.[14] It would have been hard to disagree, had he meant the seizure of power, rather than the victory of socialism. Shortly thereafter, he set forth one of his fundamental theses even more forcefully, namely that 'socialism cannot conquer simultaneously *in all* countries'.[15] This, too, would have been a rational assertion, but for the minor matter of what it was he meant by 'socialism', and the question of which were the lucky countries that might enter the promised land in splendid isolation. Lenin had the answer: those which were the weakest link in the imperialist system. It was here that the absurdity began. It appears that Germany, Great Britain, the USA and other developed capitalist states had less chance of social and economic advance than, say, Russia. And yet Lenin himself had written that the material base for socialism was already in place in Europe. Despite his attempt to smooth over the inconsistency by asserting that socialism would never arise in Russia without a certain level of capitalist development,[16] his position remained absurd, and had nothing in common with socialism. The possibility of 'building socialism in one country' boiled down to the chance of seizing power. It was easier in a country where conditions were 'ripe', and where the appropriate 'organization' was present, even if the state and the level of democracy were less ready to climb the next step up the pyramid of social progress.

After his return to Russia on 16 April 1917, when he was whipping up a mood of frenzy, harnessing the masses' impatience, promising peace and land in exchange for support for his party, Lenin bent every effort to turn that party into a combat organization, capable of seizing power. Soon after the February revolution, when all the 'illegals' emerged from hiding, he was still declaiming, 'we will create our *own* party as before and we will *definitely* combine our legal and our illegal work'.[17] This had nothing to do with socialism. The society which Lenin and his adherents began to build had to resort to unrestrained violence, in accordance with the leader's views, in order to survive. As the highest principle of revolutionary development, the dictatorship trampled and subordinated everything to its own will. Having once espoused the idea of socialism in one country, Lenin pushed questions of morality well down the Bolshevik agenda. In May 1919 the Politburo gave routine authorization for a collection of valuable jewellery to be made available to Comintern. The list of this jewellery runs to many pages and is valued in many millions of roubles, with items marked 'for England', 'for Holland', 'for France', and so on.[18] In November 1921 the Politburo unanimously rejected an appeal from a special commission for the improvement of children's rations.[19] The difficulties faced by the new regime do not justify the refusal to meet this need. While millions were dying of hunger and disease, the Politburo was lavishly disbursing tsarist gold to ignite revolution in other countries.

It is not difficult to find evidence in Lenin's writings of the idea that the dictatorship of the proletariat is compatible with full democracy, as indeed Soviet propaganda insisted for decades. It is, however, hard to reconcile the idea with the practice, where it is difficult to understand what Lenin meant by democracy. How can the dictatorship of one class – or more accurately one party – be reconciled with the principles of people's power, liberty and the equality of all citizens? It smacks of social racism. A letter from Lenin to the Bolsheviks in Penza, not far from Simbirsk, written in August 1918, illustrates this point:

Comrades! The kulak uprising in [your] five districts must be crushed without pity. The interests of the whole revolution demand it, for the 'final and decisive battle' with the kulaks everywhere is now engaged. An example must be made. 1) Hang (and I mean hang so that the *people can see) not less than* 100 known kulaks, rich men, bloodsuckers. 2) Publish their names. 3) Take *all* their grain away from them. 4) Identify hostages as we described in our telegram yesterday. Do this so that for hundreds of miles around the people can see, tremble, know and cry: they are killing and will go on killing the bloodsucking kulaks. Cable that you have received this and carried out [your instructions].

   Yours, Lenin.

   P.S. Find tougher people.[20]

Clearly, not all Bolsheviks were up to the task.

Even after this telegram, Lenin frequently discussed 'democracy and the dictatorship'. It is, however, unclear what rôle democracy was to play. The document cited above is a total condemnation of Lenin's 'theory' of socialist revolution. What did he mean by '100 known kulaks, rich men'? Who were these condemned individuals? Today we know them to have been the hardest-working, most capable of the peasantry. If the circumstances were invoked to justify the crime, then they could be invoked to justify anything at all. In what way were Lenin's orders to 'shoot on the spot', 'arrest or shoot', 'apply extreme revolutionary measures', etc., preferable to the 'Cossack whips' and 'bloody massacres' of Nicholas II? Compared to the bestialities of the civil war, the tragedies of tsarist Russia pale into insignificance.

Nor was it the 'iron logic' of a revolution that had gone out of his control that forced Lenin to apply these monstrous methods. In an earlier time, from the peacefully ordered world of Geneva in October 1905, he wrote a series of articles for publication in St Petersburg which were in effect instructions for staging an armed uprising. One such, entitled 'Tasks for the Ranks of a Revolutionary Army', discusses 'independent military actions', as well as 'managing crowds'. He recommended that 'units arm themselves as best they can (with rifles, revolvers, bombs, knives, knuckledusters, sticks, paraffin-soaked rags, rope for rope-ladders, spades to dig barricades, gun-cotton, barbed wire, nails (to stop the cavalry) and so on and so forth)'. Places and people, even if unarmed, must be made ready 'to throw stones down onto the troops and pour boiling water from top storeys, to throw acid over the police and steal government money'. It was, he wrote, of the utmost importance to encourage the 'murder of spies, policemen, gendarmes, Black Hundredists', while it would be 'criminal' to trust the 'democrats', who were only good at running a liberal talk-shop.[21]

Lenin's 'theory' of revolution proposed nothing other than these inhuman terrorist methods. Even when Nicholas II published his Manifesto of October 1905, leading to the creation of the State Duma and possibly opening the way eventually to constitutional monarchy, and offering perhaps the chance of a move towards democracy, Lenin did not alter his position. To the tsar's proposal to give 'the population stable foundations of civic freedom on principles of true inviolability of the person, freedom of conscience, speech, assembly and union', the Bolsheviks responded with a signal for renewed violence. Lenin called for 'the pursuit of the retreating enemy', an 'increase in pressure', while voicing his confidence that 'the revolution will finish off the enemy and wipe the throne of the bloody tsar from the face of the earth'.[22]

The evolution of the Bolsheviks' attitude to the Constituent Assembly of 1918 – the first such body to be elected on a fully democratic basis in Russia's history – demonstrates their extreme pragmatism. As long as it appeared possible to exploit this nationwide institution in their own interests, Lenin had supported the idea of the Assembly. But as soon as the elections produced a Bolshevik minority, he abruptly changed course. An All-Russian Commission had been formed before the Bolshevik seizure of power in October 1917 to manage the election, and when that seizure of power took place the Commission declared it 'a sad event' that would 'bring anarchy and terror'.[23] When the Commission declared that 'it found it impossible to enter any sort of relations with the Council of People's Commissars', i.e. Lenin's government,[24] its members were arrested. On the orders of the Bolshevik leadership they were locked in an empty room in the Tauride Palace for four days without food or bedding, in the hope that they would 'see sense' and cancel the election. The election went ahead regardless.

Realizing that the new Assembly, in which they had won only a quarter of the seats, would not bow to them, the Bolsheviks simply dispersed it during the night of 6 January 1918, after its first and only day of existence. Since the overthrow of the tsar in February 1917, the revolutionary bodies, the workers' strike committees, and the soldier's and peasants' representatives had been forming their own councils, or soviets, and through these had been applying pressure on the successor (Provisional) government to bring the war to an end and to introduce radical reforms. After seizing power in their name in October, Lenin declared that 'the Soviets are incomparably superior to all the parliaments in the world', and therefore 'there is no place for the Constituent Assembly'. He added, 'The people wanted to convene the Constituent Assembly, so we convened it. But the people at once sensed what this notorious assembly represented. So now we have carried out the will of the people.'[25] 'The people' had been given one day in which to make up their minds. This device, of speaking in the name of the people, would become a firm tradition, whereby every activity was authorized by the mythical 'will of the people'.

Lenin's theory of socialist revolution made no room for any representative elected institutions or direct democracy. Instead, he said, the socialist revolution 'cannot but be accompanied by civil war'.[26] Neither he nor any of his accomplices were troubled by the fact that the people had not empowered them to decide its fate. As the Socialist Revolutionary émigré Boris Savinkov wrote in 1921, in a Warsaw publication: 'The Russian people do not want Lenin, Trotsky and Dzerzhinsky, not merely because the Bolsheviks mobilize them, shoot them, take their grain and are ruining Russia. The Russian people do not want them for the simple reason that . . . *nobody elected them.*'[27]

On the eve of the Bolshevik coup d'état, in August–September 1917, Lenin wrote his famous work *State and Revolution*, in which he laid out his ideas on the future socialist state. According to Lenin, 'when *everyone* has learned to govern and is in practice independently governing social production, independently accounting for and controlling the spongers, the layabouts, crooks and similar "preservers of capitalist traditions", then to evade this accounting and control will become so unbelievably difficult, such a rare exception, and will be accompanied, no doubt, by such speedy and serious retribution (for the armed workers, the people who live practical lives, are not sentimental intellectuals and will not permit anyone to fool around with them), that the *need* to observe the simple, basic rules of any human community will soon become a *habit*'.[28] Lenin placed special emphasis on social control, believing that when it 'became genuinely universal, general, nationwide', it would be impossible to refuse to serve the state, 'there would be no place to hide'.[29]

Lenin apparently never asked himself why, before 1921, the Bolsheviks were incapable of giving the people anything but chaos, civil war, hunger and terror.[30] The fact is, the Bolsheviks had achieved their goal: the Party had power. The revolution was for Lenin a social experiment. If it failed in 1905, it would succeed in 1917, and if not, there was always the future. In an article entitled 'For the Workers' Attention', Gorky wrote in November 1917:

Life in all its complexity is unknown to Lenin, he does not know the masses, he hasn't lived among them, but he found out in books how to raise the masses onto their hind legs, how to enrage the masses' instincts easily. To the Lenins, the working class is like iron-ore to a metal-worker. Is it possible, given present circumstances, to cast a socialist state out of this ore? Evidently not. But why not try? What does Lenin risk if the experiment fails?[31]

To achieve power, the Bolsheviks became wedded forever to violence, while liberty was buried in the marriage. Lenin's address 'To the Citizens of Russia', following his coup, and his decrees promising peace and land, say nothing about liberty as the main aim of the revolution. They were not the Bill of Rights of the English revolution of 1689, nor the American Declaration of Independence of 1776. The Russian revolution, which formally gave the people peace and land, cunningly replaced the idea of liberty with that of the abolition of the exploitation of man by man. In giving the people the spectre of hope, Lenin had found and trapped man's most robust and vital element, that of faith. He thus condemned the Russians for decades to contenting themselves with hope alone.

What, if any, was the philosophical foundation of Lenin's approach? He has, after all, been called the most powerful philosopher of the twentieth century by Soviet scholars (the present author included). Had Lenin not come to power, his *Materialism and Empiriocriticism* (1908) would have been known only to the narrowest circle of experts on the theory of knowledge, and even they would have found it excessively scholastic: 'Everything in it "corresponding" to the position of dialectical materialism,' wrote the Russian émigré philosopher Vasili Zenkovsky, 'is accepted without qualification, while whatever does not, is discarded *for that reason alone.*'[32] Indeed, Lenin himself wrote in this work: 'Following the path of Marx's theory, we shall approach closer and closer to the objective truth (while never achieving it); following *any other path* we shall come to nothing but confusion and lies.'[33]

In other words, only those who employ Marxist methodology are philosophers and scholars. The peremptory nature of his arguments, his hallmark as a politician, organizer and philosopher, puts one mentally on guard. Lenin's philosophy was designed to separate the 'pure' thinkers from the 'impure', the materialists from the idealists. His aim was to demonstrate that a school of philosophy which accepted the existence of religion could not be scientific.

Whether or not Lenin's reasoning is accepted as plausible or implausible, the principle of Party-mindedness, which he proclaimed as necessary for the philosophical study of scientific knowledge, places the reader beyond the pale of science and in the sphere of ideological opposition to Bolshevik values. After the failure of the 1905 revolution, an upsurge of interest in idealist philosophy occurred in Russia, as it did also in Western Europe, for different reasons. Disappointment with socialist, that is materialist, ideas was driving Russian intellectuals towards a spiritual philosophy which emphasised individual self-perfection as the path to social improvement, rather than the other way round, which was the message and purpose of socialism. In an effort to counter this trend, the Bolshevik intellectuals Alexander Bogdanov and Anatoly Lunacharsky had become interested in the works of the contemporary Austrian physicist and philosopher Ernst Mach (the creator of the measurement of the speed of sound) and his mentor, the nineteenth-century Swiss philosopher Richard Avenarius. According to Mach, the attributes of the material world – colour, shape, texture – are conferred on objects by the human mind. In other words, man makes the world as he knows it. The object of this theory was to eliminate the distinction between the spiritual and the physical world, since the world according to Mach is a physical entity given shape by consciousness. Marxist materialism posited the opposite proposition: the physical world, the environment, is what forms and conditions the human mind. Marxists are realists, or materialists, and Machists are idealists.

Bogdanov, a trained biological scientist, took Mach further by asserting that not only the physical world, but society itself, is a product of the human mind, that without the human will to form communal life, society would not have come into being. Society therefore is the expression of consciousness. The object of this line of reasoning was, as has been suggested, to counter the corrosive effect new idealist thinking was having on socialist life in Russia, by showing that Marxist philosophy was sufficiently flexible to absorb such an apparently idealistic notion.

At around this time, 1906 to 1909, Lenin was engaged in complicated relations with Bogdanov and other intellectuals associated with his Bolshevik organization. Partly in competition for intellectual leadership, partly in order to keep control of the organization and its finances, Lenin chose to make an assault on Bogdanov and his allies, by challenging their orthodoxy as Marxists. In order to do so, he read exhaustively in philosophical literature.[34] Having accepted Marx's social-political and philosophical teaching without qualification, Lenin confined himself to nothing more than commenting on it. No social-political theory can be universal, yet that is what Lenin made of Marxism. As for such new idealists as Berdyaev and his fellow thinkers, Lenin's hostility in the end saved their lives: when in March 1922 he read a collection of articles by Berdyaev, Fedor Stepun, Frank and others, entitled *Oswald Spengler and the Decline of Europe*, Lenin wrote to N.P. Gorbunov, general administrator of the Council of People's Deputies (Sovnarkom), describing the book as 'White Guardist' and ordering Gorbunov 'to speak to the Deputy Head of the GPU, I.S. Unshlikht, about it...'[35] Philosophers were not yet being shot for 'White Guardist' views, but were merely deported from the country.

The philosophical side of Lenin's mind was strong on conviction, but dogmatic. He was absolutely certain that 'Marx's philosophy is consummate philosophical materialism',[36] and the only true theory. In one of his last works, criticizing the Menshevik Sukhanov, he wrote: 'You say that to create socialism one must have civilized behaviour. Fine. But why couldn't we create the prerequisites for civilized behaviour from the start, by expelling the landowners and expelling the capitalists, and then start the movement to socialism? Where have you ever read that such changes in the usual historical order are not acceptable or impossible?'[37] In other words, if the Marxist books have not prohibited it, any 'historical order' is permissible.

The aesthetic side of Lenin's mind was less despotic, perhaps because art was less closely associated with politics than law and philosophy, or perhaps because he did not feel as confident in this sphere. Berdyaev may have exaggerated in calling Lenin backward and primitive in art, but only slightly. His taste was extremely conservative, while his range of knowledge of literature was more extensive. He cited and used Chernyshevsky more than any other writer – more than 300 times in his collected works, indeed – but he also quoted from a range of nineteenth-century Russian writers whose interests and themes tended towards the social and political. He wrote an article on Tolstoy, but he cited Dostoevsky only twice in all of his works.[38] Preferring the classics to contemporary writing, he nevertheless much admired Gorky's novel *The Mother*, which dealt with social and political problems on an accessible artistic level.

His earlier friendship with Lenin did not prevent Gorky from attacking the Bolsheviks fiercely in 1917 and 1918 in his Petrograd newspaper *Novaya zhizn'*. Under the heading 'Untimely Thoughts', he managed to publish forty-eight of these articles before the paper was closed down on Lenin's orders in July 1918. Soon after the Bolshevik coup, on 7 (20) November 1917, Gorky had written: 'Lenin and his comrades-in-arms think they can commit any crime, like the massacre at Petrograd, the storming of Moscow, abolition of freedom of speech, the senseless arrests – all the abominations that used to be committed by Plehve and Stolypin.* This is where today's leader is taking the proletariat, and it should be understood that Lenin is not an omnipotent magician, but a cold-blooded trickster who spares neither the honour nor the lives of the proletariat.'[39]

Needless to say, these and many other articles which Gorky wrote at the time were not included in the thirty-volume edition of his works. Soon, however, Gorky altered his tone, aware that the regime was enduring and that he could not manage without its help and that of Lenin. In April 1919 he called on Lenin to ask him to release the Left SR N.A. Shklovskaya, secretary of the poet Alexander Blok. She was set free six months later. In September 1920 he asked Lenin to

---

* Vyacheslav Plehve, Nicholas II's Interior Minister, was assassinated in 1904. Peter Stolypin was the Prime Minister from 1906 until he was assassinated – in the tsar's presence – in 1911.

allow the publisher Z.I. Grzhebin to emigrate. Given Lenin's personal magnetism, these visits had an effect, and soon Gorky was virtually tamed.

While Lenin himself approached art and literature as a consumer, as Party leader he saw in them a powerful instrument of political influence. It was perhaps for this reason that he was so hostile to Futurism and the other modernist trends in art. And no doubt when he urged the closure of the opera and ballet it was because he thought they were 'court arts remote from the people', and he could not see how singers and dancers might inspire the detachments that were carrying out food requisitioning. For him, the chief purpose of art was in developing 'the best models, traditions, results of *existing* culture from the point of view of the world outlook of Marxism and the conditions of proletarian life in the epoch of the dictatorship'.[40]

Many biographers and people who met Lenin attest to the enormous 'physical force' of his mind. Perhaps this was because he usually crushed his opponent in argument with his absolute refusal to compromise; perhaps it was the uncompromising convictions themselves, the one-dimensional, virtually fanatical conviction. In any event, many people began to stress the force of Lenin's mind, and to relate it to the shape of his head. Lunacharsky, for instance, remarked that 'the structure of his skull is truly striking. One has to study him for a little while to appreciate its physical power, the contours of the colossal dome of his forehead and to sense something I can only describe as a physical emanation of light from its surface.'[41] No one is able to confirm whether light really did emanate from Lenin's forehead. Instead, we must make do with the five editions of his collected works, the forty volumes of the Lenin miscellanies, thousands of unpublished documents, thousands of works of hagiography and a handful of dispassionate, honest books about him. We do, however, have his plans and blueprints, and above all his actions, to judge him by.

## The Phenomenon of Bolshevism

Every Soviet schoolboy knew the story of the Second Party Congress of 1903 and the difference between the Bolsheviks and the

Mensheviks: Lenin and his 'rock-hard' followers 'saw the Party as a
combat organization, every member of which had to be a selfless
fighter, prepared for everyday pedestrian tasks as well as to fight with
a gun in his hand', while Martov, 'supported by all the wavering and
opportunistic elements, wanted to turn the Party into an assembly
room'. 'With such a party,' Lenin's official biography informed us,
'the workers would never have been victorious and taken power into
their hands.'[42] If a student should add that Plekhanov, though wavering and indecisive, sided with Lenin, he would earn an extra mark.
Such a student would not, however, be told that it was in fact Martov's
more loosely defined formula for membership that was passed by the
Congress, nor that it was only because Lenin obtained a majority in
elections to the Party central organs that he could call his group the
Majorityites, or Bolsheviks, while the 'opportunists' naturally became
the Minorityites, or Mensheviks.

This laundered version migrated from book to book and became
a fixed dogma in the public mind. In the years following October
1917, the term Menshevik became synonymous with opportunist,
bourgeois conciliator, White Guard ally, foreign spy, enemy of
the people. Naturally, this fundamentally affected attitudes towards
the Mensheviks. When the Politburo discussed 'the Menshevik
question' on 5 January 1922, it instructed Iosif Unshlikht, deputy
chairman of the Cheka, to find two or three provincial towns, 'not
excluding those on a railway', where Mensheviks could be settled.
He was further told not to obstruct Mensheviks who wanted to
leave the country, and that where a subsidy for fares was needed, he
should apply to the Politburo.[43] The days of mass execution had
yet to come.

By concentrating on the organizational factor as the wall dividing
the two wings of the Party, aspects of far greater significance were
pushed into the background. In fact the true line dividing Bolsheviks
and Mensheviks was not the issue of organization. The only true
social democrats were the Mensheviks: they recognized democracy,
parliament and political pluralism as values that could avert violence
as a means of achieving social development. Democracy for them was
a permanent value, not a political front. The Bolsheviks, by contrast,
became increasingly convinced of the value of violence. And when
they came to power, they believed they had conquered not only the

bourgeoisie, but also their former Party comrades, the Mensheviks. 'October,' Stalin declared, 'means the ideological victory of Communism over social democracy, of Marxism over reformism.'

Why did the Bolsheviks win? What was the appeal of their programme? Why did they survive, when it became clear they represented only the interests of the 'professional revolutionaries'? The answers to these questions will lead to an understanding of the phenomenon of Bolshevism itself.

The First World War provided the key. The news that war had broken out at first caused shock among the Russian émigrés, followed by intellectual confusion, and finally the rapid growth of a defencist mood. A volunteer movement also sprang up as soon as war was declared. Many Russian émigrés in Paris, among them about a thousand Social Democrats, including Bolsheviks,[44] were seized by patriotic fervour and rushed to join the French army. Most were drafted into the Foreign Legion, or languished in difficult circumstances because the French government did not know how to deal with them.[45]

On the other hand, a large group of Social Democratic internationalists, from both wings of the Party, soon emerged and began agitating against the imperialist war altogether. Prominent among them was Julius Martov, then living in Paris and editing a newspaper called *Nashe slovo* (Our Word). He called for the unification of all progressive forces in the struggle against the militarism of the imperialist powers and for an end to the war without reparations or annexations.[46]

The orthodox Bolsheviks took up a different position. When Lenin heard on 5 August 1914 that the German Social Democrats in the Reichstag had voted for the war budget, he declared, 'From this day I am no longer a Social Democrat, I am a Communist.'[47] The Bolsheviks would not formally change the name of the Party until their Seventh Congress in March 1918, when they became the Russian Communist Party (Bolshevik). In 1914, however, Lenin was dissociating himself from the mainstream of European socialism, which in practical terms had suspended its political programme until the war was over, and was giving notice that he was bent on revolution, now more than ever. He did not, however, decline the help of the Austrian Social Democrat leader, Victor Adler, to get out of Austrian Galicia, where he had lived since 1912, in order to be physically closer to events in Russia, and to make his way to Switzerland, where he launched into a spate of writing. His first significant response to the war was a manifesto entitled 'The Tasks of the Revolutionary Social Democrats in the European War'. In it he penned the phrase that was to become sacrosanct in Soviet historiography: 'From the point of view of the working class and the toiling masses of all the peoples of Russia, the lesser evil would be the defeat of the tsarist monarchy and its troops, which are oppressing Poland, the Ukraine and many other peoples of Russia.'[48] He went further in November 1914 when he wrote, 'Turning the present imperialist war into civil war is the only proper proletarian slogan.'[49]

He was calling for the defeat of his own country, and for making an already hideous war into something even worse: a nightmare civil war. With the seizure of power in mind, this may have been a logical position to take, but from the moral point of view it was deeply cynical. Desiring the defeat of the Russian army was one thing from the safety of Berne; it was quite another for those lying in the blood-soaked mud of the trenches on the Eastern front. What Lenin wanted was to turn the whole of Russia into a theatre of war. No one took any notice of his call, no one wanted to think about civil war, and in any case nobody then believed in the socialist revolution. True, Martov had warned at the outbreak of war that out of factional fanaticism Lenin wanted 'to warm his hands by the fire that has been lit on the world arena'.[50] But no one had taken heed.

In a letter of 17 October 1914 to one of his most trusted agents, Alexander Shlyapnikov, then in Sweden, Lenin wrote: '. . . the least evil now and at once would be the *defeat* of tsarism in the war. For tsarism is a hundred times worse than kaiserism . . . The entire essence of our work (persistent, systematic, maybe of long duration) must be in the direction of turning the national war into a civil war. When this will happen is another question, it isn't clear yet. We have to let the moment ripen and "force it to ripen" systematically . . . We can neither "promise" civil war nor "decree" it, but we are duty bound to work – for as long as it takes – *in this direction*.'[51] Articles embodying this message began appearing in the émigré press over Lenin's signature. Despite his sideswipes at 'imperialist Germany', there were those in Berlin who realized that they had a new ally living in Switzerland. Seeing that there was no realistic way by which to seize power, Lenin took the side of Russia's enemy, while clothing himself in the garb of internationalism.

When the Russian people had been driven to the limit by the war, and state power in effect lay on the streets of the capital, the Bolsheviks obtained power with remarkable ease, in exchange for the promise of peace. Lenin's call to civil war was forgotten, but having gained power, he felt he had to go further; socialism seemed so close. If yesterday's men could be swept away, one could go on with the great experiment unhampered. Having given the people peace (however unreal and shortlived) and land (which would soon be taken back when Russia's peasants were turned into twentieth-century serfs), Lenin also took back the liberty, such as it was, that he had promised.

The Bolsheviks survived because of their leader and because of their commitment to unbridled force. Lenin was the ideal leader in the situation. As Potresov was to write in 1937:

Neither Plekhanov nor Martov, nor anyone else, possessed the secret of Lenin's hypnotic power over people, or rather his dominance over them. They respected Plekhanov, they loved Martov, but unswervingly they followed only Lenin as the sole undisputed leader. Lenin represented that rare phenomenon in Russia, a man with an iron will, indomitable energy, who poured fanatical faith into the movement and the cause, and had no less faith in himself ... Behind these great qualities, however, there lurked great deficiencies, negative qualities, more appropriate perhaps in a medieval or Asiatic conqueror.[52]

What Lenin thought of Potresov he revealed in a letter to Gorky: 'Such a swine, that Potresov!'[53] Potresov had once been a close comrade of Lenin's, and Lenin always kept his most savage invective for those who had deserted him.

In 1921 the Socialist Revolutionaries illegally published a pamphlet, at a time when it was just still possible to do so in Moscow. Entitled 'What Have the Bolsheviks Given the People?', it pointed out that the new masters had not fulfilled a single promise of their programme. Instead of peace, the country had been plunged into a bloody civil war lasting three years, and had lost some thirteen million people through the fighting, disease, terror or emigration. Famine raged, and the peasants were not sowing because they knew their grain would be confiscated. Industry lay in ruins. Russia had been cut off from the rest of the world and was shunned by almost everyone. A one-party dictatorship had been installed. The Cheka was a state within a state. The Constituent Assembly had been dispersed. The regime was conducting a war with its own people.[54]

One reason the Bolsheviks were able to survive was that their leader was himself capable of setting an example of merciless terror. For instance, in the autumn of 1920 he wrote to Krestinsky, a secretary of the Central Committee: 'I suggest a commission be formed at once (one can do it secretly to start with) to work out extreme measures (in the way Larin proposed. Larin is right.) What about you plus Larin plus Vladimirsky (Dzerzhinsky) plus Rykov?* The preparation of terror in secret is necessary and urgent.'[55] What need had the country of a regime that sought to achieve its aims by means of terror as state policy? Force was the style of the Bolsheviks and their leader. The paradox of Bolshevism – the Majorityites – was that theirs was a dictatorship of the minority, a fact observed by Martov in 1919 when writing a book on the intellectual and psychological origins of Bolshevism, which was published before completion by Fedor Dan in Berlin in 1923.

In 1923 Martov, who was terminally ill, wrote that Lenin had promised to bring in immediately all the measures detailed by Marx and Engels, namely election and recall of the government, workers' pay to be the norm, everyone to carry out the functions of control and supervision, so that none would become bureaucrats. 'Reality has harshly dashed all these hopes,' he wrote. 'The Soviet state has revealed a tendency towards the extreme strengthening of state centralism, the maximum development of hierarchical and coercive principles in the community, and the growth and super-abundance of all the special organs of state repression.'[56]

The slogan 'All Power to the Soviets' had been replaced by 'All Power to the Bolshevik Party', while the Politburo possessed powers beyond those of any emperor. In 1919, it ordered that hostages should be shot if there were any more incidents of bombs being thrown at the civilian population;[57] that anyone failing to hand in weapons within an allotted period should be severely punished, even executed.[58] In

---

* Larin, whose real name was Mikhail Lurie, was a top official in the economic apparatus. Alexei Rykov was in charge of the Council for the National Economy.

April 1920 Lenin and Stalin (as People's Commissar for Nationalities) signed a cable to their emissary in the Caucasus, Sergo Ordzhonikidze, forbidding self-determination for Georgia.[59] Lenin also ordered the arrest of the delegates at an All-Russian Zionist conference being held in Moscow, as well as the publication of compromising material on them.[60] The list is endless. It is noteworthy that the Politburo, which at times had up to forty items on its agenda, rarely dealt with strictly Party affairs. The Party had become a state organ.

The system created by Lenin in turn soon created a new type of man in whom, in Berdyaev's words, the motives of strength and power displaced those of love of truth and compassion.

This new man, perfectly suited to Lenin's plan, became the material of the Party organization and took over the vast country. Alien to Russian culture, their fathers and grandfathers had been illiterate and devoid of all culture, living solely by faith. The people had sensed the injustice of the old order but had borne their suffering meekly and humbly ... But the time came when they could take no more ... Their mildness and humility became savagery and fury. Lenin could not have carried out his plan of revolution and seizure of power without this revolt in the soul of the people.[61]

Lenin's political approach was the negation of traditional democratic institutions, such as parliament, the resort to purely revolutionary methods, the idolizing of force. Combined with a powerful mind, strong will and the conviction that he was right, it was an approach that exerted a powerful attraction on those who believed in the possibility of making a leap from the kingdom of want into the kingdom of liberty. In 1904, in 'Forward or backward?', replying to Lenin's 'One Step Forward, Two Steps Back', Martov wrote:

Reading these lines, breathing as they do a petty, at times senseless personal malice, amazing narcissism, blind, deaf, unfeeling fury, endless repetition of the same old meaningless 'fighting' and 'scathing' little words, one becomes convinced that this is a man who is fatally compelled to slide further down the slope onto which he stepped 'spontaneously' and which will take him straight to the full political corruption and shattering of social democracy.[62]

The Party went on splitting itself, expelling 'factions', 'deviations' and 'platforms', incapable because of its fanaticism of seeing these as differences of opinion rather than obsessions, as creative endeavours rather than fossilized dogma. The splits continued until, by the beginning of the 1930s, all that was left was a Stalinist monolith that was utterly incapable of changing. The situation could only lead to disaster.

## Lenin and the Mensheviks

When the Third Party Congress opened in London in April 1905, with Lenin as its chairman, he paid particular attention to questions of combat: he believed that tsarism was 'rotten through' and that it must be helped to crash to the ground. He made a long speech about armed uprising, tabled a motion on the issue, and tried to convince the delegates that a revolution was a real possibility.[63] Throughout this time, he kept up his criticism of the Mensheviks. When they called for active exploitation of a proposed assembly, Lenin insisted on a boycott, since in his view any parliament was nothing more than a 'bourgeois stable'. When he read Martov's article 'The Russian Proletariat and the Duma', published in the Vienna paper *Rabochaya gazeta*, he became enraged at his former comrade's call to the Social Democrats to take part in elections to the tsarist parliament, and gave his reply in an article entitled 'At the Tail of the Monarchist Bourgeoisie or at the Head of the Revolutionary Proletariat and Peasantry?'[64] The very notion of achieving socialist, democratic and progressive goals by means of reforms, parliament and legal social struggle was blasphemy. Lenin could not see the colossal possibilities of parliamentary activity. His speeches breathe hatred for the liberals and reformists, among whom the most dangerous in his view were of course the Mensheviks.

Lenin's reaction to the October Manifesto, like that of Soviet historians thereafter, was that it was merely a tactical manoeuvre by the tsar and the bourgeoisie, engineered by the tsar's brilliant prime minister, Count Witte. According to eye-witnesses, the tsar realized that in signing the document he was taking a step towards constitutional, parliamentary monarchy. The autocracy had retreated and given a chance for democratic development. Had the Social Democrats – not only Lenin – not at once labelled the Manifesto a 'deception', and had they instead fought to make it a reality, history might have been different. Instead, the Manifesto was interpreted as a sign of weakness, and Lenin prepared to return to Russia to help bury the autocracy. He was convinced the moment was approaching. His articles now bore such titles as 'The Approach of the Dénouement', 'On the New Constitutional Manifesto of Nicholas the Last', 'The Dying Autocracy and the New Organs of People's Power'.

The differences with the Mensheviks were temporarily pushed to one side. They, meanwhile, like all the liberals, were having second thoughts about changing the existing political structure by force. Even relatively conservative, intelligent politicians like Witte were saying, 'Russia has outgrown her existing structure. She is striving for a legal structure based on civil liberty.' Witte proposed that the tsar 'abolish repressive measures against actions which do not threaten society and the state'.[65]

The government's concessions were, however, dismissed, tension rose, and the Bolsheviks forced events by exploiting the workers' discontent. Lenin's espousal of widespread violence and terror, however, pushed the Mensheviks further away from the idea of Party reunification. In September 1908, Martov wrote in exasperation to his friend and Menshevik comrade Pavel Axelrod: 'I confess that more and more I think that even nominal involvement with this bandit gang is a mistake.'[66] They were both unwilling to make peace with sectarianism and conspiratorial methods. While keener on reunification than the Bolsheviks, they also wanted to retain democratic principles within the Party. As for Plekhanov, he had long decided that true reunification was impossible. In his view, Lenin regarded reunification as his faction swallowing up and subordinating all the other elements of Russian social democracy, and thus depriving the Russian revolutionaries of any democratic basis. Plekhanov pointed out that instead of underlining the common features shared by the two wings (which both had their roots in the labour movement), Lenin emphasized their differences, and was an incorrigible sectarian.[67]

As the culmination of the Russian drama of 1917 approached, with defeats at the war front, hunger and chaos, the Bolsheviks concentrated all their energy on preparing the armed uprising. The Mensheviks meanwhile focused on peace and liberty, the Constituent Assembly and a new constitution, a strategy Lenin regarded as treacherous, for it weakened the revolutionaries' chances of a victorious uprising. In the final analysis, the difference between the two factions boiled down to the Bolsheviks' wanting socialism on the basis of a dictatorship, and the Mensheviks' wanting it on the basis of democracy. In Fedor Dan's words: 'Menshevism stood for turning the struggle for "bourgeois" political democracy and its preservation into its first priority; while Bolshevism put the "building of socialism" at the top of its agenda, throwing overboard and attacking the very idea of a "routine democracy".'[68]

Dan, who outlived Lenin by nearly a quarter of a century and who knew him well, spent a good part of his life as the political and ideological leader of Menshevism, together with Martov, who died in 1923. Repeatedly arrested and exiled by the tsarist regime, he exerted great energy to preserve the democratic ideals of the RSDLP. His star reached its zenith in June 1917 when he co-chaired the Executive Committee of the All-Russian Soviet of Workers' and Soldiers' Deputies (Ispolkom) with N.S. Chkheidze, was chief editor of *Izvestiya*, and with I.G. Tsereteli and A.R. Gots was one of the spokesmen of the democratic wing of Russian social democracy. Symbolically, it was Dan who opened the Second Congress of Soviets on 25 October (7 November) 1917, and when the Bolsheviks and Left Socialist Revolutionaries voted approval of the seizure of power that had just taken place, Dan protested by leaving the Congress together with the other Mensheviks.

For the next three years, the Menshevik leadership represented the democratic opposition, within the legal means permitted. Lenin, meanwhile, missed no opportunity to launch insulting attacks on his former comrades. Nevertheless, until 1920 the Mensheviks led a more or less legal existence, even if the term 'Social Democrat' became a dirty word. Then the Politburo launched open persecution, beginning with 'semi-harsh' measures. On 22 June 1922 it was decided that the political activity of 'these accomplices of the bourgeoisie' must be 'curtailed', and that this should be achieved for the time being by exile: 'All People's Commissars should be informed that Mensheviks, at present employed in commissariats and capable of playing any political role, should not be kept in Moscow, but dispersed in the provinces, in each case after enquiries have been made at the Cheka and Orgburo.'[69] At the same time, Mensheviks were being arrested throughout the country. Protests and appeals for release were sent to

Lenin and the Politburo. On 14 October 1920, for instance, the Polit-buro unanimously voted against an appeal for the release of a group of Mensheviks.[70] The arrests continued.

Lenin was especially interested in Martov's activities. In July 1919, in an article entitled 'Everyone into the Struggle with [White General] Denikin!', he wrote: 'Martov and Co. think themselves "above" both warring sides [in the civil war], think themselves able to create a "third side". This desire, even if sincere, is still an illusion of the petty bourgeois democrat who even now, seventy years after 1848, hasn't learnt the alphabet, namely, that in a capitalist milieu there can only be the dictatorship of the bourgeosie, for the dictatorship of the prolet-ariat cannot coexist with any third option. It seems Martov and Co. will die with this illusion.'[71] When Martov and Dan were elected with other Mensheviks to the Moscow City Soviet in 1918, Lenin wrote on Kamenev's report: 'I think you should "tire them out" with practi-cal tasks: Dan for *sanitary work*, Martov can look after *canteens*.'[72] When, in the same year, Martov submitted the manuscript of his memoirs for publication through Gorky – there was still some latitude in such matters – Lenin had it censored.[73] Martov was under constant threat of arrest, but Lenin, perhaps because of their earlier friendship, held back. At the first sign that Martov wanted to go abroad, however, permission was granted, thus releasing Lenin from the dilemma, and enabling him to say 'We willingly let Martov go.'[74]

There had never been close relations between Dan and Lenin, and Dan was arrested in February 1921, and held in the Petropavlovsk Fortress in Petrograd (as St Petersburg had been called since 1914) for nearly a year. He was no stranger there, having 'sat' (i.e. been imprisoned) in 1896 before being exiled under the tsar. He was now accused of instigating the anti-Bolshevik uprising of soldiers and sailors on the fortress island of Kronstadt in the Baltic, once the spearhead of Bolshevik support, and faced possible execution. Instead he was sentenced to internal exile, in the words of the special Politburo resolution, 'to some distant non-proletarian district where he can work in his speciality'.[75] Dan began a hunger strike, demanding the right to go abroad, and since the inflexibility of the Stalin era had yet to come, the request was granted.

Any real or imagined threat which arose in those years was invariably attributed to some 'counter-revolutionary activity of the Mensheviks', thus ensuring harsher treatment for them as a whole. On 28 November 1921, for instance, Trotsky reported to the Politburo that he had information about a counter-revolutionary coup being prepared in Moscow and Petrograd. It was headed by Mensheviks, SRs and 'surviving bourgeoisie'. Trotsky was immediately appointed 'Chairman of the Moscow Defence Committee', and it was decided that 'Mensheviks should not be released, and the Central Committee should be told to intensify arrests of Mensheviks and SRs'.[76] Whenever the Politburo returned to the subject of the Mensheviks its position hardened. On 2 February 1922 Stalin reported on imprisoned Mensheviks, as a result of which the Politburo issued a special order to the GPU, the successor to the Cheka, 'to transfer to special places of imprisonment the most active and important of the leaders of anti-Soviet parties. Mensheviks, SRs and Anarchists at present held by the Cheka should continue to be kept in imprisonment.'[77]

The Mensheviks tried appealing to Social Democrats in the West. The Cheka intercepted one such letter to the International Berne Conference and reported it to Lenin. He read it, and underlined the words: 'the prisons are overflowing, the workers are shooting each other, many of our Social Democrat comrades have been shot'.[78] The Mensheviks' Central Bureau also wrote to Lenin, asking for the 'honest legalization' of their party, but Lenin's only response was to consign their appeal 'to the archives'.[79] All that was left for the Mensheviks was to try, even from afar, to save something of the values of the revolution of February 1917 through their journal *Sotsialisticheskii vestnik* (Socialist Messenger), published first in Berlin, then in Paris and, when the war came, in New York, where it closed in 1965, as there were no more old Mensheviks left to run it.

The Bolsheviks meanwhile tightened the screws. It was not only the Menshevik leaders who were being imprisoned and exiled; rank and file members of the Party, most of them of the intelligentsia, were suffering various punishments and persecution. The radical wing of the revolution was finishing off the democratic wing. Not that the Mensheviks were blameless. They had not done well in the election to the Constituent Assembly, they had failed to rally significant numbers of liberal forces, and they had failed to get across the ideas they had advocated for decades. Theirs was a sad fate. With the help

The house in Simbirsk where Lenin was born in 1870.

The town centre of Simbirsk, 1867.

*Above left*: Lenin's maternal grandfather, Alexander Dmitrievich Blank, who died the year Lenin was born.

*Above right*: Lenin's father, Ilya Nikolaevich Ulyanov (1831–86), at the age of thirty-two.

*Right*: The Ulyanov family in 1879. Vladimir is sitting in front on the right, his elder brother Alexander is standing between his parents, Dmitri is sitting in the centre, Anna is standing on the right, Olga is on the extreme left, and Maria on her mother's lap.

*Above left*: Alexander Ulyanov in his teens. He was hanged in 1887 at the age of twenty-one for taking part in an attempt on the life of Alexander III.

*Above right*: Lenin aged seventeen in 1887.

*Left*: Lenin's sister Olga, born a year after him in 1871, died of cholera as a student in 1891.

Lenin's sister Anna (1864–1935).

Lenin's brother Dmitri (1874–1943) as an army doctor in the First World War.

*Above left*: Sergei Nechaev (1847-82) at the age of twenty-two. Nechaev was a fanatical revolutionary, chiefly remembered for his 'Catechism of a Revolutionary', which inspired Lenin.

*Above right*: Lenin at the age of twenty as a student in Samara.

*Left*: Lenin, photographed by the police after his arrest in St Petersburg in 1896.

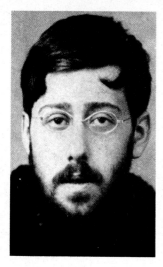

*Above left*: Yuli Martov in the police photograph taken when he was arrested with Lenin in 1896.

*Above centre*: Georgi Plekhanov (1856–1918), the 'father of Russian Marxism', was in exile in Western Europe from 1880 until he returned to Russia in March 1917. He died in Finland, a sworn enemy of Bolshevism.

*Above right*: Alexander Helphand, alias Parvus, under arrest in St Petersburg in 1905. Parvus conducted international trade during the First World War to raise funds for the revolutionary movement, and was also instrumental in channelling money from the German government to the Bolsheviks in 1915–17.

*Right*: Inessa Armand in her study on her family's estate at Yeldigino, near Moscow, in 1902. She met Lenin in Paris in 1910 and thereafter until her death in 1920 was his close confidante, and for some time also his lover.

*Above*: Lenin (yawning) playing chess on Capri in 1908 with his Bolshevik colleague Alexander Bogdanov, watched by his friend and benefactor, the writer Maxim Gorky.

*Left*: Lenin in Paris, 1910.

*Right*: Nicholas II and the Empress during the tercentenary celebrations of the Romanov dynasty in St Petersburg, 1913. The heir to the throne, Alexei, is being carried on the right.

*Below*: The Mensheviks Axelrod, Martov and Dan in 1915, probably in Switzerland.

of Lenin and the Bolsheviks, Russian Social Democracy died both inside and outside the country quietly and unnoticed. Some of the Social Democrats, it is true, changed direction under the impact of international events. For instance, in 1936, in Paris, Dan recognized the Soviet Union as the main bulwark against fascism. He published *Novyi mir* (New World), and then after escaping in March 1940 to New York, aged seventy, he retired as chairman of the Foreign Delegation and as editor of *Sotsialisticheskii vestnik* and launched *Novyi put'* (New Way). His break with Menshevism was complete by 1943. In *Novyi put'* he as it were rehabilitated Stalin. In his last book, *The Origins of Bolshevism*, published in 1946, the old adversary of totalitarianism suddenly saw something positive in the forced collectivization of agriculture, and found himself unable fully to condemn the show trials of the 1930s, or the Hitler–Stalin Pact of 1939. He even stated that 'the internal organic democratization of the Soviet system was not curtailed at its emergence'.[80] Dan's capitulation was complete.

Thus ended the Bolshevik–Menshevik struggle. The Mensheviks had seen democracy as an end, the Bolsheviks merely as a means. The Bolsheviks wanted to create a mighty, enclosed party, while the Mensheviks had wanted a party or association of liberally thinking people who rejected coercion.

## *The Paradox of Plekhanov*

Georgy Valentinovich Plekhanov was the acknowledged 'father of Russian Marxism'. Like Lenin, he was of gentry origin. Born in 1856 in Gudalovka, Tambov province, his father was an army captain who insisted his son follow in his footsteps, and Georgy duly entered military school in Voronezh. Soon after receiving his cadet badge, however, he left to become a student at the St Petersburg Mining Institute, from which he was expelled two years later, in 1877, for taking part in a student demonstration.[81] He never lost his military bearing, however, and it was perhaps this that led Lenin to say of him in 1904: 'Plekhanov is a man of colossal stature who makes you want to shrivel up,' adding in typical caustic fashion, 'still, I think he's a corpse already, and I'm alive.'[82] A Populist in the 1870s, Plekhanov left Russia in 1879, and by 1883 was a convinced Marxist. Thereafter he devoted himself to formulating doctrine for the Party and programmes for the future of Russia. When Lenin first met him in 1895, the effect of the older man was inspirational. Their next meeting in 1900, however, revealed that leadership ambitions had developed in both men which augured ill for their future collaboration, and when the Party split in 1903, Plekhanov joined the Mensheviks. The mutual hostility between the two men was reinforced by the diametrically opposed positions they took on the war, Lenin as a defeatist, Plekhanov as a defencist.

Plekhanov was abroad, in Switzerland, for thirty-seven years from 1879. He returned at last to Petrograd on 31 March 1917. This was two weeks before Lenin arrived, and is explained by the fact that the Allies were happy to facilitate the return of so ardent an advocate of the war effort. Plekhanov, who was suffering a serious chest condition and resting in the comparatively mild climate of San Remo when Nicholas II was overthrown, was eager to get back to Russia and to show his support for the revolution. He travelled through France to England and from there, on a French passport, was transported via the North Sea to Russia. Despite his warm reception, within a year he would be virtually running away from the revolution he had preached and waited for all his life. In an article, 'On Lenin's Theses and Why Delirium can be Interesting at the Time', published in the late summer of 1917, Plekhanov wrote that Lenin's call for fraternization with the Germans, for the overthrow of the Provisional Government and the seizure of power, would be seen by the workers for what they were, namely 'an insane and extremely dangerous attempt to sow anarchic chaos in the Russian land.'[83] His words fell on deaf ears. After the October seizure of power, with Vera Zasulich and Lev Deich he wrote an 'Open Letter to the Petrograd Workers', declaring that those who had seized power were pushing the Russian people 'onto the path of the greatest historical calamity', and that this step would 'provoke a civil war which in the end would force them to retreat far from the positions accomplished in February and March'.[84] Next day, a unit of soldiers and sailors burst into the apartment where Plekhanov was living with his wife, Rozalia Markovna. Pressing a revolver into his chest, one of the sailors demanded, 'Hand over your weapons freely. If we find any, we'll shoot you on the spot.' 'You're likely to do that, even if you don't find any,' Plekhanov responded calmly. 'But I don't have any.' The search did not end in immediate tragedy, but Plekhanov had to go into hiding, first in a clinic in Petrograd, then in Finland, at Pitkejarvi, near Terioki, where he died on 30 May 1918.

Lenin's relations with Plekhanov went through a full cycle, from deep regard – 'for twenty years, from 1883 to 1903, he gave the masses superb writings' – to complete ostracism – 'brand the chauvinist Plekhanov'. In fact, Marxism in Russia was raised on Plekhanov's articles. No one, including Lenin, had noticed that Plekhanov, for all his orthodoxy, did not include in his vision of Marxism the distorted features which pepper Lenin's writings. Plekhanov did not point out the 'counter-revolutionary essence' of the liberals, he did not reject parliamentarism, he accepted with reservations the idea of 'proletarian hegemony', and he accorded an enormous rôle to the intelligentsia in social movements. All this was later condemned as opportunism, liberal bootlicking, chauvinism, and so on. His particular sin was not merely 'to accommodate himself to Menshevism and liberalism', but to interpret the essence of class war in an 'opportunistic fashion'.

Indeed, in the introduction to his unfinished work 'The History of Russian Social Thought', Plekhanov had written: 'The development of any given society, divided into classes, is determined by the development of those classes and their mutual relations, that is, first, their *mutual struggle* where the internal social structure is concerned, and secondly, their more or less friendly *collaboration* when the defence of the country from outside attack is concerned.'[85] He suggested that class relations of this type were especially characteristic of Russia, and that this had left an indelible imprint on Russian history. This view may have prompted his 'defencist outlook', but despite being labelled a 'defencist' and 'social patriot' by the Bolsheviks, he retained his views on the war until the end of his life. To Lenin's call for Russian soldiers to fraternize with Germans, because Russia was conducting a predatory war, he responded ironically: 'forgive us, good Teutons, for the fact that our predatory intentions made you declare war on us; made you occupy a large slice of our territory; made you treat our prisoners with arrogant bestiality; made you seize Belgium and turn that once flourishing country into a bloodbath; made you ruin many French provinces, and so on and so forth. It's all our fault! Our terrible fault!'[86]

When he returned to Russia after more than thirty years of exile abroad, Plekhanov soon realized that being a Marxist theorist was not the same thing as being a revolutionary politician. He came out strongly against the idea of socialist revolution, accusing Lenin of forcing events for which Russia was not prepared,[87] and was firmly convinced that Russia was not ready for 'anything but a bourgeois revolution'.[88] He was not understood. Was this the chief paradox of Plekhanov? All his life he had written about the class struggle, the dictatorship of the proletariat, the leading rôle of the working class in restructuring society, and socialist revolution, as the goals of Marxist teaching. Yet when his own country raised its foot to cross the threshold of that revolution he staked all his authority on open protest. Perhaps this was not the real paradox. Plekhanov was too orthodox to depart from classical Marxist blueprints and to assent to leapfrogging stages. He regarded such an approach as 'Leninist delirium'.

Plekhanov in a sense reflected the drama of the Russian nobility and intelligentsia. Realizing that only gradual change would put Russia on the path of genuine progress, one part of this social élite believed that such changes could be achieved by revolutionary methods, while another believed in the path of accommodation, adaptation and appropriate reordering of the existing system. It is therefore not surprising that Plekhanov, a noble from Tambov province, whose mother was related to Belinsky, the famous radical philosopher of the 1840s, should have a brother, Grigory, who was a police superintendent. When the then Bolshevik Nikolai Valentinov asked Grigory if the statues of Catherine the Great would be pulled down when the revolution came, the police superintendent replied, 'What rubbish! When the revolution comes? There isn't going to be one. There can't be one in Russia. We're not in France.'[89] Georgy saw things differently, although for him the revolution, which was inevitable, must be the bourgeois one, which would last a long time. On the eve of the October revolution in 1917 he had the political courage to proclaim loudly that the coming regime must not be based on the narrow foundations of the dictatorship of the proletariat, but 'must be based on a coalition of all the vital forces in the country'. In a series of articles published in August and September in the newspaper *Yedinstvo* (Unity), he declared that a coalition would represent a consensus of the nation. 'If you don't want consensus, go with Lenin. If you decide not to go with Lenin, enter the consensus.'

In his desperate efforts to prevent the dictatorship of the 'professional revolutionaries', Plekhanov consciously went about his own political self-destruction: 'Are the interests of the workers always and in every respect opposed to the interests of the capitalists? In economic history has there never been a time when these interests coincided? Partial coincidence generates cooperation in certain areas. Socialist and non-socialist elements can realize this limited agreement in *social reforms*.'[90] All this was complete heresy to Lenin and the Bolsheviks.

In effect, Plekhanov's last articles, on the eve of the October coup, represent a new conception of socialism. Having for decades defended the class approach of the dictatorship of the proletariat at congresses of the Second International, he was now revising many of his previous principles. He had become not only a 'defencist', but also a 'reformist', terms of Leninist abuse which were equalled in derisiveness only by that of 'plekhanovist'. In March 1920, when Lenin was informed that a revolutionary tribunal in Kiev had sentenced one I. Kiselev to death and that he was appealing to Lenin for help, Lenin wrote to Krestinsky, the local Bolshevik in charge: 'The sentence of death on Kiselev is a very urgent matter. I used to see him in 1910–14 in Zurich, where he was a *plekhanovist* [Lenin's emphasis] and was accused of several vile things (I never knew the details). I caught a glimpse of him here in Moscow in 1918 or 1919. He was working on *Izvestiya* and told me he was becoming a Bolshevik. I don't know the facts.' In the end Lenin left it to Dzerzhinsky to telephone Krestinsky and decide the issue. Dzerzhinsky replied with a note for the file: 'I'm against interfering.'[91]

Coming face to face with Russian reality, Plekhanov must have shuddered; after all, he himself had penned the clause on the dictatorship of the proletariat in the Party programme, and he had uttered the famous maxim 'The good of the revolution is the highest law', in effect opening the sluice gates of unmitigated violence. Nor could he live down the fact that at the beginning of the century he had said that if after the revolution the parliament turned out 'bad', it could be dispersed 'not after two years, but after two weeks'. In essence, it was Plekhanov's formula that the Bolsheviks applied when they dispersed the Constituent Assembly in January 1918.

Valentinov recalled that when Plekhanov came to Moscow, he went on an excursion to the Sparrow Hills outside the city with a small group of friends. The photographs taken of him with Vera Zasulich are both beautiful and sad. Valentinov recalled that Plekhanov was moved and, taking Zasulich's hand, recalled a moment in the lives of two other revolutionaries: 'Vera Ivanovna, ninety years ago virtually on this spot Herzen and Ogarev took their oath. Nearly forty years ago, in another place, we also swore an oath that for us the good of the people would be the highest law all our lives, do you remember? We are obviously going downhill now. The time is coming soon when someone will say of us, that's the end. It'll probably come sooner than we think. While we are still breathing, let us look each other in the eyes and ask: did we carry out our oath? I think we did, honestly. Didn't we, Vera Ivanovna, carry it out honestly?'[92] Eight months later Plekhanov died, and shortly thereafter, so did Zasulich.

At a meeting of the Politburo in July 1921, Public Health Commissar Nikolai Semashko raised the question of erecting a monument to Plekhanov in Petrograd. The Politburo's response was both neutral and positive, leaving it to Semashko to discuss the matter with the Petrograd Soviet, since it was in a sense also a municipal matter.[93] Then the question arose of help for Plekhanov's family, which was living in straitened circumstances abroad. On 18 November 1921 Lenin proposed that 'a small sum' of 10,000 Swiss francs be given to the family as a one-off payment. At the same time it was decided without explanation that the much larger sum of 5000 gold roubles be paid to the family of Karl Liebknecht, the German Social Democrat assassinated in Germany in 1919.[94] Perhaps it was because Liebknecht's widow Sofia, a Russian by birth, had been more insistent in her appeals to Lenin. She had written that her 'father had had an estate at Rostov on Don, including three houses and shares worth about 3 million roubles. I should have had about 600,000 roubles, but the house was nationalized. Give me about 1,200,000 marks for myself and my children. I must free myself of material dependence ... I'm choking with cares ... Give us security once and for all with this round sum, I beg you! Oh, free me from dependency, let me breathe freely. But don't give me half, only the whole sum.' After agreeing to 5000 roubles in gold, Lenin wrote on the file: 'Secret, for the archives.'[95] In fact, Zinoviev had already sent Sofia Liebknecht a box of stolen gems worth 6600 Dutch guilders and 20,000 German marks.

Nikolai Potresov, who had been close to Plekhanov for much of their lives as revolutionaries, marked the tenth anniversary of Plekhanov's death with an essay. It seemed, he wrote, that Plekhanov had gone home only 'to see with his own eyes Russia being chained up again. And with what chains! Forged by the proletariat! And by whom? By his former pupils! It is hard to imagine a worse punishment . . . like King Lear, he was thrown out and betrayed by his own children.'[96] Rather than as the Master of the Order, or as the leader of the Party that he had created with Lenin, Plekhanov entered history as the prophet of the Bolshevik disaster.

## The Tragedy of Martov

It was common for Russian revolutionaries to adopt aliases and pseudonyms, often choosing them randomly or perhaps for dramatic effect. 'Lenin', as has been noted, probably derived from the River Lena in Siberia; Iosif Dzhugashvili, a Georgian, adopted 'Stalin', which suggested a man of steel; Lev Bronshtein chose 'Trotsky' because it was the name of one of his prison warders. Often a new name was a matter of simple security, to obtain a new passport, to evade capture or to throw the police off the scent. Aliases were particularly prevalent among revolutionaries of Jewish origin, since a Russian name might provide a more effective disguise. Thus it was that Julius Osipovich Tsederbaum was to become known as 'Yuli Martov'.

Martov died in Berlin in 1923, but his political death came on the night of 25 October 1917, during the Second Congress of Soviets. The Soviets were perceived as non-Party bodies, general assemblies of socialist opinion where deputies from workers', soldiers' and peasants' committees gathered to formulate their resolutions calling on the Provisional Government to leave the war, to delay sending troops to the front, and similar demands, including of course to hand over power. In the course of 1917, however, as war-weariness grew and the Bolshevik message generated a greater response, the Soviets remained non-partisan in name only: in effect, they became almost wholly Bolshevik bodies, especially in Petrograd and Moscow.

When the Second Congress of Soviets met, the Provisional Government under Kerensky had just been overthrown by the Bolsheviks, though they had ostensibly acted in the name of the Soviets. Any hope that the Congress would produce a solution to the crisis, preferably by forming a broad socialist coalition government, was dashed before a word was spoken. The composition of the Congress was probably a fair reflection of the situation in the country at large: of 650 delegates, about three hundred were Bolsheviks, while another eighty or ninety were Left Socialist Revolutionaries. The other Socialist Revolutionaries and Mensheviks amounted to about eighty each, and the remaining hundred were either unaccounted for or were genuinely non-partisan.

Fedor Dan opened the meeting, and the Bolsheviks and Left Socialist Revolutionaries – a splinter from the main Party and more in harmony with the Bolsheviks – took up their places on the platform in proportion to the number of their delegates. The Mensheviks refused to occupy the four places allotted to them, in protest against the Bolshevik seizure of power that had taken place the previous night. Martov called out that it was a time for common sense to prevail, for the coup to be repudiated and for talks to take place to form a coalition government. It looked as if the Congress might swing his way, but then Trotsky made a speech which saved Lenin's line, and the delegates swung sharply to the left. His voice hoarse from a cold and from his incessant smoking, Martov's nerve snapped and he declared: 'We're leaving!' His supporters shouted and stamped their feet in the face of their defeat. It was not the Bolsheviks who had snuffed out Martov's candle: it was his own decision to leave the Congress.

There had never been a place for Martov in the order created by Lenin at the beginning of the century. Lenin personified the leadership of an iron vangard; Martov was a Russian Don Quixote who expected a following not of Party troops but of an amorphous association. Lenin had proved the better leader, always with his eye on the political goal, while Martov, a naive romantic, had been sustained by the idea of injecting democratic values into the socialist programme.

Widely regarded as one of the most intelligent, and most approachable, of the best-known members of the RSDLP, Martov was born in 1873 into a middle-class Russian Jewish family in Constantinople, where his father was engaged in commerce and acting as the Turkish correspondent for two leading St Petersburg journals. His mother was Viennese, and the atmosphere in the Tsederbaum household was one of liberal enlightenment and tolerance. In 1877 the family moved back to Odessa.

The early 1880s in Russia was a time of mounting hostility to all things foreign, as the assassination of Alexander II in March 1881 had prompted the widespread belief that Russia's new social evil was of foreign, Western origin. As a child Martov witnessed the atmosphere of hatred against the Jews when a pogrom was unleashed in Odessa, and however wholeheartedly he was to become a part of the Russian revolutionary movement, he never lost the sense that he had come from, and would remain part of, an oppressed and despised minority. The family moved to St Petersburg in 1882, and in 1889, when he was sixteen, Julius entered high school, where he formed strong bonds of friendship with the sons of the intelligentsia he found there.[97]

He was already a committed Populist when he was admitted to St Petersburg University in 1891, and he was soon arrested for voicing seditious ideas. Released after several months, he was expelled from the university, and in 1893 was rearrested and sentenced to two years' exile from St Petersburg and any other university city. He spent 1893–95 in Vilna (Vilnius), which was both the centre of traditional East European Jewish culture and a hotbed of working-class organization. Martov arrived just at the moment when the leaders of Jewish workers' groups were changing their tactics from intensive teaching circles to mass agitation. That is, instead of raising the general educational level of a few workers, who then tended to want to enter the ranks of the intelligentsia themselves, or to exploit their new-found culture to acquire professional qualifications, the idea was to gather large numbers of workers at secret meeting places and to convey one or two simple ideas, such as the injustice of low wages or poor conditions, and thus hope to 'agitate' them sufficiently to take strike action or to demonstrate for better conditions.

The new approach was highly successful, and when Martov returned to the capital in 1895, he spread these ideas. With Lenin, whom he met at that time, he formed the Union for the Struggle for the Liberation of the Working Class, but in 1896, like his new comrade, he was arrested and exiled to Siberia. Released in 1900, he went abroad and collaborated with Lenin, Potresov, Plekhanov and Axelrod on their new newspaper, *Iskra*. Until 1903 it seemed Martov and Lenin were the perfect team. They each brought to the partnership experience in the organization of illegal groups and the formulation of ideas for wide consumption which, together with Plekhanov's more sophisticated writing, created a newspaper that many workers, intellectuals and local organizers were eager to read, risking arrest and Siberian exile for the privilege. What Martov did not know, however, was that during these years of preparation Lenin had been encouraging his agents to use any means necessary to detach local social democratic committees from their existing loyalties, and to make them acknowledge *Iskra* as the sole ideological and organizational centre of Party activity. Martov naturally wanted *Iskra* to prosper, but he conceived of the forthcoming Second Party Congress as an opportunity to bind all of the existing social democratic elements into a single, broad-based party. It was only in the course of the Congress itself that he realised that Lenin's idea was to exclude from the Party all but those elements which acknowledged the editors of *Iskra* as the leadership.

At the Second Congress, which took place in Brussels and London in the summer of 1903, it appeared that Martov's prospects were bright. After Plekhanov, he emerged as the most significant delegate, although Lenin's voice became more confident as he gained supporters. Millions of Soviet citizens, schooled in a history smoothed beyond recognition, believed that the split in 1903 into Bolsheviks and Mensheviks was over the organizational question – or, more precisely, point one of the Party Statutes on membership. Schoolmasters, professors and army commissars all parroted, 'Lenin wanted to create a party-citadel, a party-fighting unit. Martov preferred to create an amorphous, diffuse formation which could never have achieved Communist aims.' Ironically, the last point was undoubtedly true. As for the 'party-citadel', that was not Lenin's aim. The real issue was whether the Party was to be an order or a democratic body. Lenin was proposing that a member would support the Party by material means as well as by 'personal participation in one of the Party organizations'. Martov's formula was less rigorous: apart from material support, a member was obliged to give the Party 'regular personal support under the guidance of one of its organizations'. According to Stalin's *Short Course* on the history of the Party, Martov wanted to 'open the door wide to unstable non-proletarian elements ... These people would not be part of the organization, nor be subject to Party discipline or carry out Party tasks, nor face the associated dangers. Yet Martov ... was proposing to recognize such people as Party members.'[98] Stalin perhaps also believed it was an 'organizational question'. Political 'softness', for Martov, meant not only a readiness to compromise, it also signified understanding the need for a union with high morality. And it was this, not the organizational question, that separated him from Lenin forever: the conflict was dominated by moral rather than political imperatives.

Martov, who had previously been in step with Lenin and had voted with him on all the points of the programme, suddenly 'rebelled' during the twenty-second session, not only over the membership issue, but on almost everything else. His rebellion was to last for the rest of his life. Although Lenin's proposal received twenty-three votes to Martov's twenty-eight, Lenin dominated in all further contests.

As we have seen, Martov virtually began his political life as an activist among the Jewish Social Democrats who were to found the Jewish Workers' Union (known by its Yiddish name as the Bund) in 1897. In terms of scale alone, the Bund was to become an impressive social force. In 1904 it could count more than 20,000 members, or more than twice the number in the 'Russian' Party organizations.[99] For Martov in the early 1890s, the Jewish organizations had seemed the most important force for attaining civil equality for the Jews.[100] By the time of the Second Congress, however, he had become strongly opposed to what he now saw as Jewish separatism. The Bund, however, supported Martov at the Congress against Lenin until the majority of the delegates voted against giving it the status of sole representative of the Jewish workers in the RSDLP. Together with the delegates of Workers' Cause, another dissident group, the five Bundists walked out, leaving Martov's side a true minority.

In his relations with the young Vladimir Ulyanov, Martov had begun to observe certain features which in the end would make the chasm between them unbridgeable. He mentioned this in his 'Notes of a Social Democrat', which was published in Berlin, remarking that Lenin 'did not yet have, or had in lesser measure, the confidence in his own strength – never mind in his historical calling – that was to emerge so clearly in his mature years ... He was then twenty-five or twenty-six years old ... and he was not yet full of the scorn and distrust of people which, I believe, is what made him into a certain type of leader.' [101]

In practice, until the revolution of 1917, Lenin strove for his main idea of creating a monolithic, centralized party. He never doubted that he would indeed come to power, and what would follow. The Party-order would already be in existence. It would not evaporate. Was this not a threat to the future? He did not think so, and anyone who did was worthy only to join Martov. All those in favour of an iron guard, and willing to fight and smash, were welcome in his party; those who were not could go to Martov's 'flabby monster'. [102]

Lenin went on disputing with Martov right up to October 1917, if a constant stream of abuse can be called disputing. Martov was intransigent. Inclined by nature to compromise, he felt no urge for conciliation. He had long ago come to believe that the socialism Lenin wanted had nothing in common with justice, or moral principles, or the humane origins of socialist thinking. Knowing he had already lost, he summed up the 'interim' accounts of 1917 in horror. He wrote to a friend, N.S. Kristi:

It is not merely the deep belief that it is senselessly utopian to try to plant socialism in an economically and culturally backward country, but also my organic inability to accept the Arakcheev-style [barracks] concept of socialism and the Pugachev-style [violent] notion of class struggle which are being generated by the very fact that they are trying to plant a European ideal in Asiatic soil. The resulting bouquet is hard to take. For me, socialism was never the denial of individual freedom and individualism, but on the contrary, their highest embodiment, and the principle of collectivism I always saw as opposed to 'the herd instinct' and levelling . . . What is happening here is the flourishing of a 'trench–barracks' variety of quasi-socialism, based on the 'simplification' of everything . . .[103]

Martov's internationalist wartime position of 'revolutionary defen-cism' contrasted markedly with Lenin's defeatism and Plekhanov's patriotism, and was perhaps a truer and more noble one to take. The outbreak of war found Martov in Paris. In his small newspaper, *Golos* (The Voice), and later in *Nashe slovo* (Our Word), his constant cry was 'Long live peace! Enough blood! Enough senseless slaughter!' He maintained this position after returning to Petrograd in May 1917, arguing against defeatism and against turning the war into a civil war, but also against chauvinism, and so he was often under attack from both sides. I.G. Tsereteli, a Social Democrat who played a leading rôle in 1917, recalled Martov saying in the summer of that year: 'Lenin is not interested in questions of war and peace. The only thing that interests him is the revolution, and the only real revolution for him is the one in which the Bolsheviks have seized power.' Martov wondered what Lenin would do if the democrats, i.e. the Provisional Government, managed to make peace: 'He would no doubt change his tactics and preach to the masses that all the post-war misfortunes were due to the criminal democrats because they ended the war too soon and didn't have the courage to carry it on to the final destruction of German imperialism.'[104]

In June 1918 the Executive Committee of Soviets (VTsIK) voted to expel the Right SRs and Mensheviks. When they were asked to leave the meeting, Martov leapt up and began shouting curses at the 'dictators', 'bonapartists', 'usurpers', 'putschists', all the while struggling unsuccessfully to get his coat on. Lenin stood, white-faced, watching in silence. A Left SR sitting next to Martov began laughing and poking his finger at Martov, who, coughing and shouting, managed at last to get his coat on and leave, turning as he did so to hurl at his mirthful tormentor: 'You may laugh now, young man, but give it three months and you'll be following us.'[105]

Martov nevertheless remained an orthodox Marxist all his life. He believed that the socialist revolution could be an innovative and refreshing act of creativity, but he could not accept the Leninist monopoly and the Bolsheviks' reliance on coercion and terror. In defeat, he naively believed that the revolution could be clean and moral and bright. When Red and White Terror clashed to produce a monstrous wave of violence, Martov wrote a pamphlet called 'Down with the Death Penalty'. In it, he stated:

As soon as the Bolsheviks came to power, having announced the end of the death penalty, from the very first day they started killing prisoners taken in battle during the civil war, as all savages do. To kill enemies who have surrendered in battle on the promise that their lives will be spared . . . The death penalty has been abolished, but in every town and district various extraordinary commissions and military–revolutionary committees have sentenced hundreds and hundreds of people to be shot . . . This bloody debauchery is being carried out in the name of socialism, in the name of the teaching which proclaimed the brotherhood of people labouring for the highest goal of humanity . . . A party of death penalties is as much an enemy of the working class as a party of pogroms.[106]

As if to prove Martov right, in November 1923, after his death, the Politburo reviewed the 'Turkestan question'. Central Committee member Jan Rudzutak, a Latvian, reported that Basmachi (anti-Bolshevik forces) chieftains had been invited to talks with the local Soviet authorities. They had been promised their lives were not in danger, and that a special conference would find ways of settling the conflict peacefully. One hundred and eighty-three chieftains had turned up. They were arrested at once, and 151 of them were sentenced to be shot. The first on the list had already been executed when Moscow intervened. The Politburo regarded the action as 'inopportune', nothing worse.[107]

If Martov's arguments were moral, Lenin's were purely pragmatic. On 31 January 1922 he wrote to Unshlikht: 'I cannot possibly attend the Politburo. I'm feeling worse. But I don't think there's any need for me. It's only a matter of purely *technical* measures to help our judges *intensify* (and speed up) repression against the Mensheviks . . .'[108] Martov had no hope of influencing the Bolshevik leadership towards humanizing their policies. If his political death was noisy, his physical death was quiet and sad, like a guttering candle. Seriously ill, in the autumn of 1920 he was allowed by the Politburo to leave for Germany, where he founded *Sotsialisticheskii vestnik*. In his last article, he foresaw that the Bolsheviks would leave the scene and be replaced in Russia by a 'democratic regime ruled by law'. He died of tuberculosis on 24 April 1923, not yet aged fifty. Perhaps it was as much the collapse of all his ideas as his constant smoking that killed him off.[109]

People like Martov wanted the course of revolution to be like a river, peaceful, smooth and broad, while Lenin's followers saw it as a waterfall, cascading from on high. The party Lenin created soon became an order, after October 1917 a state order. Not a monastic or chivalrous order, but an ideological one, and until his death nobody had the slightest doubt that Lenin had the absolute right to be the master of this order. He had not, however, taken account of the fact that a party such as his could survive only within a totalitarian system, a fact demonstrated by the events of August 1991.

# 3

## The Scar of October

On the evening of 1 August 1914, Germany declared war on Russia. When mobilization was declared, the whole nation rallied to the tsar. Plekhanov expressed a strong desire to defend the fatherland, and even Trotsky, who was not a defencist, wrote in the Paris newspaper *Nashe slovo* (Our Word) (formerly *Golos*, The Voice) that to preach the defeat of tsarist Russia made no sense, since that would mean advocating the victory of reactionary Germany. Only Lenin sensed intuitively the improbable, fantastic chance of achieving his hopes.

As patriotism sank in the mud and blood of the trenches, and hopes for victory faded, Lenin grew confident that neither Tsar Nicholas nor Kaiser Wilhelm would emerge from the war without a revolution. The intelligentsia, both in Russia and Germany, cursed the war and called for peace. But while each side hoped that its own army would not be defeated, only Lenin saw the war as an indispensable ally.

Unlike the peasant in his soldier's cloak, enduring gas attacks, or the prisoner of war in Saxony, or the impoverished family in the city, Lenin observed the war from the Russian émigré's grand circle, at first in Poronino and Vienna, and then in the neutral comfort of Berne and Zurich. How did the leader of the future Russian revolution fill the time during its prologue? Did he prepare himself for the rôle he was to play? Was he confident of the outcome? Until the February revolution, he led the quiet life of a man used to living far from home and not very much concerned with domestic cares. Life for Lenin in those years meant writing hundreds of letters to a relatively limited circle of people, among them his close Bolshevik associates Alexander Shlyapnikov, Alexandra Kollontai, Karl Radek, Grigory Pyatakov, S. Ravich, Grigory Zinoviev and Lev Kamenev, and his friend and benefactor Maxim Gorky. A large part of his correspondence was with Inessa Armand, he being in Zurich, she in Clarens on Lake Geneva near Montreux. It was an emotionally charged exchange between two very close people who, though they discussed revolutionary matters, tried to give each other something more than routine reports, more than confirmation of the posting of books or organizing links between Russia and Scandinavia.

Lenin spent a lot of time studying the works of Hegel, Aristotle and Lassalle, as well as Napoleon and Clausewitz, he read Victor Hugo's poetry and occasionally took Krupskaya to the local theatre. They were able to relax at a moderately priced spa in the mountain resort of Flums in St Gallen. When he was not writing letters, resting, holding meetings, travelling or rowing with his opponents, Lenin wrote articles, pamphlets and more substantial works such as 'Imperialism as the Highest Stage of Capitalism'. Since the post from Russia was slow, he got his news from *The Times*, *Neue Zürcher Zeitung* and *Le Temps*, and he gained the growing impression that an earthquake was approaching in Russia. The nation's weariness of the hardships imposed by the war and constant defeats was reaching a critical point, although what lay beyond even Lenin did not suspect.

In early January 1917 he gave a lecture at the People's House in Zurich on the twelfth anniversary of the 1905 revolution. The audience, mostly students, was sparse, and the lecture was boring, prolonged and largely descriptive. Lenin emphasized the fact that in 1905 the scale of civil unrest had been insufficient to topple the autocracy: 'The peasants burned up to 2000 estates and divided the livestock among themselves . . . Unfortunately, this was only one-fifteenth of what they ought to have destroyed . . . They did not act with sufficient aggression, and that is one of the main causes for the failure of the revolution.' He rushed on speedily through his notes, expressing the view that 1905 would remain 'the prologue to the approaching European revolution'. He did not mention Russia as the scene of imminent rebellion, and also declared that the revolution would not come soon, concluding: 'We old folks may not live to see the decisive battles of the coming revolution.'[1]

## Democratic February

The two chief causes of the February revolution were the unsuccessful progress of the war and the weakness of the regime. Ostensibly, the Russian state collapsed suddenly, but its foundations had been eroded long before. As for the war, despite strategic failures, Russia's position was not hopeless. The front had been stabilized far from the Russian capital and other vital centres. A breakthrough by General Brusilov in the summer of 1916 had given the people hope in the possibility of an honourable outcome. Far-sighted politicians saw that Germany could not win, especially as the United States seemed likely to enter the war on the Allied side.

To be sure, Social Democratic agitation had its effect on the war-weary army, and the Germans managed to get Bolshevik-style propaganda into the Russian trenches, which would help the Kaiser rather than Russia. President of the Duma Rodzianko wrote in his memoirs that 'the symptoms of the army's disintegration could be felt already in the second year of the war ... Reinforcements from reserve battalions were arriving at the front with a quarter of the men having deserted ... Sometimes, echelons bound for the front would halt because they had nothing left but officers and subalterns. Everyone else had scattered.'[2] Socialist agitation among the peasants who were unwilling to fight was extremely effective, and the Bolsheviks were making their own independent contribution to the disintegration of the Russian army. On the whole, however, Russia had not yet exhausted her material and human resources on a war that came to seem increasingly just as the German occupation of her territory endured, especially since it was Germany that had started the war.

But the regime proved incapable of governing in a critical situation. Nicholas II's decision on 6 August 1915 to assume the post of Supreme Commander did not help. Almost the entire cabinet of ministers had protested that the tsar's decision could threaten both him and the monarchy.[3] Nicholas was adamant, however, and departed for Staff Headquarters, leaving the capital to the hostile and venal groupings that had formed in his own entourage. In a country accustomed to one-man rule, the 'domestic peace' proclaimed by the Duma when war broke out soon evaporated.

Events in the capital developed their own momentum. On 27 February (12 March New Style) 1917, crowds broke into the Tauride Palace, where a Provisional Committee of the Duma was meeting. By the evening of the same day another claimant to power had emerged, namely the Soviet of Workers' Deputies, hastily convened by the Party organizations. Paul Milyukov, the leader of the Constitutional Democrats, and soon to become Foreign Minister in the post-tsarist government, later wrote: 'The soldiers appeared last, but they were the masters of the moment, even if they did not realize it themselves.' They did not behave like conquerors, but rather like men fearful of the consequences of having disobeyed orders and killed their commanding officers. 'They were even less sure than we that the revolution had succeeded. They wanted recognition and protection.'⁴

In the words of Alexander Solzhenitsyn, a 'long fatigue' began which finally knocked away the foundations of the state, social stability and national unity. The main question was who would exploit the new situation. The dominant thought in the public mind was that only drastic measures of a revolutionary character could provide an outcome. Some figures close to the tsar believed that the situation had arisen out of weakness on the part of the regime. Grand Duke Alexander Mikhailovich had written bitterly to the tsar less than one month before his abdication: 'We are present at the unprecedented spectacle of a revolution from above, not from below.'⁵

Isolated in Zurich, Lenin had no feel for the nuances of the situation, and when on 2 (15) March he heard that the revolution had succeeded, he was amazed. He first heard of it from Moisei Bronsky, a quiet, retiring Polish Social Democrat from Lodz. Bronsky did not know much himself, except that telegrams had come from Russia. With Bronsky, Lenin wandered all around Zurich trying to find out something more definite, but all they heard was that there'd been a revolution in Petrograd, the ministers had been arrested and crowds were packing the streets. Lenin returned home in a state of excitement: he must do something. Pacing restlessly up and down, he exclaimed to Krupskaya, who was sitting quietly in her old armchair: 'It's staggering! Such a surprise! Just imagine! We must get home, but how? It's so incredibly unexpected! Amazing!' When he had calmed down somewhat, he wrote his first letter after hearing the news. It was to Inessa Armand, telling her what he had heard and describing the general state of agitation in Zurich. 'If the Germans aren't lying, it has happened. Russia must have been on the brink of revolution for the last few days. I'm so excited I cannot possibly go to Scandinavia!!'[6] Having only two months earlier predicted a long wait for such events, Lenin was now possessed of perfect hindsight, and like so many politicians, felt no need to recall what he had recently asserted.

He cabled Zinoviev in Berne suggesting he come to Zurich immediately, and simultaneously wrote to his most trusted agent, Yakov Ganetsky: 'We must at all costs get back to Russia and the only possible plan is as follows: find a Swede who looks like me. But as I can't speak Swedish he'll have to be deaf and dumb. I'm sending my photo, in any case.'[7] It was an order almost as tall as starting the world revolution, and was soon dropped in favour of a more practical one.

Meanwhile, the news from Petrograd was more and more staggering. The tsar had abdicated on 2 (15 New Style) March 1917, and so had his brother Michael, having first called on the people to submit to the Provisional Government, which had been 'initiated by the State Duma and invested with full powers' until a Constituent Assembly could be convened to determine the nature of government according to the will of the people.[8] When Lenin read the list of names in the Provisional Government, he remarked sarcastically, 'the bourgeoisie has managed to get its arse onto ministerial seats'. He had no doubt that these liberals were not one whit better than the tsar, and he regarded their adherence to democratic ideals as nothing better than an attempt 'to make fools of the people'. In his first 'letter from afar' Lenin, accurately from the Bolshevik point of view, caught the flavour of the moment: apart from the Provisional Government there had emerged another 'plaything' of the regime, the Petrograd Soviet of Workers' and Soldiers' Deputies, headed by N.S. Chkheidze, A.F. Kerensky and M.I. Skobelev. Only two Bolsheviks, Shlyapnikov and P.A. Zalutsky, were members of its executive committee. Lenin, however, saw in the existence of the two centres of power a unique opportunity for the Bolsheviks. In his view the Soviet was the prototype of the future dictatorship of the proletariat, while the Provisional Government, which might have introduced the principles of bourgeois democratic popular power, he saw as nothing other than the target of his frenzied attacks.

Less than a week after it had been formed, and without the slightest idea of what was happening in Petrograd and Russia, Lenin pronounced: 'The government of Octobrists and Kadets, of the Guchkovs and Milyukovs . . . cannot give the people peace, bread or liberty.'[9] The Octobrists had taken their name from the tsar's October 1905 Manifesto, and had been the political party most committed to attempting reform within the limits permitted by the tsar, rather than in constant opposition. The Kadets, that is the KDs, or Constitutional Democrats, were a fairly broad coalition of liberals, ranging from former Marxist revolutionaries to moderate reformers, who had spearheaded the criticism of the tsar's handling of the war effort and were effectively the dominant successors to the old regime. To attack the Provisional Government would undermine the possibility of a peaceful alternative to further revolution. It was therefore consistent for Lenin to tell the Bolsheviks, as they departed for Russia: 'Our tactics are complete distrust, no support for the new government; we especially suspect Kerensky; we arm the proletariat as the only guarantee; we call for immediate elections to the Petrograd city council; we make no friendships with other parties.'[10] It was a typical reaction: mentally Lenin had applauded the revolution, as his letter to Inessa Armand had shown, but power was in the hands of the bourgeoisie, and there were moderate socialists – Mensheviks – heading the soviets. None of this suited Lenin, who had shown he was incapable of compromise with such people. The only way forward was to arm the proletariat. Since the Bolsheviks had played no noticeable part in the February revolution, he had to change the scenario.

Before leaving Zurich, on 27 March Lenin made a speech in which he declared, with evident satisfaction, that 'the transformation of the imperialist war into a civil war in Russia has *begun*'.[11] The February revolution was merely the first stage. 'The unique historical situation of the present moment is as a moment of transition from the first stage of the revolution to the second, from the uprising against tsarism to the uprising against the bourgeoisie . . .'[12] He ended his speech by declaring, 'Long live the revolution! Long live the world proletarian revolution that has begun!'

In his first 'letter from afar' Lenin had described the present moment in Russian political life as 'a bloodstained bundle'. But it was the Provisional Government that believed, rightly as it turned out, that remaining loyal to the Allies, rather than consciously assisting in the defeat of its own army, would cause less loss of Russian life. It would be hard to find a precedent in history when a political party, for the sake of gaining power, worked as consistently and as zealously for the defeat of its own country as the Bolsheviks were to do. It was, however, an essential link in the chain: the collapse of the state through military defeat would be followed by the seizure of power. The democratic forces of February were not capable of withstanding such a plan.

More surprising than Lenin's cynicism and anti-patriotism was the fact that he gained enough supporters to achieve his plan in so short a time. Whether he dreamed up the idea of a separate peace with Germany in Zurich, or whether he was entirely preoccupied with the question of getting back to Russia, or whether uppermost in his mind was how to exploit the ardent desire for peace of millions of people, it is not possible to say. With the imagination of the creative writer, Alexander Solzhenitsyn has suggested, probably rightly, that all these thoughts were jumbled together in Lenin's mind in the days following February and before his return to Russia in April.[13] During that time, most politicians in Russia felt that February had opened up a great new chapter in their history, a chapter of democracy. Lenin, however, was convinced that if the country remained at that stage, he and his party would at best occupy an insignificant place among the opposition in the forthcoming Constituent Assembly. All the shrill revolutionary speeches of his followers would be seen as nothing but the sort of extreme leftism to which Western parliaments had become blithely accustomed. If the February revolution were to stick to the aims pro-claimed by its leaders, there would be an opening for Lenin's old rivals, the Mensheviks, and that was unacceptable to him. He must get to Russia. Having invented and nurtured a tribe of 'professional revolutionaries', he now intended to make use of them. The chance might not come again, and he was already forty-seven.

## Parvus, Ganetsky and the 'German Key'

Lenin wrote urgently to his most trusted agent, Yakov Ganetsky in Stockholm, to find a way for him out of his Swiss blind alley. He asked Robert Grimm, a Swiss socialist, to test the possibility of travelling through Germany, but there was no rapid response there. Ganetsky, meanwhile, expeditious and resourceful as always, sent five hundred roubles for the journey,[14] but there was still no plan, and Lenin began to wonder if he had missed the train of history. He wrote to Inessa: 'It looks as if we won't get to Russia! England *won't let us.* [The idea of] going through Germany isn't working.'[15] It is possible that the journey might indeed not have taken place at all, since Lenin was frankly afraid of either being arrested in England or sunk by a German U-boat. Perhaps, had he remained in Switzerland writing his 'letters from afar', the October revolution would never have happened. Trotsky was to write that without Lenin, October was inconceivable.

Besides the Bolsheviks, however, the German High Command was also interested in getting Lenin back to Russia. For some time they had not only been watching the Bolsheviks with interest, they had also been giving them substantial financial help through various front-men. German Chancellor Theobald von Bethmann-Hollweg had been encouraged to do so both by the General Staff and some German Social Democrats, but in particular by Alexander Helphand, then the publisher of *Die Glocke*. In conversation with the German ambassador in Copenhagen, Count von Brockdorff-Rantzau, Helphand insisted that there was danger in a separate peace with Russia, for the tsar would survive to stamp out the revolution. Only a German victory was acceptable. Helphand did not know that Lenin would soon state publicly that he had always been opposed to a separate Russo–German peace. In an article entitled 'Where is the Regime and Where is the Revolution?', published in July 1917 in *Listok Pravdy*, Lenin stated categorically that he had 'always and unconditionally repudiated separate peace with Germany in the most decisive and irrevocable way!!'[16] As we have seen, Lenin wanted the defeat of Russia and a civil war. It was a position the German High Command found deeply sympathetic, for their own 'defeatists' were hardly to be heard. As First Quartermaster General Erich von Ludendorff, the 'military brain of the German nation', was to write of this episode: 'In helping Lenin to travel to Russia, our government accepted a special responsibility. The enterprise was justified from a military point of view. We had to bring Russia down.'[17] The Bolshevik revolution, when it came, would offer Germany a unique opportunity to win the war. Ludendorff would declare frankly that the Soviet government 'exists thanks to us'. It is worth noting that in May 1920, when the Politburo discussed the publication in Russian of Ludendorff's memoirs, it was unanimously decided that 'only those sections dealing with the Brest negotiations should be translated and published'.[18] Being in power, the Bolsheviks were not especially afraid of exposure, but it would nonetheless be embarrassing. Having secured the defeat of Russia, they had not only served their own interests, but also those of German militarism.

The 'German factor' in the Russian revolution has been extensively treated, especially in non-Soviet literature. The Russian Marxists preferred to say nothing, following Lenin's request (which curiously was not published immediately) 'again and again to all honest citizens not to believe the dirty slander and dark rumours'.[19] The Bolsheviks never attempted to disprove the accusation that they had made a deal with the Germans to 'bring Russia down'. While the financial connections had evidently been indirect, it was impossible to deny the call for Russia's defeat. It was best either to say nothing, or simply 'Don't believe the slanderers.'

The question that remains to be answered is whether there was a Bolshevik–German understanding on 'peace propaganda', as the Germans preferred to refer to this touchy question. Did the Bolsheviks receive German money for the revolution? The historian S.P. Melgunov claimed that one should look for the 'German golden key in the pocket of Parvus [Helphand], who was connected both to the socialist world and the [German] foreign ministry and representatives of the German General Staff', and that this explained the extraordinarily rapid success of Lenin's propaganda.[20] The matter is one of the many secrets surrounding the revolution, and although I have examined a vast number of hitherto inaccessible documents, it is still far from clear. Much was decided within a small circle of Bolsheviks by word of mouth, many documents were destroyed after the revolution, and Lenin was very good at keeping secrets.

In order to lift the veil further, we must concentrate on two figures. The first is Alexander Lazarevich Helphand (also known as Parvus and Alexander Moskovich). The second, who is even more obscure, is Yakov Stanislavovich Fürstenberg (also known as Ganetsky, Hanecki, Borel, Hendriczek, Frantiszek, Nikolai, Marian Keller, Kuba . . .). In 1917 these two shadowy figures played the rôle of unseen levers. They did not agitate the masses: their rôle was to help Lenin and his group secure the funds needed to do so.

Helphand was born three years before Lenin to a Jewish artisan in Berezicho in the province of Minsk. He went to school in Odessa and university in Berne, where he obtained a doctorate in philosophy. In the West he made the acquaintance of such grandees of the revolutionary movement as Plekhanov, Axelrod, Zasulich, Zetkin, Kautsky and Adler, and he met Lenin and Krupskaya before the 1905 revolution. He acquired a reputation for great erudition, a paradoxical turn of mind, radical judgments and bold predictions. In a series of articles published in 1904 under the title 'War and the Revolution', he forecast Russia's defeat at the hands of Japan, which duly came to pass the following year, and, as an inevitable consequence, a revolutionary conflagration at home. Lenin had long kept an eye on Parvus, but always kept his distance. He might have been thinking of Parvus (or perhaps himself?) when he said to Gorky: 'the clever Russian is almost always a Jew or has Jewish blood in him.'[21] Kautsky introduced Parvus to journalism, a profession at which he excelled.[22] Trotsky was captivated by him, and fascinated by his theory of 'permanent revolution'. After leaving Russia, Parvus joined the German Social Democrats and for a long time edited the Dresden paper *Arbeiter Zeitung*.

Like Trotsky, Parvus played a prominent part in the 1905 revolution – unlike Lenin, who was little more than an extra. Both Trotsky and Parvus were arrested in St Petersburg and exiled, separately, to Siberia, whence they both escaped, first to St Petersburg and then abroad. Despite his talent as a writer, Parvus left only a small literary record, including a book of recollections of his spell in the Peter-Paul Fortress after the defeat of the 1905 revolution. Most of his time was taken up with his favourite occupation, commerce, in which he did extremely well. He was Gorky's literary agent, and also represented his financial interests in Germany, where at one time his play *Lower Depths* was playing to full houses. According to Gorky, Parvus took his agreed twenty per cent of the profits for himself, dividing the rest one quarter to Gorky and three quarters to the German Social Democratic Party. Parvus amassed some 100,000 marks, but instead of sending Gorky his money, he wrote to him frankly admitting that he had spent it on a trip to Italy with a female companion. Gorky, who thought 'it must have been a very pleasant holiday' to have consumed only his quarter of the earnings, complained to the Central Committee of the German Social Democratic Party. A Party court made up of Kautsky, Bebel and Zetkin condemned Parvus morally, and he left Germany for Constantinople. There he became an advisor to the Young Turk movement, and carried on highly successful commerce between Turkey and Germany.[23]

When the war began, Parvus, now a rich man, became consumed by the idea of helping Germany by bringing about revolution in Russia, although there was more to his idea than this. In January 1915, Parvus explained his plan to Wangenheim, the German ambassador in Constantinople: 'The interests of the German government are identical with those of the Russian revolutionaries. The Russian Democrats can only achieve their aim by the total destruction of Tsarism. On the other hand, Germany would not be completely successful if it were not possible to kindle a major revolution in Russia. However, there would still be a danger to Germany from Russia, even after the war, if the Russian empire were divided into a number of separate parts.'[24] Here lay the essence of the German interest in the revolution, and its coincidence with Lenin's desire for revolution via the defeat of Russia. While it is clear that the plan existed and that the Germans were interested in it, it is not clear quite how the German government intended to carry it out, or how the Bolsheviks would achieve their part of it without losing face.

Western historians have asserted that Lenin met Parvus in Zurich or Berne in May 1915. David Shub claims that 'at first Lenin listened attentively to Parvus's plan, but gave him no definite reply. To maintain contact with him, however, he sent Ganetsky-Fürstenberg to Copenhagen with orders to work in Parvus's Institute and to keep him systematically informed about Parvus's activities.'[25] The official Soviet chronicle of Lenin's activities in May 1915 states that he ordered from Berne Library a guide-book of resorts and *The Influence of High-Mountain Climate and Mountain Excursions on Man*, but says nothing about a meeting with Parvus. For his part, however, Parvus described their meeting in detail in a pamphlet entitled, 'In the Struggle for the Truth', confirming that it took place in Zurich. Shub asserts, on the basis of Parvus's own testimony and other documents, that Parvus arrived in Switzerland in the company of Yekaterina Groman and took up residence in the most luxurious hotel.

Through Groman, Parvus distributed largesse among needy Russian émigrés. One day in May he unexpectedly entered a restaurant where émigrés ate, and went straight to a table where Lenin, Krupskaya, Inessa Armand and Kasparov, another close friend, were sitting. After brief conversation, Lenin and Krupskaya accompanied Parvus to their apartment, where they talked until evening.

Parvus wrote of this meeting: 'I told Lenin my views on the social-revolutionary consequences of the war and also drew his attention to the fact that, as long as the war was going on, there would be no revolution in Germany: revolution was possible only in Russia which would blow up as a result of a German victory.' The meeting was confirmed by the Bolshevik, Arthur Zifeldt, who saw Lenin and Parvus leaving the restaurant together.[26]

Parvus made it known that he was setting up a new institute in Copenhagen to study the causes and effects of the war, and he succeeded in recruiting a number of Russian Social Democrats, among them some Mensheviks and some Bolsheviks, including, most notably, Yakov Ganetsky, Lenin's most trusted agent.[27] Parvus had frequent meetings with another of Lenin's close associates, Karl Radek, who in 1924 wrote a sketch of him, based on personal recollections. Radek quoted Parvus saying of himself: 'I'm Midas in reverse: whenever I touch gold it turns into garbage.' Twenty years after the events, in an article entitled 'Parvus–Lenin–Ganetsky', Kerensky wrote: 'The Provisional Government firmly established that Ganetsky's "financial affairs" with Parvus were continued in Petrograd by the Bank of Siberia, where in the name of a relative of Ganetsky called Madame Sumenson, and also the not unknown Kozlovsky, very large sums came from Berlin via the New Bank in Stockholm through the mediation of the same Ganetsky.' Kerensky could rightly claim that the first historical research into Bolshevik–German links was carried out by his government.

Materials in the Special Archive frequently record that in 1916 a special section was created in Berlin under the name 'Stockholm', headed by a certain Trautmann, who maintained contact with Parvus and Radek through Ganetsky. The archives also hold the addresses in Copenhagen where Parvus and Ganetsky lived not far from each other.[28] An Austro-Hungarian diplomat in Copenhagen, one Grebing, also recalled that 'Parvus and Fürstenberg-Ganetsky carried on trade between Scandinavia and Russia with German help. The export of German goods into Russia went regularly and in significant quantities through the firm of Parvus-Ganetsky in the following manner: Parvus would receive goods from Germany, including surgical instruments, medical and chemical products, contraceptives, and clothes which were needed in Russia, and Ganetsky, as the Russian agent, would forward them. None of the money realized from the sale of these goods in Russia was, however, paid to the Germans, but was instead used to finance Lenin's propaganda from the first day of the revolution.'[29] The system worked superbly to screen the financial connections. Similarly, Bolshevik abuse of Parvus as a 'renegade', 'social chauvinist' and 'revisionist' also provided intermittent camouflage and an impression of their distance from him.

Commentaries in the Special Archive show that Parvus's political activity was based on an extremely broad range of commercial speculation: 'His deals in Denmark, Turkey, Romania, Bulgaria and Russia in food, grain, coal, medicines, his participation in German propaganda, his supplying the German General Staff with both Bolshevik and anti-Bolshevik literature, speculation on freight contracts in Scandinavia, all brought Parvus capital worth several tens of millions, which he deposited in Zurich banks.'[30]

Although Lenin was not personally involved in any of these dealings, he was well informed about them. Moreover, they could not take place without his agreement, although in the event of their public failure, he would have remained in the clear. Among a collection of purely financial documents, showing the delivery of goods and payments to Madame Sumenson from Ganetsky (the majority having long been destroyed),[31] are various cables of summer 1917 to and from Lenin on such issues as the planned International Socialist Congress in Stockholm (which did not take place).[32] The cables themselves are often couched in enigmatic language, obviously coded to screen a hidden purpose.

The money, meanwhile, was much needed. A former tsarist counter-intelligence agent, recruited by the Provisional Government to investigate Bolshevik links with the Germans, found that one of the channels for financing the Party on the eve of the revolution ran from Ganetsky to Sumenson.[33] Evidently this channel functioned uninterrupted for a long time – one cable informing Ganetsky that Sumenson had deposited 100,000 roubles is numbered '90'.[34]

The historian Sergei Melgunov, who did not know of the existence of these documents, was nevertheless able to assert that Yevgeniya Mavrikevna Sumenson had a large account with the Bank of Siberia: 'Financial experts later ascertained that there was about one million roubles in this account, of which about 800,000 was removed on the eve of the revolution . . . Kozlovsky would go round the banks in the morning, taking out money in some and opening new accounts in others.'[35]

When on 8 July 1917 Sumenson was arrested by the Provisional Government's counter-intelligence service, she confirmed all these facts, and more. The handwritten notes made by the assistant chief of the counter-intelligence branch of the Petrograd military district show that in all 'two million thirty thousand and forty three roubles' had passed between Ganetsky and Sumenson,[36] a huge sum for the time. Sumenson also declared that on Ganetsky's orders she had 'given Mecheslav Yulyevich Kozlovsky money as soon as he asked for it (without taking any receipts from him), as he was [Ganetsky's] first deputy . . .' The documents also show that she 'transferred 230,000 roubles to a firm in Switzerland via the Azov-Don Bank'. She stated that she had received 288,929 roubles for the first delivery of medicines sent from Stockholm by Ganetsky in December 1915.[37] Whether or not this was connected with Lenin's meeting with Parvus in Switzerland in May, the fact is that in July 1915 von Jugow of the German foreign ministry requested the treasury to transmit five million marks to intensify revolutionary propaganda in Russia, and the request was granted on 9 July.[38] It seems reasonable to conclude that the 'German money' began to work actively for the Bolsheviks in 1915, after the meeting in May.

When the Provisional Government's investigator interrogated Ganetsky's brother Vikenty in August 1917, it emerged that Ganetsky had suddenly become rich and was running a big business. Vikenty resisted all attempts to determine the nature of this 'business': 'Every time I began talking about his brother's wealth and his enterprises, [Vikenty] immediately tried to change the subject . . . During our conversation, the lawyer Kozlovsky came in; they spoke very quietly . . . Vikenty also revealed that among the family his brother would talk only about politics, but "we never found out anything about his commercial affairs".[39] This was quite a significant admission. Ganetsky was a 'professional revolutionary', and therefore capable of keeping a secret, especially one that involved the entire Party, even if it was known only to a handful of people. Lenin valued Ganetsky, and in the summer of 1917 defended him from attack in the Central Committee and the Politburo over the government's accusations in connection with the German money. In June 1918, in a letter to Adolf Ioffe, his emissary in Berlin, Lenin emphasized that 'Krasin and Ganetsky, being businesslike people, will help you and everything will be all right'.[40]

The Provisional Government's investigation was disorganized, and clearly the case was beyond it. As Kerensky later claimed, 'all further events in the summer of 1917, indeed the entire history of Russia, would have been different had the commission managed to complete the difficult task of exposing Lenin completely, and had it been possible to prove with documents in a court of law the monstrous crime, which no one wanted to believe, precisely because it seemed so utterly unlikely psychologically'. Kerensky himself believed the link between the Bolsheviks and the Germans went as far as complete understanding, 'far beyond payment of money for the collapse of Russia, as some saw it, and the achievement of social revolution, as others saw it'. [41] Kerensky was correct in assuming such an 'understanding' existed. The Bolsheviks, indeed, came to an understanding with the Germans over several issues. For example, in late August 1918, in a handwritten note to Vorovsky, the Soviet envoy in Sweden, Lenin, speaking of a supplementary treaty just signed with the Germans, declared: 'Nobody ever asked the Germans for "help", but we had an understanding about when and how they, the Germans, would carry out their plan to attack Murman and [General] Alexeev. There was a coincidence of interests. We would have been idiots not to have taken advantage of it . . .'[42]

Lenin did not deny the possibility of coming to an understanding with the Germans. If they could agree to exploit the fact of a German attack on General Alexeev's forces in August 1918, they could have had an 'understanding' about a joint effort to bring down tsarism a year earlier.

The huge rise in Bolshevik publications after the February

revolution did not come about by chance. By July 1917 the Party was bringing out forty-one newspapers with a daily circulation of 320,000, twenty-seven of them in Russian and the remainder in Georgian, Armenian, Latvian, Tatar, Polish and other languages. Ninety thousand copies of *Pravda* alone were printed each day. Membership fees could never have sustained such a volume of publication. After February the Party paid 260,000 roubles for a press,[43] and the Party leaders were receiving their salaries, even if irregularly. The Bolshevik coffers were not empty.

When some meagre information supplied by Alexinsky, Yermolenko, Burtsev and others raised a furore in the press over Bolshevik links with the Germans, Lenin published an article in *Listok Pravdy* entitled, 'Where is the Regime and Where is the Counter-Revolution?'. Dismissing the accusations laid by Alexinsky, a former member of the Second Duma, as 'slanderous filth', he advanced two arguments which, he believed, would demolish the 'shoddy work of the newspaper slanderers'. First, Ganetsky 'was recently given free entry into Russia and allowed out again'.[44] This, however, had taken place before the furore arose, and, more important, since Ganetsky travelled on several different passports, he could have arrived under any one of his many aliases. On this point Kerensky recalled that all the facts relating to Lenin's financial connections with the Germans had been collected by the commission in early May, and that although they were of a very serious nature from the security service's point of view, they would not have stood up in court. The case was to be incontrovertibly confirmed by the anticipated arrest of Ganetsky at the border. The publication of some of this material in the press, however, 'put the Bolshevik headquarters on guard. Ganetsky's trip was postponed and the government lost the opportunity to prove with documentary evidence the chief facts compromising Lenin and Co.'[45]

Lenin's second argument was intended to be the main one: 'Ganetsky and Kozlovsky are not Bolsheviks, but members of the Polish Social Democratic Party . . . The Bolsheviks have received *no money whatsoever* from either Ganetsky or Kozlovsky. It's all lies, lies of the crudest kind.'[46] In 'Reply', an article Lenin published in *Rabochii i soldat* on 26 and 27 July 1917 – that is, after the government had issued the decree for his arrest and when he was already in hiding in Finland – he wrote that Parvus had employed other émigrés besides

Ganetsky. 'The prosecutor is playing on the fact that Parvus is linked to Ganetsky and Ganetsky is linked to Lenin! But that is a dirty trick, as everyone knows that Ganetsky had financial dealings with Parvus, while we had none with Ganetsky.'[47]

Who was telling the truth? Whose tricks were 'dirty'? Lenin's assertion that Ganetsky and Kozlovsky were not Bolsheviks was entirely untrue. When Ganetsky was arrested in 1937, his interrogator noted that he had been 'a member of the Bolshevik Party since 1896'.[48] Leaving aside the fact that the Party did not come into existence until 1898, the point was that Ganetsky had been involved in Russian revolutionary politics almost as long as anyone. In fact, he had been a prominent figure in both the Polish and Russian revolutionary movements at the same time. He was a delegate at the Second, Fourth and Fifth Congresses of the Russian Social Democratic Workers' Party, and at the Fifth this 'non-Bolshevik' was elected to the Party Central Committee, while in 1917 he was a member of the Party's Foreign Bureau, in effect its central committee abroad. Much the same could be said of Kozlovsky, who in 1917 was a member of the Executive Committee of the Petrograd Soviet. And what are we to make of Lenin's assertion that he had no financial dealings with Ganetsky, and still more, of his claim that 'everyone knows' that Ganetsky had financial links with Parvus?

After the February revolution, Lenin's correspondence with Ganetsky was exceded in quantity only by that with Inessa Armand. At the beginning of March he cabled Ganetsky that he was about to send him 'an important letter'.[49] A further cable of 15 March referred to Lenin's planned return to Russia, and in the following weeks, until his return, Lenin sent cables or letters to Ganetsky almost every day, including one with instructions 'to set aside two or three thousand crowns for the journey from Switzerland to Russia'.[50] He would soon inform Inessa that the money had been received from Stockholm,[51] adding a little later that 'we have more money for the journey than I'd thought',[52] which suggests there may have been more than one remittance from Ganetsky. Why, then, did he declare that he had never had any financial relations with Ganetsky? He knew Ganetsky had money at his disposal when he asked him to send it. How could he accuse the Provisional Government of 'dirty tricks'?

The decision to travel through Germany was taken quickly. Parvus involved not merely the German High Command and foreign ministry in the affair, but the Kaiser himself, and the Germans were perfectly frank in their intentions. The German ambassador in Copenhagen, Count von Brockdorff-Rantzau, advised the foreign ministry to 'back the extremist elements, as this ... would lead more quickly to some conclusion. In all probability, we should, in about three months' time, be able to count on the disintegration having reached the stage where we could break the power of the Russians by military action.'[53]

French counter-intelligence, not to be left out, reported in the spring of 1917 that Lenin, together with Angelica Balabanova, a Swiss socialist called Mueller and Henri Guilbeau, the French editor of the journal *Demain*, met a representative of the German embassy called Dallenvach at Scioppa's restaurant in Berne. The meeting concerned Lenin's forthcoming journey through Germany to Russia.[54]

Lenin was well aware that the Germans were just as interested in allowing Russian revolutionaries to pass through Germany as he was, and through the Swiss socialist Fritz Platten he set certain conditions which he hoped would provide the Bolsheviks with a political and historical alibi. He strengthened his own cover by refusing to meet Parvus in Stockholm. Parvus recalled the incident: 'I was in Stockholm when Lenin was passing through. He refused a personal meeting. Through a mutual friend I conveyed to him that the main aim now was peace, and hence the conditions for peace. I asked what he intended to do. Lenin replied that he was not involved in diplomacy, his business was social revolutionary agitation.'[55] Not suprisingly, once he had achieved his aim, Lenin rejected Parvus with contempt. The deed was done. The machine, started by Parvus, required no further personal contact.

Finally, Lenin established his alibi by giving pride of place on the journey to Mensheviks. In 'How we Arrived', published simultaneously in *Pravda* and *Izvestiya* on 18 April 1917, he wrote that it had been Martov's idea to travel through Germany.[56] The problem for Lenin had been a simple one: he wanted to get to Russia, all other routes were closed to him, he was concerned about what his enemies would say, and he knew the Mensheviks would be unable to attack him if their leader also returned by the same route.[57]

When their Swedish ferry docked at Trolleborg, Lenin was met by Ganetsky, who travelled with the party on to Malmö and Stockholm, where Lenin managed to find time to buy footwear and a pair of trousers. Ganetsky provided the Bolsheviks with everything they needed, including tickets for the rest of the journey. Yet Lenin would later insist he had had no financial dealings with Ganetsky.

The press and the Swedish social democrats took a great interest in Lenin during his stopover in Stockholm. A dinner in his honour was held in the Hotel Regina, he was filmed, gave press interviews, and was welcomed by the mayor, K. Lindhagen. Feeling that he was entering a phase for which he had waited and worked all his life, he spoke like a leader, like the brain and nerves of the revolution. And he was impatient to move ahead: socialism was no longer a distant utopia.

On the way to the Russian border he sent a cable to Karpinsky in Geneva, expressing satisfaction with the way the Germans had observed the agreed conditions. He also cabled Petrograd, suggesting his arrival be announced in *Pravda*: he was not returning like an ordinary émigré, but like an instant leader.

When Lenin's connections with the Germans were being investigated by the Provisional Government, and the order for his arrest was issued in July 1917, no less than twenty-one volumes of evidence were collected. But the case fizzled out because Kerensky thought the main threat to his regime was coming from the right, and that he needed support from the left, including the Bolsheviks. After the seizure of power, Lenin at once set about dealing with all this compromising evidence. He took personal charge of finding, confiscating and apparently destroying it. On instructions from Trotsky, as foreign commissar, on 16 November 1917 F. Zalkind and E. Polivanov reported that the materials of the incomplete investigation had been confiscated. They reported as follows:

To the Chairman of the Soviet of People's Commissars: In accordance with the resolution passed by . . . Comrades Lenin, Trotsky, Podvoisky, Didenko and Volodarsky, we have done the following:

1) In the Ministry of Justice archives, from the files on 'the treason' of Comrades Lenin, Zinoviev, Kozlovsky, Kollontai and others, we have removed German Imperial Bank Order No 7,433 dated 2 March 1917 authorizing payment of money . . . for peace propaganda in Russia.

2) We have examined all the books of the New Bank of Stockholm . . . opened on order No. 2,754 of the German Imperial Bank . . .[58]

The materials collected by the Provisional Government include a number which mention the Bolshevik leaders, but their authenticity cannot be established beyond doubt. They are surveys prepared by the investigators. The instructions to finance individuals engaged in peace propaganda are too flagrant to take seriously. It has been shown that a large number of documents disappeared without trace, and it would be surprising if the Bolsheviks had not taken such steps to destroy compromising material.

The investigation was intended to show that Lenin and his comrades had simply been bought by German intelligence, but this does not seem likely. A more realistic picture emerges from the circumstantial evidence. Parvus, and possibly also the Estonian Keskula, with the agreement of the German foreign ministry and General Staff, 'fed' the firm of Ganetsky, Sumenson and Kozlovsky in their commercial ventures. Without Parvus's German help Ganetsky would never have been able to start his 'business'. According to his brother, in 1914 he had been so poor he couldn't afford to buy milk for his child.[59]

A significant part of the money handled by Ganetsky reached Bolshevik coffers by various routes. As the historian of the 'Russo-Scandinavian revolutionary connection', Michael Futrell, has concluded: 'Surveying [Ganetsky's] previous career, it is difficult to imagine that he would devote himself to money-making for any other principal purpose than aiding the revolutionary cause.'[60] This seems a reasonable assumption. Ganetsky engaged in commerce because it answered Lenin's political needs. Before and after the revolution, millions of roubles and a vast quantity of valuables passed through his hands. For instance, he engaged in lengthy negotiations with the Poles over reparations following the Riga Peace Treaty in 1920, and he was deputed by the Politburo to sell huge quantities of the tsar's diamonds, gems, gold and jewellery abroad. Yet when he was arrested in 1937, all that was found in his apartment was two dollars, and not a single valuable object.[61] Either nothing had 'stuck to his fingers', or it is still salted away in Swiss accounts, or it all went into Party funds. As Lenin himself said, Ganetsky was a man of intellectual conviction. Commerce was his Party job.

After the revolution, one of the first to try to unravel the secret of the German money was the German Social Democrat Eduard Bernstein. In 1921, he published an article in the Party newspaper, *Vor-*

*wärts*, in which he stated that it was known, and had been confirmed by General Hoffmann, that the Kaiser's government had allowed Lenin and his comrades to pass through Germany so that they could carry on their agitation in Russia. 'Lenin and his comrades received vast sums of money from the Kaiser's government for their destructive agitation.' Bernstein wrote that he had known about this in December 1917, and that it had been confirmed by someone who knew about it because of his job. Bernstein did not know the amount of money Lenin had received, nor who the contacts between Lenin and the government had been. He went on: 'From absolutely reliable sources I have now ascertained that the sum was very large, an almost unbelievable amount, certainly more than fifty million gold marks, a sum about the source of which Lenin and his comrades could be in no doubt. One result of all this was the Brest-Litovsk Treaty. General Hoffmann, who negotiated with Trotsky and other members of the Bolshevik delegation at Brest, held the Bolsheviks in his hand in two senses, and he made sure they felt it.'[62]

A week later Bernstein published a second article in *Vorwärts* in which he challenged the German Communists and Russian Bolsheviks to take him to court if they thought he had libelled Lenin. The Central Committees of both parties, however, maintained their silence, virtually confirming Bernstein's assertions. The question arises of whether the German funds were as great as was suggested. Bernstein seems to have been referring to all the money transferred since 1915. On 3 December 1917 German State Secretary Richard von Kühlmann reported to the German Military High Command: 'It was not until the Bolsheviks had received from us a steady flow of funds through various channels and under different labels that they were in a position to be able to build up their main organ, *Pravda*, to conduct energetic propaganda, and appreciably to extend the originally narrow base of their party . . . It is entirely in our interest that we should exploit the period while they are in power, which may be a short one, in order to attain firstly an armistice and then, if possible, peace. The conclusion of a separate peace would mean the achievement of the desired war aim, namely a breach between Russia and her allies.'[63]

Similarly, on 3 June 1918 – a month before he was assassinated – Count Mirbach, the German ambassador in Moscow, cabled that he needed three million marks a month, and maybe more, to counter

Allied propaganda in Russia. A few days later Counsellor Trautmann of the German Foreign Ministry informed the Treasury that Mirbach had been spending large sums to counter Allied propaganda: 'The fund which we have so far had at our disposal for acquisitions in Russia is exhausted. It is therefore essential that [the Treasury] put a new fund at our disposal. In view of the conditions set out above, this fund will have to amount to at least forty million marks.'[64]

While the documents show many varied figures from both the German and Russian sides participating in this affair, Lenin stood in the wings and watched while the play, created with his involvement and agreement, was performed. He was very cautious, made very few slips, such as claiming that he'd had no financial dealings with Ganetsky, and left few traces on the affair. Having approved this enormously important anti-Russian operation, he made the maximum use of the opportunities presented by the Germans. They both sought the defeat of tsarism, and they were both satisfied.

The Bolsheviks did not want to expatiate on the 'German key', although they never let any mention of it pass without exploiting it. At the end of January 1919, for instance, Foreign Commissar Chicherin cabled Trotsky: 'The radio has just reported that the Paris newspaper *Le Populaire* is carrying a report from the New York evening *Times* to the following effect: the legend about contacts between the Bolshevik leaders and the German empire has finally been refuted. In January 1918 Russian counter-revolutionaries sent Colonel Robbins a number of documents showing there was a link between the German government and Lenin and Trotsky. Robbins conducted an investigation and questioned Galperin who admitted that many of the documents had been in the hands of the Kerensky government and are obvious forgeries . . . The former publisher of *Cosmopolitan Magazine*, Versta Sisson, agreed with Robbins, but later changed his mind. After being passed around for a long time, the documents were finally sold to the Americans for 100,000 [probably US dollars].'[65]

After the Bolshevik seizure of power, Parvus decided to test himself again in the arena of revolution, as he had in 1905. In mid-November 1917, he met Radek in Stockholm and asked him to pass a personal request to Lenin, namely to give him permission to return to Russia to do revolutionary work. He had experience, a good brain, plenty of money, and he still had his strength. He added that his reputation had been stained by collaborating with 'social patriots', and Lenin had called him a 'chauvinist', but everything he did had been for the success of the revolution in Russia. In wishing for a German victory, he had wanted to bring the Russian revolution closer. He was even prepared to face a Party court. Three weeks later, Radek returned to Stockholm with Lenin's reply: 'The cause of the revolution must not be sullied by dirty hands.' Parvus was deeply disappointed. Were the Bolshevik hands that had taken his money any cleaner? His name, however, could only compromise Lenin. His appearance in Petrograd would only confirm the accusation of treason against the Bolsheviks.

The German government also cooled towards Parvus, and cut off his credit for new commercial ventures, upon which Parvus demanded a million marks not to publish compromising documents. Whether or not the blackmail worked or the contretemps was resolved some other way, there was no scandal.[66] He then set out to write a large book of memoirs, and he had plenty to say. The last two decades had been tumultuous: women, wine, audacious financial operations and fantastic plans. After October 1917, now grossly overweight, Parvus continued to live as if he was still thirty, but the fountain of youth was rapidly petering out. In December 1924, ten months after Lenin's death, Parvus's heart failed, and what had been said at the notorious May 1915 meeting died with him. His memoirs were never written.

Although Parvus's son, Alexander Gnedin, officially condemned his father's political position, it did not save him. He was arrested in 1939, and amazingly survived sixteen years in the camps. In 1977 he published a book dealing chiefly with his long-drawn-out effort – on the orders of the Soviet government – to acquire his father's estate on behalf of the USSR.[67] But Parvus had been surrounded by clever individuals who had ensured that his money should go elsewhere. Gnedin did, however, manage to retrieve his father's library and some of his papers, both of which had first been 'examined' by Chekists, in accordance with normal procedure. Naturally, they left nothing that could compromise Lenin and the Bolsheviks.

Ganetsky's fate was more tragic. He did not die, like Parvus, in his own bed. At first, thanks to Lenin's patronage, he held important posts in the commissariats of finance and trade and the economy. Lenin often gave him delicate and sometimes personal missions. In April 1921 he asked him 'to be so kind as' to buy items on a list for

Krupskaya, and in May he asked him – 'using the Swiss money I gave you' – to buy 'flour (rye, if possible), sausage, canned goods (but not delicatessen), meat and fish . . .' And on another occasion, shoelaces for Krupskaya and French bread rolls.[68]

The dozens of documents signed or seen by Lenin and associated with Ganetsky are almost invariably about money. For instance, Ganetsky reported that they had received 83,513 Danish kroner from Karl Moor, a Swiss Social Democrat of German nationality. What was he to do with the money? Lenin could not recall why they had received it. Zinoviev had a suggestion: 'I think it should be handed over to Comintern. After all, Moor will only drink it up.'[69]

Lenin knew Moor well. As a member of the cantonal parliament and government in Berne, he had issued residence permits to Lenin and Krupskaya, as well as to Inessa Armand. What Lenin did not know, and what only became known after the Second World War, was that Moor was also a paid agent of Berlin. Under the name of Baier, he had been sending regular reports on Bolshevik activities and intentions to the German embassy in Berne. And he was well informed, since he knew Lenin, Radek, Shklovsky, Zinoviev and other revolutionaries. In September 1917 he suddenly decided to give the Bolshevik Central Committee a large sum of money. He explained that he had unexpectedly inherited a substantial estate. In fact the estate had come to him in Germany in 1908, and the money he now wanted to give the Bolsheviks came from the German High Command. His paymasters hoped that by this move Moor would earn the special trust of the Bolshevik leadership. To be sure, the Central Committee had its doubts about the source of the money, and as there was unease about the Provisional Government's investigation of Bolshevik links with Berlin, it decided to decline the 'gift'. Ganetsky told the Central Committee that the 83,513 Danish kroner was in fact 'the remainder of the money already received from Moor'.[70]

Moor was just one of the channels by which German money entered Bolshevik coffers. He remained in Soviet Russia and continued to inform Berlin about the Bolshevik leadership. He met Lenin several times, and despite the suspicions that existed about him, he managed to carry on as Baier. When he died in Berlin on 14 June 1932, aged almost eighty, Radek wrote an obituary in *Izvestiya* in which he made the unexpected admission that Moor had helped the Bolsheviks financially. Only a few people, including Radek, knew that this money had come from the German General Staff.

After Lenin's death, Ganetsky disappeared into the shade, though he continued to work in the middle ranks of government. In 1935 he was appointed director of the State Museum of the Revolution, his last job. On 18 July 1937, together with his wife, Giza Adolfovna, and son Stanislav, he was arrested as a German and Polish spy. Books and pamphlets by the now-disgraced Trotsky, Zinoviev, Kamenev, Radek, Bukharin and Shlyapnikov, seventy-eight works in all, were found in his apartment, providing ample evidence of his 'treachery'. During the search he managed to write to the chief of the NKVD, Nikolai Yezhov, with a pencil that kept breaking: 'A nightmarish tragic accident has occurred: they have arrested me tonight! They're already calling me an enemy! What's going on? How could such a ghastly mistake be made? I ask you, I beg you: 1) Stop all repression against my family. 2) Tell them to interrogate me at once. *Summon me yourself* and you'll see what an obviously horrible misunderstanding it is!' At the top of the page he scrawled feverishly: 'I ask for this to be delivered at once!'[71] It was a cry in vain.

The charge against Ganetsky was that, during a visit to Poland on Stalin's orders on 20 September 1933 to retrieve a Lenin archive, he had held a number of unauthorized meetings with Polish military intelligence officers. The NKVD naturally concluded he had been engaged in espionage. His interrogator also informed him that he had been a German spy since the war – which was not far from the truth. Ganetsky could not mention his work for Lenin, as he feared that it would bring instant punishment, and instead he counted on Stalin's intervention. Unlike the Provisional Government, which sought hard evidence, the NKVD simply assumed that anyone who had had so much contact with foreigners must be a spy. Moreover, anyone who knew as much as Ganetsky was regarded as dangerous. Before the fate of such people was decided, however, Stalin was always consulted. As in this case, he usually gave the laconic response 'Liquidate.'[72]

At Ganetsky's trial one witness, the Bolshevik Maximilian Gustavovich Valetsky (executed in September 1937, i.e. immediately after giving evidence), testified that Ganetsky had been a close companion of Parvus, itself an incriminating circumstance. Valetsky accurately described their operations in 1916–17, adding that they had been helped by Kozlovsky and Sumenson. During his own interrogation, Ganetsky reminded his torturers that the reason he had gone to Poland in 1933 was to retrieve a Lenin archive, but it did not help. As he wriggled to save himself, another witness, his assistant Petermeier, stated that when he had travelled to Berlin he had collected German marks from a certain Mr Senior on Ganetsky's instructions.[73]

Despite appalling torture, Ganetsky did not break, and never confessed to spying. Few were as tough. In a 'trial' lasting precisely fifteen minutes, from 11 to 11.15 a.m. on 26 November 1937, he was condemned to death as a spy and Trotskyist by the Military Collegium of the USSR Supreme Court, chaired by Nikitchenko. His last words to the court were 'I consider myself guilty of nothing.' The record shows that he was shot the same day, as were his wife and son.[74] His surviving daughter, Hannah, was later informed that he had died of heart disease on 21 January 1939, that her mother had died of stomach cancer on 29 December 1938, and that her brother Stanislav had died of pneumonia on 24 November 1941.[75]

Thus ended the life of one of Lenin's most trusted agents, the man who knew too much about the Bolsheviks' secret financial links with the 'merchant of revolution' for his own good.

## Lenin and Kerensky

Alexander Kerensky was born in Lenin's birthplace, Simbirsk, on 22 April 1881. His father, Fedor, was the headmaster of the high school where Alexander and Vladimir Ulyanov were educated. Kerensky obtained his secondary education in Tashkent, Central Asia, where his father became head of the educational administration, and subsequently graduated from St Petersburg University with a degree in law. In 1905 he joined the Socialist Revolutionary Party, which retained an element committed to terrorism, and it was this aspect of the Party's activities Kerensky had hoped to promote. He was, however, arrested, and spent a short time in prison and exile between 1905 and 1906, before returning to St Petersburg to set out on his career as a defence lawyer. He acquired a considerable reputation as a successful advocate in political cases.

In 1912 he was elected to the State Duma as a member of the Labour Group (Trudoviks) of the Socialist Revolutionary Party. The popular press had blossomed in the aftermath of the 1905 revolution and the considerably widened margin of freedom granted by the tsar, and soon Kerensky, a brilliant and imaginative orator, had a popular following among the working class. At informal meetings of the Duma opposition, where Russia's bleak fortunes in the war were the subject of endless debate and plotting, he called for the assassination of the tsar. When the tsar abdicated in March, Kerensky became Minister of Justice in the Provisional Government that came to power. He was responsible for abolishing ethnic and religious discrimination and also the death penalty.

Like many socialists, Kerensky often had the French Revolution in mind. The Provisional Government chose 'The Marseillaise' as its national anthem, it appointed 'revolutionary commissars', planned a 'Constituent Assembly', and before long there would be talk of 'Russian Marats and Robespierres'. Somewhere between the left and right in his political disposition, and a man of compromise, Kerensky had contacts across a wide political spectrum, from conservative to liberal to socialist. Just before the February revolution he had become secretary of an important branch of the Russian political Freemasons, and it was on the basis of this network that many of his political alliances were founded.

Shortly after Lenin's arrival in Petrograd in April 1917, Kerensky expressed a desire to see him. Meeting Lenin, he felt, might reinforce support from the left. The executive secretary of the Provisional Government, Vladimir Nabokov – father of the writer – noted in his memoirs that Lenin was hardly ever mentioned at government sessions. 'I remember Kerensky, in April after Lenin had returned, saying that he'd like to meet and have a chat with him and, in reply to the puzzled questions that followed, explaining that the Bolshevik leader was "living in a completely isolated atmosphere, he knows nothing and sees everything through the lens of his own fantasies, and he has no one to help him get his bearings on what's going on".'[76] Kerensky believed he was the one to help Lenin 'get his bearings'. Through intermediaries, Lenin declined a meeting. He had dismissed Kerensky as nothing more than the hero of the moment, and would make no compromises with him. Kerensky had no future.

In a sense, Lenin was right: Kerensky did not want to unite openly either with the Bolsheviks or the White generals. He always imagined there was a 'third way'. While the civil war was raging, he wrote: 'Social justice, liberty and free men have all been trampled by Red and White sergeant-majors alike. But a decisive third force will yet prevail against them.'[77] The third force he had in mind was the people's democracy, or people power, born in February. Throughout all the subsequent years he spent as an émigré, Kerensky claimed that the tsarist generals were the counter-revolution of the right and the Bolsheviks the counter-revolution of the left.

Kerensky remained either inside Russia in hiding or in nearby Finland throughout the civil war, and in 1922 he left for Berlin and subsequently Paris. When France fell in 1940 he left for New York, where he remained until the mid-1960s, when he moved to the Hoover Institution at Stanford University in California. He died in New York in 1970, at the age of eighty-nine.

Russia indeed lost a historic opportunity when the February revolution was demolished. For Kerensky the rule of law was paramount. Even when the Provisional Government, pressed by public opinion, issued orders in the summer of 1917 to arrest Lenin and others suspected of links with the Germans, Kerensky stressed that 'they must face the law. Only the law.' Yet history was not kind to him. After eight months in government, he was confined, chiefly but not exclusively by Soviet historians, to the margins of history as a political lightweight. Even the code name given to him by the NKVD was 'The Clown'.[78]

Lenin was merciless towards Kerensky. In his so-called Complete Works he mentions him no less than two hundred times, inventing more and more colourful epithets, dubbing him 'the braggart' and linking him with 'the idiot Romanov' as the men most responsible for bringing ruin and disorder to Russia.[79] Lenin had never been tolerant towards his political opponents. In Paris in 1911, he growled, 'One should push such people up against the wall, and if they still don't give in, trample them into the mud.'[80] Such expressions often substituted for political argument. Kerensky abstained from replying in kind. Even as an old man, knowing how savagely Lenin had dismissed him, he refrained from abusing the man who had cast him into oblivion, leaving it to history to make the final judgment.

For Kerensky, Bolshevism was 'the socialism of poverty and

hunger', and there could be no socialism without democracy; social liberation was 'impossible in a state that did not respect the personality of man and his rights'.[81] It was a view he extended to the former monarch. He wrote that Nicholas should not be made a martyr. At the Moscow Soviet on 20 March 1917, he responded to cries of 'Death to the tsar, execute the tsar,' by saying, 'this won't happen as long as we're in power. We have taken responsibility for the personal safety of the tsar and his family. We will bear this responsibility to the end. I will take him to Murmansk [en route to England] myself.'[82] The British government, however, refused to receive the royal family, and the Provisional Government transferred them instead to Tobolsk, which was regarded as the safest place in Russia.

The balance Kerensky tried to maintain between left and right during the eight months of the Provisional Government's life was ultimately tipped in the Bolsheviks' favour by General Kornilov, commander-in-chief of the government's own forces. Kerensky was aware that his generals wanted to restore order, and even welcomed this, as long as control remained with the government. But he wavered and manoeuvred, and then, on 27 August 1917, when he read a proclamation by Kornilov, he realized the general intended to 'save Russia' without the government, and without him. Kornilov declared that 'the Provisional Government, under pressure from the Bolshevik majority in the Soviets, is acting in complete accordance with the plans of the German General Staff', and that it was his, Kornilov's, firm intention, after winning the war, to bring the people to the Constituent Assembly, where they themselves would decide the future structure of the new state.[83] When Kerensky heard that Kornilov was taking full military and civil powers into his own hands, and already moving his troops on the capital, he ordered that they be halted and returned to their previous positions. Kornilov refused to obey, and ordered his troops to continue.

Kerensky's orders had failed, but the Bolsheviks and units under their influence intervened. Their Central Committee, together with other socialist bodies, appealed to the soldiers and workers to repel Kornilov. The generals' revolt was not unlike that of August 1991, especially in relation to the country's leaders. In 1917 Kerensky lost all his influence at once, just as Gorbachev would seventy-four years later. The balancing act that may be required at certain moments cannot serve as the basis of a long-term policy. After the Kornilov movement was extinguished with Bolshevik help, Kerensky issued orders for Generals Kornilov, Denikin, Lukomsky, Markov and others to be brought to justice. The attempted coup was a life-saver for the Bolsheviks, and after it their prestige rose, while Kerensky's fell. His Military Commissar later recalled that, when he returned from GHQ to Petrograd in early October, the Prime Minister struck him as 'empty, strange, uncharacteristically calm. He was not surrounded by the usual crowd of people, there were no delegations or spotlights ... He now had a lot of strange free time, so that I could converse with him for hours, revealing in him a strange unhurriedness.'[84]

As long as the February revolution was on a rising tide, Kerensky enjoyed glory, popularity and influence, but once the tide began to turn, all his expressiveness, impulsiveness and feverish activity drained from him, and he even began to lose his self-esteem. He had got on badly with the generals, who treated him with ironic condescension, and when he visited the front he had felt their unfriendly gaze on him. He had a last chance in late October, when he had already fled the capital. This time he relied on General Krasnov, commander of the 3rd Cavalry Corps. Kerensky ordered the cavalry to ride on Petrograd with the aim of regaining power, but again the Bolshevik agitators did their work when the troops were still far from their objective. The Bolsheviks arrested Krasnov, then released him once he had given his word that he would not engage in politics. In fact he carried on the fight, ending up in Germany, where he published a novel called *From the White Eagle to the Red Banner*. According to General Yepishev, who heard it from Stalin's aide, Poskrebyshev, Stalin described this novel as 'Shit, just like the general himself.'[85] Krasnov, then aged seventy-eight, was captured by the Red Army in 1945, and ordered by Stalin to be tried in Moscow for collaboration. During the trial, conducted by the Chairman of the Soviet Supreme Court, V. Ulrikh, Krasnov was reminded of his early collaboration with Kerensky, and he responded with a detailed account of the events. He was sentenced to be hanged on 16 March 1947. He did not ask for clemency, and the sentence was duly carried out the next day.[86]

Kerensky wrote prolifically in exile. In the early 1930s he published *Dni* (Days), a Russian-language weekly in Paris, and at the end of the decade a journal called *Novaya Rossiya* (New Russia), in which he published the views of a wide range of former politicians, writers, philosophers and ordinary citizens. Stalin always wanted to know what Kerensky was up to and whether it was possible to use him in some way. First Yagoda and then Beria ordered their special agents to 'work on the Clown', and in 1942, at the height of the war, Beria instructed Fitin and Sudoplatov, head of the NKVD's partisan administration, to 'get the low-down on the group around Kerensky and Chernov' in the USA. Agent 'Alligator' reported to Moscow that Kerensky was supported by his elder son, an engineer, and the Czechoslovak government, while his journal was funded by a wealthy Jewish woman called Benenson. Kerensky frequently visited England, where his former wife, Baranovskaya, lived with their two sons. He occasionally toured the European capitals to lecture in support of democracy and against dictatorial regimes. According to 'Alligator', Kerensky enjoyed great support among the Jews, who never forgot April 1917, when the Provisional Government gave them equal rights.[87] After the war, Gusakov, a senior NKVD officer, wrote on one of the reports: 'Kerensky's coming to the fore again. We must think of a way to render him harmless.' Nothing was done, however, and Kerensky was allowed to live to a ripe old age.

Interestingly, in June 1930 Kerensky raised an important question in one of his speeches, namely, 'Is Russia threatened by disintegration?' By this time, on Lenin's initiative, the Bolsheviks had long altered the face of the country. As early as 1919 they had proclaimed provinces and districts 'obsolete'.[88] No one then could have imagined that by artificially creating the new national formation, they were planting a mine of devastating power under the country. The Politburo passed a resolution on 22 June 1920 according to which 'Russian kulaks must be smashed and deported from Turkestan. All former members of the police, gendarmes, secret police and tsarist civil servants are to be deported from Turkestan to concentration camps in [the Russian Federation].'[89] In a similarly arbitrary fashion, the Politburo decided in 1923 to transfer more than a dozen districts to Belorussia, to create the Tatar Republic, to dispose of 'Bashkir affairs', and so on.[90]

The Bolsheviks drew a new political map which they called a Union, but which was in fact no less a unitary state than the Russian empire had been. Paradoxically, in this unitary society the national feeling of the Russians was suppressed, and the build-up began of the centrifugal forces that would one day smash the Union that Lenin had created and that had been held together by the Party-state. The abolition of the provinces and the formation of artificial national units, given the absence of democracy, could only lead to the build-up of national discontent and the eventual break-up of the Union.

While he was the head of the Provisional Government, Kerensky had advocated 'supra-tribal unity, the voluntary unification of the peoples not on an ethnic, but on an economic, geographical, administrative and political basis'. The Bolshevik coup of October 1917 effectively put an end to such ideas, which, with many others generated by the February revolution, might have spared the country much suffering.

## The July Rehearsal

Among the slogans Lenin contrived in the weeks after his return, one of the most simple was that all that was needed was 'to expropriate a couple of thousand banking and industrial big-shots . . . and break the resistance of a few hundred millionaires'.[91] He knew that the idea of expropriation would appeal to the semi-literate, exhausted and confused masses as a simple solution to age-old problems. Slowly but steadily the Bolsheviks consolidated Lenin's strategy in the space created by the dual power, the gap between the Provisional Government and the Soviets, for only they were prepared to promise immediate and certain peace, land and liberty.

While he offered the 'revolutionary masses' the opportunity of undermining the government, personified by 'banking and industrial big-shots', Lenin continued to attack the Soviets for their lack of revolutionariness: 'All the blame for the crisis, for the approaching catastrophe, rests on the Populist and Menshevik leaders, for they are the present leaders of the Soviets.'[92] When the Socialist Revolutionary S. Maslov condemned the unauthorized seizure of land by peasants, Lenin defended them, declaring that estate land 'should be handed over to the local peasants *at once* . . . The Bolsheviks want to give the land to the peasants without mortgages, *without any payment*.'[93] This simple message immediately made the soldier-peasants the allies of the Bolsheviks. At the First All-Russian Congress of Peasant Deputies in May 1917, Lenin drew an idyllic picture of future agricultural life: 'It will be a Russia in which free labour will work on free land.'[94] When the Leninist Politburo set about realizing Lenin's cooperative plans in 1930, however, the picture was less than idyllic. 'Counter-revolutionary' kulaks were to be incarcerated in concentration camps, or to be executed in the case of physical resistance; rich and 'semi-landowner' kulaks were to be deported to remote areas; while the least of the kulaks were to be resettled on new land beyond the limits of the collective farm areas.[95] The Bolsheviks would not mention 'free labour' once they had gained power.

Equally, Lenin's calls for peace found an enthusiastic echo among the war-weary. He proposed a simple solution at the First Congress of Soviets on 22 June 1917: 'How in fact do we see a way out of this war? We say the only way out . . . is through a revolution . . . When people say we want a separate peace, that's not true. We say: no separate peace.'[96] Revolution in the midst of war meant, of course, the defeat of the country. As for a separate peace, within a few months the Bolsheviks would have concluded just that. Who could have known that, after making their separate, defeatist, peace, the Bolsheviks would start liquidating not several hundred millionaires, but hundreds of thousands of private owners, middle and upper bourgeoisie, and intellectuals. This would lead to the civil war which the Bolsheviks had also planned. Before October, however, Lenin's calls for peace and the 'free land' promise lit a fire of hope, visible to the weary traveller from a distance.

It seems unlikely that the Bolsheviks gave any thought to the fact that giving a promise while in opposition is a different thing from fulfilling it as a government. On every point – peace, land, liberty, Constituent Assembly, freedom of the press and all the rest – their promises rapidly changed into coercion, limitation, alteration, a different 'reading', or outright denial. Even the land, which they did give, they made undesirable by confiscating everything it produced. In other words, although Lenin labelled his opponents 'demagogues', it was he who used demagogy as a way to achieve popularity, making maximum promises to a population which had very low political awareness.

Liberty was especially hard hit. Soon after the seizure of power,

Lenin's government pointed to 'special conditions', 'the civil war', 'the threat of counter-revolution', and soon also intervention by Allied forces, as excuses to install a regime of terroristic dictatorship. Inevitably, those with most to lose responded with force. Lenin's preference for extreme measures (embodied in the Cheka, a name derived from the first two initials – che-ka – of the Extraordinary Commissions for Combating Counter-revolution) quickly led to police control of the new state. When, in June 1917, the Provisional Government, alarmed by rumours of an impending attempt by the Bolsheviks to seize power, banned all demonstrations for three days, Lenin at once protested that 'in any constitutional country organizing such demonstrations is the incontrovertible right of every citizen'.[97] In a few months he would have forgotten the meaning of 'citizens' rights', and any meeting or collective activity would require the permission of the political police.

In June 1922, on Lenin's initiative, the Politburo examined the question of anti-Soviet groups among the intelligentsia, and produced a ruling reminiscent of the medieval Inquisition. 'Screening' was to be introduced for university applicants, meaning that there were to be 'strict limits on the admission to university of students of non-proletarian background and there should be police evidence of political reliability'. All printed publications were to be carefully vetted, 'no congress or All-Russian meeting of specialists (doctors, agronomists, engineers, lawyers, and so on) may be convened without NKVD permission', while local meetings would require the authorization of the equivalent local organs, and 'existing specialist sections of trade unions should be specially registered and put under special observation'.[98] The contrast with Bolshevik tactics in 1917 could not have been more striking or cynical.

On 11 June 1917, the day after a Bolshevik demonstration had failed to take place, Irakli Tsereteli, one of the Menshevik leaders, told the assembled delegates of all the factions of the Congress of Soviets that 'the counter-revolution can come through only one door, namely the Bolsheviks. What they are engaged in now is not propaganda, it is a plot. The weapon of criticism [of the government] is being replaced by criticism with the aid of a gun.'[99] Tsereteli was not exaggerating: on the same day, Lenin was telling the St Petersburg Committee of his Party – the Social Democrats rejected the change of the capital's name in 1914 to Petrograd as a nationalistic reflex – that 'the days of peaceful demonstrations are over', and that 'the workers should soberly consider the fact that there can be no more talk about such demonstrations'.[100]

Despite the horrific loss of men at the front since the outbreak of the war, and the fact that hideously maimed soldiers crowded the streets of the capital, and despite the rising tide of agitation in favour of an early end to the conflict, Kerensky and the Provisional Government, which now included a number of other socialist (Menshevik and Socialist Revolutionary) ministers, believed that a way out of their domestic weakness lay in a large-scale offensive at the front in June. Galicia was the chosen area, no doubt because there the Russian army was facing the half-hearted troops of Austria-Hungary, rather than the more vigorously led Germans. As Minister of War, Kerensky dropped everything in the capital and toured the front. Dubbed 'supreme persuader-in-chief', he harangued the troops until he was hoarse, and proclaimed that the fate of the revolution depended on the forthcoming offensive.

His claims, however fragile, were not unrealistic, and were widely shared. A victory at the front could well have altered the position in the government's favour in the capital, if not elsewhere in the country. The army was in no condition to accomplish major operational and strategic tasks, but it could have achieved partial success. Before the offensive, however, regiments which had been influenced by the Bolsheviks held long meetings, demanded conditions from their commanders and presented ultimatums. One resolution, for instance stated that 'we will occupy the Austrian trenches if half the regiment is given two weeks' home leave'. Colonel Stankevich recalled that at one regiment Kerensky was met by the fierce resistance of a Bolshevik called Captain Dzevaltovsky, who cleverly demolished every one of his arguments. 'Some of the soldiers applauded Dzevaltovsky, and no fewer applauded Kerensky, but the majority listened in silence, thinking their own thoughts.'[101]

Despite its disorganized state, the army scored an initial tactical success. The Austrians and Hungarians – barely better led than the Russians – fell back without offering serious resistance. News of this advance aroused a burst of rejoicing in Petrograd, but it was not consolidated. The soldiers' committees demanded leave and a change of commanders, among other ultimatums. The Germans transferred a few corps to the south-western front and mounted a strong counter-attack, which led to the rapidly escalating retreat of the demoralized Russians. The Bolsheviks could once again assert that the main enemy was not in the German trenches, but in the seat of government. The army had now completely disintegrated, and thousands of deserters flooded in crowds to the rear.

After the collapse of the Galician offensive the political weathervane turned sharply left. It seemed there was no other way out of the war and the crisis than those offered by the Bolsheviks. Seeing his life's goal approaching, Lenin worked harder than ever. Articles appeared in *Pravda* almost every day, and he had meetings with members of the Central Committee's military organization and soldiers' and sailors' deputies from Kronstadt, the island fortress off Petrograd. Still, most of his work was on paper, a virtual propaganda conveyor-belt, preparing the Party for the coup d'état.

In his speeches to the First Congress of Soviets in the second half of June 1917, Lenin had totally dismissed the path of 'reformist democracy', acknowledging only 'revolutionary democracy'. He explained what he meant: 'It has been said here that there is no party in Russia which would say it was ready to take power entirely by itself. I answer: There is! No party should refuse this, and our party does not refuse: we are ready at any minute to take power entirely.'[102] His words were greeted by the thin applause of the 105 Bolsheviks and the hollow laughter of the remaining nine hundred deputies. But Lenin had not concealed his cards: he was ready to take power at any minute, and since no one was about to hand it to him on a silver dish, he made his intentions perfectly clear. First, he must strengthen his influence in the factories, among the troops and on naval ships.

Every night for a month, hardly bothering to undress, he fell into an exhausted, troubled sleep. Brief naps no longer refreshed him. He had been used to a more free and easy life, unburdened by routine, but he had to make an effort now. Every day he was writing articles and making speeches at countless venues. He would wake with a dull headache, but would nonetheless take up his pen to write yet another article, and then go through the morning post. Finally, on 12 July, he took family advice and set off, with his sister Maria and two trusted

workers, for a five-day rest beyond the revolutionary tumult of Petrograd, in the nearby village of Neivola, near Mustamyaki. He stopped
to see the poet Demyan Bednyi on the way, and also stayed with the
Bolshevik Vladimir Bonch-Bruevich. Recalling the visit, Bonch-
Bruevich wrote that Lenin 'was suffering from headaches, his face was
white, and his eyes showed great fatigue'.[103] Lenin sat for long periods
on the verandah, staring at the blue sky, while the peaceful countryside
and lush foliage of the surroundings had their customary beneficial
effect.

News of the defeat of the Galician offensive aroused first despair and
then anger towards a government which seemed utterly incompetent.
Lenin and his entourage at once sensed a change in the public mood,
and he decided to speed things up. *Pravda* fiercely castigated the
government for 'throwing thousands of men into the meat grinder'.
Bolshevik influence grew rapidly. The Party Central Committee
agreed that what was needed was a powerful, mass action that would
force the Provisional Government to resign in favour of the Soviets,
where the Bolsheviks stepped up their efforts to gain control. The
idea quickly caught on in factories and among troops who did not
want to go to the front, and therefore supported the Bolsheviks.
'Taking power' in the capital was far more appealing than the filthy
trenches and the lice.

On the night of 16 July, M.A. Savelyev, a staff member of *Pravda*,
travelled to see Lenin at Neivola. Awoken early in the morning, Lenin
heard what the messenger had to say, and set off for Petrograd at
once, where he began organizing the tens of thousands of workers
who had been called out to demonstrate. All Soviet textbooks say of
this event that Lenin's main object was to turn the demonstration
into a peaceful expression of labouring Petrograd. But he had declared
two weeks earlier that peaceful demonstrations were 'a thing of the
past', and had said so much more than once.

Meanwhile, workers were streaming into the centre of the city,
along with sailors from Kronstadt and soldiers from the numerous
barracks of the garrison. As the liberal leader Paul Milyukov recalled,
the government's weakness was so obvious that 'one could understand
the temptation to try something more than the postponed demonstration of 10 (23) June'. Thus, the events of 17 July could, in Milyukov's words, be called the first real attempt at revolution by the

Bolsheviks: 'Lenin was already on his notorious balcony at Kshesin-skaya's house and was welcoming the soldiers and giving them instructions. The entire military intelligence of the Bolshevik Central Committee was there; military units came and went from there. In a word, it was the military headquarters of the uprising.'[104]

Oddly enough, of all the countless speeches he made, the one from the balcony does not appear in any edition of Lenin's collected works, even though he had notes for it in his hand. The fact is that it was after the dispersal of the demonstrators, many of them armed, that the authorities launched their case against the Bolsheviks, and against Lenin personally, accusing him of incitement to armed insurrection. His speech was later described by the Bolshevik press as peaceful. The Socialist Revolutionary Nikolai Sukhanov, who kept a detailed diary of events, wrote that it was not likely that the Bolsheviks had a detailed plan, 'but the chances of an uprising and revolt were quickly raised'. It was simply that the Bolshevik leadership wavered. 'Lenin's speech on the balcony was extremely ambiguous. It seemed as if he was not demanding any concrete action from the impressive force assembled before him; he did not even ask his listeners to continue their street demonstrations, even though they had just shown their readiness for battle by their cumbersome procession from Kronstadt to [Petrograd]. Lenin merely criticized the Provisional Government and the "Soviet of social traitors" and called for the defence of the revolution and loyalty to the Bolsheviks.'[105]

Lenin later claimed that the demonstration had been an attempt to take power by peaceful means, but who could have expected the government to lay down their authority merely in response to a request? Moreover, Sukhanov noted that disorder was breaking out in the city. Lenin watched as events unfolded. Crowds of armed soldiers were looting and raiding liquor stores. Shooting was heard in various districts around midday. Messages were coming in of chaotic clashes and unorganized confrontations, of troops loyal to the government being deployed at strategic points. There was growing talk of robberies, searches, pogroms. Lenin realized that a half-spontaneous action was not capable of bringing down even a weak regime. There was the *desire* to seize power, but not the *organization*. Having brought out half a million people, the Bolsheviks had acted without a clear plan or precise direction. Lenin decided it was best to terminate the action and retire with the minimum of political losses. He had to protect both his social ammunition and his revolutionary face. The 'July Days' served as an indicator of the unstable balance, with a microscopic advantage to the government.

On 23 July Lenin wrote that the Menshevik and SR leaders in the Soviet had betrayed the revolution and that it was now time for the Bolsheviks 'to gather their forces, reorganize them and firmly prepare for armed uprising'.[106] He sensed that if he slipped now he would not reach the 'second stage' of the revolution. One piece of bad news after another was coming in: *Pravda* had been closed, the government was bringing back troops from the front, activists in the July events were being arrested, the press was full of 'evidence', 'documents' and announcements about the 'espionage' activities of Lenin and the Bolsheviks. What had happened at the front could now be understood: there were spies in the capital! Expecting to be arrested at any moment, Lenin decided to go underground. The government was indecisive, having issued the order to arrest him and a number of others only on 20 July.

The same day, accompanied by Yakov Sverdlov, Lenin and Krupskaya left their in-laws, the Yelizarovs, and began migrating from one 'safe' Petrograd apartment to another: to that of a certain S.L. Sulimov, where they spent less than a day before moving on to that of a local worker and Bolshevik, V.N. Kayurov, and from there to the guardhouse at the Russian Renault factory, then to the dwelling of the Bolshevik N.G. Poletaev, and finally for a stay of two or three days at the apartment of an old revolutionary called S.N. Alliluev. It was there that Stalin first saw the high-school girl Nadezhda Allilueva, whom he would marry in 1919. There also Lenin heard that he was being hunted as a state criminal. At first he declared he would give himself up if the Executive Committee of the Soviet decided he should stand trial. But he knew that would not happen. Then he held a meeting with his Bolshevik comrades V.P. Nogin, G.K. Ordzhonikidze, Yelena Stasova, Stalin and Yakov Sverdlov to discuss his position. None of them trusted in the impartiality of a court, and they came to the unanimous decision that Lenin must leave the capital for a safe hiding place.

Lenin was in his element. All the Russian revolutionaries loved the secrecy and conspiratorial atmosphere of the 'underground'. Even

Plekhanov, who spent most of his life in the safety of Europe, used a number of aliases: Beltov, Valentinov, Volgin, Kamensky, Ushakov. Sometimes a pseudonym was replaced by a nickname: Fotieva was 'Kiska', Bauman was 'Ballerina', Krasin 'the Horse', Essen 'the Beast', and so on. But no one could compare with Lenin for the sheer number of pseudonyms and nicknames he dreamed up. Besides 'Lenin' itself, he was also 'Peterburzhets', 'Starik', 'Ilyin', 'Frei', 'Petrov', 'Maier', 'Iordanov', 'Richter', 'Karpov', 'Mueller', 'Tulin', and still more. The tradition was even carried on long after the revolution. During the Korean War, Stalin used the names 'Filippov' and 'Fyn Si' when corresponding with Mao Tse-tung and Kim Il Sung respectively.

In any case, the question of Lenin appearing in court was purely academic: he had decided to go into hiding even before the arrest order was written. On 21 July he wrote an article, not published until 1925, entitled 'On Whether the Bolshevik Leaders Should Appear in Court', in which he asserted that had there been a Constituent Assembly, 'a proper government, and a proper court', it would have been possible to talk about an 'appearance in court'.[107] Instead, he claimed, there was a 'military dictatorship', a resounding phrase he himself cannot have believed. Nor did anyone else. Addressing the Sixth Party Congress in August 1917, Stalin proposed (in Lenin's absence) that Lenin should appear in court if guarantees of his personal security were given. 'At the moment,' he added, 'it is not clear who holds power'.[108] Hardly the description of a military dictatorship.

Perhaps the court would not have been impartial. The government's authority was waning fast. But it was not the charges associated with the 'July Days' that Lenin feared most, it was the consequences of the allegations being printed by Alexinsky and Pankratov in *Zhivoe Slovo* (The Living Word) about Bolshevik 'espionage'. As we have seen, there is evidence suggesting that Lenin did not know the extent of the government's information about the Bolsheviks' financial links with the Germans. One point he would not have been able to refute was the existence of a strategy to help bring about the defeat of Russia in the war and its transformation into a civil war. The evidence was there in countless articles and speeches and proclamations.

Lenin called upon the people to man barricades and to revolt, but he himself stayed well away. Unlike other Social Democrats, he was not seen marching at the head of a column of demonstrators, he did not visit the trenches or battleship crews. He exercised his 'leadership from afar' via the pen. The literary facet was perhaps his strongest feature. Even when he was moving from one apartment to another in early July he managed to write three articles rebutting the accusations of his financial connections with the Germans.

Nobody ever saw Lenin frightened, depressed or confused. Enraged, irritated, excited or surprised, certainly, but in general he was able to control his emotions, even when he felt everything was hanging by a thread. This was true in August 1918, when an attempt on his life almost succeeded, and also earlier that year when the Germans launched their advance deep inside Russia. He may have experienced fear when he went into hiding in the summer of 1917; certainly he wrote to Kamenev with the request that 'if I am bumped off' his comrade should ensure the publication of his blue exercise books, containing chapters of his *State and Revolution*.[109] Trotsky recalled meeting Lenin on 4 or 5 July. 'The offensive had been repelled' – Trotsky had no qualms in calling the Bolshevik action an offensive. 'Lenin said, "Now is the best time for them to shoot us down." He was thinking we should beat a retreat and if necessary go underground.' Later, in 1919, Lenin told Trotsky: 'We committed a lot of stupidities in July.' Trotsky went on: 'It is quite likely that had the army officers managed to capture Lenin soon after the July demonstration, they would have dealt with him the way the German officers dealt with Liebknecht and Rosa Luxemburg. Lenin wanted to make the assault with a sound plan: take the enemy by surprise, seize power and then see what happens.'[110] (In 1919, Sverdlov kept 108,525 gold roubles, jewels and seven passports, including his own, in a fireproof safe, discovered in 1935 and consigned to the archives. Lenin and his closest aides were prepared to re-emigrate in the event of a White victory.)

Lenin in the heat of 1917 was a gambler – 'seize power and then see what happens'. He was not a god. He was capable of hoping, of deluding himself, of making mistakes, suffering and simply experiencing the normal human sense of fear, though he managed to curb it. Fear helped him escape danger. He rarely took risks. Neither when he returned to Russia via Germany and Scandinavia, rather than England, where he would have risked arrest and the German U-boats in the North Sea, nor when Denikin's White forces were within a breath of Moscow – too much of a risk to go to the front. Nor would he appear in the Provisional Government's court, although Trotsky gave himself up in order to use it as a platform for refuting the charges and making propaganda. Lenin's personal safety came first, and great care was taken to protect him, especially following the attempt on his life in August 1918. Several times, Stalin placed 'guaranteeing the security' of the leader on the Central Committee's agenda.[111] Seventeen body-guards were assigned to protect Lenin, according to the Cheka official who after the attempt reported on the errors committed by R. Goba-lin, Lenin's head of personal security. Stalin insisted the number be increased.[112]

The events of July 1917 turned out to be an unintentional rehearsal for the coup d'état. Lenin had to leave the political scene for a while, but although he called Kerensky's government a 'military dictator-ship', he knew the regime was weak. He had to prolong the period of this weakness, of the army's disintegration and the discredit of the parties in the government. The moment might come when the state power of the once great empire, which had been taken over by liberals and democrats, would, in Trotsky's words, simply be lying on the streets of the capital. Then Lenin's hour of triumph would come.


## October and the 'Conspiracy of Equals'

We have noted that Lenin found his inspiration in the French Revol-ution. 'The example of the Jacobins,' he wrote in his article 'The Enemies of the People', 'is instructive. It is not obsolete, but needs to be applied to the revolutionary class of the twentieth century, the workers and semi-proletarians. The enemies of the people for this class are not monarchs, but landowners and capitalists, as a class.'[113] And the 'égalité' of the famous trinity emerged in Soviet Russia soon after the Bolsheviks had seized power, when Lenin decreed that 'one warm blanket and one warm item of clothing (either a jacket, or felt boots, gloves, warm underwear, warm socks, or a scarf) should be requisitioned from each rich apartment in Petrograd'.[114] For the time being, it was only warm clothing. Soon everything that could be taken would be, while the *burzhui* themselves – the bourgeoisie – would be sent off to clear snow from the railway tracks, dig ditches, cut firewood. The *burzhui* were being thrown out of their apartments, or packed in with others, and deprived of their ration cards as early as 1917. This practice continued for several years. On 20 April 1921 the Politburo again determined to 'improve the life of the workers at the expense of the bourgeois element'.[115] It was not that the Bolsheviks were repeating the past; rather that, like the Blanquists and Babouvists and Jacobins of the French Revolution, they believed that power could only be taken by force, and that it was not possible to make the people happy without using coercion.

On the night of 22 July, soon after publication of his arrest order, Lenin set off for Razliv on the Gulf of Finland, where he hid in the now famous fisherman's hut with Zinoviev, disguised as Finnish farmworkers. Rebuilt in granite in 1927, the site became a shrine for the Soviet masses. Propagandists recited the story of Lenin, as he prepared the October revolution, working day and night on the Marxist theory of the state. Indeed, it was here that he completed the major work he had begun two years earlier in Switzerland, *State and Revolution*, a study as utopian as any by Owen, Saint-Simon or Fourier.

Lenin and Zinoviev – one of the people who had become closest to him – would spend whole evenings sitting in their hut, talking and reminiscing. They spent one evening talking about Roman Malinovsky, who had also once been close to Lenin but had later been suspected of working for the police. A Party commission had been formed under Ganetsky to investigate the charges, and Lenin had declared that Malinovsky was 'a politically honest man'. Later, when Malinovsky turned up as a prisoner of war in German hands, Lenin corresponded with him, sending him warm clothes and encouraging him to agitate among the other prisoners. After the October coup, Okhrana archives would reveal that Malinovsky had indeed been a police agent, and that Lenin was expected to give evidence. After returning from German capitivity in 1918, Malinovsky was arrested.

He was interrogated for nine days and then tried in closed court. No transcript of the trial has been found, but parts of it were reproduced either in the press of the day or in subsequent memoirs.[116] In a six-hour speech, Malinovsky claimed he had been blackmailed into becoming a provocateur by the police, and that Lenin must have known of his dual rôle. He plainly expected that the Bolshevik leader would intervene and save him. It appears that Malinovsky wrote to

Lenin from prison, requesting clemency, but the letter has not been found. Lenin is said to have attended the trial briefly, but gave no evidence, and left muttering 'What a swine he was!' Malinovsky was executed on 6 November 1918.

During the time at Razliv, Lenin was visited by several Bolshevik organizers. Periodically a woman worker, A.I. Tokareva, would come out with a trunk full of clean laundry, food and newspapers, which Lenin would read carefully, sending back new articles in reply to his opponents' or 'orders' to his comrades. The rest of his time he devoted to *State and Revolution*.

For many years this work, of no more than 120 pages, was regarded as a masterpiece. In the USSR alone it was published in more than seven million copies and forty-seven languages, while Communist parties abroad made it a best-seller. The editors of Volume 33 of Lenin's Complete Works assert that 'this work, in which for the first time the Marxist teaching on the state is fully and systematically expounded, represents a scientific illumination of the theory of the state which is unsurpassed in its depth and complexity'.[117] The revolution 'prevented' Lenin from writing the final chapter on the revolutions of 1905 and 1917, and he noted in the Afterword, 'it is pleasanter and more useful to create the experience of revolution, than to write about it'.[118]

Why did this book become the bible of Russian Bolshevism for so many years? The answers are very simple. The entire work is an extended commentary on equally extended quotations from Marx and Engels. It is a panegyric on class war, the dictatorship of the proletariat and anti-parliamentarism. It claims, by referring to the works of Marx and Engels, that the highest form of democracy is the dictatorship of the proletariat, that it is essential to smash the old state machine, that violent revolution is inevitable, that classes will disappear and that following the revolution the state will wither away. Lenin completely ignored the humanitarian aspects of Marx's early works. For him, democracy itself was a form of violence. It was 'an organization for the systematic violence of one class over another, by one part of the population over another'. He continued: 'Only when the state has disappeared can we speak of liberty.'[119] Unlike Marx, who used the term 'dictatorship of the proletariat' only a few times, Lenin regarded it as the foundation of the universe: there were only workers and the bourgeoisie.

*State and Revolution* described the Communist utopia in a most convincing way. Citing a number of unquestionably true propositions – which were well known before Lenin 'discovered' them – about the rise of the state and its functions at different periods, he came to conclusions which, however 'unsurpassed in their depth', were scholastic, contrived and detached from life. En route he demolished all his real and potential opponents, asserting that the workers of 'advanced' parliamentary countries 'had come to loathe their "socialist" leaders'.[120]

Had this work simply been the fruit of theoretical exercise by a man researching anti-worlds, anti-societies, anti-humans, and been known only to a small group of bibliophiles, no harm would have been done. Unfortunately, whole generations were raised on such books, millions of 'builders of Communism', many of whom took Lenin's propositions literally. For example: 'When the majority of the people begin to produce independently . . . the monitoring of capitalists (converted into office-workers) and gentlemen intellectuals, who haven't lost their capitalist ways, will become genuinely universal, general, nationwide, and it will be impossible to escape from it in any way, there will be nowhere to hide.'[121] There would indeed be nowhere to hide, neither from the sort of intellectual nourishment provided by such works as *State and Revolution*, nor from the ubiquitous police presence, from being shadowed, from 'Party influence', from the clutches of the bureaucracy.

From his Helsinki hiding place in the summer of 1917, Lenin continued to influence the course of events, as usual, 'from afar'. Meanwhile, the search for him was still on. A rumour circulated that he was hiding on the battleship *Zarya svobody* (Dawn of Freedom), and the Petrograd prosecutor ordered a search of the ship.[122] Newspapers carried reports that he was hiding in the capital, and the chief of the city police circulated a secret instruction to all commissars 'to capture V.I. Ulyanov (Lenin) and deliver him to the authorities'.[123]

At the end of September Lenin moved from Helsinki to Vyborg (Viipuri), close to Petrograd on the Baltic coast, to facilitate contact with the Central Committee and other local Party bodies. Having survived the Kornilov threat, when he felt compelled to support Kerensky, he was now becoming impatient, and was convinced that the critical moment for seizing power was fast approaching. At the end of August the issue had emerged in stark clarity: who would Russia follow, Kornilov, Kerensky, or Lenin? Kornilov would mean a military dictatorship, police, army, the Cossacks and the Kadets who supported them in practical terms; Kerensky would mean the supremacy of the parties Lenin called compromisers or appeasers, the SRs and the Mensheviks. The defeat of Kornilov had brought the greatest gains to the Bolsheviks, and their influence had grown extremely fast. As Lenin produced one article after another and a stream of letters, he conveyed to the Central Committee his growing confidence that an uprising would succeed. He demanded that a headquarters be organized at once, without losing another minute, that the General Staff and government be arrested, that the workers be mobilized and the post offices occupied. 'We will take all the bread and all the boots from the capitalists. We'll leave them only crumbs and we'll give them felt boots to wear ... There's a ninety-nine per cent chance that the Germans will at least give us an armistice. And an armistice now would mean winning the entire peace.'[124] As Lenin knew, the Germans had assisted the Bolsheviks precisely in order to take Russia out of the war, so enhancing their own chance of victory on the Western Front. Only three months earlier he had sworn that the idea of a separate peace would never enter his head, and yet now he was fully confident that he could achieve it. He was pragmatic to the marrow of his bones. Nothing was sacred beyond the revolution and power. As Machiavelli wrote in *The Prince*, 'we know from experience that great affairs have only been achieved in our time by those who have not striven to keep their word, once given, and were able when necessary to twist others round their fingers'.[125]

Lenin was in a nervous and excitable state, and the indecisiveness of his partners was irritating him, as a long article entitled 'The Crisis is Ripe' shows. Written at the end of September in Vyborg, it declared that the whole world was ready for revolution. 'Mass arrests of the Party leaders in free Italy, and especially the start of army risings in Germany, are unmistakable signs of the great turning point, signs of the eve of revolution on a world scale.'[126] As for Russia, 'the crisis is ripe. The whole future of the revolution is on the cards ... The whole future of the international workers' revolution is on the cards. The crisis is ripe.'[127] As for the opinion of the country, the Provisional Government had already agreed to hold elections for the Constituent

Assembly, but Lenin was not willing to wait for that. Nor would he rely on the Congress of Soviets: 'To wait for the Congress of Soviets is lunacy, for the Congress *will do nothing*, it cannot do anything! First beat Kerensky, then convene the Congress.' He had a plan: 'The Bolsheviks are now *guaranteed* victory in an uprising: we can (if we don't "wait" for the Congress of Soviets) strike *suddenly* from three points, from Peter [Petrograd], Moscow and the Baltic Fleet . . . we're ninety-nine per cent sure to win with fewer casualties than on 3–5 July, because *the troops won't oppose* a government of peace'. If the Central Committee refused to accept his plan, Lenin threatened to resign from it. He commented that he had already detected in the committee's response 'a subtle hint to keep one's mouth shut, and for me to drop my proposal'.[128]

The last part of the article was intended for the Central Committee's eyes only. In early October, Lenin asked for the figures on Party membership nation-wide. When the Finnish Bolshevik E. Rahja delivered them to him, they were an inspiration: 23,000 in February 1917, 100,000 in April, 240,000 in August, and 350,000 at the beginning of October. Entire army units and factory workforces were on their side, the government was paralysed; their time had come, they must not miss it. Sukhanov noted in his diary that the administration had ceased to exist, on the local no less than the central level. Meanwhile the people were demanding a government. 'Even the debate on land has come to a standstill at the top, while the discontent of the lower orders has reached fever pitch. In St Petersburg we have gone beyond the point where famine would start with all its consequences . . . If not today, tomorrow the army will begin its headlong escape from the front . . . The situation on the railways is threatening. All the newspapers . . . are loudly crying out about an impending economic disaster.'[129]

The Central Committee read Lenin's shrill letters, nodded their heads, but did nothing more than agree to discuss tactics 'soon'. His letters went no further. The Central Committee was shocked by his radicalism. Moreover, they resolved to destroy all his letters dealing with the uprising, except one.

On 14 September Kerensky, to show his solidarity with the left-wing parties and to appease their impatience for peace, unilaterally and without waiting for the Constituent Assembly proclaimed the

Russian Republic. On 27 September the Executive Committee of the Petrograd Soviet convened a Democratic Conference of all socialist and liberal parties which led to the formation of the fourth and last coalition Provisional Government, including ten socialist and four liberal ministers. The Democratic Conference also agreed to establish a Provisional Council of the Russian Republic, or 'Pre-parliament', which would express the views of the parties until the Constituent Assembly met.

All these measures had the effect of cooling the ardour for an armed uprising among some of the leading Bolsheviks: perhaps, they thought, their chance was coming through non-violent means. This infuriated Lenin. Merely by taking part in the Democratic Conference, he wrote, 'the Bolshevik leadership has blunted the growing revolution by playing at spillikins'.[130]

Slowly but surely the Central Committee was driven to a radical position by Lenin. They let his threat to resign pass in silence. Excessively militant paragraphs or sentences were deleted from some of his articles before publication. Lenin felt he ought to be in Petrograd, among the Central Committee members who were really holding the Party reins, as well as those of other mass organizations. He had the Central Committee's permission to return, but he did not want to take risks. He paused to survey the possibilities, and carefully worked out a route and a way to return with Rahja. They considered every possible detail and circumstance that might wreck the operation.[131] Lenin continually reminded his escorts that they should have a fallback plan for a rapid departure from the capital, preferably to Finland, should he be threatened with arrest.

In something of an anti-climax after the excitement generated by all this elaborate planning, he finally decided to take the suburban train, and duly arrived at the apartment of the woman Bolshevik M.V. Fofanova in the Vyborg district of Petrograd.

Here the security was maximized, as Lenin wanted to exclude the slightest mistake on the eve of the decisive event. When it suited him, he would proclaim such maxims as: 'To be successful, an uprising must not rely on a conspiracy or a party, it must rely on the leading class.'[132] But what he was planning was precisely a gigantic conspiracy, concealed and masked with difficulty, and not organized in the manner of the plotters in the French Revolution, but using more perfected methods. This emerges from the confidential passages of his letters to the Central Committee. His instructions about creating head-quarters for the uprising, on the deployment of forces, the arrest of the government, neutralizing the Caucasian 'Savage Division' of the army and so on, were all basic Blanquist tactics for organizing an uprising in a conspiratorial manner.[133]

On his arrival in Petrograd, Lenin insisted the Bolsheviks withdraw from the Pre-parliament 'in order not to sow illusions' among the masses. He was determined not to yield his main trump – the promise of immediate peace – to anyone else. Judging correctly that there were no viable arguments against his position, he recognized that it was not the Bolsheviks the people would follow, but the promise of peace, in which they saw the cure for all their present miseries. No one wanted to see that Germany was on the brink of defeat, and that peace might be more quickly achieved by the combined efforts of the Allies. The idea of immediate peace had been so deeply etched into the public mind by the Bolsheviks that the question of what would happen after it was achieved was left unasked.

Lenin's pressure for an immediate uprising began to tell, and a closed session of the Petrograd Party Committee on 5 October approved his proposal, followed two days later by the Moscow Com-mittee.[134] In a letter to the Central Committee, written on 8 October but not published until 7 November 1920, Lenin formulated a new slogan: 'The transfer of power to the Soviets now would in fact be an armed uprising'. Of course, there was still a need to occupy the post offices, railway stations, bridges and so on, but a new feature was Lenin's attitude to the price to be paid. He wrote that after the stra-tegic targets had been seized, the slogan 'We may all perish, but the enemy shall not pass' should be broadcast.[135]

An armed uprising will always cost lives, but the extremism of Lenin's dictatorial instruction is striking: the goal must be attained, no matter the cost. This attitude to human life became the hallmark of Bolshevik practice. Reading what Lenin wrote in October 1917, one is inevitably reminded of Stalin's calls during the Second World War 'to spare no forces and not to halt whatever the casualties'.[136]

On 10 October, soon after Lenin's return in the capital, at his insistence an extremely important session of the Central Com-mittee was held to discuss the uprising. By a chain of accidental

circumstances, the meeting took place at the apartment of the Menshevik and chronicler of the revolution N.N. Sukhanov-Gimmer, whose
wife, G.K. Flakserman, was a Bolshevik working in the Central Committee secretariat. Sukhanov himself was not at home that evening.
Of the twenty-one members of the Central Committee, twelve were
present, including Lenin, Zinoviev, Kamenev, Trotsky, Stalin, Uritsky, Dzerzhinsky, Alexandra Kollontai and Sverdlov, who was chairman. Discussion of the uprising was concealed on the agenda under
the heading 'the present moment'.

In his report, Lenin asserted that 'the matter was politically fully
ripe', and that they had only to discuss military preparations. Lenin
knew he could not count on support from the majority of the population: 'To wait for the Constituent Assembly, which will obviously
not be on our side, is senseless, and just means complicating our
task.'[137] He condemned those who thought that preparing for an uprising was some sort of political sin, though he was indulgent towards
those who were made uncomfortable by the conspiratorial nature of
his plan. He made plain the anti-democratic character of the uprising
when he said the Constituent Assembly would 'obviously not be on
our side'.

He waited for objections, but most of those present accepted his
proposal to begin preparations and to carry out the coup as soon as
possible. Only Zinoviev and Kamenev voted against. Their arguments,
which were already known, were that the Bolsheviks had little support
in the provinces, and that they might win more through the Constituent Assembly than by a military coup. By referring to the Constituent
Assembly, Zinoviev and Kamenev were in effect proposing a parliamentary path, although they showed some inconsistency after the
meeting by declaring publicly that 'the Party has not been asked. Such
questions are not settled by ten people.' Next day they stated: 'It is
said 1) we already have the majority of the people of Russia with us
and 2) we also have the majority of the international proletariat. Alas,
neither is true, and that's the whole trouble.' When Zinoviev and
Kamenev were arrested and tried in 1936, the court reminded them
of their 'sins of October', their 'villainous treachery'. In any case, they
'confessed' to 'espionage and terroristic' and 'subversive' activities, as
well as their 'anti-Leninist behaviour' in 1917. Once they had been
sentenced to death they appealed to the Central Executive Committee,

where they knew any decision would be taken by Stalin, who had secretly promised them clemency if they made full confessions.

Their appeals were brief, and are worth reproducing in full. Zinoviev wrote: 'I told the proletarian court everything about my crimes against the Party and the Soviet regime. They are well known to the presidium of the Central Executive Committee. I hereby appeal to the presidium of the Central Executive Committee for clemency.'[138] Kamenev's appeal was equally short: 'Deeply repentant for the most serious crimes I have committed against the proletarian revolution, I ask the presidium to save my life, if it does not think this conflicts with the future cause of socialism, the cause of Lenin and Stalin.'[139] Their appeals were turned down the same day by Kalinin and Unshlikht, as everything had already been decided by Stalin. The resort to unbridled violence had boomeranged and struck the creators of the revolution themselves. As Potresov commented earlier in his 'Notes of a Publicist': 'it had always seemed to ... Lenin that the end sanctified the means ... But it was not the end that sanctified the means in the present case: the means has demolished the end without trace.'[140]

The meeting of 10 October 1917 also formed a Political Bureau (Politburo) of the Central Committee, consisting of Lenin, Zinoviev, Kamenev, Trotsky, Stalin, Sokolnikov and Bubnov, but since the management of the planned coup was in the hands of the Military-Revolutionary Committee of the Soviet, under Trotsky's leadership, the new body was in effect the shell of the supreme authority it would become after the Eighth Congress in March 1919. In October 1917 it was a group of the people closest to Lenin and holding most influence in the top echelons of the Party.

Nevertheless, within a couple of days Lenin sensed that, despite the decision to prepare the uprising, the Party committees were still wavering. Some said the matter should be left to the Congress of Soviets, while others even wanted to wait for the Constituent Assembly. Lenin was beside himself, and demanded another session of the Central Committee. An enlarged session took place on 16 October at a house on Bolotnaya Street in the Vyborg district. The argument went on until morning, and the minutes of Lenin's speech, which he took himself, and the debate on it, show that nothing new was said. As Trotsky would write in his memoirs, in essence three distinct groupings had crystallized in the Central Committee: there were the opponents of an armed uprising – Zinoviev and Kamenev; there was Lenin, who was frenziedly demanding an uprising before the Congress of Soviets; and there were those, led by Trotsky, who wanted to obtain a mandate for the uprising from the Congress.[141] For now, Lenin got his way, adding to the resolution that the Central Committee would indicate a 'suitable moment' for the start of the uprising.

Lenin's notes show the task he faced in changing opinions at the meeting: members were saying 'we dare not win'; Zinoviev claimed 'the fatigue among the masses is obvious'; others feared that 'the central committee of the Party has replaced the Soviets'; and Nogin urged that 'we find a solution by political not military means'.[142] Lenin spoke three times. It was clearly not easy for him to defend the policy of armed uprising. The Petrograd Soviet had already formed its Military-Revolutionary Committee and controlled the garrison of 150,000 men. To it would be added the Military-Revolutionary Centre, created by the Central Committee.[143] The original purpose of this committee, chaired by the Left Socialist Revolutionary P.Y. Lazimir, was to mobilize the population to defend the city. Instead, the Bolsheviks used it as the headquarters of the coup, or, as they put it, for preparing the uprising: they were 'arming themselves against a counter-revolution'. The headquarters of the uprising was thus in effect created legally on 12 October, but was controlled illegally by members of the Bolshevik Central Committee, notably Trotsky.

During the last ten days before the uprising Lenin stayed in close touch with the heads of the military organization, V.A. Antonov-Ovseenko, V.I. Nevsky and N.I. Podvoisky, urging them to speed things up. But most of the time he spent writing notes and endless letters to the Central Committee. After the meeting of 16 October he wrote a twenty-page 'letter to the comrades', in which he said nothing new, but simply repeated his arguments for an early uprising over and over again. It had become, in Melgunov's words, an obsession, and it was not surprising that many of these letters, written 'in a paroxysm of irresponsibility', were burnt by the Central Committee. Leaders of mass movements of Lenin's type, Melgunov wrote, 'who are generally fanatics, rather than prophets of genius, lack a sense of historical perspective and moral responsibility for their actions'. And Lenin's mood gradually infected the rest of the leadership.[144]

While he was in hiding in Petrograd, Lenin wrote two letters, one to the members of the Party, the other to the Central Committee, which contained devastating attacks on Zinoviev and Kamenev, accusing them, among other things, of 'swindling', 'slanderous lies', 'endless dirty tricks' and 'shamelessness'. He demanded their expulsion from the Party, declaring, 'I no longer consider them as comrades'.[145] The cause of these outbursts was a statement by Kamenev, published in *Novaya zhizn'* (New Life), disagreeing with the Bolsheviks' tactics of trying to come to power by means of a coup. Lenin regarded this as treachery, as one of the cardinal rules of the revolutionary conspiracy is total secrecy. Lenin himself, however, had said on 16 October that since 'the uprising is ready, there is no need to talk of conspiracies'.[146] And Trotsky, addressing the Petrograd Soviet on the Military-Revolutionary Committee, had declared: 'They say we are setting up a headquarters for the seizure of power. We make no secret of it.'[147] At mass meetings, however, the Bolsheviks took a different line. Speaking on 21 October to Cossacks stationed in the capital, Trotsky said: 'They're telling you the Soviet is planning some sort of uprising on 22 October, that there's going to be a fight with you, shooting on the streets and a blood-bath. The people who say so are scoundrels and provocateurs.'[148]

On the eve of the coup, as the Provisional Government sat late into the night, Kerensky hurried from the Pre-parliament to the headquarters of the military district and back to his residence in the Winter Palace, trying to gather support and mobilize any available force to help suppress the impending Bolshevik uprising. His power was by now a ghost of its former self. Had his government succeeded months earlier, or even as late as October, in finding an end to the war, and sought a separate peace with Germany, the uprising might have been averted. Some timid efforts were made in this direction, but Kerensky was unwilling to renege on the Allies. Had he done so, he might have preserved his regime and its democratic achievements, as well as deprived Lenin of his main trump card, and thus spared Russia decades of suffering.

Leaders in transitional times, like Kerensky and Gorbachev, are often only suited to the beginning of the new phase, and seldom to carrying the venture through to its end without disasters. They are heroes of the moment, but their contribution should not be under-rated for that. Kerensky stumbled over the question of peace, while Gorbachev could not free himself from his idealization of the October coup. He made the false assertion that 'the choice between socialism and capitalism was the chief social alternative of our era, that it was impossible to go further in the twentieth century without rising to a higher form of social organization, to socialism'.[149] Gorbachev was incapable of seeing that it was anachronistic to divide societies into capitalist and socialist. Far deeper levels of change create the move-ment from bureaucratism and totalitarianism to democracy and civil-ized values. Neither Kerensky nor Gorbachev could step outside their time, and each in his own way made momentously important contri-butions: Kerensky did not destroy tsarism, and Gorbachev did not destroy Stalinism, but neither of them prevented the self-destruction of those systems.

There are moments in history when it seems that future develop-ment may depend on one man. Trotsky was certainly right when, in exile, he asserted that had Lenin not been in Petrograd in October 1917, the coup would not have taken place.[150] There was, however, another individual whose part in these events has been neglected, but who might have made a difference. This was Pavel Nikolaevich Malyantovich, who from 25 September to 25 October 1917 served as Minister of Justice and Chief Prosecutor for the Provisional Government.

As we know, following the unsuccessful attempt by the Bolsheviks to seize power in July, the government launched an investigation into the affair. P.A. Alexandrov, an investigator 'for especially important cases', signed an order for the arrest of Lenin on the grounds of his ties with Germany and as an enemy of Russia in the war. As Alexandrov told the NKVD when he was interrogated in 1939, 'coun-ter-intelligence put a number of cupboards full of documents and correspondence at our disposal'.[151] In November 1917, after the Bol-sheviks had been through these documents, only twenty-one volumes remained, and successive inspections and 'weedings' up to 1940 reduced the contents still further.[152] Thus the evidence establishing Lenin's links with the Germans remains circumstantial, however sub-stantial.

Having been appointed Minister of Justice in September 1917, Malyantovich cabled all prosecutors that the order to arrest Lenin for the armed uprising of 3–5 July was still active and must be carried out.[153] He had, however, underestimated Lenin's skills as an underground operator, and in any case by this time the steam had gone out of the investigation. As Alexandrov testified in 1939, they were expecting Lenin to turn up personally to refute the 'slander' of his secret German connections, as he had said he would. 'Prosecutor Kadinsky,' Alexandrov said, 'told me to show up on a certain day and time, in the evening, to interrogate Lenin, having said that Lenin himself would appear, in secret so as to avoid trouble. Lenin did not appear and so not only was he not arrested but also not questioned.'[154] Lenin, meanwhile, was busy preparing the coup.

Malyantovich was arrested several times by the Soviet authorities. On 10 May 1931 he was sentenced by the OGPU to ten years' imprisonment, reduced to three years' exile thanks to the intervention of Maxim Gorky and a small group of senior Party officials. The last time he was arrested was in 1937 together with his sons Georgi and Vladimir. The chances of his escaping Stalin's meatgrinder were minimal, but his son Vladimir had hastened the dénouement when he incautiously told a group of close friends: 'The Provisional Government ministers made a big mistake. There was only one brave man among them who acted decisively, even if it was too late, and that was my father . . . who wanted to arrest Lenin. If he'd done it, there wouldn't be all these horrors.'[155] Inevitably, his words were immediately reported to the 'organs', and the Malyantoviches were arrested.

To his credit, Malyantovich, then aged seventy, resisted the long interrogations and physical torture with unusual courage. When on 10 November 1937 he was asked about the struggle he had waged 'against the proletariat, the Bolshevik Party and its leaders', he replied: 'Yes, as a Menshevik I entered the Provisional Government, accepted the post of Minister of Justice and Chief Prosecutor, being an implacable enemy of the Bolshevik Party and the proletarian revolution. I, Malyantovich, published the decree, made arrangements, signed the telegram to all prosecutors to arrest Lenin, so that the order to arrest him which had been issued long before should be carried out. By this step I wanted to decapitate the workers' and soldiers' rising that was aimed at seizing power by the proletariat.'[156]

The investigator seems to have recorded Malyantovich reasonably accurately, especially his words about 'decapitating' the rising, and in any event Malyantovich signed the deposition. Two years or so later, when at last he was put on trial – lasting less than an hour – his final words were that he had sanctioned Lenin's arrest on the orders of the government so as to avert the armed uprising, which was entirely unnecessary as the Constituent Assembly had already been scheduled. Malyantovich understood the situation he was in, but was unwilling to distort history: the arrest of Lenin in the summer or autumn of 1917 would have changed the course of the Russian drama, for Lenin was of fundamental importance to the Bolsheviks. He was their brain and their mainspring.

A military court consisting of Orlov, Romanychev, Detisov and a secretary, Mazur, sat briefly on 21 January 1940 – the anniversary of Lenin's death, as it happened – and handed down the usual sentence of the time: execution by firing squad. The sentence was carried out the next day. No account was taken of the fact that before the revolution Malyantovich had acted as defence counsel for Russian Social Democrats in countless cases; in 1906 he had played a major part in the Bolshevik cause, as a result of which they received 100,000 gold roubles from the estate of S.T. Morozov; nor was he saved by his friendship with Gorky, Lunacharsky and Krasin, all long dead. The Bolsheviks could plainly not forgive the man who had tried to halt the course of events in the autumn of 1917. But why had his trial been delayed for over two years? From circumstantial evidence, it appears that Stalin was hoping proof would be found that efforts had been made in 1917 to arrest him as well, thus enhancing his own revolutionary image.

Malyantovich's family were to share his tragedy. His son Vladimir was savagely tortured in an effort to make him inform on his father. While Malyantovich was under investigation, his wife, Anzhelika Pavlovna, did everything she could to improve his situation, and finally, after countless petitions, she managed on 7 March 1940 to gain entry to the reception room of the Military Collegium, where she was told that 'on 21 January 1940 her husband had been sentenced under Article 58 to ten years' exile in the Far East camps without the right of correspondence'.[157] She died in December 1953, having waited in vain for thirteen years for news from her husband, unaware that he had been shot in January 1940. Not until August 1991, when Malyantovich was finally rehabilitated, did his grandson K.G. Malyantovich learn the truth.

Lenin was insisting not only on an armed uprising, but also that it be timed not to coincide with the opening of the Second Congress of Soviets. Trotsky remarked that 'as in June, when Lenin . . . expected "them" to shoot us down, so now he thought the best thing from the [government's] point of view would be to take us by surprise, disorganize the revolution and then smash it piece by piece. As in July, Lenin overrated the enemy's shrewdness and determination, and possibly also his material possibilities.'[158] The day before the coup, when he heard from Trotsky that the garrison troops were obeying the orders of the Military-Revolutionary Committee, Lenin 'was in ecstasy, laughing and rubbing his hands with joy. Then he fell silent, paused and said: "That's fine, as long as we take power."' For Trotsky, this was the moment when Lenin finally accepted that they would seize power not by a conspiracy, but through the ostensibly democratic means of the Congress of Soviets.[159] Yet the tone of Lenin's last letter to the Central Committee was desperate: 'The government is wobbling. We must *smash* it whatever the cost! It would be death to wait.'[160]

Kerensky had left the capital on 25 October (6 November) to rally armed resistance. The small force of Cossacks he managed to muster was, however, soon disarmed by local Bolshevik troops, and Kerensky himself just managed to escape capture.

Meanwhile, back in Petrodgrad, the signal was given for the bombardment of the Winter Palace, where Kerensky's ministers were awaiting his return. About thirty shells were fired from the Peter-Paul Fortress, but only two landed, one of them on a cornice. No one was even wounded.[161] The cadets were disarmed, and the regime appeared completely incapable of response. Even the ineffectual bombardment and symbolic siege had paralysed the will of the Palace's defenders.

It was not a revolutionary cohort of the Bolshevik army that burst in, but a raggle-taggle mob who behaved in the violent and outrageous way of such mobs.[162] At 2 a.m. the Winter Palace was in the hands of the insurgents, and government ministers were in the hands of the commander of the Military-Revolutionary Committee, Vladimir

Antonov-Ovseenko. There was no resistance. As Sukhanov recorded, beginning at 2 a.m. small groups of troops gradually took over the stations, bridges, power stations, post offices and telegraphs. 'It was more like the changing of the guard . . . The city was completely quiet. The centre and the suburbs were sleeping soundly, quite unaware of what was happening in the silence of this cold autumn night.'[163] Kerensky failed to find any help among 'loyal troops from the front', and the regime lay prostrate on the boulevards of Petrograd.

At a special session of the Soviet at midday on 26 October (8 November), Trotsky took the chair: 'In the name of the Military-Revolutionary Committee of the Soviet I announce that the Provisional Government no longer exists. Some ministers are under arrest, the rest will follow in the next days or hours.' Interrupted by loud applause and cries of joy, Trotsky concluded by saying, 'in our midst is Vladimir Ilyich Lenin, who was unable to appear before owing to various circumstances. Long live Comrade Lenin who has returned to us!' Sukhanov recorded of this moment: 'When I entered the hall, there was a bald, clean-shaven man I didn't know standing on the podium and talking excitedly in a rather hoarse, stentorian voice, somewhat guttural and with a very particular emphasis at the end of his phrases. Ha! It was Lenin.'[164]

That evening, at 10.40 p.m., the Second Congress of Soviets opened in the Smolny Institute. More than sixty per cent of the delegates were Bolsheviks, reflecting the changes that had taken place in the country. New Bolshevik and SR faces appeared on the platform. Martov, supported by the SR Mstislavsky and the Bolshevik Lunacharsky, demanded that a new government be created without force or military action. It looked as if a unique moment of compromise might be at hand at this crucial turning-point in Russian history. But the moment passed. The Right SRs and the Mensheviks read out a joint declaration demanding that the Bolshevik coup be condemned and that immediate talks take place with the Provisional Government on the question of forming a new democratic government. The hall erupted.

The democratic wing of the Social Democratic Party then made a false step: they left the Congress, or, more precisely, conceded the political scene to the Bolsheviks and their supporters among the Socialist Revolutionaries. Sukhanov noted: 'We left not knowing where or why, cutting ourselves off from the Soviet, getting mixed up with elements of the counter-revolution, discrediting and debasing ourselves in the eyes of the masses . . . Moreover, in going, we left the Bolsheviks a totally free hand and complete masters of the situation.'[165] Lenin was too overcome with emotion to enter the meeting during the first session. Instead, he and Trotsky lay on blankets thrown on the floor in an adjoining room and talked quietly. Lenin smiled with fatigue and said: 'The move from the underground to power has been too fast. My head is spinning.'[166]

When Lenin appeared at the evening session, he was greeted enthusiastically as the personification of the new regime. Since February the Soviets had represented the workers, soldiers and peasants throughout the country in what had had to pass for a democratic process, given the chaos and the absence of formal institutions. The voice of the Soviets in the capital had been the All-Russian Central Executive Committee of Soviets, or VTsIK. Now, having seized power from the Provisional Government in the name of the Soviets, one of Lenin's first tasks was to replace that VTsIK with a body that would reflect Bolshevik policy. The Congress elected a new VTsIK in which the Bolsheviks had sixty-two seats, the Left SRs twenty-nine, the Mensheviks six (which they refused to take up), and Ukrainian Socialists three. The new Executive Committee became the supreme legislative (and for a time also administrative) body in Russia, and would remain so, under various names, throughout the entire Soviet period, until the demise of the USSR in December 1991. Its task would in fact be to rubber-stamp decrees issued either by Lenin's Council of People's Commissars or, in due course, the Political Bureau of the Communist Party. In other words, the Soviets were retained by the Bolsheviks as an ostensibly democratic tool of the Party.

Lenin read his decrees on land and peace, and his new government was established as the Council of People's Commissars under his chairmanship. He could now proceed to realize all the abstract plans he had based on the 'founding fathers of Marxism'. Russia was to undergo an experiment that was unprecedented in its scale and its consequences. What had taken place had not been a classic conspiracy. The Bolsheviks were prepared to seize power by any means – peaceful, conspiratorial, or by mass uprising. Reading the situation correctly, they saw that a conspiracy was not required. Lenin had been putting the components of a conspiracy in place as a safeguard: if a rising did not succeed, the conspiracy would be mobilized, but it would be a conspiracy of the 'united'. Unity had come to play the decisive rôle. What had been a small clutch of illegals in February 1917 had swollen to a mighty force by October.

Lenin did not yet know if the defeated elements would accept the position. They were demoralized and disoriented, but three days after the coup, he was delighted to read in *Rabochaya gazeta* (The Workers' Newspaper) of the dying gasp of the Pre-parliament, which until its dispersal had been meeting in the Mariinsky Palace: 'To the citizens of Russia! The Provisional Council of the Russian Republic, yielding to the pressure of bayonets, was forced to disperse and temporarily cease work on 25 October (7 November). With "freedom and socialism" on their lips, the insurgents are resorting to casual violence. They have arrested members of the Provisional Government, including the socialist ministers, and imprisoned them in a tsarist casemate. Blood and anarchy threaten to overwhelm the revolution, to drown liberty and the Republic, and to culminate in the restoration of the old order . . . This regime should be seen as the enemy of the people and the revolution . . .'[167] At the same time the Chief of the General Staff, General Dukhonin, appealed to the army to remain loyal to the Provisional Government and to put an end to Bolshevik violence, calling for the Constituent Assembly as the only body capable of saving the country.[168] This was the first breath of the civil war for which Lenin had agitated.

## Commissars and the Constituent Assembly

Terms such as 'commissars' and 'plenipotentiaries' now entered Russian life, and soon commissars and Cheka officials came to embody the Soviet regime itself.

Once the government had been formed, Trotsky recalled, the question arose of what to call its members. 'Not ministers,' Lenin stipulated: 'that's a vile, worn-out title.' Trotsky suggested: 'Maybe commissars, though there are too many of them right now.' He then proposed 'supreme commissars', but discarded that, then came up with 'People's Commissars', which Lenin liked. As for the name of the government itself, Trotsky proposed 'Soviet of People's Commissars', to which Lenin replied enthusiastically: 'It smells of revolution.'[169]

The first political crisis to strike the new government came after only a few days. Representatives of the All-Russian Executive Committee of the Railwaymen's Union (Vikzhel), in which the Mensheviks and SRs were dominant, demanded a 'homogenous socialist government', that is, one made up of all the socialist parties, to be called the 'People's Soviet'. This demand was supported by four Bolshevik People's Commissars: Milyutin, Nogin, Rykov and Teodorovich, as well as by some members of the Party Central Committee, which had been elected at the Sixth Congress in August 1917. At the same time, the Mensheviks and SRs were making it a condition for their entering the Soviet of People's Commissars that it first rid itself of the 'organizers of the military conspiracy', Lenin and Trotsky, and replace them with the SRs Chernov and Avksentiev, both of whom had been associated with the Provisional Government and were therefore seen as more genuinely 'coalition-minded'.

On 1 (14) November Lenin summoned a meeting of the Party Central Committee. With some support, Kamenev, who was heading the talks with Vikzhel, proposed a compromise, permitting further talks. Lenin would brook no opposition: 'Kamenev's policy must cease forthwith. We will not talk to Vikzhel now . . . They are on the side of the Kaledins and Kornilovs.'[170] In protest against their leader's undemocratic ways, Kamenev, Zinoviev, Rykov, Milyutin and Nogin left the Central Committee, and Milyutin, Nogin and Teodorovich also resigned as People's Commissars. Lenin and the rest of the Council of People's Commissars (Sovnarkom) then sent an ultimatum to the protesters, accusing them of conciliationism and disorganizing tactics, and warning them that 'the fate of the Party and the revolution' depended on their accepting his demands.[171] He wanted a purely Bolshevik government, and by exerting personal pressure he managed to persuade the protesters to give up the fight.

At first, Lenin plunged into the work of government with enormous enthusiasm. The Sovnarkom met almost daily, and Lenin enjoyed chairing government meetings, which sometimes lasted five or six hours. He was a stickler for keeping to the allotted time for speeches, and would cut off anyone who overran. Sometimes he would scan the hall with a hand shielding his eyes as if he were looking for someone. He would send notes to participants, request information, clarify details, ask for advice and propose decisions. Those who worked for him soon found him to be strict, though he had a ready smile. He had to have the room kept at a cool temperature, and if it was very warm he would gasp for breath. He did not like soft chairs, and preferred sending notes to using the telephone. He spent more time working on the political content of documents than on their literary style, with the result that his orders were often rough and clumsy, as were his letters in general. He worked hard, but as soon as he felt tired he dropped everything and went for a rest. It would be difficult to count all the holidays he took during his six years in power.

Unused as he was to the demands of a working routine, Lenin's physical strength soon began to flag. But he never let the cares of government prevent him from writing for the Party press. As a result of overwork, he began quickly to wear himself out and to age visibly. The rôle of leader had turned out to be prosaic, bureaucratic and thankless. From 27 July 1918 until his death, out of 173 Sovnarkom sessions he attended only seven.[172]

The Bolsheviks set out to build a socialist society, detailing, monitoring, ordering and regulating the widest possible spectrum of the great state's activities themselves. In November and December 1917 alone the People's Commissars examined about five hundred questions of state, social and economic life. They started with the confiscation, division and distribution of assets, the revolutionary court and the fight against sabotage. After breaking the resistance of the SRs and their own democratically-minded comrades, on 4 (17) November the Bolsheviks on the Central Executive Committee of the Soviets (VTsIK)* managed to pass a special resolution giving Lenin's 'cabinet', the Sovnarkom, not only executive, but also legislative powers.[173] In effect, it was the Party Central Committee that ran the new administration, and decrees originating in the Sovnarkom were enacted with extraordinary speed, the only significant criterion being 'revolutionary expediency'.

---

* Not to be confused with the Central Committee of the Bolshevik Party, the VTsIK was ostensibly the supreme organ of Soviet government.

Lenin had never worked in industry or state administration, and his experience of agriculture had been minimal. Despite an exceptional mind and broad theoretical knowledge, his knowledge of the various functions of state was superficial, and many of his orders and counsels were confused and obscure. Addressing deputies from the Petrograd garrison on restoring order in the city, he said: 'Our task, which we never lose sight of, is the universal arming of the people and the dispersal of the regular army. If the working population can be involved, the work will be easier. The comrades' proposal to assemble every day is a practical one ... Each unit must work together with the workers' organizations to make sure everything required for this war of yours is stocked up, without waiting for orders from above. This task should be begun this very night independently.'[174] This puzzling speech was published in *Pravda*.

A letter from Ioffe to Trotsky confirms that many of Lenin's judgments were based on lack of experience combined with a reliance on commissars whose zeal far outweighed their abilities: 'The day after Krasin had been appointed Transport Commissar, a post for which, despite his many qualities, he was entirely unsuited, I happened to be leaving the city and went to see Vladimir Ilyich before doing so. He asked me when I was leaving. I replied that I didn't know when the train was departing. "Call up Krasin," he said. In his view, a Transport Commissar was supposed to know the entire railway timetable, even if he'd only been given the job the day before and had never had anything to do with railways. It was the same with everything else.'

Ioffe went on: 'On the financial question, if you please, Krestinsky was asked, but since when was he a financier? And Chicherin for foreign affairs, though everyone knows what sort of diplomat he is. Perhaps this is the way it should be in a "well-endowed" state, but with one prerequisite, namely that only specialists in a given field should be appointed, as used to be the case in tsarist times, where the finance minister would be someone who had earned his haemorrhoids in a finance department; the foreign minister someone who had knocked on the doors of all the foreign embassies, first as an attaché, then as envoy and finally ambassador and so on. With us, when they appoint someone straight "from the plough", so to speak, or some Lutovinov is made a Member of the Collegium of the People's Commissariat of the Workers' and Peasants' Inspectorate, it isn't because he knows something about the Inspectorate or was ever interested in it, it is only because his job is either to shut mouths or "workerize"* the Inspectorate.'[175]

Ioffe's letter is an eloquent illustration of the way class considerations took precedence over professionalism in Lenin's government. Lenin himself rarely gave reports at Sovnarkom sessions, restricting his rôle to speaking on the most crucial political matters, giving general guidance and ensuring that the government's actions bore the clearest possible signs of its revolutionary direction. At a meeting of the Sovnarkom on 28 November 1917, for instance, he proposed a decree on 'the arrest of the most prominent members of the central committee of the party of the enemies of the people [i.e. the Constitutional Democrats], and their trial by Revolutionary tribunal'.[176] The only member of the government to oppose this measure was Stalin, perhaps in an effort to establish an autonomous presence.

Sovnarkom meetings usually took place in the morning and evening, and sometimes ran on beyond midnight. Items were not debated extensively, as Lenin usually pushed decisions through in a hurry, demanding members be brief, interrupting the garrulous and admonishing latecomers. He even introduced sanctions: lateness by half an hour would incur a fine of five roubles, lateness by up to an hour ten roubles. 'Only People's Commissars who give proper notice and reasons for being late will be excused the fine.'[177] He also introduced a scale of punishment for absenteeism and lateness in all government institutions: 'Lateness by ten minutes for a meeting without good reason will incur a reprimand; a second such offence, loss of one day's pay; a third time, a reprimand in the press . . . Arriving more than fifteen minutes late will incur a reprimand in the press or compulsory labour on days off.'[178]

In this way the leader of the revolution tried to oil the huge machine of administration. He would be sharp with anyone whispering during meetings, or scribble a 'barbed note' to them. On 2 December 1917, for instance, when L.A. Fotieva, one of his own secretaries, muttered an explanation to the stenographers, Lenin was so irritated that he sent her a note saying: 'If you're going to chatter, I swear I'll throw you out.'[179] On another occasion, Fotieva was absent when Lenin

* i.e. Maximize the number of officials of working-class origin.

needed her, and he wrote angrily: '*To Fotieva:* I'm giving you a reprimand. You're not to sleep, but organize things so that *everyone* can
easily locate you and *always* [underlined three times] when it has to
do with me.'[180]

An abbreviated agenda and account of decisions taken during the
session of 19 November 1917 reads:

1) Draft decree on civil marriage, to be passed to Justice Commissariat; 2)
Draft decree on divorce, as above; 5) Stalin's report on trade with Finland
and Finnish currency, ask Pyatakov to explain question of Finnish currency;
8) Stalin's proposal to delay elections to Constituent Assembly, postpone this
matter to 20 November 1917; 9) Stalin's report on Ukraine and the Rada
[the Ukrainian government], instruct Stalin to convene a special commission
by 20 November; 11) Special request from mining and metallurgical workers
of Zenteev district for 500,000 roubles, pass to interdepartmental commission
for review; 13) Inquiry to Stalin about credits for commissariats. If it tran-
spires employees have received pay up to January 1918, they are to return it
forthwith: arrests and revolutionary tribunal not excluded; 15) Proposal by
Ulyanov [Lenin] to appoint Comrade Essen Temporary Deputy People's
Commissar for State Control, [agreed]; 18) Request from extraordinary Peasants' congress for 200,000 roubles out of the funds allocated for expenses,
issue 200,000 roubles, the remaining 250,000 to come from Pre-parliament
money; 21) Report by Glebov on rise for post and telegraph employees (grant
of 500,000 roubles); 25) Report by Trotsky on war ministry (a secret order
for purging the ministry and discharging officers from Latvian
regiments . . .); 26) Inquiry to Petrovsky about arrests in Ministry of Internal
Affairs, arrest them if Petrovsky agrees; 27) On 'purging' the ministries, all
People's Commissars are to compile a daily report on the 'purge' of their
ministries.

Signed V. Ulyanov (Lenin).[181]

Even in abbreviated form, this agenda gives an idea of Lenin's work
as chairman of the government. The main task of the People's Commissars was to distribute resources, delegate work, arrest people and
carry out 'purges'. Anything requiring action was given to the commissariats, commissions and committees to do. The old state machine
had been broken and the new one was primitive, inefficient and from
its very inception markedly bureaucratic. Perhaps even Lenin did not
then realize that the new structures being erected were in fact the
foundations of a vast totalitarian system. He ceaselessly preached that

the state must be run by the people, yet increasingly he himself regulated and limited the autonomy of the social and state agencies of everyday life which arose spontaneously. He had always seen, and would until the end of his days see, state, social and workers' control as the panacea of all ills.

Such a view of the virtues of control quickly led to the creation of a police state. As early as 26 October (8 November) Lenin personally penned a draft decree on workers' control in which 'negligence, the concealment of supplies, accounts and so on will be punished by the confiscation of all property and up to five years' imprisonment'.[182] He also introduced special control of the press, and by December 1917 many non-Bolshevik publishing houses had been closed down, and Lenin had authorized the Cheka to exercise 'preliminary censorship of the periodical and non-periodical press, photography and cinematography, blueprints, illustrations . . . correspondence of the posts and telegraph'.[183] This only months after he had been lamenting the severity of the police regime of the tsarist autocracy and the bourgeoisie. The sole argument he employed to justify the lawlessness and arbitrary rule of his own regime was that it was 'in the interests of the masses' and was being carried out by the 'most advanced class', the proletariat.

Lenin felt entitled to alter or supplement the Sovnarkom's instructions at will. For instance, he added in his own hand the following amendments to a Sovnarkom decree entitled 'The Socialist fatherland is in danger!':

2) All members of the rich classes are to supply themselves immediately with a *work book* in which weekly reports will be entered showing whether or not they have performed the allotted amount of military or administrative work . . . Work books will cost the wealthy 50 roubles each; 3) Non-possession of a work book or incorrect and especially false entries are to be punished under martial law; anyone in possession of firearms must obtain new permission, a) from their house committee, b) from their institution . . . Possession of firearms is prohibited unless both permissions are obtained; punishment for breaking this rule is execution. The same punishment applies to the concealment of supplies.[184]

Of course a regime subjected at its inception to the pressures of a civil war such as that faced by the Bolsheviks will seek and find rationalizations for its harsh policies. The question is, how clearly did Lenin and his followers distinguish, in their own minds, between the force and coercion required to combat their armed enemies, and that which they used against their purely political foes, real and potential? The promise to create a new society without oppression, police rule and terror, so adamantly expressed by Lenin as late as the summer of 1917 in *State and Revolution*, was swallowed up by the imperatives of Bolshevik survival, and never retrieved. On the contrary, the new government depended on special, 'extraordinary', punitive commissions. Those with eyes to see at once perceived the terrible threat. Gorky, who did not 'accept' the revolution straight away, was quite direct: 'Lenin, Trotsky and their fellow-travellers are already intoxicated by the foul poison of power, as they show by their disgraceful attitude to freedom of speech, the person and to all the rights for which the democracy fought . . . The workers must not let the adventurers and madmen heap shameless, senseless, bloody crimes on the heads of the proletariat, crimes for which it will not be Lenin who will pay, but the proletariat itself.'[185]

It was not only intellectuals and academics who sensed that a terrible new regime had come to power. Lenin received letters from ordinary people who complained of spiritual suffering. A certain Yemelyan Pavlov wrote that the commissars, 'all the people in leather jackets who worship you, are doing their best to put you onto a pedestal so high that you won't see anything but will be seen by the people as an unattainable god'.[186] In another letter written at the same time, a certain N. Vorontsov wrote: 'All your reforms have boiled down to the following: 1) universal hard labour with the typical marks of a regime which abolishes the right of free movement, brings in a system of permits, coercive feeding and teaching and so on; the ultimate perfection of the Security Section (Cheka) and its spread to cover all citizens: a system of general search and the absence of courts.' The writer ended by predicting that 'they'll tear your corpse apart on the streets of Moscow, like the Pretender'.*[187] There is no evidence that these letters were actually seen by Lenin, but they do show that, from

---

* The death of Tsar Boris Godunov in 1605 had triggered a period of strife, foreign intervention and anarchy, known as the Time of Troubles, lasting until 1613, when the first Romanov ascended the throne. Dmitri, who claimed to be Ivan the Terrible's murdered son, captured Moscow in 1605 and was murdered the following year.

the very outset, many ordinary people were horrified by the prospect of life under the Soviets.

Occasionally Lenin resorted to populist measures in order to increase the authority of the new regime. He set new wage scales for members of the government, fixing the salary of a People's Commissar at five hundred roubles a month plus one hundred roubles for each non-working member of the family.[188] This was probably about the wage of a skilled worker, since it was Party policy to remunerate its officials at roughly that rate. It was, however, no more than a part of a commissar's income. Commissars were given special rations, in Moscow they soon took over the country villas of the bourgeoisie, and they had access to their own special physicians. As early as 1918 the practice of going abroad for medical treatment and rest had been instituted, and top Party officials would not let such privileges slip through their fingers. In any case, after 1918 money quickly lost all meaning, as galloping inflation rendered it worthless. The only transactions of value were conducted by barter, and the only wages of value were those received in kind.

Although the government had proclaimed that the army was to be replaced by a people's militia, a regular army, it turned out, was still needed, and had to be created, fed, clothed and led. Within a few days in November 1917, Lenin signed a number of orders concerning the army. All ranks, titles, medals and officers' organizations were abolished with the proclamation that 'the army of the Russian Republic now consists of free and equal citizens who bear the honourable title of *soldier* of the revolutionary army'.[189]

Simultaneously, another decree introduced the elective principle and prescribed the organization of power in the army, underlining that the army was subordinate to the will of the people as embodied by the Sovnarkom, that all power in the army was vested in soldiers' committees, and that commanders, (i.e. officers) and all other officials were to be subject to election.[190]

As he pursued his abstract schemes, Lenin succeeded in destroying what remained of the old military organization, something he could not have contemplated had he not come to power with the intention of leaving the war. Having no notion of the peculiarities of military hierarchy, with the principle of single command, Lenin's commissars brought chaos to the regiments and naval ships. The Bolsheviks did, however, quickly master the arts of terror and requisitioning. If a complaint was received that a certain unit was badly supplied, a decree would be issued increasing soldiers' rations, quickly followed by an order 'to confiscate the resources from the rich by revolutionary means'.[191] Within a short time the new regime would, however, turn its attention to rebuilding military force, and the Red Army would be the result.

On 30 November 1917, at the suggestion of Trotsky and Bonch-Bruevich, the Sovnarkom issued a decree requisitioning gold, with a reward of one per cent of its market value for anyone who 'discovered' any.[192] In signing such decrees, Lenin was encouraging social disorder, spreading corruption, pushing the dispossessed towards organized resistance and igniting local beacons of a civil war that would soon spread into one fearful conflagration. He was assisted in these 'initiatives' by the Left SRs, to whom, after debate in the Central Committee, he decided to give several portfolios. The matter was reviewed by the Sovnarkom on 9 December, and the decision was taken to make it a condition that the Left SRs 'must follow the general policy of the Sovnarkom', that is, the Bolshevik Central Committee. After a night of negotiation between Sverdlov and Left SR representatives, it was announced at the Sovnarkom that 'full agreement' had been reached. Agriculture was given to A.L. Kollegaev, Justice to I.Z. Shteinberg, Posts and Telegraph to P.P. Proshyan, Local Self-Government to V.Y. Trutovsky, State Property to V.A. Karelin, and V.A. Algasov was made People's Commissar without portfolio but with voting powers.[193] Most of these – if they did not, like Proshyan, die of typhus or other affliction of the civil war, or emigrate, like Shteinberg – were dealt with as enemies of the people in the mid-1930s.

Although the Left SRs were hardly less radical than the Bolsheviks themselves (they tended to stress peasant interests), this interval in Soviet history represented a rare moment of socialist pluralism and, had the Mensheviks also been invited to join the government, it is just possible that a measure of moderation might have taken root. To be sure, despite Lenin's claim at the Third Congress of Soviets in January 1918 that 'after two months of working together, I can definitely say that most of the issues we dealt with were settled unanimously',[194] friction occurred straight away. Shteinberg was demanding that his commissariat be given control of the Cheka and the investigation commission of the Revolutionary Tribunal, but Lenin turned him down flat. Trutovsky wanted to retain local institutions, which the Bolsheviks saw as a stronghold of the old ways. In the course of their brief cohabitation, the two parties were in conflict more than a dozen times. It is nevertheless possible that over a period of years the coalition could have led to mutual restraint, which might in due course have mitigated the worst features of totalitarianism. There was, it is true, a moment when the Left SRs wanted to merge with the Bolsheviks, but, as Trotsky recalled, Lenin decided to 'let them wait'.[195]

But, for a time, the collaboration was a fact. Of the twenty members of the Cheka Collegium, seven were Left SRs, including Dzerzhinsky's deputies Alexandrovich and Zaks. In April 1918 the Left SRs helped the Bolsheviks to crush the Anarchists (who were splintered into a host of groupings, some of them supporting the Bolsheviks, most opposed to Lenin's strong, centralized form of government), and also helped to spread Bolshevik influence in the countryside by supporting the infamous decree of 13 May 1918 which legitimized the confiscation of grain from the peasants. Before the introduction of the New Economic Policy in 1921, force was virtually the sole means employed by the regime to bring the peasants under its control.

It soon became clear, however, that the Bolsheviks did not want to share power with any party. When the Left SRs opposed the Brest-Litovsk Treaty, under which Lenin withdrew from the war at huge cost, and resigned from the government, the Bolsheviks heaved a sigh of relief, and smashed them as a party on 6–7 July 1918 by mass arrests and deportations to prisons and concentration camps.

Lenin was less concerned with unstable allies like the Left SRs and drop-outs from Vikzhel than he was with the impending Constituent Assembly. He had already stated on 10 October 1917 that 'to wait for the Constituent Assembly, which will obviously not be with us, is senseless and will only make our task harder'.[196] His warning had gone unheeded: the Assembly was still some way off, and if the Bolsheviks seized power its fate would be uncertain. Now power was indeed in their hands, yet the Constituent Assembly, given the chance, would take it away from them. Despite his promise of land, Lenin knew that the peasants would not vote for the Bolsheviks, but would support the Socialist Revolutionaries as the more familiar party. Perhaps he also recalled Thomas Carlyle's comment to the effect that any assembly consisting of twelve hundred people was good for nothing but agitation and self-destruction. Indeed, seven decades later, a Congress of People's Deputies, in its way a Constituent Assembly, would destroy the Union Lenin had created. A vast gathering of ambitious people, standing above parliament, the regime and the courts, is more likely to act destructively than constructively.

For Lenin, it was not important that the Constituent Assembly might begin the process of creating a representative and capable parliament which could have put the country onto the path of civilized development. What mattered to him was that the Constituent Assembly could deprive him of the prize he had sought for so long. He would not have been Lenin had he reconciled himself to such an outcome, and he was resolved to throw this relic of 'dead bourgeois parliamentarism' out of the revolutionary train. And yet in January, while still in Switzerland, he had called for the Constituent Assembly 'to be convened immediately', and in April he had exclaimed indignantly: 'They say I am against the earliest possible convening of the Constituent Assembly!!! That's what I call "delirium".'[197] (He was referring to Plekhanov's comment on the position he had taken on his return to Russia in April 1917.)

Until the beginning of October, the Bolsheviks continued to parade as supporters of the Constituent Assembly, and the day after the coup *Pravda* proclaimed: 'Comrades! With your blood you have ensured that the master of the Russian land, the Constituent Assembly, will be convened on time.' The Provisional Government had determined that elections would take place on 17 (30) September 1917 and that the Assembly would convene on 30 September (13 October). The decree had been signed on 14 June, and six million roubles had been allocated to cover the costs of the election. Later, under Kerensky's prime ministership, the election had been postponed until 12 (25) November and the Assembly for 28 November (10 December), and the scale of representation had been determined by September.[198]

It was not possible to complete the election in one day – in some places it took the entire month of December. 703 deputies were elected, of whom only 168 were Bolsheviks. The SRs won 299 seats, the Left SRs 39, the Mensheviks 18, the Popular Socialists 4, the Kadets 17, and 158 were elected from various national groups.

Trotsky recalled that Lenin raised the issue of the Assembly 'days, if not hours' after the coup. 'We have to put off the elections,' he said. 'We have to have the opportunity to renew the electoral lists.* Our own lists are no use whatever, they include a lot of intellectuals who got on by accident, whereas we need workers and peasants. We have to declare Kornilovites and Constitutional Democrats outside the law.' There were objections that this was not a good moment to postpone the election, that it would be seen as the liquidation of the Constituent Assembly, especially as the Bolsheviks had accused the Provisional Government of delay. 'Rubbish!' Lenin retorted. 'Why isn't it a good moment? What if the Constituent Assembly turns out to be a Kadet–Menshevik–SR one, will that suit us?' Trotsky added that Lenin, isolated in his view, kept repeating, 'It's a mistake, an obvious mistake for which we shall pay dearly. It could cost the revolution its head.' On balance, Lenin was for dispersing the Assembly, and his only concern was how the Left SRs would react. They, however, agreed with him, yet Lenin was not content: 'It's an obvious mistake: we have already won power, and yet we have to take military measures to win it all over again.'[199]

The 'military measures' in question were the transfer of one of the most loyal Bolshevik Latvian regiments to the capital. Should the Assembly prove 'disobedient', force was to be used. On 23 November, the very eve of the elections, the electoral commission was meeting, as usual, in the Tauride Palace. At midday the palace commandant, Prigovorovsky, walked in and announced that he had been empowered to arrest the 'Kadet-defencists'. Blind to their protests, he marched the professors, lawyers, doctors and politicians into an empty room and locked it. They were held there for four days without food, water or beds, and threatened with worse. Their crime had been to publish a statement ten days earlier to the effect that, despite the disruption of the electoral process caused by the 'attempt to seize power', the Provisional Government had determined not to delay further and was announcing the date of the Constituent Assembly as 28 November (10 December).[200] It was this 'arrogance' that prompted Lenin to

---

* The electoral law passed by the Provisional Government in July 1917 had given the right to vote to all citizens, male and female, over the age of twenty (excepting convicts, deserters, the insane and the royal family).

liquidate the commission and to appoint Mikhail Uritsky as commissar for the election.

A number of the commissioners who were still at large burst in on Stalin and demanded to know why their colleagues had been arrested: 'Isn't it because the Commission doesn't recognize the People's Commissars?' M.M. Dobranitsky asked.

'We don't care what the commission thinks of us,' Stalin replied. 'The matter is more serious. You've been engaging in forgery and falsification.'

'That's a lie!'

'Can you be so sure,' Stalin retorted, 'that the Kadets and defencists haven't been having meetings and keeping them secret from you?' He ended the meeting with: 'We won't allow the counter-revolution to use the Constituent Assembly as a smokescreen for its own ends.'[201]

The arrest of the commission was a challenge to the whole democratic process, and on 28 November the liberal Constitutional Democrats (Kadets) and Right (i.e. moderate) Socialist Revolutionaries staged a demonstration at the Tauride Palace. There was an attempt to break in and 'open' the Assembly, but with the help of armed sailors the Bolsheviks dispersed the demonstrators. That evening the Sovnarkom discussed a report by Trotsky on the events. He defined what had happened as an attempt at an armed uprising and the Kadet leadership as a permanent source of counter-revolution. Lenin proposed they be arrested as 'enemies of the people and put before a revolutionary tribunal'.[202] The commission was arrested next day and, where elections had yet to be held, Uritsky was put in charge. When the remaining members of the commission refused to disperse on Uritsky's orders, the Sovnarkom decreed the commission's liquidation.

As deputies had by now been elected, the VTsIK passed a decree recalling deputies who 'had not earned the trust of the people', i.e. all those who did not accept Bolshevik authority. In a noisy campaign, orchestrated by the Bolsheviks, many deputies at congresses of peasants and soldiers were denounced as 'counter-revolutionary elements' and deprived of their mandates.

Lenin went still further. The Bolshevik section, which was to represent their interests at the Assembly, and which included the 'Vikzhel rebels', whom Lenin had not forgiven, declared that the Constituent

Assembly was an important stage in the socialist revolution. It too was swept away.

In mid-December Lenin radically revised the Bolshevik line on the Assembly, arguing that the Soviets were not merely 'a higher form', they were the 'only form of democracy', and that the results were outdated, since the population had not yet had time to assess the Bolsheviks' achievements on the questions of peace and land.[203] If Lenin thought the elections had not reflected the 'new disposition of class forces', it was open to him to correct the position by democratic means, i.e. new elections. But the Bolsheviks had lost in the November elections, and they would have lost in new ones. Lenin's decision was therefore to convene the Assembly and propose that it approve the fundamental decrees agreed by the Bolsheviks. Knowing that the Right SRs and Mensheviks would resist, there would be nothing more to do than close the Assembly down. As Lenin told Trotsky: 'Of course, it was taking a risk, a big risk, not to put off the date of the Assembly. But in the end it was for the best. The dispersal of the Constituent Assembly by the Soviet regime is the full and open liquidation of formal democracy in the name of the revolutionary dictatorship.'[204]

The Bolsheviks therefore decided to observe the formalities and convene the Assembly on 5 (18) January, setting a quorum of four hundred.[205] They even went through the motions of allocating government funds: '71,000 roubles for salaries, 8,000 for typists, couriers and guards, 10,000 for couriers' journeys, 5,000 for the restaurant . . . A round sum of 233,000 roubles.'[206] The campaign against the Assembly began in December. Trotsky proposed a motion at the Sovnarkom 'to intensify the watch on the bourgeois press for foul insinuations and slander against the Soviet regime'. Petrovsky was instructed to set up a special body at the Commissariat of the Interior to do this.[207] Here was the embryo of the future censorship, the ideological roadblock on the road to truth in the Soviet Union.

The Assembly, which bore the hopes of so many, finally opened to the accompaniment of public demonstrations of support on 18 January 1918. The Bolsheviks were prepared, and their troops barred the way to the Tauride Palace. There were clashes, and blood flowed. Meanwhile, 410 deputies had assembled. The meeting was opened by one of the oldest of them, S.P. Shevtsov, but no one heard his short speech, for the moment he began, the Bolsheviks and Left SRs struck up a cacophony, banging their desks, stamping their feet, whistling and whooping. 'Lenin,' the Menshevik Vishnyak, who was secretary of the Assembly, recalled, 'who was sitting in a box to the left of the chairman, at first listened, then sank back into his chair apathetically and finally disappeared altogether.' The leader of the Socialist Revolutionaries, Viktor Chernov, gained most votes for the position of chairman, but was prevented from taking his seat by the tumult. Vishnyak recalled Bukharin declaring: 'The dictatorship is laying the foundations for the life of mankind for a thousand years.'[208]

Sverdlov proposed that the Assembly approve the decrees issued by the Soviet regime. The SR majority rejected this as arrogance, at which the Bolsheviks, following Lenin's plan, left the hall, followed by the Left SRs. Vishnyak remembered that 'the sailors and Red Army men in the hall now lost their restraint. They leapt into the boxes and pushed deputies towards the exits with their rifle-butts, and swirled up into the balconies where the public was close to panic. The deputies meanwhile remained stationary in their seats, tragically silent. We had been isolated from the world, just as the Tauride Palace had been isolated from Petrograd and Petrograd from the rest of the world.'[209] The remaining deputies attempted to preserve the forum, and continued making speeches, despite the physical threat. At five a.m. the Bolsheviks simply proposed that the deputies leave.

In a twenty-minute speech at the All-Russian Executive Committee of Soviets on the night of 19 January 1918, Lenin stressed that civil war was an inevitable accompaniment of the socialist revolution. To loud applause, he went on: 'The people wanted us to convene the Constituent Assembly and we did. But now the people know what it represents.'[210] This despite the fact that no newspaper or other source of information had reported its proceedings, even in the capital. It was, in other words, the Bolsheviks who expressed the will of the people.

Like many other members of the Assembly, if they did not perish in the civil war, Chernov, its chairman, was to spend the rest of his life in exile looking back on 5 (18) January 1918 as a great opportunity missed. Referred to as 'The Gypsy', he was tailed throughout his life by the OGPU–NKVD, and his every move was reported back to Moscow. Agent 'Lord' stole some of his papers from his residence in

Prague, including the original minutes of the opening session of the Assembly.[211]

Trotsky later wrote derisively: 'In the form of the SR [Assembly] the February revolution had the occasion to die a second time,' adding, 'Chernov followed the old revolutionary intelligentsia tradition, while Lenin completed and overcame it fully.'[212] He ought to have said 'distorted, repudiated and destroyed it fully'. The old Russian intelligentsia, bearing the cross of spiritual rebellion, had a conscience. It was honest and idealistic. Lenin 'overcame' these 'weaknesses' and revealed himself as the new intellectual of the Marxist type, a utopian fanatic, believing himself to have the right to perform any experiment so long as the goal of power was served. Chernov, Martov, Dan and other Russian socialist intellectuals differed from Lenin in that they wanted to attain a better world for mankind without the use of force, and by learning from the experience of democracy elsewhere. Lenin was not thinking about 'mankind', but the mass, for whom he wanted to build a life of communism conceived in his head.

In 1918 Vladimir Medem, the Bundist, wrote: 'There are impatient people who think that without the Constituent Assembly it will be easier and quicker to make everyone happy. But no one has ever been made happy by *force*.'[213]

The story of Lenin's part in the sad history of the Constituent Assembly might have ended here, except that in the autumn of 1918 Karl Kautsky wrote a pamphlet, which Vorovsky sent Lenin from Scandinavia, entitled 'The Dictatorship of the Proletariat'. In it Kautsky wrote frankly about the dictatorship of the Bolsheviks. Lenin was indignant; he had never been able to accept personal criticism. He was quite comfortable lashing out at all and sundry, but he could not bear jibes at himself, especially if they were justified. Kautsky's analysis, balanced and well-argued, exposed the deeply anti-democratic nature of Bolshevism and of Lenin himself, and Lenin could not let it pass. Battles might be raging on all fronts, the Soviet regime might be under real threat, the Republic suffering severe famine, banditry, terror, but the insult must be answered. Lenin, pushing aside the endless tasks of government, set about writing a reply, 'The Proletarian Revolution and the Renegade Kautsky'.

The hundred-page work is typical of Lenin's 'scientific' style:

pragmatic and categorical in its judgments, attuned to politics rather than theory, accompanied by such abuse as to make one wonder if this really was a Russian intellectual who was writing. Kautsky, one of the most revered figures of international socialism, is repeatedly called 'the Judas Kautsky', 'renegade', 'swindler', 'blind puppy', 'sycophant of the bourgeoisie', 'swine', 'yes-man of scoundrels and bloodsuckers', 'philistine'. Lenin accuses him of 'despicable tricks' and 'foul lies', and describes him as fit for the 'cesspit of renegades'.

# 4

## *Priests of Terror*

Lenin had gained power with incredible ease. Without barricades, bloody encounters or intervention, state power had been transferred to the party that had promised to make the people happy by bringing them peace, land and liberty. According to the Marxist canon, everything was going to be simple: private property would be abolished, the bourgeois state smashed, the army replaced by an armed militia, the workers ('even the cooks') put in charge, secret treaties published, self-determination of the nations proclaimed, strict social control established, and the dictatorship of the majority confirmed. Everything, or so it seemed, had been foreseen by Lenin. All that remained was to build the socialist edifice according to the blueprint.

In reality, there was famine, factories went on strike, gangs held sway in many parts of the country, the peasants hid their grain, and the army disintegrated of its own accord. As far as the war was concerned, the Germans had moved in September to consolidate their position on the Baltic, and posed a certain threat to the Petrograd region, but since their strategy of removing Russia from the war in order to be able to concentrate on the western front looked like being successful, the war on the Russian front virtually came to a standstill at the time of the Bolshevik seizure of power. In any event, an armistice was quickly agreed, in December 1917, and the Germans' ambitions in the east could wait until they had settled accounts with the Allies in the west, or so they hoped. Meanwhile, Russia descended into chaos.

Lenin soon realized that 'victory over the old world' was impossible 'without the dictatorship of the proletariat and an iron hand'.[1] To this end, labour conscription was introduced, the bourgeoisie were subjected to repeated requisitioning, their apartments were packed out with new tenants, they were 'purged' from institutions and put under constant threat of new and worse punishments. A barracks mentality gradually took over in the endless commissariats, offices, Soviets and proletarian bodies.

Trotsky recalled that when Shteinberg, the Left SR Commissar of Justice, protested against the use of violence and repression as a means of settling social problems, Lenin exclaimed: 'Surely you don't think we'll come out as the winners if we don't use the harshest revolutionary terror?' Lenin took every opportunity to ram home the message that terror was inevitable. A dozen times a day he would fire off tirades against anyone suspected of pacifism: 'If we can't shoot a White Guard saboteur, what sort of great revolution is it? Haven't you seen what the bourgeois garbage are writing about us in the press? What sort of dictatorship is this? All talk and no action.'[2]

With typical persistence, Lenin hammered home the need to toughen the dictatorship 'to save the revolution', until gradually his regulations for using the iron hand became standard Bolshevik practice. To be sure, he was often pushed into adopting harsh measures by the disasters which threatened, above all the famine, caused by the dislocation of Russia's supply system as a result of three years of war, together with reduced production. In effect, Lenin believed that terror would save the country from starvation. The food 'must be taken from the rich'. Black marketeers must be shot. He also urged the masses to act independently, by which he meant they should carry out their own searches and confiscate food: 'As long we do not use terror – i.e. shooting black marketeers on the spot – we'll get nowhere.' Looters should be similarly dealt with, while 'the better-off should be left without food for three days, as they have stocks'.[3]

There would seem to be three elements which explain why a man with Lenin's understanding of humanitarian principles could embrace violent methods. First, he simply lost his head when confronted by an avalanche of problems. Nothing more than an émigré intellectual a few months earlier, with no practical experience beyond controlling a Party faction, he had been cut off from the grim realities of life in Russia. As his first acts show, he had no idea how to deploy his time and responsibilities: personally authorizing an apartment for an old Bolshevik, or sending aid to a village outside Moscow, setting up the management of the Sovnarkom canteen and making endless propaganda speeches. The levers of the state machine, such as it was, were in harsh but inexperienced hands. Many of Lenin's telegrams portray his loss of control, even if only temporary. For instance, he cabled Antonov-Ovseenko and Dzerzhinsky in Kharkov: 'For God's sake, take the most energetic and *revolutionary* measures to send *grain, grain and grain!!!* Otherwise [Petrograd] could expire. [Use] special trains and troops. Collect and load. Escort the trains. Inform us daily. For God's sake!'[4] This was a cry of desperation, loss of control and panic, the partners of coercion.

The second element is that the Bolsheviks observed their own scale of moral values. Lack of pity, class hatred and Machiavellianism were to them the highest revolutionary virtues. Lenin even stooped to hostage-taking, decreeing that 'in every grain-growing district, 25–30 rich hostages should be taken who will answer with their lives for the collection and loading of all surpluses'.[5] The effect on the middle classes was utterly demoralizing.

The third element was that Lenin intended to use fear as a weapon. Terror would break the will to resist of millions. When V. Volodarsky, the People's Commissar for Press, Propaganda and Agitation, was assassinated by a Socialist Revolutionary in Petrograd in 1918, Lenin cabled Zinoviev: 'This is *im-poss-ible*! The terrorists will think we're milksops. We have an extreme war situation. We must encourage energy and wide-scale terror against the counter-revolutionaries, especially in [Petrograd] as a *decisive* example.'[6]

Lenin cannot be accused of personal cruelty. His was more the social, philosophical cruelty of a leader. His main argument for the use of terror was that it was in the interests of the proletariat. In an article entitled 'Plekhanov on Terror', he wrote with seeming frankness about the difference between bourgeois and Bolshevik terror: The bourgeoisie 'practised terror *against the workers, soldiers and peasants* in the interests of a small group of landowners and bankers, whereas the Soviet regime applies decisive measures against landowners, plunderers and their accomplices *in the interests of the workers, soldiers and peasants*'.[7] Such an argument could be used to justify any crime perpetrated by the state. The leaders of the revolution had become priests of terror.

## *The Anatomy of Brest-Litovsk*

To add to Russia's hunger, chaos and the rise of class terror, a new torture threatened: the possibility of a German advance, which could only be halted by signing the 'indecent' peace of Brest-Litovsk, a solution which in turn pushed Russia to the edge of a new time of troubles.

On 3 December 1917 the Bolsheviks established contact with the Germans, and by 22 December peace talks began. This was, after all, what the Germans had wanted when they helped Lenin. By early January the German side expressed its willingness to sign a peace treaty in exchange for major territorial concessions by Russia, namely the part of Poland held by the Russian empire until the war, the provinces comprising present-day Lithuania, and parts of what later became the Belorussian and Latvian republics, amounting to more than 150,000 square kilometres. The loss of territory in itself was bad enough, but it was the physical and human resources within that territory that more than anything else earned the treaty its title of 'the indecent peace'. Soviet Russia gave up thirty-four per cent of her population, thirty-two per cent of her agricultural land, fifty-four per cent of all industrial plant and eighty-nine per cent of her coal mines.[8] Lenin was in favour of signing such an accord, but at this point the Party became virtually split between the supporters of Lenin and the so-called Left Communists, led by Bukharin, who regarded the signing of this predatory treaty as a betrayal of the revolution.

Neither Lenin nor Bukharin was concerned by the loss of territory as such. Indeed, in the end Russia would be compelled to yield about one million square kilometres. In addition to the earlier demands, Russia would recognize the independence of Ukraine and cede three districts in the Caucasus to Turkey. Lenin's chief aim was to preserve his regime, or, in his words, the 'gains of the revolution'. He would have been willing to give up Petrograd, and even Moscow itself, as long as his regime survived. 'I want to yield territory to the present victor to gain time. That's what it's all about, and only that . . . Signing a treaty in defeat is a way of gathering strength . . . If we were to wage a revolutionary war, as Bukharin wants, it would be the best way to get rid of us right now.'[9] As for the Left Communists, they believed that by rejecting peace and calling for a revolutionary war, they could exploit the situation in Europe and provoke a continental conflagration. 'The Russian revolution will either be saved by an international revolution, or it will perish under the blows of international capital,' Bukharin said. He proposed 'cancelling the peace treaty, as it gives us nothing, and then setting about proper preparations' for a revolutionary war.[10]

The crisis was played out at the Seventh Party Congress in March 1918, at which Lenin was subjected to criticism as never before. Two reports were given, one by Lenin, the other by Bukharin. Lenin's speech contained little that he had not already said, with the same arguments about world revolution, the opinion that they might have to give up Petrograd and Moscow, that war with Germany was inevitable, and that the treaty was necessary to obtain a breathing-space of a day or two – even if it was going to cost a million square kilometres. It was above all the 'breathing-space' that was targeted by the Left Communists. Bukharin declared that it was not worth the candle, that the time would not suffice to discuss the sort of thing Lenin had in mind. 'It won't be a breathing-space ... but our own self-destruction as the vanguard of the international socialist revolution. We should not pay such a price for a two-day breathing-space that will give us nothing.'[11] Among Lenin's opponents, the Marxist theorist David Ryazanov remarked that Tolstoy had proposed making Russia into a peasant country of idiots, and now Lenin wanted to make it a peasant country of soldiers: 'And we are tasting the fruits of that policy.'[12]

Lenin replied to his critics that 'the treaty is not a capitulation', but merely a manoeuvre, a tactical device to gain time and save the regime. In the end, he won the day by thirty votes to twelve. Had Trotsky, whose position was crucial, supported the Left Communists instead of remaining neutral, more of the delegates might well have swung behind the 'revolutionary war' platform. Undoubtedly, Lenin's personal authority played a great part. In any event, he added an important amendment which the Congress passed unanimously, namely that the Central Committee was empowered to annul the treaty should it see fit. He ensured that both the decisions of the Congress and all materials related to it be kept secret, and he even had all the delegates sign an undertaking not to talk openly about the

The Tsar awarding decorations, 11 April 1916.

Lenin (with rolled umbrella) and the other political émigrés who travelled with him from Switzerland through Germany, in Stockholm before continuing their journey to Petrograd, April 1917. Zinoviev is seen holding his adopted son's hand (in Soviet publications this part of the picture was invariably deleted).

*Above*: Alexander Kerensky
(second from right)
presiding at a meeting in the
War Ministry, Petrograd,
21 August 1917.

*Right*: Alexander Kerensky,
Minister of Justice, then
War Minister and Prime
Minister of the Provisional
Government between
February and October 1917.
He fled abroad after the
Bolshevik seizure of power,
and died in the USA in 1970.

The false factory pass in the name of Konstantin Petrovich Ivanov, used by Lenin to cross the Finnish border in August 1917 to escape arrest by the Provisional Government.

Trotsky with other members of the Soviet delegation during the peace negotiations at Brest-Litovsk in January–February 1918.

Nadezhda Krupskaya disguised as a female worker for her trip to see Lenin in hiding in Finland in the summer of 1917.

Two leaders of the Menshevik Party, Yuli Martov and Fedor Dan (his brother-in-law), in Petrograd in late 1917. Before the October revolution, they led different camps, Martov the internationalist, Dan the defencist, joining forces after the Bolshevik seizure of power.

A demonstration in favour of the Constituent Assembly, Moscow, winter 1918. The Assembly had been elected by universal suffrage with a Bolshevik minority. It was dispersed by Bolshevik force at its first and only session in January 1918.

The first Soviet government, the Council of People's Commissars (Sovnarkom), in session in the Smolny Institute, Petrograd, 30 January 1918.

*Above*: Lenin in January 1918.

*Right*: Lenin making a speech at the temporary monument to Marx and Engels on Voskresensky Square (renamed Revolution Square), Moscow, 7 November 1918.

*Above*: At the Kremlin Wall,
7 November 1918. Lenin
is in the centre, Kamenev
is talking to Sverdlov
(in leather coat).

*Right*: The Tsar, his son
the Grand Duke Alexei,
and daughter the Grand
Duchess Tatiana in 1916.

Former tsarist army officers perform compulsory labour service in Petrograd in 1918.

The destruction of Annunciation Cathedral, Petrograd, 1929, one of the many thousands of churches destroyed or converted to other uses.

*Above left*: Patriarch Tikhon at the Nikita Gate of the Kremlin. Vasili Ivanovich Belavin was appointed as Patriarch by the Provisional Government in 1917 – the first since the post was abolished by Peter the Great in 1721.

*Above right*: An 'anti-Easter' tram in Leningrad, 1932. The poster reads, 'The church is the true support of counter-revolution'.

*Right*: Lenin with his sister Maria in Moscow, 1 May 1918.

debate in detail, apart from the single point that 'Congress is in favour of the peace treaty'. He plainly did not want the criticisms of his position exposed, knowing that to the ordinary citizen it would appear unpatriotic, especially as only months earlier he had been labelled a German spy.

Lenin also proposed that the capital be transferred from Petrograd to Moscow, a clear sign of retreat before the threat of German occupation. Zinoviev added that the move was only temporary, 'for the Berlin proletariat will help us move it back to Red Petrograd'. Prudently he added that, 'of course, we cannot say when that will happen. Maybe we'll have to move the capital to the Volga or the Urals; it's a matter that will be determined by the state of the world revolution.'[13] On Saturday 9 March 1918[14] all senior government officials received messages informing them that the departure for Moscow would take place the next day at 10 a.m. sharp from the Tsvetochnaya platform. Details for finding the point of departure were most precise: 'Tsvetochnaya railway halt is located beyond the Moscow Gates. After one block past the Gates, turn left onto Zastavskaya Street, then at the canvas-covered fence turn right. Near this turning is the Tsvetochnaya platform, where the train will be waiting. Try as far as possible to bring your baggage to the station before departure, using telephone number 1–19 in good time in case of emergencies; use motor cars . . .' The order was signed by the Sovnarkom Administrator of Affairs, Vladimir Bonch-Bruevich.[15]

Ignoring protests from the left and from some local workers, the government moved to Moscow on 10 and 11 March. This was in effect a signal to Germany that Russia would not defend her frontier.

While the Central Committee of the Communist Party, dominated by Lenin's Council of People's Commissars, or the Sovnarkom, was the real seat of power, in theory the country was being governed by Soviets (themselves dominated by Communists), and it was therefore the Extraordinary Congress of Soviets that ratified the decision to transfer the capital that had already been planned for 14 March. Lenin travelled by special train with his own security guards, while the government members went in another train. On their arrival, Lenin and Krupskaya moved into a two-room suite at the National Hotel. The writer Arthur Ransome, in Russia at the time as the correspondent for the London *Daily News*, recalled seeing Lenin sitting in the hotel lobby surrounded by trunks, bundles of bedding and clothes and parcels of books.[16] A few days later, Lenin and Krupskaya moved across the road to a government apartment in the Kremlin, where they had three large rooms, a servants' room and kitchen. Lenin's study was in the building where the law court establishment used to be housed.

Lenin had barely arrived in the new capital before he decided to address the proletariat. His first speech, to the new municipal government in Moscow, the local Soviet, on 12 March, was confused and shapeless. He kept harking back to 'the idiot Romanov' and 'the braggart Kerensky', whom he blamed for 'destroying the army'. From such routine accusations he then moved on to the gloomy prediction that 'war is going to start, inevitably, even though our country is in ruins'. The silent audience could not fathom what their leader was driving at, until he at last came to the point: 'We have no army, and the country that has no army has to accept an unprecedentedly shameful peace.'[17] Only four months earlier Lenin had stated with conviction that the Bolsheviks' task, 'which we will not lose sight of for a second, is the universal arming of the people and the dismantling of the standing army'.[18] He now said nothing about mass demobilization.

Lenin could not but feel the ground trembling under his feet. He had to make a supreme mental effort to find arguments to justify the division of the great country, and he knew that if he faltered now, it was not only the regime and the revolution that would fall, but he, too. He returned home from the Moscow Soviet to work on the speech he must now make at the Congress of Soviets that would either ratify his treaty or see him off. But he found nothing to add to the 'breathing-space', 'gaining time', 'gathering strength', and more pointless attacks on Kerensky, Chernov and other members of the defunct Provisional Government. He even dredged up 'the predator Napoleon', 'the predator Alexander I', 'the predatory English monarchy' and 'the Paris Commune'. On his feet for more than an hour and a half, he was unperturbed by the occasional shouts of 'Lies!' But when he declared that the newspapers were full of counter-revolutionary propaganda, and a delegate called out, 'You've shut them all down,' Lenin reacted fiercely, drawing applause from part of the audience: 'Not all of them, yet, unfortunately, but we will.'[19]

He called on the delegates to ratify 'this difficult and shameful

treaty', reminding them that 'we are expecting the international socialist proletariat to come and help start the second socialist revolution
on a world scale'.[20] Without the customary 'noisy applause', he managed to get the ratification he came for: the Congress of Soviets voted
724 in favour, 276 against, with 118 abstentions.[21] The treaty was
duly signed on 3 March 1918 by the Soviet delegation, consisting
of its chairman, Grigory Sokolnikov, Foreign Commissar Georgy
Chicherin, Interior Commissar Grigory Petrovsky, and Deputy
Foreign Commissar and secretary of the delegation Lev Karakhan.

The Bolsheviks had entered negotiations with the Germans at
Brest-Litovsk with the intention of making peace 'without annexations
or reparations' – that is, having adopted the slogan of the Socialist
International. Yet, by the time the treaty was signed, Soviet Russia
had agreed to give up nearly one million square kilometres of her
western territories, including Ukraine, whose independence she reluc-
tantly recognized, but where the Germans expected to exercise their
own authority. In addition, she was obliged to demobilize her army
and navy, including the recently formed units of the Red Army, and
to pay Germany 300 million gold roubles in reparations. As far as the
Germans were concerned, all of these gains would prove illusory, but
in the spring of 1918, with the German army in occupation of the
territory under consideration, the Treaty of Brest-Litovsk looked like
a major victory for them, and a humiliating defeat for the Bolsheviks
who had done so much to facilitate the German strategy.

As for the opponents of the treaty, whatever their party or politics,
for years they were called adventurist, destructive, and even mad. In
one of the many letters Bukharin sent to Stalin while awaiting
execution in 1938, he wrote: 'I genuinely believed that Brest was the
greatest misfortune',[22] and many thought as he did. Lenin was quite
cynical about the treaty he had just agreed. When one of the delegates,
from Yekaterinoslav, asked him sadly how she was going to tell the
workers that their city was being given to the Germans, he played his
last trump: 'Revolution is inevitable in Germany. It will discard the
Brest Treaty.'[23]

During this time, Lenin was having the apartment in the Kremlin
refurbished. The work was dragging on, and the Ulyanovs meanwhile
moved out into two rooms in the Cavalry building within the Kremlin
precinct. A week later, Lenin wrote angrily to the Deputy People's

Commissar of Public Property: 'I should very much like to have the name and address of the person you entrusted to complete the work on the apartment . . . It's dragging on inordinately, and the person guilty of such unbelievable delays must be found.'[24] The threat had its effect, and two days later the family, including Lenin's sister Maria, moved into the newly finished accommodation.[25]

Meanwhile, the German forces were pressing further and further into Russia, entering the central provinces, moving on Petrograd and Pskov and Sevastopol. Alarmed messages were pouring in. The Russian people could not understand how it was that the Kaiser's troops were arriving in passenger trains, like tourists, and occupying town after town without a fight. Lenin tried to pacify the population with another decree, stating that in view of the treaty ratified on 15 March 1918 by the Fourth Extraordinary Congress of Soviets, equivalent to unconditional surrender, there was to be no armed resistance offered to the Germans.[26]

In their semi-underground paper, the Mensheviks wrote, half in sarcasm, half in sorrow: 'The Soviet regime has had to pay for the right to exist by carrying out all the orders and wishes of German imperialism. By all its latest measures, the Soviet regime has added its own stamp to Wilhelm's bondage of [Russia]. Soon we won't know whether we have a Soviet regime or a Mirbach* regime.'[27]

The Commissariat of Foreign Affairs was meanwhile sending cautious notes in an effort to stop the Germans from advancing beyond the agreed line. Foreign Commissar Chicherin cabled Berlin that the German army should not cross the Ukrainian border: 'We repeat our proposal to the German government that it express itself more clearly as to where it places the frontier of the Ukrainian Republic.'[28] Here was a once great state asking a foreign power to determine its own frontier.

Lenin, prepared to do anything to preserve his regime, accepted an exchange of ambassadors, Count Wilhelm Mirbach coming to Moscow, while Berlin received Adolf Abramovich Ioffe, a member of the VTsIK, candidate member of the Central Committee and personal friend of Trotsky. After his arrival, Ioffe cabled Moscow that he had failed to persuade the Germans to stop their advance towards the

---

* Mirbach was the German envoy in Moscow.

Caucasus. He reported that they were demanding the return of their naval ships in the Black Sea at Sevastopol before they would halt their advance: 'I advise we accept their ultimatum and return the ships at Novorossiisk and Sevastopol . . . and declare that Russia accepts responsibility not to cross the indicated demarcation line . . . We must insist on preserving the frontiers of the Brest treaty.'[29] Moscow, having long forgotten its 'revolutionary determination', again begged Germany not to infringe the understandings.

The Brest-Litovsk treaty had not been an inevitability; it was the price paid for the disintegration of the Russian Imperial Army and the Bolsheviks' acceptance of German help. Russia was now in a militarily hopeless condition. In 1917 the task had been a simple one: to hold fast against an enemy who was no less exhausted and maimed. It had been clear that America's entry into the war in April 1917 would soon bring dividends to the Allied side. When they came to power, however, the Bolsheviks had debts to repay, and this could only be done by way of national defeat. Lenin's decrees of land and peace in November 1917 had had the desired effect of disintegrating what remained of the Russian army, as the largely peasant soldiers departed from the front and the garrison towns to the villages to claim their share of land. When the Bolsheviks went to Brest-Litovsk, therefore, they had little if any bargaining power. Yet, only two or three months after the treaty was signed, Lenin's attitude was shifting. Ioffe was reporting growing difficulties in Germany, increased disorder in the army, and awareness that Germany could not beat the Western powers. Meanwhile the Bolsheviks were pouring money into making revolutionary propaganda in Germany. Just as the Germans with Bolshevik help had undermined Russia in 1916–17, so now the Bolsheviks, their secret allies, were replying in kind.

As early as the Fifth Congress of Soviets on 5 July 1918, Lenin, heckled and almost howled down by the SRs, began to sound a new note. His pathological fear that the state was about to perish had subsided, and he permitted himself to speak about Germany and the other 'imperialist plunderers', in a different way, admittedly without naming them: 'The maimed beast has torn off a great chunk of our living organism . . . but it is [it] and not we who will perish, because the speed with which [its] resistance is failing will quickly take [it] to the abyss.'[30] The main threat to Lenin's regime, however, was not the

Germans, but domestic discontent with the Bolsheviks. Starvation was strangling the cities of European Russia, where the Bolsheviks' main support was located. Opposition was growing. After the euphoria of October, the realization emerged that slogans and appeals and decrees would not deal with the mountain of problems. A contemporary who knew Lenin recalled the words of a Soviet diplomat in Berlin: 'We are doomed and must hang on till the last chance . . . Our endeavour will end in failure and severe punishment awaits us. We made this bed and we're going to have to lie in it.'[31]

The summer of 1918 saw a strange political metamorphosis: the Bolsheviks sensed the weakening of Germany, while the Germans were no less aware of the situation in Russia and the Bolshevik agony. The Germans had seen the Bolsheviks as their unofficial allies, and had helped them undermine the Provisional Government and get into power. The main German objective in removing Russia from the war, however, had been to release troops needed to crush the West. But by the summer of 1918, as the Russian civil war began to escalate, the Germans found themselves becoming increasingly drawn into the complexities of local political and military relations, especially in Ukraine. Their hopes for a rich supply of grain from 'Russia's bread-basket' foundered because the agrarian economy was disrupted, while their hopes for the transfer of large numbers of troops westwards were submerged in the quagmire of Ukrainian politics. As the historian of the Brest-Litovsk Treaty, John Wheeler-Bennett, wrote: 'A million troops immobilized in the east was the price of German aggrandize-ment, and half that number might well have turned the scale . . . in the west. [Only] a few cavalry divisions were necessary in March and April 1918 to widen the gap between the French and British, thus severing the two armies. These were not available on the Western Front, but at that moment three cavalry divisions were propping up successive puppet governments in Kiev.'[32]

The Germans nevertheless sensed that the Bolsheviks were acting convulsively, that they were bending under the strain of the problems heaped on them. After visiting Lenin in the Kremlin for less than one hour on 16 May, the German Ambassador, Count Mirbach, was convinced that 'Lenin firmly believes in his star' and remains 'inexhau-stibly optimistic'.[33] A month later, however, he reported that, in view of 'the Bolsheviks' growing instability', Germany should 'prepare to regroup our forces'. He wrote that the monarchists and Constitutional Democrats 'might form the nucleus of a future new order', and suggested that, 'with the proper precautionary measures and appropriately disguised, we might begin supplying these circles with the financial means they require . . . the Bolshevik system is in its death throes'. This notion was not supported in Berlin, where it was judged, realistically, that Russian monarchists and liberals were more likely than Lenin to be interested in reuniting their country, whereas it was in Germany's interest to prevent Russian consolidation.[34] Mirbach's opinion at the end of June was more emphatic: 'Today, after more than two months of careful observation, I can no longer give a favourable diagnosis of Bolshevism; we are undoubtedly standing at the bedside of a terminally sick patient; despite possible moments of apparent improvement, in the last analysis he is doomed.'[35]

Mirbach might have said the same of imperial Germany. By the late spring of 1918 the effect of the US entry into the war was being felt on the Western Front, and by late summer the German High Command privately recognized that victory was not possible. Austria-Hungary's war effort virtually ground to a halt at the same time, and on 3 October the Central Powers were ready to parley. In Germany itself the tide of revolution was also rising, demands for an end to the war grew more strident, and the governnment's will was flagging.

Thus, the summer of 1918 saw both unspoken allies suffering mutual frailty, and consequently reassessing their tactics. Lenin began taking the line set by Trotsky during the negotiations at Brest-Litovsk, 'neither peace nor war', when the intention had been to procrastinate by refusing the proffered terms of the treaty and threatening further military action, of which Soviet Russia was barely capable.

The Left SRs, especially in Ukraine, where armed clashes with the German forces and their local allies among the nationalists were a frequent occurrence, were openly campaigning to repudiate the Brest-Litovsk Treaty, to break off diplomatic relations with Germany and to resume the fight to free the country of its presence. Mirbach was depicted as Lenin's master, the Bolshevik regime as his pawn. On 6 July 1918, in an act characteristic of Socialist Revolutionary history, the Left SRs assassinated the representative of German militarism in Russia.

Two hours after Mirbach's assassination, Lenin and Sverdlov arrived at the German embassy on Denezhnaya Street to convey their condolences and their displeasure. Lenin cabled Ioffe to 'call on the German foreign minister and express the Russian government's indignation'. Lenin was keen to show his loyalty to the treaty, and the assassins would be tried by a revolutionary tribunal.[36] A week later, however, while resting at Kuntsevo, he was informed by Chicherin that Berlin was requesting the Sovnarkom's agreement to the transfer of a battalion of German troops to defend their embassy in Moscow. Lenin was adamant that this would not happen. Without convening the Sovnarkom, he told Chicherin to send back a note of refusal. He was now ready for the worst.

Speaking on 15 July at a session of the VTsIK in the Metropole Hotel in Moscow, Lenin was virtually ready to tear up the Brest-Litovsk agreement. To allow a German battalion to enter the city, he exclaimed, would be tantamount to 'the beginning of the occupation of Russia by foreign forces'. Ignoring the obvious fact that the Germans had been in occupation of vast tracts of Russian territory since the first months of the war, he announced 'there are limits' beyond which the Republic would not go, and it would be ready 'to a man to defend the country with arms'.[37] Lenin was repeating what his opponents, the Left Communists and Left SRs, had been saying only four months earlier, and was revealing that he had plainly exaggerated the danger: Germany was in no better a position than Russia.

The refusal to allow German troops into Moscow did not provoke a harsh response from the Germans; they merely moved their embassy to Revel (Tallin), the capital of newly independent Estonia. Lenin was at last coming to realize that he was dealing with a changed, weaker Germany, and he soon altered his attitude towards Berlin, as was to be shown in his famous 'Letter to the American workers'. Written on 20 August 1918, it makes it clear that he was no longer afraid of Germany, but was thinking instead of 'the predatory beasts of Anglo-French and American imperialism'. He declared that in the event of an attack by 'these sharks . . . I will not hesitate for a second to make a similar treaty with the predatory German imperialists.'[38] In other words, he was ready to help Germany against the Entente. Russia's payments and her deliveries of grain and metals helped Germany resist the superior force of the Western powers. In return, Germany promised not to give help to the White movement.

The Treaty of Brest-Litovsk turned Russia into a second-rate power. Her incompetent leaders miscalculated the strength of Germany, and were willing to sacrifice almost everything to remain in power. The fate of the Black Sea Fleet illustrates the point. According to the terms of the treaty, Russia was obliged to bring her warships into port and disarm them forthwith.[39] Commissars, committees, soviets and extraordinary commissions held endless meetings and countless votes, and sent telegrams to Moscow and Kiev for a decision on how to deal with the fleet. At the time the treaty was signed, the bulk of the warships were anchored at Sevastopol, and as a German naval force approached – albeit mostly small units with no heavy weaponry or logistical support – Lenin and Trotsky ordered the Soviet ships to move to Novorossiisk on the Black Sea. On 27 April 1918, Red Army commander F.F. Raskolnikov reported to Lenin that eight mine-layers, four transporters and five cruisers had left Sevastopol for Novorossiisk. Next day two battleships, the *Volya* and *Svobodnaya Rossiya*, together with the mine-layer *Derzky*, weighed anchor for the open sea. Meanwhile, Lenin took further, more drastic measures to evade the Brest terms on naval shipping. In a secret directive to the commander and chief commissar of the Black Sea Fleet, he wrote: 'Upon representations by the Supreme army council, the Sovnarkom orders you on receipt of this to destroy all the ships of the Black Sea Fleet and commercial shipping at Novorossiisk.'[40] As a few advanced German units approached Novorossiisk, Lenin's order to scuttle the fleet was carried out on 18 June 1918. Still awaiting the Germans in Sevastopol, however, were the crews of Soviet mine-layers and cruisers, as well as the entire submarine fleet, aircraft, battle equipment, stores, workshops and port facilities. Later, the *Volya* and six mine-layers returned to Sevastopol and were seized by the Germans. Raskolnikov accused Commissars Vakhromeev and Avilov-Glebov of treason.[41]

The whole affair took place because Lenin had misjudged the condition of an enemy who was himself being bled white. It took him three or four months to realize that Germany's position was no better than his own. Clearly, his attitude to the Brest-Litovsk treaty was more complex than might appear, and it was still evolving. The final part of this process Lenin expressed by concentrating all his political, diplomatic and ideological efforts into creating a revolutionary situation in Germany. Large sums of money were dedicated to the task.

In a letter which Lenin wrote while resting in Gorki in the late summer of 1918 and which Sverdlov read to the Central Committee, the Bolshevik leader claimed that 'a political crisis has broken out in Germany, the government is wobbling, it has no support among the masses. It will end with the transfer of power to the proletariat. Bolshevik tactics have been justified. We will not break the Brest treaty now, but we will raise the question of giving help to the German workers in their difficult struggle with their own and English imperialism.'[42] Lenin was thus arguing in favour of instigating revolution in Germany, but was against denouncing the Brest treaty for the moment. He was afraid of the West – Britain, France and America – but had again miscalculated, since they adopted a wholly passive position towards Russia's domestic concerns.

The results of Bolshevik influence in Germany and Austria were marked. German-language anti-war and anti-government propaganda, printed in Russia, was distributed by the Soviet envoy to all corners of Germany, and to the front.[43] Ioffe reported that, through front-men, the Soviet legation had established a fund of ten million marks to supply German workers with arms and food. Berlin sent notes protesting against Bolshevik interference in Germany's domestic affairs, finally expelling Ioffe and the other Soviet representatives at the beginning of November 1918, and withdrawing their own from Russia. The game was up, however, and a year after the Bolshevik seizure of power, on 9 November 1918, Kaiser Wilhelm was overthrown, and on 11 November the Social Democrats Phillipp Scheidemann and Friedrich Ebert signed the Armistice with the Allies. The Bolsheviks could now announce that the Brest-Litovsk Treaty of 3 March 1918 was totally devoid of force and meaning. The Entente had saved Russia from its humiliating conditions, ending the dangerous game played by Lenin and the Germans.

The first partition of Russia had lasted a mere nine months. Lenin had shown himself to be a wily and resourceful tactician, but not a strategist. In the final analysis, it may be that history has justified his actions, since the 'indecent peace' was short-lived. This was not thanks to Lenin, however, but to the Allies who indirectly served his purpose. Strategically, Lenin had consistently overrated Germany's strength. Bewitched by the magic of power, he had been willing to accept the debasement of a great nation, and had lacked the vision to see that Germany's situation on the Western Front was hopeless.

### White Raiments

In her *Petersburg Diary*, published in Munich in 1921, the poet Zinaïda Gippius wrote: 'The whole population of Petersburg have been "put on the books" . . . Practically all the intellectuals who were left were working as Bolshevik clerks. They were paid just enough to die of hunger, but slowly. By the spring of 1919 nearly all our friends had become unrecognizable . . . People with swollen bellies were advised to eat their potatoes unpeeled, but by the spring potatoes themselves had vanished, as had our one delicacy, potato-skin flat-cakes.' Gippius noted that among the intellectuals who had been 'driven into service by hunger and the lash', only a handful had become Bolsheviks, and these 'worked zealously, made dirty deals with the commissars and waxed eloquent about the "people's wrath"'. Another group which adapted was from the lower-middle class, who worked as sweated labour and thought only of their next meal. 'The overwhelming majority of the Russian intelligentsia, to their credit, are those who have "given in", suffering greatly and gritting their teeth, and bearing life's cross of cast iron. Among them are almost *all* the officers of the Red Army, the former officers of the Russian Army.'

Gippius recorded that at the mobilizations that were taking place almost monthly in 1918, former tsarist officers were being arrested, together with their families 'and even their uncles and aunts'. The whole family would be kept in prison until the authorities were satisfied that the officer was a 'compliant hero', when they would be released, the officer into the army, the rest into constant surveillance. 'And should an army commissar report adversely on this "military specialist", his uncles and aunts, not to speak of his wife and children, will be sent somewhere to do forced labour, or back to prison.'[44]

On 2 December 1918 Trotsky, as People's Commissar for War and the chief organizer of the Red Army, cabled V.I. Mezhlauk, a Red Army commissar, urging greater discipline to halt the rate at which Red Army men were surrendering to the Whites: 'The eleventh division has shown its total bankruptcy. Units are still surrendering without a fight. The root of the trouble is in the command staff. Evidently . . . attention has been paid to the combatant and technical side of the business, while forgetting about the political. I advise special attention be paid to the recruited officers, and that command duties only be given to former officers whose families are living within the borders of Soviet Russia, and they must be made to sign a personal undertaking that they will answer for the fate of their families.'[45]

Lenin's promise to turn the imperialist war into a civil war was succeeding monstrously. The bourgeoisie, now classed as 'ex-people', and having been deprived of a place in the sun because of their class origin, were simply condemned to resist. As early as May 1917, the Commander-in-Chief of the Imperial Army, General M.V. Alexeev, declared at an officers' congress at Mogilev: 'We must all unite on the single great platform that Russia is in danger. As members of the Great Army, we must save her. Let that platform unite you ... A united family must be formed from the body of Russian officers.'[46] Alexeev was immediately relieved of his post by the Provisional Government, but it was plain that the Russian officer corps could become the backbone of military opposition to the revolution, should they begin to feel that things were going too far.

In rejecting the path of reform and the evolutionary development of the country, the Bolsheviks had predetermined that civil war must follow. In September 1916, Lenin had declared unequivocally that 'whoever recognizes class war must recognize civil wars, which in any class society represent the natural and, in certain circumstances, inevitable continuation, development and sharpening of class war'.[47] This 'natural' continuation began with the coup in October 1917, but in the summer of 1918 it acquired a terrible, destructive and utterly inhuman form. At its height in December 1919, Lenin tried to blame it on international capital, which he accused of dragging out the conflict.[48] Certainly the imperialist powers did much to assist the counter-revolution, but their efforts were uncoordinated and unplanned, and were not the cause of the appalling Russian civil strife.

At the heart of Lenin's strategy was the aim of destroying the old order, the norms and ingrained customs of Russian life. He initiated a policy of violence against millions of people, and himself took a daily hand in applying the measures, giving advice and instructions on how the policy should be carried out. In one of his fundamental works of the revolutionary period, 'How to Organize Competition', printed later but immediately put into daily practice, he made it plain that communes and Party cells in town and village must devote themselves 'to one general aim: the *cleansing* of the Russian land of any harmful insects, swindler-fleas, wealthy bugs and so on and so on. In one place, they should imprison a dozen wealthy people, a dozen crooks, half a dozen workers who shirk work ... In another they should be put to work on cleaning [farming equipment]. In a third place they should be given yellow cards when they come out of lock-up, so that all the people can keep an eye on them as *dangerous* individuals until they have improved. In a fourth place, one out of every ten people guilty of parasitism should be executed on the spot. In a fifth ...'[49]

Such were the measures that ignited the fires of the Russian civil war. Lenin cannot have imagined that his attack on the better-off peasantry – the kulaks – would not spark off civil strife. He was aware that of the fifteen million peasant households, only some two million were 'kulaks', or 'wealthy'. These he called bloodsuckers, spiders, leeches and vampires, and it was against them in August 1918 that he hurled the war-cry: 'Merciless war against these kulaks! Death to them!'[50]

When Stalin set about collectivizing agriculture five years after Lenin's death, he had no need for new slogans – they had already been prepared for him. The 'cleansing' or purging of the Russian land became one of the chief sources of social disorder, and it was bloody indeed. Lenin did not restrict himself to the methods he had proclaimed after the October coup, but improved them constantly. For example, in November 1922 he scribbled in pencil to Stalin:

On the matter of expelling the Mensheviks, Popular Socialists, Kadets and so on, I would like to ask some questions, since this operation, which was begun before my holiday, hasn't been completed yet. Has it been decided to 'uproot' all Popular Socialists? Peshekhonov, Myakotin, Gornfeld, Petrishchev and the others? I think they should all be expelled. The SRs are the most dangerous, because they're smarter. Also A.N. Potresov, Izgoev and all the people working on *Ekonomist* (Ozerov and many more). The Mensheviks Rozanov (a physician and smart), Vigdorchik (Migulo or somesuch), Lyubov Nikolaevna Radchenko and her younger daughter (I hear they're vicious enemies of Bolshevism); N.A. Rozhkov (he has to be expelled, he'll never come round); S.L. Frank (the author of *Methodology*). The Commission under Mantsev, Messing and the others, should compile lists and several hundred of such gentlemen must be expelled abroad without mercy. *We will cleanse*

*Russia for a long time to come.* This has to be done at once. By the end of the
SR trial, no later. Arrest several hundred even without giving any reasons:
you may leave, gentlemen!'[51]

Lenin did more than merely invent the notion of 'cleansing Russia'.
He also compiled lists, and kept a constant eye on the process. In
1922 he wrote to Unshlikht: 'Please be so kind as to arrange to return
to me all the attached papers with notes: who has been expelled, who
is in prison, who (and why) has been exempted from expulsion. Make
short notes on this page.'[52]

The Russian civil war developed into one of the bloodiest in history.
As early as December 1917 Generals Alexeev and Kornilov began
forming their Volunteer Army in the south. The Bolsheviks, realizing
that either they must rapidly create a battle-worthy force or see their
enterprise fail, soon forgot their promises to disband the army and
create a people's militia. In giving Trotsky the task of creating the
Red Army, Lenin showed good judgment. Despite lacking military
knowledge or experience, Trotsky was a brilliant organizer, and as
tough and unforgiving as any Bolshevik leader. In September 1918
he organized the Revolutionary War Council of the Republic, serving
until 1925 as its chairman, responsible for operational and strategic
planning, political control, revolutionary tribunals and inspection.
The Council met rarely at first, since most of its members were
engaged in the field, but after the summer of 1919 it functioned as
the highest body for managing the defence of the country, under the
ultimate sanction of the Party Central Committee.

A number of fronts formed as early as 1918, with numerous different
armies. Their military councils were appointed by Trotsky himself,
and charged with the task of keeping an eye on the former tsarist
officers now serving as Red Army commanders, and of nipping in the
bud any sign of panic as well as any hint of counter-revolution. Trotsky
told his commissars 'not to take their hands off their revolvers'. Lenin
was concerned about possible betrayal. 'We'll put each one under a
commissar,' Trotsky reassured him. 'Maybe it would be better to put
them under two who can use their fists,' Lenin replied. 'Surely we
have some Communists who can use their fists.'[53]

Trotsky's orders were invariably blunt and to the point. He cabled
Raskolnikov, the commander in Kazan: 'In case of dubious com-

manders, put tough commissars over them with revolvers in hand. Give senior commanders the choice: victory or death. Don't take your eyes off unreliable commanders. In the event of desertion by a member of the command staff, the commissar pays with his head.'[54] He cabled Lenin at the same time to report the disastrous situation in Kazan: 'The absence of revolvers creates an impossible position at the front. It's impossible to maintain discipline without revolvers. I suggest Comrades Muralov and Pozern requisition revolvers from all persons who are not on combat duty. At the same time, Tula [where arms were manufactured] must be tightened up. We can't fight without revolvers.'[55]

The Bolshevik use of force in virtually all sectors of state policy was bound to provoke protest, open resistance and a widespread refusal to cooperate. In the army this manifested itself as mass desertion, the peak being reached in the second half of 1918 and early 1919. Men who had been forced to fight for the Bolsheviks against the White forces were declining the honour at an astronomical rate. In May 1919, when the government formed special units to deal with this problem, nearly 80,000 men were arrested, according to the Revolutionary War Council's own figures.[56] After an amnesty was announced in June for those who returned to the ranks, and severe punishment for those who did not, 98,183 men presented themselves to the authorities, and in the course of the year 1,761,000 men were either detained or registered as voluntary returnees. If to this figure we add the 917,000 who evaded call-up in the second half of 1918 and early 1919, the scale of the boycott becomes apparent.[57] Lenin's appeal of February 1918, entitled 'The Socialist Fatherland is in Danger' (written in fact by Trotsky), had been formulated as a Sovnarkom decree, and called on Soviets and revolutionary organizations to defend all positions to the last drop of blood.[58] Clearly, if the proletariat and committed citizens were expected to go this far, then any bourgeois resisters, counter-revolutionary elements and deserters could only expect to be executed.

From Lenin's vast civil war correspondence, nothing connected with Trotsky was published except criticism or material showing him in a negative light. Such telegrams as that sent from Lenin to Trotsky in autumn 1918 were never made public: 'Thank you, my convalescence is progressing well. I am sure that the crushing of the Czechs and White Guards at Kazan, and the kulak-bloodsuckers who support them, will be carried out in an exemplary, ruthless manner. With ardent greetings.'[59]

In the conduct of the civil war, Lenin was somewhat overshadowed by Trotsky. Lenin confined himself to instructions of a general political nature, and to making demands which often betrayed his anxiety. He cabled one front council in May 1919: 'If we don't conquer the Urals by the winter, it'll be the end of the revolution, I'm sure.' In another cable, this time to Zinoviev, demanding that more Communists be sent to the front, he warned, 'Otherwise, we'll collapse.' And to Rakovsky and Ioffe in Kiev: 'The demise of the entire revolution is absolutely inevitable if there is no rapid victory in the Donbass.'[60]

Unlike other members of the government, Lenin showed no desire to go to the front, where he believed the fate of the revolution was being decided. At any rate, he never raised the question at the Central Committee or the Sovnarkom. In the strict sense, there were no fronts as such. Lenin was often shown maps on which he gazed at various ovals, arcs, arrows and dotted lines, but there never was an unbroken 'ring of fire' that corresponded to a front. Indeed, it was of the greatest strategic advantage to the Bolsheviks that the White forces of Admiral Kolchak in Siberia, General Denikin in the south and General Yudenich in the Baltic region, and the other anti-Bolshevik formations were so scattered. However hard they tried to unite and coordinate themselves, they never succeeded, despite the help of the Allied intervention.

Lenin, while rarely involving himself in strictly military issues, dealt with the political and social context in which such matters arose. The civil war was fought not only in strictly military theatres, but also in dozens of enclaves where peasant risings were constantly flaring up, occasionally in areas where intervention forces had appeared. It was necessary to stamp out these uprisings, and Lenin made it one of his special concerns. He mobilized local Party bodies, sent reinforcements and despatched orders on how to deal with the insurgents, speculators and saboteurs. On 29 August 1918 he cabled the Party authorities at Penza in southern Russia to express his 'extreme indignation that absolutely nothing definite has been received from you about what serious measures have been taken to suppress the kulaks remorselessly and to confiscate their grain in the five districts run by you. Your inaction is criminal.'[61]

In the same month he advised the Party boss in Saratov 'temporarily to appoint your own army commanders and shoot conspirators and waverers without asking anyone or any idiotic red tape',[62] and in December 1918 he told Shlyapnikov to 'catch and shoot the Astrakhan speculators and bribe-takers. These swine have to be dealt so that everyone will remember it for years.'[63] He cabled Sokolnikov on the southern front that delay in suppressing a Cossack uprising was 'the height of disgrace ... Whatever happens, this uprising has to be stamped out to the last ... If you are not absolutely sure you have forces for a ferocious and relentless reprisal, cable us immediately and in detail.'[64]

Lenin's orders and exhortations streamed out of the Kremlin, all of their varied contents boiling down to one essential consideration: achieve your aim at any cost, regardless of losses. The Lenin who seemed externally so gentle and good-natured, who enjoyed a laugh, who loved animals and was prone to sentimental reminiscences, was transformed when class or political questions arose. He at once became savagely sharp, uncompromising, remorseless and vengeful. Even in such a state, however, he was capable of black humour. Trotsky recalled that when he heard the news of Mirbach's assassination, he called on Lenin: '"What a business!" I said, digesting the rather unusual news. "Still, we mustn't complain that life's monotonous." "Yes, the routine knocking-off of a petty bourgeois," he replied with a disquieting laugh. We had to go to the embassy to express our "condolences". It was agreed that Lenin, Sverdlov and, I think, Chicherin would go ... Lenin tried to recall the appropriate phrase in German. He nearly got it wrong ... He almost started laughing under his breath, got into his coat and said firmly to Sverdlov, "Let's go." His face changed to a stony grey.'[65]

Lenin's language was becoming that of the inquisitor, the prosecutor and the executioner. In the summer of 1918 he ordered the commander at Penza to 'carry out relentless terror against the kulaks, the priests and White Guards, put any doubtfuls into a concentration camp outside the town'.[66] He cabled Trotsky in August: 'Shouldn't we tell [the commanders] that from now on we're applying the model of the French Revolution and putting on trial and even executing [the army commander and] the senior commanders if they hold back and fail in their actions?'[67] To Trotsky again the following month he cabled that he was 'surprised and alarmed by the delay in operations against Kazan. In my opinion, you shouldn't spare the city and delay any further, because what is needed is remorseless destruction.'[68] To an unknown addressee he cabled on 3 June 1918: 'You can tell Ter* that if there is an offensive, he must make *all* preparations to burn Baku down totally, and this should be announced in print in Baku.'[69]

During the civil war Lenin told his commanders to shoot miscreants for a widening range of offences: for taking part in a conspiracy, resisting arrest, concealing arms, disobedience, backwardness, carelessness and false reports. Despite the fact that he preferred to remain either in the Kremlin or in his comfortable villa outside Moscow, where he could not see the horrors of the war, by the orders and instructions he disseminated Lenin did much to exacerbate the cruelty. How he might have reacted had he seen the carnage in person cannot be guessed. It is true that in the many articles he published and the many public speeches he made during this period, he rarely called for the shooting of counter-revolutionaries or traitors. He preferred to issue his harsh instructions in coded telegrams, confidential notes or anonymous decrees in the name of the Sovnarkom. He cared about his reputation, and did not want to stain it with the notoriety of a hangman. In this he was moderately successful, as history has not on the whole judged him badly in this light.

In 1918 the greater part of the Russian population rejected the Bolshevik revolution, yet ultimately the Bolsheviks won the day. This was in part because their opponents had no clear or appealing ideas, and by responding to Red terror with White terror they alienated the simple peasant and ordinary citizen no less than did the Reds. In the summer of 1919 Kerensky, who was for neither the Reds nor the Whites, told foreign journalists: 'there is no crime the [White] agents of Admiral Kolchak would not commit ... Executions and torture have been committed in Siberia, and often the population of whole villages have been flogged, including the teachers and intellectuals.'[70]

---

* Saak Ter-Gabrielyan, the Commissar for Oil in the Caspian oil centre of Baku and head of the local Cheka.

White terror was just as repugnant as Red terror, but its chief difference was that it emerged spontaneously from below, and locally, while Red terror was applied as an instrument of state policy, and was therefore bound to be more effective.[71]

The Bolsheviks succeeded in defending the 'gains of the revolution' and, despite desertion of fantastic proportions, in creating an army of three million men. Using systematic terror, coercion, compulsion, hostages, a wide-ranging system of punitive measures and propaganda on a scale never before seen in Russia – or anywhere else – they forced the peasants and workers to fight for the Soviet regime in the hope that at least some of the generous inducements promised by the commissars might be realized. Lenin viewed Trotsky's line on 'military specialists' with mistrust at first, and when Trotsky told him in the middle of 1919 that there were already 30,000 former tsarist officers serving in the Red Army, he did not believe him. When he did become convinced, he had no illusions – he knew that only an insignificant number of former tsarist officers had joined the Reds out of conviction. The majority were hostages – or their families were. It would not be possible to beat the Whites with 'closet' Whites.

Trotsky also persuaded Lenin that they would get nowhere without compulsion: 'If we wait for the peasant to understand what's happening it'll be too late.' Lenin agreed, but was concerned that even committed units might lack steadfastness. 'Russians are too kind, they lack the ability to apply determined methods of revolutionary terror.'[72] With Lenin's approval, on 12 August 1919 Trotsky instructed military councils to create surveillance units: 'Before we get the chance to create a kulak who will fight the enemy, we must at least have a mini-kulak who will tackle unruliness and shirkers among our own troops.'[73]

As well as unruliness and shirking, anti-semitism was also widespread in the Red Army. Among the consequences of the civil war in Ukraine in particular, where armies of bewildering political loyalties swept back and forth, was the near-destruction of Jewish village life. But anti-semitism in the Red Army as such was a separate issue. When Lenin was sent reports of ethnic vandalism by his own forces, he saw it as just another evil of civil war. In November 1920, Zilist, a Cheka official, reported on pogroms by the First Cavalry Army (immortalized in the 'Red Cavalry' stories of Isaac Babel):

A new wave of pogroms has swept through the district. The number of those killed cannot be established ... As they retreated, units of the First Cavalry Army (and the 6th Division) destroyed, looted and killed the Jewish population. In Rogachev, more than thirty were killed, in Baranovichi – fourteen, in Romanov – unknown, in Chudnov – fourteen. These are new pages [in the history] of pogroms in Ukraine. All the villages named have been pillaged. The district of Berdichev has also been destroyed. Gorshki and Chernyakhov have been totally plundered.[74]

Lenin never demanded that the perpetrators of these atrocities be brought to account.

In July 1921 it was reported to Lenin that bandits were committing pogroms in the provinces of Minsk and Gomel on 'a Ukrainian scale', and that their activities were spreading with 'catastrophic speed'. Examples were given of villages where those killed numbered between forty-six and 175, and where 'the [provincial Party secretaries], military commissars and special units are doing nothing to fight against it'.[75]

The barbarities committed by both sides were tainted with anti-semitism. The propaganda pumped out by ultra-right-wing bodies, claiming that the Bolshevik revolution was a Jewish revolution and that the commissars were all Jews, found an echo among the masses. Lenin seemed to feel no need to pay special attention to this problem. The reports he received on the subject invariably bear his usual laconic scrawl: 'For the archives'. On the other hand, when it was suggested he make sixteen three-minute gramophone records for propaganda purposes, he chose as one of his themes 'On pogroms and the persecution of the Jews'. He naturally assessed the question from a class point of view. 'It is not the Jews who are the labourers' enemies,' he said, 'it is the capitalists of all countries. Among the Jews, workers and labourers are the majority. They are our brothers being oppressed by the capitalists, our comrades in the struggle for socialism. The Jews have their kulaks, their exploiters and capitalists, just like the Russians, just like all nations.'[76] According to Lenin, it was 'capitalists who inflamed hatred against the Jews', not individuals and organizations. While condemning anti-semitism in general, Lenin was unable to analyse, let alone eradicate, its prevalence in Soviet society.

The civil war enabled the Soviet regime to make its hallmark the severe limitation of the rights and freedoms that had been proclaimed after the October coup. Speaking in April 1919 at a plenary meeting of the Central Committee of Trade Unions, Lenin dispelled any illusions that might still linger among its members: 'We never promised liberties right and left, on the contrary . . . [Clause 23 of the RSFSR Constitution] states plainly that we deny liberties to socialists if they used them to harm the socialist revolution.'[77] Henceforth the Bolsheviks would imprison 'several dozen or several hundred instigators, whether they are guilty or innocent, conscious or unwitting', as long as the interests of the revolution were protected. At the First All-Russian Congress on Adult Education in May 1921, Lenin made a two-hour speech in which he stated, among other things, that 'we do not recognize either freedom or equality or labour democracy, if they conflict with the interests of the emancipation of labour from the oppression of capital'.[78] The civil war gave the Bolsheviks the excuse to realize the dictatorship of the Party in full, even though they called it the dictatorship of the proletariat.

It was therefore not surprising that the great mass of Russian army officers, entrepreneurs, intelligentsia, peasantry and ordinary citizens, realizing that they would never enjoy basic rights and liberties under this regime, would rise up against the Bolsheviks. Having been put virtually outside the law and condemned to perform only work which the commissars permitted them to do, these people had no choice. The Whites, though they did not make the most of their opportunities, lost chiefly because they lacked a compelling idea which might have united them. The democratic case that might have been made by such as Kerensky and his sympathizers was virtually commandeered by the Bolsheviks and their high-powered propaganda machine. Slogans in favour of restoring the throne made no impact. Simple anti-Bolshevism prompted the response, 'Why are you any better?' Replacing the Bolsheviks with a White dictatorship was unappealing, especially to the peasants.

The White movement also failed because it was led by military men and not by politicians. The White generals did not understand that the only possible unifying idea that was acceptable was one which advanced the development of Russia – namely, the idea that was born in February 1917 and culminated in the Constituent Assembly. They could not rise above a military and strategic understanding of the situation. Lenin outplayed and beat them above all politically, by able manoeuvring, altering his tactics and his slogans, by rabble-rousing when necessary and by using violence as a universal instrument of policy. Whatever doubts he might have had at the beginning of 1917, by now he was convinced that the future of Communism was assured in Russia. On May Day 1919, he declared to the assembled crowds on Red Square: 'Most of you who are not yet thirty–thirty-five years old will see the flowering of Communism . . . the edifice of the social- ist society which we have founded is not a Utopia.'[79] Few realized at the time that this had been a Pyrrhic victory. But then, Lenin, despite his powerful intellect and mighty will, lacked historical perspective. He deeply and sincerely believed that the path he was blazing and cementing with violence would lead to the desired end.

The Whites did not want a barracks-style society, and though in a sense they were proved right historically, they lacked political and practical ability. Writing of the origins of their weakness and the defeat of their cause, Zinaida Gippius lamented: 'We know why the White movement perished . . . The leaders miscalculated the strength of the enemy. Yes, some units harboured an ill-considered, blind affirmation of the old, a yearning for the past, a failure to realize that the past would not come back. But the main reason the Volunteer Army failed was that it was totally abandoned. Both internally and externally. It was abandoned not only by the Russians, but also by its perfidious allies of yesterday.'[80]

Be that as it may, long before the end of the civil war Lenin had good reason to feel he had won, and he set about reviving the dying fires of world revolution.

## Regicide

On 18 July 1918 the Sovnarkom held an extraordinary session, attended by thirty-three members and chaired by Lenin. A special statement was read by the chairman of the All-Russian Central Execu- tive Committee of Soviets (VTsIK), Yakov Sverdlov. Thin-faced, and sporting a goatee beard, moustache and pince-nez, Sverdlov read a note from the minutes of the VTsIK, which had already met, to the effect that Nicholas II had been executed in Yekaterinburg.

Adjusting his pince-nez, Sverdlov – who would himself die of Spanish 'flu within a year – read that, following the discovery by the Cheka of an extensive White Guard plot to abduct the former tsar and his family, on the night of 16 July the Yekaterinburg Soviet had ordered the execution of Nicholas Romanov. The rest of the family had been evacuated to a safe place. Sverdlov raised his head and surveyed his audience. There was no reaction, everyone remained calm. Chicherin was writing, Sklyansky was whispering something in Karakhan's ear. They accepted the information as a routine event on the revolutionary agenda. Sverdlov went on to say that in the name of the VTsIK he regarded the Yekaterinburg Soviet's action as correct. He and two others were then asked to compose a statement for the press.

Lenin paused from writing a note to Chicherin and asked in his guttural voice: 'Any questions for Comrade Sverdlov?' Someone might have mentioned that on 29 January 1918 they had decided to transfer Nicholas Romanov to Petrograd for trial,[81] or that in early May Sverdlov himself had reported the transfer of the Romanovs not to Petrograd but to Yekaterinburg, and in this very month, July, the Party Central Committee had discussed what to do with the ex-tsar, and had determined that he must be put on trial. Now, however, only one quiet voice was raised to ask, 'And the family was taken away?' No reply was recorded.

Lenin asked, 'What decision should we take?' There could be only one, namely to approve what had been done by the Bolsheviks in Yekaterinburg. The brief minute reads that Sverdlov's report on the execution of Tsar Nicholas II had been received and noted.[82] Lenin then moved briskly on with his agenda of more than twenty items, which included a decree on the People's Commissariat for Health, the reorganization of the Red Cross and government statistics.[83]

Lenin knew that in fact the entire royal family had been executed. He, Sverdlov and Trotsky had discussed the issue several times. It had not been complicated: the Russian emperor must be liquidated. The Bolsheviks could not put the revolution at risk, with so many royalists raising their heads. But it had taken them a long time to decide to have him shot: they would have had a long list of charges with which to face him at a trial. But then the Cossacks had risen, as well as the old tsarist officer corps. How could there be a trial? According to the Bolsheviks, history had long ago given its remorseless verdict on the tsar.

Lenin's motives are not hard to understand. His elder brother, Alexander, had set out to assassinate a Romanov emperor and had been hanged for it. As has been seen, Lenin greatly admired Sergei Nechaev, the revolutionary who had ended up mad in prison. Bonch-Bruevich recalled Lenin telling him: 'People have completely forgotten that Nechaev possessed a special talent as an organizer, an ability to establish particular skills in illegal work ... It's enough to recall the precise reply he gave in one of his pamphlets to the question, "Who should be killed in the royal family?" It was, "The whole *ektenia*,"* So, who should be killed? The entire House of Romanov, as any reader would understand. That was pure genius!'[84]

Furthermore, Lenin regarded the extermination of the monarch as natural not only because the French Revolution had set a precedent, but also because the Social Democrats took it as axiomatic. As early as 1903, when they debated the abolition of the death penalty at their Second Congress, some of the delegates had called out, perhaps mockingly, 'And what about for Nicholas II?' Even the Mensheviks in 1903 had not dared to oppose the death penalty for the tsar.[85] And not long after Lenin's return from Switzerland, on 21 April 1917, the Central Committee passed a resolution written personally by Lenin: 'We regard Wilhelm II as much of a crowned bandit, deserving of the death penalty, as Nicholas II.'[86]

From mid-1916 to mid-1919, Lenin mentioned the tsar more than a hundred times in his articles and speeches, digging deep into his treasury of abuse to describe him, but never once attempting a serious analysis of the man or his office. When the tsar was down, Lenin went on calling him a half-wit, weak-minded, an idiot-monster.[87] Before the coup he had complained that 'the Provisional Government, which arrested Nicholas II under pressure from the left parties, is keeping him in too privileged conditions'.[88]

The day on which the royal family was killed was a routine one for Lenin, except for a piece he was shown in *National Tidende*, a Copenhagen newspaper, asking how he would reply to rumours that the former tsar had been shot.[89] It seemed that premonitions were afloat

---

* i.e. The entire list of Romanovs read out in part of the Orthodox service.

about the impending crime. Lenin scribbled that he did not comment on rumours, and that the story was bourgeois propaganda.

That evening the Sovnarkom met for a long session, after which, late at night, Lenin signed an instruction to form a Cheka on the eastern front.[90] He and Sverdlov had already been shown a prepared statement that 'White Guards are preparing to attack Ipatiev's house where Romanov, his family and company are being held under guard.' The Sovnarkom's instruction was all the more urgent, since the tsar was in the eastern front zone.

Next day, Lenin received a letter describing the situation in Yekaterinburg.[91] He was, however, already aware of it. Sverdlov had told him earlier that an order had been sent from Moscow via Perm to 'close the question'. On this command, the Urals Regional Soviet would take the previously agreed step of 'liquidating the Romanovs'. This account of events was confirmed in a conversation between Trotsky and Sverdlov after the capture of Yekaterinburg by the Red Army, which Trotsky recalled in 1935 and committed to his diary:

Talking to Sverdlov, I asked in passing: 'Oh yes, and where is the Tsar?' 'It's all over,' he answered, 'he has been shot.' 'And where is the family?' 'And the family along with him.' 'All of them?' I asked, apparently with a touch of surprise. 'All of them!' replied Sverdlov. 'What about it?' He was waiting to see my reaction. I made no reply. 'And who made the decision?' I asked. 'We decided it here. Ilyich believed that we shouldn't leave the Whites a live banner to rally around, especially under the present difficult circumstances.'[92]

The murderers in Yekaterinburg were merely carrying out orders issued from Moscow.

17 July was another ordinary day for Lenin. He chaired meetings, dictated telegrams, wrote notes, received commissars and so on. He also read a report from Deputy People's Commissar for Education M.N. Pokrovsky calling for the erection of fifty monuments to outstanding revolutionaries and 'progressive' writers and artists. Hardly had they come to power than the Bolsheviks destroyed dozens of monuments to 'persons of the exploiting classes' in order to obliterate the memory of the past, while hastening to fill the empty pedestals with 'proletarian heroes'. Within a few years thousands, indeed tens of thousands, of stone, bronze, iron and concrete idols would fill the squares, parks and palaces of the country.

This was not the first time Lenin had had power over the lives of members of the Romanov family. At the end of 1917 he had received an application from the tsar's brother Michael to adopt his wife's name and become plain 'Mr Brasov' and, he hoped, to go abroad. Lenin knew that Michael had been in favour of the February revolution, indeed had even worn a red ribbon in his buttonhole, and had in no way been involved in the fight against the Bolsheviks. Pushing the application away, Lenin snapped that he would not deal with the matter.[93] Had he granted the petition, he might have saved Michael's life – for a time, at least. Rejecting it was tantamount to a sentence of death.

Michael was arrested and sent to Perm. On the night of 11 June 1918 a group of Bolsheviks under the command of V.A. Ivanchenko took Michael and his English secretary, Johnson, out of the town and shot them. There was of course no trial. A few years later, two members of the execution squad, A.V. Markov and I.G. Novoselov, started a dispute as to which of them could claim the glory for this act. Novoselov wrote a letter to the History Section of the Central Committee, in which he gave a detailed account of the execution, and of the way the executioners had stripped the dead men of their personal belongings.

A month after Michael's death came the tragedy of Yekaterinburg. Russia and the world were informed that 'one Nicholas Romanov had been executed' because 'a major plot to effect the former tsar's escape had been uncovered. In the conditions of civil war this could mean a further danger for the proletarian revolution. The Romanov family have been moved to a safe place.'[94]

At the end of 1921 a miscellany entitled *The Workers' Revolution in the Urals* was published in Yekaterinburg. The entire edition of 10,000 copies was seized at once and removed from circulation as 'class-harmful'. The collection included an article by P.M. Bykov called 'The Last Days of the Last Tsar', in which the author stated that 'the question of executing Nicholas Romanov and all those who were with him had been decided in principle at the beginning of July. The leadership of the [Yekaterinburg] Soviet had been ordered to organize the executions and fix the date.'[95] Bykov was writing with a relatively free hand, and following relatively fresh tracks. As to the initiative for organizing the execution and fixing its date, from the available evidence it appears that the local Soviet did not meet at all in July. The orders, therefore, could only have come from Moscow.

Much later, the deputy commandant of the 'house of special purpose', G.P. Nikulin, asked whether 'Lenin, Sverdlov and other members of the ruling centre had been given prior notice of the execution of the royal family', replied: 'As Goloshchekin [military commissar of the Urals region] went to Moscow twice to discuss the fate of the Romanovs, it naturally follows that this is what they talked about.'[96] Even if the formal decision to proceed with the execution was taken by the Yekaterinburg Soviet, it is inconceivable that the action could have been carried out without the sanction of the Central Committee, and of Lenin personally. The Bolsheviks paid particular attention to Party hierarchy, and the only thing that could have restrained Lenin from dealing with the tsar as he did was the wish to do so by means of a 'proletarian trial'. As the civil war was moving towards Yekaterinburg, however, and given the shakiness of the Bolshevik regime, such considerations of even fake legality were cast aside. Lenin knew perfectly well what was in store for the Romanovs, and he approved it. Further proof can be found in the unfinished memoirs of Adolf Ioffe. In a section entitled 'Lenin and our Foreign Policy', Ioffe wrote:

I was in Berlin when the tsar and his family were executed. I was officially informed only of Nicholas II's execution; I knew nothing about his wife and children and I thought they were alive. When representatives of Wilhelm II and the brother of the former empress, the Duke of Hesse-Darmstadt, and other princes came to see me with various questions about the fate of [the empress] Alexandra Fedorovna (Princess Alix of Hesse) and her children, I always told them what I knew and believed. But finally I began to doubt the truth of my information, because I had been hearing various rumours. Despite all the queries I sent to Moscow, however, I could not get any sense out of them. Finally, when the late F.E. Dzerzhinsky was in Berlin *incognito*, en route to Switzerland, I made him tell me the whole truth, whereupon he told me that Vladimir Ilyich had categorically forbidden that I be told anything. According to Dzerzhinsky, Lenin had said: 'Better if Ioffe knows nothing. It'll be easier for him to lie to them, there in Berlin.'[97]

Until very recently, almost everything that has been written about the end of the Romanovs was published outside Russia. The subject was taboo, like the Bolsheviks' links with the Germans, or Lenin's family origins, the truth about his illness, the Party's financial affairs, Lenin's personal involvement in the origins of the terror, and many others. Despite their mastery of propaganda, the Bolsheviks were here forced onto the defensive. All the documents relating to the extermination of the tsar and his family were kept in the most inaccessible, secret repositories.

The summer of 1918 in Russia was abundant in killings. The murder of the tsar, however, represented a landmark, for with it the Bolsheviks abandoned even the pretence of legality. Even if it were supposed that they might have had charges to bring against the tsar and the empress, what possible accusations could have been made against the thirteen-year-old Alexei, and his sisters, the four young princesses, Olga, Tatiana, Maria and Anastasia? Violence against children was not a rarity at the time. In November 1920 Dzerzhinsky reported to Moscow: 'Today in Orel 403 Cossack men and women aged between fourteen and seventeen have arrived without any papers from Grozny for imprisonment in concentration camp for taking part in an uprising.' Lenin merely marked the report 'for the archives'.[98] These were merely the anonymous children of Cossacks, unknown to anyone in London or Paris. In the case of the Romanovs, however, the Bolsheviks needed to present their action under the guise of 'revolutionary initiative' and 'special circumstances'.

Indirect evidence shows that the order to execute the royal family was given verbally by Lenin and Sverdlov. The object of 'exterminating the entire Romanov kin' is confirmed by the almost simultaneous murders of Grand Duchess Yelizaveta Feodorovna, Grand Duke Sergei Mikhailovich, Prince Ivan Konstantinovich, Prince Konstantin Konstantinovich, Prince Igor Konstantinovich and Count Vladimir Paley (son of Grand Duke Paul Alexandrovich), all of them in Alapaevsk, a hundred miles from Yekaterinburg.

The Bolsheviks ascribed great importance to the extermination of the Romanov dynasty. Not only were they intent on removing the possibility of the monarchist banner reappearing on the scene and reviving the hopes of White survivors, they were also determined to force the population to become accustomed to the idea that there was not going to be any chance of a restoration. A trial, however obvious its outcome, would still have left the offspring alive and, even were they to remain in Bolshevik hands, they would have presented a threat.

Thus – leaving aside the still contentious issue of whether one or more of the children survived – in one fell swoop the Bolsheviks destroyed the direct line of a dynasty that had come into being at the Ipatiev Monastery in Kostroma, when Michael Romanov ascended the throne of Muscovy in 1613, and ended by an ironic twist of fate in the house of the merchant Ipatiev in Yekaterinburg.

An investigative commission, established by the Whites when they entered Yekaterinburg in the summer of 1918 and headed by one Sokolov, ascertained that on the morning of 16 July the draft report on the execution of the former tsar had been sent by telegraph from Yekaterinburg to Sverdlov in Moscow for his approval before the execution was carried out. The perpetrators themselves confirmed that they received a 'signal from above'. The fact that approval and confirmation of the execution was given by the VTsIK on the very next day speaks not only of coordination between Moscow and Yekaterinburg, but also of the planned nature of the crime. When the Central Committee discussed the question of Nicholas on 19 May 1918, Sverdlov proposed 'that nothing be decided yet'. The leadership was divided over whether to try the tsar – but then what should be done with the children? – or whether to exterminate him without a trial, and yet preserve the regime's 'good name'.[99]

It was agreed that for the moment no action should be taken, but that a solution should be found which would permit the extermination of the Romanov line of descent without the Bolsheviks' losing face. That solution was found in July in the form of the local 'revolutionary initiative' of the Yekaterinburg Bolsheviks. Moscow, meanwhile, was merely *awaiting* news of the executions, which it approved at once.

The recollections of the murderers lay for decades in the Kremlin's secret archives. They exemplify the machine of terror created by the Bolsheviks, and illustrate the way in which the psychology of violence became embedded in the social consciousness of the country. It rarely occurred to Soviet citizens to consider the fact that the seeds of the murderous collectivization, or the appalling purges of the 1930s and the end of the Second World War, and the post-war 'punishment' of entire nations, had been sewn by post-October Bolshevik practice. It is appalling to read the accounts by the perpetrators of the murders, the Yekaterinburg Bolsheviks Yurovsky, Medvedev (Kudrin), Radzikhovky, Nikulin, Yermakov and others, and to reflect that their action was for decades regarded as the highest revolutionary service, worthy of official commendation and reward. The deputy chief of the execution squad, Nikulin, complained in the 1940s that Yermakov was 'improperly claiming all the credit for himself'. To the indignation of the others, who also claimed primacy, Yermakov had written in his memoirs that he had personally shot the tsar, the empress, the tsarevich Alexei, and one of the princesses, while 'carrying out my duty to the people and the country'.

Yurovsky wrote in his 1922 memoirs that, as the newly appointed commandant of the House of Special Purpose, he established a harsher regime 'until a definite decision came from the centre' about the fate of the tsar.[100] For example, the empress 'used to take the liberty of glancing at the window often and going close to it. Once she took the liberty of going up to the window and was threatened by the guard with a blow of his rifle-butt.'[101] He went on:

On 16 July 1918 at 2 p.m. Comrade 'Filip' arrived and informed me that the [local] Executive Committee had given the order to execute Nicholas. A comrade would arrive at night with the password 'Chimney-sweep' to whom we would have to hand over the corpses which he would then bury and finish the job ... I called out the internal guards who had been deputed to shoot Nicholas and his family, and told each one of them whom he was to shoot. I gave them Nagan revolvers. When I was telling them their parts, the Latvians told me to leave them out of shooting the girls, as they wouldn't be able to go through with it. I thought it was best to leave them out of the shooting, as they would not be capable of fulfilling their revolutionary duty at the crucial moment ... At 1.30 a.m. there was a knock at the door. It was 'Chimney-sweep'. I entered the room, woke Dr Botkin [the family's physician], and told him they must all hurry and get dressed, as there was unrest in the town and I had to move them to a safe place.

At 2 a.m. I escorted the group down to the lower part of the house. I told them to arrange themselves in a particular order. I led the family down on my own. Nicholas was carrying Alexei in his arms. The rest, some of them carrying pillows, some with other things, made their way down into the cellar. Alexandra Fedorovna sat down. Alexei also sat down. I told everyone to stand. They all stood up, filling one whole wall and one of the side walls. It was a small room. I announced that the Executive Committee of the Soviet of Workers', Peasants' and Soldiers' Deputies had ordered their execution. Nicholas turned questioningly towards me. I repeated what I'd said, and then gave the order: 'Fire!'

I fired the first shot and killed Nicholas outright. The shooting went on a very long time ... It took me a long time to stop the shooting which had become disorderly. But when I tried to stop the shooting, I realized many of them were still alive. Dr Botkin for instance was lying propped up on his right elbow, as if he was relaxing. I finished him off with a shot from my revolver. Alexei, Tatiana, Anastasia and Olga were still alive. So was Demidova. Comrade Yermakov wanted to finish them all off by bayonet. But we couldn't. We discovered later the reason for this was that the daughters were wearing armoured bodices sewn with diamonds. I had to shoot each one in turn. To our great misfortune, the Red Army men had seen the things and decided they would have them.[102]

Another of the participants, Nikulin, also left an account:

Before the shooting started, Yurovsky said something like, 'Your friends are advancing on Yekaterinburg and so you're sentenced to death.' They didn't even know what was happening, you know, because Nicholas only said 'Ah!' and at that moment there was a volley, one, two, three. Some weren't quite dead. Well, I mean, some had to be finished off later ... Anastasia and another one ... We had to take the pillow off Davydova and shoot her. Yes, the boy was still alive, twisting and turning a long time, but then he was done for ... In my opinion, we did the job humanely ... I reckoned that if I was taken by the Whites and they dealt with me the same way, I'd be happy ... I doubt if the Urals [Soviet] would've taken the responsibility themselves, you know, for the shooting, without an order from Lenin or Sverdlov or one of the other leaders, or at least their unspoken agreement.[103]

Radzikhovsky was another who took part:

I know all about it. The shooting was all over the place. I know that ... Medvedev took aim at Nicholas. He just shot at Nicholas ... Anyway, it was just another sentence that had to be carried out, we looked on it as just another chore* ... Of course, you start to think about its historical importance ... In fact, the whole thing was badly organized. Take Alexei, it took a lot of bullets before he died. He was a tough kid ... We had a meeting after it. The townsfolk came ... Goloshchekin who spoke suddenly said, 'From Nicholas right down to the little one,' which he shouldn't have said, of course. Anyway, the people didn't seem to understand. The factories took the news well. In the Red Army it gave them a big revolutionary lift.[104]

---

* This group had not long before executed Prince Dolgorukov, General Tatishchev, Countess Gendrikova and Yekaterina Schneider, who had been accompanying the Romanovs.

Finally, Medvedev, who wrote on the first page of his recollections, 'For history. Not for publication. Party member since 1911':

The Romanovs were completely calm, they suspected nothing . . . Yurovsky rushed in and stood next to me. The tsar looked at him inquiringly . . . the empress crossed herself. Yurovsky stepped a half-pace forward and addressed the tsar: 'Nicholas Alexandrovich! The attempts of your supporters to save you have not been crowned with success. And so in this difficult year for our Soviet Republic . . . we have been charged with the mission of finishing off the House of Romanov!' The women cried out, 'My God! Ah! Oh!' Nicholas muttered, 'My God, my God! What's going on?' 'This is what's going on,' Yurovsky said, taking his Mauser out of its holster. 'Aren't you going to take us somewhere?' Botkin asked in a thick voice. Yurovsky was about to reply, but I had already cocked my Browning and I fired the first bullet at the tsar. At the same moment, the Latvians fired off their first volley . . . Yurovsky and Yermakov were also firing into the tsar's chest at point blank. At my fifth shot Nicholas II fell onto his back, dead. The women were screaming and moaning; I saw Botkin fall, the butler had fallen by the wall and the cook was on his knees. A white pillow moved from the door to the right side of the room. A woman's figure rushed from the group of screaming women through the gunsmoke towards the closed door and fell, struck down by Yermakov's shots . . . You could see nothing for the gunsmoke, the shooting was still going on at barely visible silhouettes of people falling.

We heard Yurovsky's voice: 'Stop! Stop firing!' It became quiet. There was ringing in my ears. Suddenly from the right-hand corner where the pillow was moving came the joyful cry of a woman: 'Thank God! God has saved me!' It was the maid, swaying as she got up. She'd been hiding behind the pillow and the bullets had been absorbed by the feathers. The Latvians had used up all their bullets, so two of them stabbed her with their bayonets. There was a moan from Alexei . . . Yurovsky went over to him and fired the last three bullets from his Mauser into him. He went quiet and slid down off the chair at his father's feet. We looked over the rest and found Olga and Anastasia still alive and finished them off with a Colt. Now they were all lifeless.[105]

That day or the next, Yurovsky and Nikulin left for Moscow to hand in their report to Lenin and Sverdlov. As well as a sack of diamonds and other precious stones, they took with them everything they had found in the Ipatiev house: diaries and correspondence, albums of the tsar's photographs showing the family in Tobolsk. Medvedev recalled that when the order to carry out the executions arrived from Moscow, 'Alexander [Beloborodov] and I hugged each other'. He concluded: 'So, the secret operation for ridding Russia of the Romanov dynasty was completed. It went off so well that up to now neither the secret of the Ipatiev house nor the burial site of the royal family have been revealed.'[106]

The perpetrators of this grisly action, who were not only proud of what they had done but even regarded the murders as a 'humane act', were possessed by a revolutionary drive that made them want to 'turn the imperialist war into a civil war'. By comparison, the tsar's decision to abdicate in the name of the country's good and tranquillity says much. And his October 1905 Manifesto had spoken of basing 'the unshakeable foundations of civil rights on the principles of the genuine inviolability of the person'. His prime minister of 1905, Count Witte, wrote long before the revolution: 'I pity the Tsar. I pity Russia. He is a poor and unhappy sovereign. What did he inherit and what will he leave? He is obviously a good and quite intelligent man, but he lacks willpower, and it is from that feature of his character that his state defects developed, that is, his defects as a ruler, especially as an autocratic and absolute ruler.'[107]

Perhaps Nicholas was not an outstanding personality, but he was at least noble and brave. He manoeuvred long and ably within the intricacies of Russia's contradictory system, but he could not imagine that he would meet the same terrible end as Louis XVI. But Louis's fate had been discussed by the Convention, and three votes had been taken. His request for three days' grace to prepare himself was denied, and he was given only twenty-four hours, but he did have the opportunity to bid his family farewell. The killing of any monarch is terrible, but the execution of the Romanovs was aggravated by the treacherous and arbitrary way in which it was carried out, without even a fictitious trial.

The extermination of the royal family symbolized the vast tragedy of a great nation which had yielded to class hatred and fratricide. The tragedy which took place in the Ipatiev house, ostensibly an episode in the deadly civil war, synthesized the hypocrisy of Bolshevik propaganda, the cruelty of the regime and the duplicity of its leaders. The murders in Yekaterinburg highlighted the inability of the Bolsheviks to handle problems without unrestrained violence or state terror. The authorities in Moscow could not admit to themselves that, even in defeat, they feared Nicholas as long he was alive. They did not believe that their revolution was irreversible, and Nicholas inspired in them a mystical fear as the symbol of the nation which might, when it had become disillusioned with the Bolsheviks, turn back to their monarch. The Bolsheviks were driven by the need to free themselves of this possibility.

There are several accounts of Lenin meeting Yurovsky and other participants in the murders. The deputy commandant of the Ipatiev house, Nikulin, was asked: 'Do you remember if Yurovsky ever met Sverdlov or Vladimir Ilyich Lenin personally?'

'Yes, he met Vladimir Ilyich Lenin,' he replied.

'Was that after the event?'

'Yes, after.'

'So he could have given him . . .'

'Yes, he gave him something, and even wrote a note or something . . .'[108]

Lenin had also met some of the perpetrators before the event. In 1917 he received F.I. Goloshchekin,[109] and spoke to him at the Seventh Party Congress in March 1918.[110] According to A.V. Markov, one of the murderers of Grand Duke Michael, Lenin chatted with him in the Kremlin: 'I was on a mission to Moscow in 1918 and my work took me to Comrade Sverdlov, and he took me to see V.I. Lenin who asked me about the liquidation of Michael Romanov; I told him the job had been done cleanly, and he said, "Well, that's good, you did it properly."'[111]

Nikulin later boasted, 'If we'd had more people in the Party the likes of Yurovsky and his boys, it would have done us nothing but good, it would have been an achievement.'[112] Men like Yurovsky and the rest would not have acted on their own, especially in view of the fact that Sverdlov had given them an order 'to guard the tsar for an All-Russian trial'. Model Bolsheviks would not have disobeyed the authorities. They constituted important cogs in the system created by Lenin, and the dictatorship did not tolerate autonomous action; on the contrary, soon after the operation, the authorities gave it their formal approval.

After the events of July 1918, the regime imposed strict censorship on everything connected with them. The Party would not permit the Romanov affair to become a topic of historical interest, and was extremely zealous in this regard. On 26 July 1975, Yuri Andropov, as Chairman of the KGB, presented a paper at the Politburo, headed 'Removal of the Ipatiev House':

Anti-Soviet circles in the West periodically inspire propaganda campaigns of various kinds about the Romanov royal family, and in this connection the former house of the merchant Ipatiev in Sverdlovsk [as the city was then called] is mentioned.

The Ipatiev house still stands in the centre of the town. It now accommodates a study centre of the regional cultural administration ... Foreign specialists have recently begun visiting Sverdlovsk. The number of foreigners may greatly increase in the future and the Ipatiev house could become an object of serious attention.

It therefore seems sensible to instruct the Sverdlovsk Regional Party Committee to deal with the question by demolishing the house as part of the planned reconstruction of the city.

The decision was not long in coming. The Central Committee approved Andropov's proposal and ordered Sverdlovsk to demolish the house 'as part of the planned reconstruction of the city'.[113] Boris Yeltsin, then the Regional Party Secretary, carried out the order with expedition.

Kerensky was far-sighted indeed when he wrote in 1920: 'The Provisional Government would not yield one iota to the hate-ridden rabble-rousing demands of the left, because not to martyr the tsar was the best way to secure republican Russia from the rebirth of the monarchical legend.'[114] The Bolsheviks, by contrast, made Nicholas II an eternal martyr and saint. Not all the bullets were to go in the same direction, however. Some were fired at the leader of the new regime, the chief organizer and ideologue of Bolshevism. But those who fired them were less successful than Yurovsky and his team of executioners.

## Fanya Kaplan's Shot

The summer of 1918 was the low-point of the Bolshevik revolution, and Lenin was making one rallying speech after another. On 1 August, at a meeting of the Warsaw Revolutionary Regiment in Moscow, before their departure for the front, he told the Red Army men that they had the great honour of 'defending sacred ideas'. The next day he addressed the Communists of the Butyrki district, spoke at a meeting of Red Army men at a club on Khodynsky Field, and finally, before an evening session of the Sovnarkom, he managed to fit in a speech to workers at the Michelson factory, in the old part of Moscow across the river.[115] At all these occasions he spoke with conviction about the inevitability of world revolution, especially as 'in Germany the same thing has started as happened with us, a defeatist movement'.[116]

The meeting at Michelson's on 2 August had gone well enough, and on 30 August Lenin returned to the factory to address a meeting on 'Two Regimes'. He was warmly received by the workers, who were hoping he would make things better for them soon. But Lenin, who was preoccupied with events on a world scale, warned them of the dangers of democracy. 'Wherever "democrats" rule you find plain, straightforward theft. We know the true nature of such democracies!' He affirmed that 'thanks to the abolition of the private ownership of land there is now a vital unification of the proletariat of town and country'. He then called on everyone to do their utmost to smash their enemies. 'We have only one way out: victory or death!'[117] He gave a hearty wave of the arm, and marched away towards the exit, pausing briefly outside the building to speak to a group of women.

Assistant Military Commissar Baturin of the 5th Moscow Soviet Infantry Division later testified when interrogated by the Cheka:

When Comrade Lenin was leaving the Michelson building, after the meeting on 'The Dictatorship of the Bourgeoisie and the Dictatorship of the Proletariat', I was at a distance of about twenty–forty paces from him. Everyone at the meeting was making for the exit and a bottleneck built up on the exit staircase, and I only managed to get outside with considerable effort. Proceeding towards Comrade Lenin's automobile, I heard three abrupt, dull sounds, which I did not take to be revolver shots, but rather as ordinary noises from the engine. After this, I saw the people who had been calmly standing by the car running in all directions, and there, lying motionless on the ground face-down next to the car, I saw Comrade Lenin. I realized an attempt had been made on his life. I did not see the person who had made the attempt. I did not lose my head, but shouted 'Catch the killer of Comrade Lenin!' and ran shouting into Serpukhovka, where people were running away singly or in groups and in all directions, scared by the shots and the general confusion.

I had reached [a certain point] on Serpukhovka, when I noticed behind me a woman standing by a tree and holding a briefcase and umbrella, and her strange appearance arrested my attention. She looked like someone who was escaping, frightened and hunted. I asked her what she was doing, and she replied 'Why do you want to know?' I then searched her pockets, took her briefcase and umbrella and asked her to come with me. On the way, sensing that she had shot Comrade Lenin, I asked her, 'Why did you shoot Comrade Lenin?' To which she answered: 'What do you want to know for?' And this finally convinced me that it was she who had shot at Comrade Lenin . . .

As I feared that sympathizers and supporters might try to get her away, or that she might be lynched, I asked armed militiamen and Red Army men in the crowd to accompany us . . . At the interrogation, which took place at the Military Commissariat of Zamoskvorechie District, the arrested woman identified herself as Kaplan and confessed to having made the attempt on Lenin's life.[118]

Lenin was lifted from the ground and put into his car. His driver, Gil, put his foot down and the car raced over the cobbles to the Kremlin. When they reached the entrance to Lenin's building, he refused help, put on his jacket and coat himself, and climbed the stairs to the third floor. His sister Maria opened the door in a great state of alarm, and a white-faced Lenin told her, with a tortured grin, 'I've been slightly wounded, just in the arm.' His physician, A.N. Vinokurov, was already there, waiting to give first aid.[119] The telephone in the lobby rang incessantly. Dr V.N. Rozanov recalled: 'It was a small room . . . A typical picture that you would see anywhere when someone has had an accident: the confused, worried faces of relatives and close friends standing round the patient, other people, perhaps not family but just as concerned, standing a little way off whispering. Four doctors stood by the bed and others were soon called in.'[120] Still more specialists were summoned later.

It was agreed that regular bulletins on Lenin's condition should be published. The bulletin of 30 August announced: 'At 11 p.m. two bullet wounds were identified; one bullet entered the left shoulder-blade, penetrated the chest cavity and damaged an upper section of the lung, causing haemorrhaging into the pleura and lodging in the right side of the neck, above the right clavicle. A second bullet entered the left shoulder, shattered the bone and lodged under the skin in the left shoulder region. There are signs of internal bleeding. The pulse is 104. The patient is fully conscious. The best specialists and surgeons have been brought in.'[121]

As the doctors descended on the Kremlin, Sverdlov and his comrades were preparing to make a general announcement.[122] Lenin's life, however, was not in danger. The physician Obukh told the Moscow

Soviet that the patient's heart function had returned to normal and
that there was no risk of a relapse. In all, some thirty-five regular
bulletins were to be published on Lenin's condition. Luck was on
Lenin's side. As Rozanov wrote, 'the bullet had taken an unusual and
fortunate path, passing through the neck from left to right just in
front of the larynx and behind the gullet and injuring no other vessels
in the neck. Had the bullet deviated by one millimetre in either direction, Vladimir Ilyich would of course be dead.'[123]

This event suddenly brought home to the Party leadership just how
much Lenin meant to them. His strong hand, his decisiveness and drive
had not only made the October seizure of power possible, it had been
responsible for creating the Bolshevik state. Lenin was the brain and
the engine of the entire totalitarian system that was coming into being.
Speaking at a meeting of the VTsIK on 2 September 1918, Trotsky
declared that 'in Lenin we have a person who was created for our era of
blood and iron . . . Any fool can shoot through Lenin's skull, but to
recreate that skull is a difficult task even for nature itself.'[124]

Trotsky was right: Lenin was made for the era of 'blood and iron'.
The concern aroused by the attempt on his life gave a powerful
impulse to his glorification. The press published a mass of articles,
appeals and addresses organized by Party committees expressing feelings of loyalty, gratitude and good wishes. This was perhaps the first
perceptible wave of the cult without which a totalitarian society cannot
exist. The leader and the masses were the two basic components of
the structure erected by the Bolsheviks after 1917. To his credit,
Lenin was too intelligent to bask in the rays of cult glory. Angelica
Balabanova, the Secretary of Comintern, whose memoirs on Lenin
do much to debunk him, nevertheless wrote: '[The] popularity and
indisputable authority that he possessed perhaps irritated him. He
avoided anything that might lead to his deification. He expressed this
attitude so clearly that no one in his presence ever attempted to flatter
him or display obsequiousness'.[125] Now that he was injured, a veritable
chorus of flattery welled up among Lenin's comrades-in-arms and
commissars at all levels, and he told Bonch-Bruevich to order the
newspapers and magazines to stop the campaign of adoration.[126]
Naturally, by refusing to be worshipped, he intensified the trend.

Lenin's assailant was taken to the Kremlin and incarcerated in a
basement room below Sverdlov's apartment. She was interrogated by

the top echelon of the Bolshevik legal and security systems, Commissar for Justice Dmitri Kursky and Cheka bosses Nikolai Skrypnik and Yakov Peters. She told them she had been born Fanya Yefimovna Roitman, the daughter of a Jewish schoolteacher in the province of Volhynia. She had four brothers and three sisters. In 1906, as an anarchist, she had attempted to commit a terrorist act with a bomb. She had been injured and sentenced to 'eternal' hard labour, i.e. an unspecified term. She first did time in Maltsev hard-labour prison near Orel in central Russia, and then in the notorious Akatua silver-mining camp near Chita in eastern Siberia, where she met Maria Spiridonova.* During her time in prison she broke with anarchism and became a Socialist Revolutionary. She was released after the February revolution. Her family had emigrated to America in 1911.[128]

Fanya (or Dora) Kaplan was made of the same stuff as Spiridonova, the same breed of recalcitrance, responding to violence with violence. Surrounded as an eighteen-year-old convict by SRs and terrorists, she emerged from penal servitude after February 1917 having lost none of her dedication. For such people, the gallows or the firing squad

---

* Spiridonova became a member of the terrorist wing of the Socialist Revolutionary Party as a girl. In January 1906 the Tambov regional organization of the party carried out the assassination of a local official, and Spiridonova was sentenced to death, the sentence being commuted to an unspecified term of hard labour. In 1917, as leader of the Left SRs after the October coup, she was at large for a few months, under the constant gaze of the Cheka. Exiled to Central Asia in 1925, she worked as an economist in a local planning office until 1937, when she was arrested for the last time, and sentenced to twenty-five years on the usual absurd charges. In September 1941, together with a large group of convicts, she was shot without trial in Orel Prison. In her reminiscences, published in Moscow in 1926, at a time when a welter of literature about prison and exile under the tsarist system was appearing and even a 'sworn enemy' of the Soviet state could make her voice heard on such matters, Spiridonova wrote about hard labour in Siberia. She described how some of her comrades had committed suicide in protest against corporal punishment: 'The comrade would lie on his bunk with one leg crossed over the other ... He would have laid all his clothes under him to prevent the blood spilling below the bunk from the veins in his arms and behind his knees which he would have cut with a blunt knife. He would gradually feel faint. His life would gradually ebb away with his blood. How long, how long would liberation take? Then gradually alarm would invade his dormant mind, death was not coming, his young body was mobilizing its own means of survival, his wounds were filming over, his blood was drying into clots and he must begin all over again. He starts cutting with a piece of glass, digging into the wound with a sharp point, removing the clots.'[127]

were the summit of their commitment, the final act of the fighter.

Kaplan was interrogated several times by the chairman of the Moscow revolutionary tribunal, A. Dyakonov, as well as People's Commissar for Justice Kursky and his two senior assistants from the Cheka, Skrypnik and Peters. Their chief concern was to discover what organization lay behind Kaplan, who had pushed her into making the assassination attempt and where they could be found.

Some of the interrogations were conducted in classic Bolshevik style, in the middle of the night. Trained long ago by the convicts in Akatua to outstare executioners and not to 'break', Kaplan sat on a stool in the middle of the room with her back bent, her gaze fixed on the Chekists in their leather jackets, with their Mausers.

Quietly, her voice full of conviction, she told them: 'I don't belong to any party.'

'Why did you shoot at Comrade Lenin?'

'I regard him as a traitor. The longer he lives, the further he'll push back the idea of socialism. For dozens of years.'

'Who sent you to commit the crime?'

After a moment's pause, Kaplan replied: 'I committed the attempt on my own behalf.'

Peters and Kursky in particular tried to obtain evidence of her connections with the SRs and their militant groups. They asked her about particular individuals. They wanted to know if she knew Bitsenko, a former woman convict at Nerchinsk who became prominent in the SR leadership and had attended the Brest-Litovsk treaty talks as a member of the Soviet delegation.

'Yes, I knew her during hard labour. I never asked her how to get at Lenin. I've only been in the Kremlin once . . . I saw Bitsenko for the last time about a month ago.'

'How did you feel about the October revolution?'

'I was in Kharkov, in hospital, when it took place. I didn't like it, I viewed it negatively. I was for the Constituent Assembly and I still am. As for my view of the SRs, I tend towards Chernov.'

'So, why did you shoot at Lenin? Who sent you to do it?'

'I made up my mind to shoot Lenin a long time ago. I was the one who shot him. I decided to take this step back in February. The idea matured in my mind in Simferopol [in the Crimea] and since that time I began preparing to do it.'[129]

These are the replies that appear in the minutes of the interrogation. Kaplan made no attempt to justify what she had done, to back away from it or to mitigate what she knew was in store. Her assertion, 'I was the one who shot him,' however, gives cause for serious doubt. Despite there being a large crowd present, not one witness testified to having seen Kaplan firing the revolver. Even the driver, Gil, who was alongside Lenin, said in evidence: 'When Lenin was at a distance of three steps from the vehicle, I saw a woman's hand outstretched from behind a number of people and holding a Browning. Three shots were fired and I flung myself towards the place they came from. The woman who had fired the shots threw the gun down at my feet and fled into the crowd. The revolver was lying at my feet. No one picked it up while I was there. Correction: it was after the first shot that I saw the woman's hand with the Browning.'[130]

Eighteen witnesses questioned at the Zamoskvorechie district military commissariat said more or less the same thing. No one had actually seen Kaplan, as distinct from a woman's hand, fire at Lenin. Kaplan, moreover, had very poor eyesight; she could hardly see anything close up, and it is extremely doubtful that she would have been recruited by any militant group. D. Tarasova, who had been with her in Akatua and who was rearrested, stated that Kaplan was practically blind. 'She was losing her sight over a long period and it has barely been restored.'[131]

The fact that Kaplan made no attempt to hide, and that she immediately affirmed at the first questioning that she had shot Lenin, gives even more ground for doubt. It seems likely that there was a plan in which Kaplan would accept the responsibility for the assassination attempt, as well as the consequences. In a personal communication to the author, Professor Litvin of Kazan University has asserted that the person who fired the shots at Lenin was in fact a certain Protopopov, who in July 1918 had been assistant to Popov, a Cheka unit leader. According to material collected by Litvin, Protopopov was arrested at the same time as Kaplan, and either that day or the next was executed. Kaplan did not know this and was playing out her tragic rôle to the end.

A statement Kaplan made when she was arrested, and studiedly repeated at her interrogations, deserves attention:

1918, 30 August, 11.30 p.m.

I am Fanya Efimovna Kaplan, the name under which I served in Akatua. I have borne this name since 1906. I shot at Lenin today. I shot at him out of my own conviction. I fired several times, I don't remember how many.

I won't say what revolver I used. I prefer not to give details. I was not acquainted with the women who were talking to Lenin. The idea of shooting Lenin had matured in my mind a long time ago. I didn't used to live in Moscow, I haven't lived in Petrograd . . .

I fired at Lenin because I regard him as a traitor to the revolution and his further existence will erode faith in socialism. What this erosion of the faith in socialism consists of I do not want to say.[132]

The 'Kaplan attempt' is another of the many mystifications of Bolshevik history. There are a number of puzzling circumstances. The Bolshevik A.V Kuznetsov, who according to his own testimony was a gun collector, did not give the Cheka the Browning that had been thrown to the ground after the shooting for a full three days. Yet a Browning was found in Kaplan's handbag when she was first searched. Whose revolver, then, was it that was handed in? The investigation declined to seek an answer to this question. Only after an interval of three days was Mikhail Yurovsky – the same Yurovsky who had organized the murder of the royal family, and who had been transferred to Moscow – ordered by Peters to search the scene of the crime, where the cases of *four* spent bullets from a Browning were found.[133] Yet every witness testified that only three shots were fired.

One other person was a victim of the attempt. This was M.G. Popova, presumably one of the women noticed talking to Lenin. According to her, she approached Lenin and said: ' "They've given permission to buy flour, but they're not lifting the roadblocks." Lenin replied: "According to the new decree, they can't lift the roadblocks. We must struggle." Then there was a shot and I fell.'[134] The Cheka medical report on Popova shows that 'a bullet entered the outer side of the elbow, passed right through the joint, exited through the inner side of the joint and scorched the left breast as it continued on its path'.

It has recently been ascertained that the bullet removed from Lenin's neck above the right sterno-clavicular joint on 23 April 1922 by the German physician Professor Borchardt was not fired from the Browning which Kuznetsov handed over to the Cheka. A further significant detail is that pages 11, 84, 87, 90 and 94 of the file relating to the shooting were missing when it was checked on 26 June 1963.

What are we to make of the evidence?

Oleg Vasiliev has suggested that there was no assassination attempt at all, merely a fake show: all the parts were prearranged, and the bullets were blanks.[135] It is hard to accept this theory, daring though it is. It is sufficient to point out that no less than eight physicians attended Lenin on 31 August, and all of them claimed to have felt the bullet lodged in his neck. And there are also Popova's injuries.

It is more likely that it was not actually Kaplan who fired the gun. In the aftermath of the shooting, the authorities were not concerned to carry out a thorough investigation. There were only a few brief interrogations, and there was no trial. The 'Kaplan attempt' gave the Bolsheviks the excuse they wanted to launch massive, overwhelming state terror. It enabled them finally to deal with their recent allies, the Left SRs, whom they now felt to be a hindrance. Terror provided them with their last chance to make power the monopoly of one party. Therefore, no investigation or trial was needed in order to exterminate Kaplan, and therefore all the materials relating to the case were kept inaccessible for decades in the archives of the Cheka-KGB.

Kremlin Commandant Pavel Malkov wrote that on 3 September 1918 he was summoned to the Cheka, where senior officer Varlam Avanesov read him an order: 'Kaplan is to be shot. The sentence is to be carried out by Kremlin Commandant Malkov.' Forty years later, Malkov recalled: 'The execution of a human being, especially a woman, was no easy thing. It was a heavy, very heavy responsibility. But I had never been ordered to carry out a more just sentence than this. I asked Avanesov: "When?" "Today. Immediately." No one commuted the death sentence on Kaplan and it was duly carried out, and it was I who carried it out, a Communist, a sailor of the Baltic Fleet, Commandant of the Moscow Kremlin, Pavel Dmitrievich Malkov, written in his own hand.'[136] Before the execution, Malkov was given instructions personally by Sverdlov in the presence of Yurovsky. He was told to carry out the shooting in a garage, with a car engine running. Kaplan's remains were to be destroyed without trace. The execution was carried out at 4 a.m. on 4 September. Kaplan had demanded neither an open trial nor clemency. The 'proletarian poet' Demyan Bedny was invited to watch the execution, for the sake of 'revolutionary inspiration'.

Lenin did not interfere in the course of Bolshevik 'justice'. As Malkov himself wrote, 'A charming fable existed that he had asked that Kaplan's life be spared, and that she was seen in a camp on Solovki Island or Kolyma, in 1932 or even 1938. But these were nothing more than stories.'

Speaking of the affair to Angelica Balabanova at Gorki, where he was convalescing, Lenin said brusquely: 'The Central Committee will decide what to do with this Kaplan,'[137] as if he was not aware that the execution had already been carried out. Not only would colleagues who visited him on 6 September have told him that his would-be assassin had been dealt with, but on 14 September he received Malkov, the executioner himself.[138] According to official published sources, they discussed the transfer of the Sovnarkom from the Justice building to the Great Kremlin Palace. The Sovnarkom did not in fact move, and it is unlikely that Lenin was not keen to know how Kaplan had comported herself in the last minutes before her execution. Lenin saw Balabanova at Gorki after 30 September, when she returned from Stockholm.[139] By then he had taken part in a Central Committee session on 16 September and a meeting of the Sovnarkom next day,[140] and was thus fully informed of Kaplan's fate.*

The entire episode illustrates that Lenin made a political error by remaining aloof from the 'judicial process'. Had he intervened publicly to spare Kaplan's life, the legend of a 'kind Lenin' would have grown and endured. Lenin's speech to the Young Communists in 1919, cited above, is illuminating: 'We do not believe in eternal morality, and we are exposing the deception of all the fairy-tales about morality.'[144]

---

* The Stalin era was not a healthy one for people bearing the name Kaplan. It was enough to be asked 'Are you a relative of *that* Kaplan?' to be in trouble. In 'T' Section of the Ministry of State Security, Kurbatov received a report: 'A Fanya Lvovna Kaplan has been found with a husband called Vladimir Aronovich Kaplan and daughter, Marianna Vladimirovna Kaplan. Informer "Asya" and source Myshkin reported it. An order has been issued to obtain all possible information on these people.'[141] And in 1949 Colonel Sharapov of the same ministry leaned from a certain Nikolaev that A.V. Kaplan was the brother of SR Fanya Kaplan. When asked how he knew this, he claimed he'd heard it from other tenants, but could not remember precisely who they were.[142] A Vladimir Natanovich Kaplan was arrested in 1938 by the 11th Department of the Moscow Regional NKVD and died six months later in prison, while his sister Flora was sent to camp.[143] There were many other unfortunate Kaplans.

Lenin's social ethics, by contrast, in the words of Dora Shturman, 'were adapted to Hitler's fateful formula, "I liberate you from the chimera of conscience."'[145]

In the torrent of violence unleashed by the revolution and its inevitable companion, civil war, it was natural that the enemies of the regime should identify Lenin as the author of their misfortunes. The SRs were conspicuous in this regard, and they were also accustomed to the use of terror as a means of settling political problems. Kaplan's attempt on Lenin's life was not the first. On 14 January 1918, in Petrograd, his car was fired on as he was driving to Bolshevik head-quarters at the Smolny Institute with his sister Maria and the Swiss socialist Fritz Platten, having given a speech in the Mikhailovsky rid-ing school to troops leaving for the front. 'They had gone only a few hundred yards,' an anniversary number of *Pravda* recalled, 'when bullets started peppering the back of the car.' Platten grabbed Lenin by the head and pushed him down. When the car was examined at the Smolny, it was found to have been holed in several places, a number of bullets having shattered the windscreen. Platten's hand was covered in blood, having been grazed by a bullet as he was shield-ing Lenin.[146]

A year later, Lenin had another close call, this time at the hands of gangsters. On the evening of 19 January 1919, Lenin, his sister and his bodyguard Chabanov were driving out of Moscow to a forest school at Sokolniki, where Krupskaya was living on her doctor's advice. As they approached a railway bridge, the car was stopped by three armed men. Lenin and his companions thought it was no more than a routine identity check, but, as Maria recorded, 'we were amazed when the people who had stopped the car made us get out right away and, ignoring the pass he showed them, started going through Vladimir Ilyich's pockets, holding a revolver to his temple and taking his Browning and Kremlin pass'.

'"What are you doing?" Maria cried. "This is Comrade Lenin! Who are you? Show us your permits!" "Criminals don't need permits." And with this, they leapt into the car, keeping their revolvers pointed at us, and gave it full throttle in the direction of Sokolniki.'[147]

Lenin was obviously satisfied with the deal he had made with the gangsters, since he referred to it as the precedent for successful compromise. 'Imagine,' he wrote in an article entitled 'Left-wing Communism, an Infantile Disease', 'that your car has been stopped by armed bandits. You give them your money, your identity papers, your revolver and the car itself. In exchange you are excused their pleasant company . . . Our compromise with the bandits of German imperialism was just such a compromise.'[148] Brest-Litovsk, in other words, was a case of 'your money or your life'.

The whole of Moscow was put on the alert after this incident. In effect, a state of martial law was declared in the capital. A week or two later, K.G. Rozental, chief of criminal investigation, reported to Lenin:

With the aim of investigating the bandit attack on you during your journey along the Sokolniki highway, and also in the interests of ending banditry, I ordered door-to-door investigation of all private furnished rooms and apartments which might be used as a hiding place for the criminal element of Moscow. All those suspected of being implicated in the assault have been arrested . . . We have succeeded in apprehending and arresting up to two hundred people, sixty-five of them wanted for many other crimes . . . Your attackers were the bandits Yashka Koshelkov, Zayats the Driver and Lenka the Bootmaker. A flat where the bandits had their meeting-place was discovered, and the landlord has since committed suicide.[149]

Bolshevik flair had been at work once again: two hundred arrested for the work of three.

Lenin's personal security was significantly increased after 7 April 1919, when Stalin sent a list of additional measures to be taken by the Kremlin commandant.[150] They included a rule that when leaving the Kremlin Lenin must always be accompanied by two cars and five security men. His driver must be a 'dedicated Party member', and there must be an armed escort. Security guards from Lenin's apartment and office must be Party members of at least a year's standing. Sentries must be given a system of signals and a floor-button to use in case of assaults. Access to Lenin's apartment was to be solely by special ticket issued by Lenin. The clerks' office was to be moved downstairs, and Lenin's study was to be moved next to his apartment and the committee room. Finally, there was to be a thorough purge of all Sovnarkom staff.[151]

The search for enemies and terrorists permitted the acceptable use of necessary measures, but it also generated an atmosphere of suspicion, mistrust and spy-mania. 'Awareness' now became a favoured attribute among revolutionaries of all levels. The Saratov military commissar, Sokolov, for instance, wrote to Lenin at the end of April 1919 requesting permission 'to report the secret military actions against the Soviet regime. Your enemies, all of whom are known to me, want to murder you and Comrade Trotsky. I pass this on to you at the persistent request of Red Army soldier Yakovenko of 12th Krasnokutsk Railway Regiment.'[152]

The Yakovenkos began to multiply, until it seemed they populated the entire country. Certainly Lenin was a target, but he was better protected after the attempts of 1918. He was also less vulnerable than other Bolshevik leaders because he ventured out of the safety of the Kremlin less often. He never visited the front, or the provinces, or toured the new republics created by the regime within the borders of the old empire, always preferring to rule by remote control from the Kremlin. He had intended to attend the Genoa Conference in April–May 1922 with Chicherin, and was only prevented from doing so by ill health.* On the other hand, Unshlikht had reported that 'information has been received from a reliable source about the preparation of an attempt by Poles on the lives of Comrades Lenin and Chicherin. [This is being done] in case Lenin and Chicherin go to the conference in Genoa. They do not want it to happen on their own territory.'[153]

The attempts on Lenin's life gave rise to solidarity with the leader and unbridled admiration of his merits, his mind and his will. The eulogies that now blossomed bore a pseudo-populist character, and were permeated with ideological motives and expressed in empty, bland and often naive rhetoric. The inveterate Russian commitment to the idea of the 'good tsar' quickly found a new object of expression. As one of Lenin's most capable People's Commissars, Krasin, wrote: 'The [Kaplan] attempt on Lenin's life made him far more popular than he had been before.'[154] The natural sympathy of ordinary people, pumped up by propaganda, gave rise to a persistent form of idolatry, which acquired ugly expression in the cult of Stalin while preserving

---

* The Genoa Conference, in which twenty-nine European nations, including Germany and Soviet Russia, took part, was the first step towards recognition of Soviet Russia by the Western democracies. At a parallel conference in Rapallo, Germany and Russia came to their own agreement for economic and military cooperation.

the 'deification' of Lenin. The earthly god created by the Bolsheviks out of Lenin's image called forth an entire culture of worship, with rules, rituals and customs of its own.

The attempts on Lenin thus enabled the regime to engage in the exaggeration of the leader's rôle which it regarded as necessary for its own survival. Lenin's lack of personal vanity was no obstacle to the development of the idolatry.

The second consequence of the attempts on Lenin's life was that they allowed the regime to adopt unrestrained violence. Mass executions were carried out before the VTsIK decree on mass terror. Soon after Kaplan's attempt, the public execution took place of a number of former ministers of the Provisional Government: Shcheglovitov (Justice Minister), Khvostov and Protopopov (both Interior Ministers), Beletsky (Head of the Police Department), arch-priest Vostorgov and a dozen others. Beletsky tried to run at the last moment, but was shot down. When they had finished their work in Petrovsky Park, the firing squad picked the corpses clean.[155]

By the autumn of 1918 the Soviet regime was at its weakest. It seemed that one more push and the 'first proletarian state' would collapse like a house of cards. Paradoxical as it may seem, Fanya Kaplan's attempt on Lenin saved the system. According to Trotsky: 'In those tragic days, the revolution experienced its inner crisis. Its "goodness" was moved to backstage. The Party sword was given its final tempering. Determination and when necessary remorselessness grew ... There was movement, a strengthening, and remarkably the revolution was saved this time not by a breathing-space but, on the contrary, by a new danger.'[156]

Trotsky was right. Threatened by danger, the Bolsheviks resorted to the most repugnant means of saving their state, mass terror against their own people. They kept Lenin's promise to turn the imperialist war into a civil war. They were assisted by many in this venture, including those who fired the shots on the evening of 30 August 1918 at Michelson's factory on 3rd Shchipovsky Street.

## The Guillotine of Terror

The attempt on Lenin's life became the point at which individual terror was supplanted by mass terror as an important component of state policy. Lenin had long strived for this. Trotsky recalled that when they were discussing the draft of Lenin's decree 'The Socialist Fatherland is in Danger', the Left SR Shteinberg argued resolutely against the idea of shooting on the spot anyone who gave assistance to the enemy. 'On the contrary,' Lenin exclaimed, 'that's precisely wherein lies the real revolutionary pathos.' He shifted the emphasis for ironic effect. 'You surely don't think we're going to come out the victors if we don't use the harshest kind of revolutionary terror?' Lenin never missed an opportunity, when discussing the revolution or the dictatorship, to remark: 'What sort of dictatorship have we got, anyway? Show me! It's a bowl of mush, and not a dictatorship.' Trotsky further recalled Lenin saying: 'If we're not capable of shooting a White Guard saboteur, what sort of great revolution is it? Nothing but talk and a bowl of mush.'[157] In his pamphlet 'Routine Tasks of the Soviet Regime', Lenin wrote with regret that 'our regime is incredibly mild, more like milk pudding than iron in every particular'.[158]

Before the attempt at Michelson's, Cheka terror was already a phenomenon to strike a chill in the heart. Like the sound of a bolt being shot, the two syllables, *Che-ka*, would stop any conversation. The Cheka – or the Extra-ordinary Commission for Combating Counter-revolution and Sabotage, to give it its full name – was founded in December 1917, under the chairmanship of Felix Dzerzhinsky, 'Iron Felix', as the revolutionary inquisition, remorseless and implacable. The attempt on Lenin came at an opportune moment. Only by the use of terror could the regime make the soldiers fight or secure the grain supply. On 5 September 1918, a week after the attempt, at a meeting of the Sovnarkom which Sverdlov chaired in Lenin's absence, Dzerzhinsky and Sverdlov raised the question of mass terror, and Dzerzhinsky read a brief report. The bourgeoisie, he said, and their accomplices had raised their heads. The hydra's head must be cut off. Still shaken by the attempt and by the wave of demands from the workers to use force to put an end to these hostile acts, the People's Commissars were willing to pass any decree if it was fierce enough. The decree 'On Red Terror', which they passed, was entirely satisfactory to Lenin when he saw it, no doubt making a change from the usual 'bowl of mush'. It deserves to be quoted in full:

The Council of People's Commissars, having heard the report of the Chairman of the All-Russian [Cheka], finds that in the present situation the security of the rear by means of terror is an absolute necessity; that to reinforce and to introduce a more systematic character into the activities of [the Cheka], it is essential that as many responsible Party comrades as possible be sent to work there; that it is essential to protect the Soviet Republic from class enemies by isolating them in concentration camps, that anyone involved in White Guard organizations, conspiracies and rebellions will be shot; that the names of all those executed should be published and also the grounds for applying this measure.[159]

In Lenin's absence, the decree was signed by People's Commissar for Justice Kursky, People's Commissar for the Interior Petrovsky and Administrator for Affairs Bonch-Bruevich. As the émigré historian Sergei Melgunov wrote: 'The moral horror of the terror, its disintegrating effect on the human psyche, lay not so much in the individual murders, or even in their number, as in the system itself.'[160] As during the French Revolution the knife of the guillotine ceaselessly reaped its doleful harvest, so now the Cheka gunned its way through the population.

The Bolshevik system set about 'systematically' creating a climate of fear and slavish obedience. In an interview in November 1918, Peters declared: 'Until Uritsky [People's Interior Commissar for the Northern Region and Chairman of the Petersburg* Cheka] was murdered in Petersburg there were no executions, but after it there were too many, often indiscriminate, whereas in Moscow the regime responded to the attempt on Lenin with the execution of only a few tsarist ministers.' In fact, as Peters knew well, hundreds had been shot. He used the interview to issue a warning that 'Any attempt by the Russian bourgeoisie to raise its head again will be met by such a rebuff and such punishment that anyone who knows the meaning of Red Terror will grow pale.'[161]

The war against the Russian people was the Bolsheviks' greatest sin. It may be objected that terror was only used against those found

---

* The name was adopted following the Bolshevik custom of calling the old capital Petersburg, eschewing the Slavic form, Petrograd.

guilty of crimes against the regime. Not so. A month before the decree
on Red Terror was enacted, Lenin recommended a decree to A.D.
Tsyurupa, the People's Commissar for Food Production, according to
which 'in every grain-producing district twenty-five–thirty hostages
should be taken from among the rich who will answer with their lives
for the collection and loading of all surpluses'. Tsyurupa was dismayed
by the harshness of this measure, and in his reply evaded the subject
of hostages. At the next meeting of the Sovnarkom, Lenin demanded
to know why he had not replied on the issue of hostages. Tsyurupa
tried to defend himself, as the very idea of hostage-taking appalled
him, and he had no idea how to organize it. Energetically, was the
answer. Lenin sent another note, to make his meaning clearer: 'I am
not suggesting that hostages be *taken*, but that they be *appointed* by
name from each district. The object of appointing them is that, being
rich, just as they are responsible for their contribution, so they are
responsible with their lives for the immediate collection and loading
of grain surpluses.'[162]

Those who like to think that such measures were prompted by
circumstances, and that they applied only to particular cases, are
simply wrong. The scale was massive, and the measures are typical of
the way Lenin operated during the civil war. On 20 August 1918 he
wrote to Nikolai Semashko, Commissar for Health and also a civil
war leader, in Livny: 'I congratulate you on your energetic suppression
of the kulaks and White Guards in the district. We must strike while
the iron's hot and not lose a minute, organize the poor of the district,
confiscate all the grain and all the property of the rebellious kulaks,
hang the kulak ringleaders, mobilize and arm the poor under reliable
leaders out of our own unit, arrest hostages from among the wealthy
and hold them.'[163]

The idea of the concentration camp system – the State Camp
Administration, or GULAG – and the appalling purges of the 1930s
are commonly associated with the name of Stalin, but the true father
of the Bolshevik concentration camps, the executions, the mass terror
and the 'organs' which stood above the state, was Lenin. Against the
background of Lenin's terror, it becomes easier to understand the
methods of Stalin's inquisition, which was capable of executing someone solely on the grounds of suspicion. Lenin did not merely inspire
revolutionary terror, he was also the first to make it into a state

institution. When M.M. Volodarsky, People's Commissar for the Press, Propaganda and Agitation, was assassinated in Petrograd in 1918, Lenin expected the local Bolshevik authorities to take strong measures. Instead, he found them slack and half-hearted, and sent off a stinging letter to Zinoviev: 'Just today the Central Committee heard that the [Petrograd] *workers* wanted to respond to the murder of Volodarsky with mass terror and that you (not you personally, but the local [Party leaders]) held them back. I resolutely protest! We are compromising ourselves: even our resolutions threaten mass terror, but when it comes to action, *we slow down* the *entirely* justified revolutionary initiative of the masses. This is im-poss-ible! The terrorists will think we're milksops. We have an extreme war situation. We must encourage energy and widescale terror against the counter-revolutionaries, especially in [Petrograd] as a *decisive* example.'[164]

The decree on mass terror was the foundation upon which the system was built and developed by Lenin's successors and by those who followed Dzerzhinsky and Unshlikht. It is difficult to fathom how a man who loved Beethoven and Spinoza, who had read Kant and who liked to tell Gorky and Lunacharsky how much the Bolsheviks valued the intelligentsia, could reconcile himself to a system permeated with police rule. How could Lenin, who claimed to be the leader of a new world, personally write the orders to hang, to shoot, to take hostages, to imprison in concentration camps, knowing that these would not remain mere words?

When the Bolsheviks first used terror, they justified it by citing 'revolutionary conscience' and the hasty decrees of the Sovnarkom which encouraged it. When, however, terror became an everyday, common and at times mass occurrence, Lenin felt the need to give it a theoretical foundation. There are many articles in which he developed his explanations. In November 1920 the journal *Kommunisticheskii Internatsional* published 'On the History of the Question of the Dictatorship'. Opening with his customary 'Whoever does not understand the need for dictatorship of any revolutionary class to secure its victory, understands nothing of the history of revolution,'[165] Lenin proceeded to list a number of propositions to justify and whitewash revolutionary terror. 'The dictatorship means – take note of this once and for all – unrestrained power based on force and not on law.'[166] Several times Lenin repeated Gorky's phrase, 'the logic of the axe', and he seemed to enjoy his own discovery that: 'Unrestrained, lawless power, based on force in the simplest sense of the word, is precisely what the dictatorship is about.'[167] He then produced a definition: 'The dictatorship means nothing other than power totally unlimited by any laws, absolutely unrestrained by regulations and based directly on the use of force.' The 'revolutionary people creates its own court and punishment, applies force, creates new revolutionary law'.[168] According to Lenin, violence meted out in the name of the dictatorship of the proletariat is 'revolutionary justice'.

It is worth noting that before the revolution, on the whole Lenin did not stoop to 'the logic of the axe', the methods of the executioner. Having seized power, he shrugged off the cape of the Social Democrat and donned the cloak of the Jacobin. All his attitudes were now conditioned by one consideration: to cling to power at any cost. He did not, however, restrict himself to establishing the theoretical foundations of terror as state policy, but was also directly involved in its application. His correspondence with D.I. Kursky, People's Commissar for Justice, is both eloquent and illuminating. Naïvely, Lenin hoped that the organs of justice would help to cut through the monstrous bureaucracy that was coming into being. He suggested to Kursky that 'absolutely by this autumn and winter of 1921–22, four to six cases of Moscow red tape must be brought to court, choosing "model" cases and making of each trial a political cause'.[169] Hoping that the Commissariat of Justice might bring some 'revolutionary order' into the mired bureaucracy, he wrote: 'Our state enterprises are in a shocking condition. And the worst culprits, the laziest idlers, are "well-meaning" Communists, who allow themselves to be led by the nose. The [Commissariat for Justice and the Revolutionary Tribunals] are primarily responsible for dealing fiercely with these idlers and the White Guards who are toying with them.'[170] He added that there were plenty of intelligent people among the idlers and advised Kursky 'to set up a political trial to shake up this "learned" swamp'.[171]

None of this distracted Lenin from the task of putting the repressive apparatus on a legal basis, even though his notion of what was legal bore little relation to justice. In 1922, Kursky set about formulating the Criminal Code of the RSFSR. With the formation of the USSR (Union of Soviet Socialist Republics) in 1922, each constituent republic composed its own criminal code, in theory independent but in practice in conformity with rules laid down by the Communist Party of the Soviet Union. Lenin took an active part in formulating the model criminal code, that of the Russian Soviet Federative Socialist Republic (RSFSR). He wrote to Kursky: 'In my opinion, we should widen the use of execution (commuted to deportation abroad).'[172] Two days later he wrote again: 'The law should not abolish terror; to promise that would be self-delusion or deception; it should be substantiated and legalized in principle, clearly, without evasion or embellishment.'[173] He could hardly have been more frank: terror must be legalized as a matter of principle, and its sphere of application be as broad as possible. Moreover, he added two possible variants showing how the 'use of execution could be broadened', only one of which we cite, since the differences between them are insignificant: 'Propaganda, agitation or participation or collaboration with organizations helping that part of the international bourgeoisie which does not recognize the right of the Communist system of ownership to replace capitalism and attempts its overthrow by force, by intervention, blockade, espionage or financing the press and similar methods, shall be sentenced to [death], commuted in mitigating circumstances to deprivation of liberty or deportation abroad.'[174] This became in all respects the basis of the notorious Article 58 of the Soviet Criminal Code,[175] as was recognized in Volume 45 of Lenin's works, published in 1970: 'Lenin's suggestions were taken into account in the Criminal Code ... in the section on counter-revolutionary crimes.'[176]

It was to Lenin that Soviet society owed the credit for having established and created a special rôle for its 'punitive organs'. In this he owed nothing to Marx and Engels, who had left no instructions about how such bodies should be created or how they were to function. Lenin himself was the patron saint of the Cheka. Established in December 1917, it was soon accorded extra-judicial status at Lenin's behest. The omnipotent Cheka had the power to arrest, investigate, pass sentences and carry them out. Tens of thousands of people were shot without trial in the cellars of the Cheka. As if this was not enough, on 14 May 1921 the Politburo, chaired by Lenin, passed a motion 'broadening the rights of the [Cheka] in relation to the use of the [death penalty]'.[177]

Cheka terror was closely coordinated with Party decisions. In June 1918, three months before the decree on Red Terror was adopted, a

Party conference of Chekists passed decrees 'to remove from circulation prominent and active leaders of the Monarchist-Kadets, the Right Socialist-Revolutionaries and Mensheviks; to register and put under surveillance generals and officers, to maintain observation on the Red Army, its command staff . . .; to shoot prominent and plainly guilty counter-revolutionaries, speculators, robbers and bribe-takers'.[178] Often, the Politburo preempted a decision of the courts. For example, it ordered the Central Asian Bureau 'under no circumstances to let go of the Basmachi leaders and to bring them to trial by Revolutionary tribunal straight away, with a view to applying the death penalty'.[179]

Lenin's absorption in the affairs of the Cheka embraced the most basic technical detail: 'custody and surveillance must be brought to perfection (special partitions, wooden partitions, cupboards or partitions for changing clothes), sudden searches; a system of double or triple sudden checks using all the rules of criminal-search art and so on'.[180] These were the words of a professional in the security service rather than a head of government. He wrote to Dzerzhinsky suggesting that it would be 'useful to carry out arrests *at night*'.[181]

Lenin was obsessed by the fear of 'secrets' being leaked, the discovery of Bolshevik plans and foreign intrigues. Even when Herbert Hoover, head of the US Food Administration, launched a relief programme in July 1921 to help distribute food and combat the famine in Russia, most of the workers being young American students, Lenin sensed danger. He wrote secretly to Molotov: 'In view of the agreement with the American, Hoover, there is going to be an influx of a mass of Americans. We should think about surveillance and being kept informed. I propose the Politburo order that a commission be created with the task of preparing, working out and operating intensified surveillance and informaton on the foreigners, through the Cheka and other organs. The Commission should consist of Molotov, Unshlikht and Chicherin. They may be replaced only by members of the Party, and only very highly placed ones, with Molotov's approval.'[182]

For decades the Soviet people were brought up on the myth of Lenin's 'goodness', and countless books regurgitated the same stories of his concern for his fellow man. His 'goodness' was special, it was 'revolutionary'. For example, when he was informed that in Tsaritsyn a certain Valentina Pershikova had been arrested by an alert Chekist for defacing a picture of Lenin, he wrote to the man: 'There's no need to arrest someone for defacing a portrait. Release Valentina Pershikova immediately, but if she's a counter-revolutionary, keep an eye on her.'[183]

Lenin gave the Cheka his personal protection. After the revolution, control over the punitive organs was exercised by the Politburo alone, and later by the head of government and Party. If a conflict arose between the Cheka and any other state organ, Lenin invariably took the side of the Cheka. In December 1917, M. Kozlovsky, a senior official in the Commissariat of Justice, wrote to Lenin objecting to the Cheka's 'unfounded executions': 'Several days have passed since I informed Stalin that I am at his service. But he is being slow. I attach eight cases which concern the protest I have made to the Cheka ... I proposed a review of the executions of all the police officials, beginning with the village constable and the police officer ... The decision "to shoot" is often taken without any investigation or foundation, ( ... one of them just because he's a monarchist).' Lenin wrote to Stalin that Dzerzhinsky had told him the Cheka was against his meeting Kozlovsky.[184] And there the matter ended.

The Cheka quickly became virtually the chief element of the state, arousing fear not only among the mass of the population, but also among the Bolsheviks themselves. N.V. Krylenko wrote that the Cheka soon became a People's Commissariat, 'terrifying in the remorselessness of its repression and the total impenetrability to anyone's gaze of what was going on in its depths'.[185]

Sensing the rise of muffled hostility to the Cheka, Dzerzhinsky, with Lenin's blessing, proposed to cease applying the death penalty in the provinces without ratification of the sentence in Moscow – by the Cheka. At the same time, he proposed that the death penalty be used more intensively against corrupt officials on the economic front.[186]

When an attempt was made to bring the repressive activities of the Cheka under the control of the Commissariat of Justice, Dzerzhinsky rebelled: '[It] will destroy our prestige, diminish our authority in the struggle with crime, and confirm all the White Guard slander about our "unlawful actions" ... This is not an act of supervision, it is an act of discrediting the Cheka and its organs ... The Cheka is under the supervision of the Party.'[187] Dzerzhinsky was wrong: already the Party was not in control of the Cheka. It was subordinate to the first man in the Party only, and this became its sinister tradition. Steadily, but rapidly, the Cheka became a state within a state, with the power to sentence any citizen at its own discretion.

Alongside the Cheka were the Revolutionary Tribunals, so named by analogy with the French Revolution. Sergei Kobyakov, a defender in these tribunals, recalled: 'There was no appeal against a sentence handed down by a tribunal. The sentence was not confirmed by any-one and had to be carried out within twenty-four hours.'[188] The tri-bunals did not compare with the Cheka, either in their effect or in the scale of their operations, but nevertheless they disposed of thou-sands of people, often merely for belonging to the 'exploiting' class.

Global figures are not available, but particular incidents are revealing. In March 1921, while the Tenth Congress of the Bolshevik Party was in progress in Moscow, the soldiers and sailors on the fortress Baltic island of Kronstadt, twenty miles from Petrograd, revolted against Bol-shevik rule and called for a government genuinely based on all-socialist Soviets. Lenin sent 50,000 Red Army troops to crush the insurgency. The exact number of those killed is unknown, but 167 sailors from the battleship *Petropavlosk* alone were sentenced to death on 20 March, and similar trials went on throughout March and April.[189]

In 1921, with the civil war winding down fast, the military tribunals carried on as before, and although fewer army personnel were executed than in 1918 or 1919, the scale of revolutionary terror among the military is startling. N. Sorokin, deputy chief of the Military Colle-gium of the Supreme Tribunal, and M. Strogovich, director of the statistical branch of the Tribunal, reported to Trotsky that in 1921 4,337 Red Army troops and commanders were executed.[190] This was in a year when the wind of victory was filling the Reds' sails and all their military defeats were behind them.

Occasionally, Lenin himself would advise on the conduct of a case. On 27 August 1921, at a small Politburo gathering consisting of Trot-sky, Kamenev, Zinoviev, Molotov and Stalin, the question of the trial of the White general Baron von Ungern-Sternberg was discussed. Lenin made a proposal which was at once accepted: 'We should aim for a solid accusation, and if there's plenty of evidence, about which there can be no doubt, we should organize a public trial, carry it out at maximum speed and shoot him.'[191] The question here is not whether Ungern deserved a trial – his record as a civil war chieftain in eastern Siberia was bloody enough – but why the Politburo was involved. Lenin's proposal amounted to a political order to the court. He was acting as investigator, prosecutor and judge. No defence lawyer was needed.

The Cheka did not restrict its executions to the bourgeoisie, workers, peasants and the Red Army. It also shot its own people if they aroused suspicion. In March 1921 a group of Chekists at the Turkestan front wrote to the Central Committee, protesting that executions had increased in the Cheka: '[Chekists] are being shot for various crimes, and none of the Communists working in these proletarian punitive organs has any guarantee that he won't be shot tomorrow under some heading or other.' The authors went on: 'Once a Communist starts to work for the punitive organs he ceases to be a human being, but becomes an automaton . . . He cannot express his own views or give vent to his needs, as there is always the threat of execution.' As a result of the work they did, and also the constant threat of punishment, the Chekists 'develop bad tendencies, such as arrogance, vanity, harshness, callous egoism and so on, and they are gradually becoming a particular caste'.[192]

It was a 'particular caste' that absorbed Lenin's particular interest. For him, the Cheka must have one quality, namely loyalty: loyalty to him, to the Party and to the revolution. Bolsheviks sensed this, and they tried to assist by making suggestions. Ganetsky, for example, proposed to Lenin that there ought to be still greater unity between the Cheka and the Party: 'It is important,' he wrote, 'to establish the closest possible ties between the Party organizations and the [Cheka] . . . All Party members in responsible posts must report to the Cheka all the information they receive, whether by private or official channels, that might be of interest in the struggle against counter-revolution.' Lenin responded by enquiring if Ganetsky had discussed the matter with Dzerzhinsky and asking him to telephone. It was a proposal very much in harmony with Lenin's own thinking. He expressed his feelings about the Cheka in the memorable phrase: 'A good Communist is also a good Chekist.'[193]

The Leninist school of terror took many forms: hostage-taking, deportation, deprivation of citizenship, execution for trivial causes, entrapment. In subsequent years, Menzhinsky, Yagoda, Yezhov and Beria would invent and refine yet new methods, based on proven Leninist experience. For instance, in April 1941 Deputy Interior Commissar I. Serov sanctioned the following recruiting 'programme'.

Under the code-name Operation Windmill, a false Soviet frontier with a false Japanese frontier-post was created in the Far East in the region of Khabarovsk. Soviet citizens were sent across the 'frontier' on special 'missions'. There, they were arrested by Chekists dressed as Japanese guards, savagely interrogated, recruited as agents by the 'Japanese' and sent back across the border, where they would immediately fall into the hands of 'real' Chekists. When it was revealed that under 'Japanese' torture they had confessed to their NKVD links, they were condemned to death. Hundreds of unfortunates were dealt with in this way, and it was only the Soviet entry into the war in June that halted Operation Windmill.[194]

Despite the appalling economic hardship being suffered by the country, there is much documentary evidence that Lenin never denied the Cheka financial help. To cite only one example: as Chairman of the Council of Labour and Defence, in November 1921 he signed an order releasing a supplementary grant of 792,000 gold roubles to the Cheka for special needs.[195] The Politburo ratified the decision on 24 November.[196]

The Cheka was under Lenin's constant gaze, and he made it plain that he regarded this body as one of the chief attributes of the system he had created. Speaking in 1922 at the Ninth Congress of Soviets, he said, 'without such an institution the workers' regime could not exist'.[197] Yet only a few weeks before the October coup, in his *State and Revolution*, he had stated that when the proletariat seized power the state machine would be smashed and the state begin to wither away. Lenin lacked the vision to see the distant horizon of social development; his eyes were usually fixed at his feet, on everyday concerns and on the experiments that would turn the great country into the homeland of the GULAG.

The guillotine of the Russian revolution was the gun, and when it became clear that the civil war had been won, the firing squads' volleys were gradually replaced by the sporadic crack of revolver fire. But the fight against counter-revolutionaries, terrorists and saboteurs could not be managed with the Chekists' revolvers alone. As early as 1918 the Bolsheviks began organizing concentration camps, and those who were spared the bullet began filling them. On 20 April 1921 the Politburo under Lenin's chairmanship approved the building of a camp for ten to twenty thousand people in the region of Ukhta in the far north.[198] A week later, Dzerzhinsky proposed that soldiers and sailors from Kronstadt – regarded in 1917 as the cream of Bolshevik support – who had rebelled against Soviet authority in March 1921, and held out against a mass Red Army assault for two weeks, should be 'settled in the penal colony of Ukhta'.[199] The Cheka then proposed building a new colony at Kholmogory, also in the north.[200] And so it went on. Soon the entire secret map of the country would be pitted by the evil pock-marks of the camps, through which millions would pass in the seventy years of the Leninist regime.

The first deportations to the camps took place during the civil war. An especially large number of women and children were 'resettled' from the Don and the Kuban following the savage reprisals against the Cossacks. Thousands of them died, either in camp or on the way there. Trotsky anticipated Stalin's Siberian 'marches' when in August 1920 he reported to Moscow: 'In the Kuban I propose to announce in the name of the government that families found guilty of collaborating with [the White general Baron] Wrangel will be deported beyond the Baikal to regions held by the Japanese, the Semenovites and others. I request to know if there are any objections.'[201] There were no objections, but there was no transport.

The former Party archives and repositories of the KGB–NKVD contain piles of letters from the forlorn inmates of countless camps. The greater part would have been destroyed by the authorities, but some survived. They are especially numerous from the collectivization period of the early 1930s when Lenin's 'cooperative plan' was being realized. A random selection of such letters may give an impression of the mood of the time:

Request by the deportees of Severo-Dvinsk Region, Kotlass District, from the mass of people at Makarikha camp. We ask you to deal with our cases, [to tell us] what we did to deserve being tormented and mocked here? How is it we reaped much grain and helped the state and now we are worthless? If we are worthless, then please send us abroad, as here we are threatened with starvation and every day a revolver is held to our breast and they threaten to shoot us. One woman was stabbed by a bayonet and two men were shot, and in six weeks 1600 people perished.

The masses ask you to send a commission to inspect us and the conditions we are living in. A good farmer houses his cattle better, whereas we have water underfoot and sand falling into our eyes from above, we never take our clothes or shoes off, there's not enough bread, they give us three hundred grammes, there's no hot water at all, and if this goes on for another month there'll be hardly anything left.

Surely Russia isn't suffering because we planted a lot of grain? We think it's the opposite. We never had losses of grain, but now we lose everything and the way we're treated is not civil, it's simply idiotic. Can't you see what's happening? They took everything away and deported us. No one is better off, and Russia is in decline.

We ask the Central Executive Committee to see the state the kulaks of Makarikha are in: our huts are falling down, we live in great danger, the huts are heaped in excrement, the people are dying, we carry out thirty coffins a day. We have nothing: no firewood for the huts, no hot water, no rations, no bath to keep clean, and just three hundred grammes of bread, and that's it. With up to 250 people in a hut, we are getting ill just from the air we breathe, especially the babies, and this is how you torment innocent people.[202]

Those still at large tried to help the exiles, and some brave souls even travelled to the north to find them. Here is an anonymous letter, dating from early 1930, 'to the authorities':

We are writing to your honour and we ask you to believe our letter, which was groaned out in the northern tundra, not in bitter tears but black blood. We arrived in a place in the northern tundra of the Nandomsk region to find deported innocent souls . . . They have been thrown out not to somewhere else to live, but to a living misery like no other place made for man. When we were in the north, we were witness to the fact that up to ninety-two people are dying every day: we even had to bury children ourselves and burials are going on the whole time. This is only a brief letter, but to spend a week there, as we did, it would be better if the land fell into the sea and with it the entire universe, and if there were no more world and everything living on it.[203]

As Lenin had promised, the plough of the revolution 'turned Russia over'. The writers of signed and anonymous letters, and even of poems, begged for relief in vain, as unnoticed by the regime as those who remained silent. In Lenin's words, they were the petty-bourgeoisie, the main enemies of the revolution. If they were not liquidated, they had to be re-educated, 'taught socialism',[204] at whatever cost. The Bolsheviks believed this movement towards socialism could not take place without the guillotine: the end justifed the means. As Lenin wrote: 'Let the lap-dogs of bourgeois society . . . yelp and whine over every unwanted pup, while we cut down the big, old forest.'[205]

# 5

## Lenin's Entourage

From the beginning of his revolutionary career, people were drawn to Lenin. They may have argued and quarrelled with him, but they could not ignore him. By the very force of his personality, he had an influence over people. But he had no bosom friends. In the early years he was close to Martov and N.E. Fedoseev – whom he met only twice – and A.A. Vaneev, and he had warm comradely relations with Zinoviev and Kamenev on the eve of the revolution. Later, at various times he was warmly disposed towards Sverdlov, Dzerzhinsky, Podvoisky and Lunacharsky. But there were no lifelong friends. If Lenin showed concern that his close associates were eating properly or getting enough rest, he was doing no more than his Party duty. He might laugh and joke, but he never crossed the line into intimacy with anyone, except Inessa Armand. He was dedicated to The Idea, and such people may have followers and sympathizers, collaborators and disciples, but rarely personal friends.

Many of those who were included in the Politburo formed by Lenin on 10 (23) October 1917 to deal with the issue of the armed uprising went on to play important rôles in creating the system and influencing its development. The Politburo was not, however, a body that manifested itself either during the coup or immediately after it. Lenin had felt that the entire Central Committee could not be readily assembled to debate everyday matters, and that instead a small group of its members should meet on a regular basis to deal with current issues. At the Eighth Party Congress in March 1919 Zinoviev, presenting the report on the organizational question, declared that if the Central Committee were any bigger it would look like a 'small [mass] meeting'.

The Communist leadership needed a Political Bureau, an Organizational Bureau and a Secretariat. No one imagined that the Political Bureau – Politburo – created at this congress would rapidly accumulate enormous authority and would in time become an organ of absolute power, concealed from the people by a cloak of secrecy and omnipotence.

The composition of the first permanently functioning Politburo, appointed on 25 March 1919, was Lenin, Kamenev, Krestinsky, Stalin and Trotsky, while candidate members were Bukharin, Zinoviev and Kalinin. All of these men, apart from Krestinsky, who remained in the Politburo only until 1921, and Kalinin, who was little more than a decoration, were Lenin's chief assistants. Krestinsky, who was both a 'Left Communist' and a 'Trotskyist', and who occupied a number of posts in the Central Committee, Sovnarkom and VTsIK, ended his life as a victim of Stalin's purges. A thick volume in the special collection of the Ministry of State Security Archives includes documents on 'the trial of Bukharin, Rykov, Yagoda, Krestinsky', with a half-page attached noting that the sentence on Krestinsky was carried out on 15 March 1938.[1]

Kalinin was more fortunate. Appointed Chairman of the VTsIK by Lenin on Sverdlov's death in March 1919, until his natural death in 1946 he played the part of a dummy head of state, and had no influence whatever on the fate of the country.

The first meeting of the Politburo, on 16 April 1919, attended by Lenin, Kamenev, Krestinsky and Kalinin only, made it plain that this was to be more of a state than a Party organ. The Politburo determined its own membership. It examined the economic position of the workers, restricted the teaching of religion to outside school hours, brought the People's Commissar for Land into the Politburo, agreed a trip by Kalinin on the agit-train 'October Revolution', ordered trials of anti-Soviet groups, and so on.

Lenin's evaluation of his entourage is best expressed and most concentrated in the famous 'Letter to Congress' that he dictated over several days between December 1922 and January 1923. On 24 and 25 December he described the political, moral and intellectual qualities of Trotsky, Stalin, Zinoviev, Kamenev, Bukharin and Pyatakov. On 24 December and 4 January he dictated a damning postscript on Stalin.[2] These notes give both a view of Lenin's appreciation of the situation in the country as a whole, and an insight into his personal attitudes to his retinue.

Lenin's inclusion of Pyatakov in his list of potential successors is somewhat surprising. He described him as a man of 'undoubtedly oustanding will and outstanding abilities',[3] and certainly Pyatakov occupied a number of important posts which could be described as ministerial, but he was never influential in the Party, as far as its strategic goals were concerned, and it is difficult to find anything in his biography that would put him on the same plane as, say, Bukharin, or indeed any of the others in Lenin's list. Perhaps it was simply Lenin's intuition that Pyatakov had great potential. None of this, however, saved him from a sad end. After expulsion from the Party, arrests and exile, he was finally put on trial in 1937. His 'outstanding will' failed him after the prolonged torture and beatings he received at the hands of Yezhov's henchmen. A secret meeting with Trotsky in Oslo in December 1935 was invented by his interrogators, as were Pyatakov's ravings in a thirty-five-page letter that he wrote to Yezhov in December 1936. In it, he cites Trotsky as telling him, 'You must understand that, without a whole series of terrorist acts, which should be carried out as soon as possible, it will be impossible to bring down the Stalinist government. I am talking about a coup d'état ... The most acute methods have to be used in preparing this coup, above all terror, wrecking and sabotage.'[4]

There was a second rank of Bolsheviks who were in close contact with Lenin, and who included such figures as Sverdlov, Dzerzhinsky, Ordzhonikidze, Uritsky, Lunacharsky and a number of others, but their rôle was rather as executors of the leader's will, his interpreters and representatives. It was the members of the Politburo who facilitated the armed uprising, carried through the economic policy of War Communism and the Red Terror, mobilized every resource for the civil war, managed the transformation to the New Economic Policy, and instigated the programme of world revolution. They, and the second-level Bolsheviks, while preserving their own personalities and peculiarities, were the bearers of Lenin's will, his inspiration and his bitter mistakes. They were the channels of the Leninist course.

The entourage was not monolithic, and many of its members were hostile to each other, especially Trotsky and Stalin, whose enmity had tragic consequences for the country and the Party. Bukharin tried to remain on good terms with everyone, often at the expense of his principles – so much so that as early as 1928 Trotsky dubbed him 'Kolechka Balabolkin' (a Russian Vicar of Bray or political weather-vane).[5] Zinoviev, who always found it hard to maintain his loyalties, described Trotsky – with some justification – as a 'phrase-monger' who had merely repeated whatever Parvus was thinking. In 1925 Zino-viev stated baldly that Trotsky 'did not know (and still doesn't know) the path to victory in the Russian revolution or the international revolution'.[6] The only stable partnership in the group was that formed by Zinoviev and Kamenev, who, apart from a serious lapse in October 1917, gave Lenin no trouble.

With rare exceptions, Lenin's entourage followed him unhesitat-ingly, supporting him, fighting among themselves and competing for a higher place on the pyramid of power. As a group, they also serve to some extent as human reflectors of their leader's image.

## *The Most Capable Man in the Central Committee*

On 24 December 1922 Lenin described Trotsky as 'the most capable man in the present Central Committee' and 'the outstanding leader of the present Central Committee'.[7] Shortly before his death, Lenin had remarked on Trotsky's superior intellect, but had also noted his weaknesses, his self-assurance and his inclination towards the 'admin-istrative side of the cause'. Lenin's assessment had been preceded by years of cooperation, as well as by fierce and at times unseemly confrontation, by careful study of each other and renewed collabor-ation. Their relationship went through several phases.

At the turn of the century it was Lenin who gave the young revolu-tionary help at a critical moment. In October 1902, Trotsky knocked on the door of Lenin's boarding house in London, having been given the address by Pavel Axelrod in Zurich, on whom he had called after escaping from exile in Siberia.

Lenin introduced Trotsky to the leading lights of the movement: Plekhanov, Potresov, Dan, Zasulich and Martov, and involved him in the work of their newspaper, *Iskra*. For his part, the twenty-year-old, who seemed to have aroused in Lenin a protective instinct, and who saw himself as a hero on the run, drank in the heady revolutionary wine fermented by the Russian émigrés. At first Lenin was keen to patronize the young man and to make him an assistant. Quickly, however, he sensed Trotsky's obstinacy, his capriciousness and his vanity. Their paths diverged at the Second Congress in 1903, when the Party split into Bolsheviks and Mensheviks, and Martov, Axelrod, Dan and Zasulich appeared to Trotsky immeasurably more appealing than Lenin.

After the 1905 revolution Lenin and Trotsky were irreconcilable political and ideological enemies. Lenin attacked Trotsky for trying to hold a centrist position, while perhaps also envying him his brilliant talent as a writer – not to be compared with Lenin's heavy-going style. Lenin heaped abuse on Trotsky and labelled him with the insulting nickname 'Judas'. In one of his letters to Inessa Armand, he wrote, 'That's Trotsky for you! Always the same, evasive, cheating, posing as a leftist but *helping* the right while he can.'[8] Trotsky, however, could give as good as he got. In the articles he wrote between 1905 and October 1917, he appropriated Lenin's rôle as a theorist, and changed his baton into a wooden club. It appeared the two must remain hostile forever. In March 1913 Trotsky wrote to the Menshevik Nikolai Chkheidze: 'The rotten squabble, systematically inflamed by that master of such affairs, Lenin, that professional exploiter of any backwardness in the Russian labour movement . . . The entire Leninist edifice is presently built on lies and falsification and carries within it the poisonous source of its own disintegration.'[9]

Right up to February 1917, Lenin regarded Trotsky as a pro-Western Social Democrat, a dreadful sin in his eyes. In July 1916 he dubbed Trotsky a hypocrite, a Kautskyite and an eclectic. ('Kautskyite' was one of Lenin's favoured insults, and he used it on Trotsky in several of his articles. Kautsky's centrism was for Lenin the very embodiment of opportunism and treachery; centrism was the betrayal of the working class. In an open letter to Boris Suvarin, Lenin explained that he reproached Trotsky 'because too often he represented the policy of the "centre" in Russia'.[10]) But, the closer the revolution approached, the less harsh Lenin became in his attitude to Trotsky, although he would still occasionally accuse him of sophistry and similar anti-Marxist crimes.

Once he was back in Russia, Lenin ceased to criticize Trotsky, now calling him 'the well-known internationalist and opponent of the war'.[11] The revolution, it seemed, was bringing them together despite themselves. If, before Trotsky returned to Russia in May, Lenin could still describe him, without reproach, as ambiguous in his attitude to the defencists,[12] on the whole after February 1917 Trotsky's position seemed clear to Lenin, and all anger ceased. In April 1917, during a speech to troops of an armoured division, Lenin castigated the British for arresting 'our Comrade Trotsky, the former chairman of the Soviet ... in 1905', while he was returning from the USA to Russia.[13] Finally, Lenin found a place in his heart for Trotsky when the Petrograd centrist organization known as the Inter-District Committee was admitted to the Party at the Sixth Congress in August 1917 (in the absence, be it said, of both Lenin and Trotsky). By this move, Trotsky brought Lenin the additional strength of 4000 socialists, as well as a powerful influx of intellectuals including Ioffe, Lunacharsky, Manuilsky, Karakhan, Uritsky and Yurenev.

It was not, however, personal considerations that brought the two men closer, but the need for radical solutions to the situation. They were both Jacobins by inclination, and were above all set on staging the uprising, establishing the dictatorship and, if necessary, using terror.

Trotsky, responding to Kautsky in the summer of 1920, wrote: 'The revolution demands of the revolutionary class that it reach its goal by *all* the means at its disposal: if necessary by armed uprising, if necessary by terrorism. Terror can be very effective against a reactionary class that does not want to leave the scene. *Fear* can be a powerful resource in both domestic and foreign policy. War, like revolution, is based on fear. A victorious war usually destroys only an insignificant part of the defeated army and breaks the will of the rest by fear.'[14] Trotsky knew that, soon after the revolution, Lenin had proposed that the Bolsheviks organize terror, and indeed echoes of Lenin's views can be plainly heard in Trotsky's article.

Lenin knew that in Trotsky he had found an outstanding organizer, able to function in any sphere of activity, who compensated for his own reluctance to stir from 'headquarters'. It suited Lenin that Trotsky had almost at once accepted second place, that he was not a rival, even if at times his popularity exceeded Lenin's own. Later, in exile, Trotsky wrote:

Had I not been present in 1917 in Petersburg, the October Revolution would still have taken place – on the condition that Lenin was present and in command. If neither Lenin nor I had been present in Petersburg, there would have been no October Revolution: the leadership of the Bolshevik Party would have prevented it from occurring – of this I have not the slightest doubt! ... The same could by and large be said of the Civil War, although in its first period, especially at the time of the fall of Simbirsk and Kazan, Lenin wavered and was beset by doubts. But this was undoubtedly a passing mood which he probably never even admitted to anyone but me.[15]

Trotsky's description of Lenin's (and his own) part in the revolution and civil war is accurate. The two high-profile leaders personified the Bolshevik dictatorship in the public mind. In November 1917 Nikolai Sukhanov wrote: 'Who cannot see that what we have is nothing like a "Soviet" regime, but is instead a dictatorship of Lenin and Trotsky, and that their dictatorship relies on the bayonets of the soldiers and armed workers whom they have deceived and to whom they have doled out worthless tattered banknotes, instead of fabulous riches that are nowhere to be found in nature.'[16] As Dora Shturman writes, Trotsky was fitted 'by his personal psychological qualities to be the number-two man, the supreme executor rather than the initiator and generator of the ideas, manoeuvres and moods'.[17]

Trotsky was more than an outstanding organizer, orator and writer; he also possessed a remarkable talent for psychological observation, and his recollections about Lenin, some of them published in his book on him, are of greater interest than many in the vast library of writings on the subject. He recalled that 'during sessions, when speeches were being made, Lenin would save time by sending notes with an enquiry or to sound an opinion. Sometimes it sounded like a pistol shot next to one's ear ... The art in his notes was in the way he would go to the root of the question.'[18] Elsewhere Trotsky noted that 'Lenin's way of dealing personally with many things cost a great expenditure of energy. Often he would write the letters himself, address the envelopes and then stick them down.'[19] Trotsky also recalled the way Lenin would 'watch every speaker from under his hand, as if he were feeling him out and weighing every word; it was a special look of interrogation'.[20]

Occasionally Trotsky depicted Lenin in broader strokes. In his article 'The National in Lenin', published in *Pravda* in April 1920, on the occasion of Lenin's fiftieth birthday, he wrote:

Marx's very style, rich and beautiful, a blend of strength and flexibility, anger and irony, the severe and the refined, bears within it the literary and aesthetic trends of all preceding social and political German literature, beginning with the Reformation and earlier. Lenin's literary and oratorical style is terribly simple, utilitarian, ascetic, like everything about him. And there is not a trace of moralizing in his powerful asceticism. It is not the result of a principle or a contrived system, nor of course of posturing – it is simply the outer expression of an inner concentration of force for action. It is prudent, peasant efficiency, but on a grandiose scale.[21]

The comparison may not have been valid, since Marx was never the head of a government and Lenin never attempted to write the equal of *Capital*, but Trotsky was right to draw attention to the simplicity that concealed a powerful, cunning and often duplicitous mind. He was also right to see Lenin as a man of action, which was a characteristic in which Trotsky himself, as Stalin observed, was relatively lacking. While Trotsky was a major leader at critical moments, such as the coup, the German offensive and the civil war, when his energy was inexhaustible, as soon as the conflagration had died down he quickly reverted to what he had always been, namely a talented and original political writer.

By the end of 1920 Trotsky began to spend more time writing, hunting and resting in Party sanatoria than at committee meetings, which he had always found tedious. While he was still enjoying the glory of having built the Red Army, and writing his multi-volume *Works*, Stalin was busy assembling his own staff of loyal placemen and gathering power. Trotsky's lack of concern and his vanity let him down at the crucial moments, when Lenin retired from active work and when he died. Once there was no 'number one', there was no need for a 'number two'. Trotsky was only needed while Lenin was alive.

The relations between Lenin and Trotsky are revealed in their correspondence. It is certain that many letters in which Lenin expressed a favourable attitude towards Trotsky were destroyed. His 'Complete Works' and the 'Lenin Miscellany' (*Leninskii sbornik*) contain every negative statement Lenin ever made about Trotsky, and not one positive one. When Lenin died, Stalin brought to light the old polemic his rival, Trotsky, had conducted with the late leader, in which he found a great deal of verbal ammunition to fire at the now isolated Trotsky. Stalin examined literally every one of Lenin's writings in search of criticism of Trotsky, and he found it in such epithets as 'sordid careerist', 'scoundrel', 'rascal' and 'swine'.[22]

Lenin's heirs managed to overlook his favourable remarks about Trotsky, and they remained unpublished until the 1960s. For example, in connection with the elections to the Constituent Assembly, Lenin wrote: 'nobody would dispute Trotsky's candidature, as, first of all, Trotsky as soon as he returned [to Russia] took up an internationalist position; secondly, he struggled among the Interdistrict members for fusion [with us]; thirdly, during the difficult July days, he was on top of the situation'.[23] When at a November 1917 meeting of the Central Committee Zinoviev proposed bringing Right SRs and Mensheviks into the government, Trotsky objected, and Lenin was highly appreciative: 'Trotsky said a long time ago that unification was impossible. Trotsky understood, and since then there has never been a better Bolshevik.'[24]

One more example of Lenin's high opinion of Trotsky is worth citing. In 1919 the Politburo was debating Trotsky's order to shoot a commander and commissar at the front for withdrawing their regiment and preparing to retreat. Lenin took Trotsky's side. The debate acquired a condemnatory undertone, and Trotsky recalled a similar incident in 1918 and retorted angrily that if it had not been for his ruthless measures at Sviyazhsk, 'we wouldn't be sitting here in the Politburo!' 'Absolutely right!' Lenin exclaimed, and wrote a note in red ink on a blank sheet that bore the seal of the Sovnarkom. He then handed Trotsky the note, which read: 'Comrades: Knowing the strict character of Comrade Trotsky's orders, I am so convinced, so absolutely convinced, of the correctness, expediency and necessity for the success of the cause of the order given by Comrade Trotsky, that I unreservedly endorse this order.' He added, 'I will give you as many blanks like this as you want.'[25] Clearly, Lenin invested the highest trust in Trotsky's ability to carry out the functions of the dictatorship. Trotsky was his 'iron commissar', and Lenin applauded his ruthlessness.

Trotsky, however, had absorbed more of the traditions of European Social Democracy than Lenin, and he was the first to sense the fatal danger of the rapidly growing bureaucracy, which ominously signalled the birth of totalitarianism. Lenin only saw it when he had neither the strength nor the time to fight against it. Later, in exile, Trotsky described the specific form of Soviet society as the 'Stalinist bureaucracy'. For Stalinist theorists, he wrote, this social stratum did not exist. They spoke only of 'Leninism', an incorporeal leadership, an ideological tradition, the spirit of Bolshevism, an imponderable general line, 'but about the fact that there is a clerk, alive and made of flesh and bones, who twists this general line the way a fireman twists his hose, you won't hear a word . . . And there are millions of these clerks, more than there were workers at the time of the October revolution. A mighty bureaucratic machine has been erected, towering above the masses and commanding them.'[26]

Trotsky was one of the few to discern the source of the cult of Lenin and Leninism. Writing in 1927, he warned: 'The real danger begins when the bureaucracy makes attitudes towards Lenin and his teaching the subject of automatic reverence.'[27] He was of course right, but lamentably he failed to apply his insight, and he was moreover also guilty of helping to create the climate of idolatry around Lenin during the latter's lifetime. At a session of the VTsIK on 2 September 1918, Trotsky declared: 'we have a figure who was created for our epoch of blood and iron . . . This figure is Lenin, the greatest man of our revolutionary epoch.'[28] Trotsky's admiration, however genuine, brought him a moral gain: history would reserve a special place for the man who was second only to the 'greatest'.

Lenin realized that Trotsky was playing a rôle beyond those he held formally as People's Commissar for the Army and Navy and Chairman of the Military Revolutionary Council, indeed, that his volcanic energy and extraordinary organizational skills made him the regime's trouble-shooter. Whenever there was another crisis, be it at the front, in the transport or food sectors, Lenin turned to Trotsky, confident that he would effect a solution. Trotsky, who was overloaded with all manner of responsibilites and commissions, often refused. In July 1921, for instance, the Politburo wanted to add to his jobs the post of People's Commissar for Food Supply. Trotsky refused and convinced Lenin, and within a few days the Politburo also, that he was right to do so.[29]

Lenin was well aware of the hostility between Trotsky and Stalin, and tried repeatedly to normalize their relations. Although he occasionally took one side or the other, on the whole he tried to remain above the fray, and at times he criticized them both publicly. At the Tenth Congress, for instance, he expressed his disagreement with Trotsky over the trade unions, though in so courtly a manner that one can barely recognize the Leninist style: 'Comrade Trotsky today debated with me especially politely and rebuked me or called me arch-cautious. I must thank him for the compliment and express my regret that I am unable to return it. On the contrary I am constrained to speak of my incautious friend.'[30]

After the October coup, Lenin and Trotsky had the relationship of equals, but when Lenin became ill in 1922, his relations with other leaders strengthened at Trotsky's expense. Trotsky visited him less than, say, Stalin or Bukharin. On the other hand, Trotsky, who talked to Lenin's physicians, seems to have realized sooner than many that Lenin was not going to be able to return to his full functions as Chairman of the Sovnarkom. And he was convinced in his heart that Lenin could pass the leader's baton to no one but him. He was psychologically prepared to replace the leader, but he was seriously mistaken. He had earned the unspoken dislike of his colleagues by his blatant show of intellectual superiority.

Believing that Lenin was finished, Trotsky was extremely sceptical about the sick Lenin's efforts to address the Party through the press. When on 5 March 1923 Lenin asked him to 'take on the defence of the Georgian affair at the Central Committee', since he could not rely on the impartiality of Stalin and Dzerzhinsky,[31] Trotsky refused on the grounds of ill health. Perhaps he wanted to avoid worsening his relations with Stalin, or already regarded Lenin's wishes as whims. In either case, he would not carry out the last wish of his leader.

Despite the good relations he enjoyed with Lenin, at times Trotsky felt that his past was not entirely forgotten, and that at any moment it might be used against him. Indeed, in his 'Testament' Lenin chose to remind the Party of Trotsky's non-Bolshevik past, even though his tone was not accusatory. There may have been political intimacy between them, but not close friendship. Trotsky's wife, Natalya Sedova, did not visit Krupskaya, and Trotsky, unlike Kamenev, Zinoviev, Bukharin and Stalin, did not visit Lenin at home. Nor was he drawn to his sick leader's bedside, where the others were frequently to be found.

It is possible that Lenin retained, consciously or unconsciously, a degree of distrust towards Trotsky, as a number of hitherto unpublished documents suggest. On several occasions he wrote personal – if enigmatic – notes to Kamenev, Zinoviev and Stalin, suggesting they should exert pressure on Trotsky to change his views on some issue or other. On 14 March 1921 Lenin wrote to Kamenev suggesting that at the Tenth Congress, 'You should say (I forgot to) that Trotsky's approach is *entirely wrong*, and that practical experience will show Trotsky his mistake (say you're in favour and that it'll go through on another point).'[32] Lenin was clearly reluctant to point out Trotsky's 'mistake' in public, but was encouraging Kamenev to do so. Similarly, during a discussion on another item at the Politburo, he wrote to Kamenev: 'Take no notice of Kalinin, leave him to me. You deal solely with Trotsky.'[33] It is plain here that Lenin was using Kamenev to influence Trotsky in a way he was himself not prepared to do.

When Trotsky heard that, despite the considerable administrative load he was already bearing, the Politburo wanted to put him in charge of the state treasury under the Finance Commissariat, he refused, sending a written explanation. Lenin reacted with a note to the Politburo: 'Trotsky's letter is unclear. If he is *refusing*, a decision of the Politburo is required. I am for not accepting his resignation.'[34] Once again, Lenin avoided open confrontation with Trotsky, preferring to leave it to other members of the leadership to reason with him. On 18 July 1922, while convalescing at Gorki, Lenin wrote to Stalin asking for his and Kamenev's opinion of Trotsky.[35] It appears that a line was being worked out by Lenin, Stalin and Kamenev either against Trotsky or about him. The initiative for these discussions may have come from Stalin, encouraged by other members of the Politburo who feared an increase in Trotsky's power, and it is likely that the question of relieving him of a post or two was discussed, as a letter from Lenin to Kamenev suggests:

I think we'll manage to avoid exaggerations. You write, '(The Central Committee) is casting or is about to cast a healthy cannon overboard'. Surely that's a gross exaggeration? To cast Trotsky overboard – which is what you're hinting at, there's no other interpretation – would be the height of absurdity. If you don't think of me as having become stupid to the point of uselessness, then how can you think of such a thing???? Blooded children before the eyes* . . .[36]

* A quotation from Pushkin's *Boris Godunov*.

Lenin evidently felt the opposition to Trotsky was going too far, and here he was defending him.

In general, Lenin used his authority to prevent the enmities within the leadership from splitting the Party, even if he was not always entirely open with Trotsky. He often expressed sincere amazement and admiration for Trotsky's military audacity. Trotsky sent Lenin and Sverdlov copies of most of his operational instructions, and many of them bear a note of Lenin's approval. In a cable of 26 November 1918 to the Revolutionary War Council at Balashov, Trotsky wrote: 'You must use an iron fist to force the divisional and regimental commanders to go over to the attack at whatever cost. If the situation does not change in the course of this week, I shall be compelled to apply stern repression against the command staff of Ninth Army. On 1 December I demand from Ninth Army Revolutionary War Council an accurate list of all units which have not fulfilled their battle orders.'[37]

At times Lenin interpreted Trotsky's cables to him as categorical demands which, knowing the critical position, even he would try to fulfil as quickly as possible. In a cable to Lenin of 28 December 1918, Trotsky declared: 'I draw the Defence Council's attention to the excessive exemption from military service of so-called irreplaceable officials . . . The difficult position on the railways is chiefly explained by the absence of good workers who are being replaced by frightened and hysterical people who cannot do anything.'[38] The phrase 'I draw the Defence Council's attention' smacks of an order from a boss to an inferior body. Lenin, however, was not offended, knowing full well that Trotsky was the key to success or failure in the civil war. Transport was a particularly troubled area, and Lenin fully supported the harsh proposals Trotsky made to relieve it. For instance, in February 1920 Lenin instructed the Defence Council: 'The individual bread ration is to be *reduced* for those not working in transport and *increased* for those who are. Let thousands more die, the country will be saved.'[39]

Trotsky was in his element during the revolution and civil war. He was not afraid to take upon himself the responsibility for measures and actions which could have far-reaching consequences. On the last day of the negotiations at Brest-Litovsk, for example, he went beyond the framework of Lenin's instructions and took what he saw as the only proper decision, thus putting Berlin and Petrograd at loggerheads for the first time. His cable to Lenin read: 'The talks are concluded. Today after final clarification of the unacceptability of the Austro-German conditions, our delegation declared that we are leaving the imperialist war, demobilizing our army and refusing to sign the annexationist treaty. In accordance with this declaration, [you may] issue the order immediately to cease the war with Germany, Austria-Hungary, Turkey and Bulgaria and to demobilize on all fronts.'[40]

Lenin was impressed by Trotsky's unflinching conviction of the inevitability of the world proletarian revolution. After two years of civil war, Lenin himself was less sanguine, and both of them accepted that it had not been possible to ignite the flames of an international conflagration immediately: it would have to be done gradually. This gradual approach was expressed in the formation of Communist parties throughout the world by the Soviet Communist Party; by organizing illegal agencies in capitalist countries, promoting labour movements and national-liberation risings. Tactics shifted from storm to siege – a siege which was to last for seventy years.

Very few people in history have had influence of a global order: a few conquerors, some great philosophers and religious figures. Among them, undoubtedly, Lenin and Trotsky have a place.

Six months before his assassination in 1940, Trotsky wrote in his will: 'Whatever the circumstances of my death, I will die with unshakeable faith in a Communist future.'[41] He never lost his belief in the Communist utopia of world revolution. As if aware that he did not have long to live, in the last year of his life Trotsky conducted a frantic propaganda war against Stalin. In his manifesto letter to the Soviet workers, entitled 'They are Deceiving You!', he wrote: 'The goal of the Fourth International is to spread the October revolution throughout the world and also to regenerate the USSR, purging it of its parasitical bureaucracy. This can only be achieved through an uprising of the workers, peasants, Red Army men and Red Navy men against the new caste of oppressors and parasites.'[42]

However different they were from each other in many ways, Lenin and Trotsky found common cause in the arena of revolution. Both believed that only force and determination could save the revolution. They each knew the other's strengths and weaknesses, and were able to work together during the revolution and civil war, setting aside their previous differences. But they were both wrong on the main point: they believed that the dictatorship they had created was capable of bringing happiness to the people. Lenin saw a danger for the regime in the weakening of the proletarian principle; Trotsky saw it in Stalin and in what he personified. Neither of them, however, understood that the danger – to the regime, to themselves, and to the future – was the system itself, the system they had designed.

A passage in Trotsky's *Diary* illustrates the bond that existed between him and Lenin:

When I was getting ready to go to the front for the first time, between the fall of Simbirsk and that of Kazan, Lenin was in a gloomy mood. 'Russians are too kind,' 'Russians are lazybones, softies,' 'It's a bowl of mush we have, and not a dictatorship.' I told him: 'As the foundation for your military units we should use hard revolutionary nuclei, which will support iron discipline from *within*; create reliable security detachments which will act from *outside* in concert with the inner revolutionary nucleus of the detachment, and which will not hesitate to shoot deserters; we should guarantee competent leadership by putting a commissar with a revolver over every [tsarist officer]; we should set up military-revolutionary tribunals and create decorations for individual bravery in battle.' Lenin answered something like this: 'That is all true, absolutely true, but there is not enough time; if we act drastically (which is absolutely necessary) our own Party will interfere: they will whine, set every telephone ringing, tug at our coat-tails – in short, interfere. Of course, revolution hardens one, but there is too little time . . .' When Lenin became convinced in our talks that I believed in our success, he supported my trip wholeheartedly, helped with the arrangements, showed great concern, kept asking about ten times a day over the telephone how the preparations were going, whether we should not take an airplane along on the train, etc . . .

When Trotsky returned from his success at Kazan and went to Gorki to tell Lenin about the first victories at the front, Lenin 'listened eagerly . . . and kept sighing with satisfaction, almost blissfully. "The game is won," he said . . . "If we have succeeded in establishing order in the army, it means we will establish it everywhere else. And the revolution – with order – will be unconquerable." '[43]

Lenin and Trotsky were not 'lazybones' and 'softies'. They were as one in believing that only terror and unrestrained violence would save the Bolshevik regime. Speaking on 12 January 1920 at a meeting of the Communist trade union faction, in a speech which mentioned terror frequently and that does not appear in his 'Complete' works, Lenin said: 'Trotsky has introduced the death penalty, and we shall approve it'.[44] Boundless faith in revolutionary violence made of these two very different men pragmatic allies, but even as the second in the hierarchy, Trotsky's position was unstable. He was alone.

## The Man with Unlimited Power

Of the three Bolshevik leaders – Lenin, Trotsky and Stalin – it pleased history that, after Lenin, it was to be Stalin who would play the most sinister part in the events of the twentieth century. Each of these three leaders had his own part to play: Lenin was the inspirer, Trotsky the agitator, and Stalin the executor, and it was Stalin who carried to its conclusion Lenin's scheme for a dictatorship of the proletariat in the land which was 'building socialism'. Trotsky, the outcast, meanwhile dreamed of spreading the scheme throughout the world in an improved form.

All three leaders assembled a phenomenal quantity of documentary material, access to which (apart from the large amount Trotsky managed to take abroad with him) was until recently strictly controlled. The countless thousands of books, monographs, memoirs, research and every kind of miscellany written either by the leaders themselves or by others, were read by astonishingly few people in the USSR. Apart from a required minimum for examinations, most of Lenin's works were of interest only to propaganda specialists. Since all other philosophies were banned, the system used Lenin's writings to give a basic political education to the people.

Lenin did not publish his works himself. This was done by his disciples. It never seems to have occurred to those condemned to read them how much trivia they included: insignificant notes, marginal scribblings, outlines of plans. For instance, Lenin's instructions on 'Sanitary rules for inhabitants of the Kremlin': 'All those arriving (by train) shall before entering their accommodation take a bath and hand their dirty clothes to the disinfector (at the baths) . . . Anyone refusing to obey the sanitary regulations will be expelled from the Kremlin at once and tried for causing social harm.'[45] There are hundreds of such examples, interesting perhaps for the historian, but essentially more in keeping with the output of a low-grade supervisor than a great revolutionary leader.

Lenin dead was even more important to Stalin than Lenin alive, for the entire Leninist heritage could then be used to work for the system. Whatever did not 'work' was kept hidden in super-secret archives. In 1933, in a letter to Stalin, one of the collectors and curators of Lenin's materials, Viktor Tikhomirnov, reported that 'the secrecy of their storage is completely guaranteed'.[46] Lenin documents were searched for and collected over decades, large sums in gold were paid abroad, masterpieces of art were given in exchange for single letters, or books with his markings, or for everyday personal notes. Entire expeditions were sent abroad to find Leniniana. The Director of the Institute of Marxism-Leninism, V. Adoratsky, wrote in triumph to Stalin in 1936: 'Comrade Ganetsky managed after several efforts to get about forty books with Lenin's markings and eighty-five books from his Cracow library (with his stamp but without markings).'[47]

Stalin replied to one request from those in charge of the archives: 'Allocations may be made. But we must know what we're getting under the guise of archives. We don't want to buy a pig in a poke. Let them give us a list of the documents in the archive with a short description of the contents, and then you can spend 50,000 roubles.'[48] A team consisting of Bukharin, Adoratsky, Arosev and Tikhomirnov reported to Stalin from Paris in April 1936, where a certain 'Roland' had offered them Lenin manuscripts for a large sum: 'Roland himself wants 3,000,000 French francs (about 240,000 gold roubles). We think it would be wiser, if the deal goes through, to set his cut at about 100,000 gold roubles, i.e. about 1,250,000 French francs. Roland has been of service apart from the purchase of the archives and could be useful in the future.'[49]

While in Paris, Tikhomirnov also had direct talks about some Lenin documents with G. Alexinsky, a former Bolshevik who had been involved in bringing the question of Lenin's German money to light in 1917. Under a 'Top Secret' stamp, Tikhomirnov reported to Stalin: 'At our first meeting Alexinsky very cautiously showed me what appeared to be letters written by Lenin. The handwriting, as far as I could judge – Alexinsky wouldn't let me read them properly – was absolutely like Lenin's. Alexinsky says Lenin wrote these letters to a [woman] writer who was on very close terms with him, but who was not a member of the Party. This person does not want to give the letters to us as long as Nadezhda Konstantinovna [Krupskaya] is alive. This woman is completely well provided for, as she has been receiving funds from us in Moscow and they have been passing either through Menzhinsky or Dzerzhinsky, and now she regularly receives an appropriate sum from a bank deposit.'[50]

The leadership spared no expense to retrieve Leniniana, and everything that fitted the scheme of Leninist and Stalinist ideology was published – with the appropriate commentary. Everything that did not was incarcerated *sine die* in the Party archives.

Stalin's archives are no less voluminous than Lenin's, and they include everything from the manuscript drafts of his first articles to Beria's reports of having carried out the orders of his 'infallible leader'. There are, for instance, the Politburo minutes of 5 March 1940, concerning the making of a new sarcophagus for Lenin's embalmed corpse, while the same meeting agreed the order – signed by Stalin and a number of other members, as was his custom – to exterminate over 20,000 Polish officers, soldiers, priests and civilians who had been interned when Poland was divided in September 1939.[51]

It is clear from the documents that relations between the leaders were not trouble-free, a fact that became especially evident when Lenin fell ill in 1922. By the following year, most of the leadership sensed that Lenin was doomed. Many of his wishes were simply ignored, while others were not handled impartially. Lenin dictated a memorandum to Kamenev about the principles of federative state organization, with the request that he acquaint the rest of the Politburo with it. Stalin read the memorandum and replied to Kamenev: 'Comrade Lenin has in my view "been too hasty" in demanding the fusion of the People's Commissariats into federal commissariats . . . Haste will only give food to the "independentists" . . . I think Lenin's amendment to Clause 5 is unnecessary . . .'[52] And so he went on, rejecting Lenin's proposals on nearly every item.

In public, Stalin continued to show loyalty right up to Lenin's death, but inwardly it seems he had buried him long before, as had Trotsky. During this time, however, Stalin used the close intimacy he had with the dying leader to strengthen his own position. He would return from Gorki – where he was the most frequent visitor – to Politburo meetings, which were being chaired by Kamenev in Lenin's absence, and convey 'greetings from Ilyich'. He would talk about Lenin's instructions and his point of view, all the while gradually, imperceptibly creating the image of himself as Lenin's particularly trusted agent. Some of Lenin's notes, written or dictated to him, he chose to convey to the others. Thus, on 19 May 1922 he read out: 'Comrade Stalin: Apropos. Isn't it time to establish one or two model sanatoria not nearer than 450 miles from Moscow? We should spend gold for this; we're spending money and we will go on spending money for a long time to go on necessary trips to Germany. But *model sanatoria* means *only* those where it is shown we have physicians and administrators who stick to the letter, and not our usual Soviet slipshod bunglers.' Having thus shown his concern for the Party leadership – only they were to benefit – in a way that would become traditional, Lenin then added a postscript, headed 'Secret': 'In Zubalovo, where you have built dachas for yourself, Kamenev and Dzerzhinsky, and where they are building one for me for the autumn, we should try to have the branch railway repaired by autumn and a fully regular rail-trolley in service. Then we can have a rapid and *secret* and cheap service all year round. Write and check up on this. Also the neighbouring farm should be put on its feet.'[53]

Lenin seemed very much concerned for the health and welfare of his comrades-in-arms. Also in 1922 he wrote: 'Comrade Stalin: I don't like the look of you. I suggest the Politburo issue instructions: Stalin must be made to spend from Thursday night to Tuesday morning at Zubalovo . . .'[54] All this served to reinforce the impression Stalin wanted to create among the members of the Politburo, namely that Lenin and his 'wonderful Georgian'[55] had a very special relationship, suggesting the possibility of succession by Stalin. For his part, after a session Stalin would often send Lenin a note, asking, for instance, when he might have twenty minutes of his time to bring him up to date on what was going on 'in the centre' – '1) either today (hardly: I'm already tired), 2) tomorrow, if there's a meeting, or will you be coming in? 3) on Saturday?' As if to underline his total loyalty, he might add, 'It's all the same to me when; you just consider *your own* convenience and only your own (*I can come out*, if you say so and *when* you say).'[56]

Lenin came to value Stalin's ardour, and relied on him increasingly.

On 10 March 1922 Stalin wrote to report that a check carried out by Yelizaveta Rozmirovich on the finances of the People's Commissariat of the Interior had revealed major omissions and that Lev Karakhan, Deputy Foreign Commissar, and Nikolai Gorbunov, chief administrator of the Sovnarkom, might be subject to criminal proceedings. 'Your opinion?' Stalin asked. Lenin replied at once: 'As long as you are convinced and there is a formal order by the investigator, then *we must* put them on trial. *We cannot* let it go.'[57]

In time the impression grew that Lenin's favoured method of managing state affairs was by sending notes. He wrote countless notes to a host of people on every subject, trivial or important, urgent or not. To Kamenev he wrote about three hundred letters and notes, to Trotsky more than one hundred, to Zinoviev about three hundred, and to Stalin more than two hundred. Many of these notes show Lenin to have been the forefather of the future Party bosses, who identified themselves with the absolutist regime and who regarded state property as their own. For instance, he wrote to the Secretary of the VTsIK, A.S. Yenukidze, asking him to make arrangements 'about speeding up the supply of firewood for A.I. Yelizarova' (Lenin's elder sister).[58]

During these early years Stalin became accustomed to carrying out personal favours for Lenin. In April 1922, for example, Lenin received a letter from G.L. Shklovsky, an old Bolshevik living in Germany, asking for a comfortable job. During the war Shklovsky had served as Lenin's special agent for many varied purposes: he had handled Lenin's correspondence and the transmission of documents, his publications, and on a number of occasions he had put his apartment at Lenin's disposal for business meetings, but chiefly he had been involved in the financial operations of both Lenin and the Party. During the prolonged tug-of-war over the 'Schmidt inheritance', Shklovsky had handled the lawyers, passing on Lenin's instructions on the preparation of arguments, and acted as his factotum. When Lenin was getting ready to leave Switzerland, it was Shklovsky he asked to recover the 100 francs he had given the Zurich police as a deposit on his residence permit.

Among the many tasks Shklovsky had carried out for Lenin were propaganda among Russian prisoners of war, ensuring that 'they come back to Russia as Bolshevik supporters', and organizing medical treatment for F.I. Samoilov, a Bolshevik deputy in the Fourth Duma. Now, after the revolution, when Shklovsky asked Lenin to set him up comfortably, Lenin deputed Stalin to deal with it: 'Shklovsky is an old Party man . . . he's worried; he's afraid of being "left out" and so on. (He has a family, with children; it's not easy for him to get used to cold, hungry Russia).' Lenin asked Stalin to find out Shklovsky's needs, and ended his letter: 'We mustn't "fritter" people away, we must deal with them attentively.'[59]

Stalin wrote to Shklovsky: 'Your letter to Comrade Lenin has been passed to me with a request to write to you to enquire where and what sort of work you would like. You may rest assured that the Party will not refuse to satisfy your desires.'[60] Shklovsky's desires turned out to be extremely practical and concrete. He wanted his family to remain abroad and to receive his present salary, while he himself was prepared to remain in Russia to do 'purely Party work', or 'to work in the administration of vocational education, or in the Land Commissariat, or Comintern, or the Foreign Commissariat'. He concluded: 'The happiest outcome for myself, however, would be to go as envoy to Switzerland.' Stalin informed Lenin that Shklovsky 'is asking to go to Switzerland . . . We have no trade representation in Switzerland, there's only the Red Cross, but I don't know if Shklovsky would want to work in the Red Cross, not being a medic. I must clarify this.'[61]

Shklovsky's wish was granted. He was engaged in diplomatic work until 1925, when he returned to become a Party functionary. However, he soon found himself labelled a Trotskyist, and in 1937, all his 'special commissions' for Lenin notwithstanding, he was shot.

Lenin wrote countless 'little notes' with requests to give assistance or support to people who had done him favours. In subsequent years the practice of appointing people to senior Party or state posts continued to depend on the will and the desire of the Party leader. To Stalin it was no more than 'hierarchical justice' to seek out a cosy place for someone who had been useful to Lenin.

By his actions Lenin taught Stalin his ruthlessness, his implacability, his cunning, his purposefulness and his ability to 'work with the cadres'. Stalin turned out to be an excellent pupil. He realized early on that Lenin was terminally ill, and also that Lenin would be more useful to him dead, but canonized, than alive. As early as 1920, on Lenin's fiftieth birthday, Stalin wrote that 'with the advance of the revolutionary epoch, when practical, revolutionary slogans are demanded of the leaders, the theorists leave the scene, giving way to new people'.[62] The examples he gave of departing theorists were Plekhanov and Kautsky, unaware as yet that among the 'new people' the little-noticed Stalin would soon emerge as a new leader. Stalin also wrote, while Lenin was still alive, that 'only those who combine theoretical power with practical, organizational experience, can hold the post of leader of the proletarian revolution and the proletarian Party'.[63]

Close association with Lenin may have taught Stalin a foul-mouthed intolerance of inadequate officials. He could hardly have forgotten a note to himself and Kamenev, dated February 1922, in which Lenin railed against the financial experts they had taken on. Lenin had written: 'We'll always be able to find shit-awful experts: let's start with some sensible ones ... you've got to straighten out these useless swine who can't present accounts ... Teach these arseholes some responsibility about producing complete and accurate figures...'[64]

Although Stalin had met Lenin for the first time in 1905, at the Tammerfors Party Conference in Finland, they were not on close terms before 1917. Indeed, in 1915 Lenin could not even recall the name of the future leader. In July he asked Zinoviev what it was, and again in November he wrote to Karpinsky: 'a big favour: find out (from Stepko [N.D. Kiknadze] or Mikha [M.G. Tskhakaya] the name of "Koba" (is it Iosif Dzh ...? we've forgotten). It's very important!!!'[65]

After they met again, when Stalin waited with other Bolsheviks for Lenin to arrive at Beloostrov on 3 (16) April 1917, and especially after the October coup, Stalin became extremely close to the leader. On the personal level, however, Kamenev and Žinoviev were closer.

During the coup itself Stalin somehow faded into the background. None of the documents of the period – apart from the falsifications of the Stalin era – say anything about his rôle in those dramatic days. It was only when on 26 October (8 November) Lenin proposed that he enter the new government as People's Commissar for Nationalities, that Stalin floated to the surface again. During the Brest-Litovsk negotiations, Stalin would not commit himself to either side of the debate. On 23 February 1918, when the German ultimatum was being discussed by the Central Committee, he attempted to take up an 'interim' position, suggesting the talks be continued, 'but we need not sign the treaty'. Lenin's response to this is well known: 'Stalin is wrong when he says we don't have to sign the treaty ... If you don't sign, then you are signing the death warrant of the Soviet regime within three weeks.'[66] Stalin was careful not to make such an error again, and henceforth he would ensure he was always on the leader's side.

After showing himself to be a diligent executor of Lenin's orders during the civil war, Stalin was appointed, on Lenin's suggestion, to the Politburo (Political Bureau) and Orgburo (Organization Bureau). These two bodies were created by Lenin in March 1919, in effect to bypass the much larger and less manageable Party Central Committee. Their functions were described in simple terms by Lenin: 'The Orgburo allocates forces, the Politburo decides policy.'[67] Plainly favouring Stalin, Lenin personally ensured that he was given an apartment in the Kremlin, checked to make sure he was getting the proper ('Kremlin') food rations, and on 15 October 1920 issued a second permit, the first having gone to Trotsky, allowing Stalin the use of a special train.[68] Lenin also appointed Stalin People's Commissar of Workers' and Peasants' Inspection, followed by other posts, culminating on 3 April 1922 in the General Secretaryship of the Central Committee. Although this appointment was proposed by Kamenev at a plenary session of the Central Committee, there can be no doubt that Stalin's candidacy had already been agreed with Lenin. The two Commissariats were largely nominal, for Stalin was too preoccupied at the front to function in them. In a letter to Ioffe, indeed, Lenin remarked that 'fate had not allowed [Stalin] *even once* in three and a half years to be *either* People's Commissar of Workers' and Peasants' Inspection *or* of Nationalities. That's a fact.'[69]

As General Secretary, Stalin was obliged to maintain even closer contact with Lenin, visiting him frequently to inform him about the situation among the leadership, and also to control access to him by other state and Party officials. Occasionally Lenin regulated the flow himself. In August 1922, for instance, he asked Stalin to arrange 'a *half-hour* meeting, either at noon or five, with Krasin, Rykov, Kamenev, [Miron] Vladimirov and [Ivan] Smilga, in any order they care to fix', and that the doctors should be informed about each meeting through Abel Yenukidze.[70]

Until the end of 1922, Stalin's relations with Lenin were extremely close. From the end of May until the beginning of October in that year, Stalin visited Lenin at Gorki twelve times, more often than any other person. As Lenin's sister Maria wrote to the Presidium of the Combined Plenum of the Central Committee and Central Control Commission of 26 July 1926:

V.I. Lenin valued Stalin very highly ... V.I. used to call him out and would give him the most intimate instructions, instructions of the sort one can only give to someone one particularly trusts, someone one knows as a sincere revolutionary, as a close comrade ... In fact, during the entire time of his illness, as long as he had the possibility of seeing his comrades, he most frequently invited Comrade Stalin, and during the most difficult moments of his illness Stalin was the only member of the Central Committee he invited.[71]

This letter was written to bolster Stalin in the savage internecine struggle going on in the leadership, but it nevertheless reflects the reality.

Even when he was seriously ill, Lenin never lost sight of his obsession with 'cleansing Russia for a long time', and he continued to give Stalin instructions to carry out his punitive orders through the Cheka.[72] Stalin was still following Lenin's advice in the 1930s, although in his own original way, sending not hundreds, but millions, and not abroad, but to concentration camps at the far ends of the huge country. He had learned much from Lenin. From the moment in May 1918 when Lenin had signed the order appointing Stalin to control food production in the south of Russia, and had vested him with 'extraordinary powers',[73] Stalin became accustomed to making decisions without regard to justice, to morals, elementary human feelings or mercy.

It was, however, not Lenin but Stalin who pioneered the new political device of assassination abroad. Stalin would bitterly regret having allowed Trotsky to leave the Soviet Union in 1929, and he set the NKVD – successor of the Cheka and OGPU – the task of eliminating his sworn enemy almost as soon as Trotsky was outside Soviet jurisdiction.[74] Stalin's assassination team pursued Trotsky, but for many years failed to hit the fatal mark.

As late as June 1937, Trotsky was still hoping for a reconciliation. From Mexico he telegrammed Moscow: 'Stalin's policy is leading to

ultimate defeat, both internally and externally. The only salvation is
a radical turn towards Soviet democracy, starting with the latest trials.
I offer my complete support for such a course.' The comment Stalin
wrote on this telegram leaves no doubt about his intentions: 'A spy's
mask! He's an insolent spy for Hitler!' Molotov, Kliment Voroshilov,
Anastas Mikoyan and Andrei Zhdanov obsequiously appended their
signatures below.[75] That same day, Stalin gave orders to intensify
the operation to liquidate Trotsky, but the mission would not be
accomplished until August 1940. The day after the event, Stalin was
shown the draft of an article for *Pravda* entitled 'The Death of an
International Spy'. He gave it his approval, but made a number of
amendments in pencil which, though few, suggest much. He described
Trotsky as 'an organizer of murders' and said that he 'taught people
how to murder behind one's back' and 'organized the villainous murders of Sergei Kirov, Valerian Kuybyshev and Gorky . . . he has the
stamp of an international spy and murderer on his brow'.[76]

While ordering the murders of millions, Stalin repeatedly called
Trotsky a murderer. The obsession with murder was becoming
characteristic. It was not a trait he was born with, but was acquired
in the process of bloody Bolshevik practice. While Lenin was alive,
Stalin was forging the character of the absolute ruler within himself.
Lenin was by education and training a lawyer and advocate, but he
behaved more like a prosecutor. The accusatory mode of thinking
was developed in Stalin under the manifest influence of Lenin, and
the actions he took later, as absolute dictator, bore the marks of that
influence – if in simplified form.

Stalin's 'Journal of Incoming and Outgoing Documents' eloquently
illustrates his style of leadership. In December 1937, concerning the
chairmanship of the Kalmyk Executive Committee, Stalin wrote to
the local NKVD: 'If Khomutinkov is a candidate for the Supreme
Soviet, there's no point in arresting him now, (you can deal with him
after the election). If he is a candidate, arrest him in two weeks.' In
the same month, having read Yezhov's report on the interrogation of
a certain Comrade Land, he wrote to officials in the Political Section
of the Red Army: 'Take note of Land's evidence. Evidently all the
people he mentions (with the exception of Meretskov) are scoundrels.'
In December 1938, replying to a note about shortcomings and distor-
tions in the work of the NKVD in Belorussia, he wrote '*personally* to

Molotov and Beria. We have to cleanse the dirt from the Belorussian organs of the NKVD; there's a lot of this dirt in all the other republics and regions.' At the same time he wrote to Beria about the 'Rokhlin spy ring': 'I've known Rokhlin was a swine for a long time. I told Bagirov a year ago that Rokhlin has to be got rid of. It's strange they've taken so long to arrest him.'[77]

Lenin kept no similar journal, but the laconic decisions, remarks and cabled orders he sent out bore a very close resemblance to those of his pupil. It is enough to recall his orders 'not to take hostages, but to appoint them by name', and that 'a ruthless military campaign is needed against the rural bourgeoisie'; or his message that 'the plan for a mass collection of grain using machine-guns is a brilliant one'; or 'we have to encourage energetic and massive terror'; or 'Draw up district lists of the wealthiest peasants who will answer with their lives for all grain surpluses'; 'hang the kulak ringleaders'; 'shoot the conspirators and waverers without asking anyone'; 'lock up the doubtful ones in a concentration camp';[78] or his note to Stalin and Unshlikht to make an example of thieves by 'catching some and shooting them'.[79]

Stalin personally ordered the execution on 27 August 1939 of Nikolai Sukhanov, the Menshevik chronicler of the revolution who had languished in Siberian exile since 1920.[80] A 'true Leninist' and a confirmed anti-Semite, it was also Stalin who initiated the 'case' against Solomon Lozovsky, an old Bolshevik and former chief of the Communist Trade Union International, and twelve other Jews on charges of espionage, and who ordered their execution (with one exception) on 12 August 1952.[81]

Lenin and Stalin were alike in their self-confidence, their belief in their infallibility, their absolute faith in the universality of the dictatorship of the proletariat, their ability in handling the masses, their caution and craftiness, their ruthlessness. But, while Lenin was Stalin's spiritual father, they were very different people in their personal behaviour. Lenin did not like to have his photograph taken, while for Stalin it was almost a necessity; Lenin had a weakness for foreign-language dictionaries and would leaf through one before going to sleep; Stalin's bedtime reading was more likely to be manuscripts of textbooks and scripts requiring his approval. The archives contain many such texts bearing his peremptory judgments. Lenin was reserved where hard drink was concerned, though he liked good beer.

Stalin preferred vodka and brandy, but towards the end of his life he drank only Georgian wine. Neither had close friends when they were in power, although that is not surprising: the moral bonds of friendship cannot withstand hierarchical restraint. Bukharin, for example, tried to save himself in endless letters to Stalin, addressing him as 'dear Koba' and signing himself in the familiar form. It was a one-sided correspondence: Bukharin pleaded, debased himself, extolled 'Koba', but it did not save him.

Lenin was cruel ideologically, politically, philosophically, and callous in the way he dealt with his political enemies, but in his personal relations he was not a cruel person. Towards Stalin he showed concern for his health, his food, his apartment and his rest. He wrote to Yenukidze, 'Isn't it possible to free the apartment allocated to Stalin more quickly? I ask you please to do this and to *telephone* me.'[82] When Stalin had to undergo some minor surgery in January 1921, Lenin wrote to his surgeon, V.A. Obukh: 'Would you please send Stalin four bottles of good port. We have to give him strength for the operation.'[83]

Holidays had been an important feature of Lenin's life abroad, but after 1917 he took time off mainly for reasons of ill health. When Stalin came to power, he took his holidays in Russia's southern resorts in the late summer or early autumn. After the Second World War, in which he felt that 'history had confirmed his judgment', he increased the number of his vacations, but even in the 1930s he would spend two to three months a year at special rest homes at Sochi, Gagry, Mukhalatka and other resorts, running the country during breaks from gazing at the sea, promenading in the parks and indulging in solitary philosophical contemplation on the terraces of ancient palaces. Between 1949 and 1952 Stalin spent up to four and a half uninterrupted months every year on holiday, from August until his birthday on 21 December.[84]

In 1922 Zinoviev wrote an article called 'Comrade Lenin on Holiday. Notes', in which he described how Lenin had enjoyed spending time before the revolution in Paris, Berne, Zurich, Cracow, Kuokkola and other places. Skating, cycling, hiking, swimming and hunting were all favourite recreations, but his preferred pastime was 'to be alone, one to one, with nature'. When they were in the Tatra mountains, Zinoviev recalled, 'he would think nothing of making us travel from our little Galician village over sixty miles into Hungary to come back with the trophy, a bottle of Hungarian wine'.[85] This article was not published. At the same time, *Pravda* asked Stalin to write a similar article, indeed with the same title.* His piece had a rather different tone: 'I met many old soldiers at the front who, after several days in constant battle without sleep or a break, came back looking like ghosts and would collapse in a heap, and then after a rest would get up and go back, refreshed, to fight again . . . Comrade Lenin made just such an impression on me.' Stalin wrote that Lenin was interested in every-thing, from the harvest to the price of the rouble, the budget, the Entente, the rôle of America, the SRs, the Mensheviks.

In December 1922 Lenin's nervous system underwent a sharp deterioration. A Central Committee plenum passed a special resol-ution making Stalin responsible for Lenin's regimen, and for helping the doctors to create the most favourable conditions for his recovery. Despite repeated strokes beginning around 20 December, Lenin asked to dictate letters and instructions. He felt he might die at any moment, and it was at this time that he dictated, among other things, his 'Letter to the Congress' and the famous 'Postscript' describing Stalin as 'crude', and stating that 'this failing, which is tolerable in our milieu and in dealings between us Communists, becomes intolerable in a General Secretary. I therefore suggest that the comrades think of a way of moving Stalin from this post and replacing him with someone who in every other way differs from Comrade Stalin in his superiority, that is, is more patient, more loyal, more respectful and more attentive to his comrades, less capricious and so on.'[87]

When Stalin heard that Lenin had been allowed by his doctors to go on dictating, he thundered down the telephone at Krupskaya. After listening in tears to this tirade, she at once sat down and wrote a letter to Kamenev: 'Because of a short letter which I wrote under Vladimir Ilyich's dictation, and with the doctors' agreement, Stalin yesterday attacked me in the crudest way.'[88] She did not tell Lenin of the incident until 5 March 1923, when he seemed to be improving. He was furious, and the following day he dictated the last letter of his life, upbraiding

---

* The object of the article was to dispel rumours that were circulating in the West and among émigrés about Lenin's death. Comrade Lenin, Stalin wrote, smiled and remarked: 'Let them lie if it gives them comfort, one must not deny the dying their final consolation.'[86]

Stalin for his behaviour towards his wife and insisting that he either apologize or break off relations with him.[89]*

Two days later, on the night of 8 March 1923, Lenin's condition worsened suddenly. He probably never saw Stalin's somewhat impertinent reply to his letter, dated 7 March. On three pages, torn out of a notepad stamped with his name and office, Stalin virtually denied what Krupskaya had reported, and concluded disrespectfully: 'if you think that to maintain "relations" I should take my words back, then I can take them back, though I refuse to understand what the problem was, where my fault lay and what it is people want of me.' It was signed simply 'I. Stalin'. [90]

Soon after Lenin died a year later, Stalin had the Marx-Engels Institute renamed the Marx-Engels-Lenin Institute. He ensured, by means of a special Central Committee decision, that all materials, documents and letters, including those of a personal nature, would be deposited in this new centre for the 'research of Lenin's heritage'. A Lenin archive of 4500 documents was created, as Tikhomirnov informed Stalin in early 1933. It would soon grow to 26,000. On Stalin's orders all Lenin material that had belonged to Bukharin, Zinoviev, Kamenev and other leading figures was transferred to it,[91] and expeditions by Ganetsky, Adoratsky and Tikhomirnov scoured Vienna, Warsaw, Cracow, Zurich, Brussels and Paris in search of more Leniniana.[92] In March 1946, for instance, Deputy Foreign Commissar A. Lozovsky wrote to Stalin that he had learned that 'in the archives of the recently deceased "Orthodox" [Lyubov Isakovna Axelrod] there are two of Lenin's letters and many from Plekhanov. I think the Marx-Engels-Lenin Institute should be instructed to obtain these letters from her heirs for some kind of compensation, [e.g.] letting them keep her apartment or a monetary payment.'[93]

Few people understood the hidden reason for the tireless search for Leniniana, especially as many of the documents vanished into the bowels of Stalin's repository the moment they were discovered. Stalin simply took control of Lenin's materials, and in this way was able at one and the same time to protect himself, to obtain an instrument of blackmail and intimidation, and to remove thousands of original documents from academic study. As has already been mentioned, in

* A fuller account of this incident is given in Chapter 7.

1991 the special repositories contained 3724 unpublished Lenin documents, and about a further 3000 official Sovnarkom papers bearing his signature. The greatest secret of Stalin's invulnerability, his diabolical strength, was his monopoly on Lenin, his monopoly on the interpretation and 'defence' of Lenin's heritage. Here was one of the roots of the stability of the totalitarian system created by Lenin, and of its inability to reform itself. Stalin ensured that it was not only Lenin's body that was embalmed, but also his ideas.

## The Bolshevik Tandem

It was 24 August 1936. The courtroom was hot and stuffy, and the summer heat seemed to solidify the atmosphere. All the windows were shut. The Chairman of the Military Collegium of the Supreme Court of the USSR, the military lawyer V.V. Ulrikh, read out the verdict in a loud voice: 'The guilt is established of 1. Zinoviev, G.Y., 2. Kamenev, L.B. . . .' and so on, until all sixteen names had been read out.

Ulrikh wiped his brow with a handkerchief and continued firing his words into the sticky, echoing silence: '. . . for having a) organized a united Trotskyite–Zinovievite terrorist centre to carry out the murder of leaders of the Soviet government and [Communist Party]; b) prepared and on 1 December 1934 through the Leningrad underground terrorist group carried out the heinous murder of Comrade S.M. Kirov; c) organized a number of terrorist groups which have been preparing to murder Comrades Stalin, Voroshilov, Zhdanov, Kaganovich, Ordzhonikidze, Kosior and Postyshev, i.e. crimes under Articles 58–8 and 58–11 of the Criminal Code of the RSFSR . . . On the basis of the foregoing . . . the Military Collegium . . . sentences 1. Zinoviev, Grigory Yevseevich, 2. Kamenev, Lev Borisovich' – and so on down to the sixteenth name – 'to death by shooting, all their personal property to be confiscated.'[94]

The condemned men were led from the court, Kamenev supporting Zinoviev, who kept muttering incoherently, 'He promised, he promised . . . Stalin promised. We must let Stalin know . . . he promised . . .' Grigory Yevdokimov, Ivan Bakaev, Vagarshak Ter-Vaganyan, Alexander Smirnov and the others, their heads lowered, were escorted out. The officials dispersed, talking to each other in whispers. Both Kamenev and Zinoviev still cherished some hope; Stalin had indeed promised to spare their lives if they would make a full 'confession' and repent. They had not realized that everything had been predetermined.

All of the sixteen condemned men, except one, wrote begging for mercy. The exception was Eduard Solomonovich Goltsman, eleventh on the list, who wrote a note declaring that he would positively not ask for mercy.[95] Perhaps it was clear to him that nothing could alter the grisly drama they were acting out. The rest were still hoping, especially Zinoviev and Kamenev. After all, they had been summoned from prison to an audience with Stalin, who had personally promised to spare their lives. Also hoping was Natan Lazarevich Lurie, who wrote in his appeal that he had 'repeatedly prepared terroristic acts against Voroshilov, Ordzhonikidze and Zhdanov, and had been armed for the purpose'. What could such a 'terrorist' expect, as he repeated under dictation the lies he had already told in court?[96]

None of the sixteen knew that in the folder containing the charge sheet lay a government order, signed by Unshlikht, to the effect that any 'petition for mercy must be rejected'. Ulrikh had only to enter the date. He signed one more document, addressed to the Commandant of the Military Collegium, Captain I.G. Ignatiev, and requiring him to carry out the sentence of death on Zinoviev and Kamenev immediately, and to inform Ulrikh that it had been carried out.[97] At 2 a.m. on 25 August, a few hours after the conclusion of the trial, in the presence of Ulrikh himself, Deputy Interior Commissar Agranov, Chief Prosecutor Vyshinsky and Ignatiev, the condemned men were duly executed in the cellar of the building in which their trial had been held.[98]

Thus ended the lives of Zinoviev and Kamenev, two inseparable comrades, who on the personal level had been closer to Lenin than anyone else. To be sure, Lenin had not forgotten their 'treachery' when they refused to support his plan for an armed uprising in October 1917. In his letter to the Bolsheviks of 18 (31) October 1917, he had raged and stormed that 'this is a thousand times more base and a million times more harmful than all of Plekhanov's speeches in the non-Party press in 1906–07 ... I would be ashamed if, out of our former friendship, I wavered in my condemnation of them. I say outright that I no longer regard them as comrades.'[99] It was this episode that Lenin recalled in his 'Letter to the Congress' of December 1922 when he wrote: 'I will only recall that the October episode with Zinoviev and Kamenev was not, of course, accidental, but also that they are no more to blame for it personally than Trotsky is for his non-Bolshevism.'[100]

The lives of this 'Bolshevik tandem' had been cut off by Lenin's successor, whom Zinoviev and Kamenev privately called 'the Asiatic'. They fell between the grinding stones of the mill they had themselves helped to build. Having been at the very peak of the Bolshevik hierachy during Lenin's life, after he died they remained there only for as long as they were useful to Stalin in his contest with Trotsky, and then for another decade they struggled desperately to get back into the top rank of the leadership.

Grigory Yevseevich Zinoviev and Lev Borisovich Kamenev were born in the same year, 1883. Zinoviev (his real name Radomyslsky) was the son of a Jewish dairy-farmer near Yelizavetgrad – renamed Zinovievsk, then (and still in 1994) Kirovograd – in Ukraine. Kamenev (his real name Rozenfeld), was born in Moscow into the family of a skilled Jewish worker. Both became Marxists early. They never associated with any of the Jewish revolutionary organizations that existed at the time, but despite their adoption of Russian aliases, there is no evidence of ethnic alienation. Like so many Russian Jewish intellectuals of their generation, they were highly secularized, and saw in the Russian revolutionary movement the broadest and most compelling arena. Like Lenin, neither of them ever did a day's paid work, dedicating themselves instead to being 'professional revolutionaries'. They both, but especially Zinoviev, had the reputation of being Marxist theorists: in an article called 'On Bolshevism', Lenin listed them among the 'chief Bolshevik writers' – a list which naturally also included himself.[101] Zinoviev's output was far greater than that of Kamenev, especially after the revolution. His collected works – in sixteen volumes, with his head embossed on the binding – were published almost simultaneously with Trotsky's. Compared to Trotsky, however, Zinoviev's writing was undistinguished, though it does possess a certain flair. The work most interesting to the historian is his memoirs, written shortly after Lenin's death but kept in the archives until 1989, in which Zinoviev describes the Prague Conference of

1912, the clashes associated with the attempts to unmask the Bolshevik double agent Roman Malinovsky, and reflects on his meetings with Lenin.[102]

Between 1918 and 1925 Zinoviev spoke countless times at the Sovnarkom, at factories, Comintern, the Central Committee and various conferences. Every word was carefully recorded by his staff and prepared for publication. The special archives contain two volumes of his notes at the Politburo. With the help of ghost-writers, he wrote bland apologetics on Lenin, *V. Ulyanov (Lenin)* in two volumes, *On the History of Bolshevism* in two volumes, and *A Year of Revolution: February 1917–1918*, as well as other books. His writings are a good example of the way in which the Party was becoming rapidly bureaucratized. For decades to come, the speeches and books of the Party bosses would be compiled by faceless assistants and speechwriters, and left unread on the shelves. At least, during Lenin's time, Zinoviev and his like did a great deal of work on their own texts. Later leaders, from Khrushchev to Gorbachev, generally did little more than adjust the tone of a speech, or sign their collected works. Intellectual prostitution was to become the norm.

Of the 'Bolshevik twins', Kamenev was undoubtedly the more appealing. He was certainly the more courageous. He opposed Lenin by publishing his protest against the planned coup in October 1917 in Gorky's newspaper *Novaya zhizn'*, and he made an attempt to oppose Stalin. At the Fourteenth Congress in December 1925 – on Stalin's birthday, as it happened – he declared:

We are against creating a 'leader' theory, we're against making a 'leader'. We are against the Secretariat standing above the political organ, by combining both policy and organization in practice. We are for our summit being internally organized in such a way that full power should reside precisely in the Politburo, uniting all the politicians of our Party, and so that the Secretariat should be subordinate to the Politburo and carry out its orders on the technical level ... Personally, I suggest that our General Secretary is not someone who is capable of unifying the old Bolshevik headquarters around himself ... Precisely because I have spoken on numerous occasions with Comrade Stalin, precisely because I have spoken on numerous occasion with a group of Leninist comrades, I say here at the Congress: I have come to the conclusion that Comrade Stalin cannot perform the function of unifying the Bolshevik headquarters ... I began this part of my speech by saying we are against a theory of one-man leadership, we are against creating a leader![103]

With the benefit of hindsight, one could say that the attempt Kamenev, supported by Zinoviev, made in October 1917 to avoid the violent accession to power by the Bolsheviks was prophetically cautious, and the speech he made in 1925 was a similar warning which went equally unheeded.

Kamenev was a less fluent writer than Zinoviev, and the articles he wrote at the beginning of his Bolshevik career, like those he wrote on the inner-Party struggle, make hard reading. In August 1909 Lenin wrote to Zinoviev of the difficulty he had in editing Kamenev's work: 'the last two-thirds of the article are altogether bad and can hardly be reworked. I've done the first third . . . but I don't feel like correcting the rest, as I can see that it's not so much a question of correcting as of rewriting the whole thing *all over again*.'[104] Perhaps Kamenev did not write well, but what he did leave does not confirm Lenin's remarks. His short book on Chernyshevsky, in the series 'The Lives of Remarkable People', reveals him to have matured as a writer, and to have been second only to Trotsky in that group.

Zinoviev and Kamenev felt a deep personal affection for each other. In moral, political, literary and some other respects, Kamenev was Zinoviev's superior, more solid and less corrupt. Zinoviev was tainted as an exponent of Bolshevik terror, while Kamenev was personally uninvolved and unblemished in this respect. Yet of the two, Zinoviev was the dominant figure, and Kamenev would follow dutifully behind.

When they were abroad before the revolution, Zinoviev was especially close to Lenin, and at one time Zinoviev's wife, Zlata Ionovna Lilina, had been close to Krupskaya, who in her memoirs recalls the couple frequently. Zinoviev distinguished himself as one of Lenin's most active and trusted agents, and it was his devotion that no doubt appealed most to Lenin: his doubts following October notwithstanding, they remained on good terms. All of Lenin's letters to Zinoviev before 1917, however, begin 'Dear friend', or 'Dear Grigory', while those written after October open with the more formal 'Comrade Zinoviev'.[105]

Notwithstanding his high profile, Zinoviev remains a somewhat enigmatic figure. Described by the Mensheviks as 'Lenin's arms-bearer', after Lenin died he went quickly into decline. Stocky and short-winded, this seemingly phlegmatic man would be transformed whenever he took the platform, speaking with tremendous animation. His strong, compelling voice could dominate a hall, and in the open air he seemed to have been made for great meetings. In Lunacharsky's words: 'Naturally Zinoviev's speeches are not as rich or as full of new ideas as the real leader of the revolution, Lenin, and he cannot compete in graphic powers with Trotsky, but with the exception of these two orators, Zinoviev has no equal.'[106] He was equally effective in German, when addressing a Comintern congress or a German Party congress, but while he wrote much and said a great deal, he cannot be described as a profound writer or commentator.

Despite their lack of colour, Zinoviev's books – or rather the materials that he published for books on Lenin – contain much of interest. In his memoirs, written in the 1920s and held in the Party archives until the late 1980s, he wrote that, even at the age of twenty-five, Lenin 'felt responsible for the whole of mankind, and plainly felt himself to be a leader (in the best sense of the word) of the working class and the Party'. He added that he felt Lenin had a genuine vocation for the rôle he had chosen for himself: 'Yes, he had it! Without it he wouldn't have become Lenin.'[107] Zinoviev's memoirs were written after he had passed the peak of his career, when Stalin was rapidly gaining strength. Marx finally died, Zinoviev wrote, when his successor, Engels, died. 'But it was different with Lenin. There was no Engels to succeed him, but he too did not die altogether . . . Yet in many ways at the same time things turned out worse than with Marx.' Then he let the cat out of the bag: there was the 'mistake' of the testament: 'he had a mistaken perception of how things would look without him'.[108]

In quite uncharacteristic style, Zinoviev was here saying that Stalin was no Engels, and that things had turned out badly. It seems that Zinoviev, like Kamenev, Trotsky and no doubt Bukharin and a few others, could not forgive himself for allowing the helm of the giant ship of state to have been seized by a pirate who, having made himself in effect Lenin's ideological successor, quickly became an absolute dictator. Zinoviev could not forget that in 1917 and later he had treated Stalin with condescension, virtually as the representative of the national minorities. Stalin, biding his time, had rarely responded to Zinoviev's patronizing remarks. When there was a discussion among the leadership about which of them should be put forward as chairman of Comintern, Zinoviev remarked: 'We want someone with European culture, a knowledge of languages'. And he it was who became the first chairman. He was a passionate advocate of the export of revolution, especially to Germany, a strategy Lenin agreed with. In January 1920 he declared in a speech: 'The Crimea must be liberated as soon as possible, as we will need our hands free, because the civil war could compel us to move to the west to help the Communists there.'[109]

While the Second Comintern Congress was in session in the summer of 1920, Lenin launched a military campaign to take Warsaw. Russia had been at war with the newly independent Poland since April 1920, when the Poles had launched a campaign to recover territory in Ukraine, which they regarded as traditionally Polish. Zinoviev had arranged for a vast political map of the world to be hung on the stage of the Bolshoi Theatre, where 'the world party of the socialist revolution' was in session. Every morning the delegates watched as little red flags were moved to show the progress of the Reds, while Zinoviev gave an excited commentary, promising that their next Congress would take place in Berlin, then in Paris, then London ... His words were drowned in a storm of applause.

Small details or anecdotes in Zinoviev's memoirs of Lenin are occasionally interesting and unexpected. He recalled that 'we heard a very funny joke of Plekhanov's: "They say Lenin is a first-class philosopher in the sense that in philosophy he's still in the first class."' Or: 'Lenin loved to frighten us: if we made mistakes, he'd say "We'll flee"' Or: 'In Paris once we were drinking to the success of his new book and we sat in the café till the small hours (though, to be honest, I couldn't imagine who would read the book, apart from a handful of Social Democrats).'[110]

Unfortunately, Zinoviev's occasional *mots* were lost in the welter of such assertions as 'Lenin was born a genius',[111] 'Lenin has the intuition of a genius', 'Lenin is the genius of world revolution', and even 'Lenin is the genius of Leninism'.[112] There were a few rare occasions after the revolution when Zinoviev allowed some criticism of Lenin into his speeches. On 27 November 1923, at an educationists' congress, when Lenin was already incapacitated, Zinoviev touched on the theme of the mistake Marx and Engels had made in estimating the time when the socialist revolution would arrive, and added, 'I have to say that V.I. Lenin made the same mistake.'[113] On the whole, though, glorifying Lenin became not merely an obligation for Zinoviev, but the mark of Party loyalty.

After 1926, when he was removed from the Politburo, Zinoviev divided his time between trying to oppose Stalin, expressing repentance, and doing the second-rank jobs Stalin gave him. In 1930, despite having no higher education, he was made the Rector of Kazan University, and in December 1931 Deputy Chairman of the State Scientific Council. But he kept alive the memory of his earlier closeness to Lenin, and always believed that sooner or later he would return to the pinnacle of power.

Kamenev had not lived with Lenin, or gone into hiding and shared a fisherman's hut with him, nor did he return to Russia in the famous 'sealed train'. Yet there are grounds for believing that Lenin's feelings for Kamenev were deeper than for Zinoviev. Not because Kamenev was his deputy on the Sovnarkom and the Council of Labour and Defence, but perhaps rather because Kamenev was endowed with more moral decency. Kamenev was a true Bolshevik, but in common with Pyatakov, Lunacharsky and Rykov, he lacked that indispensable harshness or cruelty which was the hallmark of Bolshevism. He was capable of raising his voice against arbitrary rule and of heeding the call of human suffering with un-Bolshevik sensitivity. When the authorities made it difficult for Kropotkin's widow to leave the country after the old Anarchist died in 1921, it was Kamenev who persuaded Lenin to grant her permission.

Lenin's meetings with Kamenev in 1921 and 1922 were numerous and extended,[114] and it is reasonable to believe that, as one of Lenin's closest associates, Kamenev's moderation, reserve and composure must have had an influence on his leader, who lacked precisely those qualities. Lunacharsky observed that Kamenev 'was regarded as a comparatively gentle person, in view of his remarkably good nature. This was praise rather than a rebuke, but perhaps it is also true that, compared to such people as Lenin, Trotsky or Sverdlov and the like, he was too much of an intellectual, responding to different influences, and was apt to waver.'[115]

Kamenev had become better known to Lenin when he was handling the negotiations with the 'trustees' of the Party funds. Despite the fact that he was married to Trotsky's sister, he became a close companion of Lenin and Krupskaya. In April 1913 Lenin wrote to him: 'So, we'll see each other this summer. Please come. We've taken a villa near Zakopane (4–6 hours from Cracow, Poronin station) from 1 May to 1 October; there's a room for you. The Zinovievs are not far away . . .'[116]

It seems that Lenin was very fond of Kamenev, for he had no difficulty after their clash in October 1917 in supporting the proposal that he be made Chairman of the new government, the VTsIK. Lenin frequently gave Kamenev difficult tasks, for example sending him, at Trotsky's suggestion, on a secret mission to England and France in February 1918, while negotations at Brest-Litovsk were in progress, to ask the Allies to help the Bolsheviks resist the Germans. The trip ended in failure. Kamenev's agreed diplomatic immunity was ignored by the British, who sequestered his diplomatic bag and a cheque for £5000 and sent him packing. The French refused him permission even to set foot in France.[117] His tasks often went well beyond the limits of Party and state concerns, embracing everyday domestic chores. Lenin wrote to him in the winter of 1920: 'Gorky arrives on the 12th or 13th. Can you make sure he has firewood?'[118] This was followed by: 'Evidently your orders for Gorky's firewood haven't been carried out. We're feeding people on promises. Comrade Guilbeau is complaining. The temperature in his apartment is 0 degrees. The person guilty of not carrying out your orders should be put on trial.'[119] And it was Kamenev whom Lenin asked to provide funds to help Inessa Armand's children to maintain their mother's grave,[120] among many other such small commissions.

The biggest service Kamenev rendered, however, was as publisher and editor of Lenin's works. As early as 1907 he undertook to publish a three-volume collection of Lenin's writings since 1895 entitled 'In Twelve Years'. He signed an agreement with the Social Democrats' publishers, Zerno, in St Petersburg, but the venture failed for various reasons, chief of which was that nobody bought the first volume when it came out. In 1920 Lenin's Collected Works in twenty volumes began to appear in Moscow, the last volume being published posthumously in 1926. Kamenev was in charge of the editing and consultations with the author as the work proceeded. The civil war was still in progress, the country languishing in darkness and chaos, but Lenin, Trotsky and Zinoviev could not wait to publish their multi-volume works.

After he was removed from the Politburo in 1926, Kamenev was posted by Stalin to various outposts of 'socialist construction': People's Commissar for Trade, envoy to Japan, then to Italy, and then member of the board of the Lenin Institute. He was the first person to see Lenin's personal archive, which formed the nucleus of the Lenin Institute's collection, and his appointment as director was a sensible one. As editor of the first edition of Lenin's works, he had already 'weeded' a good deal of material that did not accord with the canon of Leninism, in effect establishing the Bolshevik tradition of showing only what portrayed Lenin in a positive light. In 1934 he was appointed director of the Institute of Literature, where it seemed he might finally be able to accomplish something. It appears from indirect evidence that he wished to embark on reminiscences of Lenin, since he was more familiar than anyone else with the late leader's literary heritage.

Kamenev himself left no 'works', although there was sufficient material for five or six volumes. The speeches he made in Lenin's memory, his prefaces to Lenin's writings, his reflections on Martov, material virtually constituting a chronicle of the inner-Party differences, and his correspondence with Stalin, are all worthy of attention. While his political articles may have lacked originality, his literary essays are of much higher quality. Apart from the book on Chernyshevsky, he wrote an article on Goethe, a preface to one of Turgenev's novels, and review articles on a number of others.[121]

In the internecine conflict that flared when Lenin died, both Kamenev and Zinoviev made poor political judgements. At first they helped Stalin to isolate Trotsky, and then themselves fell under the wheels of Stalin's chariot. The destruction of the Bolshevik 'old guard' cannot be explained solely in terms of different policies, the contest of 'deviations' or platforms. Lenin had created a system which could tolerate only one leader at its summit. In the beginning, however, there was a host of claimants. When Stalin came out on top, they served to remind him that Lenin had tried to avoid having favourites, and had kept all his entourage in roughly the same position. Nor could Stalin come to terms with the fact that in many respects Zinoviev, Kamenev and the other 'October leaders' had had closer relations with Lenin than he. He saw them as potential rivals, and this decided their fate. The absurd invention of conspiracies and secret centres was merely the outward form of a process that finally confirmed Stalin's monopoly on Lenin and his heritage.

At first, the 'twins', especially Zinoviev, believed they would return to favour. When on 6 November 1929 the Communist cell of the Central Union of Consumers' Societies was interviewing Zinoviev for membership, he declared: 'I think that in time (and I hope it will not be far off), the Central Committee will give me the opportunity to apply my efforts in a wider arena.'[122] He had obviously failed to study the methods of Lenin's best pupil. Stalin could not overlook the fact that Zinoviev had been praised far more than he during Lenin's life. In September 1918 Trotsky had concluded a speech at the Petrograd Soviet: 'We are pupils of Lenin, we strive, however minimally, to be like this flaming tribune of international Communism, like the greatest prophet and apostle of the socialist revolution.' He sat down to 'stormy applause'. But then the chairman of the meeting, a certain Zorin, exclaimed: 'Long live the best pupil of Comrade Lenin, Comrade Zinoviev!', and the minutes show that the meeting erupted into a 'stormy ovation'.[123] Not even Trotsky could praise Lenin as Zinoviev could. When the leader died, Zinoviev declared: 'Lenin is Lenin. As mighty as the ocean; as stern and inaccessible as Mont Blanc; as tender as the southern sun; as great as the world; as humane as a child.'[124] It was intolerable to Stalin that others should try to commandeer the dead Lenin and his 'Leninism'.

As Zinoviev felt Stalin's grip tightening, he ceased to fantasize about regaining his former glory, concentrating instead on finding ways merely to survive. His (and Kamenev's) requests for an audience with Stalin were ignored, and he felt he had little choice but to join in the chorus of adoration for the new leader, a rôle for which he had proven talent. On the tenth anniversary of Lenin's death, in January 1934, Zinoviev wrote an article on the subject which he could not get published. He had cited Lenin and added: 'Comrade Stalin, the continuer of Lenin's cause, could in early 1933 reinforce this quotation with the facts of the victoriously completed First Five-year Plan.' He had then inserted the word 'great' before 'continuer'.[125] When Stalin's book *Marxism and the National-Colonial Question* was published, Zinoviev at once wrote an article entitled, 'From the Gold Reserve of Marxism-Leninism'. It began on a high note: 'There are in the treasury of Marxism-Leninism a number of books which no Marxist can do without, and which constitute the gold reserve of World Communism. Such books are few in number. Indeed, quantity is here unimportant. Few though they may be, these books represent the most valuable possession of the world labour movement. Among this "mighty pile" one of Comrade Stalin's works has for long – and rightly so – occupied a leading place. We are of course referring to *The Foundations of Leninism*. Now a new book will with equal merit take its place among the most outstanding works of Marxism-Leninism . . .'[126] This piece also failed to find a publisher.

After the assassination of Leningrad Party chief, Sergei Kirov, on 1 December 1934, both Zinoviev and Kamenev were arrested. Kamenev tried to dissociate himself from Zinoviev, hoping in this way to mitigate his lot. When he was asked by the investigator, Rutkovsky, about his friendship with Zinoviev, he replied: 'There has been a distinct cooling in my relations with Zinoviev. However, a number of domestic circumstances (a shared villa) has made it impossible for me to break with him entirely. I think it necessary to mention that living in one villa in the summer of 1934 we led completely separate lives and met rarely. We were visited by different people and we spent the time separately. Yevdokimov and possibly Kuklin, who visited him, were his guests, not mine. Finding this situation nevertheless unacceptable, at the first opportunity I started building myself a villa on another railway line. At the time of the inner-Party struggle, I never regarded Zinoviev as fit to run the Party; the recent years have confirmed my conviction that he possesses no leadership qualities.'[127]

Zinoviev meanwhile tearfully begged for mercy in letters to Stalin, Yagoda and Agranov. In one letter to Stalin, he wrote: 'I have no illusions. Already at the beginning of January 1935 in the Leningrad holding prison, Central Committee Secretary Yezhov, who was present during one of my interrogations, said to me, "Politically you've already been executed." . . . I beg you to believe this: I did not know, I absolutely did not know anything, nor did I hear anything, nor could I have heard anything about the existence of any anti-Party group or organization in Leningrad.' He declined to say anything about Kamenev.[128] Whether or not this last fact affected the court's decision, on 16 January 1935 Ulrikh read out the verdict: 'As a result of the counter-revolutionary activity of the "Moscow Centre" in various branches of the Zinovievite counter-revolutionary underground, purely fascist methods of struggle have made their appearance, and a terroristic mood aimed against the Party leadership and the government has grown stronger, leading to the murder of Comrade S.M. Kirov.'

As 'chief organizer and most active leader of the "Moscow Centre"' – a fiction created to add flesh to the invented plot – Zinoviev was given ten years' imprisonment. Kamenev, described as 'one of the leading members of the "Moscow Centre", but in recent years not having taken an active part in it', was given five years.[129]

Ten days later Zinoviev was sent to Verkhne-Uralsk camp, and Kamenev to Chelyabinsk. This, however, was not the end of their odyssey, and they were soon to be brought back for the next phase of their torment. Stalin was determined that there should be no witnesses to the movements of Lenin's former comrades, and as a result various instructions were cabled to their keepers. The Moscow NKVD chief, Molchanov, ordered the prison chief at Verkhne-Uralsk to 'send Zinoviev to me in Moscow in a separate railcar and under reinforced escort under the command of your deputy. Two days later, with you personally accompanying and following the same procedure, send me Kamenev. It is your personal responsibility to ensure that the dispatch of Zinoviev and Kamenev is kept totally secret, both from the other prisoners as well as prison staff, and to maintain careful observation on the journey. Cable me the time of departure and the train and railcar numbers.'[130]

At their second trial in August 1936, the 'Bolshevik twins' were more compliant. In exchange for Stalin's promise to spare their lives, they had agreed to confess to all the fantastic charges. They were both brought to the Kremlin at the start of the investigation, but the content of their conversation with Stalin can only be surmised. There was speculation in the West that at the first trial they may have scared Stalin into thinking that, if they were condemned, 'their friends abroad would publish compromising documents about him'.[131] Either Stalin was not afraid of this, or there were no such documents: in any event, the drama was acted out according to his scenario.

Under interrogation on 28 July 1936, Zinoviev was asked: 'It has been established by investigation of your case that the organization's centre carefully worked out a plan of the conspiracy. What evidence can you give us about this?' He replied: 'The political aim of the plot was to overthrow the Central Committee and the Soviet government and to create our own central committee and our own government, which would have consisted of Trotskyites, Zinovievites and Rightists. In concrete terms the plan for the coup was the following: we calculated that the murder of Stalin (and other Party and governmental leaders) would cause confusion in the Party leadership. We intended that Kamenev, Zinoviev, I.N. Smirnov, Rykov, Sokolnikov, Tomsky, Yevdokimov, Smilga, Mrachkovsky and others would in these circumstances return to leading Party and governmental posts . . . According to the plan, Trotsky, I and Kamenev were to have concentrated in our hands the entire leadership of the Party and state . . .'[132], and so on in the same vein.

In his letters to Stalin from prison, Zinoviev sank to the lowest depths of humiliation: 'I am at the point where I sit for long periods and stare at your portrait in the newspapers and those of other members of the Politburo thinking: my dear ones, look into my heart and surely you will see that I'm no longer your enemy, that I am yours, body and soul . . .' He signed his letters, 'With all my soul, I am now yours, G. Zinoviev.'

Leninist was eating Leninist, the system was remorselessly consuming its creators. Who would be left to be told in June 1988 of the decision to 'set the case aside in the absence of *corpus delicti*'? While no trace of Zinoviev's relatives has been discovered, a grandson of Kamenev and also his younger son have been found to have survived.

## The Party's Favourite

Lenin's assessment of Nikolai Ivanovich Bukharin is odd, despite the obvious fact that he valued him highly. He dictated it to M.A. Volodicheva, one of his four stenographers, on the grey wintry evening of 24 December 1922. Far from clarifying the situation, his opinion only muddied it:

Of the younger members of the Central Committee, I would like to say a few words about Bukharin and Pyatakov. They are in my view the most outstanding forces (of the very youngest forces) and the following should be borne in mind regarding them: Bukharin is not only the most highly valued and important Party theoretician, he is also legitimately regarded as the favourite of the entire Party, but it is very doubtful if his theoretical outlook can be considered as fully Marxist, as there is something scholastic about him (he has never studied dialectics and never quite understood it, I think).[134]

How can one reconcile the view that Bukharin was the Party's 'most highly valued and important theoretician' with the qualification that he had neither studied nor understood dialectics? How could one of the Party's 'most outstanding forces' at the same time be suspected of not being 'fully Marxist'? How could the 'scholastic' Bukharin also be the 'favourite of the entire Party'? The statement tells us more about Lenin than Bukharin. Lenin's own political 'dialectics' gave him the license to turn the dictatorship of a class into the dictatorship of a party, and then the dictatorship of one man. Bukharin's failure to understand dialectics boiled down to nothing more than the fact that he was probably the gentlest of the Bolshevik leaders, and gentleness had no place in Lenin's philosophy. As for his being the Party's favourite, it is doubtful if most rank-and-file members even knew of his existence: his lively mind, his energy as a political writer, his dedication to Communist ideals, and above all his loyalty to Lenin were enough to earn him Lenin's accolade.

Bukharin was born in Moscow in 1888 to highly cultivated parents, who were both schoolteachers. He became politically active during the 1905 revolution, and in the following year joined the Bolsheviks, attracted by their militancy and the fact that were more active in Moscow than their rivals, the Mensheviks. From 1907 to 1910 he studied law at Moscow University, but was frequently arrested, and finally exiled to the far north in 1911, whence he escaped, eventually reaching Germany. During his years in exile abroad, he spent time in Germany, Austria, Denmark, Sweden, Norway and the USA.

He first met Lenin in 1912, when the latter was living in Cracow, in Austrian Poland. Their relations were on the whole harmonious, although they differed on the national question, which Lenin raised in 1915. In New York when the February revolution occurred, Bukharin found his way back to Russia in May 1917, and his militant left-

Bolshevik views soon put him in the front rank of the Party hierarchy, where he was to remain until the end of the 1920s, when his espousal of ideas condemned as a 'right-wing deviation' brought isolation and ultimately, in 1938, execution.

In the early years after the 1917 coup, Bukharin was an exponent of Left Communism, which laid emphasis on world revolution and the boundless effectiveness of the dictatorship of the proletariat. A decade later he was the leader of the Right Communists, stressing gradualism, compromise and moderation. The switch between these two poles could not come overnight. What were his views in the intervening years? A convenient answer is to be found in his little-known work of 1924, 'On the World Revolution, Our Country, Culture and so on'.[135] It is in the form of replies to Academician Ivan Pavlov, who was developing his theory of conditioned reflexes in the early 1920s, and its sixty pages convey Bukharin's theoretical views.

Pavlov, with the courage of the genuine scientist, had stated in his introductory university lecture that 'Marxism and Communism are not the absolute truth, they may be partly true and partly untrue'. He doubted the chances for world revolution and saw nothing positive in the revolution in general, warning that the regime was heading into blind alleys that would lead to the degradation of culture. He opposed civil war as a means of achieving a political goal.

Bukharin set out to demolish Pavlov's position, itemizing what Pavlov had called the Bolshevik 'blind alleys'. Doubt about world revolution was Pavlov's 'blind alley number one'. Bukharin argued:

It is perfectly obvious that the world revolution is a *fact*. Its present phase of development, when the proletariat has seized only one sixth of the world's surface, and not six sixths, is, however, also a fact.

A profound reflection by 'the Party's outstanding theoretician', indeed.

Pavlov's 'second blind alley', namely, that the Russian revolution lacked positive content, Bukharin dismissed by pointing out that

the Bolshevik revolution saved the country from defeat and from being turned into a colony ... Merely the exit from the war and non-payment of [tsarist] debts were two factors which defined the country's life.

In other words, the positive content of the revolution was too obvious to require proof, and the non-payment of the country's debts was supposed to convince Pavlov that the revolution had brought a benefit. Here Bolshevik bandit logic was speaking through Bukharin.

Pavlov had asked whether the civil war was not appalling. Bukharin replied to this 'third blind alley':

Without the destruction of the power of capital we shall perish – that is what must be burned into every thinking mind. And for the sake of the salvation of mankind we *must* make the sacrifices demanded by the revolution.

This was simply Lenin's argument in favour of revolutionary violence 'for the sake of mankind', but Bukharin could not know that between 1929 and 1953 Soviet Russia would create 21.5 million 'sacrifices', i.e. political victims, or that he would be one of them.

Was the revolution, as Pavlov asserted in his 'fourth and last blind alley', taking the culture nowhere? Bukharin was especially annoyed by some of the examples Pavlov cited, for instance, that Soviet Russia was giving 'vast sums to foment revolution in Japan, while our laboratory gets three gold roubles a month'. 'How,' Bukharin asked, 'does Academician Pavlov know about these "vast sums for Japan"?' In fact hundreds of millions of roubles were being dispersed with Bukharin's knowledge to dozens of countries, besides Japan, for the purpose Pavlov had identified. Bukharin lectured the academician: 'If a positive outcome of the struggle is a necessary precondition for *everything else*, then there is no choice: we have to sacrifice *everything*.' Everything, in other words, must be sacrificed for the sake of clinging to power. It is unclear how culture made its appearance in this fourth blind alley. The argument was about sacrifices, all of them justified, according to Bukharin. Pavlov was made despondent, for instance, about the class basis of admission to higher learning, but here, too, Bukharin gave a nimble explanation: if not, we would slide 'towards the goals of the liberal bourgeoisie', and that would be nothing other than 'degeneration'.

Bukharin called the questions and doubts of the academicians and professors 'the ideology of the stone age'.[136] His replies to Pavlov were quintessentially those of Bukharin the theoretician, views he defended in 1918 and still held in 1929. His attractive personality, his wit and lively intelligence, coupled with the dignity with which he faced the court in 1938, have made some believe that his theoretical views were of a similar, liberally-inclined nature. But this was to mis-judge him. We may now well ask whether it was Pavlov who was in a blind alley, or Bukharin.

Arrested in March 1937 for espionage and wrecking, for three months Bukharin refused to provide the evidence needed to prove the existence of a conspiracy. Finally, in June, he was forced to make the following statement:

After prolonged hesitation I have come to the conclusion that I must fully confess my guilt before the Party, the working class and the country and finish once and for all with my counter-revolutionary past. I confess that until recently I took part in an organization of Rights and was, with Rykov and Tomsky, a member of the organization's centre, that this organization aimed at the violent overthrow of the Soviet regime (by coup d'état, uprising, terror), and that it was part of a bloc with the Trotskyite-Zinovievite organiz-ation. I will give details about this.[137]

He began with theoretical confessions, which ought to have shown him that his fate, like that of millions, was not an accident, but was profoundly systematic, and prompted by Marxism-Leninism, which grounded his crimes in theory. Bukharin's 'personal evidence' makes astonishing reading as a human document. He was prepared to confess to anything under the interrogation of State Security Captain Kogan. As the Chekists were themselves incapable of penetrating Bukharin's theoretical 'errors', they told him to write them down himself. He did so in the form of a philosophical treatise: '1. My general theoretical anti-Leninist views; 2. The theory of the state and the theory of the dictatorship; 3. the theory of class struggle in conditions of the proletarian dictatorship; 4. the theory of organized capitalism...' Only at the end of this 'treatise', composed in an NKVD prison, did he speak of political issues: his struggle against the Party, the origins of his 'school' with its counter-revolutionary aims and so on.

Bukharin's voluminous 'theoretical evidence', is perhaps unique as an occasion when an accused man assisted his interrogators by writing in his own hand a deposition that sought to trace the sins of his own theoretical views. 'As is known,' he began, 'Lenin's "testament" indicates that I did not understand dialectics and had never studied it seriously. This was entirely true ... [My] abstract schematism strove to keep up with the "latest generalizations", detaching them from multiform, rapidly moving life, and in this moribund approach to the processes of history and historical life lies the root of my huge political mistakes, becoming under certain circumstances political crimes.' Bukharin confessed to being not merely 'scholastic', but also anti-Leninist. 'As is known, V.I. Lenin accused me of concentrating all my attention on the destruction of the bourgeois state, on the one hand, and on the classless society, on the other ... It was precisely here that lay one of the roots of the recent ideology of the Rights ... The might of the state apparatus of the nascent and strengthening dictatorship of the proletariat was underrated.'[138]

It is true that Bukharin had underestimated the monstrous power of the terroristic dictatorship. The system was now operating according to the laws of totalitarian society. Now that his clever head was under the knife of Stalin's guillotine, he could better understand the satanic force of the 'state apparatus'. Nevertheless, he could still parrot Lenin's utterances on the withering away of the state: 'My fundamental error was to argue that, after the destruction of the landowners and capitalists, would come a phase of "balance" between the proletariat and the peasants in which the class struggle would die away. Hence, instead of [calling for] the destruction of the kulaks came its peaceful conversion into the slogan: "enrich yourselves".'[139]

Of course, what Bukharin wrote in prison was not what he believed. The system had no need of theory; it wanted a sectarian religion and inquisitors who would guard its purity. If only Lenin could have seen and heard the State Security captains ordering their prisoner to 'coordinate your theory with your political crimes'! It must be said that Bukharin made his 'confessions' most professionally. The several dozen pages of his 'personal deposition' are more important than many of Lenin's works, for they reveal the collapse and the tragedy of the entire Bolshevik enterprise. They show a highly intelligent man dedicating himself to the service of a utopian idea. And there were millions of such people.

Perhaps the most honest period of Bukharin's life was the time of the Brest-Litovsk treaty. He and his supporters, the Left Communists, no doubt trembled when Lenin repeated in March 1918 that General Hoffmann might not take Petrograd or Moscow 'this minute': 'But it is quite possible that he could do it tomorrow ... We are facing an epoch of severe defeats, it is here and we must take account of it, we must be ready for stubborn work in illegal conditions, in conditions of certain slavery under the Germans.'[140] Lying on his prison bunk, Bukharin might have recalled how he had cried out at the Seventh Party Congress: 'It is not a price to pay for a two-day breathing space that will do nothing for us. That's why we say, comrades, that the prospect offered by Comrade Lenin is unacceptable to us.'[141] He had been true to himself then, as he wrote to Stalin from prison on 15 April 1937: 'I sincerely thought that Brest [would cause] the greatest harm. I sincerely thought that your policy of '28–'29 was dangerous in the extreme. I proceeded from the policy to the person, not the other way round. But what did I do wrong, what let me down? Anti-dialectical thinking, schematism, striving for literary effect, abstraction, bookishness.'[142]

Lenin had said he was at odds with the dialectic, and now Bukharin repeatedly repented of his 'anti-dialecticism' before his prison guards, before the failed priest Stalin and before the cretin Yezhov at his interrogation. It was not only the circumstances that broke the man, it was the naive belief that by repenting of non-existent sins he might obtain a pardon. Lenin after all had loved him. He had written less to him than to the other members of his entourage only because he had preferred talking to him. Often he had displayed simple paternal concern for the younger man.

The Bolsheviks had hardly settled in Moscow, and had barely realized that they would stay in power, than they began to start looking after their own health. By 1920 the leaders were making regular trips to Germany for medical treatment, summoning German specialists or ordering expensive medicines from abroad. They were also already taking leave of two to three months at a time. Among those who were especially fond of long breaks were Trotsky, Zinoviev, Bukharin and Ioffe. Lenin would write to the Soviet envoys with instructions to keep an eye on the treatment and rest being given to Party leaders and to keep him informed. Bukharin and his wife took a trip to Germany in the spring of 1922, and on 26 April Lenin wrote to Nikolai Krestinsky, Soviet ambassador to Germany, in a letter marked 'top secret, copy to Stalin':

Thank you very much for the medicine you sent. I'd like to say something about Bukharchik. Smilga tells me he's behaving disgracefully. He's not taking his treatment sensibly. Rumours about attempts (being prepared) on his life have driven him crazy and so on. An attempt is a distinct possibility and the enemy has plenty of opportunity. I therefore suggest the following:

Bukharin should be summoned here. In a month (or six weeks) we'll send him back, to his wife.

During that time we should:

1. Transfer his wife to a different sanatorium where there are fewer Whites and more German Communist workers in the neighbourhood. No doubt such a place can be found in Saxony.

2. Prepare two or three German Communist workers, not blabbermouths, and settle them *without Bukharin's knowledge* near his sanatorium as security. This is hard to do because they are blabbermouths, windbags and braggarts, *one and all*. But it must be done.

3. Bukharin's wife must revert to her maiden name. She has the right to do so under our laws.

I ask you earnestly to manage all this *sensibly and seriously*.[143]

Lenin was planning this whole operation solely to ensure that Bukharin and his wife should have a good rest in a German sanatorium, and this while Russia was still in smoking ruins from the civil war.

In his way, Bukharin was a Party aristocrat. He had prepared himself well, possessed broad knowledge, knew the Marxist 'classics', and could not but feel himself to be the intellectual superior of the Voroshilovs, Molotovs and Kaganoviches around him. Early post-revolutionary Bukharin had, like Lenin, been 'orthodox'. In his *Theory of the Proletarian Dictatorship*, written in 1919, he had also been sweepingly uncompromising: the members of the Second International were 'vacantly chattering dead corpses'; Kautsky, who was one of them, was a 'general's bootlicker'; the League of Nations was 'rubbish'; 'the proletariat not only gives no freedoms to the bourgeoisie, it exercises the severest repression against them, closes their newspapers, their unions, and smashes their sabotage by force'.[144] Like Lenin, Bukharin extolled the principle of class war, the one-party monopoly, the illusory nature of the bourgeoisie. He was in favour of a strictly centralized, planned economy. In no way did he depart from Lenin.

The more mature Bukharin of the late 1920s introduced a new, near-liberal element into his social and economic views, thus further aggravating his political position and diminishing his prestige in the Party hierarchy. While defending and developing Leninism in a speech on Lenin's political testament, delivered on 21 January 1929, he added that the industrialization of the country should not be carried out 'by overtaxing the peasantry', but 'the peasantry should be engaged through their self-interest', their 'own benefit' must be taken into account.[145] It is not surprising that Bukharin never managed to throw off the accusation that he 'defended the kulak', 'inflamed personal property interest' and advocated a policy of 'personal enrichment'.

Bukharin was neither a heretic nor an opportunist. He merely saw the absurdity of repudiating, as Marxism did, the engine of economic progress, namely self-interest. He wanted to make 'some slight adjustments' to the traditional views but, more than that, he then wanted the Party line to follow suit. He thus quickly became a 'deviationist' and, according to the logic of Bolshevik thinking, 'went over from theoretical to political and then to terroristic struggle'. He tried in every way to break out of his difficult position, defending not merely his gradualist heretical views but himself as well. His defence was also traditionally Bolshevik: he attacked Trotsky, taking as his target Trotsky's July 1928 declaration about the 'danger of the Right', which he described as 'unprecedentedly slanderous and hysterical'.[146] Struggling to stay afloat, he ruthlessly kicked Trotsky when he was down and about to be deported.

For his own part, Trotsky was condescending towards Bukharin, although he also mocked him in insulting and sarcastic terms. 'Bukharin's struggle with the opposition,' he wrote in autumn 1927, 'reminds one dreadfully of the way a soldier fires his rifle when he's frightened to death: he screws up his eyes, waves his rifle above his head, fires off rounds at a crazy rate and hits precisely nothing. The same furious chatter at first deafens and may even frighten the target, who does not know that the one doing the firing ... is Bukharin, who is himself frightened to death.'[147] Later, in exile, Trotsky wrote an interesting comment on Bukharin, observing him through the prism of Lenin's attitude to him.

'There was something childish in Bukharin's character,' Trotsky wrote, 'and it was this which made him, in Lenin's words, the favourite of the Party. He had frequently and very passionately polemicized against Lenin, who replied severely but benevolently. The sharpness of their arguments never breached their friendly relations.' Trotsky then recalled an incident at the Politburo.

When England suddenly changed her attitude towards the Soviets, going from intervention to proposing a trade agreement . . . everyone, as I remember, was seized by one thought: this is a serious turning point . . . Suddenly up piped Bukharin: 'What a thing! Events are standing on their heads!' He looked at me. 'Stand, then,' I retorted. Whereupon Bukharin got up, dashed over to a leather sofa and stood on his head. After a minute or two, he returned to the table in triumph, we all laughed and Lenin resumed the meeting. That was Bukharin, in theory and in politics. Frequently, with all his exceptional abilities, he stood with his legs in the air.[148]

Like so many of Lenin's comrades-in-arms, Bukharin's was a sad fate. Perhaps it was this, together with his moderate image, that led many to think that his ideas were progressive. Closer attention to what he wrote, however, and a less frenzied approach to the discoveries of the past, reveals that Bukharin's ideas hardly differed from the official line, except perhaps over tactics and pace. As the editor of *Izvestiya*, he intuitively sensed that a policy of rapid industrialization and forced collectivization was disastrous, but he could only hint at this with extreme obscurity.

For some years after the 'Rights' had been smashed, Stalin allowed Bukharin to remain, if not the 'Party's favourite', then at least someone who was useful to it. In the 1930s until his arrest, and of course after it, he tried to return to Stalin's favour, sometimes sinking far below his dignity, even writing a poem to the leader. Invariably addressing Stalin as 'Koba' almost to the end of his life, hoping by familiarity to restore their good relations, Bukharin occasionally saw a glimmer of hope, as Stalin relaxed his grip. Then sinister omens portending persecution and arrest followed. Bukharin again wrote a long (undated) letter of explanation, expressing his sincere good feelings towards the leader:

Dear Koba,
. . . Among other things you said that I hardly appear in the editorial office. In fact I'm there every day. Recently I've been leaving after working all night . . . I haven't been in Moscow in fact for the last two days. I was commissioned to write a pamphlet on Kalinin* in three days . . . I enclose the pamphlet I've just finished as concrete proof. It seems you're being informed by some of my friends with a special interest. Don't be angry that

---

* The city, now known again by its original name of Tver.

I'm writing to you frankly and openly. If you think I'm being 'over-familiar', and that I am not behaving properly towards you, please tell me.[149]

Bukharin wanted to bring back the old days of Lenin, when the leaders addressed each other in the familiar form, intrigued against each other only politically, and had yet to learn Stalin's methods of entrapment. Bukharin's one-sided correspondence with Stalin is remarkable both for its sheer volume and also for the passion Bukharin showed in begging for forgiveness. He wrote not only to Stalin, but also to his other former comrades-in-arms. On 1 September 1936, after the trial of Zinoviev and Kamenev, he wrote to Voroshilov:

You [familiar form] no doubt received my letter to the members of the Politburo and Vyshinsky: I wrote it tonight in Comrade Stalin's secretariat with the request that it be circulated: it contains everything of substance connected with Kamenev's monstrously base accusations ... I'm terribly glad the dogs were shot ... If I'm still alive when the war breaks out, I'm going to ask to be sent to the fight ... and you're going to have to do me a last favour and fix me up in the army, even as a private. Excuse this confused letter: a thousand thoughts are galloping like wild horses, and I have no strong reins. I embrace you, because I'm clean.[150]

Bukharin lay on his prison bunk for long nights, staring at the ceiling of his cell; Lenin had trusted him, Stalin had not. The whole struggle slowly flickered through his confused, fevered mind. Before his arrest, he had written: 'Yet again and again I declare, 1) that neither by word, nor act nor thought have I ever had nor do I now have anything to do with any terrorists of whatever stripe. I regard even a hint at such a thing as monstrous ... 2) Under all and any circumstances I will protest my full and absolute innocence, however many slanderers give their slanderous evidence against me.'[151]

Following this letter, the criticism seemed to die down. Bukharin hardly dared hope: perhaps Koba had taken notice. He would never know that Stalin had sent his letter to L.Z. Mekhlis, the chief editor of *Pravda*, having scrawled on it: 'The matter of the former Rights (Rykov, Bukharin) has been postponed until the next Central Committee plenum. Therefore the abuse of Bukharin (and Rykov) should cease until the matter has been resolved. It doesn't take much intelligence to understand this elementary point.'[152] Nor did he know that Stalin was operating according to a programme. When, in February 1937, on the eve of the Central Committee plenum, a new wave of attacks struck him, Bukharin fell to pieces. He could not understand that it had been precisely he, with Lenin, Trotsky, Stalin and those who were now preparing to judge him, who had built this unfeeling system. It was ritual slaughter; there had to be enemies, spies and terrorists, preferably among the highest ranks of the regime. The system, in order to exist as a besieged fortress, must be engaged in permanent struggle, it must seek out and destroy all who would undermine its walls and its towers. And Bukharin had helped to build this fortress.

He recalled that on 20 February 1937 he had gathered all his strength and written once more to the Politburo, addressing them as 'Dear Comrades': 'I sent the Central Committee a "declaration" of nearly 100 pages in reply to the heap of slander contained in the depositions ... As a result of everything my nerves are utterly shattered. The death of Sergo [Ordzhonikidze], whom I loved passionately like a brother, drained my last strength ... I swear to you once more with the last breath of Ilyich, who died in my arms ...' This last phrase was underlined in thick blue pencil by Stalin, with a marginal note, 'He's lying'.

What was the truth about this? In the last months of Lenin's life, very few of the leaders visited him. Deprived as he was of the power of speech, it was almost impossible to conduct a conversation with him, and moreover he was reluctant to receive visitors. In Krupskaya's 'top secret' memoirs, which remained inaccessible for decades in the Party's secret archives, she recalled: 'When he was asked if he wanted to see Bukharin, who had earlier been a more frequent visitor than others, or than any of the comrades connected with our work, he shook his head in refusal, knowing that it would be unbearably hard.'[153]

But, as the press reports of January 1924 showed, Bukharin did indeed visit Lenin at Gorki on 21 January 1924. That afternoon, Professors O. Foerster and V.P. Osipov had attended Lenin. They examined him carefully, and found no worrying symptoms,[154] although Lenin in fact had less than two hours to live. When he started having convulsions, it was decided to allow Bukharin into the room.

Bukharin referred to this episode in his letter in the hope that the memory of the dead leader would protect and save him at this critical moment. He went on: 'All that is left for me is to be rehabilitated or leave the scene. In these highly extraordinary circumstances from tomorrow I am going onto a full starvation diet, until the accusations of treason, sabotage and terrorism have been lifted . . . if I have to go to the end of this doleful way, then let me die and let me die here, don't drag me away anywhere else, and forbid them to pester me. Farewell. Be victorious.'[155]

Of course, he would not be permitted to go the way he had chosen. Perhaps he now remembered September 1919, when the Politburo discussed the question of arresting the Kadets and the bourgeois intelligentsia. Appeals had been pouring in, and Lenin had deputed Bukharin, Dzerzhinsky and Kamenev to deal with them. As Lenin's letter to Gorky of 15 September 1919 witnesses, however, he still regarded his tough policy as appropriate: 'We have decided to appoint Kamenev and Bukharin to check the arrests of bourgeois intellectuals of the near-Kadet type and to release anyone they can. For it's clear to us that some mistakes were made. It's also clear that in general the arrest of the Kadet (and near-Kadet) people was both necessary and correct.'[156]

Six weeks after his arrest, during the night of 15 April 1937, Bukharin wrote yet again to Stalin, this time a letter of twenty-two pages, marked 'Personal'. He began with a request that the letter be sent to Stalin 'without any preliminary reading by anyone else'. He wrote:

At the plenum I felt like an innocent man nailed to the pillar of shame. In desperation I swore by Ilyich's hour of death. After all, you well know that I loved him boundlessly, heart and soul. I *appealed* to his memory. But they said I was taking advantage of his name, even that I had *lied* about being there when he died, and they even produced a 'document' (an article of Zinoviev's), but the fact is that after Ilyich had died I left Gorki for Moscow and then returned with everyone else, as the article says. I will not hide the fact that I *dreamed* of great intimacy with the leadership and with you. I *missed* important people, I missed broader work. Is that a sin? Is it a crime? I learned not just to respect you personally again, but to love you earnestly (again, let anyone who doesn't believe me giggle all they like, it is true). I was delirious for you to trust me. All this happened, and it's all come to dust, and I wriggle like a worm on my prison bunk.

. . . The time we lay together on a divan at your place, was I supposed to be plotting against you? Rubbish. I'll tell you what was really going on as we approached 1928. I genuinely believed that *you* were acting in a Leninist way; I cited many references to Ilyich. So, what was going on? The fact is I took Ilyich's testament (not about personalities but its line) *literally* and *formally* . . . A *special* situation had been created by 1928, which had not entered Ilyich's field of vision . . . But, like a schoolboy, I grasped only the letter, ignoring the spirit. In 1928–29 I saw in you the embodiment of *anti-Leninist* tactics. It was foolish, but that's how it was.

Bukharin was saying that Lenin had not been able to give advice for the future, and thus he acknowledged that Stalin, in 'developing' Lenin, had been right. He capitulated on every front. When he referred to Lenin and his own mistakes, Bukharin inevitably returned to Stalin: 'It was often extraordinarily nice when I managed to be with you. I really began to feel towards you as I had felt towards Ilyich, a feeling of family intimacy, a great love, boundless trust, as for a man one can say everything to, write everything to, share everything with, and complain to about everything.'

Bukharin mentions the book he was finishing and wanted to dedicate to Stalin, for now he felt that he was 'your pupil'. He asserts once more that 'nothing will make me commit shameful slander against myself', and ends on a tormented note: 'the cells are dark and the electric light is on night and day. I scrub floors, I clear up, I slop out and so on – it's all familiar. But it breaks my heart that this is in a *Soviet* prison, and my grief and my yearning are boundless . . . Be healthy and happy.'[157]

Stalin circulated Bukharin's letter to the other members of the Politburo. Each one signed it and added their own comments: Molotov: 'I've read it. In my opinion a crook wrote it.' Kaganovich: 'The same old underhand refrain: Who, sir? Me, sir? No, sir!' Mikoyan: 'Bukharin is still doing his provincial stage-act and his hypocritical sharp practice.' Andreyev: 'Typical Bukharin-style lying.' And so on.

Though he was crushed, Bukharin had one more letter to write to Stalin. This time he did not mention Lenin. Lenin was now in the dim and distant past. He wanted so much to live, and perhaps, having surrendered, he saw a glimmer of hope. Now, both 'Koba' and the familiar form of address had gone, and were replaced by 'Greetings, Iosif Vissarionovich':

I have been hallucinating (I've had such periods) that I was talking to you for hours on end – you were sitting on my bunk, you gave me your hand. Unfortunately, it was just an illusion . . .

I wanted to tell you that I'd like to clear everything up with you for the last time in my life, but *only* with you. I know it's unprecedented. I cherish not the slightest hope that it will happen. But at least you know that that was what I was waiting for, like the Israelites waiting for manna from heaven. I will take nothing back, I don't want to make any complaints about anyone.

I'm not writing this because ... I'm trying to bargain something for myself. I look at myself as someone who is politically dead. I've written (apart from a scholarly book) a big book of poems (250–300 pages long). My first pieces seem childish to me now (but I'm going to go over them) with the exception of 'A Poem about Stalin', which I sent you before I was arrested. I can say that as far as *content* is concerned, nothing like it has been attempted in our literature.

He then returns to *The Transformation of the World*, the book he has been writing in prison (which has not yet surfaced in the archives). Chapters on 'The Epoch of Great Works' and 'The Future (Communism)' occupy a special place: 'I wrote it mainly at night and literally with the blood of my heart ... Iosif Vissarionovich, you are such a specialist on style and you love literature so much, please don't let this book perish ... My words may seem monstrous to you, but it's a fact that I love you with all my soul!'[158]

The finale of the Bukharin drama was his letter, dated 13 March 1938 and addressed to the Presidium of the Supreme Soviet, from 'N. Bukharin, sentenced to death'. It was a plea for clemency:

I regard the sentence of the court as just retribution for the heavy crimes I have committed against the Socialist motherland, her people, Party and government. There is not a single word of protest in my soul. I should be shot ten times over for my crimes ... I am firmly convinced that in the years to come great historical boundaries will be crossed under Stalin's leadership, and you will not regret the act of charity and mercy I request: I will strive with all my might to prove to you that this gesture of proletarian magnanimity was vindicated.[159]

Bukharin's fate had, however, already been decided. The appeal was turned down, and on 15 March he was executed.[160]

To his credit, long before his death, Bukharin had foreseen where unrestrained state violence could lead. In December 1924 he had written to Dzerzhinsky – 'Iron Felix' – hoping to correct a view of his attitude to the GPU which had been presented at the Central Committee in his absence:

I believe we must *more quickly* go over to a more 'liberal' form of Soviet power: fewer arrests, more legality, more discussion, more self-government (under Party leadership, naturally) and so on. This line is theoretically argued in my article in *Bolshevik*, which you approved. Therefore I sometimes speak against widening the powers of the GPU and so on. You must understand, dear Felix Edm[undovich] – you know how much I like you – that you have no grounds for suspecting me of any bad feeling towards you personally or the GPU as an institution. It is a question of *principle*, that's what it's about.[161]

To write a letter like this to Dzerzhinsky, the personification of state violence, took some courage, as well as insight. Dzerzhinsky, however, forwarded it to Menzhinsky, his sinister deputy, with a personal note – 'No copy' – asking for Bukharin's letter 'to be returned to me after reading', then addressed the principle raised:

We must necessarily take account and give thought to such moods in leadership circles of the Central Committee. It would be the greatest political error if, on a question of principle like the GPU, the Party gave, or might give, a 'springtime' to the philistines, either as the line, the policy, or in a declaration. It would mean giving in to the Nepmen, to the philistines who tend towards denying Bolshevism. It would mean victory for the Trotskyites and the surrender of our positions.[162]

Dzerzhinsky was not called 'Iron Felix' for nothing. It is nevertheless likely that the majority of the Central Committee shared his views, rather than those of Bukharin. Such, however, had often been his fate. In early 1921, for instance, when a powerful peasant uprising erupted in Tambov Province, Lenin gave Bukharin the job of analysing the circumstances and reporting to the Politburo on the measures needed to put it down. In his report on 2 February 1921 Bukharin tried, and to some extent succeeded in getting, at least as an expression of intent, a reduction in the confiscation of produce in order to relieve the peasants. The Politburo approved this measure, but Lenin also proposed sending out Antonov-Ovseenko to ensure that alongside the economic measures, there should be military back-up.[163]

The rising nevertheless spread. Bukharin's 'moderate' measures did not work. As Lenin and the others in the Politburo had expected, economic measures accomplished nothing, and only punitive steps would do. The next time the Politburo met, on 27 April, it was without Bukharin. It decided to appoint Mikhail Tukhachevsky – who was to rise to the rank of Marshal in 1935, only to be executed as a spy in 1937 – as commander of the forces in the Tambov district, responsible for both the military and political spheres, with the task of wiping out resistance within one month, and 'not to allow interference in his work'.[164] The uprising was crushed in a sea of blood.

Bukharin was simply not cut out for such actions, but when the regime abandoned the policy of war communism, his influence grew. His views were aired again at the Fourteenth Party Congress, where he said 'we shall build socialism even on our impoverished base, we shall drag ourselves along at snail's pace, but we shall build social-ism'.[165] He suggested that the New Economic Policy in the country-side was a widening of the base of the well-off peasantry, that it was a transition from civil war to civil peace, that it was gradualism and consistency.

He put his views even more plainly at the Moscow regional Party conference on 17 April 1925: 'Our policy in the countryside must develop in such a way that the limitations holding back the growth of the well-off and kulak economy fall away and are partly destroyed. We have to say to the peasants, all the peasants: enrich yourselves, develop your economy and don't be afraid that pressure will be put on you.' How often would these 'heretical' words be thrown in his face, and how many times would he have to justify his 'bourgeois degeneration'? In 1925, however, his views were shared by many, including Stalin. On 9 May, speaking at a meeting of Moscow Party members, the General Secretary stated unequivocally: 'Some com-rades, seeing the differentiation in the countryside, have come to the conclusion that the Party's main task is to ignite class war in the village. That, comrades, is wrong. It is empty chatter.'

For a short time, then, Bukharin's interpretation of the New Econ-omic Policy was in the ascendant, but soon enough the Politburo reverted to a policy of harsh class war in the countryside, squeezing the kulak and finally going over to outright collectivization. Now, with Trotsky out of the way, in effect Stalin took over his radical concept of building socialism in town and country. Bukharin was prepared to support the disastrous Stalinist course, but Stalin, seeing him as a hindrance, removed him from the Politburo in 1929.

Bukharin took this very badly, and was desperate to restore his former relations with Stalin by repudiating his own earlier views on the economy and by seeking audiences – but it was too late. In this respect, Lenin's judgment of him was not far off the mark: 'He is an engaging economist, and we always supported him *in this*, but as a politician he is diabolically *unstable*.'[166] Bukharin, in fact, was typical of the kind of weak man who does not even want to look strong. His exceptional mind was compromised by his weakness of will. In the system Lenin had created, Stalin could only have people around him who were capable of agreeing with him and of approving his 'wise decisions'. Senior members of the Communist Party vied with each other to find new and more unctuous ways to praise him, but members of the Politburo were required to make a special effort; they, after all, were fortunate enough to be part of the 'Leninist HQ'.

## The Leninist Politburo

For decades the Politburo personified a mysterious, secretive, mighty and at times sinister body. When a Central Committee plenum took place, the population waited anxiously to hear the names of the new members, as if it was going to make a noticeable difference to their lives. When the long black limousine of a member passed by, the militia would stop all traffic a long way ahead and would stand eagerly to attention until it had gone. The country villas of these top officials, behind their tall green fences and electrically operated gates, were like princely estates, with security guards, staff, swimming pools, tennis courts, and even the occasional indoor cinema. The legends abounded among the half-destitute population about the food consumed in these establishments. And yet it all began so simply.

At a meeting of the Central Committee in Petrograd on the evening of 10 (23) October 1917, it was agreed to form a 'political bureau . . . to consist of seven members: Len., Zin., Kam., Tr., Sok., St., Bubn' (Lenin, Zinoviev, Kamenev, Trotsky, Sokolnikov, Stalin, Andrei Bubnov).[167] The meeting took place at 32/1 Karpovka Embankment, apartment 31, a site soon made into a museum. It was here that Lenin made his first appearance after going into hiding. But neither in the rising itself, nor in the aftermath, did this body make its mark, and indeed it might have faded from memory had Lenin not felt that the

Central Committee was too unwieldy as an instrument of leadership. He decided it needed a nucleus which would function on a permanent basis.

At the Eighth Congress in March 1919, Zinoviev proposed that the Central Committee be enlarged to nineteen members, a number, he suggested, that would make it possible to form a political bureau, an organizational bureau, a secretariat and group of roving representatives. There were no objections, and on 25 March the new bodies were duly instituted.[168]

The Politburo, in the form in which it was to become known, first met on 16 April 1919. Several resolutions were passed about the bureau's creation and its system of operation, but there was never a debate about its powers. It was always taken for granted that they were unlimited. It was Krestinsky's idea that its meetings should be regular, and it was agreed that they would take place on Thursdays. Despite attempts to change the time to Wednesdays at 11 a.m., Thursday meetings remained the 'Leninist tradition'.[169]

This small group of people, none of whom had any governmental experience, and dealing as they were with a vast range of issues – social, economic, political, Comintern, Cheka, military, diplomatic, financial, food production and cultural – many of which they could not understand, were determining the fate of millions and millions of people. Trotsky made an attempt to regulate the number of questions tabled by the Politburo every week, but in general he preferred to avoid office work and took off more time than the others for public speaking, rest and writing.

Despite a decision of 20 January 1922 that the Politburo would only consider issues from high-level bodies if they were themselves incapable of dealing with them,[170] it in fact became the decision-making body on every question, and it acquired from the very beginning the status of the highest state organ, while inner-Party questions (which ought to have been its main preoccupation) always took up an extremely small part of its agenda. On 3 April 1922 a Central Committee plenum resolved to establish the post of General Secretary and two Secretaries, appointing Stalin General Secretary and Molotov and Kuybyshev Secretaries, and from that moment the regulation of the Politburo's work was strengthened: 'Accepting Comrade Lenin's proposal, the Central Committee orders the Secretariat to fix and keep strict control of the hours of official audiences ... Comrade Stalin is instructed to find deputies and assistants for himself immediately, thus releasing him from work in government institutions (apart from policy control).'[171]

It was not yet obvious that the new proletarian state would draw its main strength from a bureaucracy as impenetrable as reinforced concrete, from the Politburo's monopoly of power and the orthodoxy of the Party members. State power had been handed over to a so-called Party organ which was in fact the main instrument of the Bolshevik dictatorship. The General Secretary quickly passed new working arrangements through the Politburo, fixing 'obligatory meetings of the Politburo on Mondays and Thursdays at 11 a.m. and meetings of the Politburo troika, consisting of Comrades Kamenev, Stalin and Molotov, on Wednesdays at 12 noon.'[172] Lenin altered this at the end of 1922 to Thursdays only for the Politburo 'from 11 a.m. and no later than 2 p.m.'. He proposed that the agenda be circulated no later than noon on Wednesdays, and that supplementary questions should be introduced on the day of a session only in case of absolute urgency, especially on diplomatic issues, 'as long as no objection is raised by even one member'.[173] It was unanimously agreed that the Central Committee would have no other permanent staff than its secretaries and that its chairman would be chosen at each session.[174] Kamenev was often chairman during the early years, especially when Lenin was absent.

In February 1923, when Lenin was too ill to carry out his duties, Zinoviev proposed a division of labour among Politburo members to manage the work of 'the major branches', such as the Presidium of the VTsIK, the Revolutionary Military Council of the Republic, Comintern, the Trade Union Council, the Foreign Commissariat, the Foreign Trade Commissariat, the cooperatives, and the National Economic Council.[175] As a Party body which had already assumed the rôle of state control, the Politburo extended its tentacles into every sphere of public life. In order to give the work of the Politburo a planned structure, Zinoviev proposed that over the next three months they should review the Finance and Food Commissariats, the export of grain, foreign trade as a whole, the Red Army, the National Economic Council, the Transport and the Education Commissariats. He proposed that the work of these main branches be made the special responsibility of individual members of the Politburo.[176]

On 14 June 1923 the Politburo adopted a three-month plan, signed by Stalin, for establishing the division of labour among its members, which resulted in a restructuring of their responsibilities. Zinoviev was given the job of preparing foreign policy materials; Trotsky would do the same for foreign trade and the commission for concessions, as well as matters relating to the struggle with the Mensheviks and SRs; all general economic issues would be prepared by Kamenev and Rykov; Stalin would prepare all materials relating to the nationalities question and education; Bukharin would be responsible for youth, press and state publishing matters; Rudzutak the cooperative movement; Molotov internal Party questions; Kalinin would keep an eye on general developments in the countryside and the peasants' mood; and Tomsky would do the same for the workers.[177]

The Politburo was often called 'Leninist', especially from the 1930s onwards. It met with exemplary regularity, even if only three members were present. On 28 May 1919, for instance, Lenin, Kamenev and Krestinsky, in consultation with Pyatakov and Bubnov, alone decided on 'universal mobilization in Ukraine', and also declined Dzerzhinsky's surprising request to release the Left SR and former Justice Commissar Shternberg, who had been arrested. It then went on to deal with a dozen other issues with equal expedition.[178] Sometimes, especially during the civil war, its decisions were those rather of a revolutionary tribunal than a political party, as for instance on 24 June 1919, when it ordered that anyone who failed to surrender a weapon within the specified time would be subject to severe punishment, including execution.[179] Or on 14 May 1921, when it drafted a law for the Sovnarkom to approve widening the powers of the Cheka to allow the death penalty for theft from state warehouses and factories.[180] On occasion the Politburo authorized such measures to be taken on a local level: on 2 February 1922 Kamenev, Molotov and Stalin instructed the Samara Cheka that it could apply the death penalty without asking the All-Union Cheka.[181] This approach greatly 'simplified' matters, and 'revolutionary repression' thus became a local institution. Within a month came the order permitting the GPU to pass sentences without trial, to 'isolate foreigners in camps' and to deal on the spot with anyone arrested in possession of a weapon.[182]

On 27 March 1922, at the Eleventh Party Congress, speaking of a planned, temporary retreat by the Party under the New Economic

Policy, Lenin drew a military analogy: 'When a real army makes such a retreat, they mount machine-guns, and when the orderly retreat turns into a rout, they give the order to fire, and rightly so.'[183] With Lenin's approval, Trotsky had indeed applied the use of blocking units at the front to prevent troops from retreating without permission. Lenin believed that the Politburo must set the tone in the harsh suppression of everyone who 'did not agree' with the revolution. On 6 July 1922, it advised the Turkestan front 'to compel the Central Asian Bureau of the Central Committee under no circumstances to let go of the Basmachi chieftains and to hand them over for trial by the revolutionary tribunal immediately, with the death penalty in view'.[184]

Increasingly, one of the dominant functions of the Politburo was that of a personnel board. Appointments from district Party instructor to deputy minister, regional military commander to manager of a large factory, would come to the Politburo for approval. The Bolsheviks had soon learned that personnel selection was of the utmost importance. The list of appointments made on 19 April 1921, for example, gives an impression of the range of detailed control exercised by the Politburo: the board of the Moscow Higher Technical School, the Council for General Financial Questions, the appointment of O.Yu. Shmidt to the board of the Finance Commissariat, Smirnov's appointment to the board of the Justice Commissariat, Lutovinov's to the Foreign Commissariat, Kryuchkov's, Skvortsov's and Freiman's to Social Security, and so on.[185] Such was a typical agenda for the Politburo. In time, every professional, specialist and bureaucrat in the country came to learn that the political, Party and ideological principle was the decisive factor in personnel selection. Loyalty to the Party was more important than ability, and this, with the active assistance of the lower Party committees, became the Soviet norm.

In 1925 the Politburo passed two special resolutions introducing 'Nomenklatura No. 1' and 'Nomenklatura No. 2'. 'Nomenclature' in this context means a list of important posts to which suitable names have to be matched.

Posts in the first category were predominantly appointed by the Politburo and ratified by the Central Committee. These included first secretaries of republic central committees, regional committees, district committees, People's Commissars, military district com-

manders, and ambassadors to important countries.[186] Candidates for
these posts were interviewed by senior state and Party figures. Stalin
thought it particularly important to look prospective district Party
secretaries in the eye, as well as regional Party secretaries, army
commanders and People's Commissars, and ask them one or two
questions such as: 'How are you personally struggling against Trotskyism?', 'Is it possible for your commissariat to fulfil the Five-Year
Plan in four?', 'How do the former [tsarist] military experts function in
your army?' The nomenklatura table, with extremely rare exceptions,
excluded former members of other parties.

Posts in the second Nomenklatura included managers of various
trusts, industrial bosses and Deputy People's Commissars. These were
appointed not by the Politburo, but by the various Central Committee
departments.

The Politburo was especially harsh in its attitude towards the Mensheviks. In his speech at the Eleventh Congress, Lenin, who spoke
calmly enough about the pros and cons of the NEP, the union with
the peasantry and competition in production, changed his tone when
he came to the Mensheviks. 'When a Menshevik says: "You're now
retreating, and I was always for retreating, I agree with you, I'm on
your side, let's retreat together," we have to reply: "Our revolutionary
courts have to shoot you for admitting publicly that you're a Menshevik, otherwise they're not our courts, but God knows what."'[187]

Lenin's hatred of the Mensheviks is striking. In several decisions
which did not relate directly to them, he nevertheless chose them for
special targeting. In November 1921 the Cheka received information
that an uprising was in preparation in Moscow and Petrograd. Lenin
at once reacted by ordering that Mensheviks in custody be kept there,
and that arrests be stepped up.[188] In March 1923, when Lenin was
seriously ill, the Politburo developed his 'programme' for dealing with
Mensheviks in the USSR on a state-wide basis. All Mensheviks were
to be expelled from state institutions and enterprises, and Menshevik
status would include even those who had left the Party after October
1917. Menshevik students were to be excluded from higher learning.
Menshevik adults were to be sent to camps in the Narym region near
Tomsk in western Siberia, while their children would be despatched
to Pechera, north of Archangel in the Arctic.[189] The Russian Social
Democratic Workers' Party was being systematically liquidated. The

Menshevik desire to impart a democratic character to socialism was as serious a sin in Bolshevik eyes as membership of the bourgeoisie, the capitalists or the royal family. One might have thought the campaign was being fought against terrorists and plotters or state criminals, rather than people who had once belonged to the same party. Had Lenin been told a few years earlier that he would be putting these people in prison or sending them into exile and handing them over to the tender mercies of the Cheka, he would have dismissed the charge as slanderous. And yet he and his 'Leninist' Politburo soon trampled on many of the principles of social democracy which they had sworn to uphold.

Lenin rarely produced a report for the Politburo. If anything, he devoted more care to the Sovnarkom than the Party body, though he left no doubt that he regarded the latter as the supreme organ of the Bolshevik regime. Frequently during meetings he would seem to be preoccupied, writing his little notes to other members, but he would come to life the moment someone seemed about to drop their 'class' guard. More than once he took Lunacharsky to task for his 'democratic licence'. For instance, he took great exception to Lunacharsky's request that the world-famous singer Fedor Chaliapine (to use the French transliteration which he himself adopted) be allowed to go abroad on a tour, dismissing it as 'frivolous'. In the end a compromise was reached: 'Chaliapine may go abroad if the Cheka can guarantee that he will return. If the Cheka objects, the matter will be reviewed.'[190] The Cheka apparently did object, but nevertheless on 31 March 1922, three weeks after the first debate on the subject, the great singer was let out of the Bolshevik cage. He was never to return, except to be reburied in Moscow in 1983.

Throughout the short time he spent at the head of Soviet government, Lenin conducted a running battle against bureaucracy and corrupt bureaucratic practice. When he was informed that a commission had confirmed allegations of corruption in the housing section of the Moscow City Council, and that the Moscow Party Committee had given protection to the culprits, Lenin was outraged, and wrote to the Politburo: 'This is not the first time the Moscow Committee . . . has *indulged* criminal Communists who should be hanged. They say it's a "mistake", but it's a gigantic "mistake". I propose . . . that the Moscow Committee be severely rebuked for *indulging* Communists.'[191] Lenin seems not to have understood that the essence of the system he had created was expressed in bureaucratic totalitarianism. He was merely battling with some of the external features of bureaucratism, while the trouble lay deep within the society he was bringing into being. His notes and instructions simply brought about a more refined version of the social defect.

Since one of the primary purposes of the regime was to promote and facilitate revolution elsewhere in the world, the affairs of Comintern and the Foreign Commissariat were a special interest of the Politburo. On such matters every member was a specialist, and debates tended to be lively. Among the most eloquent illustrations of Bolshevik *Realpolitik*, as well as its historical consequences, was the Politburo's unanimous agreement to a request from Germany to establish German officer-training courses in Soviet Russia, in order to evade the terms of the Versailles treaty. Trotsky and Dzerzhinsky were deputed to find suitable locations outside Moscow.[192]

Comintern affairs were treated by the Politburo as an adjunct of foreign policy, and an area in which there was barely any attempt to observe even a pretence of democratic methods. As an example of the way Comintern was involved with foreign affairs, on 27 July 1922, when discussing diplomatic talks with Japan, it was decided that as Japan was 'living through a revolutionary period', the Communists 'must try to use the talks for agitational purposes'.[193] In an action which typified the Politburo's cavalier attitude towards the international bodies, it simply asserted, without any pretence at form, that 'Comrade Rudzutak be appointed General Secretary of Profintern', the Communist Trade Union International,[194] and even fixed the day and the hour (Wednesdays at 11 a.m.) of its meetings.[195]

Typical of the triviality of many of the issues dealt with by the Politburo are the following: should Deborin, Lyubov Axelrod and Bazarov be allowed to give lectures on Marxist philosophy? The former, yes, the latter two, no;[196] a request from Krasin to 'publish abroad the letters and diary of the former empress, Alexandra';[197] 'developing Soviet diplomatic etiquette, entirely excluding lunches, breakfasts, suppers, teas and so on'.[198] The Politburo also dealt with matters of leave and rest, trips abroad for its members and for the entire top echelon.

In effect, as soon as it began to meet regularly, Lenin's Politburo

Lenin, with Sverdlov to his left, in Moscow, 7 November 1918.

Lenin with Kamenev, left, and Trotsky, circa 1918.

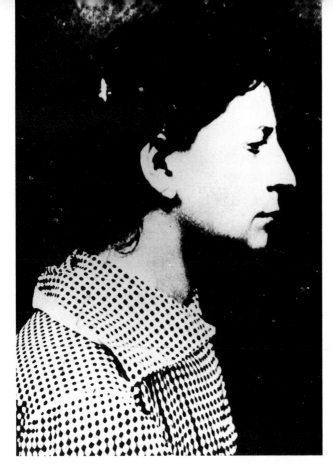

*Left*: Fanya Kaplan, arrested and executed for the attempt on Lenin's life in August 1918. This photograph was taken by the Kiev Provincial Prison Inspectorate in 1907 after her arrest for a terrorist act.

*Below*: A procession in support of Red Terror, Moscow, winter 1918.

A German army patrol in Kiev in 1918. Kiev was captured by numerous sides during the civil war, enduring perhaps as many as eighteen different occupations.

Zinoviev making a speech, possibly at a meeting of the Communist International Comintern, no date.

Lenin at the First Congress of the Comintern, March 1919.

Lenin with Krupskaya and his sister Maria outside the Kremlin, 25 May 1919.

Lenin at a military parade on Red Square, 25 May 1919. The speaker is Tibor Szamuely, the refugee leader of the failed Hungarian Communist revolution.

Lenin on the same occasion.

*Above left*: Lenin talking to
Yelena Stasova between
sessions of the Second
Comintern Congress,
Moscow, August 1920.
Stasova, nicknamed
'Comrade Absolute', was
a Central Committee
Secretary and an important
Party organizer.

*Above right*: Lenin during
an interval at the Second
Comintern Congress.

*Right*: Trotsky speaking.

Lenin speaking in Moscow on 5 May 1920, with Kamenev and Trotsky standing on the steps of the podium to his left. After Trotsky's deportation from the USSR in 1929, his figure was erased from the photograph.

*Above*: Nikolai Bukharin speaking at the funeral of the American journalist John Reed in Moscow, 1920.

*Left*: Baron Peter Wrangel, chief of the White forces in southern Russia, with his chief adviser, Alexander Krivoshein, on his right, and his chief of staff, Pavel Shatilov, on his left, Crimea, August 1920. Wrangel's forces, and several tens of thousands of civilian refugees, were evacuated to Constantinople by French and British naval ships later that year.

Corpses of some of Admiral Kolchak's White forces shot by Reds at Omsk in Siberia, 1919.

Red victims of the Japanese intervention at Vladivostok, November 1920. British, French, American and Japanese forces landed at Vladivostok in August 1918 and were engaged to various degrees in armed conflict with Red troops in the Far East. The Japanese were the last foreign forces to leave the territory, in October 1922.

became a super-government. Party affairs took second place. Many of the features of Lenin's style of work became a tradition to be scrupulously observed by all future General Secretaries. First and foremost, this meant that the decisions of the Politburo were supreme, higher than the law or the Constitution, which for this body were mere auxiliary instruments. For the citizens of the great state, the Politburo itself embodied the law. It also acquired from Lenin the rule of total secrecy. Who, for instance, knew that the Politburo planned the massacre at Katyn, or the creation of domestic and foreign terror units, how it dealt with the Berlin crisis, the Cuban adventure, the invasion of Hungary, Czechoslovakia or Afghanistan, or that it prepared to invade Poland in 1981? Much has become known since the dramatic changes that have taken place in recent years, but far from everything.

As we have seen, even in Lenin's time the Politburo had already become a super-government, and over the years this status was only intensified. By a special resolution of 8 February 1947 (by which time the People's Commissars had been renamed Ministers), 'Questions relating to the Foreign Ministry, the Foreign Trade Ministry, the State Security Ministry, the circulation of money, hard currency, and also important issues relating to the Armed Forces Ministry, will be concentrated in the Politburo'.[199] Since then, following decisions by Brezhnev, Andropov, Chernenko and Gorbachev, the spheres of Politburo members' activities were successively defined and redefined, in terms of 'the preliminary examination, preparation and supervision of a specific number of issues'.

The Politburo functioned in different ways at different times. Under Stalin it was an obedient, 'consultative' body of yes-men whose job was to sanctify the actions of the leader. To the outside world, it was still the revolutionary inner sanctum, but for Stalin it was nothing more than a convenient assembly which gave legal force to his will. Acting on the age-old precept of dictators, he had liquidated all his old comrades who had known his weaknesses and his failings, and in their place he had put new 'comrades-in-arms' who owed their promotion to him, all of them zealous executives. Lenin had transformed the dictatorship of the proletariat into the dictatorship of the Party, and Stalin went further by making the dictatorship of the Party into that of one man. The Politburo meanwhile remained the chief instrument for maintaining in the public mind some semblance of collective, or collegial, leadership, while in reality it was utterly subservient, its members vying with each other to invent some new epithet with which to praise The Leader.

This situation came about as a direct result of Lenin's having concentrated all power in the hands of the Party. Stalin finished building Lenin's totalitarian pyramid, and under him the Politburo came to resemble a court of the Inquisition. On 3 December 1934 it agreed that the security authorities be empowered to speed up their work in connection with 'terrorists', and that the courts be told 'not to allow petitions for mercy to delay the carrying out of death sentences, since ... it is not thought possible to examine such petitions'.[200] This decision echoed Lenin's order to 'shoot plotters and waverers without asking anyone and without any idiotic red tape'.[201] Lenin, however, had resorted to such summary measures in wartime, while Stalin was prepared to do so in time of peace. His 'Leninist' Politburo went even further: on 5 July 1937 it decided 'henceforth to establish a procedure whereby all the wives of unmasked Right-Trotskyite spy traitors should be sent to camps for not less than 5–8 years'.[202] But this was in effect merely the continuation of a practice established in the civil war, as when Trotsky demanded that commands be given only to those former tsarist officers whose families had remained within the limits of Soviet Russia, and that they be told that they bore responsibility for their families' lives.[203] Lenin had no objection to this measure, since he himself had introduced hostage-taking – again, however, in a war situation, while Stalin had no such excuse. Stalin was indeed, as the slogan had it, 'the Lenin of today'.

Shortly after Hitler's invasion of the Soviet Union in June 1941, the Politburo was ready to conclude a second Brest-Litovsk treaty with Germany. Stalin was willing to repeat his master's example. He ordered Beria to contact the Bulgarian ambassador, Stamenov, who was a NKVD agent, and through him to establish contact with Berlin and to propose to Hitler that the USSR would on the cessation of military action 'cede Ukraine, Belorussia, the Baltic States, the Karelian Isthmus, Bessarabia and the Bukovina'. Beria deputed his agent Sudoplatov to negotiate with Stamenov.[204] The Politburo was proposing to throw tens of millions of people into slavery under the Nazis.

No measure was too extreme, no method too dirty for the Politburo to contemplate. It is enough to recall that when it felt most threatened by the Nazis, it appealed for support to the Russian Church which it had all but destroyed, to scholars and designers whom it had cast into the oblivion of the camps, and to the Jewish population which had suffered the full measure of Soviet anti-semitism. Yet, after Hitler had been defeated, the Politburo felt that too many concessions had been made during the war, especially to the Jews. While publicly showing sympathy for Jewish causes, including the foundation of the state of Israel, behind the scenes the Politburo was rewriting its script. As early as September 1946, the dictator of Soviet culture, Andrei Zhdanov, instigated an assault on Jewish theatre critics, and thereafter anti-semitic policy ranged through attacks on Zionist sympathizers, arrests, executions, street murder and the closing down of Jewish institutions.[205]

To be sure, Stalin's power was so immense and unrestrained that often he did not even trouble to camouflage his actions with the fig-leaf of the Politburo. Astonishingly, apart from Stalin, only Molotov was privy to the negotiations with Ribbentrop on 23 and 28 August and 28 September 1939, that culminated in the cynical carve-up of several countries. Frequently, during night-long carousals at his dinner-table, Stalin would have ideas and make plans which he would share with his fellow-drinkers. Next morning it would only remain for Malenkov to formulate the 'wise decision' as an order of the Politburo.

Among the countless crimes committed by Stalin's Politburo, one stands out for its cruelty and utter cynicism – the massacre at Katyn.* On 5 March 1940 the Politburo instructed the NKVD: 'the cases of 14,700 former Polish officers, civil servants, landowners, police, intelligence officers, gendarmes, settlers [i.e. Polish farmers from Western Ukraine and Belorussia], and prison guards; and the cases of 11,000 members of various counter-revolutionary espionage and sabotage organizations, former landowners, factory-owners, civil servants and deserters, now being held in prisons in the western provinces of Ukraine and Belorussia, should be reviewed in a particular order and the death penalty by shooting be applied.' It further ordered that: 'Cases should be handled without summoning those being held under

---

* The author was a member of the four-man commission which sought and found the complete proof of this.

arrest and without prior notice of the charges, or an order to end the investigation or formulate the charges.'[206] The men to whom this was applied were not prisoners of war, nor had they committed any known offences against the Soviet Union. Like so many others, they were simply perceived as a potentially anti-Soviet force that must be eliminated.

No Politburo minutes of the discussion of this issue appear to exist. Moreover, despite their repeated denials that there were any documents which proved the Politburo's involvement, all of the subsequent leaders were familiar with them. Khrushchev examined them in March 1959, Andropov in April 1981, and Gorbachev's assistant V.I. Boldin in April 1989, presumably with the intention of informing the General Secretary of their contents. There are about a dozen different instructions, emanating from the Politburo and starting in 1971, to cover up or camouflage the crime. They involved Brezhnev, Andropov, Chernenko and Gromyko, as well as other Party leaders who are still alive today.[207]

It was Khrushchev who brought back into fashion the term 'true Leninist', as an antidote to 'true Stalinist'. After the debunking of Stalin at the Twentieth Party Congress in 1956, a silent struggle was going on in the top echelon of the Party between the supporters of classic Stalinism and those who wanted to preserve it in a more liberal form. It all ended at a plenum in June 1957 which condemned the so-called anti-Party group, consisting of Malenkov, Molotov, Kaganovich, Bulganin, Pervukhin, Shepilov and others. The minutes of this meeting, extending to 344 pages, represent a unique document, anatomizing both the morale of the Communists and the morality of the Central Committee.[208] Accusing Molotov and Kaganovich of taking part in the repressions of 1937–38, Marshal Zhukov read out a document according to which they, together with Stalin, had sanctioned the execution of 38,679 senior officials, cultural figures and army leaders. They had marked on the lists where the death penalty was to be applied, and it was left to the Military Collegium merely to carry out its duty. Zhukov cited as an example one day, 12 November 1938, when Stalin and Molotov ordered the execution of 3167 senior figures.[209] Another Central Committee member, Dudorov, described how many Party secretaries, summoned by Malenkov, were arrested as they entered his office, and as many were arrested following audiences with him.[210] The Party 'HQ' was not only organizing terror against the people, it was itself an organ of the political police.

Yet, even having heard the chilling facts of Stalin's regime, there were those who could still say, as did Kaganovich: 'I loved Stalin, and he was something worth loving – he was a great Marxist ... We should be proud of him, every Communist should be proud of him ... We have uncrowned Stalin and without realizing it we have uncrowned thirty years of our own work.'[211] Leninism in its Stalinist form had become a part of the Soviet character, a deeply fanatical outlook, a way of thinking and acting. This could be seen to some degree in the huge flourishing of dogmatism in the country at large. And the path of dogmatism is the shortest way to dictatorship.

After the dramatic Twentieth Congress, when Khrushchev courageously stripped the cloak of secrecy off the crimes of the special services, there came a new era in the life of the 'Leninist' Politburo. Its tactics changed: only Stalin, Beria and the NKVD had been guilty of 'violating revolutionary legality', while the Party, and still more the Politburo, were blameless. Any attempt to examine the origins of the terroristic regime was severely curtailed.

Khrushchev himself felt the effects. When he was removed from power in a palace coup in 1964, he was, perhaps without realizing it, a beneficiary of his courage in 1956, for he was not arrested, shot or exiled, but was left to live out his days in peaceful retirement. But once the former First Secretary of the Central Committee – the post of General Secretary was renamed in 1953 and revived again in 1966 – had drawn a bracing breath of freedom, he abandoned any intention he may have had of fading out gracefully. Like many old men who have led a stormy life, he decided to write his memoirs. With little schooling or culture, but much native wit and no little courage, he set about dictating his reminiscences.

This soon became known to the Politburo, of course. On 25 March 1970, KGB Chairman Yuri Andropov reported to the Central Committee in a top secret note:

N.S. Khrushchev has recently started work on memoirs of the period of his life when he occupied senior Party and state posts. These dictated memoirs contain detailed information constituting exclusive Party and state secrets on such specific questions as the defence capability of the Soviet state, the development of industry, agriculture, the economy in general, scientific and technical achievements, the security organs, foreign policy, relations between the CPSU and the fraternal parties of socialist and capitalist countries, and so on. He reveals discussions at closed meetings of the Politburo ... Under these circumstances, it is imperative that urgent operational measures be taken to permit the monitoring of Khrushchev's work on his memoirs, and to prevent the entirely likely leak of Party and state secrets abroad. With this aim in view, it seems sensible to establish operational secret surveillance of Khrushchev and his son, Sergei ... We also think it would be desirable to summon N.S. Khrushchev to the Central Committee again and to warn him of his responsibility for the publication and leak of Party and state secrets and to demand that he draw the necessary conclusions.[212]

The Politburo was worried. Khrushchev had presented them with an unprecedented situation. On 27 March I.V. Kapitonov and Andropov were deputed to inform Khrushchev about the 'exchange of opinions at the Politburo'.[213] This had little effect, except to make Khrushchev and his son Sergei act with greater caution. Nevertheless, the KGB managed to get hold of more than 2000 pages of transcribed dictation. It was, however, only a copy, the original having been spirited out to the West by Sergei and another relation, without even Khrushchev himself realizing it. When it became clear that it was going to be impossible to prevent publication, it was decided to put pressure on the old 'Leninist' publicly to denounce the material as a forgery.

This time the Chairman of the Party Control Commission, A.Y. Pelshe, and two other members, S.O. Postovalov and R.E. Melnikov, confronted their recalcitrant ex-comrade. The hour-long conversation, scrupulously taken down by two stenographers, reads like a film script, and although it is far too long to reproduce in full here, it is worth quoting extensively as evidence of Communist morality, the climate of political investigation cultivated by the Politburo, and Khrushchev's independent and bold behaviour.

PELSHE: According to Ambassador Comrade Dobrynin, on 6 November [1970] representatives of the American *Time* publishing house officially announced that they were in possession of the 'memoirs of N.S. Khrushchev'. Perhaps you would tell us straight to whom this material was handed over for publication abroad.

KHRUSHCHEV: I protest, Comrade Pelshe. I have my human dignity and I protest. I gave material to no one. I am no less a Communist than you.

PELSHE: I have to tell you that the material is there.

KHRUSHCHEV: You tell me how it got there. I don't think it has. I think it's a provocation.

PELSHE: You are in a Party building . . .

KHRUSHCHEV: I have never given any memoirs to anyone and would never have permitted it. As for what I dictated, I regard it as the right of every citizen and Party member.

PELSHE: We already said in a conversation with you that this method, this writing of memoirs which a wide circle of people are attracted to do, is not appropriate . . .

KHRUSHCHEV: Go ahead, arrest me, shoot me. I'm fed up with life. When people ask me, I say that I'm not happy to be alive. I heard today on the radio that de Gaulle died. I envy him . . .

PELSHE: Tell us how we can get out of the situation.

KHRUSHCHEV: I don't know. It's your fault, not yours personally, but the whole leadership's . . . I know that before I was summoned, they despatched agents . . .

PELSHE: A lot of people in Moscow know you're dictating.

KHRUSHCHEV: I'm seventy-seven. I still think clearly and I answer for all my words and actions . . .

PELSHE: How are we going to get out of this?

KHRUSHCHEV: I don't know. I'm totally isolated, virtually under house arrest. Both gates are watched. It's very shaming. I'm fed up. Relieve my suffering.

PELSHE: No one is trying to hurt you.

KHRUSHCHEV: Moral torture is the worst kind.

PELSHE: You said when you had finished you'd hand it over to the Central Committee.

KHRUSHCHEV: I didn't say that. Comrade Kirilenko suggested I stop writing. I said I couldn't do that, it was my right.

PELSHE: We don't want you to die.

KHRUSHCHEV: I want death.

MELNIKOV: Maybe someone has let you down?

KHRUSHCHEV: Dear comrade, I answer for my words and I'm not mad. I gave no one any material, nor could I have.

MELNIKOV: Your son wasn't the only one to handle the material, there was also the typist, whom you don't know, and the writer, who isn't a Party member, and whom you also don't know, and others.

KHRUSHCHEV: These are all Soviet people, trusted people.

MELNIKOV: No need to stamp and shout. You're in the CPC [Party Control Commission] now and you should behave accordingly . . .

KHRUSHCHEV: It's my nerves, I'm not shouting. I'm in a different situation and a different age.

PELSHE: Never mind about age and nerves, every Party member has to answer for his actions.

KHRUSHCHEV: You're absolutely right, Comrade Pelshe, and I do. I'm ready to take my punishment, even the death sentence.

PELSHE: The CPC doesn't sentence to death.

KHRUSHCHEV: It used to be the practice. How many thousands of people perished? How many were shot? And now they're putting up monuments to 'enemies of the people' . . .

PELSHE: On 23 November, that's in thirteen days, [the memoirs] will be published, they're with the printer now . . .

KHRUSHCHEV: I'm willing to declare that I have given no memoirs either to any Soviet or Western publisher and have no such intention. Please write that down.

POSTOVALOV: We have to think, and you above all, of what kind of announcement you should make, and to make them . . .

KHRUSHCHEV: I will say only one thing, and that is that everything I dictated is the truth. Nothing made-up, nothing amplified, if anything the opposite, it's rather toned down. I expected to be asked to write. They published Zhukov's memoirs, after all. His wife rang me and said: '[Zhukov] is ill and can't talk to you himself, but he wants to know your opinion of his book . . .' I told her I hadn't read it, but people had told me about it. I said what he had written about Stalin was disgusting and I wouldn't read it. Zhukov is an honest man, a military man, but he's a hothead . . .

POSTOVALOV: But you said you hadn't read his book.

KHRUSHCHEV: People told me about it.

POSTOVALOV: We're not talking about Zhukov.

KHRUSHCHEV: Comrade Pelshe didn't let me finish what I was saying. It's Stalinist style to interrupt.

PELSHE: That's your habit.

KHRUSHCHEV: I was also infected by Stalin, but I liberated myself, whereas you . . .

MELNIKOV: Comrade Khrushchev, you may make a protest if you're offended.

KHRUSHCHEV: I'm telling you, don't push me into lying in my old age.

PELSHE: We heard today that the American *Time* publishing house has the memoirs of Khrushchev which will be published there. That's a fact. We would like you to define your attitude to this affair, without talking

about the substance of the memoirs, by saying you're indignant and that
you gave nothing to anyone . . .

KHRUSHCHEV: Let the stenographer take down my statement. From
reports in the foreign press, chiefly in the United States of America and
other bourgeois countries, it has become known that the memoirs or
reminiscences of Khrushchev are to be published. I am indignant at this
fabrication because I have given no memoirs to anyone, neither *Time*
nor any other publisher, not even Soviet publishers. Therefore I regard
this as lies, a forgery which the bourgeois press is capable of
publishing . . .[214]

To his credit, Khrushchev would only admit, despite the arm-twisting,
that he had not given his memoirs to anyone. He did not disavow the
contents of the memoirs. The long dialogue between the disgraced
'Leninist' and the Party inquisitors highlights the way Party morality
had been intensively cultivated by the Politburo. Since the time of
Lenin, falsehood had become one of the Party's chief political assets.
Khrushchev's words, 'don't push me into lying in my old age', reflect
on the individual level the rule of untruth, falsification and lying that
were the Communist Party's stock-in-trade. It has to be said, however,
that the vast majority of the people believed the lies, and helped to
spread them.

Thus, after the Twentieth Congress the Politburo lost none of its
power, but merely altered the form of its influence. Instead of openly
using physical terror, it now resorted to mental terror, the manipulation of public opinion and the 'perfecting' of the totalitarian bureau-
cratization of society. It still remained the super-government, the
supreme organ, which decided everything.

The Politburo relied on the vast apparatus of the Central Committee. While the Central Committee itself had in the order of three
hundred members, and half as many candidate-members, its many
thousands of officials stood above the government, the ministries,
universities, industry, culture, sport, diplomacy, the army, the secret
police and intelligence services. And this was true in every region
and district. The Central Committee organization had over twenty
sections and as many sub-sections, further subdivided into 180–190
sectors.[215] There were sectors for Ukraine and Belorussia and the
other republics, an international department to handle relations
with other socialist countries, newspapers, Party cards, philosophy,

work among foreign students, the cinema, general and specialized defence engineering, defence electronics, collective farms, state security, Soviet institutions in capitalist countries, and so on and so forth. By the end, the Party apparatus – that is its working organization, as distinct from Party members – numbered as many as 100,000 to 150,000 people. This pyramidal structure, from the smallest cell at grassroots level up to the Politburo itself, stood like a scaffold around the nominal governmental, or Soviet, administrative structure, controlling, energizing, directing and manipulating it, through the Party members who everywhere saturated the Soviets, to ensure that the Politburo's policies were carried out.

Lenin's invention of the one-party system in effect led to the liquidation of the party in the usual sense of the word. It became an order of privilege which observed hierarchy more strictly than an army, and at its peak was the Politburo, a clan of inviolable, unanswerable individuals. But just as they could rise, so they could be lowered rung by rung down the ladder of authority to the very bottom – sometimes with a bang – by the General Secretary, invariably with the unanimous support of the rest. This was put succinctly in an exchange on 17 June 1971: Politburo member Gennadi Voronov proposed that regional Party secretaries and chairmen of soviets should be confirmed in office by the Council of Ministers, 'or at least that it give its agreement'. Stalin had changed People's Commissars into Ministers in 1943, and the Council of Ministers ostensibly occupied the same place as the Sovnarkom had done (this is not to say that it had the same authority – far from it, since Stalin needed none of these bodies in order to rule, preferring his own personal Secretariat and the security organs). Voronov's colleague Andrei Kirilenko at once spoke up: 'I would like to help Voronov and tell him that in Russia we have the Central Committee of the CPSU and it decides all such questions, including personnel questions. It was never otherwise, so why rearrange things now so that such questions should go through the Council of Ministers?' Podgorny added: 'Why put these things through any other organs?'[216]

On 7 January 1974, during a two-hour discussion on the dissident writer Alexander Solzhenitsyn, Brezhnev declared: 'According to our overseas representatives and the foreign press, a new work by Solzhenitsyn, called *The Gulag Archipelago*, is being published in France and the USA. No one has read it yet, but its contents are already well known. It is a crude anti-Soviet libel. We must now discuss what to do about it. Our laws permit us to put Solzhenitsyn in prison right away, for he has encroached on the holiest of holies, on Lenin, on our Soviet system, on the Soviet regime.' After speeches by Kosygin, Andropov, Kirilenko and Suslov, the Politburo confronted the dilemma of whether to try Solzhenitsyn or to put him out of the country. They chose the latter course.[217] For them, an intellectual danger was no less threatening than a nuclear one.

Even when faced with a humanitarian problem, they were incapable of rising above their Bolshevik prejudices. On 31 August 1983 Soviet aircraft shot down a South Korean passenger airliner that had violated Soviet air space in the Far East. The Politburo session of 2 September was a long one, as member after member exclaimed: 'This was a crude anti-Soviet provocation', 'Our pilots acted in strict accordance with the regulations', 'We must show resolve and presence of mind', 'We must stick to the version announced in the press', and so on. All their thoughts were bent towards concealing the truth of the matter. Only Solomentsev and Gromyko said, *inter alia*, 'Perhaps we could say we sympathize with the families of the victims?' Gorbachev took the view that 'We cannot say nothing, we have to take an offensive position.'[218]

What is so striking about this exchange is that, while the whole world was shaken by the deaths of the 269 innocent victims, and by the senselessness and savagery of the action, the only concern shown by members of the Politburo was to find a way to save face, to justify themselves, and to take up an unassailable 'offensive position'.

Even during the period of *perestroika*, when it seemed that everyone had at last recognized the urgent need for fundamental reform, the Politburo's main objective was to find a way to renew the system cosmetically, to change its façade while preserving its essence. It never occurred to them that the totalitarian system, created by Lenin, was not amenable to reform. With this in mind, Gorbachev's historic rôle appears in a different light. It was not so much that he destroyed the totalitarian system, but rather that he did not prevent its self-destruction. The three-hour Politburo session of 15 October 1987 concerned itself entirely with a discussion on the question of the draft report to be given at a ceremonial session of the Central Committee on the seventieth anniversary of the October revolution, a significant date in the Communist calendar in any year, but especially so now, with change in the air.

RYZHKOV: I think the report gives a correct rebuke to a certain group of people who are trying to exploit democracy to harm our Party and the general interests of the state.

GORBACHEV: We don't need any kind of bourgeois pluralism. We have socialist pluralism, for we take account of people's different interests and different points of view.

RYZHKOV: That should go into the report . . . After all, every word is going to be used as ammunition: 'Aha, pluralism! Let's have a second party, a third party,' and so on.

LIGACHEV: I would like once more to stress: it is very important that precisely now a correct, principled Marxist-Leninist evaluation be given of the Party's ideological struggle with Trotskyism . . .

GROMYKO: There can be no argument about how things would have been if we hadn't had collective, socialist agriculture. How would the country have looked during the war and what state would it have been in at the end of it? . . . We should say that without Lenin the Party faced a very difficult problem of gaining victory over the dark forces which wanted to destroy the Party . . .

GORBACHEV: . . . here Lenin's genius was revealed, in that all his comrades-in-arms were of an order beneath him. I can say here in this circle that, until Lenin's return to Petrograd, Stalin and all the rest who were in Russia were getting themselves ready and thinking that things were fine now, there will be a legal opposition. And they would be in the opposition. They were already preparing themselves to be a legal opposition party. That was the view of rather senior figures in the Party. And then Lenin appeared and, without pausing, said: 'Long live the socialist revolution!'

SHEVARDNADZE: I'm a bit worried about one phrase, although it's correct in principle. It says in the report: 'The policy of liquidating the kulaks as a class was the correct one . . .' Maybe we could drop 'liquidating' and find some other word . . .

CHEBRIKOV: A group has emerged, they don't reflect the mood of the people, of course, but they're distributing leaflets about the need for a new constitution. Here's one of them. It says our Constitution doesn't correspond to *perestroika*, that it's the constitution of a totalitarian regime, more like army regulations, and that the country is like a barracks. They also attack Article 6, on the leading rôle of the Party.

The rest of the members spoke in similar vein. The population was freeing itself slowly enough from Bolshevism, from socialism which levelled downwards, from hostility to those who thought differently, but the Politburo was even more backward. In this respect the Politburo was keeping the Leninist tradition alive.

Similarly, it was keeping alive the tradition of looking after itself. A special session of 28 July 1966 decided that Politburo 'members and candidate members, Central Committee Secretaries and Deputy Chairmen of the Council of Ministers would start work at 9 a.m. and finish at 5 p.m., with an obligatory break for lunch', and that they would have a six-week summer holiday and a four-weeks winter break.[219] On 24 March 1983 the additional privilege of starting work at 10 a.m. was agreed for members and candidates over the age of sixty-five – at that time virtually all of them qualified.[220] Three years later, members' pensions were reviewed and set at eight hundred roubles a month (a skilled worker earned about two hundred), plus the dacha and staff of five, the Chaika and Volga limousines, and so on.[221] All this information was kept in 'special files' which could be opened 'only with the permission of the General Secretary of the CPSU'.[222]

All power is vicious, but Bolshevik power was especially so. A glimpse into the doings of the Politburo confirms that. They represented the apocalypse of the regime in the twilight of the revolution.

# 6

## The One-Dimensional Society

Bolshevism destroyed everything in Russia, starting with the weak and ineffective Provisional Government, followed by private property, the peasant commune and the Church. Everything connected with Lenin was anti-capitalist, anti-democratic, anti-liberal, anti-reformist, anti-human and anti-Christian. There can scarcely have been another man in history who managed so profoundly to change so large a society on such a scale.

Perhaps the single most characteristic feature of the new society was its one-dimensionality, its uniformity. The infinite variety of social and intellectual life, culture, historical tradition and the creative potential of millions of people was reduced to the harsh, uniform, uncompromising ideological paradigm of Leninism. Dogmatic thinking, totalitarian bureaucracy, authoritarianism and irrational fear became the characteristic features of the new society.

The pages of Soviet history after 1924 are filled with the invariable call: 'Back to Lenin!' Society was gripped by the idea of him, and at critical moments his successors raised their eyes to this icon of Soviet godliness and called for his spirit to come to their aid. In October 1927, as he was defeating the Trotskyist opposition at the Fifteenth Party Conference, Stalin summoned Lenin as an ally: 'You know,' he said, 'in 1921 Lenin proposed to expel Shlyapnikov from the Party ... just because he dared to make some critical remarks about the Council of National Economy inside a Party cell.' That had been a good enough reason for Stalin, and he went on: 'People are talking about the arrest of disorganizers who were expelled and who are now carrying on anti-Soviet work. Yes, we are arresting them, and we're going to go on arresting them, if they don't stop undermining the

Party and the Soviet regime.' His remarks were greeted by shouts of 'Quite right! Correct!'[1] The lesson Stalin wanted to convey was that he, and they, must be just as merciless to their enemies as Lenin had been.

The return to Lenin and his aggressive form of 'defence' became the Communist norm and the rule of Party life: 'Lenin bequeathed . . .', 'it says in Lenin . . .', 'the Leninist way to do it is . . .'. When on 25 February 1956 Khrushchev made his famous speech in the Kremlin, 'On the Cult of Personality and its Consequences', Lenin's shade hovered in the hall. Indeed, Khrushchev, his head thrown back, pronounced: 'Lenin taught . . .', 'Lenin always stressed the rôle of the people . . .', 'Under Lenin, the Party Central Committee was a genuine expression of collective leadership . . .'.

The nub of the cult of personality was that Stalin had forgotten Lenin's teaching. Even Lenin's cruelty, according to Khrushchev, was of a different order from Stalin's: 'And who will say that Lenin did not resort to the cruellest measures against the enemies of the revolution, when really necessary? No, no one can say that. Vladimir Ilyich called for the harsh punishment of enemies of the revolution and the working class and when the need arose he used such methods with utter ruthlessness. Just recall V.I. Lenin's struggle against the SR organizers of anti-Soviet risings, against the counter-revolutionary kulaks in 1918 and others . . . But Lenin was using such measures against real class enemies . . .'[2] If the class enemy was a 'real' one, everything was permitted.

On 27 April 1921, the Politburo under Lenin's chairmanship appointed Tukhachevsky as commander-in-chief of the Tambov region. He was given one month to put down a peasant rebellion, and told to report in writing every week on his progress. Tukhachevsky could not meet his deadline, but he did his level best. On 12 June 1921 he issued the following orders:

The remnants of the defeated bands and individual bandits . . . are gathering in the forest and carrying out raids on peaceful inhabitants. 1. The forest where the bandits are hiding must be cleared with poison gas; careful calculation must be made to ensure that the cloud of asphyxiating gas spreads throughout the forest and exterminates everything hiding there; 2. The artillery inspector must immediately release the required number of poison gas balloons and necessary specialists to the localities.[3]

It is hard to imagine what sort of peasants could be designated as 'real class enemies' by the regime, but similar measures taken elsewhere were known to and approved by the Politburo.

Khrushchev's 1956 speech continued: 'Stalin showed irreverence for Lenin's memory. It is no accident that the Palace of Congresses, which was agreed on thirty years ago as a monument to Vladimir Ilyich, was never built and was constantly postponed and the idea forgotten. We must correct the position and build this monument to Vladimir Ilyich.' At this point the assembly interrupted the speaker with 'stormy and prolonged applause'[4] – as if the country were not already inundated with Lenin monuments. It would have been hard to find a village, however out of the way, in which the farm-manager's office or the club or the square did not have a plaster, concrete or bronze Lenin. There was a dense network of Lenin museums, Lenin rooms, Lenin memorial sites, routes, libraries, streets, collective and state farms, one-horse towns and regions. The gigantic Central Lenin Museum had branches everywhere; a vast number of house- and apart-ment-museums where Lenin or members of his family had stayed were set up: a ship museum on the Yenisei, a barn museum and fisherman's cottage museum at Razliv, a funeral train museum. Lenin memorial sites were also established abroad, in Paris, Prague, Leipzig, Helsinki, Cracow and elsewhere. Even places Lenin had never visited were included: Bratislava, Ulan-Bator, Aden, Havana. No saint, auto-crat or military leader was ever accorded such attention. Many people, hypnotized by the sheer scale of his greatness, believed in the holiness of the Bolshevik leader.

*Perestroika* was already a well-established idea when the Politburo debated its report for the seventieth anniversary of the October revol-ution. General Secretary Gorbachev, extolling Lenin's genius, said: 'We wanted to build a bridge from Lenin, to connect Leninist ideas and Leninist approaches to the events of those years with the affairs of our own day. After all, the dialectic which Lenin used to solve problems is also the key to present-day tasks.'[5] So, we Russians, above all the leadership, had held the alleged key in our hands, and yet somehow we had never managed to open the door to freedom, abund-ance and respect for human rights, and thus lagged farther and farther behind the caravan of civilization.

At the beginning of the century Lenin had said: 'Give us an organization of professional revolutionaries and we will turn over all of Russia.' The organization was given, and Russia and everything in it was 'turned over'. The immoral became moral, the base became the elevated, catastrophes were proclaimed as great achievements, the defeat of the country as a huge revolutionary victory. As a result, there emerged the one-dimensional society with a one-dimensional personality. The means of accomplishing this had been the destruction of private property. Lenin had not understood that private property is in itself a complex and universal mechanism for the self-regulation of the economy. The shift to the Communist management of the economy inevitably demanded the replacement of economic levers by administrative ones, and thus was created the source of totalitarian bureaucracy. And since bureaucracy cannot manage without dogmatism, the most important pillars of the one-dimensional society were erected. Every facet of society suffered, and it should not be forgotten that the same thing was planned for the whole world. As Lenin put it in 1920, the advance on Warsaw was to be an attempt 'with the bayonet to probe Poland's readiness for social revolution',[6] after which eruptions in Germany and then the rest of the world were to follow.

## *The Deceived Vanguard*

'From A. Zedmidko to Comrade Beria: In order to develop the site, I request that another camp be organized for 5000 people, with 30,000 metres of tarpaulin for tents and fifty tonnes of barbed wire. 22 March 1947.'[7] Beria, like other ministers, was accustomed to signing such orders for an additional allocation of the slaves who were building 'the socialist society'. Behind miles of barbed wire, millions were trudging the Leninist path and making roads, building bridges, sinking mines and erecting power stations, working in scientific laboratories and design bureaux. Beria, as Interior Minister, was virtually the country's biggest 'producer'; he employed the largest army of workers, all of them totally without rights. His reports to Stalin flowed in a constant stream: 'On 13 April at 1700 hours the Magnitstroy NKVD commissioned Unit no. 4, consisting of sixty-five ovens, for industrial production at the chemical-coke factory at Nizhne-Tagilsk. It will

provide 450,000 tonnes of metallurgical coke a year for Soviet industry. Construction is being completed of blast furnace no. 3, with a
capacity of 1,050 cubic metres and an annual output of 450,000 tonnes
of cast iron, to be commissioned in the last ten days of April 1944.'[8]

The archives teem with such reports, almost giving the impression
that the entire working class had been resettled in the NKVD's miserable concentration-camp system. At the cost of millions of lives, this
forced labour often achieved amazing results. In the year of Stalin's
death, the hundreds of thousands employed in the gold fields raised
the Soviet Union's gold reserves to 2,049.8 tonnes, the highest figure
ever attained. Stalin's successors were never able to come anywhere
near such figures, and they merely consumed what had been accomplished by the efforts of slaves – by 1991 the reserves were down to
about 250 tonnes.

Opening the Twelfth Party Congress on 17 April 1923, Kamenev
declared:

With the working class under Vladimir Ilyich's leadership, we have travelled
a long, unprecedented path, unique in history . . . We are the only Communist Party which is no longer struggling for power but which is organizing
the regime of workers and peasants, the only party with the chance to put
the age-old tools of oppression at the service of the working class and all
toilers. Our state is the first attempt to turn all these tools, the national
wealth, the land, schools and education – everything that was created by
labour and that was until now in the hands of the ruling classes and served
only to oppress – to turn all this into tools for the emancipation of the toilers
and to hand it all over to the working class. (Applause)[9]

Was it true that the working class had been made into an instrument
of universal emancipation? Had everything been put into its hands?
Was it really the vanguard of the revolution? Lenin, of course, had not
given affirmative replies to these questions. In his *State and Revolution*,
written on the eve of October 1917 and published in 1918, he had
extolled the proletariat as a 'special class' which alone was 'capable of
being the leader of *all* the toiling and exploited masses . . . but the
proletariat is not capable of struggling for its emancipation *independently*'.[10] As a perceptive politician, he knew he must take the working
class with him if his plans were to be realized. And indeed, on the
eve of the October coup, eighty per cent of the Petrograd Bolshevik

organization consisted of workers. It was their choice of the Bolsheviks to lead them that made it possible for Lenin to convert a seemingly hazardous plot into reality, and it remained only for him to use the enormous force of the workers, who had come to believe that their fate was now in their own hands. Writing to Pavel Axelrod on 19 November 1917, Martov admitted that 'nearly the entire proletariat is on Lenin's side and expects that the coup will lead to their social emancipation'.[11] The workers believed in the Bolsheviks, they believed in Lenin, and it was this that predetermined the success of the coup.

Did the proletariat become the 'dominant force'? What did the working class gain from the 'dictatorship of the proletariat'? First, it should be noted that as a rule they were to be led by members of the intelligentsia, whom Lenin so disliked and whom he now ordered about as he chose. Virtually all the key posts were held by people who had never been inside a factory or workshop, and who had spent much of their lives abroad. Most of the 'professional revolutionaries' were not proletarians, and once they were in power they made haste to bring 'representatives' of the working class onto the Central Committee as a sort of political entourage. In fact, from October 1917 until August 1991, the Party and the country were led first by 'professional revolutionaries' and later by 'party officials' of the *nomenklatura*. To be sure, people with a working-class background, commonly factory engineers, often managed to rise to these high-ranking positions, but the system was so structured that such people quickly lost their proletarian character and were assimilated into the Party bureaucracy. The working class had as it were involuntarily delegated its power to a tenacious, imperious and all-seeing stratum of professional Leninist Party members.

On countless occasions Lenin had talked of the transfer of the industrial potential of the state into the workers' hands, claiming that 'the workers, having won political power, will smash the old bureaucratic machine, reduce it to its foundations, and will replace it with a new one consisting of these same workers and employees, but taking immediate measures to ensure they do not become bureaucrats'.[12] The naivety of this notion was quickly revealed when the workers, having taken over the factories, became enslaved to an even greater degree. Everything was declared state property, and ordinary workers had only one right: to work and to keep on working, without striking ('bourgeois sabotage'), and unable to advance any social or economic demands. Lenin and his party completely alienated the workers from the means of production. Meanwhile, the bureaucratic machine, created anew, surpassed the old one in its totality and cruelty.

It had seemed that the 'dictatorship of the proletariat' would give the workers opportunities to acquire a dominant position in the running of industry and the state. That indeed was what Lenin had meant by revolutionary democracy. This democracy, he declared, was a form of state whose essence was 'the organized, systematic use of coercion'.[13] Here he was a prophet, indeed: coercion and violence used on the working class there would be in abundance. His successor would put workers in prison for absenteeism and lateness, confiscate the peasants' identity cards in case they should try to escape from the countryside to the towns, and take away the right of a worker to move from one job to another.

It was not long after the revolution before the 'vanguard' was being exploited even more than under the tsarist regime. The constant reiteration by Lenin and his comrades of the workers' right to rule and to take decisions was nothing but political camouflage. It was the 'professional revolutionaries', the Party functionaries, who ruled, and who were the real high priests of the notorious dictatorship of the proletariat. The working class thus served as the most important mass instrument for the forced introduction of socialism in Russia. As Karl Kautsky wrote, however: 'Soviet socialism is not socialism at all, for it arose not out of abundance and the "development of productive forces", but out of scarcity and backwardness; militarized Communism is the result not of a revolutionary process, but of the disintegration brought about by domestic and foreign war.'[14] Lenin in effect used the working class as the main force to reconstruct Russia in the social-ist mode.

The very word 'worker' seemed to act like magic on Lenin. The formula 'of working class origin' aroused in him the highest level of trust in a man. On occasion he was seriously disappointed. The story of Roman Malinovsky is a case in point. Malinovsky, head of the St Petersburg metal-workers' union on the eve of the First World War, enjoyed Lenin's utter confidence. On Lenin's recommendation this talented speaker and organizer was appointed to the Party Central Committee at its Prague Conference in January 1912. Together he and Lenin travelled to Leipzig, and, as Zinoviev recalled, on his return Lenin expressed the highest opinion of Malinovsky. So impressed was he that he proposed that Malinovsky stand as a Bolshevik candidate in the forthcoming elections to the Russian parliament, the State Duma. In fact, in May 1910 Malinovsky had been recruited by the Okhrana, the tsarist secret police, and had been informing them regularly about the situation in the Bolshevik camp. His reports had led to the arrest of several Bolsheviks, including Stalin. It was the Okhrana who cleared the way for his election victory later that year, entrusting him with the task of maintaining the split between the Bolsheviks and Mensheviks in order to keep them both weak.

When suspicions were raised about Malinovsky, however, a commission consisting of Ganetsky, Zinoviev and Lenin could find no compromising evidence. In an article on the subject, Lenin wrote that the scoundrels who had cast a shadow on Malinovsky were 'letting blackguards and vermin and skunks, ignored with contempt by the working class, root around in all this!'[15]

During the war Malinovsky fought in the Russian army. He was taken prisoner in 1915, and from his prisoner of war camp he quickly established contact with Lenin in Switzerland. After the February revolution, when ample proof of Malinovsky's treachery came to light, Lenin gave evidence to the Provisional Government's investigative commission, claiming that the secret police had accomplished nothing, except to help consolidate the ties between the Bolsheviks' underground operations and their legal newspaper, *Pravda*.[16] In October 1918 Malinovsky returned voluntarily from captivity and was arrested. Lenin's only comment was: 'What a swine! He really put one over on us. The traitor! Shooting's too good for him!'[17] But in November 1918 that is what he got. The episode might have taught Lenin that a working-class background was no guarantee of dependability.

The Politburo continually sought ways of increasing the Party's influence among the workers, and in fact the construction of the industrial base of socialism bore a coercive character from the outset. Many sites – if not the majority – were built by prisoners who, from the late 1920s, always numbered several million. In August 1933, for instance, after the completion of the White Sea–Baltic Canal, it was agreed that the NKVD should take over the entire zone by settling it with new contingents of prisoners and exploiting mineral deposits and barge and tug-boat construction.[18] More than ninety per cent of the projects in the canal zone were carried out by convict labour.

First Menzhinsky, then Yagoda and Beria, as the commissars responsible, maintained a constant demand for more and more people, and each project – the canal itself, roads, bridges and mines – cost thousands of lives. Stalin was especially concerned that this particular cauldron of hell should be kept on the boil. When Commissar of Heavy Industry Ordzhonikidze complained to him that Yagoda was not keeping up an adequate supply of labour, Stalin at once corrected the situation.[19]

In August 1937 the Politburo agreed to the construction of the Baikal–Amur railway line, and a year later confirmed the exact route the immense project would follow. Once again it was the NKVD that was to shoulder the responsibility for conducting the surveys, doing the work, and even for supplying thousands of horses.[20] In the same way, it was the NKVD that oversaw the building of the Norilsk mining plant, the huge Dnieper and many other similar hydro-electric stations.

Lenin is not commonly regarded as the originator of the use of slave labour, yet it was he who resorted to it as a means of rapid conversion to a socialist economy. Confronted by the chaos created by the revolution, Lenin saw no other solution than harsh regulations, coercion and control, policies presented as a new structure called 'War Communism'. War Communism has always been associated with the civil war, and considered as a temporary policy which could be abandoned and replaced by the New Economic Policy as easily as it had been adopted. In fact, it was the basis and essence of Lenin's policy, and only its total collapse forced him to grab the lifebelt of NEP. War Communism, however, did not completely die, but survived in various forms even until the end of the 1980s.

The dominance of the state over society which Lenin approved, despite his repeated insistence on the 'withering away of the state', ensured the adoption of War Communism. Lenin believed that the concentration of industry and finance, and a total state monopoly on production, trade and prices, would bring socialism closer. Instead, it only brought closer a barracks form of War Communism, and despite the temporary phase of the NEP, Stalin returned to it when he applied Lenin's ideas to the collectivization of agriculture, the militarization of industry, the imposition of the GULAG on the national economy and the application of coercive management as absolutely socialist.

In Lenin's view, War Communism would lead to the future commune-state, a commune imbued with the proletarian consciousness he was to impart to it – although he hardly believed in it himself. The picture of the future he painted in his *State and Revolution* is shocking even today:

The more democratic the state, consisting of armed workers, the faster will *any* state begin to wither away. For then everyone will learn to run the economy independently, and independently monitor and control the spongers, the sons of the wealthy, the crooks and other 'defenders of capitalist traditions', then it will be so unbelievably hard to evade national accounting and control, it will be such a rare occurrence, and will no doubt be accompanied by such swift and harsh punishment (for the armed workers know about real life, they're not sentimental intellectuals and won't let anyone fool them), that the need to observe the simple and basic rules of any human society will quickly become a *habit*.[21]

Lenin was right at least in one respect: the Russian people did indeed soon come to regard the methods applied as natural, they did become a habit. It is for this reason that the notion of War Communism as a short-term stage in Soviet construction is unsustainable. After the brief flowering of the NEP, Stalin reapplied Lenin's War Communism in modernized and adapted form to his own 'Leninist' strategy. Even Stalin's monstrous assertion that 'the further we move forward, the more we succeed, so the more embittered the remnants of exploiting classes will become, and the more quickly will they resort to more acute forms of struggle',[22] appears as the logical consequence of War Communist thinking.

Despite the collapse of War Communism, Lenin, and then Stalin, viewed it as a natural phase of the revolution. Even in the summer of 1917, Lenin had stated publicly that the move to socialism would be impossible without the kind of coercion and force characteristic of War Communism. In an interview with the bourgeois newspaper *Den'*, he had stated frankly: 'Historians of the proletariat see in Jacobinism one of the highest upsurges of the oppressed class in the struggle for emancipation.'[23] Others had seen in Lenin's policy a militaristic future for Russia, and not only 'capitalist encirclement'. In his 'Reflections on the Russian Revolution', Peter Struve, the former Marxist revolutionary who then became a liberal politician and finally a religious philosopher, wrote in 1921: 'It is important to note that Soviet Communism is in some respects a direct heir of what it was customary to call the war economy, war socialism or war regulation . . . War socialism regulated more or less relative scarcity.'[24]

It was in the military sphere alone that Soviet Communism was able to compete with the Western democracies, for the most important indicator of the state's greatness was its might, and above all its military might. The boomerang always returns, however, and the military way of thinking and acting became one of the sources of erosion of 'Lenin's cause'. In order to provide some sort of stimulus to efficient production, an effective substitute for personal material interest had to be found. Lenin found it in socialist competition, and indeed for as long as the people still genuflected before The Idea, for good or ill this stimulus worked. Millions believed they were accomplishing a 'feat', struggling 'for honour', carrying out 'Lenin's bidding'. In the 1930s, by relying on and indeed by arranging individual examples and models of labour, Stalin enticed millions to fulfil and over-fulfil their appointed tasks. This was perhaps the moral peak of War Communism in its efforts to find non-economic stimuli for raising production.

The example of Alexei Stakhanov is well known. In 1935, at the Central Irmino coal mine, he established a fantastic record of production. With the assistance of the local Party organizers, Stakhanov's efforts were used as a means to whip up enthusiasm in other sectors. Soon A. Busygin, a smith, achieved a new record, then P. Krivonos, a machine-worker, followed by M. Mazai, a metal-worker, and so on. For Stalin, it did not matter if the quality of output was falling, if accidents and breakages rose rapidly, even though he was to denounce this at the plenum on 3 March 1937 as sabotage. Stakhanov was important as a symbolic founder of the new Communist movement. The Central Committee set its propagandists to work writing books and pamphlets with such titles as 'My Method', 'A Year in the Homeland of the Stakhanovite Movement', 'A Tale about Myself', 'The Story of My Life', all of them signed, but in fact not even read, by Stakhanov. This was Stalin's way of replying to Lenin's question, 'How to organize competition?'

The Stakhanovite movement was an attempt to use non-economic methods, plus ideological means and Party pressure, to raise industrial production rapidly. No doubt Stakhanov and his followers deserve respect, believing as they did that they were bringing the bright future closer. Not many then realized that the deep economic flaws in the system could not be hidden forever by such efforts, and although for many years the Party functionaries did their utmost to revive and resuscitate 'socialist competition', they failed. Economic laws, like the laws of nature, cannot be flouted forever.

Resorting again to Lenin's teaching, Stalin shifted the accent from material to moral incentives. There now appeared countless medal-bearers, Heroes and Heroines of Labour, shock-workers. It was reported in 1939 that for their 'Stakhanovite labour' 18,519 people in industry had been decorated, while 4318 village schoolteachers received medals, as did 1147 artists and 205 sportsmen. As official propaganda put it: 'This could only happen in our country, where the toilers work for themselves, for their class ... The leader of the people, Comrade Stalin, has said of the Stakhanovite movement that "it contains the seed of the cultural and technological rise of the working class, that it is showing us the way by which alone we can achieve the highest indicators of labour efficiency".'[25] By stressing the importance of the Stakhanovite movement, Stalin was exposing his own crisis mentality. Such methods – exploiting enthusiasm, patriotism and moral exhortation – could only produce transient results. Material arguments were bound sooner or later to replace The Idea.

History is a dispassionate judge. Its mills grind slowly, but ceaselessly. The 'grain of Communism', which Stakhanov and his like thought they were growing, produced no burgeoning shoots; despite the fact that millions of honest people, led by the 'vanguard of the revolution', laboured for it, the utopia remained a fairy-tale. Even the rational nucleus of the idea of social justice found no worthy expression. The policy of levelling down meant that even the small gains that were made were reduced by the periodic deductions from wage-packets, disguised as 'income redistribution', that became common practice.

The working class had become the servant of the Party oligarchy. The peasantry got even less. Speaking at the Fourth Comintern Congress on 13 November 1922, Lenin was frank: 'The peasants understand that we seized power for the workers and our goal is to create the socialist order with the help of their power.'[26] Frank, but disingenuous. He had not seized power for the workers, but for the Party oligarchy.

## Peasant Predators

After Stalin's death, his successors made the purchase of grain from abroad one of their regular priorities. It was not that more grain had been produced under Stalin – on the contrary – but he had been able to keep the country on low rations and in general to regard the shortage of grain as of little significance. Khrushchev, Brezhnev and the other 'true Leninists', however, having repudiated Stalin's excesses, could not take the same cavalier attitude towards a basic source of the nation's nourishment and food for livestock. From 1957 on, vast quantities of grain were purchased from the USA, Canada and elsewhere.

On 16 August 1975, Brezhnev studied a note from the head of the Foreign Economic Trade Department, N. Patolichev. It was the kind of note Khrushchev had also received many times when he was in charge: 'In addition to the 15.95 million tonnes of grain (which we reported to you last week), we have been able to buy another 1.95 million tonnes. This means that as of today we have bought 17.9 million tonnes.' Patolichev added that, apart from the USA, grain had been purchased from Canada, Argentina, Romania and Australia, and that talks were in progress for further purchases from France, West Germany, Hungary, Yugoslavia, Argentina, Brazil and Australia. The aim, Patolichev concluded, was to bring the total amount purchased abroad to thirty million tonnes.[27] A further note explained that the grain would cost US$4.934 billion, and suggested that the sum could be raised by the sale of fifteen million tonnes of oil, 1.6 million tonnes of diesel fuel, petrol, fuel oil and, above all, 397 tonnes of gold. In the previous year the purchase of grain had been covered by the sale of only 265 tonnes of gold.[28] Meanwhile, Soviet financial managers were complaining that 'selling the gold in the present situation is extremely difficult. There has been a marked fall in prices on the world's gold markets as demand has sharply diminished. While an ounce of gold was selling at $180–200 in December 1974, today it is worth only $141–146.'[29]

The purchase of grain had become such an everyday matter for the Party leaders that it was being planned years in advance. For instance, in June 1977 the Politburo received a programme of foreign grain purchases, based on estimates supplied by the State Planning Agency, Gosplan, calling for a total of 47.4 million tonnes over the next four years. Over the same period, the country was expected to produce 362 million tonnes of its own grain. Together with imported grain, the authors of the report concluded, 'we will be in a position to maintain the release of grain for consumption and seed requirements, as well as deliveries to Cuba, Vietnam, the Mongolian People's Republic, North Korea, and for processing in the quantities envisaged in the Five-Year Plan'. The report is embellished by the signatures of every member of the Politburo, from Brezhnev and Suslov to Romanov and Shcherbitsky.[30] The output of grain over these years was, of course, lower than predicted, while purchases abroad were considerably greater.

These figures go some way towards explaining where all the state's hard currency reserves went. According to memoranda approved by the Politburo, in the Five-Year Plan prior to 1977, 1214 tonnes of gold were sold for grain.[31] This had evidently been insufficient, for it had been supplemented by the sale of fuels, copper, zinc, magnesium, chromium ore, aluminium, cellulose, coal, industrial diamonds, cotton, cars, tractors, machinery and much, much more.

It is obvious enough from all this that the Bolsheviks' plans for agriculture had failed. Russia had been turned from a large-scale exporter of grain into a regular importer. In the last twenty-five years during which the USSR bought grain abroad, Moscow was in effect financing the development of agriculture in other countries, instead of its own. In that time, the USSR transferred about 9000 tonnes of gold to Western banks. Only part of this was for grain – it was also buying meat, butter and other agricultural products. In 1977 alone, for instance, and only for 'supplementary' deliveries of meat, the Politburo had to sell an additional forty-two tonnes of gold abroad.[32] Virtually all the gold the country produced, plus its hidden reserves, was being sold abroad to buy food. If the economic system had not been so distorted, these astronomical sums might have been used to make the country's own agricultural sector a model of balanced and profitable production. If, as has been seen, the highest volume of pure gold reserves was reached in 1953 at 2,049.8 tonnes,[33] then all the gold mined after that date, between 250–300 tonnes annually, was sold for grain.

Significantly less grain was produced before 1953 than after that year. The highest output of grain achieved during Stalin's rule had been 34.7 million tonnes, in 1952. No large foreign purchases were made during that time, despite the fact that in 1945 and 1946 there was near-famine in many regions. (For instance, the Interior Commissar of the Tatar Republic, Gorbulin, reported to Beria that 46,000 people were suffering from malnutrition and needed help.[34]) Under Stalin, the only grain that came from abroad was a certain amount sent by the USA at the end of the Second World War. Stalin had other ways of maximizing the grain supply. In July 1947 he received a report that '22,678 people had been put on trial for the theft, wasting and spoiling of grain'. They were chiefly collective farm managers, managers of collecting points and elevators. 'A particularly large number of thefts took place and evidence of waste was discovered in Ukraine. In July alone the Ukrainian Ministry of the Interior put 10,511 people on trial.'[35] In effect, this was one way of covering up the shortage of grain: arrests, keeping quiet about the problem, and strict rationing.

After 1953, less grain was produced than was consumed in eighteen of the twenty-four years to 1977, the shortfall being covered by huge foreign purchases, at the cost of the national reserves. In 1975, for instance, 50.2 million tonnes were produced, while consumption amounted to 89.4 million tonnes.[36]

On 16 October 1978 the Minister of State Procurement, G.S. Zolotukhin, submitted a report to Leonid Brezhnev exposing the entire sorry picture of grain supply from 1940 to 1977. Brezhnev read the report, which was nothing less than a condemnation of the whole Bolshevik farm system, and simply signed it. Either he did not understand it, or he was used to reading about such failures.

Stalin had no intention of selling his large gold reserves for grain, because it was a matter of indifference to him if half the population died of starvation: he would never bend his knee to the capitalists. In 1953, moreover, there were millions of slave labourers in the GULAG: Soviet gold was stained with the blood of Soviet prisoners whose lives had been trampled in the frozen wastes of Kolyma. Considering the vast consumption of the country's reserves, whether in material or human resources, it is not surprising that all the figures cited above were hidden away as top state secrets. They were indeed an indictment of the system, and of 'Lenin's cooperative plan'.

When on 8 November 1917 (New Style) Lenin reported on the land and his decree on land to the Second Congress of Soviets, he stated that the question 'can be determined only by the Constituent Assembly'. He was compelled to declare that 'until the great land changes have been carried out, until their final solution by the Constituent Assembly, the following peasant mandate, compiled on the basis of 242 local peasant mandates, must apply'.[37] He then proceeded to list the eight points of this decree, which included abolition of the right to own land privately. Land was to become national property, to be distributed by local and central government, and the land fund would be subject to periodic repartition, according to the growth of the population. There were disapproving noises in the hall. Lenin faltered, but then retorted: 'It is being said here that both the decree and the mandate were composed by the Socialist Revolutionaries. So what? What does it matter who composed it, but we as a democratic government cannot ignore a decree that has come up from the grass roots.'[38]

Lenin could scarcely conceal his dissatisfaction that the SR programme, while socialist in essence, said nothing about the dictatorship of the proletariat, and put the land problem in the context of the traditional peasant commune. The SRs saw the state as an auxiliary element. Lenin would speak his mind on the subject at the Third Congress of Soviets, where, admittedly, he was also compelled to say that the union of Bolsheviks and Left SRs 'had been created on a firm base and is getting stronger, not by the day, but by the hour'.[39] He nevertheless made it plain that the peasants must understand clearly that 'there is no other path to socialism than by the dictatorship of the proletariat and the ruthless suppression of the supremacy of the exploiters'.[40] Having just thrown off one halter, the peasants were now going to have to put on another, a proletarian, or rather Bolshevik, one.

In the final analysis, it was their attitude to the peasants that led the Bolsheviks into a blind alley. In one of his last works, 'On Cooperatives', Lenin defined his concept of bringing the peasants to socialism. The article contains some valid propositions and sensible ideas, for example, that the NEP was a way of combining private and general interest, or that cooperative agriculture was a gradual affair that would take one or two decades. Lenin also talked of the need for a cultural revolution. He devalued all of these ideas, however, by stressing his old Jacobin motives: 'securing the proletariat's leadership of the peasantry', 'the ownership of the means of production to be in the hands of the state', and so on. In effect, he abandoned common sense when he asserted that it was vulgar and fantastic to imagine that 'by simple cooperativism we can convert our class enemies into class collaborators and the class war into . . . so-called civil peace'.[41]

All the good intentions of the revolutionaries foundered as soon as the Bolsheviks started singing their favourite tune about class war, the dictatorship of the proletariat, coercion in the village. They left no room for political and economic freedom, the voluntary principle or age-old traditions of non-Bolshevik communal life. Lenin revealed his approach to the peasant question most completely during the civil war. In effect his policy was one of decimating the peasants, of igniting civil war in the villages. Not even the worst food shortages could justify Lenin's cruelty towards the most productive element among the peasants. He always spoke the word 'kulak' with seething hatred. Yet, had he not sold the family estate at Alakaevka, he would have been among the first to suffer 'dekulakization'.

In May 1918 Lenin wrote the fundamental points of his decree on food. He demanded that the decree include ideas on 'the ruthless and terroristic struggle and war against the peasant and other bourgeoisie who are holding back surpluses'. He insisted on 'making it clearer that grain owners, who have surpluses and are not bringing them to stations and places of collection and loading, must be declared *enemies of the people* and subject to a prison term of not less than ten years, with confiscation of all their property and permanent expulsion from the commune'.[42] He wrote of those he called kulaks with open hatred: 'Sated and self-satisfied, their money-boxes stuffed with huge amounts which they made out of the state during the war, the peasant bourgeoisie is obstinately deaf and indifferent to the cries of the starving workers and peasant poor . . . We must put an end to the obstinacy of greedy village kulaks – peasant predators – and the well-off.'[43] It might have seemed that this element ought to have been preserved in order to support and help the poor, whether by economic, financial, fiscal or other means. Why reduce them to the level of the poorest? Because that would have undermined Lenin's dictatorship of the proletariat and class war. He made that clear at the Third Congress of Soviets when he said: 'To imagine that the socialists are going to serve up socialism on a plate, all dressed up, is wrong, it isn't going to happen. No question of the class war has yet been resolved in history other than by force. Force, in the form it issues from the toiling, exploited masses against the exploiters, yes, we are for such force!' (Stormy applause.)[44]

It was in the war waged against the kulaks that Lenin introduced the term 'enemy of the people', created the taking of hostages, organized penal units in the army and concentration camps. He was, in Victor Chernov's words, 'a virtual Robespierre'.[45] Continually calling for 'shooting on the spot',[46] he would make it lawful to give half the value of grain found as a reward for revealing the existence of a surplus, or simply for informing on one's neighbour.[47]

The full weight of the Bolshevik experiment fell on the peasants, above all the better-off peasants. The countryside responded at first by silent mass resistance, and then numerous uprisings which were ruthlessly drowned in blood. Raids on villages by food detachments became routine, leading to the famine of 1921–1922. A particularly big uprising – there were many others – was that in Tambov, which began in August 1921. Moscow had to use large forces and, as we have seen, poison gas to suppress it.

Curiously, Lenin was more restrained in relation to the Allied intervention, and even to the White leaders Kolchak, Denikin and Wrangel, than he was towards the peasants or the Cossacks, towards whom he became maniacally ruthless in his use of unbridled violence. For instance, on 11 June 1921 the following order was issued with the approval of the Politburo:

Antonov's band [in Tambov] has been smashed by the decisive action of our troops, it has been scattered and is being captured piecemeal. In order finally to tear out all the SR-bandit roots ... the All-Union Executive Committee orders as follows: 1. Citizens who refuse to give their names are to be shot on the spot without trial; 2. The penalty of hostage-taking should be announced and they are to be shot when arms are not surrendered. 3. In the event of concealed arms being found, shoot the eldest worker in the family on the spot and without trial. 4. Any family which harboured a bandit is subject to arrest and deportation from the province, their property to be confiscated and the eldest worker in the family to be shot without trial. 5. The eldest worker of any families hiding members of the family or the property of bandits is to be shot on the spot without trial. 6. If a bandit's family flees, the property is to be distributed among peasants loyal to the Soviet regime and the abandoned houses burnt or demolished. 7. This order is to be carried out strictly and mercilessly. It is to be read at village meetings.[48]

The Politburo fully approved the massacre that was being conducted in the provinces. Only rarely did it register a faint voice of protest. In September 1921 Vera Figner,* head of the Moscow Committee of the Red Cross, wrote to the Revolutionary Tribunal of the Republic:

There are at present in Moscow detention centres a large number of peasants from Tambov province, expelled ... as hostages for their relatives before the liquidation of Antonov's bands. There are fifty-six people in Novo-Peskov camp, thirteen in Semenov, 295 in Kozhukhov, including twenty-nine men aged over sixty, 158 young people under the age of seventeen, and forty-seven under ten years old, and five not yet one year old. They all arrived in Moscow in pitiful condition, ragged, half-naked and so hungry that the small children are rooting in rubbish dumps to find a scrap to eat ... The Political Red Cross is petitioning for the relief of these hostages and for their return home to their villages.[49]

The regime was utterly deaf to such pleas.

In May 1921 Tukhachevsky had at his disposal more than 50,000 regular troops, three armoured trains, three armoured units, several mobile machine-gun units, about seventy field guns, hundreds of machine-guns and an aircraft unit. In the event of resistance, the troops would burn whole villages, firing point-blank into the peasants' huts and taking no prisoners. After his defeat, Antonov tried again to revive resistance, and continued for several months to keep the Bolsheviks busy. In May 1922, however, he was betrayed to the Cheka, and was trapped in a hut with his brother a month later. They held

---

* Vera Figner was the grand old lady of terrorism of the 1870s and 1880s. She was condemned to death in 1884, but the sentence was commuted to life imprisonment, and she remained for twenty years in the Schluesselberg Fortress in St Petersburg. Released in 1904, she was briefly an SR, but devoted most of the rest of her life to women's causes. She died in Moscow in 1943, aged ninety.

out for an about hour, but when the army set fire to the hut they made a break for the forest and were shot down as they ran. Many executions followed, as the army took its revenge on those suspected of having helped Antonov.

Less widespread uprisings than that led by Antonov had been flaring in many provinces. In 1921 the Red Army lost 171,185 men in internal disorders, not including troops of the Cheka or Special Purpose units. In the course of 1921–22 a war situation existed in thirty-six provinces.[50]

The ruined countryside was incapable of feeding the population. Famine was beginning to break out in many provinces, and the workers in the towns were receiving a miserable ration of bread. Yet the government continued to sell grain abroad. At the end of 1920, for instance, the Foreign Commissariat suggested that 'a second shipment of grain be sent to Italy'. The Central Committee decided 'to acknowledge that it was politically necessary to give Italy a further quantity of grain. The precise amount and conditions of the delivery are to be worked out by the Food Commission and Foreign Trade Commissariat.'[51]

Thirty-six million people were starving, thousands dying every day, and yet on 7 December 1922 the Politburo under Lenin's chairmanship took the decision to export almost a million tonnes of grain.[52] As Berdyaev put it: 'There is something other-worldly in the Bolsheviks, something alien. That is what makes them terrifying.'[53] The country was starving, the civilized world was sending food aid to Russia, and yet the government was selling vast quantities of grain abroad.

The famine grew. In the summer of 1921, the US government had decided to send help to the starving through its American Relief Administration, headed by Herbert Hoover. The quantities of aid were huge, and the feeding programme continued until the summer of 1923, supporting no less than twenty-five million people in the Volga region alone. The lives of millions of Soviet citizens were saved. Yet while the American Relief Administration was bringing aid, the Politburo was requisitioning valuables from the middle classes, robbing the churches and using tsarist gold reserves, ostensibly to purchase grain from abroad, but in reality to finance revolution throughout the world and to force the creation of more and more new Communist Parties. On 15 October 1921, it decreed that 'not one expenditure of the gold reserve may be undertaken without a special order of the Politburo'.[54] The number of agents abroad to whom very large sums of money in local denominations were sent – virtually from the moment the Bolsheviks took power – is countless. A typical monthly statement begins with Hungary and continues with Czechoslovakia, Germany, Italy, America (including US$1.008m for John Reed), England, the Balkans, Sweden and Switzerland. Such allocations went on month after month.[55]

Meanwhile, Lenin seemed to view the international aid organizations more as 'intrigues of the imperialist bourgeoisie' than humanitarian agencies. A note in his own hand to Molotov, dated 23 August 1921, reads: 'Comrade Molotov, in view of the agreement with the American, Hoover, there is going to be an influx of a mass of Americans. We should think about surveillance and being kept informed. I propose the Politburo order that a commission be created with the task of preparing, working out and operating intensified surveillance and information on the foreigners, through the Cheka and other organs. The Commission should consist of Molotov, Unshlikht and Chicherin.'[56] The very next day, the appropriate orders were issued.

Many documents, signed by Stalin, Trotsky and Kamenev, show that obstacles were deliberately placed in the path of the Americans, such as limiting the quantity of food to be distributed to private citizens and organizations, and imposing cash levies for the use of Russian roads and warehouses.[57] The Bolsheviks seemed incapable of understanding the humanitarian motives of foreigners. The Americans were 'bourgeois', and nothing good could be expected of them.

The SRs, who were regarded as the defenders of the peasants' interests, bitterly criticized the Bolsheviks. In 1921 their Central Committee published an underground pamphlet entitled 'What Have the Bolsheviks Given the People?' It stated:

From the start of their accursed empire the Bolsheviks have shown themselves to be enemies of the peasants. They sent armed detachments into the countryside to get grain ... The peasant cannot breathe freely: it's either confiscations or loading duties, or tree-cutting or the army, and bring your carts with you, or bring your last livestock for slaughter. There are ninety million peasants in Russia, that is, the huge majority. But what part do they have in running the state?[58]

The SRs, however, could do nothing. The liquidation of the uprisings meant also the liquidation of the SR Party. The Bolsheviks, having formally reconciled themselves to the SR agrarian programme and virtually taken it over, never accepted its central point, that the land was the property of the commune. The Bolsheviks regarded the land as the property of the state alone, and indeed their Land Code stated this plainly. As for the peasants, they would become merely a living appendage of the state's property. The ground for collectivization was being prepared. By making the peasant and the commune into state property, Lenin was preparing them for a new form of social enslavement, one based on 'socialist principles'. The New Economic Policy was no more than a chance for a few last gasps of freedom before the peasants were incarcerated into the collective farm system of virtual serfdom, where their daily lives and their working practices were controlled, not by the demands of agrarian production, but by the dictates of the Communist Party.

The coming collectivization began according to methods essentially formulated by Lenin. Force was both permissible and inevitable. It was to be cooperative agriculture, but under the dictatorship of the proletariat. Lenin was able to take over the countryside chiefly because the Bolsheviks managed to ignite conflict between the peasants themselves, by setting the landless, the weak and the indolent against the well-off. They also took the civil war into the villages, and at the cost of millions of lives pacified the countryside and set it 'on a new path'. Speaking at a combined plenum of the Central Committee and Party Control Commission on 7 January 1933 about the achievement of the Five-Year Plan in agriculture in four years, Stalin invoked Lenin:

Lenin said that 'If we go on in the old way with small farms, even if we're free citizens on free land, we shall still face inevitable disaster.' Lenin said that 'Only with the help of common ... comradely labour can we get out of the crisis which the imperialist war put us in.' Lenin said that 'It is essential to go over to general cultivation in large model farms; without this we won't get out of the disorder, out of the frankly desperate position Russia is in.'[59]

He declared that the Five-Year Plan for agriculture had been over-fulfilled three times, and also revealed what Bolshevik logic ought to have meant keeping a state secret: 'The Party has managed to ensure that, instead of the [eight–ten million tonnes] of marketable grain produced during the period of individual farming, we now have the possibility of delivering [ten–twenty million tonnes] of marketable grain annually.'[60] Why, if this was true, should the country be starving? The fact is that the collectives were useful to the state because it could choose to take all the grain, if it wished, and at a symbolic price. It was only a matter of giving the order. This 'Leninist' form of management became a unique way of acquiring all the surplus product – and often more – at no cost. Stalin explained that the main aim of the rural Communists must be 'to drive the grain procurement campaign all-out'. The only obstacles were the 'peasant predators', as Lenin had described the kulaks, who had been 'smashed', Stalin said, 'but not yet finished off'.[61] That, however, would be a simple matter, he con-cluded, 'for *we* are in power, *we* dispose of the state's resources, it's up to *us* to run the kolkhozes, and *we* must bear all the responsibility for the work in the countryside'.[62]

Even as Stalin was giving this speech on the kolkhoz, the kulaks were being 'finished off'. On 16 January 1933 he approved a proposal from Kaganovich and Balitsky to deport five hundred kulak families from Odessa province;[63] on the same day he signed a proposal from Kosior to evict three hundred kulak families from Chernigov. Similar orders dealt with seven hundred families in Dnepropetrovsk and four hundred from Kharkov;[64] a thousand families of 'malicious peasant farmers' from Bashkiria, three to four hundred 'of the most malicious saboteurs' from the Lower Volga, and in addition to 30,000 kulaks from Northern Caucasus, another four hundred families to be deported to concentration camps in the north of Russia.[65] Any Com-munists who had been expelled from the Party for sabotage of grain supplies were to be sent to the north 'like the kulaks'.[66] The documents show that the Politburo ordered the resettlement of another one mil-lion people to the northern territories of Siberia. The only requests that came from the local authorities were for more GPU troops and for the right to apply the death penalty at their own discretion.[67]

Responding to Shevardnadze's unease in 1987 about the term 'liquidating the kulaks', Gorbachev declared: 'The liquidation of the kulaks as a class was the correct policy. Why change the words? That's what happened. What we cannot agree with are the things done during dekulakization. The competition [between activists] and the forced pace of the collectivization meant that a large number of middle peas-ants were affected. These were different things. But as far as the kulaks were concerned, it was the correct policy.'[68] The words of a reformer who, it seemed, had yet to free himself of Leninist dogmatism.

It was the peasants who suffered most in both the civil war and the 'socialist transformations'. Lenin's slogans were utterly incomprehensible to them, but it was also they who were most often sent to the front, who had the most requisitioned and taken from them, who were the most arrested and exiled group of all. The Bolsheviks appeared to be alarmed by the thought of the least improvement in village life. Any sign of wealth was taken as a tendency towards the 'bourgeoisification' of the countryside, an increase in the number of kulaks. Dogma deprived the Bolsheviks of common sense. Preobrazhensky, for instance, asserted that middle peasants were turning to individual farming as a way of raising productivity, but that this was the path to kulakism. He could not have made it plainer that productivity and the creation of wealth in the countryside was emphatically not the Bolshevik purpose for the peasants.

At the same time, the Bolsheviks saw the peasants as the source of funding for industrialization, a fact which Lenin's successors did not conceal. On 9 July 1928 Stalin addressed a Central Committee plenum: the peasant, he said, 'is paying the state not only the usual direct and indirect taxes, but he is also over-paying through relatively high prices for industrial goods, that's first; and on the whole he receives less for his agricultural produce, that's second. This is an additional tax on the peasantry in the interest of raising industry. It is a sort of "tribute", a super-tax.'[69]

Invoking Lenin as an ally, Stalin spoke of the need 'to apply extreme measures' in the villages. He called the kolkhoz revolution 'the most profound revolutionary change, equal in its consequences to the revolutionary change in October 1917'.[70] In carrying out this 'kolkhoz revolution', i.e. collectivization, Stalin created a state of emergency throughout the country which was to last several years – he had learned from Lenin that a crisis called for radical measures. In the spring of 1918, for instance, when grain supplies ceased to arrive from German-occupied Ukraine, Lenin had proposed converting the War Commissariat into a War Produce Commissariat, 'to concentrate nine tenths of the work of the War Commissariat on preparing the army for a war for grain and for fighting that war'. He proposed that breaches of discipline in such a war should be punished by execution. 'Food detachments must be formed and sent to the war for grain.'[71]

When the time came, Stalin, too, gave the signal for a war in the countryside. On 27 December 1929, at a conference of Marxist agronomists, he declared: 'We have moved from a policy of *limiting* the kulaks' exploitative tendencies to a policy of *liquidating* the kulaks as a class.'[72] And yet only two years before he made this speech, the kulaks had produced more than eleven million tonnes of grain, almost eight times as much as that produced by the state and collective farms. However, kulak grain had to be purchased, whereas it could simply be taken from the kolkhoz.

At the time of this speech, Stalin was preparing documents for the Politburo which included a directive 'on methods for the liquidation of kulak farms in districts of total collectivization'. It was a lengthy and detailed document, the implementation of which would put an end once and for all to the most productive and hardworking part of the Russian peasantry. Stalin personally wrote a treatise on the urgency of these measures.

The Politburo defined three categories in its policy on the kulaks: 'a) First category: counter-revolutionary kulak activists are to be liquidated at once by means of imprisonment in concentration camps, using the death penalty if necessary; b) Second category: the remaining activists ... who are to be deported to remote regions of the USSR; c) Any kulaks left over.' The directive gave the OGPU a schedule of numbers to be deported to the north and east of the country, depending on their place of origin, but since only the heads of families were counted, the real figures would have been between five and seven times those shown:

| Place of origin | Camp | Exile |
| --- | --- | --- |
| Middle Volga | 3–4,000 | 8–10,000 |
| Northern Caucasus | 6–8,000 | 20,000 |
| Ukraine | 15,000 | 30–35,000 |
| Black Earth region | 3–5,000 | 10–15,000 |
| Lower Volga | 4–6,000 | 10–12,000 |
| Belorussia | 4–5,000 | 6–7,000 |
| Urals | 4–5,000 | 10–15,000 |
| Kazakhstan | 5–6,000 | 10–15,000 |

As far as remaining *oblasts* [provinces] and republics are concerned, the OGPU should apply an analogous schedule in agreement with the corresponding local Party secretaries and the Central Committee. Uninhabited or under-inhabited locations should be selected for exile ... Deported kulaks should be distributed in these localities in small settlements to be run by a commandant. [Land] confiscated from kulaks is to become part of the indivisible assets of collective farms ... For the duration of the campaign the OGPU shall have full powers of extra-judicial handling of affairs.[73]

According to this schedule, nearly two million men, women and children would have been affected. But taking into account other similar data, my own reckoning is that between eight and a half and nine million were thus 'dekulakized'. About a quarter of them died within a few months, and another quarter within a year.

The version of this horrible business that Stalin gave to Churchill, during the latter's visit to Moscow in August 1942, paints a very different picture: 'It was fearful. Four years it lasted. It was absolutely necessary for Russia, if we were to avoid periodic famines, to plough the land with tractors ... Many peasants agreed to come in with us ... Some of them were given land of their own to cultivate in the province of Tomsk or the province of Irkutsk or farther north, but the great bulk were very unpopular and were wiped out by their *batraks* [i.e. the poorest peasants].'[74] A large part of the population – and not only Bolsheviks – believed that this drastic measure would solve many problems in one fell swoop. Such was the monstrous price paid for Stalin's plan to 'introduce socialism into the countryside'. The peasants were made into a semi-slave 'socialist' estate, while the more professional, active and efficient part of the rural population – Lenin's 'peasant predators' – were liquidated.

Already debilitated by the confiscations and other hardships imposed by the regime, the peasants were in no condition to resist. Yet there were outbursts here and there. In response to one in Dagestan, Stalin told the Politburo, 'it would be sensible to carry out the gradual liquidation of the disturbances by isolating the region from the outside world and taking it apart from within. Yagoda must be told to order the OGPU to demand the surrender of the chiefs.'[75] As in Tambov and elsewhere, so here the affair ended in arrests, exile and prison camp.

The peasants were finally crushed by the famine that struck them in the closing stage of collectivization. The state, as we have seen, was now able to extract every last ear of grain, including seed-grain. In 1932 the harvest was less than in previous years, but the state took virtually the same amount as before from the collectives, using all available means. The Central Committee of the Ukrainian Communist Party kept a blacklist of villages that were 'maliciously sabotaging grain procurements'. Six such villages were named on 6 December 1932 alone,[76] and once a village was named it could expect punishment to follow: sale of its produce prohibited, deliveries to the farm halted, immediate payment of credits and, of course, a visit from units of the OGPU to 'cleanse the kolkhoz of alien and hostile elements'.

In 1932–33 Ukraine, the Central Black Earth region, the Kuban, the Northern Caucasus, the Volga region and Kazakhstan were gripped by famine. Meanwhile, kulaks and 'hostile elements' continued to be removed in order to settle the White Sea–Baltic Canal zone, as well as new sites in Siberia and the north.[77] In places the famine was worse than during the civil war. Thousands tried to flee to the towns, but the roads and railway stations were blocked by Chekists. Also, in December 1932 the regime had imposed another restriction: peasants were deprived of their identity papers, without which they were finally made into Soviet serfs.

The peasants and their children were reduced to eating grass, nettles and the stubble left after harvesting. The state, however, was keeping a watchful eye, and on 7 August 1932 an order, known to the population as 'the stubble law', was issued, according to which: 'For the misappropriation (theft) of kolkhoz and cooperative property, the highest form of social defence is to be applied as a measure of judicial repression, namely execution, with confiscation of all property or not less than ten years' loss of liberty and confiscation of property in mitigating circumstances.'[78] Taking stubble was not usually a shooting offence, but several thousand peasants were given ten years. Apart from the tens of thousands of peasants who were despatched to the camps, another three and a half million starved to death. Meanwhile, grain was being sold abroad by the hundreds of tonnes.

Yet Stalin, the chief organizer of Lenin's 'cooperative plan', remained confident. The propaganda machine was working at full blast. At the height of the famine, in February 1933, a congress of

1500 kolkhoz shock-workers, loyal to the OGPU, was convened. Speeches were given by Molotov, Kaganovich, Kalinin and Voroshilov, as well as Red Cavalry commander Budenny. The main speech was given by Stalin on 19 February. He mentioned the famine only indirectly. Noting that his comrades had said that the workers had achieved far more than the kolkhozniks, he went on: 'But you know what these achievements cost the workers of Leningrad and Moscow, what privation they suffered.' There had been times, he said, when the workers got only 'two ounces of black bread, half of it husks. And that went on not for a month or half a year, but for two whole years.'[79] By his demeanour Stalin made it plain that he regarded such privation as the norm, even necessary and inevitable. The workers had stuck it out, but that was as far as he would go in mentioning the famine.

The famine was incidental. The important thing was that the shock-workers should remember their duty: 'You are only asked to do one thing, and that is to work honestly, divide the kolkhoz income according to the work done, protect the kolkhoz goods, take care of the tractors and machines, see the horses are well looked after, carry out the tasks of your workers' and peasants' state, strengthen the kolkhoz and throw out any kulaks and their henchmen who might have got in.'[80]

While the congress was in session, regional Party secretaries in Ukraine were attempting to do something to help the thousands of starving people. The Kiev regional Party secretary ordered that 'all people, children and adults alike, who are swollen or prostrate from starvation' must be got on their feet by 5 March, and he transferred them to special accommodation and arranged restorative feeding. At the same time, 'kolkhoz funds are not to be squandered on pain of severe punishment'. On the basis of his orders from Moscow, this official saw the cause of the famine as 'abuses in the kolkhozes, idling, a fall in labour discipline and so on'.[81] With such contradictory orders, famine was being manufactured in Ukraine, the land of plenty.

Lenin said that 'the simple growth of cooperative farming is the same for us ... as the growth of socialism',[82] and Stalin called the kolkhoz the most acceptable form of cooperative farming. It was, after all, able to destroy the peasant commune and turn its inhabitants into state serfs, and the Communist system tried with amazing persistence to make the obligatory labour of the kolkhoz the equivalent of free labour. But however many 'historic' Central Committee plenums were held, however much investment and technology was sent to the villages, or stratagems employed to make the kolkhoz managers happy, the desired result was never achieved.

The country which before the revolution had been the world's fourth largest exporter of grain had become a major importer. This alone was a condemnation of the Bolshevik experiment. Stalin would not of course buy grain from abroad: the death of millions of his citizens from starvation was no more than an incident along the great path to the shining future. Khrushchev and his successors became big buyers of grain, but every year they had to rack their brains wondering what they could sell for the necessary hard currency, on top of the two to three hundred tonnes of gold they sold annually. Only once did Brezhnev ask for a report on the supply and consumption of grain over an extended period. It came stamped 'Especially Important' and was at once tucked away in a 'special file'. In two pages, and with merciless clarity, it revealed a huge Party secret: throughout the whole Soviet period, the country had suffered a shortage of grain in practically every year.[83] The situation had been dealt with in two ways: under Stalin the people had starved, and after him the government had bought grain from the capitalists who, contrary to Lenin's prophecy, had not suffered a 'collapse'.

Brezhnev pondered the two pages for a long time. Did this mean the collective system could not feed the country? Lenin's intention to liquidate the 'peasant predators' had long been fulfilled, yet still there wasn't enough grain. And the Soviet Union had been buying it every year from the capitalists. What about socialist competition? The virgin lands? The millions of medals given away? Only recently he had received a proposal from Kiev to create a new one, 'Hero of Communist Labour', with himself as the first recipient, of course. Since 1957, the country had been buying and buying abroad. Hundreds, thousands of tonnes of gold, oil, gas, metal – all for grain.

Normally Brezhnev marked files 'For circulation', i.e. to the rest of the Politburo. This time, he managed only to sign his name and add the date, 17 October 1978. He did not want to discuss the issue at the Politburo. What good would it do for such information to leak beyond the Kremlin walls? No one else needed to see it. He put it aside and set about signing a thick pile of orders giving decorations to the victors of socialist competition in honour of the Great October Revolution.

## The Tragedy of the Intelligentsia

Lenin was both a demon of destruction and a demiurge of creation. He wanted to 'introduce' socialism in a few months, and to 'build' communism in a few years. His ideas were radical and impulsive. At his suggestion, on 12 April 1918 the Sovnarkom approved a decree 'to remove monuments erected in honour of the tsars and their servants and to prepare plans for monuments to the Russian socialist revolution'. It was expected that models would be ready by 1 May. It proved, however, much easier to remove the tsars and their servants from their pedestals than to replace them with new idols. At the end of July Academician Pokrovsky presented a report to the Sovnarkom in which he called for the erection of 'fifty monuments in the field of revolutionary and social activity, in philosophy, literature and art'. Lenin proposed that lists of candidates be presented to the Sovnarkom 'in five days' time'.

A report was sent to Lunacharsky, expressing 'the desirability of urgently fulfilling the Sovnarkom order to embellish the streets, public buildings and so on with inscriptions and quotations'. Two days later the list was approved. Two months later Lenin wanted to know how far the Sovnarkom's order had been implemented, and he was extremely dissatisfied with the response. Almost nothing had been done. He called Lunacharsky, discovered he was in Petrograd, and cabled him at once: 'I heard Vinogradov's report today on busts and monuments, and I am indignant to the bottom of my soul; nothing's been done in months; up to now not a single bust. There's no bust of Marx for the street, nothing's been done to make propaganda inscriptions on the streets. I'm admonishing you for your criminal and negligent attitude, I demand you send me the names of all the responsible people to be put on trial. Shame on the saboteurs and scatter-brains.'[84]

With the country in ruins, the people starving, widespread crime and social chaos, Lenin wanted to discard the old as quickly as possible and inspire the crucified population with new cast-iron idols. He seemed not to understand that nothing disappears in history, and try as he might to obliterate the memory of, for example, 'the idiot Nicholas II', seventy-five years later the tsar would overtake Lenin in popularity, and that thanks to the Bolsheviks' own efforts. Memory and public awareness function according to their own laws, not those of a Politburo or Sovnarkom.

The episode of the monuments serves to illustrate that Lenin regarded the country's spiritual culture in strictly pragmatic terms: everything must serve the revolution, and to this end revolutionary education and agitation stood at the head of the list.

Replying to a questionnaire from the Institute of the Brain in 1935, Krupskaya remarked: 'He [Lenin] loved the theatre very much, it always made a strong impression on him.'[85] This assertion was, however, at odds with other reminiscences she had previously produced, in which she had noted that while they were living abroad before the revolution, 'we'd go to the theatre and leave after the first act'. Lenin went to the theatre only rarely in Moscow, and Krupskaya recalled that, in the middle of a dramatized version of Dickens's *The Cricket on the Hearth*, he became bored and left early. His 'love' for the theatre did not prevent him from agreeing to close the Bolshoi Theatre. The Politburo discussed this issue on several occasions, and was in favour.[86] Lunacharsky protested even before the question came to the Sovnarkom, but Lenin was insistent. He wrote to Molotov:

Having heard from Kamenev that the Sovnarkom has unanimously accepted Lunacharsky's obscene proposal to save the Bolshoi opera and ballet, I propose the Politburo issue the following orders: 1. The Presidium of VTsIK must rescind the Sovnarkom order; 2. Keep just a few dozen artistes for Moscow and Peter[sburg] to perform (as singers and dancers) on a self-financing basis, that is, avoid any large expenditure on scenery, etc.; 3. Give not less than half the billions thus saved for the liquidation of illiteracy and for reading rooms; 4. Summon Lunacharsky for a five-minute hearing of the accused's last words and to be reprimanded.[87]

This last remark confirms Lenin's tendency to humour and indulge the cosmopolitan Lunacharsky, but the burden of the message was plain. Who would oppose a campaign against illiteracy, but at the price of the Bolshoi and other great repositories of national culture?

Lenin was unconcerned: a lowering of the nation's intellect would be the price for raising the general population's awareness to a standard that would make it easier to rule them.

In December 1918 Lenin personally wrote an instruction:

The task: within two weeks to compose a book for peasants and workers to read ... Themes: the building of the Soviet regime, its domestic and foreign policies. For example, what is the Soviet regime? How is the country governed? The law on land. The Economic Councils. The nationalization of the factories. Labour discipline. Imperialism. The imperialist war. The secret treaties. How we proposed peace. What we are fighting for now? What is Communism? The separation of church and state. And so on.[88]

Even the campaign against illiteracy was politicized. Nothing was to be said about the past, as if it had been confiscated and consigned to the scrapheap. The workers and peasants must know above all else what Communism was. As someone with a powerful intellect of his own, Lenin knew that the mind was the strongest of bastions. It would not be easily captured, even with the help of the OGPU. It would be necessary to mobilize the Party and the small section of the intelligentsia which had accepted Bolshevism. Lenin's general line was therefore to bring the intelligentsia under Party control, and make them work for the revolution. When the Politburo discussed the question of the Proletcult* congress, Lenin, Stalin, Kamenev, Krestinsky and Bukharin unanimously advocated 'the subordination of Proletcult to the Party'.[89]

Trotsky, who was more deeply involved in literature and art than were the other leaders, told Moscow writers and poets in 1925: 'We have a factory for creating new proletarian poets and artists, but it is not any MAPP or VAPP, it is the RKP† ... The Comrades should sit in the Party and study. The Party educates the proletarian poet, it creates the genuinely artistic writer. Therefore the Communist

---

* An organization, founded by Bolsheviks and supported by Lunacharsky as Commissar for Education (Public Enlightenment), to encourage the artistic and creative endeavours of the workers in a Communist spirit, but also autonomously. It effectively represented a pluralist trend in Bolshevism and its fate was therefore highly significant as an indicator of things to come.

† MAPP: Moscow Association of Proletarian Writers. VAPP: All-Union Association of Proletarian Writers. RKP: Russian Communist Party.

writer, as a member of the Party, must concentrate his attention on creativity within his Party.'[90]

The tragedy of Russian culture and the intelligentsia was on its way. Their Party-mindedness would deprive them of creative freedom. The mind is not only a fortress, it is also the last oasis of freedom. In order to form a nation capable of thought at an elementary level, the Bolsheviks fed the people a generous diet of primitive intellectual nourishment. The field of literature banned to Soviet readers widened to absurd proportions over the next seventy years. The education of the Soviet intelligentsia would be one of the Bolsheviks' chief tasks, and the programme for it was devised in an article Lenin had written as early as 1905, entitled 'The Party Organization and Party Literature'. This made it plain that literature must be the business of the Party, that newspapers must be under the control of Party organizations, and that writers must be Party members.[91] Once Lenin was in power, this view was made into a policy.

First, the intellectuals had to be screened. Those – perhaps the majority – who were incapable of responding to the demands of the revolution, became exiles. Many paid with their lives, or fled abroad, or were driven there, as were tens of thousands of the best of them. In June 1922 the Politburo discussed a report on 'anti-Soviet groupings' by Iosif Unshlikht, Dzerzhinsky's top aide, which proposed that those who thought differently from the Party should be deprived of their homeland. The report proposed the formation of a special commission, consisting of representatives of the NKVD and Justice Commissariat, which would have the right, when there was no possibility of resorting to stronger measures, of commuting such measures to exile abroad or to defined places in the Russian Federation.[92]

The omnipotent GPU set about singling out those it regarded as a danger to the revolution, in practice the élite of Russian society. On 2 August Unshlikht was already able to report to Stalin with a list of 'the anti-Soviet intelligentsia of Moscow . . . and Petrograd. All notable individuals will be arrested and offered the chance to leave the country at their own expense. If they refuse, the GPU will pay.' At the same time, the 'counter-revolutionary newspapers *Agricultural News*, *Thought* and *Economic Rebirth* will be closed for publishing anti-Soviet and idealistic views'.[93]

The GPU evidently knew its business: the names it selected were the brightest of the Russian intellectual élite, but it was also guided in its choices by Lenin's personal intervention, for the policy of draining society of its best intellectual resources was very much his. The lists were submitted to him several times for corrections, additions, remarks and questions, before going on to the GPU, to Dzerzhinsky, Stalin and Unshlikht for completion. Even when the first contingent was ready for deportation, in the autumn of 1922, when Lenin was recovering from illness, he was still concerned about similar such events in the future. On 17 September 1922 he wrote to Unshlikht: 'Please be so kind as to arrange for *all* the documents to be sent back to me with *comments* as to *who* has been deported, who is in prison, who has been excused deportation and why. Make short comments *on this letter*.'[94] The following night, Unshlikht being away, his deputy, Yagoda, replied: 'In accordance with your instructions I enclose your lists with comments on them, and the names of people (listed separately) who have remained in Moscow or [Petrograd] for one reason or another.' He added that 'the first contingent leaves Moscow on Friday 22 September'.[95]

Lenin's lists were extensive, and bore such sub-headings as: Professors of 1st Moscow University; Professors of Petrovsko-Razumovsky Agricultural Academy; Professors of Institute of Railway Engineers; [those involved in] the case of the Free Economic Society; anti-Soviet professors of the Archaeological Institute; anti-Soviet figures connected with Bereg publishing house; people involved in case no. 813 (Abrikosov group); anti-Soviet agronomists and cooperativists; physicians; anti-Soviet engineers; writers; Petrograd writers; and a special list of Petrograd anti-Soviet intellectuals.

The first contingent numbered 120 people. The document ordering their expulsion was first signed on 31 July 1922 by Kamenev, Kursky and Unshlikht. Following the list of distinguished names came a comment by Yagoda: 'According to a decision of the Politburo, the Commission chaired by Comrade Dzerzhinsky examined petitions to cancel the deportation of individuals considered irreplaceable in their fields and for whom the appropriate institution had requested permission to remain at their posts.' As an example of the sort of comment made by the GPU, the entry on the philosopher Nikolai Berdyaev reads: 'He is close to Bereg publishing house, has been investigated in connection with the tactical centre, monarchist, right-wing Kadet,

Black Hundredist [ultra-right-wing], religious, involved in church counter-revolution. Exile.'[96]

It is worth noting that Lenin was making these decisions only a month after Krupskaya had been helping him to do the simplest mental exercises, such as double-figure multiplication. He had covered a twenty-one-page notepad with childlike scrawls in the process.[97] The future of an entire generation of the flower of the Russian intelligentsia was being decided by a man who could barely cope with an arithmetical problem for a seven-year-old. No mention of this police activity is to be found in the official twelve-volume chronicle of Lenin's life, which only depicts the sunny side of his life. On the day he was going through the lists for deportation, according to the Chronicle, he ordered 'envelopes and best quality glue'.[98]

Two days earlier, on 15 September, Lenin wrote a long letter to Gorky, who had written anxiously from Germany concerning the arrests of intellectuals. Lenin's letter expressed the essence of his attitude to the intelligentsia, and no doubt inspired his successors to reduce Soviet intellectuals to performing the rôle of obedient servants. According to Yelena Kuskova, formerly a leading liberal, in 1922 an émigrée and sharply critical observer of the Soviet scene, Gorky was wavering; he was drawn to his homeland, but was hearing terrible news about the continuing execution of his people.[99] Under great pressure from Moscow to return, Gorky, whose life reflected in its own way something of the tragedy of the Russian intelligentsia, was still holding out. To retain his artistic freedom he had to remain abroad, but it was more than he could stand. His letter to Lenin, protesting and begging him to protect the intelligentsia, sounded like the last spasm of his freedom.

Lenin's reply was dogmatic, angry, peremptory and harsh. It was as if he already knew that Gorky, and with him the remnants of the intelligentsia still left in the country, would be broken and won over. Having admitted that 'mistakes were made' during the arrests, Lenin nevertheless concluded that it was also 'clear that the arrest of the Kadets and near-Kadets was both necessary and correct'. He lectured Gorky:

It is wrong to confuse the intellectual forces of the people with the forces of the bourgeois intellectuals. I take [the writer Vladimir] Korolenko as an example: I recently read his pamphlet 'War, the Fatherland and Mankind', which he wrote in August 1917. He's probably the best of the 'near-Kadets', practically a Menshevik. Yet what a vile, mean, disgusting defence of the imperialist war it is, and coated with sugary phrases! He's a pitiful philistine, trapped in bourgeois prejudices! For gentlemen such as this ten million dead in the imperialist war is something worth supporting . . . while the death of hundreds of thousands in a *just* civil war against landowners and capitalists makes them oh! and ah! and sigh and go into hysterics.

Lenin continued: 'The intellectual forces of the workers and peasants are growing and getting stronger in the struggle to overthrow the bourgeoisie and their accomplices, the intellectuals, the lackeys of capital, who think they're the brains of the nation. In fact, they're not its brains, they're its shit.' Lenin could scarcely have expressed his feelings for Russia and the intelligentsia more graphically or forcefully. He could not end his letter without striking a smarting blow at Gorky himself:

More than once, on Capri and later, I told you that you allow yourself to be surrounded by the worst elements of the Russian intelligentsia and that you give in to their whining . . . I completely understand, completely, completely understand that it's possible to write oneself into saying that the Reds are just as much enemies of the people as the Whites (the fighters for the overthrow of the capitalists and landlords just as much enemies of the people as the landlords and capitalists), and also into believing in God Almighty or the Tsar, our Little Father. I completely understand.

Truly, you'll perish [here Lenin added a note: 'Because you're not writing. To waste yourself on the whining of rotten intellectuals and not to be writing is the same as death for a writer, isn't it a shame?'] if you don't tear yourself away from this environment of bourgeois intellectuals! From my heart I wish you would tear yourself away as soon as possible.

With best wishes.

Yours, Lenin.[100]

For an individual to hold such a poisonous view of the Russian intelligentsia was one thing, but in the head of the new Soviet state and leader of the Bolshevik Party it spelled disaster. Lenin had long ago made it plain that he did not trust the intelligentsia, and that 'the business of literature must become a component part . . . of Party work'. Once he had accepted Marxism as an absolute truth, he denied every other point of view the right to exist. His outlook became the expression of a secular religion and, like a religious fanatic, he could not countenance the sort of intellectual balancing of arguments, for and against the Reds and the Whites, of which he accused Gorky. And of course, as the architect of the October experiment, he had the authority to demand that others follow his line.

In an extensive memorandum to Stalin in the autumn of 1922, Lenin targeted individuals who were either associated with anti-Bolshevik publications or whom he regarded as especially perceptive opponents of his régime. The memorandum conveys the tone of Lenin's obsessive concern to rid himself of such people:

On the question of expelling Mensheviks, Popular Socialists, Kadets, etc., I'd like to ask a few questions, as this matter, which was started before I went on leave, is still unfinished. Has it been decided to 'uproot' all Popular Socialists? Peshekhonov, Myakotin, Gornfeld? Petrishchev and *the others*? I think they should all be expelled. They're more dangerous than any SR, because they're more cunning. Also A.N. Potresov, Izgoev and *all* the people on [the journal] *Ekonomist*, *(Ozerov and many many more)*. The Mensheviks Rozanov (a physician, cunning), Vigdorchik (Migulo, or some such), Lyubov Nikolaevna Radchenko and her young daughter (allegedly the most malicious enemies of Bolshevism); N.A. Rozhkov (he has to be expelled; he's incorrigible); S.L. Frank (the author of *Methodology*), the Mantsev-Messing commission should compile lists and several *hundred* such gentlemen should be deported from the country without mercy. We'll cleanse Russia once and for all.

As for Lezhnev . . . we should think about it: shouldn't we expel him? He'll always be utterly *crafty*, as far as I can judge from his articles. Like *all* the people on *Ekonomist*, Ozerov is the most relentless enemy. All of them must be chucked out of Russia. It should be done all at once. By the time the SR trial is over, not later, and with no explanation of *motives* – leave, gentlemen!

All the authors in Writers' House and [Petrograd] *Mysl'* ['Thought']; Kharkov must be ransacked, *we have no idea what's happening there*, it's 'abroad' to us. It must be cleaned out *quickly*, *not later* than the end of the SR trial. Pay attention to the writers in [Petrograd] (their addresses are in *Novaya russkaya kniga*, No. 4, 1922, p. 37) and also to the list of private publishers (p. 29).'[101]

Lenin's police instructions, disconnected but written in indelible pencil, as it were in a single breath, are remorseless and cruel, and a note in Stalin's hand shows that they were despatched at once to Dzerzhinsky as the leader's orders. For twenty-five years after the Twentieth Congress the Russian people asked themselves where Stalin had acquired the cruelty which he inflicted on his fellow-countymen. None of us – the present author included – could begin to imagine that the father of domestic Russian terrorism, merciless and totalitarian, was Lenin. Where Lenin acquired his own cruelty is another question: unlike Stalin's, his childhood had been benign, and he had spent a pleasant enough life in prosperous countries and cities abroad. It can only have been from the philosophy of 'revolutionary law and morality' that Lenin absorbed the notion that everything is allowed in the name of the goal. As Machiavelli had written: 'Leaders are judged by results, therefore they should try to maintain their power and win victory. Whatever means they use to achieve this, they will always be thought worthy and approved.'[102] The fanatical belief that history would justify whatever means he employed, if he reached his goal, was firmly fixed in Lenin's mind when, quite unexpectedly, power fell into his hands.

The Party leader, in the manner of the head of the secret police, was setting an example to the Chekists on how to deal with neglected Party directives. He returned to the theme of deportations at the end of 1922, when he telephoned an order to Stalin, via his chief secretary, Lydia Fotieva, about another free-thinker, N. A. Rozhkov: 'I propose, first, that Rozhkov be expelled abroad, secondly, if this doesn't go through (for instance, on the grounds that his age deserves consideration), then . . . send him to Pskov to live in bearable conditions and with adequate means and work. But he must be kept under strict surveillance, for he is and will no doubt remain our enemy to the end.'[103]

Thus, Lenin was personally involved in realizing his sinister formula: 'We shall cleanse Russia for a long time to come.' Cleanse it, that is, of intellectual conscience. He was not deterred by the notion of pointing the finger at his victims, despite the fact that he was personally acquainted with many of them. If his letter to Gorky expressed his attitude to the intelligentsia, then his note to Stalin was a concrete instruction. In August 1922, the Politburo followed his lead when it approved Unshlikht's proposal to 'expel abroad counter-

revolutionary elements among the students' and to 'form a commission consisting of Kamenev, Unshlikht and Preobrazhensky'.[104]
The Bolsheviks were looking ahead, and were uprooting the green
shoots of the next generation of intellectuals.

Lenin had refined his view of the creative artist in 1908, when
analysing Leo Tolstoy.[105] His article 'Leo Tolstoy as the Mirror of
the Russian Revolution' is extremely illuminating, in that it shows
Lenin as capable of seeing the great author only in terms of the
revolution. He wrote:

On the one hand, he is an artist of genius who has given not only incompar-
able pictures of Russian life, but also first-class works of world literature. On
the other hand, he is a landowner, an idiot in Christ. On the one hand, he
makes a remarkably strong, direct and sincere protest against social lies and
hypocrisy, on the other hand, he is a 'Tolstoyan', i.e. a worn-out, hysterical
sniveller, called a Russian intellectual, who beats his breast and says: 'I'm
foul, I'm vile, but I am practising moral self-improvement; I don't eat meat
anymore and now feed on rice cutlets.'[106]

Lenin remained bogged down in his class dug-out, with his superficial
view of Tolstoy, while the great writer espoused the imperatives of
universal human values. Tolstoy, however, had been necessary to
Lenin, to show him the pointlessness and insignificance of the Russian
intelligentsia. The intelligentsia was, of course, multi-faceted, and to
see it, as Lenin did, as a body of 'worn-out, hysterical snivellers', was
to take a narrow, class viewpoint.

A significant number of writers, academics, engineers, and others,
finding themselves in desperate straits, tried to leave the country under
their own steam, but the Politburo and GPU were quick to react.
Yagoda wrote to the Central Committee that his agency had 'statements by a number of writers, notably, [Zinaïda] Vengerova, [Alex-
ander] Blok, [Fedor] Sologub, about leaving the country'. Yagoda
warned: 'taking into account the fact that writers who leave carry on
the most active campaign against Soviet Russia and that some of them,
like [Konstantin] Balmont, [Alexander] Kuprin, [Ivan] Bunin, stoop
to the most vile initiatives, the Cheka does not think it proper to
approve these applications'.[107]

The treatment of well-known artists and intellectuals became a matter of great sensitivity – and public relations importance – when the Soviet Union was seeking diplomatic recognition and acceptance by the outside world in the early 1920s, and therefore in due course most of those named above were permitted to leave. The Ukrainian intelligentsia were to be treated somewhat differently: the Politburo accepted Unshlikht's proposal that, 'instead of expulsion abroad, they should be deported to remote regions of the RSFSR'.[108]

Many wanted to leave, especially those who saw no prospect of continuing their creative work in Soviet Russia. Indeed, there soon emerged in emigration a regeneration of Russian literature, characterized by originality, love of liberty and honesty, and continuing the tradition of literary Russia. The critic Gleb Struve could justifiably ask: 'What has Soviet Russian literature to compare with Bunin's *The Lives of Arsenyev*, Remizov's work as an émigré, Shmelev's best efforts, the historical-philosophical novels of Aldanov, the poetry of Khodasevich and Tsvetaeva, or the highly original novels of Nabokov?'[109] The names of many other writers and philosophers could be added to the list, but the thought of their exclusion from their homeland inevitably prompts the reflection that, had Lenin not expelled them, they would surely have succumbed to Stalin's guillotine a decade or so later.

People also tried to leave the country in groups. In May 1921 the Politburo discussed an application to go abroad from the First Studio of the Moscow Arts Theatre, and decided to postpone a decision until Lunacharsky had reported on how many people from the scholarly and artistic world, who had already been allowed to go abroad, had actually returned home.[110] Most traffic was, indeed, one-way, and it was westward. By 1921–22, artists who had welcomed the revolution as a unique moment of creative freedom were ready to leave for a more tolerant environment, often in Paris and Berlin. Once again, some of the best-known names of the Russian artistic world were to be found outside their native country: Chagall, Kandinsky, Soutine; Diaghilev and his Russian Ballet; the composers Prokofiev and Stravinsky.

This large-scale emigration of leading Soviet citizens was surely clear proof that the system was fatally flawed. Even in Lenin's day the Bolshevik government sensed that the exodus of the intelligentsia would harm wide areas of the economy. On 9 August 1923 the Politburo, chaired by Kamenev, discussed a memorandum by Dzerzhinsky, who wrote: 'There are several quite important Russian specialists living abroad in difficult circumstances who would like to return to Russia to work. And we lack specialists. The best ones we have are those we got from Kolchak, Denikin and Wrangel, who were for some reason not shot. They [those abroad] should make individual application and be given Soviet citizenship.' It was decided that 'Russian specialists should be allowed to return from abroad and be given work'.[111] But if during the civil war the intelligentsia had left the country in an avalanche, those who returned formed a mere trickle. But of course there remained those who were 'for some reason not shot'.

In 1923 the Politburo instructed the Cheka 'to organize the disintegration of the White Guard emigration and to use some of them in the interests of the Soviet regime'. In due course, a special Foreign Section of the OGPU was created, and carried out extensive operations among Russian émigrés, including the 'liquidation' of 'especially dangerous enemies of the Soviet regime'. The voluminous files of reports from agents in Western capitals show how the authorities first expelled masses of intellectuals, then did their utmost to 'disunite' them, using scandal, bribery and playing off one group against another. Files were opened on leading scholars, writers and, of course, political figures, in which their every move and utterance was recorded, all collected under the general heading 'Russian emigration'.

Interestingly, the Soviet secret service made an attempt to insinuate itself into Berdyaev's confidence and to use his name and influence. According to agent Kal, however, Berdyaev would be of no use, for 'he criticizes Communism, is a determined enemy of materialist philosophy and only wants to discuss teleology'. It was perhaps for this reason that Berdyaev appears in the files of the Foreign Section under the name 'Confessor'.[112] After several attempts, Menzhinsky's agents gave up and left the philosopher in peace.

The Soviet regime was also troubled by the fact that the Russian émigrés, despite having lost their homeland and often having to survive in poverty, had quickly established their own publishing houses and periodical press, in which the leading lights participated. Preventive measures were taken to ensure that the Soviet citizenry was protected from the 'putrid bourgeois influence' that would ensue should such publications filter into the country.

For the expelled intelligentsia the greatest tragedy was the loss of their homeland, while for those who remained in Soviet Russia it was the loss of creative freedom. Those who did not accept the revolution tried to change things in the country, while also attempting to adapt themselves to the bitter new reality. In this connection, the 'Case of the Doctors'* is pertinent.

In the early summer of 1922, the All-Russian Congress of Physicians met in Moscow. Health Commissar Semashko reported to Lenin and the Politburo:

> The recent Congress of Physicians revealed such important and dangerous trends in our lives that I believe it essential not to leave the members of the Politburo in further ignorance ... A campaign was waged at the congress against Soviet medicine, while local government medicine and health insurance were eulogized. Delegates debated efforts to support the Kadets and Mensheviks, and to create their own periodical. As for removing the doctors' leaders, Granovsky, Manul, Vigdorchik and Livin, the GPU should be consulted. Wouldn't arrest increase their popularity?[113]

Lenin saw something more dangerous in the doctors' independent thinking, and wrote a note on Semashko's report: 'To Comrade Stalin. I think this ought to be shown to Dzerzhinsky and all members of the Politburo, *in strict secrecy* and without making copies, and an appropriate directive should be issued.'[114] Two sessions of the Politburo were devoted to the 'Case of the Doctors', the first on 28 May and the second on 8 June. Only Tomsky abstained from voting for repressive measures, declaring that 'the matter of the physicians' congress requires a different approach. We are in many ways guilty.' Lenin's resolution was nonetheless passed on 'anti-Soviet groupings among the Soviet intelligentsia'.[115]

These outright police and punitive measures heralded the further strengthening of totalitarian tendencies. The Party began determining everything in intellectual life: what could be written, who could be praised, who was to be hated, who could be published and who rewarded. Thus, on 13 September 1922 the Politburo under Lenin's chairmanship debated a question from Pokrovsky on who was to be allowed to give lectures in the Institute of Red Professors. It was

* Not the notorious 'doctors' plot' of 1953, but the lesser-known events of 1922.

decided that 'Deborin and [Lyubov] Axelrod be permitted to give lectures on Marxist philosophy, but Bazarov should not be allowed to lecture on capital'.[116] In February 1921 the Politburo had devoted more time and attention to Krasin's question about selling the late empress's letters and diaries abroad than it did to the famine in Russia.[117] Whatever had even the smallest ideological dimension was regarded by the Bolsheviks as a strategic matter. The return from abroad of White General Slashchev was permitted with the proviso that he write 'memoirs on the period of his struggle with Soviet Russia',[118] naturally with the aim of 'unmasking' the White movement. Even shorthand typists were provided – not that any of this prevented the assassination of the general himself in 1929, probably with the connivance of the secret police.

The intelligentsia were ultimately the bearers of the indestructible idea of liberalism, and liberalism, for as long as it retained any political influence, was a guarantee against the worst excesses of the proletarian dictatorship. Lenin understood this better than most, and hence, long before the events of October 1917, he had launched savage attacks on the liberal bourgeoisie. As early as the beginning of 1905, in an article entitled 'The Workers' and Bourgeois Democracy', he had written that social democracy consisted of two wings: the first was proletarian and intellectual, while the second was liberal and incapable of taking decisive revolutionary action. Liberalism was a movement of the bourgeoisie, and that was all that need be said of it. And liberal intellectuals were capable only of making an alliance with the bourgeoisie.[119]

Since it was the Mensheviks among the social democrats who were closest to liberalism, it was they who were above all branded 'conciliators'. Lenin was perfectly aware that a radical doctrine like Bolshevism would have no chance in 'normal' parliamentary political struggle, or within the framework of a functioning Constituent Assembly. The latter would inevitably become the expression of liberal moderation, and was therefore anathema to Lenin, and he and his Politburo therefore continued to rain blows on liberalism and its bearers, the Russian intelligentsia. On 11 January 1923 the Politburo formulated an order for the GPU 'to intensify surveillance of individuals in the liberal professions and simultaneously to take measures to render enemies of the Soviet regime harmless'.[120]

The expulsion of members of the intelligentsia abroad, and the deportations to remote regions were systematic attacks, yet the intelligentsia, however trampled upon, did not as a rule reply in kind: it behaved like an intelligentsia. In 1931 the first editorial of a new liberal journal, *Novyi grad*, published in Paris, declared: 'A generation raised in bloodshed believes in the saving power of violence.' The authors called upon their readers not to yield to feelings of vengeance, but to defend the eternal truth of freedom of the individual and humanitarianism. 'We see no future for the hangmen of Russia. Only by the path of Christianity is social justice possible.'[121] It was inconceivable that Lenin, the personification of the proletarian dictatorship, could have found a common language with the proponents of such a view. The tragedy of the intelligentsia was predetermined by the incompatibility of the Bolshevik dictatorship and liberty. The regime needed an obedient, compliant intelligentsia.

In both the Leninist and post-Leninist periods, these characteristics were achieved by very simple and, it would seem, effective methods. On 15 July 1937, for instance, Yezhov wrote to Stalin: 'I am sending you a report of 4 July 1937 from Comrade Dmitriev, head of Sverdlovsk regional NKVD on the writer V.V. Kamensky. I think it essential to arrest V.V. Kamensky. I request your approval.' Dmitriev had reported that 'Kamensky is sympathetic to the Futurists [avant-garde poets and writers]. Bukharin was enthusiastic about him. His distant relations were shipowners. He was friendly with Govin who has been unmasked as a Trotskyist.'[122] After such devastating arguments, Stalin could only agree to Kamensky's arrest.

After the Twentieth Congress, to be sure, other ways of holding human thought captive had to be found, if the intellect was to remain under the vigilant control of the Party and special services. The system Lenin created remained in being for decades as he had made it, and the slightest attempt to move beyond the permitted limits raised a mighty outcry from his heirs. The following abbreviated extracts from a session of the Central Committee Secretariat of 26 April 1983, are illustrative. The meeting was discussing the play *Dear Elena Sergeevna*, by Lyudmilla Razumovskaya.

GORBACHEV: This is a serious matter. I have asked the heads of the
   Central Committee sections, representatives of the Ministry of Culture of

the USSR and RSFSR and the Council of Ministers of the Russian
Federation to remain so that we may go over the matter thoroughly.
Comrade Barabash, please tell us how it could happen that a play that
is so ideologically harmful could be shown on the stages of our theatres
for so many months? How is it that the question of taking it off was
raised not by the Ministry of Culture, but by the Committee for State
Security [KGB]?

BARABASH (FIRST DEPUTY MINISTER OF CULTURE OF THE USSR):
The staging of L. Razumovskaya's play, *Dear Elena Sergeevna*, was a serious
omission by the Ministry of Culture of the USSR, its organs in the
republics and in the localities ... We have taken into consideration the
fact that the RSFSR Ministry of Culture ordered its local organs to
examine the question of whether there should be any further staging of
Razumovskaya's play. The play is being rewritten at present, and so there
is no question of its being staged in its present form.

GORBACHEV: The fact that this matter has been brought to the attention
of the Central Committee Secretariat is already abnormal ... We in the
Party Central Committee are not going to debate the staging of every
play. Those who have made such mistakes should be severely punished.

BARABASH: It should just be noted that in most of the theatres, the text
of the play was somewhat corrected, altered and reworked.

PONOMAREV: What could possibly be reworked in such a squalid play,
and why rework it at all?

GORBACHEV: The Ministry of Culture has ducked out of handling the
difficult issue of the training of playwrights. But for how long are we,
Communists, going to shrink from defending our Party positions, our
Communist morality?

PONOMAREV: Who is this L. Razumovskaya, anyway?

BARABASH: She's a woman of thirty-five who teaches in a technical school,
a non-Party member. She wrote four other plays before this one, but none
of them has been put on ...

GORBACHEV: Yet the Ministry of Culture said nothing for a whole year
while the play was being put on in the country's theatres.

RYZHKOV: Has anything appeared in our press about this play?

BARABASH: Viktor Rozov came out in defence of it in *Literaturnaya gazeta*.
And *Sovetskaya kultura* carried a positive review of it.

ZIMYANIN: This business of *Dear Elena Sergeevna* is not the only one.
There have been other attempts to criticize negative phenomena in our
life which have gone as far as to blacken Soviet reality ... It is the Party's
policy to nip such phenomena in the bud, to work with the writers and
playwrights and correct their work as they write it ... When a play is

ready, we have repertoire commissions to evaluate it, and finally there's Glavlit whose job is to make sure nothing anti-Soviet is published . . .

SOLOMENTSEV: The staff at the Ministry of Culture don't want to spoil their relations with the playwrights and writers. They want the Party Central Committee's cultural staff to spoil these relations . . .

SHAURO (CHIEF OF THE CULTURAL SECTION OF THE CENTRAL COMMITTEE): The USSR Ministry of Culture and the Ministry of Culture of the Russian Federation, Lithuania, Estonia, Georgia, unfortunately, still work badly with the playwrights . . . They need help to understand complicated phenomena of reality from a Party point of view. *Dear Elena Sergeevna* has been staged in all ninety-eight times, and about 50,000 people have seen it. In my view there is no need to rework this play. It is not reworkable.

GORBACHEV: So a view of our disorders is being opened up in a very important sphere of ideological work.

KOCHEMASOV (DEPUTY CHAIRMAN OF THE COUNCIL OF MINISTERS OF THE RSFSR): Actually, there have been articles not only in the central press, but also in the local papers. They were mostly positive. Only the Irkutsk Komsomol paper sharply criticized Razumovskaya's play as ideologically harmful . . .

GORBACHEV: Why didn't you pick up on that article, why didn't you draw the proper conclusions?

KOCHEMASOV: That, I'm afraid, is my fault. It's high time we restructured our work with the people in culture, and raised responsibility.

GORBACHEV: Since you understand this, why don't you restructure yourselves?

KOCHEMASOV: This was simply a case where our system of control broke down.

GORBACHEV: But still how could it be that a play that is ideologically harmful could have received positive support in our newspapers?

STUKALIN (HEAD OF PROPAGANDA SECTION OF THE CENTRAL COMMITTEE): We knew nothing about this in our Section, nor did we take any note of Rozov's article in *Literaturnaya gazeta*.

SOLOMENTSEV: When Viktor Rozov comes out in defence of any work, one should be on one's guard.

ZAMYATIN: I completely agree with the view that the people in the [Chief Repertoire Commission] don't want to quarrel with the playwrights. There are nine plays that have been taken off in Moscow right now. Yet they were all passed by the Repertoire Commission.

BOBKOV (DEPUTY CHAIRMAN OF THE KGB): The main reason why such an ideologically defective play could be put on is the absence of control.

But it should be noted that sometimes a play gets well vetted and the text is not bad, and yet it turns out to be ideologically harmful when it's staged, that's to say it's so altered by the director . . .

SOLOMENTSEV: This question has to be seen in a wider context. This isn't the first time we've come across an ideologically harmful work that has been dragged onto the stage or the cinema, aimed at an immature public, at young people . . . For instance, who needs a play like the one on now at the Moscow Arts Theatre, Vampilov's *Duck Shoot*? It blackens our entire system.

GORBACHEV: Without turning this incident into an absolute, it must frankly be said that we have an obligation to fight against such phenomena and not let our foot slip off the brake. Just listen to what one of the characters says in a dialogue with the father: 'I ask you, Dad, what are these ideals that are just making the people laugh at you? Well, name one of them? They're shaking with laughter. I tell you, the people have become swine. Bourgeois and cattle. They live without laws. Well, never mind, I say, it's the times we live in.' How can we ignore such a speech? If I may say so, such a statement is enough to put any Soviet person on guard. And especially anyone in the cultural sphere or a censor. We have to conclude that there is a lack of control and an absence of political alertness.[123]

After decades of control, the intelligentsia was still capable of protest and intellectual resistance, even if only in a passive way. As in earlier years, the Party leadership was still bent on maintaining its monopoly not only on power, but also on thought, even on the threshold of *perestroika*. Even Gorbachev, who could see farther and deeper than his colleagues in the Politburo, was still constrained to do everything, as before, in the 'Leninist way'.


## Lenin and the Church

'Electricity will take the place of God. Let the peasant pray to electricity; he's going to feel the power of the central authorities more than that of heaven,' Lenin said in 1918, during a discussion with Leonid Krasin on the electrification of Russia.[124]

The peasant accepted electricity readily enough, but it did not replace God for him. He had carried God in his heart since childhood, nurtured there by the popular culture, by the splendour of religious ceremony and the beauty of the liturgy. Perhaps God's hold on the Russians would have been even stronger, had He not been so closely associated in the public mind with the tsar. Once the tsar fell, the people's faith in God was also shaken. Lenin took careful account of the Russian duality of religion and monarchy. Unlike the former Marxists Struve and Berdyaev, he did not engage in agonized meditation on the question, but he summed up his views on religion in society in some propaganda pamphlets early in the century and in a few Party directives.

G.M. Krzhizhanovsky related that Lenin told him that 'already in the fifth class in high school [at the age of sixteen], I broke sharply with all questions of religion: I took off my cross and threw it in the rubbish bin'.[125] Despite (or perhaps because of) the fact that both his parents were devout believers,[126] and that his school required church attendance, Lenin was certainly a convinced atheist by the time he left school.

In principle, Lenin recognized freedom of conscience – but not freedom of belief, for he saw religion as 'a form of spiritual oppression' and, parroting Marx, 'the opium of the people'.[127] Since he had never closely embraced religion, the move from a tenuously held faith in his school years to materialism was easy and unmarked. Untroubled by the thought that life's problems cannot be explained by economic determinism and dialectical materialism alone, Lenin never wondered why Marxism's 'simple' explanations often bordered on mystical incantations, demanding almost as much faith as formal religion.

Religion, he declared, must be a private matter. Sounding like a true liberal, he wrote: 'We demand the complete separation of Church and state in order to combat religious fog with purely ideological and only ideological weapons, with our press, with our words.'[128] In 1905, nobody paid much attention to what Lenin had to say on this issue, but once in power he set about putting his ideas into practice. The Church was indeed separated from the state. The Bolshevik press was predictably abusive about the clergy – 'counter-revolutionaries in cassocks' – but it seemed that that was as far as it might go; after all, Lenin had promised to use ideology alone to combat the Church's influence. Given his other policies, it is surprising that he did not launch his fatal blow against the Church until 1922, when his own physical resources were ebbing away. The Church, moreover, had maintained a low profile. The Provisional Government had re-established the position of Patriarch of Russia, abolished by Peter the Great in the eighteenth century, and the new Patriarch, Tikhon, was a man of independent spirit. He had refused to bless the White movement in 1918, perhaps sensing the approach of the Red Terror, perhaps the failure of the Whites. In any event, he presented a manifestly neutral image.

The Patriarch had wanted to meet Lenin to discuss the question of the Troitsky-Sergievsky Monastery outside Moscow, which Lenin had ordered to be converted into a museum of atheism. Tikhon protested, begged, wrote letters, all in vain. The Bolsheviks apparently believed that even a business contact with the clergy would compromise them, and Lenin wanted to demonstrate the way in which they should behave towards the Church. He refused to meet either the Patriarch or other Church elders who were seeking a *modus vivendi* with the new authorities. He did not want to hold talks with the very people he was only awaiting the opportunity to liquidate.

There were some 80,000 churches in Russia, most of them Orthodox. Several times Unshlikht reminded Lenin of the 'fabulous treasures' to be found in them. Finally the opportunity to deal with the Church presented itself: namely, the famine of 1921–22. If the Stalinist famine of the early 1930s was artificially created by the regime and carefully concealed from the outside world, and even from much of the Russian population, the Leninist famine was there for all to see. Even Comintern was mobilized, appealing to the workers of Europe to give one day's pay a week for famine relief to Russia. The first to sound the tocsin, however, was Patriarch Tikhon. In an appeal to the people, he wrote: 'Carrion has become a delicacy for the starving population, but even this "delicacy" is not to be found. The cries and moans are to be heard on all sides. It has even brought cannibalism. Of thirteen million starving, only two million have received aid. Stretch out your hands to help your starving brothers and sisters! With the agreement of the believers, you can use the treasures in the churches to help the starving (rings, chains and bracelets that adorn the holy icons, silver and gold staves).'[129]

The Politburo discussed the Patriarch's initiative on 7 July 1921, and agreed to broadcast his appeal on the radio. Of the senior leadership, only Lenin, Trotsky and Molotov were present, and the debate was lively. Trotsky also wanted to publish Tikhon's appeal in the Bolshevik press, but Lenin was thinking beyond the moment, and was looking for a way to exploit the crisis in order to confiscate the Church's riches and thus clip its wings once and for all.

In August, Tikhon again appealed to the public and Orthodox Christians. An All-Russian Church Committee was formed to help the starving, and priests were asked to give up those church treasures 'which have no liturgical use'. At the same time, a public committee for famine relief was created by liberals. Headed by S.N. Prokopovich, Y.D. Kuskova and N.M. Kishkin, it earned the nickname 'Prokukish', and the files relating to it the label 'Kukish', a derisive term of contempt.[130] On 27 August 1921 Lenin ordered the immediate arrest of Prokopovich and all the other non-Communist members of the Aid Committee.[131] He could not allow any leeway to 'the wilful bourgeoisie' who, according to Unshlikht's reports, were linked with the SRs and carrying on anti-Soviet propaganda. The Bolsheviks were uncomfortable enough with the idea of famine relief coming from the Church and Western charities, and would not countenance such aid being organized by the bourgeoisie.

According to incomplete data, in 1921–22 there were about twenty-five million people starving in Russia. During this time the Party leadership was sending vast sums of money, and a large quantity of gold and treasure, to foreign Communist Parties to help ignite world revolution. Again according to incomplete data, in the course of 1922 gold and treasure, much of it of Church origin, to the value of more than nineteen million gold roubles were thus transmitted. Moscow's emissaries carried money to China, India, Persia, Hungary, Italy, France, England, Germany, Finland and elsewhere in a bid to give a new impulse to the revolutionary process.

The famine meanwhile was appalling. People were eating carrion and dead bodies, although the Politburo banned any mention of cannibalism in the press. On 23 February 1922 the public learned from their newspapers that a government decree had been issued on the forcible confiscation of *all* valuables from Russian churches. It was not stated that this decree had first been personally approved by Lenin and confirmed by the Politburo.

Party organizations, the GPU and specially formed units began to burst into churches, where they read out the decree and demanded the voluntary handing over of all treasure. The priests were willing to surrender everything but Eucharistic objects. Local atheists either pushed the clergy aside or arrested them, and carried out their own confiscations. It was systematic robbery, perpetrated with the widespread support of criminal elements.

In many places believers offered resistance. In mid-March Lenin received a GPU report that mayhem had broken out in the small town of Shuya, near Ivanovo. After three small churches had been stripped and an inventory taken of valuables in the Shuya synagogue, a local Party commission, accompanied by militia, had arrived at the church. A large crowd had gathered, fighting broke out, and someone started ringing the church bells. A half-company of the 146th Infantry was called out. Machine-guns were fired, blood flowed, people were killed. That evening the congregation of the church took about a hundred pounds of silver valuables to the local Party committee. The confiscation commission was not satisfied, and removed a further 360 pounds of silver and a quantity of gold objects and precious stones.

The Cheka reported that the disturbances had been organized by the 'Black Hundreds clergy', even though, as elswhere, it was plain that the protest had been spontaneous. Lenin was outraged. Usually able to control himself, now he stormed and cursed – until he realized that a golden opportunity had presented itself to finish off the clergy in one fell swoop, especially Patriarch Tikhon, who had responded to the confiscation decree with another appeal to the people. Reiterating the Church's commitment to famine relief, Tikhon described the acts of confiscation as sacrilege. The Church, he wrote, 'allowed the surrender of church objects if they were not used for the Eucharist . . . But we cannot approve the removal from churches, even voluntarily, of holy objects, the use of which for non-Eucharistic purposes is prohibited by the canons of the Universal Church and is punishable as sacrilege, with excommunication for laymen and expulsion from holy orders for priests.'[132]

Lenin took Tikhon's appeal as a call for organized resistance and a challenge to the regime, and personally set about formulating the Party's policy to crush the Church. He was taking one of his numerous breaks, this time at the village of Korzinkino near Troitsko-Lykovo in Moscow province, and Krupskaya recalled that during their walks Lenin talked frequently on anti-religious themes. He also wrote a major article for the journal *Pod znamenem marksizma* (Under the Banner of Marxism), titled 'On the Meaning of Militant Materialism'. He was completely geared up for his campaign against the Church.

On 11 March 1922 he wrote to Trotsky to ensure that the Politburo had issued instructions for the collection of figures on the number of churches that had been 'cleansed', i.e. stripped.[133] At the same time he requested regular information on the number of clergy being arrested and executed. The Cheka sent him several reports in the second half of March on 'the revolutionary repression of priests and other religious functionaries'. The Politburo had already followed Lenin's proposal to 'provide information on attempts by rebellious priests' and to shoot ringleaders,[134] and on 4 May formally passed a decree ordering 'the death penalty for priests'.[135]

The contents of a six-page letter Lenin wrote on the events at Shuya, to Molotov as Secretary of the Central Committee and for perusal by the Politburo, were concealed even from true Leninists. In a mere five lines the 'Biographical Chronicle' notes that he 'regards it as essential that the VTsIK decree of 23 February 1922 on the removal of church valuables be carried out resolutely'.[136] In the Complete Works the letter received six lines, in an appendix of a more frank nature: 'Lenin in his letter to the members of the Politburo wrote of the need to crush clergy resistance to the decree . . .'[137]

In his latter years, Lenin usually confined himself to notes and comments and hastily scribbled papers. This long and carefully thought-out letter, written on 19 March, was an exception. Lenin was always careful that such materials should remain classified, and on this letter he wrote an important preliminary note: 'I request that under no circumstances should copies be made, and members of the Politburo (including Comrade Kalinin) should write their comments on the letter itself.' He knew that what he was writing could not be justified by any 'revolutionary expediency'. His pen was guided by the hand of an inquisitor. The letter, moreover, went far beyond expressing his attitude to the Church alone: it mirrors his political and moral personality. It is too extensive to reproduce in full, but extracts suffice to convey its message.

Concerning events in Shuya, which are to be discussed by the Politburo, I think a firm decision should be taken right now in connection with the general plan of struggle on this front ... If what the papers are reporting about the clergy's attitude to the decree on removing church valuables is combined with what we know of Patriarch Tikhon's illegal appeal, it becomes perfectly clear that the Black Hundreds clergy, under their leader, are carrying out a premeditated plan to offer decisive battle precisely at this moment.

Typically, Lenin spoke in terms of war. He also garbled the intent of Tikhon's appeal. It was of course he, not the Church, who was planning to launch a crushing blow. The measures he regarded as essential were listed later in the letter.

There is a ninety-nine per cent chance of smashing the enemy on the head with complete success and of guaranteeing positions essential for us for many decades to come. With the starving in the localities eating people and the roads littered with hundreds if not thousands of dead bodies, it is now and only now that we can (and therefore must) carry out the removal of church valuables with furious and pitiless energy ... We can secure for ourselves a fund of several hundred million gold roubles (think of the riches of some of the monasteries). Without such a fund no state work in general, no economic construction in particular, and no defence of our position at [the Genoa Conference in 1922, where Soviet Russia and the Allied forces unsuccessfully attempted a reconciliation] is at all thinkable. We must at all costs take into our hands this fund of several hundred million roubles (maybe even several billion).

No mention here of aid to the starving. And how, it may be asked, had Lenin intended to 'build socialism', if he could now declare that economic construction would be unthinkable without the confiscated wealth of the Church? During all his years in power, Lenin seems to have been obsessed with confiscation and requisition: factories, banks, grain, roads, personal valuables, houses, clothes (there were special decrees for removing warm clothes and footwear from the bourgeoisie), theatres, schools, presses – one vast process of dispossession.

The letter continued:

... a wise writer on state questions has rightly said that, if one has to commit a number of cruelties to gain a certain political aim, then it is essential to carry them out in the most energetic way possible and in the shortest possible time, for the people will not endure the long-drawn-out application of harsh measures.

Lenin was wrong. The people he was leading to Communism endured incredibly harsh measures for decades. The civil war alone cost Russia thirteen million lives. In the period between the civil war and the collectivization, during the 'happy years of NEP', about one million died in camps or in the crushing of anti-Soviet resistance in the interior. And between 1929 and 1953, when 'the first Leninist' died, another 21.5 million perished.

In his letter Lenin remarked that the international situation was favourable for a general punitive operation against the Church 'of such ferocity that it will not forget it for decades to come'.[138] This undoubtedly was to be the case: the Church was made into a servant of the Party, with a huge number of Party agents infiltrated among its personnel. From about 80,000 churches in 1905, by 1950 the number had been reduced to no more than 11,525, despite the revival that had taken place during the Second World War, when Stalin turned to the Church for support.[139]

Lenin's onslaught on the Russian Church is comparable with Stalin's war on the peasantry. It probably caused more spiritual and physical damage to the Church than it had suffered at any other time in its history. According to a variety of data, between fourteen and twenty thousand clergy and active laymen were shot. This was not a large bag by Lenin's standards, particularly as in his letter he had demanded that 'the greater the number of reactionary clergy and reactionary bourgeoisie shot over this issue, the better'.

As for Shuya, Lenin recommended that the Politburo issue a directive, 'so that the trial of the Shuya rebels, who were opposed to famine relief, should be carried out with maximum speed and should conclude in no other way than by the shooting of a very large number of the most influential and dangerous of Shuya's Black Hundredists, and if possible not only of this town, but also of Moscow and a number of other spiritual centres'.[140]

Lenin dictated the draft of his letter over the telephone to his secretary, Lydia Fotieva, on the day of the Politburo meeting, as he was not planning to attend. The Politburo devoted several sessions to the letter, since the Church question was of such importance. On 20 March Kamenev, Stalin, Trotsky and Molotov discussed a decree drafted by Trotsky, as chairman of the Revolutionary War Council, and the seventeen-point decree was approved, with some amendments.

A central commission was formed, consisting of Yakovlev, Sapronov, Unshlikht, Krasikov, Vinokurov and Bazilevich. It would be under Trotsky's supervision. Similar commissions would be created in the regions. Care should be taken to see that 'the ethnic composition of these official commissions does not give grounds for chauvinistic agitation'. For this reason, although he chaired it, Trotsky, a Jew, was not an official member of the central commssion.

It was decided to develop the broadest possible agitation and to create a split in the Church by giving support to the so-called 'Living Church', or Renovationist wing, which opposed Tikhon's alleged refusal to give famine relief. The campaign was to be carried out in the shortest possible time and followed by the arrest of prominent clergy. During the confiscations, troops, Communists and special-purpose personnel should remain in the vicinity of the given church.[141] The pillage had barely begun when Trotsky informed Lenin: 'The main work of removals up to now has taken place in abandoned monasteries, museums, repositories and so on. The booty is enormous, but the work is far from finished.'[142]

The trial in Shuya was set up at lightning speed. A session of the Politburo of 22 March had decided that 'we should state that the arrest of the Synod and the Patriarch was necessary, not now but in fifteen–twenty-five days. The facts about Shuya should be published, the accused Shuya priests and laymen should be tried within a week. The ringleaders of the rebellion should be shot.'[143] Unshlikht insisted on the immediate arrest of the Patriarch. In a GPU note to the Politburo, it was stated that: 'Patriarch Tikhon and his pack . . . are carrying on open operations against the removal of church valuables . . . There is sufficient evidence to arrest Tikhon and the most reactionary members of the Synod. The GPU finds: 1) the arrest of the Synod and patriarch timely; 2) The selection of a new Synod should not be allowed to proceed [the existing one had been arrested]; 3) Any priests who oppose the removal of valuables should be sent to the most starving districts of the Volga as enemies of the people.'[144]

In an effort to step up the rate of the confiscation, the Politburo allocated five million roubles to the commission to pay for more 'technical assistance'.[145] Many of the commission's new assistants were ex-convicts who had done time for armed robbery.

Throughout the country military-style expeditions were mounted against churches and the clergy. Jewish synagogues, Muslim mosques and Roman Catholic churches were not spared. At night, in the cellars of the Cheka or in nearby woods, the dry crack of revolver-fire could be heard. Executed priests and laymen were piled into gullies and ravines. The church bells fell silent throughout the land. Local Party leaders, Chekists and commission members hastily counted the gold and precious objects as they stuffed them into boxes.

The total quantity of valuables collected is unknown, but the contents of one list of items collected up to 1 November 1922 provides an idea of the scale of operations: 1220 pounds of gold, 828,275 pounds of silver, 35,670 diamonds, 71,762 items of unspecified valuables, 536 pounds of gemstones, 3115 gold roubles, 19,155 silver roubles, 1902 'various precious objects'. 'In addition to the church valuables listed above, 964 antique objects were collected and will be valued.'[146] Once in Moscow, the boxes were sorted before despatch to the State Repository: part of the loot was put at the immediate disposal of the Politburo for the Comintern fund, for the needs of the GPU and 'state construction', while only a small part was allocated for the purchase of food. The Politburo ordered that a substantial amount of the material collected should remain in the regions for use by local authorities. Much of it was allocated to the needs of the Party hierarchy: thousands of houses requisitioned from the bourgeoisie in the Moscow area were now embellished with confiscated furniture.

The pillage reached beyond Church treasure to sacred objects. For instance, P. Krasikov, a Justice Commissariat official concerned with Church affairs and a close associate of Lenin, reported from Kostroma that the silver tomb containing the relics of St Barnabas of Vetluga should be confiscated: 'The opening [of the tomb] should be done with the definite intention of removing these so-called relics. If major complications are expected, the GPU should be informed at once.' The Politburo approved the removal of the tomb,[147] and Lenin ordered the Justice Commissariat to issue a decree on 'the liquidation of the relics'.

St Barnabas was only one victim of the treasure-hunters' zeal. The same treatment was meted out to the relics of St Sergius of Radonezh, the fourteenth-century Church leader who embodied the Russian spirit of resistance to the Tatars, and in whose memory the very centre of the church at Zagorsk was named. Krasikov wanted to make a propaganda film of the exhumation of St Sergius. Patriarch Tikhon begged and protested against this sacrilege, but in vain. Similarly, the eleventh-century Monastery of the Caves in Kiev, one of the Church's holiest places, was pillaged. The local Ukrainian commission wanted to retain the treasure under the guise of relief for children, but the order immediately came from Moscow: confiscated valuables must be handed over to the central authorities, and only twenty-five per cent retained 'for the children'.[148]

Lenin meanwhile was hastening the trial of the senior clergy, and in early May the Politburo ordered the Moscow tribunal, '1) to put Tikhon on trial at once, 2) to sentence the priests to death.'[149] It had been hoped to carry out the trial with all despatch, but an international protest was raised: telegrams were sent by the Pope, by German socialists and Swedish pacifists, and by Fridtjof Nansen, the Norwegian explorer/politician whose chief occupation was now as the League of Nations' High Commissioner for Refugees. The Politburo decided to postpone the trial and prepare its case more carefully. The Party's chief atheist, Yaroslavsky, proposed that if Tikhon were to repent, he could be sent to the Balaam church hostel and allowed to engage in Church work.[150]

Meanwhile, on 8 May the trial of the Shuya priests and laymen was concluded, with the death sentence for eleven of them and various terms of imprisonment for the rest. Of the pleas for clemency addressed to the Politburo, six were granted and five rejected. Those who were executed joined the list of the many thousands already shot without trial.

On 8 October 1922 Tuchkov, the GPU 'curator' of Church affairs, head of the 6th department of the secret section of the GPU, reported to the Politburo:

On the Tikhon question. A group has been formed of the so-called 'living church', consisting chiefly of 'white clergy' [i.e. married priests, as distinct from monks, who were known as 'black clergy'], and this has given us the chance to cause a quarrel between the priests and the bishops, like soldiers against generals, for there was hostility between the white and black clergy. We are working to push the Tikhonites out of the patriarchate and the parishes. We are creating groups of 'adherents of renovationism'. Following the priest Krasnitsky's speech in the Church of Christ the Saviour, twelve laymen joined the group.[151]

Tikhon, imprisoned in Donskoi Monastery, was being subjected to the standard treatment: interrogation, threats, pressure and bribes. The interrogations went on even after Lenin had lost his faculties, as his instructions on Church affairs continued to be carried out to the letter. In the summer of 1923, the Politburo accepted Yaroslavsky's proposals: '1) That the investigation of the Tikhon case be continued until further notice; 2) That Tikhon be informed that his sentence could be altered if: a) he makes a statement of repentence of his crime against the Soviet regime; b) recognizes the court; c) distances himself from White Guards and other counter-revolutionary organizations; d) declares a negative attitude towards the Catholic Church. If he agrees, he will be freed.'[152]

Before this, however, the GPU's 'Renovationists' had held their Second All-Russian Assembly and voted to remove Tikhon from his holy orders, a move he and his entourage repudiated as illegal. His GPU handlers, however, had by now done their work, and on 16 June 1923 the Patriarch signed a declaration, manifestly written or dictated by them. It read:

From Patriarch Tikhon, Vasili Ivanovich Belavin, being held under guard. Raised as I was in a monarchist society and before my arrest being under the influence of anti-Soviet persons, I was decidedly hostile to the Soviet regime ... my hostility at times going over into active deeds, for instance, an address on the Brest-Litovsk Treaty, anathema of the authorities in that year, and, finally, an appeal against the removal of church valuables in 1922. With a few amendments, all of my anti-Soviet actions are detailed in the sentence of the Supreme Court. While recognizing the court's decision in bringing me to justice as correct, I wish to make the following statement: I repent of these crimes against the state order and I ask the Supreme Court to alter my sentence, that is, to release me from custody. Furthermore, I declare to the Supreme Court that henceforth I am no enemy of the Soviet regime. I utterly and decisively dissociate myself from the White Guardist counter-revolution both abroad and at home.[153]

Several months elapsed before the Politburo reacted to Tikhon's statement, and on 18 March 1924, that is, after Lenin's death, it was decided to close the case.[154] Tikhon died only a year later, under virtual house-arrest, a broken man. His death was announced by the head of the OGPU secret section, Deribas: 'On 7 April 1925 at 23.45 Patriarch Tikhon died from an attack of angina pectoris in the

Bakunins' Hospital at 19, Ostazhenka, while being attended by Doctors E.N. Bakunina and I.S. Shchelkan and his own attendant Paskevich. The burial took place in Donskoi Monastery.'[155] Lenin's instructions had been clear: 'the more reactionary clergy and reactionary bourgeoisie are shot . . . the better', and 'the priests must be sentenced to death'. Since it had proved impractical to execute Tikhon, the Cheka had had to find other ways of ensuring that the sixty-year-old Patriarch should not long survive his sojourn in their company.

The greater part of the money realized from the sale of the confiscated valuables went to the Party for its own purposes. The Central Committee combated the famine with the help of the American Relief Administration and the journal *Bezbozhnik* (Atheist). *Bezbozhnik* catalogued the dark deeds committed by the Church, which it practically accused of having caused the famine. The Central Committee's commission for the separation of Church and state instructed each of its members to 'write not less than two articles a month for the journal'.[156]

The Church neither forgot the massive blow Lenin had dealt it, nor recovered from it. Instead of functioning as a Church, it became a decorative embellishment of the state – to keep the West quiet – deprived of spiritual freedom and infiltrated by agents of the GPU. Its tribulations were not over, however, and the pillage was to continue for a long time to come. Decapitated and disfigured, from the start of collectivization the Church was kept on a short leash by the Bolsheviks. Point 8 of the Politburo order of 30 January 1930 on 'Measures to liquidate kulak farms in districts of full collectivization' reads: 'The legislation on religious communities should be urgently revised to ensure that the leading organs of such communities (church councils, sectarian communes and so on) cannot under any circumstances become kulak strongholds. The Orgburo is ordered to issue a directive on the closure of the churches.'[157]

On the initiative of the Council of Labour and Defence, and with Politburo approval, the removal of church bells began. Every year a plan was launched calling for the collection of a specific quantity of bronze. On May 1933, for instance, the Politburo confirmed that, 'with the aim of securing bell bronze for the tractor industry, the annual plan for bronze should be increased from 5200 tonnes to 6300 tonnes', and the amount to be collected region by region was given.[158]

The churches were gradually closed. Cathedrals were deserted. Disfigured buildings, their cupolas stripped and dismantled, stood forlornly on their hillocks, silent and doomed. Occasionally, to be sure, from the depths of the desecrated religious consciousness, perhaps out of sheer desperation, a rebellious protest sparked.

In September 1938, Deputy People's Interior Commissar Beria reported to Stalin that the Nekrasov District Party Committee of Yaroslavl *oblast* had taken the decision to close the church in the village of Chernaya Zavod and to remove its bells. The district chiefs arrived, a crowd gathered, shouts rang out of 'Guard!', 'Robbers!', 'The drunken bandits have come!' The Church authorities put a twenty-four-hour guard round the church. Stalin, without even reading the whole document, scribbled a note on it: 'Comrade Malenkov, Please check up and report. Arrest the organizers.'[159]

On the eve of the Second World War, the regime hastened to take control of the newly annexed territories in Western Ukraine, Moldavia and the Baltic republics of Estonia, Latvia and Lithuania. All were well known for their religious observance. In October 1940, Khrushchev, Secretary of the Ukrainian Party Central Committee, sent a report with a request to Stalin: 'According to ancient Jewish tradition, for ten days a year God takes stock of every Jew's actions in the previous year . . . For nine days the Jews pray to God and ask forgiveness for their sins. They are forbidden to work during this time. On the tenth day, the "Day of Atonement", which in 1940 falls on Saturday 12 October, the Jews never work . . . The Secretary of the Lvov District Party Committee, Comrade Grishchuk, has received many requests from inhabitants of Jewish nationality for permission not to work in factories and institutions on Saturday 12 October. I request instructions on how to proceed.' On 11 October, one day before 'zero hour', Stalin, in a rare moment of comparative religious tolerance, magnanimously ordered: 'Let them not work. Tell Khrushchev.'[160]

Rule over the new diocesan provinces was established, naturally, by means of the secret services. As an illustration of the process, the following report was received by Stalin in March 1941 from B. Merkulov, People's Commissar for State Security of the USSR:

There are at present in the territories of the Latvian, Estonian and Lithuanian republics autocephalous [autonomous] Orthodox churches, headed by local metropolitans who are placemen of the bourgeois governments.

In the Latvian SSR there are 175,000 Orthodox parishioners. Anti-Soviet elements, former members of the Fascist organization 'Perkanirust', are grouped around the head of the Synod, Augustin.

In the Estonian SSR there are 40,000 Orthodox. The head of the eparchy has died. Archbishop Fedosi Fedoseev, who heads an anti-Soviet group of churchmen, is trying to grab the job.

The NKGB has prepared the following measures:

1) Through an NKGB agency we will get the Moscow patriarchate to issue a resolution on the subordination of the Orthodox churches of Latvia, Estonia and Lithuania to itself, using a declaration from local rank and file clergy and believers for the purpose.

2) By a decision of the Moscow patriarchate we shall appoint as eparch Archbishop Dmitri Nikolaevich Voskresensky (an agent of the NKGB of the USSR), using for the purpose appropriate requests from the local clergy, which are to be found in the Moscow patriarchate.[161]

This document clearly demonstrates the reasons behind Lenin's confident assertion that 'our victory over the clergy is fully assured'. So complete, indeed, was that victory that even Stalin and his accomplices were at times at a loss to know if someone was a priest or an NKGB agent in a cassock. While boasting loudly of freedom of conscience and quoting copiously from Lenin's hypocritical statements on how humanely socialism treated religion, the Bolshevik regime, through the widespread use of violence, had turned the dwelling-place of the spirit and faith into a den of thought-police.

In July 1937, the Politburo ordered the raising of 'all taxes on priests as persons receiving unearned income'. And churches and monasteries were in addition taxed in kind – grain, potatoes – as though they were private farms.[162] These measures virtually stifled the last vestiges of the parishes. Just before Stalin's death there were no more than 12,499 priests left in the USSR.[163] The Church had been killed off as if by a plague unleashed by Lenin. His record in anti-Church affairs is monstrously impressive: soon after the October revolution came the closure of the monasteries, then the attempt to split the Church, the exhumation of relics, and finally the confiscation, the pillage of Church holy objects and the mass physical annihilation of the clergy.

The post-war condition of the Church is depicted in a memorandum dated July 1953 to Khrushchev from Karpov, the Chairman of the Council for Orthodox Affairs, under the Council of Ministers.

Karpov reported that 19,000 inactive churches had survived total destruction and removal. Of these, 13,000 were being used as warehouses, the rest as clubs and industrial workshops; about 3000 had retained their religious equipment, but were under lock and key and not used for services. Karpov went on to say that 'the Council's many years of practice have established that when the buildings of inactive churches are left standing or even when they are used for undesignated purposes (as warehouses, etc.), and the question of their refurbishment is not raised, we see no great activity from groups of believers, but as soon as there is any question of refurbishing or removing the building of an inactive church, the activity begins'.[164]

The disaster of the Russian Church was not entirely the work of Lenin and the Bolsheviks, although they were certainly responsible for the culmination of the tragedy. The Orthodox Church in Russia had traditionally been in the hands of monarchs, its independence illusory. The Church at times simply identified itself as a part of the monarchy, a fact which partly explains the deep crisis the Church experienced after 1917. The collapse of the autocracy rendered the Church at once impotent and defenceless. The rapid decline of the Church in Soviet Russia created a sudden vacuum in the public mind, into which the myths of materialism were pumped. Atheism was an important component of the new state religion, Bolshevism, and generations were raised in the new faith, in a spirit of class antagonism and an absence of faith in the eternal values which the Church had always upheld.

## The Prophet of Comintern

23 July 1920 was a typical day, full of tension and problems, and Lenin, neither ill nor resting, was working alone in the Kremlin. But the main event later that evening was to be the meeting of the Second Comintern Congress, which he would chair.[165] He could envisage the growth of revolution in other countries, the creation of new Communist Parties, the rise in international support for the great cause he and his Party had begun. Already the blood-red banner was being raised in many capitals. Only three years earlier it would have seemed

an impossible, fantastic idea, although in July 1918, in an article entitled 'Prophetic Words', he had written: 'No one believes in miracles anymore, thank God. Miraculous prophecy is a fairy-tale. But scientific prophecy is a fact.'[166] The approaching world revolution was no fairy-tale. For Lenin it was a fact that was about to happen.

Inspired by the Comintern Congress that had just opened in Moscow, by reports from outside and his own analysis of the world situation, and above all by the Red Army's march towards Warsaw in the opening Soviet campaign of the war with Poland, that evening Lenin sent a coded cable to Stalin in Kharkov: 'The situation in Comintern is splendid. Zinoviev, Bukharin and I, too, think it is time to encourage revolution in Italy. My view is that for this to happen, Hungary must be sovietized, and maybe also the Czech Lands and Romania. This has to be carefully thought out. Send your detailed conclusions. The German Communists think that Germany is capable of mobilizing 300,000 riff-raff against us.'[167]

By this time the decision had been made, as Trotsky put it, 'to take the risk, on Lenin's initiative, of feeling out bourgeois-landowning Poland with the bayonet'.[168] In September of the same year, Lenin would put it more frankly: by attacking Poland 'we will help the sovietization of Lithuania and Poland' and the revolutionizing of Germany. To be sure, in his political report to the Ninth Party Conference, he warned: 'I would ask you not to take too many notes: this must not get into the press.'[169] But even failure in Poland, he concluded, must not stop them: 'It will teach us about offensive war.' 'We will help Hungary, Italy, and at each step we will remember where to stop.'[170]

All this was an effort to fulfil Lenin's own prophecy. He believed in world revolution, though he did not care to expatiate on his failures. The campaign against Poland (and the onward march of the Red Army to the German frontier in order to revive the revolution there) was undertaken on Lenin's initiative and his determined insistence. He never publicly spoke of the fact that his decision ended in the humiliating defeat of the Red Army at Warsaw in September 1920. Under the terms of the Treaty of Riga, signed by Soviet Russia and Poland in March 1921, Russia lost western territory containing nearly four million inhabitants, and was required to make substantial financial restitution to Poland. When the time arrived for the first instalment of the compensation, Moscow decided to pay it in the form of precious stones, having first raised their nominal value several times. Warsaw was furious, and the Foreign Commissar, Georgy Chicherin, informed Lenin:

On 1 November 1921 we were obliged to pay and ought to have paid Poland ten million roubles in gold and diamonds. The diamonds we handed over were valued by Polish experts at 2.5 million gold roubles. We have no more stones ready to hand over. The Pole Olszewski warns that finding us out in such a monstrously false valuation would be widely exploited in the press ... we would be monstrously compromised.

Another solution would be to pay the difference at once in gold, but it is too hard to throw away 7.5 million in gold. Another way would be to start collecting the rest in stones. We have a lot of stones, but they are not sorted or valued ... We haven't got the people ... The former head of the loan bank, Levitsky, is in prison. Alexandrov, the valuer, is also in prison. We need a decision of the Politburo to accommodate them in normal conditions.[171]

Lenin agreed, but seems to have suffered no pangs of conscience over the Polish adventure. He was as unconcerned by the loss of millions of roubles of the country's wealth as he was by the pointless loss of thousands of lives, all sacrificed to satisfy his revolutionary whim.

In the summer of 1917, while hiding from the Provisional Government, Lenin had deluded himself into fixing a time for the arrival of Communism.[172] Two years later, on 1 May 1919 at Red Square, he declared: 'Most of you here who are not older than thirty to thirty-five will live under Communism.'[173] Eighteen months later, he was no less sanguine as he wound up his speech to the Third Congress of Communist Youth: 'The generation that is now fifteen will in ten to twenty years from now live in a Communist society.'[174]

Soviet Marxism has traditionally and invariably described Lenin as a prophet, and claimed that the twentieth century developed 'according to Lenin', thereby proving him a genius. Yet neither Soviet historians nor philosphers ever officially confronted the fact that not one of his epoch-making predictions has ever come true. Not one. The end of capitalism? Nobody can take it seriously. Many 'capitalist' countries, moreover, have developed more 'socialism' than Lenin ever imagined possible. If Marx were to rise again and visit, say, Stuttgart, and Chita in Eastern Siberia, and were then asked where he found more 'socialism', his answer would be plain enough: there is more social provision in the capitalist West than was ever given to the Soviet people. The idea of the creation of a World Soviet Federation has died quietly, in conditions entirely different from those prophesied by Lenin. To be sure, he himself declared that 'any attempt to calculate future opportunities with complete accuracy is either charlatanism or hopeless pedantry'.[175]

As a theorist, Lenin was profoundly contradictory, a fact for which his successors were silently grateful, since they were always able to find the appropriate quotation, the 'Leninist proof', to support a diametrically opposite line to the one they had just been defending. Lenin could predict with certainty that 'socialism will shorten the working day, raise the masses to a new life, create conditions in which *everyone* without exception will carry out "state functions"',[176] and not long afterwards assert that 'we do not claim that Marx and the Marxists know the path to socialism in all its detail. That's nonsense.'[177] Thus, while his utterances were a rich seam for his successors to mine, considerable judgment had to be exercised in deciding what was 'a wise precept' and what was 'nonsense'.

The fullest expression of Lenin's prophetic rôle was in relation to the question of world revolution, a matter to which he devoted unprecedented effort. A world revolution, however, needed a world instrument. Apart from the Russian Communist Party, in Europe only Germany could boast another such party, those in other countries still being in a relatively embryonic stage. Lenin ordered his Foreign Commissar, Chicherin, to broadcast an invitation to all Communists in Europe and Asia to assemble for a conference in Moscow in March 1919. Chicherin's summons received a weak response, as there was hardly anyone to take notice of it: a few prisoners of war remaining in Russia and some foreign nationals attended, and Hugo Eberlein came from Germany to represent the German Communist Party. For nearly a week this small group, barely exceeding thirty in number, debated. They decided that 'the international Communist conference would create the Third Communist International', known henceforth as Comintern. Seventeen delegates, most of them completely unknown and chosen more or less at random, signed the manifesto, and Lenin set them their task: to struggle for the world dictatorship of the proletariat.

From its inception, this body became a cover and a tool of the

Russian Communist Party's activities in the international arena. Appointed president of the new organization, first by the Politburo and then 'confirmed' by the Executive Committee of the Communist International (ECCI), Zinoviev claimed time and again that the victory of Communist revolution in Europe was guaranteed, and that the Red Flag would soon be flying over all continents. He saw his primary task as helping to ferment armed uprisings wherever 'the revolutionary situation was ripening'. When it proved impossible to do this, however, as for instance in Germany in 1921, when strikes and attempts at armed uprising petered out for lack of effective Communist leadership against a determined government, the putsches and plots ended in complete disaster. While the German police and troops were rounding up scattered conspirators, Zinoviev was in Moscow, shouting from the platform: 'Arm yourselves, German proletarians! Wherever you can get hold of a gun, take it! Form soviets! Build a Red Army! Long live the proletarian revolution in Germany and the whole world!' And he was trying to convince the Politburo that 'the leaven of world revolution' was already at work in the main capitalist countries.

The Central Committee, meanwhile, was preparing the programme for new parties, formulating the 'Twenty-one Conditions' for admission to Comintern,[178] and sending trunkloads of gold and other valuables to Germany, Italy, Hungary and elsewhere in order to foment revolution. The Bolshevik leadership believed fanatically that, the torch of revolution having been lit in Russia, the ancient edifice of civilization would soon be engulfed in flames and burn to the ground like an old wooden barn.

On 6 March 1920, at a ceremony marking the first anniversary of the founding of Comintern, Lenin gave a 'guarantee that the victory of the Communist revolution is inevitable . . . and that it is not too far off'.[179] Don Quixote, tilting at windmills, and Khlestakov, Gogol's fantasist, were scarcely more short-sighted or irresponsible. The Bolsheviks planned not merely to control but also to create revolutionary situations through Comintern. For this purpose, from the very beginning, Lenin had to shift the entire financial burden of the 'international Communist Party' onto the shoulders of plundered, starving, half-stifled Soviet Russia. As early as 8 October 1918, Lenin and the Central Committee had created a Russian Communist Party Bureau for 'foreign work', consisting of Balabanova, Vorovsky, Bukharin and Axelrod.[180] This enabled him to say in May 1919 that the Third International had really been created in 1918, when parties in a number of countries had needed coordinating.[181] The fact was, as Ioffe wrote, that 'the wager on world revolution, even if plainly delayed, was the keystone of Lenin's entire tactics during Brest-Litovsk and after'.[182]

All financial operations were conducted through the Bureau, under Zinoviev, although the Commissariat for Foreign Affairs also exercised a degree of patronage. Comintern affairs were, however, removed from the Foreign Commissariat by the Politburo when Zinoviev complained to Lenin of Chicherin's 'rivalry', and the Bureau acquired financial independence. It was, of course, subordinate to the Bolshevik Central Committee, and this financial dependence made Comintern an obedient tool of Bolshevik plans. The Politburo determined practically everything: where and when Comintern congresses should take place, what should be on their agenda, and such trivial questions as whether Karl Radek, who was in charge of Bolshevik relations with foreign Communist delegations, should be given twelve extra rations 'for the needs of the delegates'; Abel Yenukidze, Nikolai Sklyansky and Efraim Bryukhanov were charged with 'taking the feeding of participants in hand', improving supplies for the workers in Comintern's printing press, and many other similar routine matters.[183]

From the start, Comintern had close links with the GPU, which created Soviet intelligence abroad. Contacts were established with Comintern sections, operations were financed, personal papers prepared, personnel recruited. The administrator of the Comintern Executive Committee, a certain D. Blake,* wrote to the Politburo on 24 November 1920 'on illegal techniques', raising the question of his committee's lack of foreign notepaper, photographic paper and related materials. Among other things, he also mentioned that 'technical personnel and their families should be looked after with secret funds from Comintern'. Before passing Blake's note on for attention, Lenin wrote on it: 'On conspiracy – Blake's report. Secret.'[184]

The national sections of Comintern, that is the non-Russian parties,

---

* Evidently an alias. It has proved impossible to establish his identity.

had the task not only of recruiting new members and producing propaganda, but also of organizing strikes, demonstrations, protest marches and uprisings wherever possible. Under the cover of Comintern, the Politburo succeeded in creating a number of bases abroad. For instance, its representative in Turkestan wrote to Karakhan, a Deputy Foreign Commissar, to ask the Politburo: '1) Whether it would sanction the formation of an Indian base in Turkestan, in collaboration with the Central Committee's own Turkburo; 2) To whom am I to transmit the 2 million gold roubles?' Lenin's answers to these questions were given orally, and only his signature, in red ink, appears on the document.[185] Until Comintern had its own proper budget – and it would soon be funded by both the Central Committee and the OGPU for its own secret operations – most decisions on financial matters were made personally by Lenin.

For example, Ivan Rahja, the Finnish Bolshevik who had helped to hide him in the summer of 1917, and who was now one of the leaders of the Finnish Communist Party, asked Lenin for ten million Finnish marks' worth of valuables for his party's use. Lenin agreed.[186] From Bengal a letter came via Chicherin asking for money and literature to help overthrow the British Raj: 'I would ask you to convey my greetings to all the brave comrades who so valiantly struggle for the liberation of mankind: Lenin, Trotsky, Chicherin. Signed Virendranat Chattopadia.' The Eastern Section of the Foreign Commissariat noted on this document: 'If we are seriously thinking of revolutionizing India, we should bank on the non-Muslim population . . . As for the funding Ch[attopadia] talks about, he has undoubtedly been corrupted by European life, having been kept for a long time on German money.'[187] There were many such 'revolutionaries' in need of Russian money, and many who received it.

Moscow was handing out money to all kinds of people, millions of gold roubles, dollars, pounds, marks, lire, crowns and so on, all raised by selling off the tsarist gold reserves, the valuables looted from the churches and confiscated from the bourgeoisie. It seems that ECCI kept no proper accounts of the financing of its illegal operations. In this connection, it is interesting to note the correspondence between Stalin and Zinoviev, on the one hand, and Litvinov, then Deputy Foreign Commissar, and Osip Pyatnitsky, who was in charge of ECCI's hard-currency chest, on the other. At issue was the money which had 'run away' through the fingers of one of the Foreign Commissariat's emissaries, Carlo, real name Lyubarsky. It seems that Carlo had handed over to the Italian Communist Party only 288,000 of the 750,000 lire he had been given, while also managing to mislay some 124,487 Czech crowns and a large amount of British pounds. Litvinov wanted him sentenced, but Pyatnitsky thought it enough to fire him.[188] It is safe to assume that there were many such people who were using the revolutionary ardour of the Bolshevik leadership to line their own pockets.

Lenin did not merely prophesy, he did all in his power to make his prophecies become reality. Efforts were made, especially in a number of Asian countries, to radicalize Comintern's influence. Karakhan proposed, for instance, the regular despatch of agitators who would be paid fixed bonuses. It seemed that these agents, while fighting for Communist ideals, preferred to receive their reward in a material rather than moral form. Karakhan wrote to Lenin: 'The proposal is to allocate 200,000 [roubles] for the first quarter of the year, January to March 1919, to the Foreign Commissariat for supporting Asian labour organizations and sending agitators to make propaganda in Asia. The cost of each agitator, plus his bonus when he returns, would be as follows: North Korea and Korea – 10,000 roubles; South China – 20,000 roubles. Similar missions are envisaged for Persia and India.'[189] Thus, before Comintern was founded, it was the Foreign Commissariat that was responsible for spreading revolutionary ideas.

Lenin wanted to incorporate Bolshevik principles in Comintern from its inception. Having seized power in Russia with a relatively small force, he thought that a centralized and disciplined party on a worldwide scale would make his prophecy of world revolution come true. At his behest, Trotsky wrote the Manifesto for the Second Comintern Congress, which Lenin approved. The style was typical of Trotsky:

We must kill imperialism so that the human species can survive . . . Belated German parliamentarism, an abortion of the bourgeois revolution, which is itself an abortion of history, suffers in its infancy from all the illnesses of an old dog . . . The Communist International is the international party of the proletarian uprising and proletarian dictatorship . . . The Soviet system is a class apparatus which in the struggle and by means of the struggle will lay waste to parliamentarism and replace it by itself . . .[190]

In these few phrases Trotsky expounded the aims and strategy of Bolshevik international policy. Their easy victory in October 1917 had induced euphoria and the conviction that they could reach their goals by any available means.

The rôle of the army and armed force in revolution played an important part in Bolshevik thinking about how to initiate world revolution. In May 1924, Trotsky addressed the Red Army Academy on the need to prepare for civil war in peacetime. A 'statute of civil war' must be drawn up which would take two factors closely into account: first, armed invasion from without and civil war within, and secondly, constant reference to Leninism, which according to Trotsky determined the political circumstances of the struggle.[191] Even though he was aware that the revolution was in retreat by 1924, he nevertheless urged that the movement should be ready for the coming battles.

While the Eighth Party Congress was in session in March 1919, the formation of the Hungarian Soviet Republic was announced. The Congress erupted in ecstasy and asked Lenin to send its greetings to Budapest, which he gladly did: 'Our Congress is convinced that the time is not far off when Communism will be victorious throughout the world . . . Long live the international Communist Republic!'[192]

Less than a month later came another joyful announcement, this time that a Communist government had come to power in Bavaria under Eugen Leviné, and that it had at once begun carrying out the urgent measures required by the proletarian dictatorship: nationalization of the banks, creation of a Red Army, introduction of the eight-hour day, arming the workers, isolating the bourgeoisie. Lenin's message this time was more in the nature of an instruction: 'have you armed the workers, disarmed the bourgeoisie, doubled and tripled the wages for farm-labourers and navvies, confiscated all paper and all printing presses . . . packed in the Munich bourgeoisie to make room for the immediate rehousing of workers in wealthy apartments . . . taken hostages from among the bourgeoisie . . . mobilized the workers to a man, both for defence and ideological work in the outlying villages?'[193]

Lenin was convinced the European revolution had begun, and he was most concerned that it should occur above all in Germany. As Trotsky was to write: 'Soviet Germany united with Soviet Russia would at once be stronger than all the capitalist countries put together.'[194]

Meanwhile, Comintern emissaries were travelling about Europe and elsewhere, their suitcases stuffed with hard currency and various treasures. Angelica Balabanova, the Secretary of Comintern, recalled that soon after the revolution she was despatched to Stockholm to set up links with left-wing organizations in Europe:

Ships arrived in Stockholm every Saturday. They brought me ... large quantities of money which I deposited in a bank. [My] office did not require such large sums, and the purpose of these transfers was incomprehensible to me ... I felt ill at ease and I took every opportunity to ask Lenin for explanations and instructions ... I received the following letter from Lenin: 'Dear Comrade Balabanova, Excellent, excellent [underlined three times, a habit of Lenin's to lend special emphasis], you are our most capable and deserving collaborator. But I beg you, don't economize. Spend millions, many many millions.'

When eventually Balabanova managed to speak to Lenin, he explained that there had been a misunderstanding. He had taken her to be a good revolutionist, even though not a Bolshevik, and assumed she approved his methods: corruption and slander to undermine opponents and dissenting organizations. She resigned forthwith, but obviously could not go public, which meant the Bolsheviks could continue to use her name.[195]

Lenin meanwhile was sending telegrams to all the places he regarded as hot spots: 'To Bela Kun in Budapest: Please let us know what concrete guarantees you have that the new Hungarian government will really be Communist, and not merely socialist, i.e. composed of social traitors?'[196] In May 1919 he addressed the Hungarian Communists through *Pravda*, warning them that they must 'be firm. If the socialists who joined you yesterday, or the petty bourgeoisie, start to waver, crush their hesitations mercilessly. Shooting is the only legitimate recourse for a coward in war.'[197] These Jacobin injunctions may have terrified the Hungarian and Bavarian Communists more than they encouraged them, but for Lenin the sound of shooting in the cellars of Budapest and on German waste land was a sign that the revolution was being 'confirmed' in those countries.

His declaration to Hungary at the Eighth Party Congress that 'the working class of Russia is hastening to your aid with all the means at its disposal' was no empty gesture. Money and propaganda literature were sent, and there were attempts also to send arms. In May Podvoisky in Kiev informed Lenin that he had begun forming an international division to help Hungary.[198] Lenin at once ordered the urgent despatch of money to assist this initiative.

While units were being prepared for shipment to Hungary, Russia was enduring mayhem, and the army itself was unstable. Excerpts from Cheka reports on the political situation in Ukraine between 1 January and 15 May 1919, in precisely the area from which units would go to Hungary, indicate the degree of chaos reigning there:

Berdichev: Attack on Cheka. Armoury burgled. Vasilkov: Uprising in town. Crushed by armoured train and 300 troops. Shpola: The local garrison is arresting people, searching and slaughtering the population. Kazatin: Red Army men of the 4th Nezhin Regiment have dispersed the Cheka. Oseter: Uprising in village of Novo-Glybovo and Svorota. Crushed by Cheka unit. Four men killed. Starodub: Uprising in village of Vitelin, crushed by unit of 400 men. Twenty killed. Krolevets: Uprising in village of Antonovka. Crushed by Cheka unit. Ten ringleaders shot.

And so on almost endlessly, including occasions where artillery had to be used, and where, as in Gomel, the Soviet authorities were put to flight.[199]

The Bolsheviks hung onto power only by the use of relentless terror, driven by the urge to carry the civil war as fast as possible to other countries. It was their firm conviction that their supporters abroad would only come to power by the use of force and terror. In the Manifesto of the Second Comintern Congress, this was clearly stated: 'The Communist International cannot admit those organizations which, while including the dictatorship of the proletariat in their programmes, continue a policy plainly aimed at the peaceful resolution of the historic crisis.'[200]

In countless speeches, the Bolshevik leaders stressed armed uprising and the need to bring armies over to their side, and they attempted to pursue this policy along the entire periphery of Soviet Russia. As their hopes for Hungary faded, they turned their attention to the East. Trotsky wrote: 'In the European sphere of world politics, our Red Army will turn out to be of rather modest size, both for offensive and defensive purposes . . . The position is quite different if we turn to face the East . . . The road to India might seem more passable and shorter for us at the present moment than the one to Hungary.'[201] He went on to advise that a powerful military base be established in the Urals from which to revolutionize the East. He predicted that 'Asia could become the arena of early uprisings' and therefore the Soviets should prepare for an assault on India via Afghanistan, and he ordered Field Commander Lebedev to deliver 'the necessary military supplies to Afghanistan'.[202]

Meanwhile, it was important not to neglect Persia, which had only recently seemed to be 'going Red'. Fedor Raskolnikov, the regional Red Army commander, had reported to Moscow, on returning from Enzel, that the situation in Persia was indescribable: 'The entire people greeted us with extraordinary enthusiasm. At first, red flags were to be seen in only a few places, but now the whole town is covered with them. The Persian Cossacks have told us they are at our disposal. I arrested the Russian officer in charge of them and appointed one of our own people in his place ... I request your instructions concerning future policy in Persia. Should I consider myself at liberty to move deeper into Persia if a revolution takes place and a new government requests help from us?'[203]

The Persian affair soon came to a standstill. Efforts were made to save the revolution there. Central Committee emissary Abukov wrote asking for urgent help to be sent to Moscow's ally, Mirza Kuchuk: 'Help is needed in arms, gold, silver ... So far Kuchuk is in control of only two towns ... Raskolnikov has promised him official recognition ... We await proper help ...'[204]

Proposals were pouring in about where to go next: revolutionary action was urged in Korea, China and India. In August 1919 the Chairman of the Kalmyk Executive Committee, Chapchaev, suggested sending armed units to India 'from the other side', i.e. through Mongolia and Tibet. Money and gold would be needed, and the units should also take arms to distribute to the local population. As cover, they should disguise themselves as a scientific expedition. Lenin immediately ordered that concrete measures be undertaken to carry out these suggestions.[205]

Lenin was more cautious with a Korean delegation that requested an audience. He told Comintern leader Matyas Rakosi – a refugee from the already defeated Hungarian Soviet – to receive the delegation and report back.[206] The Koreans wanted Moscow to give direct aid to them in their struggle against the Japanese. Chicherin was opposed: 'We shall not throw down a challenge to the Japanese. Of course, we bear a grudge against them; of course, we can and should give covert aid to the Korean partisans. But there should be no open, still less, demonstrative action on our part.' Lenin noted on the report: 'Comrade Molotov, I agree with Chicherin completely. No open, still less, demonstrative action. More in secret. Give this instruction as from the Central Committee.'[207]

As Russia writhed in starvation, civil war and disease, millions of gold roubles were disappearing into the sands of the world revolution. As we have seen, much of it went by haphazard channels, while Lenin received equally casual reports on the sale of valuables. It was not until September 1921 that the Politburo created an ECCI budget commission, comprising Zinoviev, Solts and Molotov, with Mikhailov as Molotov's deputy.

Lenin took a close personal interest in the financing of organizations and individuals abroad. In November 1921 P.I. Stuchka wrote asking for his help in fixing the budget for the Latvian Communist Party, 'as the issue has been dragging on since 1 August and our comrades are not getting anything, except a refusal.' Lenin noted: 'Comrade Molotov, This red tape is shameful. Prepare the question for Thursday's meeting of the Politburo.'[208]

An excerpt from the Comintern budget commission's meeting of March 1922 gives an idea of its workings:

1 Budget for the German CP: Brandler, Popov, Humbert-Droz and Pyatnitsky voted for a grant for 1922 of 446,592 gold roubles (42,872.832 German marks); Solts and Molotov voted 400,000 gold roubles.

2 Budget for French CP: unanimous vote for a grant of 100,000 gold roubles (638,000 French francs).

3 Budget for Italian CP: 360,842 gold roubles or 4,306,000 lire.

4 Budget for Czechoslovak CP: (Humbert-Droz having left) Popov, Brandler and Pyatnitsky in favour of 250,000 gold roubles (7,910,000 Czech crowns), Solts and Mikhailov for 200,000.

5 Budget for English CP: unanimous vote for 200,000 gold roubles.[209]

The list goes on.

Lenin and the Bolsheviks supported all the parties that accepted the

Comintern's programme and conditions. Regular payments topped up the coffers of the Communist Parties of the USA, Poland, Austria, Switzerland, Sweden, Hungary, Yugoslavia, Romania, Luxemburg, Holland, Greece, Turkey, Persia, India, China, Korea, Japan, Germany, Belgium, Spain, Argentina, Italy, South Africa, Estonia, Latvia, Lithuania, Finland, Norway and elsewhere. The Comintern commission also distributed large sums to international youth organizations, Communist trade unions, publishing houses and other bodies, with the most frequent contributions going to Germany. Fixed budgets were supplemented by extra payments, as Moscow on the whole satisfied the constant flood of requests. The money committed by the session cited above alone amounted to some 5,536,400 gold roubles, a huge sum. According to the available data, in that year the Politburo spent no more than a third of that sum on feeding the starving people of Russia – and the river of gold for Comintern, be it noted, would continue to flow for a long time to come. Moscow was to be especially generous in the post-war period, paying out huge amounts, of which the following list is only a small part (all figures in US dollars): in 1945, to Bulgaria (Kostov) – $100,000; in 1946, to China (Chou En-lai) – $50,000; to Romania (Gheorgiu Dej) – $500,000; in 1947, to Greece (Zachariades) – $100,000; in 1948, to France (Thorez) -$258,350; to Italy (Secchia) – $40,000; to Holland (Groot) – $50,000; to Greece (Zachariades) – $100,000.[210]

From the revolution onwards it became common practice for Soviet diplomats, representatives of various kinds and 'plenipotentiaries' to demand from the Kremlin more and more funds to revolutionize the political process abroad and to consolidate Soviet Russia's position in different countries. In January 1920, for instance, Ioffe, who had aspired to manage the revolutionary process in Germany in 1919, wrote to Chicherin complaining of the waste: 'Having overpaid Estonia by 15 million, we'll send the money back extremely quickly.' He reminded Chicherin that 'when Kolchak carried off more than 800 million of our gold roubles, we hardly winced ... I saw the way our agents in Lithuania and Belorussia are throwing away millions . . .'[211]

In April 1922, the Politburo approved Comintern's budget, and the order signed by Stalin was duly sent to the Finance Commissariat for action.[212] As we have seen, however, the official budget was only a part of total expenditure, as constant requests for further payments were met out of the 'reserve fund', the Politburo fund and the OGPU's budget. Thus, Karakhan reported to Stalin in April 1922, the very month when the budget had been fixed, that on behalf of the Foreign Commissariat he had transferred two payments of 600,000 gold roubles and four million roubles in tsarist notes to the Koreans, to help them establish printing presses in Shanghai and Peking, and to help with their underground work against the Japanese in Korea, including organizing for an armed uprising.[213] (For several years, the Politburo continued to use tsarist paper money for its secret operations in the East.)

Lenin waited impatiently for some result to come from all these financial inputs, but in vain. Soon after the budget commission was formed, report after report began to come in of corruption, embezzlement and the disappearance of large sums of Comintern money. Safarov reported to Stalin that money and valuables were being handed over 'to irresponsible people from different groups', and cited the case of 200,000 gold roubles having been given to a certain Jun Hu-nam and Lee Ko-chi to support the national movement in Korea, whereas the money was in fact used to keep the squabbles alive among the various Korean émigré organizations in Manchuria.[214]

Concerned to tighten up the organization, Stalin wrote a personal note to Zinoviev asking him to explain just what 'this Frankfurt fund' in Germany was. Who was financing it? What for? Zinoviev, who did not know, promised to find out when Pyatnitsky and Fotieva turned up.[215] It transpired that Comintern's financial affairs in Germany were being handled by one James (Yakov) Reich, known in the Party as 'Comrade Thomas', into whose hands Moscow was placing vast sums. For the German Communist Party's armed uprising of February 1921 alone, some 620,000 gold roubles, in currency and valuables, was transmitted. And for the whole of 1921 Comrade Thomas disbursed 1.22 million gold roubles in Germany, of which he retained some 500,000 under his control in the 'Frankfurt fund'.

When Pyatnitsky looked into Comintern's finances, the mysterious Comrade Thomas could not account for several million marks.[216] A female Comintern operative who worked in Thomas's organization later recalled: 'The money was usually kept at Comrade Thomas's apartment. It was in trunks and suitcases, cupboards and occasionally in thick files, left lying on his bookshelves or behind books. The money was doled out in our apartments late at night in cardboard boxes weighing as much as ten to fifteen kilogrammes each.'[217] When a commission, established by Stalin and headed by Krestinsky, was unable to find any receipts for some very large sums, it was decided that 'no further matters connected with financial operations should be entrusted to Comrade Thomas'.[218] It later transpired that 'Comrade' Thomas was not even a member of the Communist Party, but was simply someone who had happened to find himself working in Comintern's financial organization in a rather important position.

At the end of the year, a Politburo commission consisting of Trotsky, Kuybyshev, Pyatnitsky and Sokolnikov, requested a further 2,196,500 gold roubles for 'additional subsidies to parties'. While he was constantly demanding executions for saboteurs, speculators and black marketeers, Lenin was utterly incapable of bringing order to the financial operations of his own organization. He simply scattered money abroad, in the vain hope that it would water the seeds of his ideas. Yet in November 1921 he published an article, entitled 'On the Importance of Gold', in which he could write: 'The RSFSR must look after its gold, it must sell it dearer and buy goods cheaper with it.'[219] This was not the first time Lenin said one thing and did another.

Only once, it seems, did Lenin explode when told of the loss of a large amount of Comintern money. He wrote a 'draft of a secret Central Committee letter' which, among other things, said: 'There is no doubt that the financial aid Comintern gives to the Communist Parties of bourgeois countries, while of course perfectly legitimate and necessary, sometimes leads to disgraceful conduct and disgusting abuse.' He then listed the Party punishments for the robbery, conceal-ment and appropriation of Comintern money, ranging from a repri-mand to removal from post, expulsion from the Party and often arrest – and demanded detailed accounts of 'every kopek spent'.[220] A naive hope, indeed.

Comintern's expenses came under more strict control during Stalin's rule, and their purposes were more precisely defined. For instance, the French writer Henri Barbusse came to Moscow and declared that he intended writing a book on Stalin. Naturally, Moscow wanted to encourage him, and an 'advance' of 40,000 francs was paid.[221] This was not a large sum, but Barbusse would be much more lavishly 'encouraged' when the book appeared in 1936. When Georgy Dimitrov, Comintern's last general secretary from 1935 to 1943, wanted to fix the budget, he had to go to Stalin, who was by then disillusioned with Comintern and was prepared to give only enough to maintain the organization. Foreign parties were now subsidized exclusively through the NKVD, bypassing Comintern. Thus, while ECCI's budget for 1937 was submitted to Stalin – 12,048,028 in hard (unspecified) currency and 18,658,762 Soviet roubles – the NKVD's expenses on Comintern were being processed under special heads, for what was at stake was no longer a Party affair, but espionage and terrorism.[222] Comintern was now more useful to the NKVD as a human resource for diversionary operations in capitalist countries than it was to the Communist movement. International Communism, to be sure, remained a lever of Soviet foreign policy, but it was a weak lever, since everyone knew what was going on behind the scenes.

When it became clear that the world revolution was not immediately going to follow the Russian revolution, the Bolsheviks started looking for new allies. Unexpectedly, a tempting situation presented itself. In January 1922 the leaders of the Socialist International – known as the Two-and-a-Half, i.e. neither the old Second Socialist nor Third Communist International – proposed holding an international congress of all three Internationals, with the aim of coordinating the joint struggle of the working class against international reaction. The Politburo discussed the issue at a long session, during which Lenin expressed the hope that they would manage to exert their influence on the other two organizations. The leaders of the Second International, however, with their long and often bitter experience of the Bolsheviks and their leader, knew perfectly well how things would go.

Lenin did not hide his intentions: 'If there are still people . . . who don't understand that the tactics of a united front will help us overthrow the leaders of both . . . Internationals, then they need to attend more popular lectures and discussions.'[223]

At a joint conference, the leaders of the non-Bolshevik Internationals demanded the legalization of the Menshevik Party in Russia, an end to the execution of SRs, and so on. A commission was formed to convene the congress, but it met only once. Lenin was sharply critical of the 'indulgence' shown by the Comintern delegation, led by Radek, and described the agreements as 'political concessions to the international bourgeoisie'. Western social democrats realized that for Lenin the term 'cooperation' meant nothing other than subordination to Comintern, and the whole initiative fizzled out.

Both the West and the East had long known what Comintern stood for, and much had been said and written about it. On 26 April 1928, therefore, Stalin and the Politburo resolved that visible signs of the direct dependence of Comintern organizations on Soviet state organs must be avoided at all costs. Bukharin and Pyatnitsky were instructed to devise a covert way of making it seem that money paid to foreign parties came not from Moscow, and not through Russian hands, but from Berlin (Zapburo – Western Bureau) and Irkutsk (Vostburo – Eastern Bureau), 'in any case via foreign comrades'. This was soon taken in hand by the NKVD, though hardly anyone was deluded, but it meant that the NKVD (and its military intelligence arm) became ever more 'organically' integrated into the fabric of Comintern.

One of the most notorious such cases was that of Richard Sorge. Born in 1895 in Baku on the Caspian Sea to a German father and a Russian mother, Sorge grew up in Germany, served in the German army in the First World War and, along with numerous other refugees from the failed Communist revolutions of Central and Eastern Europe, became a Comintern operative in Moscow in the 1920s. In 1929 he was transferred to Soviet military intelligence and sent abroad as a journalist. From Shanghai between 1929 and 1932, and then from Tokyo between 1933 until his arrest by the Japanese in October 1941, he sent highly valuable reports back to his masters in Moscow. Yet, like so many competent and audacious operatives, whether working for Comintern, the NKVD or military intelligence abroad, Sorge became enmeshed in the web of murderous intrigue that was being woven in Moscow in the middle of the 1930s.

In the process of building up a case against Bukharin and Radek, and to bring down Jan Berzin, the former head of military intelligence, and Pyatnitsky, the head of the Communist Trade Union International, a former military intelligence agent called Valin-Gailis was arrested in the summer of 1937. In his deposition of 19 August 1937 he was made to say that Sorge was 'undoubtedly a German or German–Japanese agent'. According to Valin's confession, Stalin had already in 1936 seen through Sorge and had cautioned that he was sending

German disinformation to Moscow. Valin described much of Sorge's information as routine material that could have been gleaned from the daily press. A drunk and a womanizer, in Valin's words, Sorge was the boon companion of Colonel Ott, head of German intelligence in Tokyo, in whose company he blabbed too much. As a result of Sorge's provocative behaviour, it was claimed that Berzin had to close the Tokyo agency, thus terminating a most valuable source of foreign intelligence.[224] In this way, Berzin could be accused of sabotage by means of a conspiracy with one of his chief agents.

Despite the fact that all the main targets of the conspiracy were liquidated in 1938, Sorge himself managed to remain in Tokyo and to continue sending his reports. In January, March and May 1941 he reported to Stalin that Hitler was preparing to invade the USSR, and then on 15 June 1941 gave the precise date. Whether Stalin ignored his warnings because he regarded him as a tainted source, or because they did not conform to his own agenda, is a question that need not detain us. In any event, Sorge and his entire network were arrested in Tokyo in October 1941 and tried in 1942. Sorge and one other were sentenced to death, ironically on charges of spying for Comintern, and the sentence was duly carried out by hanging, again ironically, on 7 November 1944, the anniversary of the Bolshevik revolution. Sorge's wife was arrested by the NKVD in September 1942 in Moscow and exiled for five years to Krasnoyarsk in Siberia, also as a spy. On 28 May 1943 she died, allegedly of a brain haemorrhage, at the age of thirty-eight.[225]

Soon after Lenin's death, Comintern had been turned into an obedient and expeditious adjunct of the special services. For instance, when it was necessary to remove Zinoviev, Stalin gave the order to 'organize support'. At once, statements of approval of the Central Committee's recall of Zinoviev as chairman of Comintern, and the liquidation of his post, began pouring in from the 'independent Communist parties'. The first to respond was the faithful Communist Party of Germany, which declared that it 'unreservedly supports the Central Committee Plenum's order and calls upon the Party mass to struggle fiercely against the new opposition . . . It regards Comrade Zinoviev's deviation from Leninism as incompatible with his further remaining at the head of the International.'[226] In November 1926 Zinoviev was relieved of his post, which once upon a time he used to think of secretly as the presidency of the World Socialist Federation. Stalin found him a new job as 'a member of the presidium of Gosplan to watch over the activity of the cultural administration commissariats'.[227]

By the eve of the war Comintern was vegetating, as Stalin had become progressively more doubtful about its potential, and only the NKVD still derived some benefit from it as a pool of new recruits for foreign intelligence. Dimitrov was reduced to begging tearfully for funds to maintain the apparatus. In 1937 he had confirmed a budget of twenty-one million roubles and 3.5 million gold roubles in hard currency, but in 1938 the budget was reduced to a third of that sum.[228] In January 1924, while Lenin was still just alive, the allocation had been more than a hundred times this. Stalin became increasingly cool towards Comintern, until finally and with little regret he disbanded Lenin's brainchild in 1943.

Stalin had changed his view of the world revolution. The aim of turning the planet red was still in place, but the methods for achieving it needed to be reviewed. When the time came to kill it off, Comintern's disappearance was barely noticed. On 31 October 1941, Dimitrov wrote to Stalin:

> Dear Comrade Stalin,
> With the transfer of ECCI to Ufa [in the Urals], a number of questions relating to the legal position of our institution arise. Is it wise, given the present situation, for everything to be done under the flag of Comintern, or wouldn't it be better if we went on existing in Ufa as a different organization? I personally think there is no need at present to over-emphasize Comintern. It would be better to do all the work under the name of a different firm, for instance, 'The Institute for the Study of International Questions' . . .[229]

By now 'the international party of proletarian revolt and the proletarian dictatorship' had become a pale shadow of Lenin's grandiose idea, and was in fact nothing more than Stalin's pawn. Before Dimitrov could fly 'for a couple of days . . . to Ufa and Kuybyshev to my organization', he had to beg humbly for Stalin's permission.[230]

To be sure, in 1947 Stalin would try once more to resurrect Comintern as Cominform (Communist Information Bureau), but that, too, proved a fruitless exercise. He had even gone as far as to propose creating the post of General Secretary of Cominform and offering it to Palmiro Togliatti, the Italian Communist leader. The response was an unexpected refusal, polite but firm:

> Dear Comrade Stalin,
>
> I have spent a long time considering the offer of the post of General Secretary of Cominform. It is very hard for me to express an opinion which does not coincide with your own. But it seems to me that the Italian Communist Party cannot agree to the proposal . . .

Togliatti then listed seven points, intended to provide decent motives for his refusal.[231] What he omitted to give, however, was the main reason: namely, that he had stopped believing in Lenin's Utopian world revolution years before. No one had spoken of it aloud for a long time. It had simply become bad form to do so.

It is extremely doubtful if even Stalin still believed in the success of the world revolution. Of all the leaders of the October revolution, only Trotsky could still claim (six months before he was murdered in 1940): 'My faith in the Communist future of mankind is no less fervent, and is even stronger than during my youth.'[232]

Stalin was holding to a different course. Step by step, tearing away one country after another from the old world, using plots and violence, subtle calculation and cunning, he exploited the consequences of the Second World War to consolidate his totalitarian dictatorship. He continued to swear by Lenin, who had been of such enormous value to him for over thirty years, but he was well aware that Lenin's plan openly to storm the capitalist citadel had been Utopian. The 'first Leninist' preferred the tactics of the long siege. He was also more cautious than Lenin about making predictions, especially about when the Russian people would see Communism in their country.

# 7

## *The Mausoleum of Leninism*

During an evening of reminiscences on 23 April 1924, Kamenev, Trotsky and Radek spoke with what now seems rare frankness, and at a time when there was as yet no cult of Lenin.

Radek, one of the most original and amusing characters among the leadership, and an alleged source of many jokes, said that Lenin was 'the first man who believed in what we wrote, not as something that would happen in a hundred years, but as a concrete thing'. Lenin's greatness, he went on, lay in the fact that he was able 'to overcome all wavering and carry the Party into the struggle for power'. As an example of this greatness, he cited a speech of 1921 in which the leader declared that War Communism had been a mistake.

I rang him and told him I disagreed with this judgment. He invited me over and said: '. . . who told you a historian has to establish the truth? The Party conducted its particular policy [War Communism] for three years, now it looks on the NEP as a sin. You can write a hundred theoretical articles, saying it is not a sin, but in your heart you're telling yourself it is a "sin". You have to say "to hell with it", and say it was a stupidity, and then a year later you'll write historical pamphlets proving that [NEP] was a policy of genius'.[1]

A more blatantly cynical attitude to politics would be hard to imagine, but there was nothing new about it: Lenin's cynicism was well known to his comrades before the October revolution. What is interesting is that they regarded his pragmatism as a sign of his 'greatness'. It was probably this characteristic that Potresov had in mind when he spoke of 'Lenin's diabolical genius'; and when Pavel Axelrod was asked, in 1910 at the Congress of the Socialist International, how one

Lev Kamenev and his wife, the sister of Trotsky, with American relief officials at a soup kitchen in the famine-stricken Volga region in November 1921.

A starving family of Chuvash refugees outside the town of Samara, 1921.

Famine refugees in a camp in the Volga region, 1921.

*Above left*: Lenin and army chief Kliment Voroshilov among Red Army soldiers who had just taken part in crushing the Kronstadt revolt, 22 March 1921. The island fortress of Kronstadt, which had been in the vanguard of Bolshevik support in 1917, had by 1921 become disillusioned and rose in armed revolt, demanding a broad-based socialist government. Fifty thousand Red Army troops crushed the rebellion, causing heavy casualties.

*Above right*: Lenin being sketched for a painting by I. Brodsky at the Third Comintern Congress, June–July 1921.

*Below*: Lenin observing the testing of the first electric-driven plough, Moscow, 1921.

*Above*: The 'triumvirate' of Stalin, Kamenev and Zinoviev in Moscow in the early 1920s, with Rykov (next to Stalin).

*Left*: Lenin and Stalin at Gorki, Lenin's country retreat. This photograph has been the subject of speculation that Stalin had it 'doctored' to reflect his intimacy with the leader. The original negative, held in the archives, shows that it was taken by Lenin's sister Maria, and is genuine.

Lenin and Krupskaya with Lenin's sister Anna Yelizarova, her son Viktor, and the daughter of a local worker, Gorki, August–September 1922.

Lenin in early August 1922.

Lenin and Krupskaya motoring around
Gorki with their chauffeur, P.S. Kosmachev,
and bodyguard, P.P. Pokaln,
August–September 1922.

Lenin and Krupskaya at Gorki with their
telescope, August–September 1922.

Lenin in the park at Gorki, accompanied by
P.P. and M.M. Pokaln, summer 1923.

Lenin at Gorki in July–August 1923, showing
clear signs of a sharp deterioration in his
condition since the previous summer. His
sister Maria is with him. The male figure
is unidentified, possibly a physician.

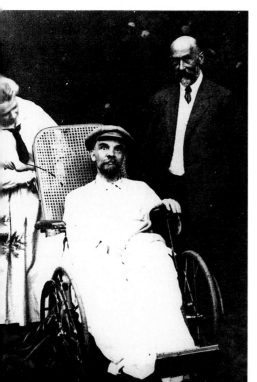

Lenin in the summer of 1923. Among the last pictures taken of him.

Lying in state, January 1924.

Lying in state. At the catafalque are secret police chief Felix Dzerzhinsky (third from left) and Voroshilov (in army uniform).

A demonstration of Leninists in Moscow, 1992.

A protest against the handing-over of the Lenin Museum to the Moscow City Council, 1993.

man could possibly cause all the splits and scandals in the Party, he replied that Lenin thought about nothing but revolution, day and night, and even dreamt about it: such a man was impossible to have dealings with.

Most significantly, Lenin was able to transmit his fanatical credo to a vast number of people. He succeeded, despite the delusionary nature of the idea. The delusion became reality, it materialized as the Soviet state, as a new way of life and new ideological institutions. Leninism, a term first used by Martov in 1904,[2] displayed remarkable durability. As for the society he set out to build, he managed to lay only the foundations of the great new edifice before he was struck down by illness. To what extent did this illness affect his judgment and his functioning, especially in 1921 and 1922?

## The Regime and the Illness

In December 1935 the head of the Kremlin medical administration, Khodorovsky, discovered in a secret archive the notes of the neurologist, the late Professor Kramer, who had treated Lenin. Khodorovsky naturally informed the authorities at once, but they had no intention of bringing the long-buried past to light, and consigned Kramer's notes to the secret archives of the Central Committee, where they remained untouched for more than fifty years.

Kramer had written that Lenin's terminal illness 'lasted all in all about two and a half years, and its general characteristics harboured signs that all the neurologists, whether Russian or foreign, dwelt on as something that did not conform to conventional disease of the nervous system'.[3] Lenin was seriously ill as early as the second half of 1921, yet he was working as hard as ever, and was under as great a strain as before. His schedule on one day, 21 June 1921, may serve as a good example. At 11 a.m. he arrived by car from Gorki and went straight to a meeting of the Politburo, where the agenda included a purge of the Party, the famine, the Third Congress of Comintern, taxes, the arrival of a US Senator, the forthcoming Moscow Party conference, a Chinese government proposal for the handing over of White Guards, the question of British representation in Petrograd, confirmation of Viktor Kopp as Russia's envoy in Berlin, and more. The Politburo usually dealt with between twenty and forty such items. Lenin listened more than he spoke, and also spent much of the time signing a pile of Sovnarkom and Party papers.

In the interval before the evening session, which began at six p.m., he had been engaged in his favourite occupation: writing or dictating notes. That day he wrote to at least a dozen government officials on matters ranging from food procurement in the North Caucasus to foreign trade, land use and educational policy; he read letters and cables, signed financial papers, mandates and permits, made numerous telephone calls, and so on. In the evening he chaired the Sovnarkom, which dealt with several dozen items. There he also wrote notes, signed documents, interrupted long-winded speakers, called for quiet, and showed signs of irritation if someone left the room or re-entered.

The stress, especially on someone who only in his forty-eighth year had discovered the meaning of state service, was enormous. Lenin's health suffered from the strain caused by having constantly to shift his attention from economic to political questions, from Party to diplomatic concerns and the endless receiving of visitors, as well as having to think about a mass of trivial daily affairs, dubbed 'vermicelli' by those inundated by them, or a tangle of incoherent problems. From having been an émigré spectator of Russian public life, and its sternest critic, he was now at the epicentre of the upheavals caused by his own policies.

His nervous system was seriously overloaded, and it had probably never been very strong. Lenin had always been excitable, losing his head and going pale when hearing of dramatic events or some new danger. Radek recalled that, when their train crossed the Swedish frontier in April 1917 and soldiers entered the compartment, 'Ilyich began to talk to them about the war, and he went horribly white'.[4] The sound of the violin put his nerves on edge, and he couldn't stand extraneous noise or bustle. Lydia Fotieva recalled that in July 1921, when his apartment in the Kremlin was being repaired, he ordered that the partition walls between the rooms be made '*absolutely* soundproof, and the floors absolutely free of squeaks'. People conversing during a meeting infuriated him.

Lenin complained about his nerves quite often. In February 1917 he wrote to his sister Maria: 'I can hardly do any work at all because of my desperately bad nerves.'[5] He had evidently known for a long time that he suffered from some sort of nervous condition, as there are among his papers the addresses of specialists in nervous disorders whom he seems to have consulted in Stuttgart in 1900.[6] When he got excited he would work himself up into such a state of bellicosity that he would be ready to take extreme, even cruel measures. During the 1905 revolution, in a state of heightened excitement, he urged the revolutionaries to adopt tactics which most people would regard as abnormal and terrible: to fight against the Cossacks, he urged the use of knives, knuckledusters, sticks, paraffin-soaked rags, nails, slabs of gun-cotton, boiling water, stones and acid 'to throw over the police'. He called for the Black Hundreds to be beaten up and killed, for Cossacks who had been accidentally separated from their troop to be attacked, and so on.[7] The range of savage tactics is so broad and carefully thought out that it is hard to believe it emanated from an educated man, a writer and journalist. Such counsels of cruelty Lenin normally issued at moments of mental stress, nervous excitement or in extreme circumstances. At such times his powerful mind became simply possessed by revolutionary remorselessness.

A few years of Bolshevik power, with its attendant pressures, and Lenin's nervous vulnerability rose to the surface. It was especially noticeable after his first stroke, in May 1922, when Professor Kramer noted: 'the basis of his illness is actually not only the overstrain of the brain, but also severe disorder of the blood vessels in the brain'.[8] Disorder of the brain's blood supply is closely associated with mental dysfunction, which explains why most of the physicians who attended Lenin in 1922 and 1923 were psychiatrists and neurologists. According to the medical literature, mental illness, when caused by deterioration of the arteries of the brain, manifests itself as persistent headaches, irritability, anxiety, depression, fixed ideas. Lenin displayed all of these symptoms.

It is unlikely that we shall ever be able to establish the precise effect or importance of Lenin's illness on his actions when in power. He was perfectly capable of issuing cruel orders before the onset of his illness, notably in 1918. Nevertheless, those decisions, too, were taken at a time of heightened nervous tension: the greater the stress, the more radical and harsh the decisions. It seems clear that vast, unmonitored, unbounded power exacerbated the pathological tendencies in his mind.

We have seen that it was in August and September 1922 that Lenin initiated the expulsion of the Russian intelligentsia. The notion of deporting – in effect extinguishing – the flower of Russian culture could have occurred only to a sick or callous person. Yet only a month or two before those events, with Krupskaya's help, the sick Lenin was re-learning how to write, trying to solve elementary arithmetical problems and write the simplest dictations. He was covering pages with barely legible, crippled handwriting.[9] After his stroke in May he was having serious lapses of memory and reacting slowly to events. He was absent-minded: 'He is unable,' Professor Kramer noted, 'to perform the simplest arithmetical functions, and he has lost the ability to recall even a few short phrases, while retaining his intellect in full.'[10]

There are certainly grounds for doubting the neurologist's assertion that Lenin had retained his intellect in full. His sister Maria recalled that when on 30 May 'the doctors asked him to multiply 12 by 7 and he could not do it, he was very depressed. But then his old stubbornness reasserted itself. When the doctors had gone, he struggled for three hours over the problem and solved it by addition instead ($12 + 12 = 24$, $24 + 12 = 36$ and so on)'.[11] Yet within a month Lenin was taking such momentous decisions as the expulsion of the intelligentsia, approving 'extra-judicial measures of the GPU, including executions',[12] and determining the tactics and strategy of Comintern.

Lenin was dangerously ill. The Politburo summoned physicians from abroad. Stalin sent instructions to the Soviet Ambassador in Berlin, Nikolai Krestinsky: 'Take all necessary measures to persuade the German government to allow the physicians Foerster and Klemperer to leave for Moscow for the summer ... Give Foerster 50,000 gold roubles (Klemperer will receive his in Moscow). They can bring their families, they'll be given the best conditions in Moscow.'[13] Once there, these doctors plagued Lenin with their methodical ways. He wrote to Stalin: 'I humbly request that you liberate me from Klemperer ... I earnestly beg you to deliver me from Foerster. I'm more than happy with my own doctors, Kramer and Kozhevnikov.'[14] His comrades, however, in their notes to each other on the matter, were not inclined to take any notice. Zinoviev suggested 'leaving the Germans alone and reassuring Ilyich by telling him that a new examination is planned of all eighty comrades previously examined by the Germans'. The Politburo agreed to this proposal.[15]

Lenin was adamant that he be kept informed about political affairs. He wrote to Stalin:

The doctors have apparently created a legend which cannot be left unrefuted. They lost their heads when I had a serious attack on Friday and they have committed a particular stupidity: they tried to forbid 'political' meetings (having little idea of what that means). I was *extremely* annoyed and sent them packing. Kamenev came to see me on Thursday. We had a lively political conversation. I had a wonderful sleep and feel marvellous. On Friday came the paralysis. I ask you urgently, in case the illness gets worse and I *don't have time* to say it. Only idiots are capable of blaming political discussions. If I sometimes get agitated, it's because of the *lack* of timely and competent conversation. I hope you understand and you'll get rid of the idiotic German professor and company. You must come and tell me about the Central Committee plenum, or send one of the participants . . .[16]

For Lenin, life was politics and politics was life.

Lenin was ill, yet there was no serious call for him to lay down the burden of office and resign. In the course of conversation in the summer of 1922 he did mention on several occasions that if he could not continue in political life, he would try agriculture. His sister Maria recalled that he talked about cultivating mushrooms and breeding rabbits, but that he was obviously not serious.

As much as the physical effects of the illness itself, being cut off from current affairs caused Lenin profound bitterness and constant irritation. He was depressed by his inactivity, and he realised that the greater his comrades' concern for his well-being, the more they distanced him from government, and consequently the more exasperated he became. Power had always been the meaning of life for him, and, however ill he might be, he was not about to give it up.

He did not, however, conceive of power in personal terms, but as something much broader than an individual's participation in government. Ioffe once wrote to him, suggesting that he personified the Central Committee. Lenin replied in emphatic terms: 'You're wrong when you say (more than once) that "the Central Committee – that's me," [a variation of "l'état, c'est moi"]. That could only have been written in a state of great nervous agitation and exhaustion.'[17] Ioffe's remark was intended to indicate Lenin's huge personal influence, and that, as Chairman of the Sovnarkom and the Council of Labour and Defence, and a member of the Politburo, his style of leadership made a marked impression on those around him. He was, in the words of V.S. Voitinsky, 'surrounded by an atmosphere of unconditional submission', and his comrades looked at the world 'with the eyes of Ilyich'.[18]

Lenin was depressed by his constant headaches, and was pessimistic about his chances of recovery. On 14 June 1922, after a brief spasm of the blood vessels in his head, he told Kozhevnikov: 'So, that's it. It'll be a stroke.' At the beginning of the winter of 1923, again following a spasm lasting several minutes, he told Kramer and Kozhevnikov: 'So, one day I'll have a stroke, just as a peasant once told me I would many years ago. "As for you, Ilyich," he said, "you'll die of a stroke." When I asked why he thought so, he replied: "It's that terribly short neck of yours."' Although Lenin tried to treat it as a joke, it seemed he feared the peasant might be right.[19]

He was oppressed by forebodings, and could not help noticing that he was losing the intellectual capacity to work as he once did. He summoned Professor Dorshkevich and told him he was suffering from insomnia and a lack of 'mental quiet'. Dorshkevich observed: 'first, a mass of extremely serious neurasthenic phenomena, depriving him totally of the possibility of working as he used to, and, secondly, a number of obsessions which cause the patient much anxiety.' 'Doesn't all that suggest madness?' Lenin asked. Dorshkevich replied: 'Obsessions are difficult for the patient to bear, but they never involve mental disorder.'[20]

The many doctors who attended Lenin after 1921 began to record a history of his illness from 29 May 1922. Kozhevnikov, a very perceptive physician, kept a record for a year; Professor Kramer maintained a diary from 6 May to 4 July 1923, while Professor Osipov, former head of psychiatry at the St Petersburg Army Medical Academy, and one of the leading specialists in the field, recorded the final and fatal phase of the illness.

As these records show, even when Lenin had been incapacitated by a second stroke, all his thoughts were of the Politburo, the Sovnarkom, the Kremlin. He could not believe that the power he had so unexpectedly and so recently acquired was now passing into other hands because of his illness. He fought back, and kept hoping to return to the summit. Notes relating to the period from 3 October 1922, a period of relative recovery, to the second stroke in December of that year, are illustrative. The dates indicate short periods of time, rather than a single day.

*10 October*: Kozhevnikov and Kramer chatted with Lenin after an evening session at the Sovnarkom. 'The toothache had nearly gone, but his nerves have been shattered by the earlier illness and he kept wanting to weep, tears were welling up in his eyes, but Vladimir Ilyich just managed to suppress them; he did not cry once.'

*29 October*: The doctors were at Kamenev's, where Stalin and Zinoviev were also present. 'Kamenev reported that at the last session of the Sovnarkom Vladimir Ilyich had criticized a point in a draft law, then did not notice that he had begun reading the same page again, though a different point, and was criticizing it again without realizing that this point had a completely different content.'

*31 October*: At 12 noon Lenin spoke at the VTsIK, his first appearance in public since the stroke in May. 'He spoke firmly in a loud voice, he was calm and did not go wrong once ... At home he listened to music, the piano, and was not upset, though he couldn't listen to the violin, as it has too great an effect on him.'

*13 November*: 'Vladimir Ilyich spoke at the plenum of the Comintern Congress and gave a speech in German lasting one hour. He spoke fluently, without faltering, and did not lose his place ... After his speech he told Doctor Kozhevnikov that at one place he forgot what he'd said and what he still had to say ...' He reported that the day before he had had 'a very brief paralysis in the right leg'.

In his speech at the Comintern Congress, Lenin had made a frank confession: 'We have committed and will still commit a vast number of stupidities. No one can see this better and more plainly than I.' After a succession of international defeats, he had obviously cooled towards the world revolution. He described its prospects as 'favourable', but did not dwell on it. At the end of his speech he made some cautious remarks about Italian fascism, which might perform 'great service' by showing the people that 'their country is not yet secure from the Black Hundreds'.[21] Nothing in the speech itself indicated that it had been written and delivered by a sick man. But it cost Lenin an enormous effort and the utmost strain, and at the end of it he was soaked in perspiration. The doctors continued their observations and treatment. The Journal of the Duty Physician continues:

*25 November*: Lenin was walking along the corridor when his legs went into spasm. He fell down. He got up with difficulty. After consultation with the doctors it was decided he should not take part in the general meetings of the Congress and should rest for an entire week.

*12 December*: He was back in his Kremlin office, where he saw Rykov, Kamenev, Tsyurupa, Dzerzhinsky and Stomonyanov. He gave his approval by telephone for the expulsion abroad of several 'anti-Soviet elements'. A normal working day.

*13 December*: 'Doctor Kozhevnikov and Professor Kramer visited Vladimir Ilyich ... he is having paralytic attacks every day. This morning he had a small paralysis in bed, and another in the hip-bath ... Vladimir Ilyich is upset and worried by the deterioration in his condition.'

*16 December*: 'His condition has worsened. He can write with difficulty, but what he writes is illegible, the letters overlapping each other. For thirty-five minutes neither the right hand nor right leg were capable of any movement. He could not touch the tip of his nose with the tip of his finger.[22]

Almost every day the doctors were recording: 'he became agitated towards evening', 'his mood is worse', 'his mood is bad', and so on. The isolation from political life was a torment, Lenin could no longer write as he used to, he was being shown practically no documents or papers to sign, even though he did attend a few more sessions of the Sovnarkom, the Politburo and some other meetings. Together, his doctors and his Party comrades protected him from the turmoil of life in Russia by wrapping him in cotton wool. The Politburo had already decided, on 20 July 1922, that 'Comrade Lenin should have absolutely no meetings' without its permission.[23] Stalin was entrusted with the task of ensuring this rule was followed. After Lenin's improvement in October, however, there were lapses, and people started visiting him again. It seemed he was re-entering the fray. But his mood was uneasy. He was aware of how much he had deteriorated.

Lenin was in a hurry. There were still things he wanted to do, things he wanted to say. He was still capable of speaking, and he set about dictating his last notes and letters from 23 December 1922 to 2 March 1923. On 23 December he dictated to M.A. Volodicheva part of his famous 'Letter to the Congress'. It opened with a drastic proposal that augured yet another sharp alteration of course: 'I would strongly advise that this congress adopt a number of changes in our political system.' In fact, Lenin was not capable of making such changes. It was this system after all that gave him power and the hope of achieving the goal of world revolution. He did not want to change anything in the Party's strategy, but only certain aspects of an operational and tactical nature, essentially to increase the number of Party members by bringing in more workers.

The next day, the doctors went to see Stalin, Kamenev and Bukharin. They reported on Lenin's condition, and on the fact that he had been dictating the day before. The trio decided, after the event, that the patient 'should have the right' to dictate every day for five to ten minutes, 'but it should not be correspondence and Vladimir Ilyich should not expect to receive replies to these notes'.[24] Lenin continued to dictate his 'Letter to the Congress' on 24, 25 and 26 December, returning to it again on 4 January 1923, when he dictated his famous postscript on the personal qualities of his comrades, especially Stalin and Trotsky.

What was it he wanted to say? He was concerned above all about unity in the Party, the danger of a split in the Central Committee, and the bureaucratic character of the administration, although he showed no awareness of the roots of this last danger. He was obsessed by one idea, namely that more workers and peasants be brought into the Central Committee and the Party organization, the *apparat*. He believed that 'workers, by taking part in all Central Committee meetings, all sessions of the Politburo and reading all the Central Committee papers, can become a body of dedicated supporters of the Soviet system'.[25] The naive idea at the heart of this proposal was that by changing personnel, one could change everything. Stalin, Khrushchev, Brezhnev, Andropov, Chernenko and Gorbachev were all of peasant or worker origin, as were nearly all the members of the Politburo and Central Committee, yet bureaucratism soon became the very essence of the Leninist system. Individuals and their social origins were not the problem.

Although Lenin's 'Letter to the Congress' does not nominate his successor, it does, however, name those who in his opinion did not fit the part. He wanted this document, which came to be known as 'Lenin's Testament', to be kept a strict secret. He ordered that five copies be kept in wax-sealed envelopes, which only Krupskaya was to open after his death, but Volodicheva did not write this instruction on the envelopes. Lenin was already being written off, not only by his comrades, but even by his administrative secretaries. Fotieva, the chief secretary of the Sovnarkom, informed Stalin, and shortly afterwards several other members of the Politburo, of the contents of Lenin's notes, thus giving Stalin the opportunity to neutralize their effect. Since Lenin was still alive during the Twelfth Congress, his notes had to remain 'secret'. Stalin, forearmed, had time to secure the support of his comrades for the Thirteenth Congress.

Even before his 'Letter to the Congress', on 21 December Lenin had dictated a note to Trotsky on the foreign trade monopoly. Hearing of this, Stalin, who since 18 December had been responsible for maintaining Lenin's prescribed regime, roundly abused Krupskaya in the coarsest language, as we have seen. On 23 December she reported the incident to Kamenev, protesting that she knew better than anyone, including the doctors, what topics it was permissible to discuss with Lenin, 'as I know what upsets him and what does not, at any rate I know better than Stalin ... I'm human, too, and my nerves are strained to breaking point.'[26] It was not until the beginning of March 1923 that she told Lenin about what had transpired.

Lenin's 'Letter' played a fatal part in intensifying the struggle for power. However one reads the text, it is plain that Trotsky, despite his excessive arrogance, was seen as 'the most capable man in the present Central Committee', while Stalin was 'too rude' and unlikely to exercise power with due caution.[27] The result was that, while seeking to avoid a split, in fact Lenin increased the likelihood of just such an outcome.

The impact of the 'Letter' was dramatic. It was brought to the attention of the delegates at the Thirteenth Congress, but with the recommendation that Stalin be left in place as General Secretary, on condition he curb the defects Lenin had mentioned. It was then buried for decades in the deepest recesses of the Party archives. The system created by Lenin would have found its Stalin in any event. The country might have been spared the monstrous experiments of Stalinism, but the one-party 'dictatorship of the proletariat' would inevitably have led to an authoritarian regime. Therefore, the importance of Lenin's 'Letter' has probably been overstated: he was not proposing 'changes in our political system'.

Up to the beginning of March 1923, Lenin dictated letters and articles on the legislative functions of the State Planning Agency, on the national question, on agricultural cooperatives, the peculiarities of the revolution and the Workers' and Peasants' Inspectorate, which Stalin controlled and which was responsible for recruitment for the Party. In 1929, on the fifth anniversary of Lenin's death, Bukharin gave a speech on 'Lenin's political testament', in which he described these last works of the leader as 'a future plan for all our Communist work' and 'Lenin's plan for socialist construction'.[28] For decades this definition was used, although its author's name was not mentioned – especially when the hapless Bukharin was awaiting execution.

While there were political and practical merits in some of Lenin's last thoughts, notably on the national question and cooperatives, and although he could even speak of 'changing our entire view of socialism',[29] much of what he had to say was devalued by his entrenched political motivation: all this was necessary because 'the whole world is now shifting towards a movement that must give rise to a world socialist revolution.'[30]

It is remarkable that Lenin was capable of dictating these lengthy works in such a short time, especially taking into account the sharp deterioration that took place in his condition during the nights of 16 and 22 December. Professor Kramer, moreover, recorded on those occasions that Lenin had shown symptoms of memory-loss. The 'undulating' form of the illness and its 'unusual course' were also noted by the other physicians, Strumpfell, Hentschell, Nonne, Bumke, Foerster, Kozhevnikov and Yelistratov.[31] It was as if nature had given Lenin one last chance to have his say, and he seized it with all his strength. Plainly, he feared political extinction more than physical death, and although his comrades regarded his last notes as little more than his political death throes, Lenin was still fighting. He could not let go of the meaning of his life – political struggle, political leadership, political ambition.

The Politburo had given Lenin extended leave, lasting in effect from the middle of 1921. After May 1922, it seems, many Politburo members no longer expected him to recover, and they threw in their lot with the new arrangement of forces. The Central Committee's rules about 'Lenin's medical regime', which virtually isolated him from political and social life, were thus not entirely altruistic in their intent. While Lenin was learning to speak and write again at Gorki, the other leaders were preparing the ground for the decisive clash over personal power and influence. Stalin, Kamenev and Zinoviev did not conceal their fears about Trotsky, who appeared to have made up his mind some time ago that he was Lenin's natural successor, that the post had been reserved for him by the logic of history.

Lenin, although still hoping for recovery, was having more frequent thoughts about death. Several times in conversation with Krupskaya he mentioned the joint suicide of Marx's younger daughter Laura and her husband Paul Lafargue in 1911; he became interested in medical literature, and he asked Krupskaya to give him poison if his condition became hopeless. He often greeted the physicians with near-hostility. Naturally, all his fears were answered by assurances of a complete recovery.

Lenin began to be interested in what people were saying and writing about him. He reread Gorky's article 'Vladimir Ilyich Lenin', asked for a copy of Trotsky's 'The National Element in Lenin' and articles by Bukharin and other comrades which praised him, and wanted to hear the messages of goodwill that were coming in from all over the country, something that had never concerned him before. He wondered how he would be remembered, what he had given the people, what he had achieved.

Lenin now had the opportunity to look back over his life with a degree of detachment, and to assess it philosophically. There is no evidence in his last conversations, his notes or his articles, that he felt repentant about anything. He regarded mistakes, miscalculations and failures as a natural part of the process. He felt no remorse at having buried the social democrats in Russia, or at the destruction of the Romanov dynasty, the execution of Fanya Kaplan, the elimination of the SRs, the banning of the non-Bolshevik press, the expulsion of the Russian intelligentsia, the destruction of the provincial administration, the squandering of a vast part of the country's wealth on the world revolution. For Lenin, the end always justified the means.

## The Long Agony

Lenin was no longer in control of his own fate. Professor Kramer recorded that hope for a recovery was sustained until March 1923, even though in February there were renewed signs 'of breaks in his speech, at first negligible, but then more significant, though always fleeting . . . Vladimir Ilyich was finding it hard to recall either a word he wanted, or he was unable to read what he had dictated to the secretary, or he would begin to say something completely incoherent.'[32] Krupskaya was his best 'interpreter', and she bore her heavy burden with remarkable stoicism.

After the unforgettable telephone conversation, Stalin bothered her no more; he simply ignored her. Evidently now certain that Lenin would not recover, he was finding his responsibilities onerous. On 1 February 1923 he read a statement to the Politburo, asking to be relieved of having 'to observe that the regime established by the physicians for Comrade Lenin is carried out'. The response was a unanimous 'no'.[33]

In early March 1923 Lenin was diverted by the so-called 'Georgian affair'. A conflict had arisen the previous autumn over Stalin's plan, as Commissar for Nationalities, to integrate the three Caucasian republics, Azerbaidzhan, Armenia and Georgia, as autonomous bodies within the Russian Federation. (The plan also included other republics, but the conflict arose in the Caucasus.) The Georgian Bolsheviks, while accepting that economic integration of the region made sense, were adamantly opposed to relinquishing their political independence. The conflict had prompted Lenin to propose an arrangement which in effect led to the foundation of the USSR in December 1922. Instead of uniting the republics to the Russian Federation, he wanted to offer them apparently equal status as federal parts of a union; a union, moreover, which would govern Russia, not the other way round. Stalin stuck to his own agenda, however, and the conflict in Georgia now became a conflict between the ailing leader and his strutting lieutenant.

By March 1923 the situation in Georgia had deteriorated to the point where Ordzhonikidze,* frustrated by local resistance and procrastination, physically assaulted a local Bolshevik. For Lenin, when he heard of it, this represented nationalist oppression at its worst: assimilated non-Russians behaving worse than Russian bullies. Lenin

---

* Ordzhonikidze, Stalin and Dzerzhinsky – two Georgians and a Pole – were Lenin's special emissaries in the Caucasus.

did not approve of Georgian Bolshevik 'nationalism', but at this moment he thought it a lesser evil than 'great state chauvinism'. He regarded the national question – i.e. the policy for holding the great multi-national country together – as a matter of primary importance, and dictated a note to Trotsky to 'take it on yourself to defend the Georgian affair at the Central Committee. This affair is at present being "prosecuted"* by Stalin and Dzerzhinsky, and I cannot depend on their impartiality.'[34] Trotsky, realizing no doubt that to accept would lead to open conflict with Stalin, declined the invitation, pleading ill health. He was content to wait.

The next day, having learned of Trotsky's refusal, Lenin dictated the last letter of his life. It was addressed to the Georgian Bolsheviks: 'I am following your case with all my heart. I am appalled by Ordzhonikidze's crudeness and the tolerance of it shown by Stalin and Dzerzhinsky. I am preparing notes and a speech for you.'[35] He would be unable to keep this promise.

The day before, however, a significant, if little noticed, event had taken place. Lenin, annoyed by Stalin's conduct of the Georgian affair, and feeling as if he was being held almost under house arrest by the high-handed General Secretary, was discussing these troubling thoughts with Krupskaya. As she listened to his disjointed complaints, she felt she could remain silent no longer, and told him about the way Stalin had abused her on the telephone two and a half months earlier. Lenin's sister Maria described that occasion in her notes: 'Stalin called her on the phone and, apparently counting on it not getting to V.I., started telling her, in a pretty sharp way, that she shouldn't talk business with V.I., or he'd drag her before the Party's Control Commission. N.K. was terribly upset by the conversation; she was quite beside herself, sobbing and rolling on the floor and so on.'[36]

Lenin was up in arms when he heard about this incident. Ignoring Krupskaya's entreaties, apparently that day he dictated a letter which indicated exactly what he thought about Stalin. The letter, which opens with an uncomradely formal address, was marked 'Top secret' and 'Personal', but copies were sent to Kamenev and Zinoviev.

---

* A pun on 'persecuted'.

Respected Comrade Stalin,

You had the gall to call my wife to the telephone and abuse her. Although she agreed to forget what was said, she nevertheless told Zinoviev and Kamenev . . . I have no intention of forgetting what has been done against me, as it goes without saying that what was done against my wife was done against me. Therefore I must ask you to consider whether you are prepared to take back what you said and apologize, or whether you would rather break off relations between us.

With respect,

Lenin[37]

Lenin had strained relations with Stalin to the limit, and unthinkingly made his wife an object of his successor's ill will for the rest of her life. The weak condition of Lenin's nervous system could not bear such stress. As Kramer noted, the constant breaks in speech function and paralysis of the extremities 'led on 6 March, for no obvious reason, to a two-hour attack, presenting as total loss of speech and complete paralysis of the right limbs'.[38] The physicians were, of course, not privy to the drama that was being enacted between Lenin and Stalin. While they were busy with Lenin, Stalin transmitted his reply to Lenin via Volodicheva, but it could hardly have been read to him, in view of his sharply worsened condition.

The letter has lain in Stalin's secret archive for decades. Handwritten on three sheets of his own General Secretary's headed paper, it opens baldly, with no customary 'Respected' or other form of address than plain 'Comrade Lenin', and its general tone is openly disrespectful:

Five weeks ago I had a conversation with Comrade Nadezhda Konstantinovna, whom I regard not only as your wife but as my old Party comrade, and I said roughly the following to her (on the telephone): 'the doctors have forbidden [us] to give Ilyich political information, as they regard this as the most important way of curing him. It turns out, N.K., that you are not observing this regimen. We must not play with Ilyich's life,' and so on. I do not regard anything I said as crude or impermissible, or aimed against you, for I had no other purpose than your earliest recovery. Moreover, I regarded it as my duty to see that the regimen was observed. My conversation with N.K. confirmed that my suspicions were groundless, nor could they be otherwise. Still, if you think that to maintain our 'relations' I should take my words back, then I can take them back, though I refuse to understand what the problem was, where my fault lay and what it is people want of me.

I. Stalin.[39]

Krupskaya wrote in her memoirs of 'The Last Six Months of the Life of Vladimir Ilyich' (published only in 1989) that 'his last illness falls into two periods. In the period lasting from July, there was further deterioration. This period was connected with much physical suffering and bad nervous upsets.'[40] On 7 and 8 March it appeared that Lenin's attack on the sixth had been transitory, especially as on the tenth he gave Krupskaya to understand that he felt better.[41] But Dr Kramer's notes show that on that evening he suffered another attack, leading to 'stable changes both in speech function and the right limbs'.[42]

As soon as the leadership heard about the stroke, Zinoviev convened a meeting, consisting, according to the minutes, of 'available members'. In addition to Zinoviev, those present were Trotsky, Molotov and Rykov. Telegrams were sent to Kalinin, Kamenev, Kuybyshev and all the members of the Central Committee, informing them of Lenin's worsening condition.[43]

A swarm of doctors was rushed to Lenin from Moscow, while telephone calls were made to Krestinsky in Berlin, urging him to send the best therapists, neurologists and psychiatrists. On 15 March the Politburo agreed to widen still further the range of physicians and 'to bring in all the medical expertise that might be at all helpful in establishing a diagnosis and cure for Comrade Lenin'.[44] Krestinsky reported from Berlin that Professors Minkovsky, Strumpfell, Bumke and Nonne were on their way, and that he was still 'working on' others. Questions were clarified as to whether they should be paid in pounds, dollars or marks.[45] It seemed these experts were not enough, as Stalin cabled a Soviet emissary in Sweden, Simanovsky, to hire the famous specialist Hentschell. He promptly demanded a fee of 25,000 Swedish crowns, to which Moscow agreed without demur.[46]

After 11 March, when regular bulletins on Lenin's state of health began being published, suggestions started arriving for yet more doctors to be called in. For instance, Clara Zetkin drew the Kremlin's attention to Professor Oskar Vogt, 'who in his time has treated Adolf Heck, Jules Guesde, Wurm and others'. He was, she said, 'a Communist by conviction and he has a world reputation'.[47] The Politburo supported Zetkin's proposal, but according to Zinoviev, when Professor Foerster was asked for a view, he was opposed.[48] The Soviet consul in Mongolia reported that the local People's Party wanted to send a Tibetan doctor, and added that, 'for political reasons it would be very desirable if he went to Moscow'.[49]

On 21 March Hentschell, Bumke, Nonne, Foerster, Kozhevnikov, Yelistratov and Kramer reported that Lenin's condition had deteriorated; he now manifested sensory aphasia, that is, he had difficulty understanding what was being said to him. By then, however, another incident had taken place, which revealed the extreme state of Lenin's mood.

Maria Ulyanova wrote in her memoir of Lenin's last six months that

in the winter of 1920–21 or 21–22 V.I. was very, very bad. Headaches and an inability to work troubled him deeply. I don't remember exactly when, but at some time during that period, V.I. told Stalin that he would very likely end up being paralysed, and he got Stalin's word that in that event he would help him get hold of some potassium cyanide. Stalin promised. Why did V.I. ask Stalin? Because he knew him to be a firm, steely man, devoid of sentimentality. There was no one else of whom he could ask such a thing.

She returns to this topic elsewhere:

V.I. made the same request to Stalin in May 1922, after his first stroke. V.I. had decided that he was finished and asked for Stalin to come to him for the shortest possible time. He was so insistent that it was decided he should be indulged. Stalin stayed for literally no more than five minutes. And when he came out, he told me and Bukharin that V.I. had asked him to get some poison, as the time to fulfil his earlier promise had arrived. Stalin had promised, they had embraced and Stalin had left. But then, after discussing it together, we decided we must give V.I. courage, so Stalin went back to V.I. again and told him that, having talked to the doctors, he was convinced that all was not yet lost . . . V.I. was visibly cheered and agreed. Though he did say to Stalin: 'You aren't fooling me?' To which Stalin replied, 'When did you ever see me try to fool anyone?'[50]

Maria's memoirs, although they are not always accurate, are nevertheless clear that the thought of suicide was in Lenin's mind from
the moment the illness struck him.

The archives, however, hold a more reliable document – a 'strictly
secret' letter from Stalin to the Politburo, dated 21 March 1923:

On Saturday 17 March in the strictest secrecy Comrade Ulyanova
(N.K.[Krupskaya]) told me of 'Vladimir Ilyich's request to Stalin', namely
that I, Stalin, should take the responsibility for finding and administering to
Vladimir Ilyich a dose of potassium cyanide. In our conversation N.K. said,
among other things, that 'Vladimir Ilyich is suffering unbelievably', that 'to
go on living is unthinkable', and she stubbornly insisted that I 'not refuse
Ilyich's request'. In view of N.K.'s insistence and also because V. Ilyich *was
demanding* my agreement (V.I. twice called N.K. to go to him during my
conversation with her in his study, where we were talking, and emotionally
asked for 'Stalin's agreement', causing us to break off our conversation twice),
I felt it impossible to refuse him, and declared: 'I would like V. Ilyich to be
reassured and to believe that when it is necessary I will fulfil his demand
without hesitation.' V. Ilyich was indeed reassured.

I must, however, state that I do not have the strength to carry out V.
Ilyich's request and I have to decline this mission, however humane and
necessary it might be, and I therefore report this to the members of the
Politburo.

The reactions of the Politburo were summed up in an informal resolution: 'I have read it. I propose that Stalin's "indecisiveness" is correct.
There should be an exchange of opinion strictly among Politburo
members. Without (administrative) secretaries. Signed Tomsky, G.
Zinoviev, Molotov, N. Bukharin, Trotsky, L. Kamenev.'[51]

Stalin had already written to Zinoviev and Kamenev, evidently on
17 March, to report on his visit: 'Nadezhda Konstantinovna just summoned me and told me in strict secrecy that Ilyich is in a "terrible"
condition, he's having fits, "he doesn't want to live and can't live any
longer and is asking for potassium cyanide, without fail. She told me
she tried to give him cyanide but had "lost her nerve", which is why
she is asking for "Stalin's support".' Zinoviev and Kamenev wrote
on Stalin's note: 'This *must not happen*. Foerster is hopeful, how
can we? And even if that wasn't the case! It mustn't, mustn't, mustn't
happen!'[52]

There are certain aspects of these letters that require elucidation.

It is unclear, for instance, quite how Lenin, who had lost the power of speech, could have requested 'a dose of potassium cyanide'. Perhaps using sign-language? Stalin emphasizes several times that Nadezhda Konstantinovna 'stubbornly insisted' he be given cyanide, and even that she had tried to administer it to him herself. But where would she have obtained the poison? Had it been prepared at some earlier date? Had Stalin delivered it? These are questions to which no answers are available.

There is another no less important circumstance: on each occasion, Stalin promised to give the poison 'without hesitation'. He considered it, moreover, a 'humane and necessary mission'. To have carried out this mission would have accelerated the process of appointing Lenin's successor, for while the physicians were busy with their patient, the Politburo was the scene of a struggle for power. No expense or effort was spared to help Lenin, but perhaps this was rather in order to demonstrate loyalty to Leninism, the idea, the leader's cause, than in any real hope of a cure. Whoever called for the most effort would look the most loyal.[53]

From the published bulletins, it was impossible to guess Lenin's real condition. On 14 March 1923 it was reported that he was having difficulty speaking and moving his right arm and leg, but also that 'his general health is improved, his temperature is 37.0, his pulse 90, steady and full'. On 17 March, 'along with the continuing improvement in speech function and movement of the right arm, there is a noticeable improvement in the movement of the right leg. His general health continues to be good.'[54]

Many thought that Lenin's condition was simply due to exhaustion. Party organizations were sending telegrams to the Kremlin asking how he really was. From Tiflis (Tbilisi), Ordzhonikidze cabled Stalin: 'Let me know Ilyich's true condition.'[55] The Central Committee was by now, however, expert at manipulating information, and only what was regarded as necessary to maintain political calm was released. Speaking at the Seventh All-Ukrainian Party Conference on 5 April 1923, Trotsky declared: 'When we discussed the first bulletin on Lenin's health in March, we were thinking not only of his health, we also thought about the impression this number of blows to his heart would make on the political pulse of the working class and our Party.' Trotsky also set the tone for judging Lenin's role: 'No one in the whole of history has had historical influence of sufficient scale to enable us to measure Lenin's historical importance.'[56]

Each leader took pains to demonstrate his own loyalty to Lenin, to his ideas and aspirations, although it was plain to all of them that his active political life was over, and that they must prepare themselves for the end.

The Journal of the Duty Physician following the stroke of 10 March 1923 gives a detailed account of Lenin's true condition:

*11 March*: Doctor Kozhevnikov went in to see Vladimir Ilyich at 11.15 a.m. His colour was pale and sallow, the expression on his face and in his eyes sad . . . He kept trying to say something, but only quiet, disjointed sounds emerged . . . Today, especially towards the evening, his comprehension of what was being said to him was worse, sometimes he replied 'no' when he should have said 'yes'.

*12 March*: Professors Minkovsky and Foerster came today. Doctor Kozhevnikov went with them from the station to the Politburo and then to see Vladimir Ilyich . . . He appears to be fully conscious, but has total motor aphasia and today can say nothing . . . He cannot understand what he is asked to do. He was shown a pen, his spectacles and a paper-knife. When he was asked to give the spectacles, he gave them, when he was asked for the pen, he gave the spectacles again (they were lying closest to him) . . . After the visit, the doctors went again to the Politburo.*

*17 March*: After the doctors' visit, Lenin ate a good dinner. After a short time he wanted to express either an idea or a wish, but neither the nurse, nor Maria Ilyinichna, nor Nadezhda Konstantinovna could understand him. He became agitated and was given a bromide and Maria Ilyinichna called Doctor Kozhevnikov . . .

*21 March*: Another consultation took place with the addition of Hentschell who arrived today. After it they all went to the Kremlin. Vladimir Ilyich greeted them all [Strumpfell, Hentschell, Bumke and Nonne], but was evidently not happy about this invasion. Strumpfell made the examination, the others merely being present. When Nonne approached Vladimir Ilyich, he made a gesture with his hand as if asking him to move back . . .[57]

---

* Although the members of the Politburo did not attend Lenin's deathbed, in assuming the rôle of controller of his medical management they set a precedent which nearly thirty years later would be repeated when Stalin was dying. For more than ten hours after suffering a stroke, Stalin lay without medical attention because no one was empowered to call a doctor without Beria's permission, and Beria was nowhere to be found. Virtually every decision of the consortium of terrified physicians attending him required Politburo approval.

The patient was losing confidence in his doctors.

In May, however, Lenin seemed to be making a slow recovery. He would be taken out onto the veranda of the Kremlin apartment, and on the fifteenth he was transported, with a team of doctors and virtually at snail's pace, to Gorki. Kozhevnikov noted that 'he has become stronger physically, has begun to show an interest in his own condition, as well as in his surroundings, he has recovered from the sensory aphasia and begun to learn to speak'.[58] S.M. Dobrogaev, a physician specializing in speech therapy, worked with Krupskaya, who then herself undertook to help Lenin recover his power of speech.[59]

According to the medical notes and the research carried out by B. Ravdin,[60] after 10 March Lenin's vocabulary was limited to a few monosyllabic words. 'Vot-vot' became a catch-all term that he used to express agreement, objection, a demand, annoyance, a request or just to keep a conversation going. As a rule, the use of individual words was accidental, and even when he repeated them, they were meaningless. Following Krupskaya's instruction, he learned to say 'congress', 'cell', 'peasant', 'worker', 'people' and 'revolution'. She used alphabet cards and basic exercises, but without her help he was incapable of saying even a single word that he had already repeated after her. His brain was dying.

The artist Yuri Annenkov, who had painted Lenin's portrait in 1921, left an interesting account of his visit to Lenin in December 1923: 'Kamenev took me to Gorki to do a portrait, or rather a sketch, of the sick Lenin. Krupskaya greeted us. She said there was no question of a portrait. And, indeed, reclining on a chaise-longue, wrapped in a blanket and looking past us with the helpless, twisted, babyish smile of a man in his second infancy, Lenin could serve only as an illustration of his illness, and not to model for a portrait.'[61]

It would appear that the numerous 'reminiscences' of meetings and 'conversations' with Lenin after March 1923 must either be mystification or politically motivated fabrications. Sometimes these were intended to show that Lenin would soon return to the helm of Party and state. As Ravdin has noted, Lunacharsky, speaking in Tomsk in May 1923, declared: 'Vladimir Ilyich's arm and leg, that have been slightly paralysed, are recovering; his speech, which was at one time unclear, is also recovering. For a long time now, Vladimir Ilyich has been able to sit in an armchair, he can converse quite calmly, whereas before he was often very upset by his unclear speech.'[62]

There were many examples, after Lenin died, of official accounts which set out to show not the human tragedy of his end, but 'the greatness of the sick leader'. For instance, one of his bodyguards, S.P. Sokolov, related that in the autumn of 1923 an armchair was delivered to Gorki as a gift from the Communist Party of Great Britain. Lenin thought for a while, and then mentioned a commissar who had lost both legs at the front: 'Let's send the armchair to him. He's not going to be walking again. And for the moment I don't need it.'[63] The production-line of myths was rolling.

After his stroke on 10 March Lenin completely lost the ability to indulge in one of his favourite pastimes, that of writing notes. Together with his loss of speech, this made communication impossible. With desperate endeavours, Krupskaya tried to revive some minimal capacity for elementary social intercourse. She gave Lenin almost daily exercises in the use of his left hand, which, like his vision, was not functioning properly (his right hand was completely paralysed). The Journal of the Duty Physician records that Lenin was 'given biscuits, but for a long time he could not put his hand straight onto the plate and kept putting it around it'.[64]

The obstacles facing the patient and his long-suffering wife can easily be imagined. A teacher by profession, Krupskaya tried to revive from scratch Lenin's ability both to speak and to write. The first words he wrote, her hand on his, were 'mama' and 'papa'. According to the official biography, 'Thanks to his exceptional willpower, courage and persistence, in a relatively short time he accomplished improvements which would normally take months.'[65] In fact, none of these 'improvements' led to the revival of either speech or writing ability.

Krupskaya's efforts, and those of the physicians, nevertheless produced some improvement in the second half of 1923; Lenin was now capable of shuffling across the room very slowly with the aid of a stick; with sign-language and gestures and his '*vot-vot*', he was able to communicate in an elementary way. Professor Kramer noted: 'In November and more so in December he was able to say a few words without prompting, he learned to write better with his left hand, he could read, or at least look through the newspaper, always pointing precisely at what interested him.'[66]

Lenin's basic abilities were returning slowly, but there was no sign that his mental strength was intact. The statements for the press and the Party organization, which had maintained an optimistic note, ceased after 16 May 1923 with Bulletin No. 35. The feeling arose among the population that Lenin must be improving, and that a complete recovery could not be far off. Behind the scenes, however, a greater frankness ruled. On 26 September Zinoviev reported at a Party meeting:

Roughly since 20 July V.I.'s health began to improve and continued to do so noticeably each day ... For three days he has been able to walk, with someone next to him just in case ... He has been out in a car ... The worst thing has been his speech, but even here there is improvement ... As for unprompted speech, that's bad ... When the improvement began, he couldn't form one syllable out of two letters. Now that's improving, too ...

The question was raised of his moving somewhere in the South. We all suggested the South, but the doctors were against it, and so was V.I., which was the main thing. [Professor] Osipov says, evidently he is conservative in his personal life and so is decisively against any [trip to the] South ...

The newspapers are read to Vladimir Ilyich, at first with cuts, now without. They read him the headlines and he chooses what he wants to have read and what not ... Nadezhda Konstantinovna told him about the [reoccupation by the Germans of the] Ruhr and then read about them to him. He expressed no great surprise. He expressed greater dissatisfaction with the news that in Ukraine rich peasants are having surpluses confiscated, and that was something he hadn't done before. He has an excellent idea of his own condition and is looking after himself very well ... he is directing his own treatment and looking after himself ...

He chases the doctors away and makes it hard for them to examine him ... At the end of July they issued extremely pessimistic reports, giving less than one per cent chance of a good outcome. But since the middle of July things have been getting better and continue to do so.[67]

This was a more or less accurate account of Lenin's condition at the time, although he was probably indicating the pieces he wanted read to him from the newspapers entirely haphazardly. His condition had stabilized, with paralysis of the right side of the body and serious brain damage. The round-the-clock medical attendance was suspended.

Several times Lenin gave indications that he wanted to go to Moscow, and finally in the evening of 18 October 1923 such a trip took place. As Krupskaya wrote: 'One day he set off to the garage, got into the car and insisted on going to Moscow.' Apart from Krupskaya, he was accompanied by his sister Maria, Professors Osipov and Rozanov, and bodyguards. The Kremlin staff were waiting. With difficulty Lenin went up to his apartment, inspected objects and books with curiosity, and soon lay down to recover from the journey of an hour and a half.

Next day, for the last time, he visited his office, which was close by, looked into the deserted Sovnarkom meeting hall, and went outside. After choosing some books from his library, he indicated that he would like to be driven around Moscow. The group set off for the All-Russian Agricultural and Handicraft Exhibition, but heavy rain prevented a viewing, and, after calling in at the Kremlin for the books, they returned to Gorki.[68]

Whether or not Lenin had been mentally able to formulate and convey the idea of coming to Moscow to say farewell to the city, as has sometimes been suggested, the fact is that his brain, when it was examined after his death, showed such severe damage that many specialists expressed amazement that he had had even a rudimentary ability to communicate. Health Commissar Semashko confirmed on the basis of the autopsy that 'the sclerosis of the blood vessels of Vladimir Ilyich's brain had gone so far that these blood vessels were calcified. When struck with a tweezer they sounded like stone. The walls of many blood vessels were so thickened and the blood vessels so overgrown that not even a hair could be inserted into the openings. Thus, whole sections of the brain were deprived of fresh blood.'[69] He had been a seriously sick man, kept alive thanks only to the unceasing attentions of a team of physicians and a numerous entourage.

Yuri Annenkov, invited in 1924 to select photographs and drawings for books on Lenin, saw a glass jar at the Lenin Institute: 'in it was Lenin's brain preserved in alcohol ... one hemisphere was healthy and full-sized, with clearly defined convolutions; the other, which hung as it were by a ribbon, was wrinkled, crumpled, crushed and no larger than a walnut'.[70]

After the stroke in March, Lenin saw his comrades only rarely. As early as December 1922 the Politburo had accepted Stalin's proposal 'to isolate Vladimir Ilyich both as far as personal relations are concerned, as well as correspondence'.[71] Even the large household of chef,

cook, gardener, cleaners, nurses and security men were not allowed
to linger in the patient's view without cause. When Lenin was being
pushed in his wheelchair around the grounds, by a nurse or by his
chief of security, P.P. Pokaln, staff members would quickly move out
of sight, in case unexpected contact upset him. Those who did meet
him at that time experienced bewildering feelings. Instead of the man
who only eighteen months or so before had been the brains and the
heart of the revolution, they saw an almost immobile figure with sad
eyes and a pitiful half-smile on his face.

In July his brother Dmitri visited, but apart from the physicians
and domestic staff, only a handful of people came to see him. 'Every
visit disturbed him,' Krupskaya recalled. 'One could see it from the
way he moved his chair after the meeting, the way he convulsively
pulled the drawing-board towards him and got hold of the chalk.
When he was asked if he wouldn't like to see Bukharin, who used to
be our most frequent visitor, or one of the other comrades . . . he
would shake his head, as he knew how incredibly hard it would be.'[72]

Some members of the Politburo and Sovnarkom visited, but only
to observe Lenin from a distance, as he was being pushed around in
his wheelchair or resting in the house. Like Stalin and Trotsky, they
were reluctant to endure a meeting in which normal contact would
be impossible. Trotsky expressed his concern by sending Krupskaya
an American proposal for treatment, adding, however, 'Personally, I
don't have much faith in it.'[73] Krupskaya was rightly perceived as
'Lenin's manager' now. She was the only one who could follow what
he wanted to say, or guess the meaning of his 'questions'. She recol-
lected that 'when you have spent your lives together, you know the
associations that are evoked. I might say "Kalmykova", and I would
know from his questioning "What?" that he wanted to know about
Potresov and his present political position. This was our own peculiar
way of communicating.'[74] This episode is recounted in the official
biography as though it had been a normal conversational exchange:
'Lenin listened with interest as N.K. Krupskaya told him about the life
and work of the well known Russian social activist A.M. Kalmykova; he
asked her about the present political position of A.N. Potresov.'[75]

Krupskaya's own mood fluctuated between hope and apathy, disappointment and total exhaustion. Her letters to Inessa Armand's
daughters, notably the elder one, Inna, are more revealing about

Lenin's last months than are her memoirs. On 6 May 1923 she wrote: 'I'm kept alive only by the fact that Volodya* is glad to see me in the mornings, he takes my hand, and sometimes we talk without words about different things which anyway have no names.' On 2 September: 'I spend whole days now with Volodya who is improving rapidly, then in the evenings I go mad and am quite unable to write letters.' 13 September: 'The improvement continues, but it's all going devilishly slowly.' 28 October: 'Every day he makes a conquest, but they're all microscopic, and we are still hanging between life and death. The doctors say that all the facts indicate that he's recovering, but I now know for sure that they don't know a damn thing, they can't possibly.'[76]

It seemed possible that Lenin's 'stabilized' condition might last a long time. In the Politburo there was an unspoken understanding that while a recovery was unlikely, so was Lenin's death while the illness remained stabilized.

In mid-January 1924, the Thirteenth Party Conference opened. Krupskaya read Lenin the conference papers. He was elected a member of the presidium *in absentia*. During the conference, Skvortsov-Stepanov, who had been to Gorki on 29 November 1923, was asked by Kamenev to telephone Krupskaya, and on the closing day he gave Kamenev a note: 'Lev Borisovich, I think the best thing would be for you to say a few words about V.I.'s health in your closing speech, but not to dwell on it,' adding that the stenographers should not record it, and that the press should not be told anything about Lenin's condition. He proposed that Kamenev say that Krupskaya had been unable to attend the conference and had issued a statement. The text Skvortsov-Stepanov wrote for Kamenev read:

The recovery is progressing satisfactorily. He walks quite well with a stick, but he cannot stand up without help ... He can pronounce individual words, he can repeat any word and clearly can understand its meaning ... He has started reading about the Party discussion. He has read Rykov's speech and a letter from Trotsky. According to Nadezhda Konstantinovna, those around him can tell from various signs how he is reacting to the disputes, but she would rather not report her own deductions on this matter.[77]

---

* Diminutive of Vladimir.

Krupskaya was only repeating what the members of the Politburo already knew. As for 'her own deductions', they would have been pure guesswork. Yet, in Krupskaya's published reminiscences, recalling that she had told Skvortsov-Stepanov that the recovery was proceeding satisfactorily, she added: 'Starting on Thursday [17 January], I began to feel something was coming; V.I. looked horribly tired and tormented. He was closing his eyes frequently and went pale, but the main thing was that somehow the expression on his face altered, his gaze became somehow blind.'[78]

On the evening of 20 January 1924 Professor M.I. Averbakh examined Lenin, who complained about his eyes, but nothing conclusive was discovered. Next day, after lunch, he was examined by Professors Foerster and Osipov. He had been extremely sluggish, had twice needed help in getting out of bed, and had then immediately lain down again. Fifteen minutes after Osipov had left him, Lenin suffered his last attack. He had been given bouillon and coffee. 'He drank thirstily, and felt slightly better, but then he started having gurgling in the chest,' Krupskaya recalled. 'The gurgling in his chest was getting more and more. His eyes looked less and less conscious, [the male attendant and the head of security] were practically lifting him bodily, he occasionally moaned quietly, a tremor ran through his body, at first I held his hot, damp hand, but then just watched as the towel turned red with blood, and the stamp of death settled on his deathly pallid face. Professor Foerster and Doctor Yelistratov sprayed camphor and tried to give him artifical respiration, but in vain, it was not possible to save him.'[79]

At 6.50 p.m. on Monday 21 January 1924, Lenin died.


## The Mummy and the Embalming of Ideas

According to an official anouncement of 23 January 1924, signed by six physicians and Health Commissar Semashko, the cause of Lenin's death was 'an incurable disease of the blood vessels'.[80] On the basis of the autopsy, the notion, sometimes suggested, that his disease was syphilitic in origin is unsustainable. Syphilis would have caused changes in the smaller vessels at the base of the brain, whereas the evidence is that it was the large blood vessels that were seriously affected, providing the physical evidence of the small strokes Lenin suffered. This interpretation is further strengthened by the atheroma, or narrowing of large vessels in the heart and aorta.[81] It is reasonable to conclude that Lenin died from a number of causes, of which the most important was an inherited predisposition to atherosclerosis. The deaths of his father, his two sisters and his brother all suggest a genetic disease of the blood vessels.

Another contributory factor to Lenin's death was his physical unpreparedness for the huge strain to which he was subjected after the October revolution. Until the age of forty-seven, when he assumed vast and unfamiliar burdens, he had lived a life free of administrative responsibility. By 1920 it was already evident that he was beginning to crack under the stress. He took holiday after holiday, but it made no difference. Virtually the entire second half of 1921 and the whole of 1922 were taken as a 'sabbatical'. Previously accustomed to literary activity, vacationing in the mountains, and to Party squabbles in exile, Lenin was completely unprepared for the new stresses. He was simply destroyed by the strains of power.

The Party leaders saw in the very act of Lenin's burial an enormous opportunity for strengthening the regime. At first, no one thought of a tomb or embalming: he was simply to be buried. The day after his death a Central Committee plenum agreed to hold a funeral meeting of the Congress of Soviets, arranged demonstrations of mourning, agreed that the funeral should take place on Saturday afternoon, that the body should be brought to Moscow accompanied by two hundred Congress delegates and Party leaders, and that steps be taken to prevent panic in the country. The lying in state would be in the House of Soviets, and the burial would take place in Red Square.[82]

The same day the Central Executive Committee formed a commission to organize the burial, consisting of Dzerzhinsky as chairman, Muralov, Lashevich, Bonch-Bruevich, Voroshilov, Molotov, Zelensky and Yenukidze.[83] Stalin notified all regional and republican Party committees of Lenin's death, and called for immediate steps to maintain order and prevent panic.[84] Among his numerous other chores, Stalin sent a coded cable to Tiflis: 'Tell Comrade Trotsky that on 21 January at 6.50 Comrade Lenin died suddenly. Death was caused by paralysis of the respiratory centre. Funeral Saturday 26 January 1924.'[85]

Every day up to the funeral the Politburo, the Central Control Commission and the Funeral Commission met in almost constant session. Resolutions were taken to disseminate Lenin's speeches and to commission biographies: even before the decision was taken to turn his body into a Bolshevik relic, measures were quite far advanced to embalm his ideas. If the attempt on Lenin's life in 1918 was used to launch the mass terror, his death became the occasion to begin the Leninization of the spiritual and intellectual life of the country. The campaign would soon be launched, and would quickly snowball, to turn him into an ideological saint. Orders were issued for the mass casting of busts; on the initiative of the Petrograd Bolsheviks the Politburo agreed to rename the city Leningrad; the order of service was worked out for the Congress of Soviets; and the funeral was postponed to Sunday.[86]*

There was still no mention of mummifying the body. Digging had begun in Red Square when the Funeral Commission proposed extending the lying in state and delaying the burial, thus providing time for the absurd idea of mummification to emerge. Soon after Lenin's death, A.I. Abrikosov carried out a normal embalming, with the aim of preserving the body for six to seven days. On 24 January the Politburo discussed various ways of preserving Lenin 'a little longer' in a temporary vault at the Kremlin Wall. Neither Krupskaya nor Lenin's sisters and brother, however, would agree to even a temporary preservation of the body. The Politburo deputed Bukharin and Zinoviev to 'persuade Nadezhda Konstantinovna: if she will agree not to insist on acceptance of her proposal, the question can be discussed again in a month'.[87] Lenin's corpse had become an object of political and ideological manipulation.

Stalin at first gave no opinion as to whether the body should be mummified, but on reflection he came to see it as the creation of a secular Bolshevik relic with huge propaganda potential. On 24 January, on the orders of the Politburo, the following instructions were issued:

1) The coffin containing V.I. Lenin's corpse is to be kept in a vault which should be made accessible to visitors;

* Trotsky, who had assumed he would not be able to get to Moscow in time for the funeral on Saturday, was thus prevented from taking part in this important political event.

2) The vault is to be formed in the Kremlin wall on Red Square among the communal graves of the fighters of the October revolution. A commission is being created today for the construction of a mausoleum (temporary for now). Academician A.B. Shchusev is commissioned to prepare drawings of the mausoleum.[88]

The funeral session of the Second All-Union Congress of Soviets opened at 11 a.m. on 26 January. The official biography states that those who spoke included Stalin, Zetkin, Narimanov, Sergeev, Krayushkin, Voroshilov, Smorodin, Oldenburg and 'others'.[89] The 'others' were Zinoviev, Bukharin and Kamenev. *Pravda* published only twenty-eight lines of Stalin's speech on the following day, less than it had of any of the other speakers. Two days later, after Stalin had had a word with them, the editors returned to the topic and published all the speeches in full. They were later published as pamphlets, while Stalin's appeared in his collected works. He described Lenin as 'a genius of geniuses among the leaders of the proletariat', evidently having decided that he himself was going to be the chief disciple of Lenin's cause: to be the heir of the 'genius of geniuses' sounded fine to him. Knowing about the plan to construct a 'temporary' mausoleum, Stalin predicted: 'In a short time you will see a pilgrimage by representatives of millions of toilers to the grave of Comrade Lenin.' Zinoviev, in an hour-long speech, confirmed that on the following day 'we shall lower Vladimir Ilyich into the grave'. He believed that the vault with access to Lenin was indeed only temporary.

What must Bukharin have thought, awaiting execution in his cell in 1938, if he recalled what he had said at the funeral session? 'A revolutionary tactician of genius, Vladimir Ilyich steered our ship of state through all the dangerous reefs and shallows, and that means that nine-tenths of the fundamental work for our country has been accomplished.' Kamenev said that Lenin had 'conquered the world' with the help of ideas. Some parts of his speech appear distinctly ambiguous when seen through the long perspective of time. He spoke at length, for instance, of the 'trail of blood' that led to Lenin's assumption of office. He meant the blood that Lenin himself had given for the cause. Today, however, we can interpret his words literally: after all, Lenin himself had said, speaking to the Communist Trade Union faction on 2 January 1920, 'we shall not hesitate to shoot thousands of people'.[90] Kamenev, like Zinoviev, thought the funeral was to be a customary one: 'now we bow our heads before the grave of our leader'.[91]

The semi-aborted edition of *Pravda* merits quotation. In its address to the country, the Central Committee declared that, thanks to Lenin, 'we stand firmly on the ground. Among the ruins of Europe we are the only country that can look boldly at its future under a workers' regime.' And ECCI confirmed that the world revolution was marching forward 'in giant strides'. In an article entitled 'Comrade', Bukharin wrote: 'We shall never again see that great forehead, the wonderful head which radiated revolutionary energy in all directions.' Lenin 'was a dictator in the best sense of the word', possessing 'a powerful mental apparatus, an iron hand' and 'a furious temperament'. Kamenev called Lenin 'a great rebel', Zinoviev remembered him as 'a rebel among rebels, a thinker among thinkers', while Trotsky, who was in the Caucasus, called on the people to take up 'Lenin's lantern'. Even the Metropolitan of Moscow, Yevdokim, was given space to say his piece. More prophetic than most, he predicted that 'this grave will give birth to millions of new Lenins and will unite all of them into one brotherly invincible family ... This grave will become a permanent rostrum from generation to generation.' The historian M. Pokrovsky, ignoring the recent expulsion of so many of his former colleagues, declared that Lenin had 'saved higher education from destruction ... by demanding that whoever did not take the special Marxist examination, would be denied an education'. Similar tributes came from a large number of other prominent Bolsheviks. The newspaper also published the decree on the construction of the vault, and of monuments to Lenin in Moscow, Leningrad and elsewhere. The Congress of Soviets took the decision to publish Lenin's selected works 'in millions of copies', while the Lenin Institute undertook to produce an edition of 'the complete works'.[92]

Articles by Zinoviev appeared in *Pravda* nearly every day. Of the 'burial' he wrote:

On a severe winter's day – as if on purpose, a hard frost of 26 degrees had struck – a million people arrived on Red Square ... It is good that we had decided to bury Ilyich in a vault! It is good that we thought of it in time! It would have been beyond endurance to have put his body into the ground ... Above the vault is the short, but entirely adequate inscription, 'Lenin'. The people's pathway here will in truth never be overgrown. A Lenin

Museum will arise nearby. Gradually the entire square will be a Lenin district
... At 4 p.m. we lower the coffin into the vault with gun salutes ... Lenin
is dead, Leninism lives ... When the proletarian revolution conquers the
world, it will above all be the victory of Leninism.[93]

A rare film taken of the funeral reveals something uniquely Russian.
Thousands, tens of thousands of people had come on that freezing
January day to bury their Soviet tsar, some bearing banners with
the unwittingly prophetic slogan 'Lenin's grave is the cradle of the
revolution'. Their faces show plainly that the people already believed
in him, the more so as an attempt had been made on his life and as
he had suffered at the end. The traditional Russian belief that their
leader had wanted to do good turned the funeral into an important
step towards creating the myth of a new, secular saint.

From the day of the funeral, the 'embalming' of Lenin's ideas also
began, possibly one of the most unfortunate consequences of his death.
The seemingly unstoppable process started of creating museums,
erecting statues and publishing countless books and miscellanies,
of renaming towns, streets, factories, palaces, ships and workshops.
Krupskaya, who had a sensitive nose for the practical, knew that Lenin
was being canonized into an earthly god. Only two days after the
funeral, *Pravda* published a brief letter from her in response to the
announcement of a Lenin Fund aimed at building monuments to him:
'I wish to make a big request: don't let your grief for Ilyich run away
into outward regard for his personality. Don't build monuments to
him, palaces in his name, grand ceremonies in his memory and so on.
When he was alive he had no time for such things, he found such
things oppressive.'[94]

These words were generally quoted to show Lenin's modesty and
simplicity, qualities that were perhaps undeniable. Lenin himself was
not responsible for the embalming of his ideas, or the aggrandizement
of his name. It should nevertheless be noted that during his lifetime
the ancient Moscow district of Rogozhskaya was renamed Ilyich Gate,
while Ulyanov Street made its appearance, as well as the propaganda
train *Vladimir Lenin*, Lenin district in Petrograd province, and so on.
Presumably the 'Leninist Politburo' of later years was not unaware of
Krupskaya's words, as it approved the making of still more monuments
and busts, year in, year out, month by month? In one decree after
another, monuments to Lenin were erected throughout the Soviet

period and throughout the Soviet Union, to say nothing of the effort that went into carrying on the practice outside the USSR. Whole studios and foundries were built and allocated hundreds of millions of roubles, supplied with thousands of cubic metres of granite, marble, stainless steel and bronze, all dedicated to this single purpose.[95]

The temporary mausoleum, as later the permanent one, soon became a place of pilgrimage not only for true Communists, but also, and perhaps primarily, for the simply curious. In time it formed an indispensable ritual stop for state visitors and other important delegations. It is not difficult to imagine the impression this made on Lenin's family, who could never reconcile themselves to it. Krupskaya was the first person to visit the temporary resting place, with Lenin's brother Dmitri, on 26 May 1924. In general she was to visit it infrequently, not even once a year, preferring to spare herself the emotional upset it caused her. The curator of the mummy, B.I. Zbarsky, recalled that the last time Krupskaya visited the tomb was in 1938, a few months before her death in February 1939. She is said to have stood by the catafalque for a while, muttering quietly: 'He's just the same, but look how I've aged . . .'

Having created their relic, the Bolsheviks had taken the first decisive step towards turning Lenin's ideas into a secular religion; a religion, moreover, comparable in the unquestioning obedience of its adherents only to the faith of fanatical fundamentalists. As Winston Churchill wrote, the Russian people had been led by the Bolsheviks and Lenin into a quagmire. 'Their worst misfortune was his birth: their next worst – his death.'[96] Lenin's death did not free Russia of him; henceforth her citizens were forced to 'carry out his commandments'.

The first decrees of the Central Committee after Lenin's death affirmed that the Party leadership 'in its struggle to build the Communist society' would make Lenin's mummy and everything associated with it one of the most important tools for accomplishing the task. A first step was the so-called 'Lenin Enrolment', or the induction into the Party of some quarter of a million factory workers. Henceforth a new element arose in people's lives: the 'struggle for the purity of Leninism' and for its 'development'. The fierce inner-Party struggle of the 1920s was a battle over the monopoly of the Lenin inheritance.

The reason was Stalin. To secure his ascendancy, Stalin probably read Lenin's works more closely than anyone else, and to greater effect. In so many respects inferior to Trotsky, Zinoviev, Kamenev and Bukharin, he succeeded in clambering to the pinnacle of power precisely because he used as his chief weapon the 'defence' of Leninism, and presented himself as the chief interpreter of Lenin's ideas. On countless occasions he used this weapon as an argument that quickly became unanswerable in Soviet circumstances. On 1 August 1927, for instance, speaking at a joint session of the Central Committee and Central Control Commission, he disabled his opponents with his Leninist rapier: 'I must first repudiate the utterly false statement of Zinoviev and Trotsky claiming that I belonged to the so-called "military opposition" at the Eighth Party Congress. It's completely untrue, comrades. It's gossip cooked up by Zinoviev and Trotsky who have nothing better to do. I have in my hands the minutes which show plainly that I then spoke together with Lenin against the so-called "military opposition".' Similar devices were used to great effect, as the Party increasingly saw Stalin as 'defending Lenin' while defending himself. As he said in the same three-hour speech: 'We are carrying out ... Lenin's commandments, while the leaders of the opposition have broken with Leninism and cast his commandments into oblivion.'[97]

The mummification of Lenin and the embalming of his ideas helped to consolidate the dogmatic mode of thought, and even the character of Party members. At first, attempts were made to explain the decision to preserve the body in rational terms. Thus, A.E. Yenukidze, Secretary of the TsIK, declared at the Commission for Perpetuating the Memory of V.I. Ulyanov-Lenin: 'We did not want to make of Vladimir Ilyich's remains some sort of "relic", as a means to popularize or preserve his memory ... We ... accorded and still accord the greatest importance to preserving the image of this remarkable leader for the rising generation and future generations, but also for those hundreds of thousands of people, perhaps even millions, who would be extremely happy to see the image of this man.'[98] It is doubtful if the 150 million people who filed past Lenin's sarcophagus over the years thought that the sight of him was intended to make them 'extremely happy'.

As the Politburo was organizing the carefully controlled publication of Lenin's writings, it was simultaneously committing great quantities of his materials to the most secret recesses of the archives. When, for instance, on 28 January 1924 the Funeral Commission applied to the Politburo for permission 'to organize as soon as possible the correct and most complete information on Ilyich's life, up to his last moment, and the history of his illness and especially the last six months of it',[99] they met a stone wall, as all such matters had already become state secrets.

Lenin himself was extremely secretive, and the state he created followed his commandments in this sphere with devotion. For instance, the cost of hiring foreign specialists to treat him was a major state secret. In all twenty-six physicians took part in numerous consultations: Professors Dorshkevich, Foerster, Klemperer, Borchhardt, Kramer, Rossolino, Minkovsky, Strumpfell, Hentschell, Nonne, Bumke, Obukh, Veisbord, Averbakh, Osipov, Bekhterev, Krol, Feldberg, Doctors Kozhevnikov, Levin, Gautier, Yelistratov, Rozanov, Dobrogaev, Popov and Health Commissar Semashko. All the foreigners, of course, had to be paid. In June 1924 OGPU chief G.I. Boky enquired what these fees had amounted to, and from Brodovsky in the Soviet embassy in Berlin he received detailed information: Borchhardt, 220,000 German marks; Foerster, £11,900; Minkovsky, £4400; Bumke, $29,000; Strumpfell, $9500; Hentschell, 25,000 Swedish crowns – the list continues in this vein.[100]

Moscow conducted an extensive correspondence with its representatives abroad over which physicians should be invited and what fees they should be paid, fees agreed to without a quibble. Soviet envoys gave advice on both scores. Krestinsky in Berlin, for instance, wrote in a letter to Stalin, Trotsky and Molotov, that 'Foerster has already received a good fee from us twice; he doesn't doubt, of course, that all three trips will be well paid . . . I think Minkovsky will be satisfied with less than you're giving Foerster . . .'[101] None of this was particularly unusual business practice, to be sure, and had the documents not been sealed in secret archives, they would have been of little interest.

After the strange funeral, the Politburo set out, with the aid of Dzerzhinsky, Krasin and the scientists, to find ways of preserving the dead leader, and even debated the technical aspects of the problem.[102] On 13 March 1924, having heard reports by Molotov and Krasin, it decided: 'In view of the absence of other methods for conserving the body of V.I. Lenin, the commission should be ordered to resort to measures for preserving it using low temperature.'[103] Soon, however, the Politburo was able to approve a system devised by V.P. Vorobiev, a chemist from Kharkov, and on 24 July 1924 it recognized his achievement by conferring on him the title of Honorary Professor.[104]

The embalming process took four months. Meanwhile, A.V. Shchusev, the architect who had been commissioned to design the mausoleum, took his inspiration from Krasin's idea of a 'tribune for the people', and all his plans took account of this, whether for the temporary monument made of pine, the more permanent one of oak, or the eternal one of granite. The Politburo nevertheless decided to hold a competition, with prizes for the four best entries: first prize was to be 1000 roubles, second 750, third 600 and fourth 500[105] – a very inexpensive initiative, compared to the fees paid to the foreign specialists called in to treat Lenin.

It was not, however, until 4 July 1929 that the Politburo, after innumerable reviews of the question, finally decided to proceed with the building of the permanent structure.[106] For all practical purposes, the preservation of the mummy had up to now been handled by political security, the OGPU, and the least hint of criticism of the matter was subject to severe suppression. For instance, in July 1929, when Lazar Shatskin, writing in *Komsomolskaya pravda* on 'Party philistinism', cast doubt on the idea of the mausoleum, the Politburo at once denounced his position as 'a crude political error', and drew the corresponding administrative, i.e. punitive, conclusions:[107] Shatskin was expelled from the Party soon after for 'factional activity', and was executed in 1937, his 'error' of 1929 no doubt figuring on the charge sheet.

Stalin was given regular reports by the NKVD on the condition of the mummy and the measures being taken to preserve it, such as its wartime evacuation to Tyumen in Western Siberia, from 1941 until the spring of 1945. Professor Boris Ilyich Zbarsky was responsible to the security services for maintaining Lenin's body in viewable condition, and in 1934 he and Vorobiev were decorated and each given the use of an automobile, an exceptional privilege at the time. In November 1939 Zbarsky was installed in a new laboratory on the personal initiative of Beria,[108] and in 1944 he was created an Academician – not that his work or his position saved him from arrest during the postwar terror.

By the early 1970s this laboratory employed twenty-seven scientists and thirty-three technicians, including three Academicians, one Corresponding Member of the Academy of Sciences, three Doctors of Science and twelve Ph.Ds. The embalming specialists watched carefully for any marks on the mummy's skin, 'peeling of the nose', 'darkening' or 'deformation of the dermis'. In February 1940, for instance, Beria had reported to the Politburo that an inspection had revealed 'deviations' on the face, 'a parting of the [autopsy] scar on the head, darkening on the nose'.[109] In 1972, salaries at the laboratory were increased by twenty-five per cent.[110] More care and attention was lavished on it than on the country's wretched public health service.

In March 1940 the Politburo approved Beria's plan for a new sarcophagus. Zbarsky was expected to submit plans and models 'of an artistic kind' by 15 April, for completion by 20 October. Special tasks were delegated to the Commissar for Power Stations and Electrical Industry, M.G. Pervukhin, and Commissar for Armaments B.L. Vannikov.[111]

An improved sarcophagus was made in the 1970s. Ninety-six people received medals and dozens more high awards for its creation.

The mausoleum was frequently under repair. In 1974, for instance, refurbishment cost 5.5 million roubles, and four hundred people received medals and awards.

Gradually an entire mechanism was put in place to manage Lenin's embalmed body, which had become vitally necessary not so much for its propaganda value, as for its effect on the psychology of the masses. They indeed became accustomed to it, seeing it as a special feature of Soviet political culture. It is plain that the mummy could only exist in a society dominated by dogmatic thinking, and in effect it became the physical expression of the 'eternal' nature of Lenin's ideas. Rehoused in 1933 in its granite mausoleum and again on view, the ideological exploitation of the mummy had its effect for an extraordinarily extended period. For the Bolsheviks it was one means of personifying the 'immortality' of Lenin's precepts, although on the eve of the twenty-first century, rather than serving as testimony of the man's greatness, it is instead a reminder of the depth of the country's historic failure. For decades hundreds of millions of roubles were spent on preserving Lenin's relics. It was of no consequence to the Soviet leadership that the remains of thousands of soldiers had not been buried after the Second World War, nor that war invalids – the victors – lived under far worse conditions than those they had defeated. Thousands of wounded veterans of the war in Afghanistan could not obtain qualified medical help or accommodation or wheelchairs, yet funds for the mummy, for the mausoleum and its laboratory were never short.

To be sure, over the years there have been some futile attempts to expose the absurdity of the mausoleum. Several times small quantities of leaflets were distributed on Red Square protesting against 'Russia's chief blasphemer' being housed at the holy Kremlin. On 20 March 1959 a visitor threw a hammer at the sarcophagus and broke the glass. He was arrested, and most probably died in a lunatic asylum. On 1 September 1963 another visitor was blown up and killed by a device he had concealed under his coat.

As early as 1925 the Politburo established a special laboratory to study Lenin's brain. They wanted to show the world that the great ideas had been born in an extraordinary mind, and that this would confirm both their special quality and their absolute truth. In 1927 the laboratory became the Institute of the Brain under Professor Vogt, and later Professor Sarkisov. In May 1936 the chairman of the Committee for the Management of Research and Teaching Institutions reported to the Central Committee that the Institute of the Brain had in ten years 'completed the fundamental and vitally important task for which it was established'. Its work consisted of 153 pages of typescript and fifteen albums containing 750 microphotographs, tables and diagrams.[112]

The Party leadership obviously hoped to be handed results which would confirm the special and superior nature of Lenin's brain compared to those of other people – despite the fact that it was manifestly diseased. In a secret report to Stalin in May 1936, Sarkisov wrote that from a series of indicators, such as the quality of the furrows and convolutions, it was possible to say that 'V.I. Lenin's brain displayed an extraordinarily high degree of organization'. Lenin's brain, Sarkisov wrote, was being compared with ten hemispheres from the brains of 'average people', as well as with the brains of the Bolshevik Skvortsov-Stepanov, the poet Vladimir Mayakovsky, and the well-known philosopher and former Bolshevik Alexander Bogdanov. Lenin's brain, the report continued, 'was preserved in formalin and alcohol, divided into blocks and set in paraffin wax. The blocks have been sliced into 30,963 sections, all kept at the Institute.' According to Sarkisov, Lenin's brain had a higher proportion of furrows of the frontal lobes than the brains of Kuybyshev, Lunacharsky, Menzhinsky, Bogdanov, Michurin (the father of Soviet genetics), Mayakovsky, Pavlov, Clara Zetkin, Academician Lulevich, the scientist Tsiolkovsky ... the list goes on. This activity continued long after Sarkisov's day, with brain after brain being delivered into the hands of his successors, including that of Stalin.

If there was any scientific value in all this, it was surely vitiated by the blatant intent to establish the superiority of Lenin's brain over those of other people. Who knows – perhaps the furrows in Mayakovsky's brain were what made him a better poet than Lenin, and if so, then in that respect his brain was superior to Lenin's.

An average human brain weighs between 1300 and 1400 grammes, and Lenin's weighed 1340. Sarkisov's report said nothing about the anomalies caused by the long illness. On the contrary, he declared that 'V.I.'s brain possessed such high organization that even during the illness, despite much damage, it remained on a very high level.' The report reeks of political obedience and predetermination.[113] In fact, in January 1994 Dr Oleg Adrianov, the most recent director of the institute, announced, 'In the anatomical structure of Lenin's brain there is nothing sensational.'[114]

A hardly less disreputable fact about the institute is that it collected the brains of many people, as 'rich anatomical material' for its purposes. Apart from those already mentioned, it analysed the brains of the Japanese Comintern official Sen Katayama, the French writer Henri Barbusse, the writer Andrei Bely, the poet Eduard Bagritsky, the composer Mikhail Ippolitov-Ivanov, the opera singer Leonid Sobinov, among others. Whether their previous owners had given permission for such tests is unknown.

The idea of a party dictatorship had been Lenin's, but a dictatorship is unthinkable without a leader, and Lenin was of course the first leader of this dictatorship. Therefore, his posthumous deification should not be seen as a deviation from the norms of Party thinking. It was rather the natural result of the pre-eminent and well-established Party dictatorship. Lenin, however unwittingly, was the creator of his own grotesque immortality. Had the Congress of Soviets of 1924, by a fortunate twist of history, included Mensheviks, SRs and Kadets, it would never have authorized the rash of funeral ceremonies, to say nothing of the mausoleum and thousands of monuments and, least of all, the creation of a new form of holy relic.

Possibly the idea of the mummy was spontaneous, even accidental, but the transformation of the leader of the Party dictatorship into an ideological idol certainly was not. It was a natural expression of totalitarian thinking. The slogan 'Lenin is more alive than all the living' was taken almost literally. At the Politburo meeting of 16 February 1973 a discussion took place on 'the question of renewing Party documents'. The 'question' was plainly raised in order to produce the following decree: 'Party card No. 00000001 in the 1973 format is to be inscribed with the name of the founder of the Communist Party of the Soviet Union and Soviet State V.I. Lenin. The signing of the card is to be done by General Secretary of the Central Committee of the CSPU Comrade Brezhnev, L.I. Members of the Politburo, Candidate Members and Central Committee Secretaries are to be present for the signing.'[115] Card No. 00000002 was issued to the other 'Ilyich', Leonid Ilyich Brezhnev.

## The Inheritance and the Heirs

Thanks chiefly to Lenin's efforts, the Bolsheviks succeeded in convincing the Russian people that the path to happiness lay through lawlessness, arbitrary rule and violence. It had been a recurrent theme in his speeches for many years. In 1906, he stated the doctrinal position from which he never departed: 'Dictatorship is nothing other than power which is totally unlimited by any laws, totally unrestrained by absolutely any rules, and based directly on force.'[116] The totalitarian Soviet state was built on Leninist principles and, although after the Twentieth Party Congress in 1956 it was liberalized to a certain extent, it never became democratic. Described by Khrushchev as an all-people's state, all the components of the political system were elements of the same Leninist dictatorship exercised by one party, the CPSU. The last Soviet Constitution, promulgated in 1977, frequently mentions the full power of the people, but the delusion of democracy was easily punctured by a simple question: why were elections always unopposed? The central idea and chief content of the Soviet state was 'the leading and guiding rôle of the Party'. Contrary to whatever he may have written in his *State and Revolution*, the essence of the Leninist state was the creation of the *partocratic* society, society ruled by a political party, with the dictatorship of the CPSU enshrined in the Constitution.

Thus, Lenin's chief heritage was a powerful partocratic system, based on a bureaucratic, military and political apparatus. Furthermore, it was official policy that the rôle of the Party would grow: 'As the Soviet people handle more and more complex and responsible tasks in the building of Communism,' Brezhnev said, 'the rôle of the Communist Party will grow yet larger.'[117] It is worth noting that Brezhnev not only renamed his own post General Secretary, but also made himself Chairman of the Supreme Soviet, i.e. President, in 1977, after removing Podgorny. All his successors followed this practice, with the interval between becoming Party leader and head of state rapidly growing shorter. In effect, the reality of the Party's control of the state was thus recognized in this personalized, non-institutional way. Party rule gradually produced an omnipotent clan of Party bosses in the centre and the provinces. State bodies, starting with the government itself, existed only to carry out the orders of the shadowy Politburo.

To become a member of this tiny inner circle meant undergoing the most stringent of checks. The General Secretary and the heads of the security service kept secret dossiers with compromising material on every member of the Politburo. Sealed in 'Special files', only the General Secretary himself was entitled to inspect these dossiers. Even the much-feared and hard-line orthodox M.A. Suslov had things to hide: as Party Secretary of the Stavropol region during the war, he had apparently escaped from the town as the Germans approached, commandeering several cars for his own use and abandoning wounded troops to their fate. In Moscow, he had abused his privileged access to restricted shops and bought large quantities of goods in short supply at nominal prices.[118]

Such compromising material was collected on every Politburo member. One had dubious clergy origins; another had uttered incautious remarks in the presence of his staff; a third disdained

Communist morality and had affairs with the female members of his staff, and so on. In fact, each and every Politburo member had something which could be used to get rid of him if he displeased the chief in any way. Alexander Shelepin, who was Chairman of the KGB from 1958 to 1961, then head of Soviet Trade Unions, was sacked from the Politburo in 1975 for displaying, in the words of Brezhnev, 'false democratism': he had taken his holiday in an ordinary rest-home, rather than one of the special villas reserved for dignitaries, and – good God! – had even eaten in the communal dining-room. The real reason for his disgrace was the large demonstration by Ukrainians and Jews that had greeted him on a trip to London earlier that year.

The minutes of the Politburo are a chronicle of Lenin's heirs, and they embrace every imaginable – and unimaginable – aspect of the life of the great state. The agenda of a single meeting might include the results of a nuclear test, practical measures to prepare defence against nuclear and biological weapons, methods to speed up the construction of the Baikal–Amur railway, reinforcing atheist education, strengthening the security organs, the sale of oil and gas, and, most often, the celebration of Lenin anniversaries and jubilees. There was always time to discuss Leninist topics. As Brezhnev declared on 20 June 1968, 'the main thing is that we must always, at all stages, defend Leninism from any attack, any assault . . . Leninism must be defended and we will defend it consistently and implacably . . . As you know, we have built our life and all our work according to Lenin. This is no empty phrase, it is our real life, it is our real work.'[119]

It would be hard to disagree: everything done in Soviet Russia after Lenin's death was done according to his blueprint, his precepts and his principles: the totalitarian state, the bureaucratic society, the dominance of a single ideology, militant atheism, the planned economy, the incredible exploitation of labour, the endless militarization of the country, the tireless search for new enemies. The ordinary Soviet citizen adapted to a life in which the state guaranteed him a barely adequate wage, a miserable apartment, some social benefits in the form of education, medicine and holidays – a beggarly minimum in a fabulously wealthy country. But the people were used to it, and knew nothing different. Their thinking was done for them, their decisions were taken for them. Even when the reins were somewhat loosened with the end of mass repression in the mid-1950s, there were those in the upper echelons of power who had to be dealt with by modified Stalinist methods, such as exile and isolation.

For instance, the Politburo discussed KGB Chairman Shelepin's report on Kaganovich, a member of the 'anti-Party group' who had been banished from Moscow to Kalinin at the time of the attempted coup against Khrushchev by the Stalinist die-hards in the Politburo led by Molotov in 1957. As the report indicated, Kaganovich had taken to visiting the capital illegally and looking up old friends, in the hope of getting help with the writing of his memoirs. His old friends, to a man, had reported these 'unauthorized contacts' to the KGB, mentioning the most trivial details: Kaganovich was complaining that 'the pension he'd been given was a small one, only 1158 roubles', and commenting ironically, 'They couldn't even go to 1200 [the state maximum], I hadn't done enough time.' He was also offended that the Central Committee had made it clear that he had permission only to reside in Kalinin.[120] The Politburo responded to Kaganovich's complaints by stepping up surveillance on him and sending him to the Urals as a factory manager, bringing him back to Moscow in 1961 for expulsion from the Party. He nevertheless succeeded in beating the system by living for the rest of his life in the capital, whose underground railway once bore his name. He died in 1991 at the age of ninety-nine, dominoes champion of his locality.[121]

It became a tradition for the General Secretary to give the Politburo an end-of-year account of the amount of work it had gone through. In December 1973 Brezhnev told his colleagues that at fifty-three sessions they had dealt with 615 questions by discussion and a further 3256 by correspondence. Of these, 2062 involved foreign policy and foreign trade. Agriculture concerned 165 items, industry 163, welfare seventy. He added that as far as ideology was concerned, 'things were not so good', and only sixty-four ideological issues had been raised. He sympathized with his colleagues that 'We are often tired, of course, we overload ourselves, but all of it, comrades, is for the sake of the good of our country, all of it is for the sake of serving our great Leninist Party.' Even in this narrow inner sanctum, ideological cant was obligatory: 'Comrades, we work in harmony, in the spirit of Lenin's commandments . . . In Lenin's times there were oppositional groupings in our Party that Lenin fought decisively against. Now we have total unity . . . For instance, sometimes I sign decrees which I

don't agree with. True, there aren't many of them. I do it because
the majority of the Politburo has voted for them.'[122]

What kind of men were Lenin's heirs? He himself had not been
General Secretary of the Party, but his authority was so great that he
was unanimously regarded as head of both the state and the Party.
Subsequently, in the Stalinist interpretation, the Party leader was also
in practice both the head of state and of government. We have already
given much attention to Stalin, as Lenin's first successor. Let us now
look at how the rest, from Khrushchev to Gorbachev, continued,
defended or developed Lenin's ideas and his methodology. It should
be noted that, unlike their ideological progenitor (and Stalin), most
of their writings on Lenin and Leninism, whether articles, collections
or even books, were not their own work, but that of anonymous
speech-writers or ghost-writers, a practice that became deeply
entrenched among the Party *nomenklatura*. Even a First District Party
Secretary who wrote his own articles was a rare phenomenon.

In this respect Lenin was far superior to his successors. Even if his
style was ponderous, impenetrable and repetitive, at least it was his
own. With the exception of Gorbachev, it appears that Lenin's successors were not well versed in his works, however fond they were of
quoting him. He was Marxist holy writ, which could be drawn on for
any occasion. A quotation from Lenin had mystical significance, but
it was above all the surest way to protect oneself from criticism for
a lack of ideas. His successors merely skimmed the surface of his
writings.

After Stalin's death in 1953, a joint session of the full Central Committee, the Council of Ministers of the USSR and the Presidium of
the Supreme Soviet of the USSR decided that Nikita Khrushchev
should concentrate on working in the Party Central Committee, and
on 7 September 1953 he was appointed First Secretary, as the General
Secretaryship was then called. Energetic, impulsive and inconsistent,
Khrushchev was, however, a courageous politician, who would be
remembered as the man who struck the first and most fatal blow
against Stalinism. As a product of the Stalinist system himself, he
condemned only the manifestations of Stalinism, not their origins and
causes. On the contrary, the speech he gave at the Twentieth Party
Congress in 1956 – written for him by Central Committee Secretary

P.N. Pospelov and his team – established Lenin as the ideal from which Stalin had departed.

Khrushchev declared that Stalin had introduced the idea of 'enemy of the people', whereas in fact it had been Lenin. 'In January 1920,' he went on, 'Lenin ordered an end to mass terror and the abolition of the death penalty.' He omitted to add that in March 1922 Lenin declared that 'the more bourgeois and Black Hundreds clergy we shoot, the better'. Khrushchev very properly exposed Stalin, but he removed only the outer layer of his political and social defects, forgetting that he himself had been among those who had made their own contribution to Stalin's cult. Speaking at election meetings in Moscow in 1936, Khrushchev repeatedly praised Stalin: 'Our Party has fulfilled Lenin's commandments under the leadership of our great Stalin ... I am proud and think myself lucky to be able to work under the leadership of our great leader, Comrade Stalin ... I swear an oath that I will not deviate one step from the line being carried out by our great Stalin.'[123] All such speeches were greeted with stormy applause. The whole nation was blinded, like Khrushchev himself, who at the time genuinely believed that with Lenin's blueprint and his wise leader the Russian people were building a radiant future.

Although he called himself an orthodox Leninist, Khrushchev – who had not read him – used Lenin to debunk Stalin, as if Lenin had not been Stalin's spiritual father. It would not have occurred to Khrushchev for an instant that Lenin could have been wrong about anything. His listeners accepted that Lenin was an infallible saint, and that it had been Stalin who had broken his commandments. Thus, when Khrushchev stated that Stalin had shown disrespect for Lenin by shelving the building of the Palace of Soviets as a monument to Lenin, his audience was hushed. And when he declared that 'we must correct this position and erect this monument to Vladimir Ilyich', his words were drowned in a storm of applause.

Much is revealed of the kind of man Khrushchev was in his talks with Mao Tse-tung on 2 October 1959 in Peking. Their conversation lasted for four hours, and when the discussion turned to the territorial dispute between China and India, Khrushchev declared: 'Whether they penetrated more than five kilometres or less than five kilometres is unimportant. I take as my example Lenin, who handed over Kars, Ardagan and Ararat to Turkey. And up to this day there are people in the Transcaucasus who are still disgruntled by these measures of Lenin's.' He went on: 'As for the Dalai Lama's leaving Tibet, had we been in your shoes we wouldn't have given him the chance to go. It'd be better if he was in his grave. But now he's in India and might go to the USA. Surely that wouldn't be good for the socialist countries?'

The talks were not going well, and Khrushchev, answering Chinese objections and ignoring diplomatic niceties, said much that was self-revealing: 'As for Hungary [in 1956] ... You must understand, we had an army in Hungary, we were supporting that idiot Rakosi, that was our mistake, not the mistake of the United States ... If the windows of the American and [West] German embassies in Moscow were broken, it was we who organized it.'

In the course of the talks, a heated confrontation took place between Khrushchev and Marshal Chen Yi:

KHRUSHCHEV: If you think we're time-servers, Comrade Chen Yi, don't give me your hand, because I won't shake it.

CHEN YI: Me too. I'm telling you, your anger doesn't scare me.

KHRUSHCHEV: Don't you try to spit on us from up there, Marshal. You haven't got enough spit. You won't spit on us ... We've shot down more than one American plane and always said they'd crashed by themselves. There's no way you're going to call us time-servers.[124]

Straightforward, harsh and tactless, Khrushchev's style had all the hallmarks of the Leninist. It was also the spirit of Lenin, however, that ejected Khrushchev from his position on 14 October 1964. The seventy-page report of the Central Committee plenum on this event is packed with quotations from Lenin, beginning with his 'Letter to the Congress' as the age-old argument against 'the newly exposed claimant to a new cult of the personality'. Quotations were found on the harm and misfortune caused by 'enthusiasts for restructuring in all or any kind of way', on the 'need for state wisdom', on the importance of 'the leader's personal qualities', the 'rôle of the Soviets', and so on. Lenin was now being mobilized against Khrushchev, no less than he had been by Khrushchev himself when he was debunking Stalin.

One experienced participant recalled: 'At a big reception, with about 2000 people, many of them foreigners, Khrushchev had declared that it was not the working class and armed troops who had carried out the October revolution (which Lenin led), but old women. What is this but an attempt to diminish the rôle of Vladimir Ilyich and raise his own? How could his tongue twist itself into making such blasphemous remarks?'[125]

The Plenum, naturally, blamed Khrushchev for everything that was wrong in the country: slower output growth since Stalin's death, slower scientific and technological progress, problems in agriculture, but above all for his endless attempts to reorganize and restructure, his reforming itch. The 'true Leninist' was mocked with particular malice for his frequent trips abroad. It was pointed out that in 1963 alone he spent 170 days out of the country – and with his wife, to boot. Then there were all the gifts he had presented to foreign heads of state, and those he had received in return. It was all too much for the Party's hypocritical morality. As they scraped away at what dignity Khrushchev might have had, they overlooked the fact that it was they alone who had put him in his post.

He was condemned for the 'colourful' language to which he commonly resorted, often on inappropriate occasions: 'Khrushchev's foul language was enough not only to wither your ears, as they say, but to make the cast-iron pillars blush: fool, idler, layabout, stench, a filthy fly, a wet hen, crap, shit, an arsehole – and these are only the printable ones. There isn't paper strong enough to bear the words he used most often, nor can the tongue bring itself to pronounce them.' His attack on Stalin was also re-examined, and in the process Stalin, with some reservations, was defended. 'Can Stalin really be depicted as having acted with the help of the axe and the scaffold? And how does it make the Party and the people look for tolerating him so long in power? One should not belittle Stalin's services, still less cancel them out.'[126]

Khrushchev was removed not because of his mistakes and omissions – of which there were not a few – but mainly out of revenge, revenge for what he had done at the Twentieth Congress in 1956, for the blow he had struck against Stalinism. Virtually all the 'Leninists' of those days longed for a Stalinist order without terror, and Khrushchev's departure meant that Stalinism was still alive and well. It was a form of Leninist Bolshevism with deep roots which Khrushchev had damaged badly, but not uprooted from their totalitarian soil.

A 'true Leninist', Khrushchev was a child of the regime. His long years of dedication to Leninism, of which he had only the vaguest understanding, were more highly regarded than his abilities, education or culture. Like Lenin, he was generous with his ephemeral, utopian prognoses, and, like his hero, he was prepared to fix the date (1981) at which the Soviet people would come into the promised land. While he was the instigator of the Cuban missile crisis of 1962, perhaps the closest the world has yet come to a nuclear catastrophe, he had the political courage to pull back. It is not for this, however, that he will be remembered by the Soviet people, but rather as their liberator from the gloomy oppression of Stalinism; incomplete, inconsistent, superficial it may have been, but still it was a liberation. Like his more fortunate successors, who remained in office until their deaths, after 1956 Khrushchev still kept his gaze zealously on Lenin, for it was clear that the system could not function without its 'holy' leader. This approach was well suited to the mediocrity who took over in 1964, Leonid Ilyich Brezhnev.

Brezhnev would take no step without consulting Lenin. He went further than any other of Lenin's successors in promoting the Comintern idea of spreading Communism throughout the world. On 16 April 1970, when opening a Lenin memorial complex in Ulyanovsk (not yet, in 1994, renamed Simbirsk), he declared that he firmly believed 'in the universal triumph of the cause of socialism', and that only a little effort was required to achieve complete victory. Thanks to Lenin, he went on, the time would come when 'there will not remain even the tiniest island in the world where exploitation will exist'.[127] Once again, the Soviet leadership was talking in terms of continents and epochs, hoping that as socialist influence spread across the political map it would be possible to constrict the capitalist world. Brezhnev's support for national and anti-imperialist movements was therefore enormous, costing the USSR fantastic resources. Egypt, Ethiopia, Yemen, Angola, Afghanistan, Nicaragua, Libya, Iraq, Syria and many other countries were all beneficiaries, as long as they adopted an anti-American stance.

Few historians of the decline of the Russian empire have been able to resist citing Nicholas II's published diary as evidence that the great country was ruled by a man of low intellectual calibre. On 10 April 1916, for instance, Nicholas wrote: 'Slept till 10 a.m. The weather was warm. Received two reports. Birilev came for breakfast. Had long walk. At 6 received Fedorov. Read. Stana had dinner with us, rode with us and stayed the night.'[128] The last tsar, it seems, did not lead a busy life. But at least he read, and was able to do so in several languages.

Brezhnev also kept a diary, and every day he wrote between ten and twenty lines in it, in a flowing, sweeping hand. Opening his diary at the same date as the above quotation from Nicholas, sixty-one years later, we find – and we reproduce Brezhnev's own punctuation and orthography: 'Was at the dacha, had lunch. Borshch made with fresh cabbage Rested went outside read some papers. Watched hockey USR Sweden – USR won 4–2. Watched "programme vremya [Time]" Had dinner – sleep.' The entry for 21 January is more informative: 'Rested at home for first half of the day lunched at home. Weight 85.200 Second half worked in Kremlin Signed PB [Politburo] minutes of 20 January. Bogolyubov reported . . .

*16 February*: Work at the house.

*18 March*: Exercise. Then talked to Chernenko. Then with C[omrades] Gromyko A.A., Andropov Ustinov – we read materials about Vance's visit – Rang Pavlov G.S. on cost [next word started and crossed out] Read all kinds of material with Galya Dorishina Went to the circus

*13 April*: Morning usual domestic chores. They took blood from a vein From 11 o'clock conversation with Daoud Question of one-to-one meeting dropped Had good rest – (lunch) Worked with Doroshina.

*14 April*: At home – Tolya washed my hair Weight 86.700 Talks with Podgorny about presenting me with Koms. card Presentation of Komsomol card No. 1 speech by Tyazhelnikov my speech Galya read serial from 'pravda' on limitation of strategic arms Who are the authors of this material Lunch and rest 2.30–4.10

*15 April*: Zavidovo 4 ducks – 33rd wild boar – 21 – dragged

*22 April*: 86.400 Five o'clock meeting devoted to his [Lenin's] birthday Talked with Grishin Gromyko Chernenko Doroshina

*23–24 April*: Days off

*3 May*: Weight – 85.300. Talk with Ryabenko. Talk on phone with Storozhev? I know what he wants. Talk with Chernenko K.U. –? About PB agenda *Tailors* – gave the grey suit, got the leather double-breasted casual jacket Rang Yu.V. Andropov – he came and we chatted Worked with Doroshina

*3 June*: Received Chernenko – signed minutes worked with Galya Doroshina Rest – flew to Zavidovo – 5 boars.

And so it goes on: 'Talked with Comrade Kopenkin A.N. – he said I've heard him with the voice of an officer, then the voice of a general, and now he's glad I hear his voice of a marshal'; 'Went nowhere – no one rang all the same – had haircut and shave in the morning and hair wash Strolled a bit – the mail Watched [Central Army Sports Club] lose to Spartak good lads played well'; 'Swam. 1 o'clock. 30 m. pool. Shave. Gossiped with Podgorny. After conversation with Ceausescu talked with Sharvanadze [sic]'; 'Hunted in Astrakhan in the evening killed 34 geese . . . Had good shower'; 'Talked with Podgorny about football and hockey and a bit about the constitution'; 'Persuaded K.U. Chernenko to cut rise in tanks out of the film Communists'.[129] The diary meanders in this way for hundreds of pages. Compared to Brezhnev's gibberish, even Nicholas II appears brilliant.

The important point is that the Leninist system of the monopoly of power facilitated and even favoured the promotion of colourless, mediocre and semi-literate people, whose intellectual potential was only half-developed. Everyone knew it, and it suited almost everyone.

Brezhnev's pathetic diary only arouses one's pity for the country. The last time I saw him was in November 1982, a week before he died. Marshal Ustinov brought him – he was practically carried by a hefty young man – into the Sverdlov Hall of the Kremlin, where all the military top brass were assembled. Unable to get up onto the platform where the chairmen were sitting, Brezhnev was led to a rostrum, papers were set before him and, clinging shakily to the edge of the speaker's lectern, he tried to read his speech. The generals in the audience lowered their heads; they were ashamed for their country and sorry for Brezhnev, a sick man who had reached the top by an organizational quirk. There followed twenty minutes of disjointed speech.

Yet this was the same man who quite recently had declared, in a speech entitled 'Lenin's Cause Lives and Will be Victorious': 'However contradictory the picture of the world is today . . . the main decisive trend of development is precisely the one predicted by Lenin. However different the component parts of the world may seem, each one of them is leading – and in the last analysis can only lead – towards Communism!' This was said not in 1919 at the Comintern Congress, but in April 1970. Lenin's successors had lost all sense of reality, living as they did in an illusory world created by the ideological myths of Leninism.

The whole country was mildly amused by Brezhnev's passion for decorations. He was a Hero in all the socialist countries that had created this order; in 1973 he was awarded the Lenin Prize 'for strengthening peace between peoples'; he received the Frederic Joliot-Curie Peace Medal; and the Karl Marx Medal, which was the highest award the Soviet Academy of Science could bestow, for 'outstanding work in the development of Marxist-Leninist theory'. He wanted very much to be a Marshal, and made himself one. He awarded himself every imaginable decoration, title and rank. His vanity became an absurdity and a public joke, while his entourage agonized over what new medal they could find to pin on him. It reached the point where more than once the Politburo awarded Brezhnev an order, and the Presidium of the Supreme Soviet only issued the decree after the fact.

Lenin had always wanted the Party leadership to include as many workers and peasants as possible. In practice it consisted of professional revolutionaries, a tradition the Party bosses jealously maintained, never letting state power slip from their grasp. Although they all came from workers' and peasants' families, in their early youth they joined the ranks of Komsomol and Party Secretaries, and worked their way steadily up the ladder to an office in the Kremlin.

In order to hang onto the East European satellites, all the General Secretaries not only relied on a common ideology and a vast army of tanks, but also had to be prepared to hand out interest-free credit, oil, gas, metals and weapons at less than world prices. When Brezhnev met Eduard Gierek, Gustav Husak, Todor Zhivkov, Jan Kadar and Erich Honecker – the leaders of the East European Communist states – in Budapest on 18 March 1975, the discussion quickly turned to oil and related topics:

HUSAK: Our planners say we need approximately another half million tonnes.
BREZHNEV: You're getting greedy. I can remember when your Slovnaft factory got three million tonnes of oil a year, now it wants six or seven.
HUSAK: We get sixteen million tonnes in all.
SHCHERBITSKY: That's the entire annual output of our Ukraine.
BREZHNEV: It's not such an easy matter to find new deposits. We're also making deliveries to Cuba. And we're clothing the Cuban army for nothing. And we're paying them for their sugar at favourable prices. We supply grain to several countries. Poland and the GDR are also not self-supporting in grain.[130]

The Comintern way of thinking was still functioning and, as before, it was costing the Soviet Union dear, at a time when the Soviet people were enduring a perpetually low standard of living.

Having reached the Party's Mount Olympus, each General Secretary had to immortalize himself by his acts, and once he was dead it was the Party's duty to continue to do so, according to the Leninist tradition. After Brezhnev's death on 10 November 1982, for instance, the Politburo strove long and hard to find a way to make the 'great Leninist's' imprint on history more visible. They wanted to rename the city of Zaporozhie 'Brezhnev', but Brezhnev's successor as General Secretary, Yuri Andropov, was wary: 'The city is connected with the Zaporozhie Cossacks and Cossack unrest and so on. Wouldn't it be better for us to call it Naberezhnye Chelny?' The meaning of this term was something like 'River Canoes', but the object of using it would be to incorporate the syllables 'berezh', and thus suggest the name of the recently departed leader. When the Politburo then suggested renaming a space centre after Brezhnev, Andropov again showed more wisdom than the others: 'Should we really connect his name with rockets? It would be better to call Zvezdny Gorod ['Star City'] in the Shchelkovsk district of Moscow *oblast* after him.'

Nikolai Tikhonov, Chairman of the Council of Ministers, then proposed giving the late leader's name to Nurek Power Station and to the Raspad Mine in Kemerovo *oblast*. Again Andropov was cautious about the associations: 'There was a big accident at the Raspad Mine recently, a lot of people were killed.' Tikhonov saw the point, withdrew his proposal and suggested instead that the ice-breaker *Arktika* be renamed the *Leonid Ilyich Brezhnev*. The Novolipetsk factory was also dropped as a candidate for renaming, but the Oskolsk metallurgical plant was so honoured. Many squares in various cities were renamed. For some unaccountable reason, Minister of Defence Ustinov thought that, while 'the name of Brezhnev could be applied to a passenger ship, for the time being we should not use it for river shipping'. Andropov sensed that the Politburo was running out of ideas, and proposed that 'Brezhnev's name be given to several more enterprises, but let's do it a bit later on'. This was agreed.[131]

Unlike his predecessor, Yuri Vladimirovich Andropov was a man of exceptional intelligence. He had given a substantial part of his life to the work of the KGB, he spent four years, from 1953 to 1957, in

Budapest doing diplomatic work, and the rest of his career was devoted to the Leninist commandments of fighting political diversion and dissidents and undermining imperialism.[132] For instance, at a session of 7 November 1974, the Politburo unanimously agreed the steps to be taken against Alexander Solzhenitsyn. As the minutes show, Andropov set the tone, which was followed by the rest of the Politburo:

BREZHNEV: We have to take account of the fact that Solzhenitsyn didn't even go abroad to collect the Nobel Prize.

ANDROPOV: When it was suggested he go abroad to collect the Nobel Prize, he asked for guarantees for returning to the Soviet Union. Comrades, I have been asking about Solzhenitsyn since 1965. Now he has risen to a new stage in his hostile activity. He is trying to create an organization inside the Soviet Union cobbled together from former prisoners. He speaks against Lenin, against the October revolution, against the socialist system . . . There are tens of thousands of Vlasovites [wartime army collaborators with the Germans] in the country, and Ukrainian Nationalists and similar hostile elements. Hundreds and thousands of people among whom Solzhenitsyn can find support . . . I think we ought to put Solzhenitsyn on trial and apply Soviet law to him . . . Suppose there is a hostile underground and the KGB has not spotted it? But Solzhenitsyn acts openly and is quite brazen . . . Therefore the necessary measures, about which I have already written to the Central Committee, have to be taken, that is, he must be put out of the country. [133]

Lenin's call to 'cleanse Russia' of the intelligentsia was clearly still being heard.

Andropov was fond of talking about democracy, as he did for instance on the occasion of the 106th anniversary of Lenin's birth, in 1976. Having made the customary obeisance to the dictatorship of the proletariat, from which the all-people's state had emerged, and stressed that 'there is no democracy as such', only 'bourgeois democracy or socialist democracy', Andropov declared that: 'the huge advances made in socialist democracy . . . have for a long time put socialism way ahead of the bourgeois democratic states'.[134]

Of all of his successors, Andropov might be considered closest to Lenin in type. He had a powerful mind, was well read, and even wrote poetry in his spare time. The spirit of battle, the constant search for enemies, a narrow class focus, a love of secrecy, personal asceticism and inventive methods all made him a 'true Leninist'.

Before Andropov became General Secretary, he frequently wrote confidential personal notes to his bosses, often of a highly idiosyncratic kind. In a note to Brezhnev during the Yom Kippur War of 1973, for instance, he wrote that the Americans were artificially fixing the world's attention on the Middle East, thereby trying to trick the USSR into neglecting its own interests. In this situation, he wrote: 'You personally cannot do anything other than to drop everything you're doing and deal with this problem until morning ... Personally, I think it is a diversion calculated to keep us fixed artificially only on the Arab–Israeli conflict, thus creating overstrain for everyone, especially for you personally. After all, in this situation you are forced to postpone many other no less important matters than the Middle East one, for example, preparing for your visit to India ...'[135]

Such notes, of which there are many, indicate that Andropov, as Chairman of the KGB, was trying to control the more simple-minded Brezhnev. Seeing spies and provocations everywhere, in typical Leninist fashion he believed that the Americans were trying to undermine the General Secretary's precious health by setting up a smoke-screen behind which they could do their dirty deeds. Perhaps he had seen Lenin's 'arch-secret' note telling Chicherin that they must support the 1922 Genoa Conference publicly, but work secretly to undermine it.[136]

Becoming General Secretary on 12 November 1982, in little more than a year Andropov made huge attempts to change things both in the Party and the country. More than anyone else in the leadership, he knew that the state and society were in a condition of deep stagnation. The main indicators were showing zero growth, and the economy was being kept afloat by billions of dollars earned from the export of oil, gas and other commodities. Having been the chief advocate of sending Soviet troops into Afghanistan in 1979, Andropov now saw that the episode had turned out to be a typical military-political trap. Party and state leadership, especially in the republics, was mired in corruption. A feeling of distrust reigned in the minds of the Russian people. Wanting to know the truth about what was happening in their own country and abroad, millions of citizens were secretly tuning in to foreign broadcasts.

Only the iron curtain, barbed wire and insurmountable obstacles prevented a vast number of people from leaving the country, the land of the GULAG, unfree Russia. When Andropov requested information about the number of Soviet citizens who had succeeded in escaping the country, even the incomplete statistics amazed him. Scientists, artists, sportsmen, intelligence officers, sailors, diplomats, writers, pilots and many others had legally crossed the frontiers, and then remained abroad. But there had also been illegal escapes – across the frontier, over the Berlin Wall, sailors abandoning naval vessels under cover of darkness, all drawn by the hope of liberty. Since 1946, the number of escaping soldiers alone was legion. Having read through the lists of names, Andropov slammed the file shut and set about taking measures to increase control of exits, legal or otherwise, to reduce the number of 'inessential' contacts to a minimum, and to intensify the work of prevention and to raise alertness.

A clever man, but an orthodox Marxist to the core, Andropov could see that drastic steps were required to arrest the collapse, break the stagnation and breathe new life into the old ideals. But as a Bolshevik of the Leninist type, he could think of no other way to stimulate the country than by 'bringing in order'. Soon after his elevation to General Secretary, patrols started arresting people for loitering, thousands of homeless beggars were picked up by the militia, discipline at work was tightened up. In general, the people had some sympathy for such measures, although they did not realize that the sickness in the system was in its very foundations: the command economy, the monopoly of power, the lack of liberty. As might have been expected, Andropov's measures produced only very temporary results. The stagnation continued, and deepened.

During his brief period in office Andropov was extremely ill with kidney disease, and rarely appeared at the Politburo, still less in the republics or provinces. He attempted instead to rule by means of notes. On 4 August 1983 the Politburo discussed his note on the deployment of US missiles in Western Europe. Andropov did not mention the fact that it had been the deployment by the USSR of SS-20 mobile missiles that had provoked a response from the US and NATO. Instead, he proposed that all available means be used to bring pressure on governments and parliaments in the NATO countries in order to create maximum obstruction to the deployment of US missiles in Europe.[137] Yet again, the country lost billions of roubles as the Party leadership strove for strategic supremacy in medium-range missiles, only to have to agree to withdraw them eventually for destruction, while yet again claiming this as a victory of 'Leninist foreign policy'.

Even while he was bedridden, Andropov continued to send his notes for discussion in the Politburo. In October 1983 he sent a particularly important one, to be regarded as a programme paper, in which he raised the question of combating 'departmentalism and bureau-cratism'. He advised his colleagues to think about 'a fundamental improvement in the organization of the management of the country'. This was to be placed at the top of the Central Committee's agenda and a commission was created to formulate the issues, headed by Mikhail Sergeevich Gorbachev.[138] Andropov, like so many others before him, was deluded by the belief that it was possible to eradicate bureaucratism by administrative means. But more and more people were coming to see that this approach was hopeless, and that citing extracts from Lenin was not helping. A total crisis of the Leninist system was becoming plain to see.

The 'true Leninist' who succeeded Andropov when he died on 9 February 1984 was Konstantin Ustinovich Chernenko, whose star flickered in the political firmament almost unnoticed. The people had expected that, with the departure of Andropov, the parade of ailing gerontocrats would come to an end, but the Politburo had other ideas. Chernenko himself opened the Politburo meeting on 13 February 1984 from the chairman's seat, then demonstratively walked across to his usual place at the long table and asked: 'Are there any proposals? I would ask the comrades to express themselves.' Here he looked meaningfully at Tikhonov, who took his cue:

Comrades, we are all feeling these sorrowful moments. General Secretary of the Central Committee of the CPSU and Chairman of the Presidium of the Supreme Soviet, Yuri Vladimirovich Andropov, an outstanding figure in our Party and state, has left this life. Our Party, however, has at its disposal a large number of well trained cadres. I think the Politburo also has worthy comrades. Therefore I propose that the next Party Plenum appoint Comrade Chernenko, Konstantin Ustinovich, as General Secretary . . .[139]

The main hurdle had been cleared, and it remained only to proclaim support. Anyone who now proposed an alternative candidate would be labelled as threatening the unity of the leadership. Following Tikhonov, who was close to Chernenko, Gromyko, Ustinov and Grishin spoke in his support. Then it was Gorbachev's turn:

The situation demands that our Party, and above all its leading organs, the Politburo and Secretariat, remain united as never before. And unmistakably all of us in the Politburo, plus Candidate Members and Central Committee Secretaries, will be preserving the principle of succession if we accept the proposal to recommend Konstantin Ustinovich Chernenko for the post of General Secretary ... The unanimity with which we have today spoken of Konstantin Ustinovich's candidature bears witness to the fact that we in the Politburo have complete unity in this respect.

Gorbachev was playing a part that had been prepared for him, as for the others, in this Party ritual. All those who spoke later had only to find different words with which to repeat the sentiments uttered by Tikhonov.

While Andropov had tried to change the fatal course of things, Chernenko, a typical example of the mediocrities to be found in the Party organization, was incapable of advancing a single new idea. Collection No. 83 in the Presidential Archives, containing 428 files, describes the career of a dedicated Party functionary. As chief of the Secretariat of the Presidium of the Supreme Soviet and director of the Central Committee General Department, Chernenko had daily access to the top level of Party and state. Endowed with little more than zeal, he became Brezhnev's favourite when no longer young and already a sick man, and towards the end of his career he had a sudden meteoric rise. In 1977 he became a Candidate Member of the Politburo, and a full member the following year. On 13 February 1984 he was made General Secretary. He was thrice a Hero of Socialist Labour, and was liberally sprinkled with decorations, including the Lenin Prize.[140] For a Party functionary of Chernenko's calibre to become head of state and Party leader was a sure sign that the Leninist system was about to disintegrate.

Chernenko's sole accomplishment was to reallocate the functions of the Politburo members. Following Central Committee tradition, he made himself responsible for defence, state security and Party personnel, and also gave himself and his old friends in the apparatus responsibility for the General Department and Administration of

Central Committee Affairs.[141] A functionary to the end, he even sent a directive, which he ordered to be distributed to all executives in the localities, specifying the precise width of margin to be used in official papers, failing which such papers would not be admitted. Every member of the Politburo had an obligation to be a 'theoretician'. The Party's publishing house, Politizdat, systematically inundated the bookshops with thick volumes written not, of course, by the 'Leninists' themselves, but by ghost-writers and speech-writers. Chernenko too made his contribution. Although his writers were well aware of their leader's own bureaucratic predilections, they dug deep into Lenin's manuscripts, hoping to find something that would show him in a 'Leninist', anti-bureaucratic light. They finally came up with a little-known letter from Lenin to Stomonyanov in September 1921 which they used to embellish an article by Chernenko on 'the Party's growing rôle'. Lenin had written: 'You are weighed down by work . . . That's not right. It's a mistake. And the mistake could become fatal. In important matters you should not work without the ability to load others with all the secondary jobs . . . Organize things so that *you only* direct and check. Otherwise you'll collapse.'[142] It was paradoxical that Lenin, who for three years had attempted to decide everything on his own, should write that a leader should know how to delegate work.

The last time I saw Chernenko was in November 1984, four months before he died. He was due to read an official text at a large government reception in the Palace of Soviets to celebrate the anniversary of the revolution. His hands were trembling, he was wheezing and finding it hard to make out the words. He could barely hold the pages. He omitted whole lines; the hall was as silent as the grave, the audience feeling a mixture of embarrassment and pity. The General Secretary was practically dying from emphysema before our eyes, and with him was dying the period of stagnation.

Gorbachev's time had come, a time of hope, even euphoria. At long last a leader had emerged who seemed worthy of the great nation. First, he stunned the Soviet people by speaking without a written text, and doing it coherently, smoothly and intelligently. Nobody could remember such a thing happening before. To be sure, there were those who felt that although Gorbachev made different speeches to different audiences and on different topics, he seemed to be saying the same thing all the time. Against this, it could be argued that he was in the grip of a single reformist idea, and wanted the whole country to understand and support it.

It is still difficult for a Soviet citizen to write about Gorbachev, the last of the General Secretaries. In the West dozens of eulogies have appeared, and will no doubt continue to do so, while in his own country harsh criticism or outright slander is currently the order of the day. Speaking for myself, I was a strong supporter of Gorbachev, and still believe that Russians will only appreciate his true rôle in history at some future time. But I was also one of the first members of parliament to criticize him for his 'contemplative' attitude to reform, for his passivity over the conflict that arose in the Caucasus in early 1988 between Armenia and Azerbaidzhan over the Armenian enclave of Nagorno-Karabakh, and on other issues. Next day, as a serving Colonel-General, I was summoned to the Ministry of Defence and asked to submit my resignation as Director of the Institute of Military History.

The term of the last General Secretary began in time-honoured fashion. The full Politburo met on 11 March 1985, but this time even conservative army generals were terrified by the thought that yet another old man might be appointed, that the era of funerals would continue. There was a genuine fear that Chernenko would be succeeded either by the elderly Moscow Party boss Viktor Grishin or, worse still, by the acting Minister of Defence Grigory Romanov, who, although only sixty-two, was regarded as a rock-ribbed bureaucrat.

As Chairman of the Funeral Commisson – always an important job and a mark of approaching elevation – Gorbachev unexpectedly asked Minister of Health Chazov to go over the facts of Chernenko's death, which everyone already knew: at 3 a.m. on 10 March he had lost consciousness, and had died at 19.20 hours. Gorbachev then addressed the assembled leaders: 'We must first of all decide the question of the General Secretaryship of the Central Committee of the CSPU. I would ask the comrades to express themselves on this item.'

Andrei Gromyko, then Foreign Minister and in June to become Head of State, was waiting, and raised his hand: 'Whatever we may be feeling at this time, we must look into the future and we must not lose one iota of our historic optimism, our faith in the rightness of our theory and practice. I will say it straight out. When one thinks about the candidacy for the post of General Secretary . . . then of course one thinks of Mikhail Sergeevich Gorbachev. That in my view would be the absolutely proper choice . . . One more thought. When we gaze into the future, and I won't hide the fact that for many of us it is hard to do that, we must have a clear sense of the outlook. And the outlook is that we do not have the right to allow our unity to be damaged in any way.'

Everything went as usual. The first to speak on the issue carried the day, and Gromyko also resorted to the customary Leninist ploy of invoking unity in the ranks. The other members could only agree. Tikhonov, as if making amends for having so recently proposed Chernenko, now gave it as his 'unqualified opinion' that Gorbachev was the right man for the job. One after the other, they all followed suit. Demichev, the Minister of Culture, supported Gorbachev because 'he has done a great deal to develop our agricultural-industrial complex'. The last to speak, Chebrikov, head of the KGB, declared: 'The Chekists told me to nominate Comrade Gorbachev . . . You understand that the voice of the KGB, the voice of our team, is the voice of the people.' In a police state, he was probably right.

Gorbachev was brief in his thanks for the nomination, which had only to go to the Central Committee plenum for rubber-stamping, but part of his five-minute speech is worth noting. He said: 'The nine years I worked in Stavropol region and the seven years of my work here have made it obvious to me that our Party has huge creative potential ; . . . We do not need to change our policy. It is a true, correct, genuinely Leninist policy. We have to raise the tempo, move forward, expose shortcomings and overcome them, and see our radiant future clearly.'[143]

At the outset, then, Gorbachev followed the pattern of all previous General Secretaries by swearing loyalty to the Leninist course. It is unlikely that at that moment, before he had been formally elected, he could have done much else. He was a Party official who, however, felt acutely that the country was crying out for major change. He also understood that to initiate excessively sharp turns would be dangerous. It seems likely, though, that Gorbachev had no intention of smashing the old system, but wanted only to carry out some fundamental repairs to it. Even that was an unusual and bold course for such a hardened, dogmatic and bureaucratic society, and indeed the first small steps he took were in their effect revolutionary.

At the end of the Politburo meeting of 4 April 1985, suddenly and without notice, Gorbachev gave a speech on the struggle against ostentation, arrogance, the glorification of leaders, and toadyism. He made his task easier by reading from a long letter from one V.A. Zavyalov, an old Communist in Leningrad, which mocked Brezhnev for his gold stars and the adoration directed at General Secretaries. Gorbachev summed up: 'Lenin talked of the authority of the leadership, the authority of the leaders, but that mustn't be confused with the authority of the Party . . . It's no secret after all that when Khrushchev took his criticism of Stalin to incredible lengths it caused only harm, and to some extent we are still picking up the pieces.'[144] This perfectly encapsulated Gorbachev's standpoint: he was for a Leninist approach, against Stalinism, and in favour of cautious criticism of an already devalued past. It is difficult to see what position he could have taken at the time other than this rather timid and equivocal one.

Gorbachev often referred to Lenin in ritual fashion, but without excessive mawkishness. Even his programme statement at the Central Committee plenum of 23 April 1985 did not contain too many examples like: 'The whole of life, the entire course of history convincingly confirms the great correctness of Lenin's teaching.'[145] Calm and unexaggerated as Gorbachev's use of Lenin may have been, there is no sign that he ever subjected the leader's inaccurate predictions to the least criticism. He understood the vital need for change, for restructuring – *perestroika* – but most of his measures were half-hearted, indecisive and sometimes ambiguous.

At times, to be sure, Gorbachev acted with admirable statesmanship. Withdrawing the troops from Afghanistan, bringing Andrei Sakharov back from exile in January 1987, taking tough decisions after the young German Mathias Rust penetrated Soviet frontier controls and landed his plane in Red Square in May of the same year. There were also occasions when his decisiveness produced dubious results. Thus, when First Deputy Minister of Finance V.V. Dementsev tried during a Politburo meeting to object to the sweeping reduction of vodka sales, Gorbachev rounded on him: 'There's nothing new in what you've said. We all know that we have nothing to cover the money in circulation. But all you can suggest is making the people into drunkards. So, present your ideas more succinctly: you're not in the Finance Ministry now, you're at a meeting of the Politburo.'[146]

Before becoming General Secretary, Gorbachev had behaved like a typical 'ideological fighter', careful to adapt to the opinion of his seniors. In September 1983, during the Politburo's discussion of the shooting down of the Korean Air Lines 747 which had strayed into Soviet airspace, with the loss of all 269 passengers and crew on board, he was vehemently indignant: 'I am sure that our actions were justified. After all, the aircraft was over Soviet territory for some two hours, so it is hard to suggest that it was an unplanned action ... we cannot keep silent now, we must take up an offensive position. We must develop the version which we are supporting at present.'[147]

Although Gorbachev remained burdened to some extent by the habits he had learned in the Party organization, he was in many ways a new kind of General Secretary who by the early 1990s was liberating himself from the more noticeable traits of provincialism. Gorbachev is commonly blamed for the break-up of the Soviet Union, but in fact he tried to save the Union to the very end.

By the summer of 1991, the hard-line Communists knew that the reformist Russian government under Boris Yeltsin was about to negotiate a new Union treaty with the republics that would guarantee the demise of the Soviet Union in its Leninist form, a treaty that would formally recognize the end of Communist rule and permit the nationalities to determine their own political futures. To prevent this, a group of conspirators, including the Soviet Prime Minister, the Defence Minister and other top officials, attempted to seize the government building by force and to declare a state of emergency. They had failed to take account of the Yeltsin government's popularity, and indeed also of the army's unwillingness to fire on Russian citizens. As the world watched the television pictures of the government building, the 'White House', surrounded by thousands of civilian defenders, the coup collapsed in confusion and demoralization. The attempt, far from halting the process of altering Russia's relations with the other republics, accelerated it to the point where, by the end of the year, the Soviet Union itself was declared defunct.

The demise of the Union was an enormous misfortune, especially as a confederation had been a viable possibility – and may yet come to pass. But it was neither Gorbachev nor Yeltsin who brought it about. Ultimately, the demolition of the Soviet Union was caused by the mine Lenin planted deep in its structure in 1920, when the Politburo began liquidating the provinces and creating national entities in their place. Under a dictatorship this was no threat to the unity of the country, but once the democratic process began, centrifugal forces came into play, and the long-repressed desire of every national republic for political independence mounted in a rising, irresistible tide. After seventy years of domination by Moscow, it was inevitable that this process should occur, but historical logic suggested that, instead of a break-up, a new arrangement ought to have been made possible between the republics – a Democratic Federation, perhaps.

## Lenin as History

Lenin at the turn of the century was almost a typical Russian social democrat. He was the Lenin-Ulyanov who could observe Russia from abroad and create his abstract scenarios, abuse the Tsar and send advice on how to organize revolutionary action. But he separated himself from the liberal trend in social democracy and set off on the more radical course. From the time of the 1905 revolution his attacks on the liberal intelligentsia became savage, as he saw in liberal politicians the chief obstacle to his plans. His anti-liberalism was a mark of his general antipathy to liberty as a political and moral value.

The 'bolshevization' of his mind then took place. It seemed as if he could not envisage himself back in Russia unless a revolution took place, yet even in January 1917 he did not believe the revolution would happen. Had it not been for the First World War and the February revolution, Lenin night have lived out his days vegetating in Zurich or Geneva. Lenin was one of the few social democrats who saw in the war an ally for his cause. It had been the chief factor of the fall of the tsarist regime, but the Provisional Government that followed did not know how to get out of it with honour. Lenin knew how to get out of it, even if there was to be no honour. He came to the conclusion that the war must be buried, even at the cost of Russia's defeat. Indeed, he staked everything on Russia's defeat, and went still further, calling for the war between nations to be turned into a war within nations, a civil war. This is crucially important to an understanding of Lenin: to achieve his goal he was prepared to transcend patriotism, national honour and common humanity.

When he took control of the revolutionary government, Lenin was armed only with theoretical plans, and had never governed anyone, other than his wife. He was simply helpless when confronted with the mountain of Russia's problems. All he could think of was to confiscate, requisition and expropriate everything. To do this he needed only one device, merciless dictatorship. A mere two or three months before, he had been talking about the withering away of the state, and now he was feverishly creating an army, tribunals, people's commissars, an inspectorate, secret departments and a diplomatic service. The new state structure could only be made to work by recourse to the despised bourgeois 'experts'.

Lenin's dispositions as founder and leader of the new state may have been superficial, haphazard and half-baked, but they were also harsh and cruel. He was not, in my view, the Janus he is often said to be: his character was of a piece. He was a total Bolshevik who combined in himself a number of traits which made him unique. He was committed to the revolution to the point of frenzy, and only what Viktor Chernov called Lenin's 'irrational common sense' saved himself and his party in hopeless situations.[148]

He was willing to commit appallingly cruel acts in the name of the revolution. Although he was not personally vindictive, like Stalin, he did believe that the revolution would fail if the millstones of the dictatorship ceased to grind for a moment. While this Jacobin outlook was little better than Stalin's brutality, it seemed to give a noble purpose, a certain revolutionary aura, to force and cruelty.

In a letter to Trotsky of 22 October 1919, Lenin wrote that the way to 'finish off [White General] Yudenich is to mobilize another 20,000 [Petrograd] workers plus 10,000 of the bourgeoisie, put machine-guns at their backs, shoot a few hundred and put real, massive pressure on Yudenich'.[149] Twenty-two years later, in the autumn of 1941, when Zhukov and Zhdanov reported to Stalin that the Germans were advancing on the defenders of Leningrad behind a living shield of Russian civilians (the old men, women and children were crying out, 'Don't shoot, we're your people!'), Stalin at once signalled back: 'My advice is don't give in to sentimentality, bash the enemy and his accomplices in the teeth . . . Give the Germans and their delegates everything you've got, whoever they are.'[150]

Believing that 'everything is moral that facilitates the victory of

Communism', Lenin readily sacrificed long-term strategy to short-term tactics. Defending the excesses of War Communism in January 1920 against the arguments of Trotsky, who was by then convinced of the need to alter course, he said: 'We sacrificed tens of thousands of the best Communists for 10,000 White officers and it saved the country. We have to apply the same methods now, or there'll be no grain.'[151] Only when hundreds of thousands more had died from execution, hunger and above all rebellion, did Lenin yield and resort to the NEP, a solution forced on him to resuscitate the basic economy.

Lenin's ideas for creating the just and equal Communist society were delusions, yet they also possessed their own iron logic. The Russian revolution, as he saw it, was only the beginning. Russia was only the detonator of world upheaval. He was ready to sacrifice Russia in order to trigger the continental conflagration. The campaign against Poland, which was his initiative, 'cost the country dear', in Trotsky's words, and its outcome, in the Treaty of Riga, 'cut us off from Germany and . . . gave a powerful impulse to the consolidation of the European bourgeoisie'. Trotsky, however, no less a Jacobin than Lenin, believed the goal was worth the risk.[152] He did not mention that the senseless policy had also cost the lives of tens of thousands of Russian soldiers, and reparations to Poland of more than thirty million gold roubles.[153] Another symptom of this senselessness was the transfer of ninety-three tonnes of tsarist gold to Berlin only two months before Germany capitulated in November 1918.

Lenin's dream of turning the planet red was based on false thinking bred by years of sitting in isolation and making up schemes for world Communist revolution, without taking account of ethnic, national, religious, geographical or cultural factors. He saw only class and economic motives, and the only value he was prepared to defend was power. There is no hint in any of the vast array of archival material to suggest that he was troubled by his conscience about any of the long list of destructive measures he took. Lenin was not personally vain, but he genuinely identified himself with the idea in which he believed. Because his delusions to some extent reflected universal values of social justice, he succeeded in converting them into a programme for millions of people, and imposing it by force.

\*     \*     \*

As we have seen, the Party kept both the delusions and the image of Lenin alive as its most valuable asset. In April 1970, his centenary was marked with special pomp. For two years before the event the Politburo discussed and refined the details of the celebration. On 20 June 1968, for instance, Politburo member Gennady Voronov complained that 'the question of Lenin's cooperative plan has been dropped, yet it was a most important stage in the life of the Party and in Lenin's commandments'; Prime Minister Kosygin thought it was a mistake to write that 'the Party has become the leading force. I think that's wrong, because it has always been the leading force'; summing up the various statements that had been made in this vein, Brezhnev said: 'We are building the whole of our life and all our work on Lenin.'[154] The centenary itself opened a floodgate of every kind of commemorative act: statues and busts, books and films, festivals, readings, conferences, tours to the Lenin sites, new medals, new museums, postage stamps, gramophone records, and so on. Top Party officials were assembled in the Kremlin to receive special decorations. As Podgorny pinned yet another gold disc onto Brezhnev's lapel, he remarked: 'I don't know for sure whether V.I. Lenin held meetings or worked in this hall, but let us think that he is among us now at this ceremonial moment.'[155] The regulation storm of applause greeted his words.

A two-day event in the Kremlin on 21 and 22 April 1970 brought sixty-six Communist and workers' delegations from the capitalist and developing countries, eighteen from the People's Democracies, a dozen from socialist parties, and many others from illegal and semi-legal organizations whose presence in Moscow was facilitated by the special services. The Soviet leadership wanted to astonish world public opinion by the sheer scale, influence and quantity of Leninists inhabiting the planet. Nothing was said, of course, of the fact that most of these parties and groups had been supported materially by Moscow for years, or that many of the 'general secretaries' had come to Moscow in the hope of receiving fresh infusions of hard currency.

In the immediate aftermath of the Twentieth Congress in 1956, the Russian people heaved a sigh of relief and waited for their emancipation. The period of post-Stalinism, however, was to last another thirty years. During that time, the people somehow adapted themselves, formally carrying out their Leninist rituals, keeping a low profile, but mainly by working and hoping. The old bureaucratic shell remained the same, while below there were increasing signs of free-thinking, internal dissidence, and attempts to point out what was wrong, often using Aesopian language. The new phenomenon of 'kitchen frankness' was born. The erosion of Leninism was under way, and the cracks in the monolith were well advanced. The leadership, at all levels, tried to halt the decay and preserve the 'purity' of Leninism.

As early as 1966, at the end of a meeting of the Central Committee Secretariat, Defence Minister Ustinov announced that he would like to discuss the nominations for the Lenin Prize for Literature and the Arts: 'The list of candidates was published recently . . . and it was strange to see the name of the poet Yevtushenko there, as well as a few others who are not worthy of this high award.' He was supported by Demichev: 'Of course, the masses won't understand it if the Lenin Prize is given to Yevtushenko. There are some unhealthy tendencies among the writers, as the meetings at the Mayakovsky monument have shown. A lot of the things being published in *Yunost'* and *Novyi mir* are having a bad effect on readers, especially the young. I think Tvardovsky [the editor of *Novyi mir*] should no longer be a member of the Central Committee.' Yevtushenko did not get his Lenin Prize, and Tvardovsky was dropped from the Central Committee.

In June 1981 the Central Committee decided it was time to start preparing a new edition of Lenin's collected works, the sixth. Since each previous edition had been between ten and fifteen volumes larger than its predecessor, the new one could have run to some seventy volumes. It is unlikely, however, that most of the 3725 documents secreted in the Party archives would have seen the light. For that to happen, Lenin would first have to be removed from his pedestal. Instead, the new edition would probably only have incorporated the material published in the 'Lenin Miscellanies' since the fifth edition of his works had appeared in the 1960s. Gorbachev, then a relative novice on Olympus, suggested 'we leave the fifth edition and publish the new materials as a collection, or as a supplement to the fifth edition'. He was overruled, and the Institute of Marxism-Leninism was instructed to start on the sixth edition, with the additional task of preparing a ten-volume collection of memoirs to be completed by Lenin's 120th anniversary in 1990: five of these volumes have been published. In a mood which anticipated *glasnost*, the publishers were also permitted to include in the collected memoirs suitably edited extracts from the reminiscences of Trotsky, Martov, Valentinov, Kautsky and a few other heretics.[156]

By this time, however, the unanimity shown by the Politburo, and its dedication to Lenin's ideals, were no longer shared by a large part of the population. Leninism had been going through a long process of erosion. The authorities were of course aware of this. While Brezhnev was in the Kremlin reading his speech about Lenin's genius, or perhaps signing his new Party card, reports of a different kind were being written in the Lubyanka. The KGB had for many years been collecting material on its struggle against anti-Leninism. Andropov's report to the Central Committee for 1982 reads in part:

10,407 anonymous documents and 770 leaflets of an anti-Soviet, nationalistic and politically harmful character, and written by 1688 people, were distributed throughout the country in the past year. Most of the anti-Soviet documents were written anonymously and with the aid of various devices, such as spray-paint, home-made printing, stencil and photo-reproduction. Among perpetrators who have been apprehended were 118 Party members and candidate members, and 204 members of the Komsomol. 498 culprits had acted under the influence of the enemy's ideological sabotage, 228 were psychologically ill, 220 were hooligans, 37 were protesting against living conditions.'[157]

The leadership could not accept that Soviet society was not merely mired in stagnation, but also in a state of psychological disaffection and doubt about values that had previously been universally accepted. The gap between what people said in public and what they thought was widening to the extent that it had become an everyday fact of life. The public mood was like Lenin's physical condition after 10 March 1923. Leninism seemed on the surface to be alive, but it was incapable of a single fresh idea. By the beginning of Gorbachev's period of *perestroika*, Leninism was entering its death throes. The Russian people had not yet understood that Leninism was not amenable to reform, that either it must remain what it had been for decades, or be totally discarded.

# POSTSCRIPT

## *Defeat in Victory*

It was widely believed by those of us who were captives of the Marxist way of thinking that, had Lenin only lived a little longer, he would have steered the proletarian ship of state onto a proper course. In the blindingly sacred image conjured by Party propaganda, we saw Lenin as a man whose life had been stolen from him at a cruelly early age, preventing him from completing the task he had begun. We were deluding ourselves.

Speaking on 23 April 1924, two months after Lenin's death, at a congress of mining engineers, Kamenev declared that future happiness would be secured 'by carrying out Lenin's revolutionary proletarian commandments precisely and rigorously . . . only by taking the path of Leninism will we live until the moment when we can go to Lenin's Mausoleum on Red Square and take the glad tidings that Leninism, and hence proletarian Communism, has conquered the world'.[1] Needless to say, no one has yet carried that message to the Mausoleum, and the mummy itself may not be there much longer anyway.

Even in the mid-1980s many of us still believed that we had only to 'return to Lenin' for the elusive Communist firebird to appear in our hands. The reforming Gorbachev, speaking at the Politburo in October 1987, declared with conviction that 'a bridge must be thrown from Lenin, connecting Lenin's ideas and Lenin's approach to the events of his time to the affairs of today. That, after all, was the dialectic by which Lenin solved problems, it is the key to the solution of our present tasks.'[2] Party propaganda had imbued us with the image of Lenin as a man who had made a historic breakthrough to a new and equitable way of life, as the creator of the New Economic Policy and the ideologue of cooperative agriculture, as the initiator of peaceful co-existence and the tireless fighter against bureaucratism. We had never been permitted to reflect on the truth of these myths.

It never occurred to us that the 'breakthrough' of October 1917 might be a counter-revolution, when compared to the events of February of that year. Nor did we realize that the NEP was not an economic strategy, but merely a tactical manoeuvre forced on Lenin by the devastating collapse of the genuinely Leninist policy of War Communism. Lenin, far from being the initiator of the NEP, was in fact its long-time foe. Speaking on 5 December 1919 at the Seventh All-Russian Congress of Soviets, he told those 'who want to trade freedom for bread' that they were wrong: 'We will struggle against that to the last drop of blood. There can be no concessions on this.'[3] This oath was forgotten by the time he was ready to introduce the NEP in March 1921.

We did not realize that, despite the common sense of some of his ideas on cooperative farming, Lenin was always profoundly hostile to the peasants. Even before he came to power, in 1916 there were no less than 10,500,000 members of cooperatives in Russia. By his dependence on the working class, Lenin condemned the peasants to be the mere building blocks of the Communist edifice that he had fixed in his mind. It was the peasants who bore the brunt of the civil war. Typically, as we have seen, he instructed the Bolsheviks in Livny 'to organize the poor peasants of the district, confiscate all the grain and all the property of the rebellious kulaks, hang their ringleaders, mobilize and arm the poor peasants and give them reliable leaders from among our own people, arrest hostages from among the rich and keep them under arrest until all the surplus grain of their district has been collected and loaded'.[4] This was the path to Lenin's cooperative plan and socialist industrialization. It was for this, according to him, that people were shot in their thousands.[5] Yet in 1916, when the Swedish socialist Zeth Höglund was arrested and put in prison for a few months for preaching defeatism, Lenin wrote to Alexandra Kollontai: 'this savagery is unprecedented, it's incredible!!!'[6]

We did not realize that peaceful co-existence with the outside world was forced on Lenin by the failure of his dream of an instant onslaught on the capitalist citadels. As Adolf Ioffe wrote in his unpublished memoirs:

The world revolution seemed (and indeed was) so close that any agreement with the bourgeoisie was regarded as extremely short-term and therefore of no consequence. What was important was not what one could obtain in talks with the bourgeoisie, but only that both the talks and the agreement itself should have the greatest possible revolutionary effect on the broad masses ... somehow to make it doubly clear that their content was immaterial and to emphasise their ephemeral character. When at the end of the talks I brought Vladimir Ilyich the bound copy of the treaty, he narrowed his eyes cunningly, slapped the cover and asked: 'Well, did you manage to write a lot of dirty tricks into it?'

In Ioffe's view, it was only the slow pace of the revolution that prompted the temporary shift to a 'peaceful offensive'. Lenin did not, nor would he ever, repudiate the future revolutionizing of the planet. Ioffe wrote: 'When the Central Committee sent me to Turkestan in 1921, in our talks before I left and in letters he sent when I was in Tashkent, Vladimir Ilyich constantly urged and stressed that: "Turkestan is our world policy. Turkestan means India ..."'[7]

Lenin seemed unable to accept that the revolution in Germany had failed not because of the treachery of 'the renegade Kautsky' and the German Social Democrats, but because the workers had not believed in it, the intelligentsia had not wanted it, and the peasants had had no time for it. Needless to say, the army and the middle classes were deeply hostile. While German gold had assisted Lenin in making revolution in Russia, the millions the Bolsheviks poured into Germany were thrown to the wind. While the revolution in Russia had succeeded in large part because Lenin had helped to undermine the Russian army, in Germany the army, although it had succumbed to the Allied powers, was still strong and determined enough to crush the revolution. One disappointment in the external sphere followed another as Finland, Hungary, Persia, India, China, Poland and other countries failed to ignite and maintain the revolutionary momentum. 'The world revolution,' Ioffe wrote, 'was held up.'[8]

There were failures in the internal sphere also: the policy of War Communism proved unsustainable, the new bureaucracy indestructible, large sections of society were silently hostile to Bolshevism, and there was none of the Party unity Lenin had struggled to maintain. The defeat Leninism was to suffer seventy years after the revolution was already prefigured while he was still alive. This is evident from the fact that from the earliest days socialist structures were replaced by state institutions. In part spontaneously, the Bolsheviks began using the vast arsenal assembled by the state: the unlimited power of the bureaucracy, strict centralization, undivided state power, regimentation of public life and ideology as a substitute for religion. The imperial style of government was thus preserved by the Bolsheviks. Having destroyed first the tsarist and then the bourgeois dictatorship, Lenin replaced them by the dictatorship of his Party. Since the historical traditions which created the Bolsheviks were incapable of evolution, one form of oppression was replaced by another, both harsher and more repugnant.

It is conceivable, as has often been claimed, that Lenin would not have exterminated his comrades in the Politburo, as Stalin did, and it is hard to imagine that he would have introduced collectivization at the cost of millions of peasants' lives, or eliminated dissidents – even potential dissidents – by the methods used by Stalin at the end of the 1930s. But even a more 'moderate' form of Communism under Lenin would still have been Bolshevik in kind. There would still have been terror and collectivization and the hunt for the 'impure'. The system he created could work no other way, the only variations being those of scale.

But the genetic origins of the system provide no basis for blaming its founder for every crime and mistake committed by his successors. Lenin cannot be blamed for the monstrous decision of the Politburo to execute thousands of Poles at Katyn in 1940 and to cast the blame on the Nazis. Perhaps this was, as some thought, Stalin's revenge on the Poles for the humiliating defeat of Soviet Russia in 1920. But it was indeed Lenin who in August 1920 ordered Sklyansky and Dzerzhinsky to 'hang kulaks, priests and landowners' and to 'cast the blame for these crimes on [General] Bulak-Bulakhovich's units in Poland'.[9]

Lenin cannot be blamed for planning a bizarre attempt on the life of Yugoslavia's Marshal Tito in 1948:

'Max' [Soviet agent Grigulevich] will obtain a personal audience with Tito during which he will remove from within his clothing a silent mechanism and release a dose of pulmonary plague bacteria, ensuring the infection and death of Tito and the others present. 'Max' himself will not know the content of the substance. In order to save 'Max's' life he will be inoculated with anti-plague serum.[10]*

But in 1920 Lenin instructed his comrades that 'it is essential and urgent to prepare the terror in secret'.[11]

Nor can Lenin be blamed for the plan to intervene in Poland in 1980 to crush 'Solidarity', the widespread movement against the Communist regime. A document signed by Suslov, Gromyko, Andropov, Ustinov and Chernenko called on the Central Committee to have a number of units placed on battle alert, and 'to mobilize up to 100,000 reservists and 15,000 automobiles'.[12] In the event, it was the Polish army and police that suppressed the opposition for another eight years.

The leadership's Leninist way of thinking was demonstrated in 1960 by an event that has never before been revealed. The Soviet ambassador to Poland, Ponomarenko, reported in May of that year that, since the Twentieth Party Congress of 1956, the Polish Workers' Party had been 'seething'. Khrushchev, Mikoyan, Bulganin, Molotov and Kaganovich decided to fly to Warsaw on the eve of the Polish party's Central Committee plenum. Ochab, Gomulka and other Polish leaders protested, but Khrushchev and the others resolved to go nevertheless. According to the notes Mikoyan kept, the discussion at a meeting in the Belvedere Palace following the plenum was stormy. Gomulka and the other Polish leaders wanted non-interference in their party's affairs, a definition of the status of Soviet troops in Poland, a reduction in the number of Soviet advisers, and the recall of Soviet Marshal Rokossovsky as Polish Minister of Defence.

Khrushchev, Bulganin and Molotov responded belligerently, shouting, 'you want to turn your faces to the West and your backs to us . . . you've forgotten that we have our enormous army in Germany'. Emotions grew heated. Mikoyan's notes continue: 'During this conversation one of the Polish comrades handed Gomulka a note. Gomulka turned to Khrushchev and said, "I'm told that your units from the western part of Poland are moving tanks right now on Warsaw." Gomulka requested that they be ordered back to their stations. We exchanged glances and Khrushchev ordered Konev [the Soviet

---

* Tito had long been wary of Stalin's efforts to subvert his authority, and was ever on his guard against the agents planted in his organization by Russia. The attempt to infect him came to nothing.

Commander-in-Chief of Warsaw Pact troops] to stop the tanks and send them back to their stations.'[13] Even in talks with their allies, the Soviet leaders used tanks as an argument.

Lenin had resorted to such violent measures as had been available to him when settling 'disputes' with his neighbours, whether by sending troops into Georgia or planning revolutionary acts in the countries bordering the Soviet Union. He had been quite explicit that Latvia and Estonia be 'punished by military means' when in 1918 they established their independence. In his own hand, he made the message clear: 'Cross the frontier somewhere, even if only to a depth of half a mile, and hang 100–1,000 of their civil servants and rich people.'[14]

Lenin cannot be blamed for the fact that the top Party leadership in the republics, regions and territories was riddled with embezzlement, corruption and disintegration. When public outrage demanded it, these people were discreetly moved to other jobs. But it had also been Lenin's custom to cover things up, to rescue and defend his lieutenants. When Ordzhonikidze was asserting Moscow's control over the local Communists in the Caucasus in 1922, Lenin wrote to him: 'Comrade Sergo, I've received a report that you and fourteen army leaders were boozing and womanizing for a week. A formal complaint has been laid . . . Scandal and shame. And there was I, boasting to all and sundry about you. You must straighten up. It's not good enough. You're giving a bad example. Greetings, Yours, Lenin.'[15]

The long war in Afghanistan between 1979 and 1989, in which the Soviet leadership had mindlessly intervened, was over, yet the Comintern way of thinking survived until the very end. In 1991 Defence Minister Dmitri Yazov reported to the Politburo on the 'results' of the ten-year campaign. No less than 546,255 members of the Soviet armed forces had served in Afghanistan. Of this number, 13,826, including 1977 officers, had laid down their lives 'performing their international duty'. The whole adventure had cost the country tens of billions of roubles.[16] Such losses were almost negligible when compared to those inflicted by Lenin's promise to turn the imperialist war into civil war. True to his mentor's teaching, Stalin saw human lives as no more than statistical units. During the Second World War, he would conclude his orders with the words, 'This task must be carried out regardless of losses.'

Such analogies and comparisons could be made without end. Lenin cannot be made to bear responsibility for his successors' acts, but plainly, there is much he might have prevented or avoided. No one has yet succeeded in creating heaven on earth, even if many have seen what hell is like. Lenin can, however, be held responsible for creating a dictatorship which functioned for many years according to his laws. Even after the Twentieth Congress, during the thaw, the inner structure of the system barely changed. While execution for political dissidence ceased, the psychiatric hospital, prison and exile to the concentration camps continued for those brave enough to voice or to publish a disapproved opinion.

Despite the fact that it was doomed to defeat, the Leninist system was extraordinarily viable. This is explained not only by social inertia and the Party's monopoly of power, but also by some of the more attractive features of Leninist 'socialism'. There was its broad base of elementary social security: free education, medicine, holiday pay, accommodation, full employment, a guaranteed minimum wage and much else. The idea of social justice seemed to have found its realization, although, to be sure, all this was accomplished at the cost of the exploitation of the workers and the country's resources.

A closer look reveals that the people's rights and liberties were negligible, and that their lives were led at a level of guaranteed poverty and total dependence on the ideological postulates of the only active political party. Nevertheless, despite all the ugliness of the Leninist system, it could not have maintained itself for as long as it did purely as a result of violence or the threat of violence.

But the life the Soviet people lived for seventy years was not socialism. Without the dictatorship, the Bolsheviks would not have been able to hold onto power and the state they created in 1917. They rejected parliamentary democracy, and Lenin installed his extreme and harsh dictatorship without a second thought. From that moment the primary features of Bolshevism were 'hatred for class enemies' and implacable hostility to imperialism and everything else that was not socialist, not Marxist, not Leninist. Here Lenin's personal characteristics played a far-reaching role. We have seen the violence of the language he used against his ideological enemies, to say nothing of his former friends. No insult was too crude or dismissive, and conscience was nowhere to be heard. We have also seen how easily this destructive approach to the opinions of others escalated into the physical elimination of all those who chose not to fall into line, and how, once absorbed as normal behaviour by the Party, this became an integral and essential feature of the regime in its post-Lenin years.

The legacy of this 'political culture' will die hard. The defeat, by those who valued Russia's fragile democratic institutions, of the attempted coup in August 1991 provided an opportunity to create a genuinely new and free society. But a background of savage invective, formerly used against external 'foes', is preventing Russian politicians from talking to each other except in terms of 'struggling to a victorious end', elevating abuse and disrespect to moral, political and aesthetic virtues, as we were taught to do by so many books with titles such as *Lenin's Language* and *On Lenin's Polemical Art*. In worshipping the 'genius of abuse' – to quote Berdyaev on Lenin[17] – we cultivated a slavish psychology in ourselves, as well as undemocratic conduct and dogmatism.

The defeat of Leninism was brought about by the change in the international climate. As soon as Gorbachev's foreign policy began to bear fruit, in the form of growing trust of the Soviet Union's traditional enemies, the erosion of Leninism accelerated. Lenin and his system could exist only by watching its opponents through the cross-hairs of a gunsight, only by digging deeper and stronger defences, only by feverishly competing for military superiority. To flourish, Communism needed a military threat, and both domestic and foreign enemies. The defeat of Leninism was programmed by history. Lenin had only one chance to save it: he could have preserved political pluralism after October 1917 and given scope to social democratic aspirations and traditions. But that would not have been the Leninist way.

One thing is certain, and that is that the 'Epoch of Lenin' is gone forever. Legend has it that Alexander the Great once read an inscription on the grave of a fallen king: 'Deny me not the handful of earth that covers my body.' Lenin's heirs, by making him into an earthly god, denied him even his handful of earth. Since then, the cosmic requiem of eternity is being sung not only for his mummy, but also for his cause.

# Notes

## Introduction

1 Russian Centre for the Preservation and Study of Recent Historical Documentation, Moscow, f.2, op. 2, d.447, l.1. This is the new title of the Party Central Committee Archives covering 1917 to 1952, hereafter referred to as RTsKhIDNI

2 RTsKhIDNI, f.2, op. 2, d.478, l.3–4

3 *Stalin: Triumph and Tragedy*, London, 1991 (Russian edition Moscow, 1990); *Trotsky*, Moscow, 1992

4 Lenin, *Polnoe sobranie sochinenii*, in 55 volumes, plus two index volumes, Moscow, 1961–1965 (hereafter *PSS*), vol.37, p. 58

5 In *Edinstvo*, 28 October 1917

6 RTsKhIDNI, f.2, op. 1, d.4269, l.1

7 Ibid., d.348, l.1

8 Ibid., d.621, ll.1–5

9 RTsKhIDNI, f.17, op. 3, d.14, l.1

10 RTsKhIDNI, f.2, op. 2, d.122, l.1

11 RTsKhIDNI, d.515, l.1

12 Geller, M., 'Lenin Today', in *Russkaya Mysl'*, Paris, 21 December 1990

13 Trotskii, L.D., *O Lenine: Materialy dlya biografa*, Moscow, 1924

14 The Houghton Library, BMS, Russ 13.1. (9508–9678), folder 1 of 14. Trotsky coll. pp. 1, 18

15 The Houghton Library, BMS, Russ 13.1 (9442–9457), Trotsky coll. p. 3.

16 Krzhizhanovskii, G.M., *Velikii Lenin*, Moscow, 1982, p. 112

17 Zinoviev, G., *Leninizm. Vvedenie v izuchenie leninizma*, Leningrad, 1925, p. 2

18 Krzhizhanovskii, op. cit., pp. 16–17

19 In *Obshchee delo*, Paris, 21 February 1921

20 Tyrkova-Williams, A., *Na putyakh k svobode*, London, 1953, p. 400

21 RTsKhIDNI, f.2, op. 2, d.125, l.1

22 *PSS*, vol.45, pp. 189–91

23 *XIV s'ezd VKP(b), Stenograficheskii otchet*, Moscow-Leningrad, 1926, pp. 600–1

24 *PSS*, vol.54, p. 160

25 *PSS*, vol.44, p. 428

## Chapter 1

1 Martov, Y., *Zapiski sotsial-demokrata*, vol.1, Berlin-Petersburg-Moscow, 1922, p. 268

2 Nikolaevskii, B.N., *Potresov, A.N., Opyt literaturno-politicheskoi biografii*, Paris, 1937, p. 294

3 Mindubayev, Z., 'Ulyanovsk', *Literaturnaya gazeta*, 10 April 1991

4   Until 1 January 1918 the Russian
    (or Old Style) calendar lagged
    behind the Western (or New
    Style) calendar by twelve days in
    the nineteenth and thirteen days
    in the twentieth century. We have
    included both dates where
    necessary.

5   *Vladimir Ilyich Lenin:
    Biograficheskaya khronika*, vol.1,
    Moscow, 1970, p. 1

6   A pun on the pay of Party members

7   Shub, D., *Lenin: A Biography*, New
    York, 1948

8   'Istorik' (Shub, D.), 'O predkakh
    Lenina', in *Novyi zhurnal*, 1961,
    no.63, pp. 286–91

9   Valentinov, N.V., 'O predkakh
    Lenina i ego biografiakh', in
    *Novyi Zhurnal*, 1960, No.61,
    pp. 219–36

10  RTsKhIDNI, f.2, op. 1, d.22, l.1

11  Ibid., d.311, l.1

12  The term in Russian is *meshchanin*,
    a legal category designating the
    urban lower middle classes, or
    petty bourgeoisie, and consisting
    generally of tradesmen and
    artisans.

13  The documents show him also as
    Ulyanin and Ulyaninov.

14  Valentinov, 'O predkakh Lenina i
    ego biografiakh', op.cit., p. 224

15  Central State Military History
    Archives (TsGVIA), f.316,
    op. 69, d.57, l.109

16  RTsKhIDNI, f.13, op. 1, d.471,
    ll.2–3

17  RTsKhIDNI, f.2, op. 2, d.125, l.1

18  RTsKhIDNI, f.13, op. 1, d.471,
    ll.5–6

19  Central State Archives of
    Literature and Art (TsGALI),
    f.631, op. 15, d.265, ll.2–5

20  Haas, L., 'O proiskhozhdenii
    Lenina', in *Posev*, Munich, 1984,
    No.1, pp. 53–4; Barnett, C. (Ed.),
    *Hitler's Generals*, London, 1989,
    pp. 319, 330

21  Valentinov, 'O predkakh Lenina i
    ego biografiakh', op. cit., p. 229

22  Shub, *Lenin*, op. cit., pp. 21–2

23  *Vladimir Ilyich Lenin: Biokhronika*,
    vol.1, Moscow, 1970, p. 25

24  *Vladimir Ilyich Lenin: Biografiya*,
    2nd ed., Moscow, 1963, p. 9

25  Krupskaya, N., 'Detsvo i ranyaya
    yunost' Ilyicha', *Bolshevik*,
    Moscow, 1938, No.12, pp. 65–72

26  Valentinov, N., 'Vydumki o
    rannei revolyutsionnosti Lenina',
    in *Novyi zhurnal*, 1954, No.39,
    p. 216

27  Ulyanova, M.I., *O V.I. Lenine i
    semie Ulyanovykh*, Moscow, 1988,
    p. 219

28  RTsKhIDNI, f.2, op. 1, d.6, l.32

29  *Lenin v Simbirsk*e, collected
    articles, Ulyanovsk, 1968, p. 478

30  Ulyanova, *O V.I. Lenine i semie
    Ulyanovykh*, op. cit., p. 78

31  Valentinov, N., 'Rannie gody
    Lenina', in *Novyi zhurnal*, 1955,
    No.40, p. 204

32  Ulyanova, *O V.I. Lenine i semie
    Ulyanovykh*, op. cit., pp. 105–6

33  Radek, Karl, *Portrety i pamflety*,
    Book 1, Moscow, 1933, p. 27

34  Churchill, W.S., *The World Crisis:
    Vol.5, The Aftermath*, London,
    1929, p. 76

35  *Biograficheskaya khronika*, vol.1,
    op. cit., p. 29

36  *Lenin v Simbirske*, op. cit., p. 29

37  'Kazan' i Samara', collected
    articles, in *Krasnyi arkhiv*, 1934,
    No.1, pp. 55–64

38  RTsKhIDNI, f.2, op. 1, d.6, l.21

39  *V.I. Lenin v Tatarii*, collected
    articles, Kazan, 1964, pp. 134–5

40  Lenin, *PSS*, vol.1, pp. 552–5

41  Valentinov, N., 'Chernyshevskii i
    Lenin', in *Novyi zhurnal*, 1951,
    No.26, pp. 198–9

42  Vishnyak, M., 'Ideinye korni
    Bol'shevizma', in *Novyi zhurnal*,
    1951, No.27, pp. 296–303

43  In September 1888 Lenin wrote

to Chernyshevsky, but received no reply. A year later, hearing of Chernyshevsky's death, he drew a cross on the writer's photograph and wrote 'October 1889, Saratov'.

44 *PSS*, vol.1, pp. 291–2

45 Ibid., p. 280

46 *Vospominaniya o Vladimire Ilyiche Lenine*, vol.2, p. 261

47 Plekhanov, 'Sovremennaya zhizn', in *Zametki publitsista*, December 1906

48 Bonch-Bruevich, V.D., in *Tridtsat' dnei*, January 1934, p. 18

49 Voitinskii, V., *Gody pobed i porazhenii*, Book 2, Berlin, 1924, p. 227

50 Plekhanov, *God na rodine*, vol.2, Paris, 1921, p. 267

51 Valentinov, N., 'Vstrecha Lenina s Marksizmom', in *Novyi zhurnal*, 1958, No.53, p. 206

52 *PSS*, vol.1, pp. 1–66

53 *PSS*, vol.7, pp. 193–4

54 In *Narodopravstvo*, Moscow, No.20, 1907, p. 2

55 *PSS*, vol.2, pp. 532–3

56 RTsKhIDNI, f.17, op. 3, d.164, l.2

57 Ibid., d.255, l.3

58 Ibid., d.195, l.1

59 Valentinov, 'Vstrecha Lenina s Marksizmom', op. cit., p. 206.

60 Nikolaevskii, B.N., *A.N. Potresov: Posmertnyi sbornik proizvedenii*, Paris, 1937, pp. 21–2

61 Plekhanov, G.V., *Sochineniya*, vol.5 (2nd edn.), Moscow, 1924, pp. 21, 83, 84

62 RTsKhIDNI, f.17, op. 3, d.290, l.4. Between 1923 and 1927, however, an edition of Plekhanov's complete works was published under the editorship of D. Ryazanov.

63 Plekhanov, G.V., *Sochineniya*, vol.19, Moscow, 1927, pp. 54–5

64 Trotskii, N., *Nashi politicheskie zadachi*, Geneva, 1904, p. 69

65 *Pis'ma Lenina Gor'komu*, Moscow, 1936, pp. 17–18

66 In *Volya Rossii*, Paris, 1924, No.3

67 In *Dni*, Paris, 1928

68 Nikolaevskii, *A.N. Potresov*, op. cit., p. 196

69 RTsKhIDNI, f.2, op. 2, d.463, l.1

70 Nikolaevskii, *A.N. Potresov*, op. cit., pp. 302–3

71 A.N. Potresov, *Ocherki*, Paris, 1927, p. 19

72 *Vospominaiya o Lenine*, vol.1, 1968, pp. 232, 233, 234

73 Fischer, L., *The Life of Lenin*, London, 1964, p. 22

74 *Leninskii sbornik*, vol.13, Moscow-Leningrad, 1930, pp. 93–111

75 Archives of the President of the Russian Federation (Arkhiv Prezidenta Rossiiskoi Federatsii) (APRF), f.3, op. 22, d.297, l.166

76 *PSS*, vol.46, pp. 450–1

77 His mother's petition to have him moved to Krasnoyarsk in August 1897 was refused

78 RTsKhIDNI, f.2, op. 2, d.1338, l.1

79 *PSS*, vol.54, p. 148

80 *Pis'ma Vladimira Ilyicha Lenina k rodnym*, Moscow, 1985, p. 41

81 Ibid., pp. 44, 46, 50, 53

82 Krupskaya, N.N., *Vospominaniya o Lenine* (2nd edn.), Moscow, 1972, p. 26

83 *Lyubyashchii tebya V. Ulyanov: Pis'ma V.I. Lenina materi*, Moscow, 1967, p. 36

84 Ibid., p. 37

85 *PSS*, vol 55, p. 93

86 *Lyubyashchii tebya V. Ulyanov: Pis'ma V.I. Lenina materi*, op. cit., p. 57

87 Ibid., p. 119

88 *Vospominaniya o Lenine*, vol.2, p. 37.

89 RTsKhIDNI, f.16, op. 3, d.20

90  *Lyubyashchii tebya V. Ulyanov: Pis'ma V.I. Lenina materi*, op. cit., pp. 91, 92, 102, 120

91  RTsKhIDNI, f.127, op. 1, d.14, l.2

92  Cited in Fischer, *The Life of Lenin*, op. cit., p. 80

93  *Leninskii sbornik*, vol.37, Moscow, 1970, p. 233

94  *Leninskii sbornik*, vol. 35, Moscow, 1945, p. 143

95  Cited in Fischer, *The Life of Lenin*, op. cit., p. 80

96  Krupskaya, N.K., *Vospominaniya o Vladimire Ilyiche Lenine*, vol.2, Moscow, 1989, pp. 144, 148, 153, 179

97  Ibid., p. 191

98  RTsKhIDNI, f.127, op. 1, d.1

99  Ibid., d.2, ll.1–2

100  Ibid., d.61, l.18

101  APRF, f.3, op. 22, d.293, ll.30–8

102  RTsKhIDNI, f.2, op. 1, d.24299, l.1

103  In a personal communication to the editor. See also Elwood's *Inessa: Revolutionary and Feminist*, Cambridge, 1992, pp. 185–6, which casts doubt on the idea that the relationship was romantic.

104  Solzhenitsyn, A., *Lenin v Tsyurikhe*, Paris, 1975, p. 24

105  RTsKhIDNI, f.127, op. 1, d.61

106  RTsKhIDNI, f.3, op. 1, d.4365

107  Ibid., d.4401

108  *Vladimir Ilyich Lenin: Biografcheskaya khronika*, vol.3, Moscow, 1972, p. 268

109  *Leninskii sbornik*, vol.11, Moscow, 1931, p. 195

110  Ibid., p. 180

111  Krupskaya, N.K., *Vospominaniya o Lenine*, Moscow, 1968, p. 260

112  *PSS*, vol.49, p. 367

113  *Leninskii sbornik*, vol.21, Moscow, 1933, p. 83

114  *Leninskii sbornik*, vol.35, Moscow, 1945, p. 108

115  Ibid., p. 108

116  Ibid., p. 109

117  RTsKhIDNI, f.2, op. 2, d.24299

118  Ibid., op. 1, d.12862, ll.1–2

119  Ibid., d.4573, ll.1–2

120  RTsKhIDNI, f.127, op. 1, d.61, ll.7–14

121  Ibid., d.52, l.12

122  Balabanoff, A., *Impressions of Lenin*, London, 1964, p. 15

123  *PSS*, vol.54, p. 67

124  RTsKhIDNI, f.127, op. 1, d.61

125  RTsKhIDNI, f.17, op. 3, d.289, ll.2–3

126  Ibid., d.290, l.3

127  *Proletarskaya revolyutsiya*, 1928, Nos.11–12, pp. 251–2. It also compares with the 25 roubles a month which a skilled artisan could earn at that time

128  Krupskaya, N.K., *Izbrannye proizvedeniya*, Moscow, 1988, p. 120

129  Valentinov, N., *Maloznakomyi Lenin*, Paris, 1972, p. 31

130  RTsKhIDNI, f.2, op. 1, d.25342, l.1

131  Valentinov, *Maloznakomyi Lenin*, op. cit., p. 34

132  *Pis'ma Vladimira Ulyanova k rodnym*, Moscow, 1985, p. 78

133  *Lyubyashchii tebya V. Ulyanov: Pis'ma V.I. Lenina materi*, op. cit., p. 108

134  *Pis'ma Vladimira Ulyanova k rodnym*, Moscow, 1985, pp. 46, 66, 126, 133, 195

135  RTsKhIDNI, f.2, op. 2, d.7, l.1

136  A.N. (A.D.Naglovskii), 'Lenin', in *Novyi zhurnal*, 1967, No.88, pp. 170–1

137  Lenin, *Sobranie sochinenii*, 3rd edn., vol.22, p. 253

138  *Vospominaniya o V.I.Lenine*, vol.2, p. 113

139  Avtorkhanov, A., 'Koba i Kamo', in *Novyi zhurnal*, 1973, No.110, p. 274–5

140  *Vospominaniya o V.I. Lenine*, vol.2, p. 113

141  Avtorkhanov, A., 'Koba i Kamo', in *Novyi zhurnal*, 1973, No.110, pp. 270–3

142  RTsKhIDNI, f.2, op. 1, d.2419; 2413, l.1

143  Ibid., d.550, ll.1–13

144  Lenin, *Sochineniya* (3rd edn.), vol.10, p. 86

145  RTsKhIDNI, f.17, op. 3, pp. 45–7

146  *Vospominaniya o V.I. Lenine*, vol.2, p. 139

147  Valentinov, *Maloznakomyi Lenin*, op. cit., pp. 128–9

148  *Vospominaniya o V.I. Lenine*, vol.2, p. 121

149  *Leninskii sbornik*, vol.XXXVIII, 1975, p. 66

150  Valentinov, *Maloznakomyi Lenin*, op. cit., pp. 115–17

151  RTsKhIDNI, f.2, op. 2, d.6, l.2. Note that first initials of names were commonly altered, e.g. N. Lenin and Yu. Kamenev.

152  RTsKhIDNI, f.2, op. 2, d.9, l.1

153  Ibid., d.12, l.1

154  Ibid., d.23. l.1

155  Ibid., d.73, l.1

156  Ibid., d.1314, l.1

157  RTsKhIDNI, f.2, op. 1, d.26325, l.1

158  Ibid., d.13, l.1

159  RTsKhIDNI, f.14, op. 1, d.175, l.3

160  *PSS*, vol.9, p. 561

161  These articles were published in collected form as *Nesovremennye mysli: zametki o revolyutsii i kul'ture*, Petrograd, 1918, and in English as *Untimely Thoughts*, London, 1970

162  *Pis'ma Lenina Gor'komu*, Moscow, 1936, p. 63

163  *Novaya zhizn'*, No.174, 7(20) November 1917

164  Lenin, *Sochineniya*, 3rd edn., vol.19, p. 276

165  *Pis'ma Vladimira Ulyanova k rodnym*, op. cit., p. 110

166  Ibid., p. 95

167  RTsKhIDNI, f.2, op. 1, d.550, l.1–15

168  Ibid., op. 2, d.741, l.1–4

169  Ibid., op. 3, d.216, l.4

170  Ibid., op. 1, d.311, l.1

## Chapter 2

1  *PSS*, vol.6, p. 112

2  Ibid., p. 124

3  Unless otherwise stated, all such publications abroad were in Russian

4  *PSS*, vol.6, p. 178

5  RTsKhIDNI, f.17, op. 3, d.290, l.4; d.291, l.2; d.293, l.12; d.194, l.1

6  *Lenin i Vecheka*, Moscow, 1975, p. 231

7  Ibid., p. 363

8  *Leninskii sbornik*, vol.37, Moscow, 1970, p. 11

9  RTsKhIDNI, f.2, op. 2, d.4, l.1

10  *PSS*, vol.9, p. 211

11  *PSS*, vol.30, p. 347

12  Ibid., p. 346

13  RTsKhIDNI, f.325, op. 1, d.403, l.84a

14  *PSS*, vol.26, p. 354

15  *PSS*, vol.30, p. 133

16  *Leninskii sbornik*, vol.11, Moscow, 1931, p. 397

17  *PSS*, vol.49, p. 399

18  RTsKhIDNI, f.495, op. 82, d.1, l.8

19  *PSS*, d.234, l.3

20  RTsKhIDNI, f.2, op. 1, d.6898, l.1

21  *PSS*, vol.11, pp. 339–43

22  *PSS*, vol.12, pp. 32, 34

23  *Izvestiya Vserossiiskogo po delam o vyborakh v Uchreditel'noe Sobranie Komissii*, No.16–17, 10 November 1917, p. 3

24  Ibid., p. 7

25  *PSS*, vol.35, pp. 240–1

26  Ibid.

27 Savinkov, B.V., *Nakanune novoy revolyutsii*, Warsaw, 1921, p. 48

28 *PSS*, vol.35, p. 102

29 Ibid., p. 101

30 Shturman, Dora., *V.I. Lenin*, Paris, 1989, p. 73

31 Gorky, M., *Nesvoevremennye mysli*, Paris, 1971, p. 113

32 Zenkovskii, V.V., *Istoriya russkoy filosofii*, vol.2, Paris, 1950, p. 285

33 *PSS*, vol.18, p. 146

34 Berdyaev, N.A., *Istoki i smysl russkogo kommunizma*, Paris, 1955, p. 97

35 RTsKhIDNI, f.2, op. 1, d.22899, l.1

36 *PSS*, vol.23, p. 44

37 *PSS*, vol.45, p. 381

38 Sharapov, Yu.P., *Lenin kak chitatel'*, Moscow, 1990, p. 185

39 Gor'kii, M. *Nesvoevremennye mysli*, Paris, 1971, pp. 102, 103

40 *Leninskii sbornik*, vol.35, Moscow, 1945, p. 148

41 Lunacharsky, A.V., *Lenin. Tovarishch, chelovek*, Moscow, 1987, p. 216

42 Pospelov, P.N. (Ed.), *V.I. Lenin: Biografiya*, Moscow, 1963, pp. 99—100

43 RTsKhIDNI, f.17, op. 3, d.249, l.6

44 Aronson, G., *Rossiya nakanune revolyutsii*, New York, 1962, p. 184

45 See Lydia Krestovskaya, *Iz istorii russkogo volonterskogo dvizheniya vo Frantsii*, Paris, no date

46 'Pis'mo L. Martova "Nashedel'tsam"', in *Proletarskaya revolyutsiya*, No.3/5, 1923, pp. 281—91

47 Bagotskii, S.Y., *Vospominaniya o Lenine*, vol.2, Moscow, 1969, p. 329

48 *PSS*, vol 26, p. 6

49 Ibid., p. 22

50 *Golos*, Paris, 1914, No.87

51 *PSS*, vol. 49, pp. 13—15

52 Potresov, A.N., *Posmertnyi sbornik proizvidenii*, Paris, 1937, pp. 301—2

53 *Pis'ma Lenina k Gor'komu*, Moscow, 1936, p. 43

54 *Chto dali bol'sheviki narodu?* Moscow, 1921

55 RTsKhIDNI, f.2, op. 2, d.492, l.1

56 Martov, Y.O., *Mirovoy bol'shevizm*, Berlin, 1923, pp. 36—7

57 RTsKhIDNI, f.17, op. 3, d.4, l.1

58 Ibid., d.13, l.5

59 Ibid., d.74, l.3

60 Ibid., d.75, l.2

61 Berdyaev, *Istoki i smysl russkogo kommunizma*, op. cit., pp. 101—2

62 Dvinov, B., 'L. Martov (Yu.O. Tsederbaum)', *Novyi zhurnal*, 1961, p. 277

63 *Leninskii sbornik*, vol.5, Moscow, 1926, pp. 244—5

64 Ibid., pp. 345—58

65 *Polnyi sbornik Platform vsekh russkikh politicheskikh partii*, St Petersburg, 1906, pp, 1, 3

66 Aronson, G., 'Bol'sheviki i Men'sheviki', in *Novyi zhurnal*, 1966, No.83, p. 255

67 Plekhanov, G.V., *Sochineniya*, vol.19, op. cit., pp. 534, 537

68 Dan, F.I., *Proiskhozhdenie bol'shevizma*, New York, 1946, p. 369

69 *Vladimir Ilyich Lenin, Biograficheskaya khronika*, vol.9, Moscow, 1978, pp. 61—2

70 RTsKhIDNI, f.17, op. 3, d.150, l.1

71 *PSS*, vol.39, pp. 6—61

72 *PSS*, vol.51, p. 150

73 *Biograficheskaya khronika*, vol.9, op. cit., pp. 61—2

74 *PSS*, vol.43, p. 241

75 RTsKhIDNI, f.17, op. 3, d.239, l.5

76 Ibid., d.136, l.1—2

77 Ibid., d.259, l.9

78 RTsKhIDNI, f.2, op. 2, d.1311, l.1

79 Ibid.
80 Shvarts, S.M., 'F.I. Dan', in *Novyi zhurnal*, 1947, No.15, p. 293
81 *Bol'sheviki*, 2nd edn., Moscow, 1918, p. 222
82 Valentinov, N., 'Tragediya Plekhanova', in *Novyi zhurnal*, 1948, No.20, p. 280
83 Plekhanov, G.V., *God na Rodine*, op. cit., p. 21
84 *Edinstvo*, 28 October 1917
85 Plekhanov, G.V., *Sochineniya*, vol.20, Moscow-Leningrad, 1925, p. 13
86 Ibid., p. 23
87 Ibid., p. 22
88 Valentinov, 'Tragediya Plekhanova', op. cit., p. 272
89 Valentinov, N., *Vstrechi s Leninym*, New York, 1981, pp. 240–1
90 Valentinov, 'Tragediya Plekhanova', op. cit., pp. 273–5
91 *Leninskii sbornik*, vol.37, Moscow, 1970, pp. 292–3
92 Valentinov, 'Tragediya Plekhanova', op. cit., p. 289
93 RTsKhIDNI, f.17, op. 3, d.190, l.3
94 Ibid., d.232, l.1
95 RTsKhIDNI, f.2, op. 2, d.482, ll.1–6
96 *Dni*, Paris, 30 March 1928
97 Haimson, L.H., *The Russian Marxists and the Origins of Bolshevism*, Cambridge, Mass., 1955, p. 63
98 *Istoriya Vsesoyuznoy Kommunisticheskoy partii (bol'shevikov). Kratkii kurs.* Moscow, 1938, p. 41
99 Rafes, M., *Ocherki istorii Bunda*, Moscow, 1923, p. 141
100 Martov, L., *Povorotnyi punkt v istorii evreiskogo rabochego dvizheniya* (1895), Geneva, 1900, p. 9
101 Martov, Y., *Zapiski sotsial-demokrata*, vol.1, op. cit., p. 268
102 *PSS*, vol.54, p. 287

103 Dvinov, Boris, 'L. Martov (Yu.O. Tsederbaum)', op. cit., p. 281
104 Tsereteli, I.G., *Vospominaniya o Fevral'skoy revolyutsii*, Paris, 1964, I, p. 242
105 Witnessed by E. Drabkina and cited by Shub, D., *Novyi zhurnal*, 1969, No.94, pp. 264–5
106 Martov, Y. O., *Doloy smertnuyu kazn'*, Petrograd, 1918, p. 7
107 RTsKhIDNI, f.17, op. 3, d.396, l.1
108 *PSS*, vol.54, p. 149
109 Getzler, I., *Martov: A Political Biography of a Russian Social Democrat*, Cambridge, 1968, p. 212

## Chapter 3

1 *PSS*, vol.30, pp. 325, 322, 327, 328
2 Rodzianko, M.V., *Gosudarstvennaya Duma i fevral'skaya revolyutsiya 1917 g.*, Rostov on Don, 1919, p. 31
3 Yakhontov, A.N., 'Tyazhelye dni', *Arkhiv Russkoy revolyutsii*, vol.18, Berlin, 1926, p. 98
4 Milyukov, P.N., *Vospominaniya (1859–1917)*, New York, 1955, pp. 455–6
5 Semennikov, V.P. (ed.), *Nikolai II i Velikie knyazya*, Moscow-Leningrad, 1925, p. 122
6 *Vladimir Ilyich Lenin: Biograficheskaya khronika*, vol.4, Moscow, 1973, p. 1
7 Ganetskii, Y., *O Lenine: Otryvki vospominanii*, Moscow, 1933, p. 59
8 Zaslavskii, D.O. and Kantorovich, V.A., *Khronika fevral'skoy revolyutsii 1917 goda*, vol.1, Petrograd, 1924, p. 288
9 *PSS*, vol.31, p. 20
10 Ibid., p. 7
11 Ibid., p. 73
12 Ibid., p. 75

13 Solzhenitsyn, *Lenin v Tsyurikhe*, op. cit., pp. 197–9

14 *Biograficheskaya khronika*, vol.4, op. cit., p. 16

15 *PSS*, vol.49, p. 414

16 *PSS*, vol.32, p. 414

17 Ludendorff, E., *Meine Kriegserinnerungen, 1914–1918*, Berlin, 1919, p. 47

18 RTsKhIDNI, f.17, op. 3, d.74, l.2

19 *PSS*, vol, 32, p. 427

20 Melgunov, S.P., *Zolotoy nemetskii klyuch bol'shevikov* (first published in Paris in 1940), New York, 1989, p. 157

21 *Russkii sovremennik*, Moscow, No.1, 1924, p. 241

22 Central State Special Archives (TsGOA), f.7, op. 4, d.127, ll.23, 47–403

23 Shub, D., 'Kupets revolyutsii', in *Novyi zhurnal*, 1967, No.87, pp. 300–01

24 Zeman, Z.A.B. and Scharlau, W., *The Merchant of Revolution*, London, 1966, pp. 136–7

25 Shub, D., 'Lenin i Vil'gel'm II', *Novyi zhurnal*, 1959, No.57, pp. 226–267

26 In *Bakinskii rabochii*, No.24, 1924, cited in Futrell, M., *Northern Underground*, London, 1963, p. 173

27 Shub, 'Kupets revolyutsii', op. cit., pp. 306–8

28 TsGOA, f.198, op. 2, d.582, ll, 19, 22; f.1, op. 33, d.33, ll.77, 78, 97 et al

29 Shub, 'Kupets revolyutsii', op. cit., p. 308

30 Central State Special Archives (TsGOA), f.1, op. 8, d.8480; f.7, op. 2, d.1534, ll.4, 25, 28, 71, 111–114, 182; f.1, op. 12, ll.264, 265

31 State Archive of the Russian Federation (GARF), f.coll.TsGAOR, d.13, ll.83–4

32 Ibid., ll.85, 88

33 Nikitin, B., *Rokovye gody*, Paris, 1937, pp. 117–20

34 GARF, f.kol.TsGAOR, d.13, l.93

35 Melgunov, *Zolotoi nemetskii*, op.cit., pp. 108–9

36 GARF, f.kol.TsGAOR, d.13, l.111

37 Ibid., l.107

38 Zeman, Z.A.B., *Germany and the Revolution in Russia, 1915–1918*, London, 1958, pp. 3, 4, 10, 14

39 GARF, f.kol.TsGAOR, f.d.9., ll.66, 67

40 *Leninskii sbornik*, vol.36, Moscow, 1959. p. 47

41 Melgunov, *Zolotoi nemetskii*, op. cit., p. 128

42 RTsKhIDNI, f.2, op. 2, d.122, l.1

43 Avtorkhanov, A., 'Lenin i TsK posle iyul'skogo vosstaniya', in *Novyi zhurnal*, 1971, no.102, p. 226

44 *PSS*, vol.32, p. 415

45 Kerenskii, A., *Izdaleka* (collected essays, 1920–21), Paris, 1922, p. 172

46 *PSS*, vol.32, p. 415

47 *PSS*, vol.34, p. 31

48 NKVD-KGB Archives, P–1073, t. 1, l.11

49 *Biograficheskaya khronika*, vol.4, op. cit., p. 2

50 Ibid., p. 31

51 Ibid., p. 35

52 *PSS*, vol.49, p. 424

53 Zeman, *Germany and the Revolution in Russia*, op. cit., p. 31

54 TsGOA, f.7, op. 3, d.394, ll.8–9

55 Parvus, A., *Im Kampf um die Wahrheit*, Berlin, 1918, p. 51

56 *PSS*, vol.31, p. 120

57 Fischer, L., *Lenin*, London, 1970, p. 168

58 RTsKhIDNI, f.2, op. 2, d.226, ll.1–5

59 GARF, kol.TsGAOR, d.13, l.65

60 Futrell, M., *Northern Underground*, London, 1963, p. 192

61  NKVD-KGB Archives, P–1073, t.1, l.5
62  Bernstein, E., 'Ein Dunkeles Kapitel,' *Vorwärts*, Berlin, 11 January 1921
63  Zeman, *Germany and the Revolution in Russia*, op. cit., p. 94
64  Ibid., pp. 130, 133.
65  Russian State Military Archives, formerly Central State Archives of the Soviet Army (TsGASA), f.33987, op. 2, d.79, l.90
66  TsGOA, f.1, op. 12, d.25023, ll.264–265; f.7, op. 1, d.953, l.341
67  Gnedin, A., *Katastrofa i vtoroe rozhdenie: Memuarnye zapiski*, Amsterdam, 1977
68  RTsKhIDNI, f.2, op. 2, d.571, ll.1–2
69  Ibid., op. 1, d.25064, l.1
70  Ibid., ll.2–3
71  NKVD Archives, p. 1073, t. 1, l.47
72  Ibid.
73  Ibid., l.11
74  Ibid., l.57
75  Ibid., l.87
76  Nabokov, V., *Arkhiv russkoy revolyutsii*, vol.1, Berlin, 1921, p. 76
77  Kerenskii, *Izdaleka*, op. cit., p. 52
78  NKVD-KGB Archives, 9 section PGU, No.85686
79  *PSS*, vol.35, p. 395
80  *Leninskii sbornik*, vol.18, Moscow, 1931, p. 33
81  Kerenskii, *Izdaleka*, op. cit., p. 40
82  Ibid., p. 189
83  Sverchkov, D.F., *Kerenskii*. Leningrad, 1925, p. 82
84  Stankevich, V.B., *Vospominaniya*, Berlin, 1920, p. 252
85  General A.A. Yepishev, who died in 1985, gave the author this information during interviews for his book on Stalin
86  Interior Ministry Archives (AMB), N–18768, t. 12, l.1–100
87  NKVD-KGB Archives, 9 section

88  RTsKhIDNI, f.2, op. 2, d.151, l.4
89  Ibid., d.90, l.5
90  RTsKhIDNI, f.2, op. 2, d.397, l.10; d.85, l.3; d.68, l.2–3
91  *PSS*, vol.32, pp. 121–2
92  Ibid., p. 129
93  Ibid., p. 132
94  Ibid., p. 182
95  Archive of the President of the Russian Federation (APRF), P 86/14-rs, l.28
96  *PSS*, vol.32, pp. 286–7
97  Ibid., p. 321
98  RTsKhIDNI, f.17, op. 3, d.306, l.6–7
99  Tsereteli, I.G., *Vospominaniya o Fevral'skoy revolyutsii*, vol.2, Paris, 1963, p. 230, citing his speech in *Pravda*, 13 June 1917
100  *PSS*, vol.32, p. 331
101  Stankevich, *Vospominaniya*, op. cit., p. 153
102  *PSS*, vol.32, p. 267
103  Bonch-Bruevich, V.D., *Vospominaniya o Lenine*, Moscow, 1969, p. 96
104  Milyukov, P.N., *Vospominaniya (1859–1917)*, vol.2, New York, 1955, pp. 387–9
105  Sukhanov, N.N., *Revolyutsiya 1917 goda*, Rome, 1971, p. 312
106  *PSS*, vol.34, pp. 2–5
107  *PSS*, vol.32, p. 433
108  *Shestoy s'ezd RSDRP(b), Protokoly*, Moscow, 1958, pp. 27–8
109  *Biograficheskaya khronika*, vol.4, op. cit., p. 277
110  Trotskii, *O Lenine*, op. cit., pp. 58–9, 61
111  APRF, f.3, op. 22, d.306, l.3
112  RTsKhIDNI, f.2, op. 2, d.700, l.1
113  *PSS*, vol.32, p. 306
114  GARF, f.130, op. 1, d.5, l.1
115  RTsKhIDNI, f.17, op. 3, d.153, l.1
116  Elwood, R.C., *Roman Malinovsky: A Life Without a Cause*,

Newtonville, Mass., 1977, provides the best account both of the case itself and the accessible sources on the trial

117  *PSS*, vol.33, p.viii
118  Ibid., p. 120
119  Ibid., pp. 83, 89
120  Ibid., p. 45
121  Ibid., p. 101
122  *Krasnaya letopis'*, 1927, no. 3, Moscow-Leningrad, p. 29
123  RTsKhIDNI, f.4, op. 3, d.45, l.1
124  *PSS*, vol.34, pp. 245, 247
125  Machiavelli, Niccolo, *Izbrannye sochineniya*, Moscow, 1982, p. 351
126  *PSS*, vol.34, pp. 272–5
127  Ibid., p. 280
128  Ibid., pp. 280–2
129  Sukhanov, *Zapiski o revolyutsii*, vol.6, Berlin, 1922–23, pp. 73–5
130  *PSS*, vol.34, p. 253
131  RTsKhIDNI, f.4, op. 2, d.3590, l.7
132  *PSS*, vol.34, p. 242
133  Ibid., p. 247
134  *Ocherki istorii Leningradskoy organizatsii KPSS*, vol.1, 1962, pp. 568–9; *Podgotovka i pobeda Oktyabr'skoy revolyutsii v Moskve; Dokumenty i materialy*, Moscow, 1957, p. 343
135  *PSS*, vol.34, pp. 383–4
136  TsAMO, f.132-A, op. 2642, d.13, l.7
137  *PSS*, vol.34, p. 392
138  Ministry of Security of the Russian Federation Archives (AMBRF), R–33833, l.257
139  Ibid., l.259
140  TsGOA, f.1345, op. 1, d.128, l.23
141  Trotskii, *O Lenine*, op. cit., p. 70
142  RTsKhIDNI, f.2, op. 1, d, 4629, ll.1–2
143  Ibid., d.4630
144  Melgunov, S.M., *Kak bol'sheviki zakhvatili vlast'*, Paris, 1953, pp. 15, 18, 20
145  *PSS*, vol.34, p. 420

146  Ibid., p. 396
147  Trotskii, L.D., *Sochineniya*, vol.3, Moscow, 1925, p. 15
148  Ibid., p. 39
149  Gorbachev, M.S., *Oktyabr' i perestroika: revolyutsiya prodolzhaetsa*, Moscow, 1987, p. 5
150  Trotskii, L.D., *Portrety revolyutsionerov*, Vermont, 1988, p. 45
151  AMBRF, N–15069, d.21790, t. 1, l.61
152  Ibid., t.1, ll.129–34
153  AMBRF, N–15318, d.14625, t.1, l.281
154  AMBRF, N–15069, d.21790, t.1, l.66
155  AMBRF, N–15318, d.14625, t.1, l.1
156  Ibid., t.1, l.20
157  Ibid., t.2, l.48
158  Trotskii, *O Lenine*, op. cit., p. 71
159  Ibid., p. 75
160  *PSS*, vol.34, p. 436
161  Ryabinskii, K., *Revolyustiya 1917 g.*, vol.5, *Oktyabr'*, Moscow-Leningrad, 1926, p. 189
162  Melgunov, S., 'Osada Zimnego Dvortsa', in *Novyi zhurnal*, New York, 1947, No.17, p. 307
163  Sukhanov, N.N., *Zapiski o revolyutsii*, Berlin, 1922–23, vol.7, p. 160
164  Ibid., p. 174
165  Ibid., pp. 219–20
166  Trotskii, *O Lenine*, op. cit., p. 77
167  RTsKhIDNI., f.325, op. 1, d.11, l.11
168  Ibid., l.10
169  Trotskii, *O Lenine*, op. cit., p. 100
170  *PSS*, vol.35, p. 43
171  Ibid., p. 48
172  *Velikaya Otyabr'skaya sotsialisticheskaya revolyutsiya*, Moscow, 1987, p. 481
173  *Dekrety sovetskoy vlasti*, vol.1, Moscow, 1957, pp. 44–5
174  *PSS*, vol.35, p. 40

175  TsGASA, f.33987, op. 3, d.46, l.144
176  GARF, f.130, op. 1, d.1, l.20
177  Ibid., ll.55–6
178  GARF, f.1235, op. 37, d.2, l.43
179  RTsKhIDNI, f.2, op. 1, d, 7597, l.1
180  GARF, f.130, op. 4, d.593, l.1
181  Ibid., op. 1, d.1, l.7–80b
182  PSS, vol.35, pp. 30–1
183  RTsKhIDNI, f.2, op. 2, d.940, l.1–3
184  PSS, vol.35, pp. 359–60
185  In Novaya zhizn', 7 (20) November 1917, No.174
186  RTsKhIDNI, f.5, op. 2, d.246, l.1
187  Ibid., op. 1, d.960, ll.30–2.
188  GARF, f.130, op. 1, d.3, ll.4–40b
189  Ibid., d.5, l.35
190  Ibid., l.33
191  Ibid., d.5a, l.3
192  Ibid., d.3, l.210b
193  Ibid., l.32–3
194  PSS, vol.35, p. 264
195  Harvard University, Houghton Library, BMS Russ 13, T–3815, p. 1
196  PSS, vol.34, p. 392.
197  PSS, vol.31, p. 65; p. 117
198  Izvestiya Vserossiiskoy po delam o vyborakh v Uchreditel'noe Sobranie kommissii, No.1, 6 September 1917, pp. 2, 6–7
199  Trotskii, O Lenine, op. cit., pp. 91–92; p. 93
200  Izvestiya Vserossiiskoy po delam o vyborakh v Uchreditel'noe sobranie kommissii, op. cit. p. 2
201  Ibid., p. 6
202  GARF, f.130, op. 1, d.1, l.20
203  PSS, vol.35, pp. 162–6
204  Trotskii, O Lenine, op. cit., p. 94
205  GARF, f.130, op. 1, d.1, l.460b
206  Ibid., d.1, l.180b
207  Ibid., d.3, l.24
208  In Anin, D., Revolyutsiya 1917 goda glazami ee rukovoditelei, Rome, 1971, pp. 456–70
209  Ibid.

210  PSS, vol.35, p. 241
211  Archives of Foreign Section of OGPU (INO OGPU), No.17458, vol.2, p. 215
212  Trotskii, O Lenine, op. cit., p. 95
213  Medem, V., Uchreditel'noe sobranie i demokraticheskaya respublika, Berlin, 1918, pp. 14–15

## Chapter 4

1  PSS, vol.35, p. 172
2  Trotskii, O Lenine, op. cit., pp. 104–5
3  PSS, vol.35, p. 311
4  PSS, vol.50, p. 30
5  Ibid., p. 144
6  Ibid., p. 106
7  PSS, vol.35, p. 186
8  Wheeler-Bennett, J., Brest-Litovsk: The Forgotten Peace, March 1918, London, 1963, p. 269
9  Sed'moy s'ezd RKP. Stenograficheskii otchet. Moscow-Petrograd, 1923, pp. 126, 129, 131
10  Ibid., pp. 33, 50
11  Ibid., p. 42
12  Ibid., p. 87
13  Zinoviev, G.Ye., Sochineniya, vol.7, part I, Moscow, 1923–26, pp. 544, 537
14  Dates following 1 January 1918 conformed to the Western calendar
15  TsGASA, f.33987, op. 3, d.2, ll.1–4
16  RTsKhIDNI, f.4, op. 2, d.2788, ll.1–4
17  PSS, vol.36, pp. 84–7
18  PSS, vol.35, p. 40
19  PSS, vol.36, p. 100
20  Ibid., p. 111
21  Vladimir Ilyich Lenin: Biograficheskaya khronika, vol.5, Moscow, 1970, p. 319
22  APRF, f.3, op;. 24, d.301, l.144
23  RTsKhIDNI, f.4, op. 2, d.3734, ll.2–3

24 RTsKhIDNI, f.2, op. 1, d.5542, l.1

25 RTsKhIDNI, f.4, op. 2, d.1927, l.7

26 RTsKhIDNI, f.2, op. 1, d.5497, l.2

27 *Novaya zhizn'*, No.2, 1918, pp. 3–4

28 APRF, f.33, op. 1, d.2, l.16

29 Ibid., ll.25–27.

30 *PSS*, vol.36, p. 497

31 Solomon, G., *Sredi krasnykh vozhdei*, vol.1, Paris, 1930, p. 85

32 Wheeler-Bennett, *Brest-Litovsk*, op. cit., p. 327

33 *Biograficheskaya khronika*, vol.5, op. cit., p. 459

34 Zeman, Z.A.B., *Germany and the Revolution in Russia*, op. cit., p. 129, citing a letter from State Secretary Kühlmann to Mirbach

35 Feltchinskii, Yu., 'Iz istorii Brestskogo mira', in *Novyi zhurnal*, no. 162, 1986, pp. 241, 243

36 *PSS*, vol.50, p. 113

37 *PSS*, vol.36, p. 525

38 *PSS*, vol.37, p. 56

39 The terms of the treaty are reproduced in Wheeler-Bennett, *Brest-Litovsk*, op. cit., pp. 403–8

40 Lenin, V.I., *Voennaya perepiska (1917–1920)*, Moscow, 1956, p. 36

41 TsGASA, f.33987, op. 3, d.13, ll.70–85; op. 1, d.572, ll.13–15

42 Sverdlov, Ya.M., *Izbrannye proizvedeniya*, vol.3, Moscow, 1960, pp. 28–9

43 Feltchinskii, Yu., 'Iz istorii Brestskogo mira', in *Novyi zhurnal*, No.182, 1986, p. 259

44 Merezhkovskii, D.S., Gippius, Z.N., et al., *Tsarstvo Antikhrista*, Munich, 1921, pp. 55–6

45 TsGASA, f.33987, op. 2, d.41, l.63

46 Golovin, N.I., *Rossiiskaya kontrrevolyutsiya*, part I, Paris, 1937, pp. 89–90

47 *PSS*, vol.30, p. 133

48 *PSS*, vol.39, p. 343

49 *PSS*, vol.35, p. 204

50 *PSS*, vol.37, pp. 40–1

51 RTsKhIDNI, f.2, op. 2, d.1338, ll.1–2

52 Ibid., op. 1, d.1245, l.1.

53 Trotskii, *O Lenine*, op. cit., p. 106

54 TsGASA, f.33987, op. 1, d.11, l.229

55 TsGASA, f.4, op. 14, d.7, l.11

56 Olikov, S., *Dezertirstvo v Krasnoy Armii i bor'ba s nim*. Moscow, 1926, p. 27

57 Ibid., pp. 29, 31, 32

58 *Direktivy Glavnogo komandovaniya Krasnoy Armii (1917–1920)*, Moscow, 1963, pp. 18–19

59 RTsKhIDNI, f.325, op. 1, d.408, l.87a

60 Lenin, V.I., *Voennaya perepiska*, Moscow, 1956, pp. 39, 133, 137

61 *Leninskii sbornik*, vol.18, Moscow, 1931, p. 209

62 Ibid., p. 189

63 *Leninskii sbornik*, vol.34, Moscow, 1942, p. 65

64 Ibid., p. 122

65 Trotskii, *O Lenine*, op. cit., pp. 117, 118

66 *Leninskii sbornik*, vol.18, Moscow, 1931, p. 202

67 RTsKhIDNI, f.325, op. 1, d.403, l.84a

68 Lenin, V.I., *Iz epokhi grazhdanskoy voiny*, Moscow, 1934, p. 44

69 RTsKhIDNI, f.2, op. 2, d.109, l.1

70 Archives of NKVD-KGB, arkh. No.501, t. 3, l.616

71 Geller, M., Nekrich, A., *Utopiya u vlasti*, Frankfurt-am-Main, 1982, p. 90

72 Trotskii, *O Lenine*, op. cit., p. 121

73 TsGASA, f.33987, op. 2, d.32, l.311

74 RTsKhIDNI, f.2, op. 2, d.454, l.1

75 Ibid., d.717, l.1

76 *PSS*, vol, 38, p. 242

77 Ibid., p. 298

78  Ibid., p. 372
79  Ibid., p. 325
80  Gippius-Merezhkovskii, Z., *Dmitrii Merezhkovskii*, Paris, 1951, p. 241
81  *Biograficheskaya khronika*, vol.5, op. cit., p. 242
82  RTsKhIDNI, f.19, op. 1, d.159, l.1
83  *Biograficheskaya khronika*, vol.5, op. cit., pp. 648–9
84  Bonch-Bruevich, V.D., *Tridtsat' dnei*, no. 1, 1934, pp. 15–19
85  *PSS*, vol.39, p. 183
86  *PSS*, vol.31, p. 310
87  *PSS*, vol 32, pp. 32, 97, 186; vol.36, pp. 85, 215, 269, 362
88  *PSS*, vol.36, p. 268
89  RTsKhIDNI, f.2, op. 1, d.6601, l.1
90  Ibid., d.6606, l.1
91  Ibid., d.6623
92  Trotsky, Leon, *Trotsky's Diary in Exile*, London, 1959, p. 80
93  *Biograficheskaya khronika*, vol.5, op. cit., pp. 165–6
94  RTsKhIDNI, f.19, op. 1, d.158, l.8
95  *Rabochaya revolyutsiya na Urale*, Yekaterinburg, 1921, pp. 3–29
96  RTsKhIDNI, f.588, op. 3, d.12, l.30
97  APRF, f.31, op. 1, d.4, l.216
98  RTsKhIDNI, f.2, op. 2, d.463, l.2
99  APRF, f.3, op. 58, d.280, l.1
100  Ibid., l.12
101  Ibid., l.10
102  Ibid., ll.12–13
103  RTsKhIDNI, f.588, op. 3, d.12, ll.18, 19, 59
104  Ibid., d.14, ll.28, 29, 30, 41
105  Ibid., ll.52–4.
106  Ibid., ll.60, 61
107  Witte, S.Yu., *Vospominaniya*, vol.1, Moscow, 1969, p. 245
108  RTsKhIDNI, f.588, op. 3, d.12, l.48
109  Goloshchekin, F.I., 'Vospominaniya uchastnikov Velikogo Oktyabrya', in *Istoricheskii arkhiv*, 1957, no.5, Moscow, p. 198
110  TsGAOR, f.130, op. 1, d.58, l.130b
111  Platonov, O., 'Tsareubiitsy', in *Literaturnaya Rossiya*, no.38, Moscow, 21 September 1990, p. 19
112  RTsKhIDNI, f.588, op. 3, d.12, l.43
113  APRF, 'Special file', Minutes of the Politburo and Central Committee Secretariat. (The designation 'Special file' indicates that a file has not yet been allocated to a collection, or has not been catalogued. All such 'Special files' have been housed in the Politburo archives.)
114  Kerensky, A.F., *Izdaleka*, op. cit., p. 189
115  RTsKhIDNI, f.5, op. 1, d.1648, l.4
116  *PSS*, vol.37, l.4
117  Ibid., pp. 83–5
118  Central KGB Archives (TsAKGB and TsMB RF), d.4–200, l.7
119  RTsKhIDNI, f.4, op. 1, d.86, l.5
120  *Vospominaniya o Vladimire Ilyiche Lenine*, Moscow, 1990, p. 309
121  RTsKhIDNI, f.4, op. 1, d.85, l.1
122  *Dekrety Sovetskoy vlasti*, vol.3, Moscow, 1963, p. 266
123  *Vospominaniya o Vladimire Ilyiche Lenine*, Moscow, 1990, p. 310
124  Trotskii, *O Lenine*, op. cit., pp. 152, 157–8
125  Balabanoff, *Impressions of Lenin*, op. cit., p. 1–2
126  RTsKhIDNI, f.4, op. 2, d.453, ll.1–2
127  Spiridonova, Maria, *Iz vospominanii o Nerchinskoy katorge*, Moscow, 1926, pp. 82, 84
128  TsAKGB, d.4–200, ll.8–10
129  Ibid., ll.8–11
130  Central Archives of the Ministry of Security of the Russian

Federation (TsAMB RF), 4–200, ll.22, 220b

131  TsAMB RF, f.4, op. 10, d.2197, l.126

132  Ibid., l.109

133  TsAMB RF, 4–200, l.12, 120b

134  Ibid., l.17

135  Vasiliev, Oleg, *Nezavisimaya gazeta*, 29 August 1992

136  Mal'kov, P., 'Zapiski komendanta Kremlya', in *Moskva*, No.11, 1958, pp. 123–61

137  Balabanoff, A., *Lenin: Psychologische Beobachtung und Betrachtungen*, Hanover, 1959, pp. 1–2

138  RTsKhIDNI, f.4, op. 2, d.3272, ll.1–2

139  RTsKhIDNI, f.86, op. 1, d.35, l.79

140  *Vladimir Ilyich Lenin: Biograficheskaya khronika*, vol.6, Moscow, 1975, pp. 127, 129, 130, 147

141  TsAMB RF, f.4, op. 10, d.2197, l.101

142  Ibid., ll.185–6

143  Ibid., d.2197, ll.191–2

144  *PSS*, vol.41, pp. 298–318

145  Shturman, Dora, *V.I. Lenin*, Paris, 1989, p. 75

146  *Pravda*, 14 January 1925

147  Ulyanova, *O Lenine i semie Ulyanovykh*, op. cit., pp. 113–17

148  *PSS*, vol.41, p. 19

149  RTsKhIDNI, f.2, op. 1, d.26388, l.1–2

150  APRF, f.3, op. 22, d.306, l.3

151  Ibid., l.1–10b

152  TsGASA, f.33987, op. 2, d.60, l.15

153  APRF, f.3, op. 22, d.306, ll.8–9

154  Krassin, L., *Leonid Krassin: His Life and Work by his wife*. London, 1920, p. 97

155  Kobyakov, S., 'Krasnyi sud', in *Arkhiv russkoy revolyutsii*, vol.7, Berlin, 1922, p. 273

156  Trotskii, *O Lenine*, op. cit., pp. 121, 122

157  *Trotsky's Diary in Exile*, op. cit., p. 82

158  *PSS*, vol.36, p. 196

159  GARF, f.130, op. 2, d.2, ll.241–2

160  Melgunov, S.P., *Krasnyi terror v Rossii*, Berlin, 1924, p. 6

161  *Utro Moskvy*, 4 November 1918

162  *Leninskii sbornik*, vol.18, 1931, pp. 145–6

163  Ibid., pp. 186–7

164  *PSS*, vol.50, p. 106

165  *PSS*, vol.41, p. 369

166  Ibid., p. 376

167  Ibid., p. 380

168  Ibid., p. 383

169  *PSS*, vol.54, p. 1

170  Ibid., p. 209

171  Ibid., p. 221

172  Ibid., p. 189

173  Ibid., p. 190

174  Ibid., pp. 189–90

175  *Ugolovnyi kodeks SSSR*, Moscow, 1938, pp. 26–32

176  *PSS*, vol.45, p. 549

177  RTsKhIDNI, f.17, op. 3, d.164, l.2

178  Ibid., op. 4, d.194, ll.3–30b

179  Ibid., op. 3, d.302, l.5

180  *PSS*, vol.52, pp. 222–3

181  *Leninskii sbornik*, vol.37, 1970, p. 114

182  RTsKhIDNI, f.2, op. 2, d.830, l.1

183  *Leninskii sbornik*, vol.24, 1933, p. 172

184  RTsKhIDNI, f.2, op. 2, d.133, ll.1–2

185  Krylenko, N.V., *Sudostroistvo RSFSR*, Moscow, 1923, p. 97

186  RTsKhIDNI, f.76, op. 3, d.149, ll.8–80b

187  Ibid., ll.30–320b

188  Kobyakov, S., 'Krasnyi sud', in *Arkhiv russkoy revolyutsii*, vol.7, Berlin, 1922, p. 246

189  AMBRF, f.114728, t.82, ll.1–2, 436

190  TsGASA, f.33987, op. 2, d.141, l.179

191  RTsKhIDNI, f.17, op. 3, d.195, l.1

192  Ibid., op. 84, d.228, ll.13–130b

193  *Lenin i VeCheKa*, Moscow, 1975, p. 231–2

194  TsKhSD, f.4, op. 16, d.157, ll.120–8

195  RTsKhIDNI, f.17, op. 3, d.239

196  Ibid., d.234, l.3

197  *Lenin i VeCheKa*, Moscow, 1975, p. 544

198  RTsKhIDNI, f.17, op. 3, d.153, l.2–6

199  Ibid., d.190, l.2

200  Ibid., l.3

201  TsGASA, f.33987, op. 1, d.392, l.108

202  GARF, f.3316, op. 1, d.448, ll.71–2

203  Ibid., ll.72–3

204  *PSS*, vol.36, pp. 255–7

205  Ibid., p. 193

*Chapter 5*

1  AMBRF N–13614, t. 1, l.100

2  *PSS*, vol.45, pp. 343–6

3  Ibid., p. 345

4  AMBRF, R–33835, d.3257, ll.237–71

5  Trotskii, L.D., *Dnevniki i pis'ma*, Paris, 1986, p. 31

6  Zinoviev, *Leninizm*, op. cit., p. 150

7  *PSS*, vol.45, p. 345

8  *PSS*, vol.49, p. 390

9  RTsKhIDNI, f.325, op. 1, d.6, l.1

10  *PSS*, vol.30, p. 270

11  *PSS*, vol.31, p. 204

12  Ibid., p. 253

13  Ibid., pp. 268–9

14  Trotskii, L.D., 'Terrorizm i kommunizm,' *Sochineniya*, vol.12, Moscow, 1926, p. 59

15  *Trotsky's Diary in Exile*, op. cit., pp. 53–4

16  In *Novaya zhizn'*, RTsKhIDNI, f.325, op. 2, d.11, l.21

17  Shturman, Dora, 'Samyi

18  RTsKhIDNI, f.325, op. 1, d.347, l.5

19  Ibid., l.6

20  Ibid., d.365, l.59

21  Ibid., d.282, ll.2–3

22  *PSS*, vol.47, pp. 187–188; vol.48, p. 11; vol.49, p. 387

23  *PSS*, vol.34, p. 345

24  Trotskii, L.D., *Stalinskaya shkola fal'sifikatsii*, Berlin, 1932, p. 119

25  Trotsky, Leon, *My Life*, New York, 1930, pp. 468–9

26  Trotskii, L.D., *Nemetskaya revolyutsiya i stalinskaya byurokratiya*, Berlin, 1932, pp. 99–100

27  RTsKhIDNI, f.325, op. 1, d.365, l.7

28  Trotskii, *O Lenine*, op. cit., pp. 152, 154

29  *PSS*, vol.44, p. 249

30  *PSS*, vol.43, p. 52

31  *PSS*, vol.54, p. 329

32  RTsKhIDNI, f.2, op. 1, d.17615, l.1

33  Ibid., d.18517, l.1

34  Ibid., d.23226, l.1

35  Ibid., d.25996, l.1

36  Ibid., op. 2, d.1239, l.1

37  TsGASA, f.33987, op. 2, d.41, l.5

38  Ibid., op. 1, d.23, l.18.

39  AMB RF, f.2, op. 4, d.133, l.10

40  APRF, f.64, op. 1, d.44, l.21

41  Trotskii, Lev, *Dnevniki i pis'ma*, New York, 1986, pp. 167–8

42  Ibid., p. 160

43  -*Trotsky's Diary in Exile*, op. cit., pp. 82–3

44  AMB RF, f.1, op. 4, d.133

45  *Leninskii sbornik*, vol.35, 1945, pp. 55–6

46  APRF, f.3, op. 22, d.297, l.64

47  Ibid., l.71

48  Ibid., l.114

49  Ibid., d.298, l.71–2

50  Ibid., d, 297, l.166

otkrovennyi amoralist', in *Posev*, Munich, No.1, 1992, p. 100

51  APRF, Politburo minutes No.P13/144, 5 March 1940
52  APRF, f.45, op. 1, d.693, ll.100-1
53  Ibid., d.694, l.2
54  *Leninskii sbornik*, vol.40, 1985, p. 100
55  *PSS*, vol.48, p. 162
56  *Leninskii sbornik*, vol.37, 1970, pp. 175-6
57  APRF, f.45, op. 1, d.694, l.31
58  *Leninskii sbornik*, vol.38, 1975, p. 417
59  APRF, f.45, op. 1, d.694, l.112
60  Ibid., l.109
61  Ibid., ll.101, 107-8
62  Stalin, I., *Sochineniya*, vol.4, Moscow, 1947, p. 314
63  Ibid.
64  APRF, f.45, op. 1, d.694, ll.3-4
65  *PSS*, vol.49, pp. 101, 161
66  *PSS*, vol.35, p. 369
67  See Schapiro, L., *The Communist Party of the Soviet Union*, London, 1970, p. 244
68  APRF, f.45, op. 1, d.694, l.36
69  *PSS*, vol.52, p. 100
70  APRF, f.45, op. 1, d.694, l.119
71  Ulyanova, M., in *Izvestiya TsK KPSS*, No.4, 1991, p. 78
72  RTsKhIDNI, f.2, op. 2, d.1338, l.1
73  *Leninskii sbornik*, vol.18, 1931, p. 193
74  Volkogonov, D., *Trotskii: politicheskii portret*, 2 volumes, Moscow, 1992, vol.2, p. 297
75  APRF, f.3, op. 24, d.163, l.179
76  Ibid., ll.222-5
77  APRF, f.45, op. 1, d.420, ll.8, 90b, 220b, 24, 250b, 64
78  *Leninskii sbornik*, vol.18, 1931, pp. 146, 163, 166, 169, 180-1, 189, 202
79  *PSS*, vol.54, pp. 32-3
80  Archives of MGB, d.7331, ll.50-3
81  Ibid., d.3208, t.42, ll.215-26
82  *PSS*, vol.51, p. 456

83  RTsKhIDNI, f.2, op. 1, d.24278, l.1
84  APRF, f.45, op. 1, d.67-117
85  RTsKhIDNI, f.324, op. 1, d.254, l.3
86  Stalin, I., *Sochineniya*, vol.5, Moscow, 1947, pp. 134-6
87  *PSS*, vol.45, p. 346
88  *PSS*, vol.54, pp. 674-5
89  Ibid., pp. 329-30, and APRF, f.3, op. 22, d.307, l.26
90  APRF, f.3, op. 22, d.307, ll.27-9
91  Ibid., d.297, ll.64, 65
92  Ibid., l.68
93  APRF, f.3, op. 22, d.299, l.87; published in *Izvestiya Ts KPSS*, No.12, 1989
94  AMBRF, archive no. R-33833, t. 41, ll.49-68
95  Ibid., l.256
96  Ibid., pp. 256-7
97  Ibid., l.91
98  Ibid., l.112
99  *PSS*, vol.34, p. 420
100 *PSS*, vol.45, p. 345
101 *PSS*, vol.22, p. 280
102 RTsKhIDNI, f.324, op. 1, d.452
103 *XIV s'ezd VKP(b), Stenograficheskii otchet*, Moscow-Leningrad, 1926, pp. 274-5
104 *PSS*, vol.47, pp. 188-9
105 Deich, G.M. *Leninskie eskizy k portretam druzei i protivnikov*, Leningrad, 1990, p. 125
106 Lunacharsky, A., *Revolutionary Silhouettes*, Translated by Michael Glenny, London, 1967, p. 76
107 Zinoviev, G.E., 'O zhizni i deyatel'nosti V.I. Lenina', in *Izvestiya TsK KPSS*, No.7, 1989, p. 171
108 Ibid., pp. 172, 175
109 AMBRF, f.1, op. 4, d.133, l.7
110 Zinoviev, 'O zhizni i deyatel'nosti V.I. Lenina', op. cit., pp. 173, 172, 178
111 Ibid., p. 173
112 RTsKhIDNI, f.324, d.246, l.2; d.267, ll.4, 5, 7

113   Ibid., op. 1, d.42, l.5

114   *Vladimir Ilyich Lenin: Biograficheskaya khronika*, vol.12, Moscow, 1982, p. 407ff

115   Lunacharskii, A. Radek, K, Trotskii, L., *Siluety*, Moscow, 1991, p. 300

116   *PSS*, vol.48, p. 175

117   Wheeler-Bennett, *Brest-Litovsk*, op. cit., pp. 284–5

118   *PSS*, vol.51, p. 10

119   *Vladimir Ilyich Lenin: Biograficheskaya khronika*, vol.11, Moscow, 1980, pp. 692–3

120   *PSS*, vol.52, p. 166

121   RTsKhIDNI, f.323, op. 1, dd.37, 45, 47 et al

122   RTsKhIDNI, f.324, op. 1, d.9, l.22

123   Ibid., d.12, l.17

124   Ibid., d.490, l.2

125   Ibid., d.489, l.12

126   RTsKhIDNI, f.324, op. 1, d.489, l.12

127   AMBRF, archive no. R–33834, t. 1, l.107

128   AMBRF, archive no. R–33833, t. 59, l.38

129   AMBRF, archive no. R–33834, t. 1, ll.120–1, 122

130   AMBRF, archive no. R–33833, t. 15, l.2

131   *7 dnei*, Paris, 19 January 1935

132   AMBRF, archive no. R–33833, t. 12, ll.40–1

133   Ibid., t. 59, l.128; Hochschild, A., *The Unquiet Ghost: Russians Remember Stalin*, Viking/Penguin, London, 1994, pp. 84–92

134   *PSS*, vol.45, p. 345

135   Bukharin, N., *O mirovoy revolyutsii, nashei strane, kul'ture i prochem*. Leningrad, 1924

136   Ibid., pp. 28, 32, 39, 43, 49, 52 et al

137   AMBRF, archive no. N–13614, t. 5, l.15

138   Ibid., t. 15, l.19

139   Ibid., t. 5, ll.20–1

140   *Sed'moy s'ezd Rossiiskoy Kommunisticheskoy partii*. Moscow-Petrograd, 1923, pp. 31, 32

141   Ibid., p. 42

142   APRF, f.3, op. 24, d.301, l.144

143   RTsKhIDNI, f.2, op. 1, d.24789, ll.4–40b

144   Bukharin, N., *Izbrannye proizvedeniya*, Moscow, 1988, pp. 1–17

145   Ibid., pp. 428–9

146   Ibid., p. 400

147   Feltchinskii, Y. (Ed.), *Portrety revolyutsionerov* (a compilation based on Trotsky's works), Vermont, 1988, p. 141

148   Ibid., pp 142–3

149   APRF, f.45, op. 1, d.710, l.48

150   TsGASA, f.33987, op. 3, d.891, ll.25–7

151   APRF, f.3, op. 24, d.262, l.29

152   Ibid., l.30

153   Ibid., op. 22, d.307, l.175

154   RTsKhIDNI, f.4, op. 1, d.142, l.476

155   APRF, f.3, op. 24, d.291, ll.18–19

156   *PSS*, vol.51, p. 47

157   APRF, f.3, op. 24, d.301, ll.135–56

158   Ibid., d.427, ll.1–5

159   TsGAOR, f.7523, op. 66, d.58, ll.1–4

160   AMBRF, archive no. N–13613, d.53, l.97

161   RTsKhIDNI, f.76, op. 3, d.345, ll.2–20b

162   Ibid., ll.1–2

163   RTsKhIDNI, f.17, op. 3, d.128, l.1

164   Ibid., d.155, ll.2–3

165   *Chetyrnadtsatyi s'ezd VKP(b)*. Moscow-Leningrad, 1926, pp. 84–5

166   *PSS*, vol.49, p. 194

167   APRF, f.3, op. 22, d.8, l.1

168   Ibid., d.23, l.2

169   Ibid., l.7

170   Ibid., d.9, ll.15–16

171    Ibid., d.8, l.78
172    Ibid., d.23, l.28
173    Ibid., ll.37–8
174    Ibid., d.8, l.7
175    Ibid., d.9, ll.51–3
176    Ibid., ll.72–3
177    Ibid., ll.74–8
178    RTsKhIDNI, f.17, op. 3, d.9, ll.1–2
179    Ibid., d.13, l.5
180    Ibid., d.164, l.2
181    Ibid., d.259, l.1
182    Ibid., d.279, ll.1–2
183    *PSS*, vol.45, pp. 88–9
184    RTsKhIDNI, f.17, op. 3, d.302, l.5
185    Ibid., d.152, ll.1–2
186    RTsKhIDNI, f.80, op. 19, d.1, ll.6–14
187    *PSS*, vol.45, p. 89
188    RTsKhIDNI, f.17, op. 3, d.136, ll.1–2
189    Ibid., d.345, ll.5–6
190    RTsKhIDNI, f.17, op. 3, d.161, l.2
191    *PSS*, vol.45, p. 53
192    RTsKhIDNI, f.17, op. 3, d.120, l.3
193    Ibid., d.305, l.6
194    Ibid., d.361, l.15
195    Ibid., d.69, l.2
196    Ibid., d.201, l.4
197    Ibid., d.132, l.2
198    RTsKhIDNI, f.17, op. 3, d.322, l.1
199    APRF, Politburo Minutes, 8 February 1947, No.P56/137
200    APRF, Politburo Minutes, 3 December 1934, No.P17/89
201    *Leninskii sbornik*, vol.18, 1931, p. 189
202    APRF, Politburo Minutes, 5 July 1937, P51/144
203    TsGASA, f.33987, op. 2, d.41, l.63
204    APRF, f.3, op. 24, d.463, ll.33, 72
205    Redlich, S., *Propaganda and Nationalism in Wartime Russia: The Jewish Antifascist Committee in the USSR, 1941–1948* (n.p.USA), 1982; RTsKhIDNI, f.17, op. 18, d.305, l.20
206    APRF, Politburo Minutes, 5 March 1940, No.P13/144
207    The 'Special files' of the Politburo relating to this issue, as to many others, have not yet been given archive numbers
208    APRF, f.2, op. 1, d.259
209    Ibid., l.9
210    Ibid., l.13
211    Ibid., l.24
212    APRF, 'Special file', KGB note of 25 March 1970, No.745-A/ob.
213    APRF, Politburo Minutes, 27 March 1970, No.P–158
214    APRF, 'Special file', Materials on the memoirs of N.S. Khrushchev
215    Centre for the Storage of Contemporary Documentation (TsKhSD, formerly Central Committee Archives), f.5, op. 61, ll.1–9
216    APRF, Politburo Minutes, 17 June 1971
217    APRF, Politburo Minutes, 7 January 1974
218    APRF, Politburo Minutes, 2 September 1983
219    APRF, Politburo Minutes, 28 July 1966, No.P12/XVII
220    APRF, Politburo Minutes, 24 March, 1983, No.P103/XII
221    APRF, Politburo Minutes, 2 October 1986, No.P30/64-OP
222    Ibid.

## Chapter 6

1    Stalin, I., *Sochineniya*, vol.10, Moscow, 1949, pp. 189–90
2    'Doklad Khrushcheva, 1956', in *Izvestiya TsK KPSS*, No.3, 1989, p. 134
3    RTsKhIDNI, f.17, op. 3, d.155, ll.2–3
4    'Doklad Khrushcheva, 1956', op. cit., p. 159

5   APRF, Politburo Minutes, 15 October 1987, p. 156

6   RTsKhIDNI, f.44, op. 1, d.5, l.15

7   TsGAOR, f.9401, op. 2, d.176, t. II, l.360

8   Ibid., d.64, t. 1, l.263

9   *Dvenadtsatyi s'ezd RKP(b)*, Moscow, 1923, pp. 2–3

10  *PSS*, vol.33, pp. 26–7

11  *Lenin i XX vek*, Moscow, 1991, p. 111

12  *PSS*, vol.33, p. 109

13  Ibid., p. 100

14  Kautsky, K., *Social Democracy versus Communism*, New York, 1946

15  RTsKhIDNI, f.2, op. 2, d.86, ll.1–4

16  Lenin's evidence was published only in *Vestnik Vremennogo Pravitel'stva*, No.8/81, 16 June 1917, p. 3, and is cited in Pipes, R., *The Russian Revolution, 1899–1919*, London, 1990, pp. 374–5

17  Zinoviev, 'O zhizni i deyatel'nosti V.I. Lenina', op.cit., p. 201

18  RTsKhIDNI, f.17, op. 3, d.928, ll.48–9

19  RTsKhIDNI, f.85, op. 29, d.357, l.1

20  RTsKhIDNI, f.17, op. 3, d.999, ll.92–3

21  *PSS*, vol.33, p. 102

22  Stalin, I., *O nedostatkakh partiinoy raboty i merakh likvidatsii trotskistkikh i inykh dvurushnikov*, Moscow, 1937, p. 29

23  *PSS*, vol.32, p. 374

24  Struve, P.B., *Razmyshleniya o russkoy revolyutsii*, Moscow, 1991, pp. 42–3

25  *Krasnoarmeiskii polituchebnik*, part 1, Moscow, 1937, p. 293

26  *PSS*, vol.45, p. 289

27  APRF, 'Special file' No.989, ll.1–5

28  APRF, 'Special file' No.1246, l.2

29  APRF, 'Special file' No.397, ll.1–3

30  Ibid.

31  APRF, 'Special file' No.583, l.1

32  APRF, 'Special file' No.21, ll.1–2

33  APRF, 'Special file' No.6403, l.1

34  GARF, f.9401, op. 2, d.68, t. V, l.383

35  Ibid., ll.334–41

36  APRF, 'Special file' No.433, ll.1–2

37  *PSS*, vol.35, p. 24

38  Ibid., p. 2

39  Ibid., p. 264

40  Ibid.

41  *PSS*, vol.45, pp. 369–73

42  *Leninskii sbornik*, vol.18, Moscow, 1931, p. 82

43  Ibid., p. 85

44  *PSS*, vol.35, p. 265

45  Chernov, V., *Rozhdenie revolyutsionnoy Rossii*, Prague, 1934, p. 404

46  *Leninskii sbornik*, vol.18, Moscow, 1931, p. 141

47  Ibid., p. 87

48  TsGASA, f.33388, op. 2, d.383, l.14

49  Ibid., l.171

50  Srechinskii, Yu., 'Kompartiya i krestyanstvo', in *Novyi zhurnal*, No.89, 1967, pp. 211–12

51  RTsKhIDNI, f.2, op. 1, d.21244, l.1

52  RTsKhIDNI, f.17, op. 3, d.325, ll.1–2

53  Berdyaev, N., *Novoe Srednevekovye*, Berlin, 1924, p. 89

54  APRF, Politburo Minutes No.68, 15 October 1921

55  RTsKhIDNI, f.495, op. 82, d.1, ll.10–100b

56  RTsKhIDNI, f.2, op. 1, d.21444, l.56

57  Ibid., l.1–4

58  *Chto dali bol'sheviki narodu?* Moscow, 1921, p. 14–15

59  Stalin, I., *Sochineniya*, vol.13, Moscow, 1951, p. 189

60  Ibid., p. 191

61  Ibid., p. 231

62  Ibid., p. 233

63  APRF, f.3, op. 30, d.196, l.106

64 Ibid., ll.109–11

65 Ibid., ll.97, 104, 105, 114

66 Ibid., l.108

67 Ibid., ll.116–18

68 APRF, Politburo Minutes, 15 October 1987

69 Stalin, I., *Sochineniya*, vol.11, Moscow, 1949, p. 159

70 *Istoriya VKP(b), Kratkii kurs*, Moscow, 1938, p. 291

71 *Leninskii sbornik*, vol.18, Moscow, 1918, pp. 93–4

72 Stalin, I., *Sochineniya*, vol.12, Moscow, 1949, p. 168

73 APRF, Politburo Minutes No.116, 31 January 1930

74 Churchill, W.S., *History of the Second World War*, vol.4, London, 1951, pp. 447–8

75 APRF, Politburo Minutes No.123, 10 April 1930

76 RTsKhIDNI, f.17, op. 26, d.55, ll.71–2

77 APRF, Politburo Minutes No.143, 2 August 1933

78 Vyshinsky, A.Y. (Ed.), *Spravochnik sovetskogo rabotnika*, Moscow, 1939, p. 89

79 Stalin, I., *Sochineniya*, vol.13, op. cit., p. 243

80 Ibid., p. 245

81 RTsKhIDNI, f.17, op. 42, d.82, ll.82–83

82 *PSS*, vol.45, p. 376

83 APRF, 'Special file' No.743, ll.1–2

84 *Leninskii sbornik*, vol.21, Moscow, 1933, p. 213

85 Cited in Krupskaya, N.K., *Vospominaniya o Lenine*, Moscow, 1989, p. 468

86 RTsKhIDNI, f.17, op. 3, d.253, l.2

87 *PSS*, vol.54, p. 110

88 *PSS*, vol.37, p. 402

89 RTsKhIDNI, f.17, op. 3, d.113, l.1

90 TsGASA, f.4, op. 14, d.3, l.27

91 *PSS*, vol.12, pp. 100–01

92 RTsKhIDNI, f.17, op. 3, d.296, l.6

93 APRF, f.3, op. 58, d.175, ll.35–6

94 RTsKhIDNI, f.2, op. 2, d.1245, l.2

95 Ibid., l.3

96 APRF, f.3, op. 58, d.175, ll.37–56

97 RTsKhIDNI, f.2, op. 2, d.1343

98 *Biograficheskaya khronika*, vol.12, op. cit., p. 378

99 Kuskova, E.K., 'Tragediya Maksima Gor'kogo', in *Novyi zhurnal*, No.38, pp. 224–45

100 RTsKhIDNI, f.2, op. 1, d.11164, ll.7–8

101 Ibid., op. 2, d.1338, ll.1–2.

102 Machiavelli, Niccolo, *Izbrannye sochineniya*, Moscow, 1982, p. 353

103 RTsKhIDNI, f.2, op. 2, d.1344, l.1

104 APRF, f.3, op. 58, d.175, l.72

105 *PSS*, vol.17, pp. 206–13

106 Ibid.

107 RTsKhIDNI, f.2, op. 1, d.11164, l.48

108 RTsKhIDNI, f.17, op. 3, d.329, l.2

109 Struve, G., *Russkaya literatura v izgnanii*, Paris, 1984, p. 7

110 RTsKhIDNI, f.17, op. 3, d.160, l.4

111 Ibid., d.370, l.13.

112 AMBRF, Archive No.32490, t. 1

113 APRF, f.3, op. 58, d.175, ll.5–50b

114 Ibid., l.6

115 Ibid., ll.6–16

116 RTsKhIDNI, f.17, op. 3, d.201, l.4

117 Ibid., d.132, l.1

118 Ibid., d.332, l.7

119 *Leninskii sbornik*, vol.16, Moscow, 1931, pp. 24–36

120 RTsKhIDNI, f.17, op. 3, d.329, l.2

121 *Novyi grad*, No.1, 1931, Paris, pp. 1–7

122 APRF, f.3, op. 34, d.188, ll.35–7

123 APRF, Zasedanie Sekretariata TsK KPSS 26.04.83, ll.1–7

124 Liberman, S.I., 'Narodnyi komissar Krasin', in *Novyi zhurnal*, no.7, 1944, p. 309
125 Krzhizhanovskii, G.M., *Lenin: Tovarishch, chelovek*, 6th edn., Moscow, 1987, p. 212
126 See Ulyanova, *O V.I. Lenine i semye Ulyanovykh*, op. cit.
127 *PSS*, vol.12, p. 142
128 Ibid., p. 145
129 RTsKhIDNI, f.17, op. 3, d.261, ll.13–14
130 RTsKhIDNI, f.2, op. 1, d.20449, l.1
131 RTsKhIDNI, f.17, op. 3, d.195, l.1
132 APRF, f.3, op. 60, d.23, ll.7–8
133 RTsKhIDNI, f.2, d.1166, ll.1–2
134 RTsKhIDNI, f.17, op. 3, d.284, l.9
135 APRF, f.3, op. 60, d.25, l.5
136 *Biograficheskaya khronika*, vol.12, op. cit., p. 244
137 *PSS*, vol.45, pp. 666–7
138 RTsKhIDNI, f.2, op. 1, d.22947
139 APRF, f.3, op. 60, d.10, l.87
140 RTsKhIDNI, f.2, op. 1, d.22947
141 RTsKhIDNI, f.17, op. 3, d.283, ll.6–7
142 RTsKhIDNI, f.2, op. 2, d.1166, l.5
143 RTsKhIDNI, f.3, op. 6, d.22, l.32
144 APRF, f.3, op. 60, d.22, ll.35–7
145 Ibid., l.53
146 Ibid., d.23, ll.76–7
147 Ibid., ll.57–8
148 Ibid., ll.80–1
149 APRF, f.3, op. 60, d.25, l.5
150 Ibid., l.49
151 Ibid., d.12, l.37
152 RTsKhIDNI, f.17, op. 3, d.360, l.9
153 *Izvestiya*, 27 June, 1923
154 APRF, f.3, op. 60, d.25, l.58
155 Ibid., ll.59–60
156 RTsKhIDNI, f.89, op. 4, d.115, l.24
157 APRF, Politburo Minutes No.116, 30 January 1930
158 APRF, f.3, op. 60, d.23, ll.97–9
159 Ibid., d.23, ll.100–2
160 Ibid., d.9, l.49
161 Ibid., ll.60–3
162 Ibid., d.10, ll.23, 58
163 Ibid., d.10, l.88
164 GARF, f.5446, op. 55, d.735, ll.51–4
165 RTsKhIDNI, f.2, op. 1, d.14802
166 *PSS*, vol.36, p. 472
167 RTsKhIDNI, f.2, op. 2, d.348, l.1
168 Trotskii, *O Lenine*, op. cit., p. 87
169 RTsKhIDNI, f.44, op. 1, d.5, ll.9–36
170 Ibid., ll.127–32
171 RTsKhIDNI, f.2, op. 2, d.1003, ll.1–2
172 *PSS*, vol.33, p. 102
173 *PSS*, vol.38, p. 325
174 *PSS*, vol.41, p. 318
175 *PSS*, vol.14, pp. 378–9
176 *PSS*, vol.33, p. 117
177 *PSS*, vol.34, p. 116
178 APRF, f.3, op. 20, d.53, ll.55–9
179 *PSS*, vol.40, pp. 209, 211
180 APRF, f.3, op. 20, d.53, l.1
181 *PSS*, vol.38, pp. 302–3
182 APRF, f.31, op. 1, d.4, l.211
183 APRF, f.3, op. 20, d.52, ll.3, 4
184 RTsKhIDNI, f.2, op. 2, d.5, l.1
185 Ibid., d.448, l.1
186 Ibid., d.1299, l.1
187 Ibid.
188 APRF, f.3, op. 20, d.64, ll.171–6
189 RTsKhIDNI, f.2, op. 2, d.1318, ll.1–3
190 Trotskii, L.D., *Pyat' let Kominterna*, Moscow-Leningrad, 1925, pp. 73–99
191 TsGASA, f.4, op. 14, d.32, ll.190–9
192 *PSS*, vol.38, p. 186
193 Ibid., p. 321
194 Trotskii, L.D., *Pyat' let Kominterna*, Moscow-Leningrad, 1925, p. 90
195 Balabanoff, *Impressions of Lenin*, op. cit., pp. 29–30

196 *PSS*, vol.38, p. 217
197 *PSS*, vol.8, pp. 384, 388
198 GARF, f.130, op. 1, d.19, l.13
199 Ibid., ll.126–30, 96–8
200 Trotskii, *Pyat' let Kominterna*, op. cit., p. 98
201 TsGASA, f.33987, op. 2, d.32, ll.279–279ob
202 Ibid., l.528
203 RTsKhIDNI, f.2, op. 2, d.293, ll.1–3
204 Ibid., d.329, ll.1–2
205 Ibid., d.183, ll.1–4
206 Ibid., op. 1, d.24832, l.1
207 Ibid., op. 2, d.653, l.1
208 Ibid., d.1019, l.1
209 APRF, f.3, op. 20, d.64, ll.34–9
210 APRF, 'Special file', Packet No.5
211 RTsKhIDNI, f.2, op. 2, d.235, ll.4–5
212 APRF, f.3, op. 20, d.64
213 Ibid., l.45
214 Ibid.
215 Ibid., ll.67–9
216 RTsKhIDNI, f.495, op. 19, d.15, l.24
217 Ibid., d.18, l.8
218 Ibid., d.15, l.24
219 *PSS*, vol.44, p. 226
220 RTsKhIDNI, f.2, op. 2, d.380, l.1
221 APRF, f.3, op. 20, d.73, l.123
222 Ibid., d.66, l.8
223 *PSS*, vol.44, p. 405
224 NKVD Archives, f.K–1, op. 1, d.17671
225 Ibid.
226 APRF, f.3, op. 20, d.58, l.91
227 Ibid., l.122
228 Ibid., d.66, l.19
229 Ibid., d.54, l.102
230 Ibid., l.114
231 APRF, f.45, op. 1, d.319, l.31
232 Trotskii, L.D., *Dnevniki i pis'ma*, New York, 1986, p. 165

## Chapter 7

1 TsGAOR, f.5459, op. 5, d.2, l.262
2 Martov, Iu.O., *Bor'ba s osadnym polozheniem v Rossiiskoy sotsial-demokraticheskoy rabochei partii*, Geneva, 1904
3 APRF, f.3, op. 22, d.307, l.135
4 TsGAOR, f.5459, op. 5, d.2, l.254
5 *PSS*, vol.55, p. 368
6 RTsKhIDNI, f.2, op. 1, d.385, l.1
7 *PSS*, vol.11, pp. 339–3
8 APRF, f.3, op. 22, d.307, l.136
9 RTsKhIDNI, f.2, op. 2, d.1343
10 APRF, f.3, op. 22, d.307, l.137
11 Ulyanova, M.I., 'O Vladimire Ilyiche', in *Izvestiya TsK KPSS*, No.3, 1991, p. 189
12 RTsKhIDNI, f.17, op. 3, d.314, l.6
13 APRF, f.3, op. 22, d.307, l.16
14 Ibid., l.17
15 Ibid., l.18
16 Ibid., l.19
17 *PSS*, vol.52, p. 100
18 Voitinskii, V., *Gody pobeg i porazhenii*, Book 2, Berlin, 1924, p. 100
19 Ulyanova, 'O Vladimire Ilyiche', op. cit., p. 185
20 RTsKhIDNI, f.16, op. 3, d.6, l.7
21 *PSS*, vol.45, pp. 278–94
22 RTsKhIDNI, f.16, op. 2, d.13, ll.180–90
23 APRF, f.3, op. 22, d.307, l.23
24 RTsKhIDNI, f.16, op. 2, d.13, l.189
25 *PSS*, vol.45, p. 348
26 *PSS*, vol.54, pp. 674–5
27 *PSS*, vol.45, pp. 345, 346
28 Bukharin, N.I., *Politicheskoe zaveshchanie Lenina*, Moscow, 1929
29 *PSS*, vol.45, p. 376
30 Ibid., p. 403
31 APRF, f.3, op. 22, d.307, l.139
33 Ibid., l.138
33 *PSS*, vol.54, p. 329
34 Ibid.
35 *PSS*, vol.54, p. 330
36 RTsKhIDNI, f.14, op. 1, d.398, ll.4–5
37 *PSS*, vol.54, pp. 329–30

38  APRF, f.3, op. 22, d.307, l.138

39  Ibid., ll.27–9.

40  Ulyanova, 'O Vladimire Ilyiche', op. cit., p. 169

41  RTsKhIDNI, f.4, op. 1, d.142, l.240

42  APRF, f.3, op. 22, d.307, ll.133–9

43  Ibid., l.98

44  Ibid., l.50

45  Ibid., l.172

46  Ibid., l.55

47  Ibid., l.77

48  Ibid., l.73

49  Ibid., l.62

50  RTsKhIDNI, f.14, op. 1, d.398, ll.3–6

51  APRF, f.3, op. 22, d.307, ll.1–2

52  Ibid., ll.1–2

53  The story of Lenin's request for poison was related by Trotsky in 1939, but in a garbled and dubious form. See Deutscher, I., *The Prophet Outcast: Trotsky – 1929–1940*, Oxford, 1963, p. 446

54  APRF, f.3, op. 22, d.307, ll.7, 11

55  Ibid., d.308, l.61

56  Trotskii, *O Lenine*, op. cit., pp. 159, 160

57  RTsKhIDNI, f.16, op. 2, d.13

58  APRF, f.3, op. 22, d.307, l.140

59  RTsKhIDNI, f.4, op. 1, d.142, ll.310–46

60  Ravdin, B., in *Znanie – sila*, No.4, 1990

61  Annenkov, Yu., 'Vospominaniya o Lenine', in *Novyi zhurnal*, no. 65, 1961, pp. 149, 141, 142

62  Ravdin, op. cit., p. 22

63  Ibid.

64  RTsKhIDNI, f.16, op. 2, d.13

65  *Biograficheskaya khronika*, vol.12, op. cit., p. 621

66  APRF, f.3, op. 22, d.307, l.140

67  Ibid., d.306, ll.127–8

68  RTsKhIDNI, f.4, op. 1, d.142, ll.406–7

69  Cited in Fischer, *The Life of Lenin*, op. cit., p. 672

70  Annenkov, Yu, 'Vospominaniya o Lenine', in *Novyi zhurnal*, no. 65, 1961, p. 144

71  RTsKhIDNI, f.17, op. 2, d.86, ll.5–50b

72  APRF, f.3, op. 22, d.307, l.175

73  TsGASA, F.4, D.17, L.290

74  APRF, f.3, op. 22, d.307, l.174, see Ulyanova, 'O Vladimire Ilyiche', op. cit.

75  *Biograficheskaya khronika*, vol.12, op. cit., p. 653

76  RTsKhIDNI, f.12, op. 2, d.254, ll.2, 3, 4, 9, 10

77  APRF, f.3, op. 22, d.308, l.141

78  Ulyanova, 'O Vladimire Ilyiche', op. cit.

79  APRF, f.3, op. 22, d.307, l.176

80  *Pravda*, 24 January 1924

81  The editor is grateful to Dr Peter Greenhall of the Neurology Department at the Radcliffe Infirmary, Oxford, for his opinion. The autopsy is cited in full in Payne, R., *The Life and Death of Lenin*, London, 1964, pp. 637–40.

82  APRF, f.3, op. 22, d.309, ll.1–2

83  Ibid., l.2

84  Ibid., l.5

85  TsGASA, f 33987, op. 3, d.80, l.587

86  APRF, f.3, op. 22, d.309, ll.15, 16, 21

87  Ibid., l.15

88  *Biograficheskaya khronika*, vol.12, op. cit., pp. 672–3

89  Ibid., p. 675

90  Archives of Security Ministry (Arkhiv MB), f.1, op. 4, No.133, l.10

91  *Pravda*, 27 January 1924

92  Ibid.

93  *Pravda*, 30 January 1924

94  Ibid.

95  APRF, f.3, op. 77, l.526

96  Churchill, W. S., *The World Crisis*, *Vol.5*, op. cit., p. 76

97    Stalin, I., *Sochineniya*, vol.10, op. cit., pp. 41, 56
98    *Pravda*, 27 July 1924
99    APRF, f.3, op. 22, d.309, l.38
100   Ibid., d.307, l.156
101   APRF, f.3, op. 22, d.307, l.49
102   See Zbarskii, B.I., *Mavzolei Lenina*, Moscow, 1944
103   APRF, f.3, op. 22, d.311, l.3
104   Ibid., l.5
105   Ibid., ll.5–6
106   Ibid., l.24
107   Ibid., l.31
108   Ibid., l.103
109   Ibid., l.120
110   Ibid., d.523, ll.1–11
111   Ibid., d.311, l.121
112   Ibid., d.310, l.53
113   Ibid., ll.54–64
114   *The Times*, 19 January 1994
115   APRF, f.3, op. 22, d.36, l.23
116   *PSS*, vol.12, p. 320
117   Brezhnev, L.I., *Leninskim kursom*, vol.6, p. 533
118   APRF, 'Special file' No.576, ll.2, 3, 5
119   APRF, 'Special file', Politburo Minutes, 20 June 1968, p. 6
120   APRF, 'Special file', Politburo Minutes No.244, 15 October 1959, pp. 36–8
121   Medvedev, R., *All Stalin's Men*, Blackwell, Oxford, 1989, p. 139
122   APRF, Politburo Minutes, 27 December 1973, pp. 1–7
123   Khrushchev, N.S., *Rechi na sobraniyakh izbiratelei Moskvy*, Moscow, 1937, pp. 3–21
124   APRF, 'Special file', Notes of Khrushchev's talks in Peking, 2 October 1959, pp. 1–33
125   APRF, 'Special file', Central Committee Plenum Report of 14 October 1964, p. 59
126   Ibid., p. 4
127   Brezhnev, L.I., *O kommunisticheskom vospitanii trudyashchikhsya*, Moscow, 1974, pp. 286–7
128   *Dnevniki imperatora Nikolaya II*, Moscow, 1991, p. 309
129   APRF, f.80, op. 11519
130   APRF, 'Special file', Meeting of L.I. Brezhnev and leaders of the fraternal parties in Budapest, 18 March 1975
131   APRF, 'Special file', Minutes of Politburo, 18 November 1982, pp. 464–5
132   APRF, f.82
133   APRF, 'Special file', Minutes of Politburo, 7 January 1974, pp. 19–34
134   Andropov, Y.V., *Izbrannye rechi i stat'i*, Moscow, 1983, p. 126
135   APRF, 'Special file', Note from Y.V. Andropov to L.I. Brezhnev, 29 October 1973, pp. 1–5
136   RTsKhIDNI, f.2, op. 2, d.1119, ll.1–2
137   APRF, 'Special file', Minutes of Politburo, 4 August 1983, p. 66
138   APRF, 'Special file', Minutes of Politburo, 20 October 1983, pp. 241–6
139   APRF, 'Special file', Minutes of Politburo, 10 February 1984, pp. 11–126
140   APRF, f.83
141   APRF, 'Special file', Minutes of Politburo, 23 February 1984
142   RTsKhIDNI, f.2, op. 1, d.20706, l.1
143   APRF, 'Special file', Minutes of Politburo, 11 March 1985
144   APRF, 'Special file', Minutes of Politburo, 4 April 1985, pp. 248–51
145   Gorbachev, M.S., *Izbrannye rechi i stat'i*, Moscow, 1985, p. 9
146   APRF, 'Special file', Minutes of Politburo, 4 April 1985, p. 212
147   APRF, 'Special file', Minutes of Politburo, 2 September 1983, p. 6
148   *Volya Rossii*, Paris, No.3, 1924
149   *PSS*, vol. 51
150   Central Defence Ministry Archives (TsAMO), f.3, op. 1156, d.2, l.252

151 Archives of the Ministry of State Security (AMB), f.1, op. 4, No.133, l.7
152 Trotskii, *O Lenine*, op. cit., pp. 87, 88
153 RTsKhIDNI, f.2, op. 2, d.1166, ll.1–2
154 APRF, 'Special file', Minutes of Politburo, 20 June 1968, pp. 1–8
155 APRF, 'Special file', Minutes of Politburo, 17 April 1970, pp. 1–2
156 APRF, Minutes of the Central Committee Secretariat, 2 June 1981, p. 2
157 APRF, 'Special file', KGB Report No.456-'Ch', pp. 162–4

*Epilogue*

1 TsGAOR, f.5459, op. 5, d.2, l.232
2 APRF, Minutes of Politburo, 15 October 1987, p. 156
3 *PSS*, vol.39, p. 408
4 *Leninskii sbornik*, vol.18, Moscow, 1931, p. 187
5 AMBRF, f.1, op. 4, d.133, l.10
6 *Leninskii sbornik*, vol.2, Moscow, 1924, p. 271
7 APRF, f.31, op. 1, d.4, ll.25, 213
8 Ibid., l.27
9 RTsKhIDNI, f.2, op. 2, d.380, l.1
10 APRF, f.3, op. 24, d.463, ll.148–9
11 RTsKhIDNI, f.2, op. 2, d.492, l.1
12 APRF, 'Special file', Note to CPSU Central Committee 682-'op', 28 August 1980, l.1
13 APRF, 'Special file', Notes of Khrushchev's conversation in Warsaw, May 1960, No.233
14 RTsKhIDNI, f.2, op. 2, d.447, l.1
15 Ibid., d.231, l.1.
16 APRF, Defence Ministry Note 04311, ll.1–4
17 Berdyaev, *Istoki i smysl russkogo kommunizma*, op. cit., p. 131

# Index